THE QUALITY OF LIFE

WIDER

Studies in Development Economics embody the output of the
research programmes of the World Institute for Development
Economics Research (WIDER), which was established by the
United Nations University as its first research and training centre
in 1984 and started work in Helsinki in 1985. The principal
purpose of the Institute is to help identify and meet the need for
policy-oriented socio-economic research on pressing global and
development problems, as well as common domestic problems
and their interrelationships.

THE QUALITY OF LIFE

Edited by

MARTHA NUSSBAUM
AND
AMARTYA SEN

*A study prepared for the World Institute for Development Economics
Research (WIDER) of the United Nations University*

CLARENDON PRESS · OXFORD

#2487117

OXFORD
UNIVERSITY PRESS

Great Clarendon Street, Oxford ox2 6DP

Oxford University Press is a department of the University of Oxford.
It furthers the University's objective of excellence in research, scholarship,
and education by publishing worldwide in

Oxford New York

Athens Auckland Bangkok Bogotá Buenos Aires Calcutta
Cape Town Chennai Dar es Salaam Delhi Florence Hong Kong Istanbul
Karachi Kuala Lumpur Madrid Melbourne Mexico City Mumbai
Nairobi Paris São Paulo Shanghai Singapore Taipei Tokyo Toronto Warsaw

with associated companies in Berlin Ibadan

Published in the United States
by Oxford University Press Inc., New York

First published 1993
Reprinted 1993, 1995, 1996 (twice), 1997, 2001

WIDER: World Institute for Development Economics Research (WIDER)—
The United Nations University, Annankatu 42c 00100 Helsinki, Finland

British Library Cataloguing in Publication Data

Data available

Library of Congress Cataloging in Publication Data
The Quality of life / edited by Martha Nussbaum and Amartya Sen.
p. cm.—(Studies in development economics)
Papers presented at a conference sponsored by the World Institute for Development Economics
Research.
Includes index.
1. Quality of life—Congresses.   2. Public welfare—Congresses.
3. Human services—Congresses.   4. Social values—Congresses.
I. Nussbaum, Martha Craven, 1947-   . II. Sen, Amartya Kumar.
III. World Institute for Development Economics Research.
IV. Series.
HN25.Q33   1992   306—dc20   91–42030
ISBN 0-19-828797-6 (Pbk)

Printed in Great Britain
on acid-free paper by
Bookcraft (Bath) Ltd., Midsomer Norton, Avon

FOREWORD

THESE papers derive from a conference that took place at the WIDER in Helsinki in July 1988. It was organized by Martha Nussbaum and Amartya Sen. The organizers wish to thank Dolores E. Iorizzo for her invaluable role in looking after every phase of the conference and the preparation of this volume of essays, and would also like to acknowledge the help received from Iftekar Hossain and Richard L. Velkley.

An important part of WIDER'S mandate—symbolized indeed in the acronym 'WIDER'—was to engage in interdisciplinary research. What is meant by the 'quality of life', and what is required in terms of social policy for improving it, has been a common preoccupation of both economics and philosophy, and an obvious focus of WIDER's work was a conference that would bring scholars together from both these disciplines. At the aggregative level, economists work with a crude measure of per capita income as indicative of human welfare, and a number of questions are begged here which require closer investigation. Similarly, at the micro level, the notion of maximizing an individual's utility underlies much of conventional demand theory. But this raises two questions: is utility measurable? And is utility the right thing to be measuring, when we are interested in assessing the quality of human lives?

Philosophers have been debating both these issues from a variety of points of view, providing sophisticated new perspectives on them. At the aggregative level, they have been critical of the single crude measure provided by per capital income, insisting that we need to consider the distribution of wealth and income as well, and that we need to assess a number of distinct areas of human life in determining how well people are doing. There have been a number of different proposals about how this should be done, and the most prominent of these are represented in the papers in this volume. At the individual level, the notion of measurable utility has been criticized in several difficult ways. Even those philosophers who would still defend utility as the best measure of quality of life argue that this notion must be refined in a number of ways, especially by discounting preferences that are formed in an inappropriate manner. Others have more profoundly criticized the notion of utility, suggesting that we should instead measure people's capabilities, that is, whatever they are able to do and to be in a variety of areas of life. Again, several prominent approaches to these questions are represented in this volume.

The introduction to the present volume by Martha Nussbaum and Amartya Sen focuses in greater detail on the way in which contributors to the conference have analysed these issues. My purpose in this foreword is to look, as it were, beyond the conference to see how far the objective of getting the two disciplines together was in fact achieved, namely, encouraging debate between philosophers and economists on the issue of improving the quality of life, and, more specifically, encouraging further co-operative inquiries between members of both disciplines so as to lead up to results assimilable by policy-makers. The conference, and its resulting papers, show that some economists are in fact becoming more sensitive to the importance of facing fundamental philosophical questions about their starting points. This sensitivity needs to become far more widespread. Especially in the area of development, it is becoming increasingly clear that an adequate approach to complex economic problems cannot be found if these questions are avoided. On the other hand, it is clear that philosophers are also becoming aware of the importance of linking their foundational and theoretical inquiries to an understanding of complex practical problems. Once again, such awareness needs to become more widespread; and such practical inquiries need to be informed by a concern for the entire world, not only for a small group of privileged and developed nations, which are frequently the point of reference for philosophical discussions of distributive justice. The examples in this volume of Finnish and Swedish approaches to the formulation of public policy — in which social scientists examine activities and not just satisfactions, and measure achievements in a plurality of distinct areas of living — point toward the sort of benefit that can be expected for both sides, if economists and philosophers continue and develop further the type of co-operative effort begun in this conference.

Such co-operation is perhaps especially necessary in two areas, on which the conference focused: the area of health, and the area of gender justice. Reflection about the complex decisions public policy must make concerning health, and the distribution of the goods connected with health, reveals the need to think about the whole issue of life quality in a way that goes beyond conventional crude economic measures. The assessment of women's quality of life is an area of special urgency in the developing world. For here, because of the ways in which people's desires can be limited and warped by a lifetime of deprivation and lack of education, so that expectations adjust to substandard living conditions, one frequently sees a very large gap between utility (construed as satisfaction) and a woman's actual ability to function in a variety of important ways. And one also sees the need to press philosophical questions about tradition and cultural relativity, in order to determine whose beliefs and judgements should be the source of the measures to be used by policy-makers. These two issues are the focus of continuing interdisciplinary research at WIDER, which will lead to the production of a further volume on human capabilities and gender justice, and to a research programme on the ethical implications of health policy.

Lal Jayawardena
Director, WIDER
27 August 1990

CONTENTS

LIST OF CONTRIBUTORS

ERIK ALLARDT, President of Finnish Academy, Professor of Sociology
University of Helsinki
Helsinki
Finland

JULIA ANNAS, Professor of Philosophy
Department of Philosophy
Columbia University
New York City
USA

CHRISTOPHER BLISS, Nuffield Reader in International Economics
 of the University of Oxford
Nuffield College
Oxford
England

SISSELA BOK, Professor of Philosophy
Department of Philosophy
Brandeis University
Waltham, MA
USA

DAN BROCK, Professor of Philosophy and Professor of Human Values in Medicine
Department of Philosophy
Brown University
Providence, RI
USA

G. A. COHEN, Chichele Professor of Social and Political Theory at the University of Oxford,
 and Fellow of All Souls College
All Souls College
Oxford
England

ROBERT ERIKSON, Professor of Sociology
SOFI
University of Stockholm
Stockholm
Sweden

WULF GAERTNER, Professor of Economics
Department of Economics
University of Osnabrück
Federal Republic of Germany

JAMES GRIFFIN, Reader in Philosophy at the University of Oxford,
 and Fellow of Keble College
Keble College
Oxford
England

SUSAN HURLEY, University Lecturer and Fellow in Philosophy
St Edmund Hall
Oxford University
Oxford
England

CHRISTINE M. KORSGAARD, Professor of Philosophy and General Studies in the
    Humanities
Department of Philosophy
Harvard University
Cambridge, MA
USA

LORENZ KRÜGER, Professor of Philosophy, University of Göttingen
Göttingen
Federal Republic of Germany

MARTHA C. NUSSBAUM, University Professor and Professor of Philosophy, Classics and
    Comparative Literature
Department of Philosophy
Brown University
Providence, RI
USA

ONORA O'NEILL, Principal
Newnham College
Cambridge
England

SIDDIQ OSMANI, Senior Research Fellow
WIDER
Helsinki
Finland

DEREK PARFIT
All Souls College
Oxford
England

HILARY PUTNAM, Walter Beverley Pearson Professor of Modern Mathematics and
    Mathematical Logic
Department of Philosophy
Harvard University
Cambridge, MA
USA

RUTH ANNA PUTNAM, Professor of Philosophy
Department of Philosophy
Wellesley College
Wellesley, MA 02181
USA

JOHN E. ROEMER, Professor of Economics and Director of the Program on Economy,
    Justice, and Society
Department of Economics
University of California at Davis
Davis, CA
USA

THOMAS SCANLON, Professor of Philosophy
Department of Philosophy
Harvard University
Cambridge MA
USA

PAUL SEABRIGHT
Fellow of Churchill College
Cambridge
England

AMARTYA SEN, Lamont University Professor and Professor of Economics and of
    Philosophy
Harvard University
Cambridge MA
USA

CHARLES TAYLOR, Professor of Political Science and of Philosophy
Department of Political Science
McGill University
Montreal, Quebec
Canada

MARGARITA M. VALDÉS
Institute for Philosophical Research
Universidad Nacional Autonoma de México
Mexico

BERNARD M. S. van PRAAG, Professor of Economics
Faculty of Economic Sciences
Erasmus University of Rotterdam
Rotterdam
The Netherlands

MICHAEL WALZER, Professor at the School of Social Studies
Institute for Advanced Study
Princeton, NJ
USA

BENGT-CHRISTER YSANDER, Professor of Economics
Department of Economics
University of Uppsala
Uppsala
Sweden

Introduction

Martha Nussbaum and Amartya Sen

'And he said, Now, this schoolroom is a Nation. And in this nation, there are fifty millions of money. Isn't this a prosperous nation? Girl number twenty, isn't this a properous nation, and a'n't you in a thriving state?'

'What did you say?' asked Louisa.

'Miss Louisa, I said I didn't know. I thought I couldn't know whether it was a properous nation or not, and whether I was in a thriving state or not, unless I knew who had got the money, and whether any of it was mine. But that had nothing to do with it. It was not in the figures at all,' said Sissy, wiping her eyes.

'That was a great mistake of yours,' observed Louisa.

(Charles Dickens, *Hard Times*)

When we inquire about the prosperity of a nation or a region of the world, and about the quality of life of its inhabitants, Sissy Jupe's problem still arises: How do we determine this? What information do we require? Which criteria are truly relevant to human 'thriving'? Girl number twenty quickly discerns that just knowing how much money is available for a given number of people (the analogue of GNP per capita, still widely used as a measure of quality of life) will not take us very far. For we also need, at the very least, to ask about the distribution of these resources, and what they do to people's lives.

The problem is actually more complex still. For if we are really to know much about the 'thriving' of Sissy Jupe and her fellow citizens, we need to know not only about the money they do or do not have, but a great deal about how they are able to conduct their lives. We need surely to know about their life expectancy (think of the miners of Coketown in Dickens's novel, who keep their families from 'want and hunger', but go to a premature death). We need to know about their health care and their medical services. We need to know about education – and not only about its availability, but about its nature and its quality (it seems likely that Mr Gradgrind's school may actually diminish the 'thriving' of its pupils). We need to know about labour – whether it is rewarding or grindingly monotonous, whether the workers enjoy any measure of dignity and control, whether relations between employers and 'hands' are human or debased. We need to know what political and legal privileges the citizens enjoy, what freedoms they have in the conduct of social and personal relations. We need to know how family relations and relations between the sexes are structured, and how these structures foster or impede other aspects of human activity. We need, perhaps above all, to know how people are enabled by the society in question to imagine, to wonder, to feel emotions such as love and gratitude, that presuppose that life is more than a set of commercial relations, and that the human being – unlike the steam engines of Coketown – is an 'unfathomable mystery', not to be completely 'set forth in tabular form'. In short, to think well about Sissy's problem, we seem to need a kind of rich and complex description of what people are able to do and to be—a description that may be more readily available to the reader of Dickens's novel than to those who confine their reading to the narrowly technical and financial documents favoured by Sissy's teachers.

Economists, policy-makers, social scientists, and philosophers are still faced with this problem of measurement and assessment. They need to know how people are doing in many different parts of the world, and they need to know what is really involved in asking that question. When they face the problem well, they face it, so to speak, with wonder (to use, deliberately, the word least tolerated in Mr Gradgrind's school); with a sense, that is, of the profound complexity of assessing a human life, and with a desire to admit, at least initially, the widest possible range of accounts of how one might go about this, of what indicators one might trust.

Of course, it is possible to wonder not at all—to stick to a mechanical formula that is easy to use and which has been used before. The unasked question does not have to be answered. This volume is an attempt to ask questions and to propose and examine some possible answers. By examining the arguments for and against a variety of different accounts of how to measure quality of life, it aims to generate a more complex understanding of alternative positions and their respective merits. The original motivation for this project lay in our perception that these issues were being debated in several different fields whose communication with one another was unfortunately slight. Most social scientists and economists would agree with Sissy Jupe that GNP per capita is a crude and incomplete measure of quality of life; and yet such measures continue to be widely used when public policy is made. Again, philosophers have for some time been debating the merits of measuring the quality of human life in terms of utility (whether understood as happiness or as the satisfaction of desires or preferences). Some philosophers continue to defend this general approach—though usually with considerable qualification, producing utilitarianisms with complex and subtle restrictions on the nature of the preferences that may be taken into account. Others have concluded that the whole utilitarian approach should be rejected—to be replaced, perhaps, by an account of the many different kinds of activity that actually make up a 'thriving' human life. (Such a programme can take various forms and some of these are explored in the papers by Cohen, Sen, Brock, Scanlon, and Nussbaum.) The philosophical debates have not had much impact on the making of public policy in much of the world; nor have they been particularly noticed in the standard works in economics. Our hope was that by getting the participants in these debates together and encouraging further debate among them, we might advance the state of the question, encourage further co-operative inquiries, and present the debate in a form accessible not only to professionals in these academic disciplines but also to policy-makers and the general public.

Lives and Capabilities

The papers in Part I address the general questions we have already described, examining how we may try to find adequate criteria for assessing the quality of life. Cohen's and Sen's papers both discuss the 'capability approach' presented by Sen, but Cohen also examines a number of other approaches, including, among others, utilitarian calculations, the Rawlsian focus on primary goods, and Dworkin's use of resources. After criticizing these approaches, Cohen argues for concentrating on what he calls 'midfare', which is fairly close to the idea of functionings used in the 'capability' literature.

The life that a person leads can be seen as a combination of various doings and beings, which can be generically called functionings. These functionings vary from such elementary matters as being well nourished and disease-free to more complex doings or beings, such as having self-respect, preserving human dignity, taking part in the life of the community, and so on. The capability of a person refers to the various alternative combinations of functionings, any one of which (any combination, that is) the person can choose to have. In this sense, the capability of a person corresponds to the *freedom* that a person has to lead one kind of life or another. Cohen's paper discusses why one has to go in this direction (rather than staying with the traditional concerns: incomes, utilities, resources, primary goods), but he ends by questioning whether the freedom-type idea of capability is the precisely correct alternative. Sen presents the capability approach and its rationale, and also attempts to answer Cohen's critique (along with a few other criticisms presented elsewhere).

The papers by Erikson and Allardt discuss some methods and strategies for measuring the quality of life that have been used by Scandinavian social scientists for a long time. Their approach has much in common with that of focusing on functionings and capabilities, and the actual measurement techniques used have obvious relevance for the use of the capability approach. The philosophical underpinnings of the capability approach, on the other hand, provide some defence of the Scandinavian practices and also some suggestions for extension. While the Swedish and Finnish approaches differ in some significant respects, they agree in focusing neither on opulence nor on utility, but on the ways in which people are actually able to function, in a variety of areas. And they insist that any adequate measure of quality of life must be a plural measure, recognizing a number of distinct components that are irreducible to one another.

Brock's comprehensive study of measures of quality of life in the area of health care shows, among other things, still another convergence, as doctors and philosophers, looking for the best way to assess the quality of patients' lives, have increasingly turned to a list of functional capabilities, not unlike those proposed in the capability literature and in the theory and practice of Scandinavian social scientists. The field of health care provides a rich ground for comparing, contrasting, and assessing different approaches.

Traditions, Relativism, and Objectivity

When standards are chosen to assess the quality of life of people in different parts of the world, one has to ask whose views as to the criteria should be decisive. Should we, for example, look to the local traditions of the country or region with which we are concerned, asking what these traditions have regarded as most essential to thriving, or should we, instead, seek some more universal account of good human living, assessing the various local traditions against it? This question needs to be approached with considerable sensitivity, and there appear to be serious problems whichever route we take. If we stick to local traditions, this seems to have the advantage of giving us something definite to point to and a clear way of knowing what we want to know (though the plurality and complexity of traditions should not be underestimated, as frequently happens in cultural-relativist accounts). It seems, as well, to promise the advantage of respect for difference: instead of telling people in distant parts of the world what they ought to do and to be, the choice is left to them. On the other hand, most traditions contain elements of injustice and oppression, often deeply rooted; and it is frequently hard to find a basis for criticism of these inequities without thinking about human functioning in a more critical and universal way. (For example, Dickens's criticism of British materialism and class injustice relies centrally on some extended reflections about what a human being is—reflections that, in their socially radical character, would not have been easy to extract from the traditions of English class relations.)

The search for a universally applicable account of the quality of human life has, on its side, the promise of a greater power to stand up for the lives of those whom tradition has oppressed or marginalized. But it faces the epistemological difficulty of grounding such an account in an adequate way, saying where the norms come from and how they can be known to be the best. It faces, too, the ethical danger of paternalism, for it is obvious that all too often such accounts have been insensitive to much that is of worth and value in the lives of people in other parts of the world and have served as an excuse for not looking very deeply into these lives.

The papers in Part II confront this difficult set of questions, exploring arguments about cultural relativism from a variety of viewpoints and showing the bearing of these arguments on questions about the quality of life. Putnam's paper attacks the widely accepted idea that questions of science are matters of fact, and ethical questions, by contrast, are questions in resolving which we can appeal to nothing beyond subjective preferences. He argues that 'fact' in science is a more anthropocentric and 'internal' matter than is frequently realized, and that the very same sort of truth and objectivity that is available in science is available in ethics as well. Walzer, by contrast, defends a qualified form of relativism, in which, however, much attention is paid to the various forms of criticism and discontent that may arise within a society. However inarticulate these dissenting voices may be, they are, he argues, to be taken as important data in understanding what a good life would be for the society as a whole.

Scanlon's paper, closely related to the debate about utility in Part I, questions the adequacy of desire as a measure of quality of life, arguing instead for exploring an approach based on a critical scrutiny of a 'substantive list' of elements that make human life valuable. Taylor examines the forms of reasoning that people use when they argue that one way of life is better for human beings than another. Although such arguments always take place in a particular historical context and do not have the deductive structure that we have come to associate with good scientific argument, they can none the less, he claims, be perfectly reasonable, and can succeed in showing that some ways of doing things are indeed better than others.

Nussbaum examines one major account of the quality of life in terms of a list of basic human functions—Aristotle's—that does claim to have validity for all human beings. She argues that although Aristotle himself did not confront the subtle arguments cultural relativists today might use against his account—for example, the argument that even such basic human experiences as reasoning and desiring are constructed and experienced differently in different societies—his account can still be made to reply convincingly to such objections. (The Aristotelian list of functions converges surprisingly, once again, with the proposals of Sen, Erikson, Allardt, and Brock in Part I, although they emanate from different intellectual traditions.)

Women's Lives and Gender Justice

In no area are there greater problems about measuring quality of life than in the area of women's lives and capabilities. The question of whether utility is an adequate measure and the question of cultural relativism take on a special urgency here. For in most parts of the world women do not have the same opportunities as men. These inequalities—and the deficiencies in education and experience often associated with them—tend to affect women's expectations and desires, since it is difficult to desire what one cannot imagine as a possibility. Desire-based approaches to measuring quality of life frequently end up, for this reason, affirming the status quo, informing us, for example, that the women of country Q have no need of literacy because, when investigated by the authorities of Q, they do not express an unsatisfied desire for literacy. An approach based on a substantive account of human capabilities would ask different questions here, and would probably arrive at a different recommendation. Again, our solution to the problem of cultural relativism will have especially clear implications where women's lives are concerned, for most local traditions oppress women. A universal account of human functioning seems to have greater critical potential here. (Current work in progress at WIDER will press these issues further, attempting to construct a non-relative account of human capabilities in the context of questions about women.)

But as we try to answer such questions, we also need to decide whether the quality of a female life has the same constituents as the quality of a male life. Some respected philosophical answers to this question (for example, that of Jean-Jacques Rousseau), while universalist rather than relativist about the good, have divided humanity into two distinct 'natures', with different norms and goals for each. If Rousseau's Emile were found leading the life that is judged best for his consort Sophie, tending the house and caring for children, Rousseau would judge his quality of life to be low indeed; so too for Sophie, were she to be discovered (*per impossible*, as Rousseau would have it) exercising the virtues of citizen autonomy. Some contemporary feminist writing tends in a similar direction. In Part III, Annas's paper examines this question, defending a single account of human functioning. O'Neill partly concurs, and describes a strategy we might use to judge that a particular practice is unjust to women. She links the question of gender justice to related questions about justice across international boundaries.

Policy Assessment and Welfare Economics

Part IV explores a number of ways in which questions about quality of life arise in welfare economics (broadly defined) and the formation of public policy. Roemer studies the criteria of resource allocation used by the World Health Organization, comparing them with some criteria proposed by economists and philosophers. The axioms implicit in practical policies can be made explicit and then illuminatingly contrasted with rival demands. Van Praag analyses the results of some empirical studies of how people perceive their well-being. He shows that perceptions are highly relative to surrounding social issues.

Seabright examines the problem of living standards in terms of the plural influences that call for accommodation. He explores the connection between contractarian justifications of social theories and pluralist conceptions of the social good.

Finally, Bliss discusses the measurement of the standard of living, arguing (against Sen) that this question should be separated from the broader question of quality of life. He presents, partly by implication, a partial defence of more orthodox measures of living standards, in particular real income, but develops his own line of departure in terms of the concept of 'life-style', the contents and implications of which he investigates extensively.

The contributions of the commentators at the original WIDER conference were, in general, of such a high order that it was decided to publish them along with the papers. Although this introduction has not commented on their contents, they are an integral part of the philosophical and practical debate of which this volume is the outcome.

PART I
LIVES AND CAPABILITIES

Equality of What? On Welfare, Goods, and Capabilities

G. A. Cohen

1 Introduction

In his Tanner Lecture of 1979 called 'Equality of What?' Amartya Sen asked what metric egalitarians should use to establish the extent to which their ideal is realized in a given society. What aspect(s) of a person's condition should count in a *fundamental* way for egalitarians, and not merely as cause of or evidence of or proxy for what they regard as fundamental?

In this study I comment on answers to Sen's question in recent philosophical literature. I take for granted that there is something which justice requires people to have equal amounts of, not no matter what, but to whatever extent is allowed by values which compete with distributive equality; and I describe and criticize what a number of authors who share that egalitarian view have said about the dimension(s) or respect(s) in which people should be made more equal, when the cost in other values of moving towards greater equality is not intolerable.[1]

The publication of John Rawls's *A Theory of Justice* in 1971 was a watershed in discussion bearing on the question, derived from Sen, which forms my title. Before *A Theory of Justice* appeared, political philosophy was dominated by utilitarianism, the theory that sound social policy aims at the maximization of welfare. Rawls found two features of utilitarianism repugnant. He objected, first, to its aggregative character, its unconcern about the pattern of distribution of welfare, which means that inequality in its distribution calls for no justification. But, more pertinently to the present exercise, Rawls also objected to the utilitarian assumption that welfare is the aspect of a person's condition which commands normative attention. Rawls replaced aggregation by equality and welfare by primary goods. He recommended normative evaluation with new arguments (goods instead of welfare quanta) and a new function (equality[2] instead of aggregation) from those arguments to values.

Rawls's critique of the welfare metric was undoubtedly powerful, but, as I

For their excellent criticism of a previous draft of the material in this article, I thank Richard Arneson, John Baker, Gerald Barnes, Will Kymlicka, David Lloyd-Thomas, John McMurtry, Thomas Scanlon, Amartya Sen, and Philippe van Parijs.

[1] I discuss conflict between equality and other values in section 1 of 'On the Currency of Egalitarian Justice', *Ethics*, 99 (July 1989). That article represents part of the contribution which I prepared for the July 1988 Helsinki WIDER symposium on 'The Quality of Life', and the present article is also drawn from that contribution. There is overlap between the articles in that a similar critique of Rawls appears in both. Discussions of Dworkin and Scanlon which appear in the *Ethics* article are not reproduced here.

[2] Or, strictly, the maximin function, which enjoins departures from equality when the worst off benefit as a result. But that complication is of no significance here.

shall argue, his motivation for replacing it by attention to primary goods was not correspondingly cogent. He did not consider, as an alternative to equality of welfare, the claims of equality of opportunity for welfare, which his criticisms of equality of welfare do not touch. What is more, those criticisms positively favour equality of opportunity for welfare as a remedy for the defects in the rejected doctrine.

But while equality of opportunity for welfare survives Rawls's criticisms of equality of welfare, arguments against the welfare metric which were later advanced by Sen also apply against its opportunity-defined cousin. Sen called for attention to something like opportunity (under the title 'capability'[3]), but it was not welfare, or not, at any rate, welfare alone, which Sen thought people should have the opportunity to achieve. Instead, he drew attention to the condition of a person (e.g. his level of nutrition) in a central sense captured neither by his stock of goods (e.g. his food supply) nor by his welfare level (e.g. the pleasure or desire satisfaction he obtains from consuming food). In advancing beyond Rawls, Sen therefore proposed two large changes of view: from actual state to opportunity, and from goods (and welfare) to what he sometimes called 'functionings'.

In my view, Sen's answer to his own question was a great leap forward in contemporary reflection on the subject. But often a thinker who achieves a revolution misdescribes his own achievement, and I shall argue, at some length, that Sen's work is a case in point. He moved away from Rawlsian and other views in two directions which were orthogonal to each other. If Rawls and welfarists fixed on what a person gets in welfare or goods, Sen fixed on what he gets in a space between welfare and goods (nutrition is delivered by goods supply and it generates welfare), but he also emphasized what a person *can* get, as opposed to (just) what he *does*. Sen's misdescription of his achievement lay in his appropriation of the word 'capability' to describe both of his moves, so that his position, as he presented it, is disfigured by ambiguity. I shall here expose the ambiguity in Sen's use of 'capability' (and cognate terms), and I shall also propose an answer to his (my title) question which departs from his own in a modest way.

2 Rawlsian Criticism of Equality of Welfare

Before examining Rawls's critique of equality of welfare, a word about what will here be meant by 'welfare'. Of the many readings of 'welfare' alive (if not well) in economics and philosophy, the present inquiry recruits two: welfare as enjoyment, or, more broadly, as desirable or agreeable state of consciousness, which

---

[3] Immediately after introducing the notion of '*capability* to function' in the Dewey Lectures, Sen shifts to the alternative language of 'opportunity' to express the same idea. See 'Well-Being, Agency and Freedom: The Dewey Lectures 1984', *Journal of Philosophy*, 82 (April 1985), 200–1. Cf. *Commodities and Capabilities* (Amsterdam, 1985), 59; *The Standard of Living* (Cambridge, 1987), 36.

I shall call *hedonic welfare*; and welfare as *preference satisfaction*, where preferences order states of the world, and where a person's preference is satisfied if a relevant state of the world obtains, whether or not he knows that it does.[4] It will sometimes be necessary to say which of those two I mean by 'welfare', but not always. Often the debates on which I comment have a similar shape under either interpretation of welfare, so that I shall have both in mind (by which I do not mean some amalgam of the two) at once. Unless I indicate otherwise, my contentions are meant to hold under either of the two readings of 'welfare' that I have just distinguished.

Rawls advances two objections to equality of welfare, and they apply against both its hedonic and its preference interpretations. I shall call his objections the 'offensive tastes' and 'expensive tastes' criticisms. I believe that each criticism can be accommodated by a welfare egalitarian through a natural modification of his original view. In the case of the offensive tastes criticism, that would probably be conceded by Rawls (and by Ronald Dworkin, who develops the criticism more systematically and at some length[5]). But the second criticism is supposed by Rawls and Dworkin to justify an abandonment of the terrain of welfare altogether; as I shall indicate, I do not think that it does. The second criticism also creates a problem for Rawls's system, which I shall describe in a brief digression.

Rawls adverts to offensive tastes in the course of his critique of utilitarianism, but, as Amartya Sen notes,[6] he is at that point really criticizing welfarism as such, where welfarism is the view that just distribution is some or other function of nothing but the welfares of individuals. It follows logically that the offensive tastes criticism also applies against a conception of justice in which equality of welfare is the only principle. And although a believer in equality of welfare who also affirms further principles need not be a welfarist other than with respect to the metric of equality in particular, it is extremely unlikely that a good criticism of welfarism proper will not also apply to that restricted welfarism which acknowledges the relevance of no information but welfare in the context of

---

[4] These two readings of welfare correspond to Sen's 'happiness' and 'desire fulfilment' readings and exclude his 'choice' reading: see 'Well-Being, Agency and Freedom', 187 ff. It is reasonable to ignore the 'choice' reading, since, as Sen shows, it reflects confusion about the relationship between preference and choice. My two readings also correspond to Ronald Dworkin's 'conscious state' and 'relative success' conceptions: see 'Equality of Welfare', *Philosophy and Public Affairs*, 10 (Summer 1981), 191–4, 204–9, 220–1. I do not consider welfare as 'overall success' (ibid., 209 ff.) because it is very hard to handle, and in any case it is, arguably, undermotivated: see my 'On the Currency of Egalitarian Justice', n. 34. I also set aside so-called 'objective theories of welfare' (Dworkin, 'Equality of Welfare', 224–6), since most philosophers would consider them alternatives to any sort of welfare theory: Thomas Scanlon, for whom welfare is preference satisfaction, would describe his theory as anti-welfarist, yet it is an objective theory of welfare in Dworkin's sense. Finally, to mention an author whose work is salient in this study, Richard Arneson has the same understanding of welfare as Scanlon and Rawls has not specified a particular conception – which is not to say that he should have done.

[5] See 'Equality of Welfare', 197–201.

[6] 'Equality of What?' in S. McMurrin (ed.), *Tanner Lectures on Human Values* i (Cambridge, 1980), 211.

equality, even if its proponent admits non-welfare information elsewhere. In any case, the offensive tastes criticism strikes me as powerful against the welfare-egalitarian claim, whether or not other claims are conjoined with it.

The offensive tastes criticism of welfarism is that the pleasure a person takes in discriminating against other people or in subjecting others to a lesser liberty should not count equally with other satisfactions in the calculus of justice.[7] From the point of view of justice, such pleasures deserve condemnation, and the corresponding preferences have no claim to be satisfied, even if they would have to be satisfied for welfare equality to prevail. I believe that this objection defeats welfarism, and hence equality of welfare. But the natural course for a welfare egalitarian to take in response to the offensive tastes criticism is to shift his favour to something like equality of *inoffensive* welfare. The criticism does not seem to necessitate abandoning equality of welfare in a more fundamental way.[8]

The 'expensive tastes' criticism *is* thought to necessitate such an abandonment. It occurs in the context of Rawls's advocacy of primary goods as the appropriate thing to equalize. Now the phrase 'primary goods' covers a set of different things in Rawls,[9] but for our purposes, we can, as Rawls does in the texts I shall quote, take it narrowly, as referring to goods in the economist's sense, or the power to purchase them.

Prosecuting his case against welfare and for primary goods, Rawls asks us to 'imagine two persons, one satisfied with a diet of milk, bread and beans, while the other is distraught without expensive wines and exotic dishes. In short one has expensive tastes, the other does not.' A welfare egalitarian must, *ceteris paribus*, provide the epicure with a higher income than the person of modest tastes, since otherwise the latter might be satisfied while the former is distraught. But Rawls argues powerfully against this implication of the welfare egalitarian principle:

as moral persons citizens have some part in forming and cultivating their final ends and preferences. It is not by itself an objection to the use of primary goods that it does not accommodate those with expensive tastes. One must argue in addition that it is unreasonable, if not unjust, to hold such persons responsible for their preferences and to require them to make out as best they can. But to argue this seems to presuppose that citizens' preferences are beyond their control as propensities or cravings which simply happen. Citizens seem to be regarded as passive carriers of desires. The use of primary goods . . . relies on a capacity to assume responsibility for our ends.

People with expensive tastes could have chosen otherwise, and if and when they

[7] *A Theory of Justice* (Cambridge, Mass., 1971), 30-1.

[8] In fairness to Rawls, one should recall that he presented the offensive tastes criticism as an objection not to equality of welfare but to utilitarianism, and for utilitarians a move to 'inoffensive welfare' would no doubt constitute a pretty fundamental shift. From the fact that the same criticism applies against both views, and that each should be revised in the same way in the face of it, it does not follow that the distance between the original and the revised view is the same in both cases.

[9] See *A Theory of Justice*, 62.

press for compensation, then others are entitled to insist that they themselves bear the cost of 'their lack of foresight or self-discipline'.[10]

I believe that this objection defeats welfare egalitarianism but that it does not, as Rawls supposes, also vindicate the claims of the primary goods metric. The right way for an erstwhile welfare egalitarian to respond to the objection seems to me to be the following: 'To the extent that people are indeed responsible for their tastes, the relevant welfare deficits do not command the attention of justice. We should therefore compensate only for those welfare deficits which are not appropriately traceable to the individual's choices. We should replace equality of welfare by equality of opportunity for welfare. It would be utterly unjustified to adopt a primary goods metric because of the expensive tastes counter-example.'

Equality of opportunity for welfare,[11] unlike equality of welfare, permits and indeed enjoins departures from welfare equality when they reflect the choices of relevant agents, as opposed to deficient *opportunity* for welfare. If a person's welfare is low because he freely risked a welfare loss in gambling for a welfare gain, then, under the opportunity form of the principle, he has no claim to compensation. Nor has a person who frittered away welfare opportunities which others seized. Nor, to take a different kind of example, has a person who chose to forgo welfare out of devotion to an ideal which (expressly, or merely as it happened) required self-denial. A person like Rawls's epicure who, *ex hypothesi*, could have controlled himself and maintained more austere tastes, has, in consequence, no grievance at the bar of equality of opportunity for welfare if his actual welfare is substandard because his tastes are expensive. The eligibility of equality of opportunity for welfare as a reply to Rawls shows that his conviction that the reasons he gives for rejecting equality of welfare are also reasons for affirming equality of primary goods is misplaced.

Before leaving Rawls, I want to indicate a serious problem for his political philosophy which his remarks about expensive tastes raise. The problem would be less interesting than it is in fact were it merely a problem in the Rawlsian architectonic and not also expressive of a general tension in left–egalitarian thinking.

The problem, as it appears in Rawls, is that the picture of the individual as

---

[10] 'Social Unity and Primary Goods', in A. K. Sen and B. Williams (eds.), *Utilitarianism and Beyond* (Cambridge, 1982), 168–9. Cf. 'Fairness to Goodness', *Philosophical Review*, 84 (April 1975), 553; 'Justice as Fairness, Political not Metaphysical', *Philosophy and Public Affairs*, 14 (Summer 1985), 243–4. For a somewhat different explanation of why justice ignores expensive tastes, with less (not no) emphasis on the idea that they are subject to the agent's control and more on the idea that it is appropriate to hold him accountable for them, see the reply to Arrow in Rawls's unpublished 'Citizens' Needs and Primary Goods'.

For interesting comment on and sympathetic development of Rawls's views on responsibility for preference, see Bruce Landesman, 'Egalitarianism', *Canadian Journal of Philosophy*, 13 (March 1983), 37.

[11] For an elegant exposition and defence of equality of opportunity for welfare, in its preference interpretation, see Richard Arneson, 'Equality and Equality of Opportunity for Welfare', *Philosophical Studies*, 56 (1989).

responsibly guiding his own taste formation is hard to reconcile with claims Rawls uses elsewhere in a fundamental way to support his egalitarianism. These claims, which are quite standard on the left, express scepticism about special effort as a ground for rewarding people unequally. Here is how Rawls formulates this fairly familiar scepticism:

the effort a person is willing to make is influenced by his natural abilities and skills and the alternatives open to him. The better endowed are more likely, other things equal, to strive conscientiously, and there seems to be no way to discount for their greater good fortune. The idea of rewarding desert is impracticable.[12]

Now there are two ways of taking this passage. One way is as I think Rawls intended it, and the other is as Robert Nozick took it, and on the basis of which he directed strong criticism against Rawls. Nozick, I am sure, misread the passage, but his misreading of it constitutes a correct reading of what many socialists and egalitarians say about effort, so it will be worth our while to pause here, to attend to Nozick's criticism. On either reading of the passage, it is hard to reconcile with what Rawls says about foresight, self-discipline, and expensive tastes. But I shall come to that point in a moment, for the passage can also be criticized independently, and I want to do that first.

The two readings of the passage divide with respect to how they take the word 'influenced' in Rawls's use of it here. On my reading of it, it means 'influenced', that is, 'affected, but not necessarily wholly determined'. On Nozick's reading of the passage, 'influenced' means something like 'wholly determined'. There is a difficulty for Rawls whichever way we take the passage, but not the same difficulty in each case.

On my reading of Rawls, in which he means 'influenced' by 'influenced', he does not say that those who make a lot of effort have no control over, and therefore deserve no credit for, the amount of effort they put in. His different point is that we cannot reckon the extent to which their above-par effort is attributable not to admirable striving but to 'greater good fortune': there is no 'way to discount' for the latter. That is a practical objection to trying to reward effort that deserves reward, not a claim that there is no such effort: see the final sentence of the passage.

If Rawls is right that not all effort is deserving, then, we might agree, not all effort deserves reward. But why should it follow that effort deserves no reward at all? The practical difficulty of telling how much of it merits reward hardly justifies rewarding it at a rate of 0 per cent, as opposed to at a rate of somewhere between 0 and 100 per cent, for example through a taxation scheme whose shape and justification escapes, because of its deference to effort, the writ of the Difference Principle. (To be sure, it is hard to tell how much effort a person supplies, but Rawls's claim is not that total effort is indiscernible, but that we cannot identify the contribution to effort of fortunate endowment.)

---

[12] *A Theory of Justice*, 312.

But that criticism of Rawls is mild by comparison with the one to which he is exposed on Nozick's reading of his remarks. The plausibility of that reading is enhanced by Nozick's careless or mischievous omission of what follows 'conscientiously' when he exhibits the *Theory of Justice* passage quoted above. Nozick thereby creates the impression that Rawls is presenting a familiar egalitarian determinist doctrine. Nozick's response to that doctrine is very powerful:

So denigrating a person's autonomy and prime responsibility for his actions is a risky line to take for a theory that otherwise wishes to buttress the dignity and self-respect of autonomous beings . . . One doubts that the unexalted picture of human beings Rawls' theory presupposes and rests upon can be made to fit together with the view of human dignity it is designed to lead to and embody.[13]

Nozick is pressing a dilemma: either people have real freedom of choice, in which case they may be credited (at least to some extent) with the fruits of their labours; or there is no such thing as free choice, in which case liberals should take the purple out of the passages in which they set forth their conception of humanity, and – we can add – socialists should stop painting inspiring pictures of the human future (unless they believe that people lack free will under capitalism but will get it after the revolution).

On Nozick's reading of the 'effort' passage, it is clearly inconsistent with the responsibility for taste formation with which Rawls credits citizens. That does not matter too much, since Nozick's reading is a misreading. But it is not easy to reconcile what Rawls says about effort with what he says about tastes, even on my less creative reading of his text. On my reading of it, effort is partly praiseworthy and partly not, but we cannot separate the parts, and the indicated policy consequence is to ignore effort as a claim to reward. Now, the passage about tastes begins with the thought that 'citizens have *some* part in forming and cultivating their final ends and preferences', though it ends by assigning a more wholesale responsibility for preferences to citizens. If we stay with the opening thought, then we can wonder why partial responsibility for effort attracts no reward at all while (merely) partial responsibility for expensive taste formation attracts a full penalty (and those who keep their tastes modest reap a welfare reward). And if we shift to the wholesale responsibility motif, then we can wonder why beings who are only in a limited way responsible for the effort they put in may be held wholly responsible for how their tastes develop.

The most natural view about these matters is that people are partly responsible and partly not, both for how much effort they put into production and for whether or not they develop expensive tastes.[14] This does not mean that it is easy to tell where responsibility begins and ends or, consequently, what the dictate of distributive justice is in particular instances – but there is no antecedent

---

[13] *Anarchy, State and Utopia* (New York, 1974), 214.
[14] I press that natural view against Dworkin's development of the theme of expensive tastes (see 'Equality of Welfare', 228–40) in section IV of 'On the Currency of Egalitarian Justice'.

reason whatsoever for supposing that judgements about justice, at a fine-grained degree of resolution, are easy.

3 Sen and Capability

a. The foregoing critique of Rawls does not prove that quantity of primary goods is the wrong metric for egalitarian evaluation; it just proves that a major reason Rawls offered for favouring primary goods points, instead, to equality of opportunity for welfare. For a more thorough refutation of the primary goods proposal, I turn to Sen's 'Equality of What?' That seminal article also argues persuasively against the welfare metric, and, while Sen did not address equality of opportunity for welfare, his argument against equality of welfare readily extends itself to the former view. After presenting and endorsing Sen's negative arguments, I shall argue that his positive replacing proposal, capability equality, suffers from a severe expositional obscurity.

Sen's argument against the primary goods metric was simple but powerful. It was that differently constructed and situated people require different amounts of primary goods to satisfy the same needs, so that 'judging advantage in terms of primary goods leads to a partially blind morality'.[15] It is, Sen rightly said, a 'fetishist handicap' to be concerned with goods as such, to the exclusion of what goods '*do* to human beings'.[16] Or, as Sen later expressed the point: 'what people get out of goods depends on a variety of factors, and judging personal advantage just by the size of personal ownership of goods and services can be very misleading . . . It seems reasonable to move away from a focus on goods as such to what goods do to human beings'.[17] The principle of equality condemns equal goods provision to a sound-limbed person and a paraplegic, because greater resources are necessary to enable the latter to achieve mobility, a desideratum to which a metric of stock of wealth is blind.[18]

Sen also used the example of the needy cripple to good effect against the welfare alternative to primary goods. For the egalitarian response to his plight is not determined by a judgement that he suffers a welfare deficiency. Perhaps, indeed, he suffers no such thing, 'because he has a jolly disposition. Or because he has a low aspiration level and his heart leaps up whenever he sees a rainbow in the sky.'[19] So while both hedonic and preference-satisfaction welfarists are free of the goods theorist's fetishistic neglect of what goods do to human beings, Sen criticized them for their too-narrow view of what people get from goods, for focusing 'not on the person's capabilities but on his mental reaction', not, for example, on how much nourishment a person gets from food, but on how much

[15] 'Equality of What?' 216.
[16] Ibid., 218; see also 'Ethical Issues in Income Distribution', in *Resources, Values and Development* (Oxford, 1984), 294; *Commodities and Capabilities*, 23; *The Standard of Living*, 15–16, 22.
[17] 'Introduction', in *Choice, Welfare and Measurement* (Oxford, 1982), 29–30.
[18] 'Equality of What?' 218.
[19] Ibid., 217.

utility, which is a matter of mental reaction or attitude, he derives from such nourishment.[20] Utility is an unsuitable guide to policy, if only because a person may adjust his expectations to his condition. The fact that a person has learned to live with adversity, and to smile courageously in the face of it, should not nullify his claim to compensation.[21]

His high welfare score is thus not a decisive reason for not assisting someone who labours under a severe disadvantage, which is recognizable as such from an objective point of view. His equanimity may, after all, reflect admirable and reward-worthy striving to overcome a natural reaction of misery. But even if no such striving is necessary, because the person is blessed from birth with an extra-sunny disposition, the requirement of compensation retains intuitive force. And that means that not only equality of welfare but also equality of opportunity for welfare falls before the case of the cripple. Consider the poor and lame but sunny-spirited Tiny Tim. Tiny Tim is *actually* happy, by any welfarist standard. And we may also suppose that, because of a fortunate innate disposition, he is blessed with abundant *opportunity* for happiness, that he need not do much to get a lot of it. Yet egalitarians would not on that account strike him off the list of free wheelchair receivers. Hence they do not think that wheelchair distribution should be controlled exclusively by the welfare opportunity requirements of those who need them. They need wheelchairs to be adequately resourced, whether or not they also need them to be, or to be capable of being, happy.

b. In the course of making the critical points reported and endorsed above, Sen used the term 'capability', and he appropriated that term to denote his own positive counter-proposal. I shall now argue that, in 'Equality of What?', Sen brought two distinct aspects of a person's condition under that single name, and that this unnoticed duality has persisted in his subsequent writings. Both aspects, or dimensions of assessment, should attract egalitarian interest, but one of them is not felicitously described as 'capability'. The identification of that latter dimension constitutes a particularly striking contribution to normative understanding, but just that dimension is hard to perceive in Sen's exposition, because of the unfortunate and ambiguous nomenclature.

As we have seen, Sen arrived at what he called 'capability' through reflection on the main candidates for assessment of well-being that were in the field when he gave his 1979 lecture, to wit, utility, or welfare, and Rawlsian primary goods.[22] Sen pleaded for a metric of well-being which measured something

---

[20] Ibid., 218. 'Mental reaction' must here cover not only a kind of experience but also a subjective valuation, to cater for the preference form of welfarism.

[21] See, for further development of this point, *Commodities and Capabilities*, 21–2, 29; 'Introduction' in *Resources, Values and Development*, 34; 'Rights and Capabilities', in ibid., 308–9; 'Goods and People', in ibid., 512; *The Standard of Living*, 8–11.

[22] A notable further candidate not yet then in print is Dworkin's equality of resources. It would be a worthwhile – and difficult – exercise to distinguish each of the two Sen dimensions I shall describe from the Dworkin resources dimension. (For pertinent remarks, see Sen's excellent rebuttal, all of which strikes me as correct, of Dworkin's criticism of Sen's view: 'Rights and Capabilities', 321–3.)

falling *between* primary goods and utility, in a sense that will presently be explained—a something which had, amazingly, been largely neglected in previous literature. He called that something 'capability': 'what is missing in all this framework[23] is some notion of "basic capabilities": a person being able to do certain basic things'.[24] But that characterization of the missing dimension was different from another which Sen offered in the same text, and which was more in keeping with his *argument* for the new perspective.

According to that argument, as we have seen, it is necessary to attend to what goods do to (or for) human beings, in abstraction from the utility they confer on them. But to call what goods supply to human beings 'capability' was a mistake. For even when utility has been set aside, it is not true that all that goods do for people is confer capability on them—provide them, that is, with the capacity to do things—or that that is the uniquely important thing they do for them, or that that is the one thing they do for them that matters from an egalitarian point of view. In naming his view 'Basic Capability Equality' Sen failed to delineate the true shape and size of one of the dimensions he had uncovered, and which I shall now try to describe.

It is indeed false that the whole relevant effect on a person of his bundle of primary goods is on, or in virtue of, his mental reaction to what they do for him. There is also what welfarists ignore: what they do for him, what he gets out of them, apart from his mental reaction to or personal evaluation of that service. I shall call that non-utility effect of goods *midfare*, because it is in a certain sense midway between goods and utility. Midfare is constituted of states of the person produced by goods, states in virtue of which utility levels take the values they do. It is 'posterior' to 'having goods' and 'prior' to 'having utility'.[25]

Midfare is a heterogeneous collocation, because goods do categorially various things for people: (1) they endow them with capabilities properly so called, which they may or may not use; (2) through people's exercise of those capabilities, goods contribute to the performance of valuable activities *and* the achievement of desirable states; and (3) goods cause further desirable states directly, without any exercise of capability on the part of their beneficiary: an example would be the goods which destroy the insects that cause malaria. Capability (properly so called) is, then, a part of midfare, for it certainly cannot be excluded from the range of things that goods confer on people, yet, equally certainly, it does not exhaust that range.

Each terminus of the goods–midfare–utility sequence has seemed to some the right focus for assessment of a person's situation from an egalitarian point of view. Rawlsians look at the beginning of the sequence and welfarists look at

---

[23] That is, the framework of discussion restricted to the rival claims of primary goods and utility as measures of well-being, and, within 'primary goods', to goods in the ordinary sense. It is that subset of primary goods which is pertinent here.

[24] 'Equality of What?' 218.

[25] *Commodities and Capabilities*, 11. Midfare is the '*state* of a person' in the sense of ibid., 23.

its end. Welfarists think that the Rawlsian measure is too objective, that it takes too little account of distinguishing facts about individuals. Rawlsians think that the welfare measure is too subjective, that it takes too much account of just such facts. The reasons each side gives for disparaging its opponent's dimension suggest that each should prefer midfare to the dimension favoured by its opponent. Welfarists draw attention to utility because, so they say, people do not care about goods as such but about the utility they provide. But, since people also care more about midfare than about goods as such (save where they are *themselves* being fetishistic), the welfarist reason for preferring welfare to goods is also a reason for preferring midfare to the latter. Advocates of goods oppose the welfare metric because, they say, the welfare consequences of goods consumption are (1) too subject to volition (Rawls, sometimes[26]), (2) too much a matter of people's (not necessarily chosen) identifications (Rawls at other times,[27] Dworkin[28]), or (3) too idiosyncratic (Scanlon[29]). On all three grounds midfare arguably scores better than utility does.

Given that each side in the foregoing division has reason to prefer the midfare dimension to the one favoured by its opponents, it is extraordinary that midfare had not been uncovered, and Sen's reorienting proposal was consequently profound and liberating, albeit remarkably simple. For it simply says that, in the enterprise of assessing a person's well-being, we must look to her condition in abstraction from its utility for her. We must look, for example, at her nutrition level, and not just, as Rawlsians do, at her food supply, or, as welfarists do, at the utility she gets out of eating food.[30]

But this significant and illuminating reorientation is not equivalent to focusing on a person's capability, in any ordinary sense. Capability, and exercises of capability, form only one part of the intermediate midfare state. *What goods do to people is identical neither with what people are able to do with them nor with what they actually do with them* (and it is also not identical with all or part of the combination of these two things). To be sure, it is usually true that a person must do something with a good (take it in, put it on, go inside it, etc.) in order to be benefited by it, but that is not always true, and, even where it is true, one must distinguish what the good does *for* the person from what he does *with* it. The colloquial question 'How are you doing?' can be used to ask after a person's midfare (especially when this pedantic rider is attached to it: 'by which I do not mean how do you feel about how you are doing'), but the usual answer will not be (just) a list of capacities, activities, and results of activities, because not all midfare is capability or an exercise of capability or a result of

[26] See pp. 12–13 above.

[27] See the reference to 'Citizens' Needs and Primary Goods' in n. 10 above.

[28] See 'Equality of Welfare', 228–40; 'Equality of Resources', *Philosophy and Public Affairs*, 10 (Fall 1981), 302–3, and, for criticism of the latter, see section IIIc of my 'On the Currency of Egalitarian Justice'.

[29] See his 'Preference and Urgency', *Journal of Philosophy*, 72 (Nov. 1975), 659–66, and see section Vb of my 'On the Currency of Egalitarian Justice' for criticism of Scanlon's idiosyncrasy claim.

[30] 'Introduction' in *Choice, Welfare and Measurement*, 30.

exercising capability. And many midfare states which are indeed a result of exercising capability have a (non-utility) value which is unconnected with their status as effects of exercising capability, and which is not clearly exhibited in its true independence of capability by Sen.

The case of food, which has, of course, exercised Sen a great deal, illustrates my claims. The main good thing that food does for people is that it nourishes them. Typically, of course, people become nourished by nourishing or feeding themselves, by exercising the capability of nourishing themselves which ownership of food confers on them. But the fact that food gives a person the capability to nourish himself is not the same fact as (and is usually less important than) the fact that it enables him to be nourished. To say that food enables him to be nourished is to say that it makes it possible for him to be nourished. That he characteristically actualizes that possibility himself is a further (and usually less important) fact. When, moreover, we ask how well nourished a person is, we are not asking how well he has nourished himself, even though the answer to the two questions will usually be the same; and we are usually primarily interested in the answer to the first question.[31]

The difference between midfare and capability (properly so called) will perhaps become more evident if we reflect a little about small babies. Small babies do not sustain themselves through exercises of capability. But it is false that, in the case of babies, goods generate utility and nothing else worth mentioning. When food is assigned for the consumption of either a baby or an adult, each is enabled to be nourished. The fact that only the adult is able to nourish himself does not mean that he alone gets midfare. The baby gets it too. Hence midfare, the product of goods which, in turn, generates utility, is not co-extensive with capability, and 'capability' is therefore a bad name for midfare.

If food does not make my case strongly enough, since babies do suck and chew, think instead of clothes. No collaboration on the baby's part is needed when its parent confers the midfare of warmth and protection on it by dressing it. Or consider the midfare supplied by the nutriment in a hospital drip, to baby and adult alike, or, for that matter, by the rays of the sun. There is no relevant exercise of capability by benefited agents in these instances, but there is an important benefit to be described in non-welfarist—midfare—terms. Hence the concept of capability is insufficiently general to capture one of the things that Sen wants to identify.

There are two powerful motivations for pointing to something other than either goods or utility when concerning oneself with egalitarian policy, but the motivations point at different things. There is good reason to look at what a

---

[31] In one place ('Goods and People', 510), Sen makes one of the distinctions on which I am insisting: 'while goods and services are valuable, they are not valuable in themselves. Their value rests on what they can do for people, or rather, what people can do with these goods and services.' But why does Sen here reject his first and, in my view, superior suggestion in favour of the second? Because, I suggest, of an interest in advocating freedom, which is a desideratum different from midfare: see subsection *d* below.

person *can* achieve, independently of his actual state; *and* there is good reason not to reduce the evaluation of that *actual* state either to an examination of his stock of resources or to an assessment of his utility level. But these are distinct points, and the language of capability felicitously covers the first one only.

The ambiguity I have tried to expose appears in a number of Sen's dictions, including the apparently harmless phrase 'what people get out of goods'.[32] On one reading of it, under which 'get out of' means (roughly) 'extract', getting things out of goods represents an exercise of capability. But 'get out of' can also mean, more passively, 'receive from', and it does not require capability to get things out of goods in that sense. Goods (and welfare) theorists ignore (some of) what people get out of goods in both senses of the phrase, but while only the first sense relates to capability, the second denotes something at least as important.

c. In Sen's discourse, to have a capability is to be capable of achieving a range of what he calls 'functionings'. But Sen characterizes functionings differently at different times, and thereby adds further imprecision to the presentation of his view.

Sometimes, in keeping with the ordinary meaning of 'functioning', and in line with Sen's original gloss on 'capability' as 'being able to *do* certain basic things',[33] a functioning is by definition an activity, something that a person does.[34] The questions 'Can they read and write? Can they take part in the life of the community?'[35] inquire into people's functionings in this familiar sense of the term. But at other times, functionings are not by definition activities but all (desirable) states of persons, and 'being well nourished', 'being free from malaria', and 'being free from avoidable morbidity'[36] are consequently entered as examples of functionings, although, not being activities, they are not functionings in the ordinary sense of the term. (Even though 'I am free from malaria now' can be part of the answer to the question 'How are you doing?' in its colloquial use.)

When Sen writes that 'Functionings are . . . personal features; they tell us what a person is doing',[37] he places his incompatible broad and narrow definitions of 'functioning' on either side of the semi-colon. For not all personal features, and not all of the personal features that Sen wishes to encompass, are things that a person is doing. Unlike reading and writing, being free from malaria is not something that one does. Elsewhere, a broader definition of 'functionings'

---

[32] See p. 16 above, text to n. 17.

[33] 'Equality of What?', 218 (italics added).

[34] ' "Functionings" are what the person succeeds in *doing* with the commodities . . . at his or her command' (*Commodities and Capabilities*, 10).

[35] 'The Living Standard', *Oxford Economic Papers*, 6 (1984), 84.

[36] Ibid., 84, and see 'Well-Being, Agency and Freedom', 197. These examples fall under the characterization of functionings as 'activities . . . or states of existence or being' (ibid., 197). (In one place, Sen describes 'being well nourished' not as a functioning but as a capability, but that is probably a slip: see *The Standard of Living*, 18).

[37] 'Rights and Capabilities', 317.

is offered, under which 'they tell us what the person is doing or achieving',[38] and it is true that being free from malaria is something that one *may* achieve. But it is surely of supreme (midfare) importance even when one cannot be credited with achieving it.

Sen himself notes that being free from malaria may be entirely due to 'anti-epidemic public policy'.[39] What he fails to note is the consequent impropriety of regarding it, in that instance, as something the person achieves, as the exercise of a capability of any kind. Yet Sen would surely not want to exclude hetero-nomously obtained freedom from malaria from the balance sheet of how a person 'is doing'. *And that proves that he has a concern to promote forms of midfare which does not derive from his concern to promote the claims of capability as such.* Indeed, one may go further: the lacks in people's lives which Sen is *most* concerned to draw to our attention are midfare lacks which are not lacks in capability proper, and the alleviation of which need not always proceed through an enhancement of the sufferer's capability. He is concerned with people who are 'ill-fed, undernourished, unsheltered and ill',[40] who lack 'basic clothing, ability to be housed and sheltered, etc.'[41] Being able to be housed is not the same thing as being able to house oneself. Entitlements to goods make desirable states possible for people. They generally realize these possibilities themselves, by exercising a capability to do so. But, with respect to the lacks which most exercise Sen, it is the possibilities that matter, and the corresponding capabilities matter only derivatively.

At one point[42] Sen extols the importance of 'a person's ability to function without nutritional deficiency' and of 'the capability of avoiding nutritional deficiency'. Such functionings and avoidings are genuine activities,[43] but the generative desideratum here is not activity but simply lack of nutritional deficiency, the fundamental desirability of which is lost in these athletic phrasings. It is not hitting the nail on the head to say that food is desirable because it enables a person to avoid nutritional deficiency, as though performing that activity is the (one) important thing here. Decent living space, to change the example, is a primary good which helps to maintain a person in good health, and it often does that when it would be false to say that it helps him to maintain himself in good health. Whether he is doing that is an exquisitely subtle question, a negative answer to which is consistent with decent living space delivering its hygienic boon. More generally, the 'kind of life I am living' cannot be identified

---

38 'The Living Standard', 84.

39 *Commodities and Capabilities*, 16.

40 Ibid., 21.

41 Ibid., 73.

42 I am embarrassed to say that I have lost my record of where these phrases occur.

43 The *ability* to function without nutritional deficiency is trickier. I have that ability if and only if there is something I am able to do and I lack nutritional deficiency. But, in general, the characteriza-tion of the result as an ability is owing to the first clause in that statement of necessary and sufficient conditions, rather than to my nutritional good order.

with what I am 'succeeding in "doing" or "being"',[44] unless we put scare-quotes around 'succeeding' as well. There are many benefits I get which I do not literally succeed in getting.

It is true that the better nourished I am, the larger is the number of valuable activities of which I shall be capable. But that capability, the important capability which food confers, is a *result* of eating it. It is not the Sen capability associated with food, which is a capability to *use* food to achieve various 'functionings': being nourished, conducting a ceremonial, entertaining friends.[45] One cannot infer from the central place in life—and midfare—of action and capacity that capability spreads across the entire space of midfare. And, as we have seen, not everything which merits attention under the broad midfare construal of Sen's contention is an activity or achievement.

We may conclude that, while Sen's focus on what goods do for people apart from the mental reaction they induce is original and illuminating, it is unnecessarily narrowed when the object of the focus is described in functioning/ capability language. Comprehending as it does everything which 'goods do for people',[46] midfare cannot be identified either with capability or with what Sen calls 'functioning', nor can it be factored into the two without a confusing stretching of the meanings of words.

d. Why did Sen use the language of capability and functioning to express claims which that language fits quite imperfectly? Because, I hypothesize, he had something in addition to midfare in mind, to wit, freedom, and he wrongly thought that attending to a person's midfare—to what he gets from goods apart from the utility upshot of getting it—is attending to how much freedom he has in the world. Both the misrepresentation of all desirable states as a result of the exercise of capability and the tendency to represent all desirable states as activities reflect an interest in freedom distinct from, but not clearly distinguished by Sen from, the move from both utility and goods to midfare.

There is a case for installing the notion of freedom within egalitarian discourse, but that is a different exercise from vindicating the claims of midfare as such. There are *two* powerful motivations for pointing to something other than either goods or utility in a comprehensive characterization of well-being, but the motivations justify two distinguishable deviations from each of those metrics: possession of goods and enjoyment or utility are not the only actual states that matter,

---

[44] *Commodities and Capabilities*, 28. Cf. ibid., 51, where 'well-being' is described as depending on 'the particular achievements of the person—the kind of "being" he or she succeeds in having'. This is entirely implausible when 'achievements' and 'succeeds' are taken literally, and (see subsection *d* below) Sen has a reason to want their literal meanings to resonate.

[45] At one point Sen writes that 'the essence of the capabilities approach is to see commodity *consumption* as no more than a means to generating capabilities' ('Goods and People', 522 (italics added), but that is either an aberration or an unsignalled change of doctrine. For elsewhere commodity *entitlement* generates capability, which is the power to use or consume the commodity in a variety of ways, each of which uses is a functioning. In the different conceptualization just quoted, capability is a consequence of what elsewhere is called a 'functioning'.

[46] See the catalogue characterization of midfare at p. 18 above.

and—here is the freedom motivation—it is not only actual states, but the range of states the agent can attain, that matter.

According to Sen, 'the category of capabilities is the natural candidate for reflecting the idea of freedom to do',[47] since 'capability to function reflects what a person *can* do'.[48] Hence 'the concept of capabilities is a "freedom" type notion',[49] and the functioning vectors accessible to a person determine her '*well-being freedom*'.[50] All that may be true of capability (more or less) strictly so called, but it is not true of 'capability' where the term is used to denote the entire midfare dimension between goods and utility. Sen intends capability to have an athletic character. He associates it with the Marxist idea of a person fulfilling his potential through activity, which is to be contrasted with the idea of a person finding his *summum bonum* in passive consumption.[51] But, in Sen's wider construal of it, as midfare, capability covers too much to provide 'the perspective of "freedom" in the positive sense'.[52]

The ambiguity between capability as a form of freedom and capability as midfare was not resolved in Sen's contribution to the July 1988 WIDER symposium ('Capability and Well-Being'), to which, with characteristic generosity, he has allowed me to refer. Instead, and as I shall explain, his ambiguous use of 'capability' was matched by an ambiguous use of 'freedom'.

At p. 5 of his 1988 typescript, Sen says that 'capability reflects a person's freedom to choose between different ways of living'. That formulation more or less identifies capability with freedom of choice (how much it does so depends on what 'reflects' means here: it might mean 'is'). In line with that characterization of capability is Sen's description of the rich faster, who 'has the capability to be well nourished, but chooses not to [be]'.[53]

Elsewhere, however, something very different from the freedom to choose whether or not to eat, namely, freedom *from* hunger, is denominated a 'capability'.[54] In fact, though, freedom from hunger is *being* well nourished. It is not the ability to choose which the rich faster has: it is what he chooses not to have. Freedom from hunger is a desirable absence or privation, the sort of freedom which even beings that are not agents can have. Healthy plants have freedom from greenfly, and sound houses are free from dry rot. (Note that a person might even be described, in a special context, as free from nourishment, for example, when he wants to fast, or by captors who want him to starve.)

---

[47] 'Rights and Capabilities', 316. Cf. 'Economics and the Family', in *Resources, Values and Development*, 376.

[48] 'Rights and Capabilities', 317.

[49] *Commodities and Capabilities*, 14.

[50] 'Well-Being, Agency and Freedom', 201.

[51] For relevant citations of Marx, see 'Development: Which Way Now?', in *Resources, Values and Development*, 497; 'Goods and People', 512; *The Standard of Living*, 37.

[52] 'Economics and the Family', 376. The sentence continues: 'who can *do* what, rather than who has what bundle of *commodities*, or who gets how much *utility*.' My point is the simple one that what people can do with their commodities is not identical with what their commodities (can) do for them.

[53] 'Capability and Well-Being', 38.

[54] Ibid., 41.

Unlike the freedom to choose whether or not to eat, freedom from hunger is not constitutively freedom to *do* anything. Sen speaks of *exercising* such 'capabilities' as freedom from hunger and freedom from malaria.[55] But they are not freedoms that are *exercised*. Sen's application of the term 'capability' *both* to the freedom to *avoid* morbidity[56] *and* to freedom *from* morbidity[57] shows that, in the attempt to bring the very different issues with which he is concerned under the single rubric of 'capability', he is led to make equivocal use of the term 'freedom'.[58]

When Sen introduced capability equality in 'Equality of What?', he was modest about its claims. It was 'a partial guide to the part of moral goodness that is associated with the idea of equality'.[59] Five years later, his claim for the new perspective was much stronger. For, in the Dewey Lectures, Sen said that 'the *primary* feature of well-being can be seen in terms of how a person can "function", taking that term in a very broad sense', and that 'the accounting of functioning vectors' provides 'a more plausible view of well-being' than competing conceptions do.[60] Elsewhere, we are advised that, in assessing 'well-being and advantage', we should focus 'on the capability to function, i.e. what a person can *do* or *be*'. His utility is only *evidence* of a person's advantage in that central sense,[61] and the goods at his disposal (here called his 'opulence') are only *causes* of that advantage.[62] The position of midfare between primary goods and utility, thus construed, is given as a reason for treating it as the central dimension of value.

These are strong claims, but they are easier to accept in that functionings are now explicitly described as 'doings *and* beings' so that both 'activities' and 'states of existence or being' come under the 'functioning' rubric.[63] What I cannot accept is the associated athleticism, which comes when Sen adds that 'the central feature of well-being is the ability to achieve valuable functionings'.[64] That overestimates the place of freedom and activity in well-being. As Sen

---

[55] Ibid.

[56] Ibid., 6.

[57] Ibid., 41.

[58] There is further evidence of the persisting ambiguity at pp. 17–19 of 'Capability and Well-Being'. At pp. 17–18, and in line with the definition of capability on p. 5, a capability set is characterized by the 'various alternative combinations of beings and doings any one (combination) of which the person can *choose*' (italics added). But at pp. 18–19, it is allowed, in seeming contradiction of that characterization, that the realized combination in a capability set may or may not be chosen. What is 'achieved' might not be 'achieved on the basis of choice' (p. 19).

[59] 'Equality of What?' 220.

[60] 'Well-Being, Agency and Freedom', 197 (italics added), 226. See further ibid., 195, where there is an implied identification of 'having "well-being"' with functionings. Cf. *Commodities and Capabilities*, 25, 51; *The Standard of Living*, 16.

[61] And often it is rather unreliable evidence, since people tend to adjust to adverse conditions: see pp. 16–17 above.

[62] *Commodities and Capabilities*, Preface. Cf. ibid., 52. (Strictly, opulence is a magnitude which *supervenes* on command of goods: see ibid., 58).

[63] 'Well-Being, Agency and Freedom', 197 (italics added).

[64] Ibid., 200.

writes elsewhere, 'freedom is concerned with what one *can* do' and 'with what one can *do*':[65] midfare fails, on both counts, as a representation of freedom.

e. I said earlier that there are two powerful motivations for pointing to something other than either goods or utility when concerning oneself with egalitarian policy: there are other actual states that count, and it is not only actual states that count. In the last section I have shown how confusion of those two points is visible in the attempt to express both in the language of freedom, which is appropriate to the second point only.

Under one exegetically plausible disambiguation of Sen's formulations, they recommend equality of capability to achieve functionings, where 'capability' carries something like its ordinary sense (and is therefore not confused with midfare), and where 'functionings' denote all desirable states, and not desirable activities only. So disambiguated, Sen's theory displays two departures from equality of welfare: there is a change of modality, in that capability or opportunity, rather than final achievement, is key; and there is an enrichment of the conception of what opportunities are *for* — not welfare alone, but more broadly conceived good states of the person. In this reconstruction, the error of forcing the concept of capability to denote both the element of opportunity and the move to a broader conception of advantage is eliminated.

When Sen first invoked capability, it was in the context of a proposal that we attend to '*basic* capability equality'.[66] The relevant capability was of a fundamental sort, capability whose absence disables the person from satisfying his basic needs. Such need satisfaction is, while clearly related to the achievement of welfare, also irreducible to the latter: one may need something for which one has no desire and one may desire something which does not constitute a need. At the basic level, we can, with some confidence, rank capabilities in importance without paying attention to people's tastes. But, as Sen points out, capability rankings are more moot once we pass beyond the basic desiderata of a normal human life:

when there is diversity of taste, it becomes harder to surmise about capability by simply observing achievement. For extreme poverty this problem is less serious. Valuing better nourishment, less illness and long life tend to be fairly universal, and also largely consistent with each other despite being distinct objectives. But in other cases of greater relevance to the richer countries — the informational problems with the capability approach can be quite serious.[67]

For capabilities which go beyond need satisfaction, it is hard to see how rankings are possible without recourse to utility valuations of the relevant states. In a critical comment on Sen, Richard Arneson tries to exploit the dependence on preference of the value of 'higher' capabilities:

[65] 'Rights and Capabilities', 318.
[66] That was the title of section 4 of 'Equality of What?'
[67] 'The Living Standard', 87.

I doubt that the full set of my functioning capabilities [matters] for the assessment of my position. Whether or not my capabilities include the capability to trek to the South Pole, eat a meal at the most expensive restaurant in Omsk . . . matters not one bit to me, because I neither have nor have the slightest reason to anticipate I ever will have any desire to do any of these and myriad other things.[68]

Arneson infers that, in so far as the capability approach claims our attention, it is only as a different way of presenting the idea of equality of opportunity for welfare. But that conclusion is hasty. For one might hold that objective (non-welfare) assessment of capability is possible at the basic level, even though, beyond that level, we evaluate capability according to the range of desires which it enables a person to satisfy. The capability which matters as such (that is, independently of its welfare consequences) is capability definitive of a normal human existence, capability whose absence spells non-satisfaction of need. This answer to Arneson is anticipated by Sen:

The index of capabilities can be sensitive to the strength of desires without converting everything into the metric of desires. The welfarist picture drops out everything other than desires. A non-welfarist over-all index of capabilities may not drop out desires and may well be sensitive to the strength of desires *without ignoring* other influences on the indexing.[69]

And, one might add, the sensitivity of the capability index to desire is inversely related to the degree of 'basicness' of the region of capability space under exploration.

Still, if capability in its higher reaches waits on utility for its significance, it is in its more basic reaches that it makes its distinctive normative contribution, as Sen acknowledges: 'The issue of capabilities – specifically "material" capabilities – is particularly important in judging the standard of living of people in poor countries – it is also important in dealing with poverty in rich countries.'[70] And even if utility and opulence offer more general, non-dependent (on other metrics) assessments of people's conditions, because of not being restricted to the basic, the notion of basic capability equality may provide an apter reading of the egalitarian impulse than they do. The problem of characterizing well-being in general is not the same as the problem of the priorities of egalitarian justice, and basic midfare, if not basic capability as such, rather than goods bundles or utility quanta, surely is the first priority of justice.

f. In the last sentence of subsection *e*, I reintroduced the equivocation between capability and midfare. Here I shall explain why I did so, and why, more

[68] 'Equality and Equality of Opportunity for Welfare', 93.
[69] 'Rights and Capabilities', 319. Not only does Sen allow strength of desire to condition capability evaluation, but, somewhat curiously, he is also disposed to classify happiness itself as a functioning. 'Being happy' is described as a 'major functioning' at p. 13 of 'Well-Being and Agency' (unpublished, 1987) and as a 'momentous' one at p. 200 of 'Well-Being, Agency and Freedom'. See also 'Goods and People', 512; *The Standard of Living*, 8, 11, 14. See, too, *Commodities and Capabilities* (15, 52) for more tentative statements of happiness's credentials as a functioning.
[70] 'The Living Standard', 85.

particularly, capability as such is not, in my view, the right thing for an egalitarian to focus on.

I have elsewhere proposed that the right thing to equalize is what I called 'access to advantage'.[71] In that proposal, 'advantage' is, like Sen's 'functioning' in its wider construal, a heterogeneous collection of desirable states of the person reducible neither to his resources bundle nor to his welfare level. And, while 'access' includes what the term normally covers, I extend its meaning under a proviso that anything which a person actually has counts as something to which he has access, no matter how he came to have it, and, hence, even if his coming to have it involved no exploitation of access in the ordinary sense (nor, therefore, any exercise of capability). If, for example, one enjoys freedom from malaria because others have destroyed the malaria-causing insects, then, in my special sense, such freedom from malaria is something to which one has access. That special construal of access is motivated by the thought that egalitarians have to consider states of a person which he neither brought about nor ever was in a position to bring about, states which fall within category (3) of midfare, as it was sub-classified above (desirable states caused directly, without any exercise of capability by the beneficiary). Under the disambiguation of Sen's position articulated in subsection e above, such states go unconsidered in the egalitarian reckoning (though Sen himself is, of course, supremely concerned about them).

Under equality of access to advantage, the normative accent is not on capability as such, but on a person not lacking an urgent desideratum through no fault of his own: capability to achieve the desideratum is a sufficient but not a necessary condition of not suffering such a lack. My own proposal strikes me as better attuned than capability equality to the true shape of the egalitarian concern with such things as health, nourishment, and housing.

Equality of access to advantage is motivated by the idea that differential advantage is unjust save where it reflects differences in genuine choice (or, more or less, capability) on the part of relevant agents, but it is not genuine choice as such (or capability) which the view proposes to equalize. The idea motivating equality of access to advantage does not even imply that there actually is such a thing as genuine choice. Instead, it implies that if there is no such thing — because, for example, 'hard determinism' is true — then all differential advantage is unjust. The fact that my view tolerates the possibility that genuine choice is a chimera makes salient its difference from Sen's. In my view, Sen has exaggerated the indispensability of the idea of freedom in the correct articulation of the egalitarian norm. No serious inequality obtains when everyone has everything she needs, even if she did not have to lift a finger to get it. Such a condition may be woeful in other ways, but it is not criticizable at the bar of egalitarian justice.

[71] See 'On the Currency of Egalitarian Justice', 920–1.

BIBLIOGRAPHY

ARNESON, R. (1989). 'Equality and Equality of Opportunity for Welfare', *Philosophical Studies*, 56.

COHEN, G.A. (1989). 'On the Currency of Egalitarian Justice', *Ethics*, 99.

DWORKIN, R. (1981*a*). 'Equality of Welfare', *Philosophy and Public Affairs*, 10.

—— (1981*b*). 'Equality of Resources', *Philosophy and Public Affairs*, 10.

LANDESMAN, B. (1983). 'Egalitarianism', *Canadian Journal of Philosophy*, 13.

NOZICK, ROBERT (1974). *Anarchy, State and Utopia*. New York: Basic Books.

RAWLS, JOHN (1971). *A Theory of Justice*. Cambridge, Mass.: Harvard University Press.

—— (1975). 'Fairness to Goodness', *Philosophical Review*, 84.

—— (1982). 'Social Unity and Primary Goods', in A.K. Sen and B. Williams, (eds.), *Utilitarianism and Beyond*. Cambridge: Cambridge University Press.

—— (1985). 'Justice as Fairness, Political not Metaphysical', *Philosophy and Public Affairs*, 14.

—— (1986). 'Citizens' Needs and Primary Goods', unpublished.

SCANLON, T.M. (1975). 'Preference and Urgency', *Journal of Philosophy*, 72.

SEN, A.K. (1980). 'Equality of What?', in S. McMurrin (ed.), *Tanner Lectures on Human Values*, i. Cambridge: Cambridge University Press.

—— (1981). 'Ethical Issues in Income Distribution: National and International', in S. Grassman and E. Lundberg (eds.), *The World Economic Order: Past and Prospects*. London: Macmillan. Repr. in Sen (1984*a*).

—— (1982). *Choice, Welfare and Measurement*. Blackwell, Oxford.

—— (1983). 'Development: Which Way Now?', *Economic Journal*, 93.

—— (1983). 'Economics and the Family', *Asia Development Review*, 1.

—— (1984*a*). *Resources, Values and Development*. Oxford: Blackwell.

—— (1984*b*). 'The Living Standard', *Oxford Economic Papers*, 6.

—— (1985*a*). *Commodities and Capabilities*. Amsterdam: North-Holland.

—— (1985*b*). 'Rights and Capabilities', in T. Honderich (ed.), *Morality and Objectivity: A Tribute to J.L. Mackie*. London: Routledge and Kegan Paul. Repr. in Sen (1984*a*).

—— (1985*c*). 'Well-Being, Agency and Freedom: The Dewey Lectures 1984', *Journal of Philosophy*, 82.

—— (1987). 'Well-Being and Agency', unpublished.

—— *et al.* (1987). *The Standard of Living*. Cambridge: Cambridge University Press.

—— (1988). 'Capability and Well-being', unpublished draft of the paper that follows in this volume.

Capability and Well-Being

Amartya Sen

1 Introduction

Capability is not an awfully attractive word. It has a technocratic sound, and to some it might even suggest the image of nuclear war strategists rubbing their hands in pleasure over some contingent plan of heroic barbarity. The term is not much redeemed by the historical Capability Brown praising particular pieces of *land*—not human beings—on the solid real-estate ground that they 'had capabilities'. Perhaps a nicer word could have been chosen when some years ago I tried to explore a particular approach to well-being and advantage in terms of a person's ability to do valuable acts or reach valuable states of being.[1] The expression was picked to represent the alternative combinations of things a person is able to do or be—the various 'functionings' he or she can achieve.[2]

The capability approach to a person's advantage is concerned with evaluating it in terms of his or her actual ability to achieve various valuable functionings as a part of living. The corresponding approach to social advantage—for aggregative appraisal as well as for the choice of institutions and policy—takes the sets of individual capabilities as constituting an indispensable and central part of the relevant informational base of such evaluation. It differs from other approaches using other informational focuses, for example, personal utility (focusing on pleasures, happiness, or desire fulfilment), absolute or relative opulence (focusing on commodity bundles, real income, or real wealth), assessments of negative freedoms (focusing on procedural fulfilment of libertarian rights and rules of non-interference), comparisons of means of freedom (e.g. focusing on the holdings of 'primary goods', as in the Rawlsian theory of justice), and comparisons of resource holdings as a basis of just equality (e.g. as in Dworkin's criterion of 'equality of resources').

For helpful discussions, I am most grateful to G. A. Cohen, Partha Dasgupta, Jean Drèze, Hilary Putnam, Ruth Anna Putnam, Martha Nussbaum, Derek Parfit, John Rawls, John Roemer, and Thomas Scanlon.

[1] This was in a Tanner Lecture given at Stanford University in May 1979 ('Equality of What?'), later published as Sen (1980). The case for focusing on capability was introduced here in the specific context of evaluating inequality. I have tried to explore the possibility of using the capability perspective for analysing other social issues, such as well-being and poverty (Sen, 1982a, 1983c, 1985b), liberty and freedom (Sen, 1983a, 1988a, 1992), living standards and development (Sen, 1983b, 1984, 1987b, 1988b), gender bias and sexual divisions (Kynch and Sen, 1983; Sen, 1985c, 1990b), and justice and social ethics (Sen, 1982b, 1985a, 1990a).

[2] Though at the time of proposing the approach, I did not manage to seize its Aristotelian connections, it is interesting to note that the Greek word *dunamin*, used by Aristotle to discuss an aspect of the human good, which is sometimes translated as 'potentiality', can be translated also as 'capability of existing or acting' (see Liddell and Scott, 1977: 452). The Aristotelian perspective and its connections with the recent attempts at constructing a capability-focused approach have been illuminatingly discussed by Martha Nussbaum (1988).

Different aspects of the capability approach have been discussed, extended, used, or criticized by several authors, and as a result the advantages and difficulties of the approach have become more transparent.[3] There is, however, a need for a clearer and more connected account of the whole approach, particularly in view of some interpretational problems that have arisen in its assessment and use. This paper is an attempt at a clarificatory analysis at an elementary level. I shall also try to respond briefly to some interesting criticisms that have been made.

2 Functionings, Capability, and Values

Perhaps the most primitive notion in this approach concerns 'functionings'. *Functionings* represent parts of the state of a person—in particular the various things that he or she manages to do or be in leading a life. The *capability* of a person reflects the alternative combinations of functionings the person can achieve, and from which he or she can choose one collection.[4] The approach is based on a view of living as a combination of various 'doings and beings', with quality of life to be assessed in terms of the capability to achieve valuable functionings.

Some functionings are very elementary, such as being adequately nourished, being in good health, etc., and these may be strongly valued by all, for obvious reasons. Others may be more complex, but still widely valued, such as achieving self-respect or being socially integrated. Individuals may, however, differ a good deal from each other in the weights they attach to these different functionings— valuable though they may all be—and the assessment of individual and social advantages must be alive to these variations.

In the context of some types of social analysis, for example, in dealing with extreme poverty in developing economies, we may be able to go a fairly long distance with a relatively small number of centrally important functionings and the corresponding basic capabilities (e.g. the ability to be well nourished and well sheltered, the capability of escaping avoidable morbidity and premature mortality, and so forth). In other contexts, including more general problems of economic development, the list may have to be much longer and much more diverse.

[3] See the contributions of Roemer (1982, 1986), Streeten (1984), Beitz (1986), Dasgupta (1986, 1988, 1989), Hamlin (1986), Helm (1986), Zamagni (1986), Basu (1987), Brannen and Wilson (1987), Hawthorn (1987), Kanbur (1987), Kumar (1987), Muellbauer (1987), Ringen (1987), B. Williams (1987), Wilson (1987), Nussbaum (1988, 1990), Griffin and Knight (1989a, 1989b), Riley (1988), Cohen (1990), and Steiner (1990). On related matters, including application, critique, and comparison, see also de Beus (1986), Kakwani (1986), Luker (1986), Sugden (1986), Asahi (1987), Delbono (1987), Koohi-Kamali (1987), A. Williams (1987), Broome (1988), Gaertner (1988), Stewart (1988), Suzumura (1988), de Vos and Hagennars (1988), Goodin (1985, 1988), Hamlin and Pettit (1989), Seabright (1989), Hossain (1990) and Schokkaert and van Ootegem (1990), among others.

[4] If there are *n* relevant functionings, then a person's extent of achievement of all of them respectively can be represented by an *n*-tuple. There are several technical problems in the representation and analysis of functioning *n*-tuples and capability sets, on which see Sen (1985b: chs. 2, 4, and 7).

Choices have to be faced in the delineation of the *relevant* functionings. The format always permits additional 'achievements' to be defined and included. Many functionings are of no great interest to the person (e.g. using a *particular* washing powder—much like other washing powders).[5] There is no escape from the problem of evaluation in selecting a class of functionings in the description and appraisal of capabilities. The focus has to be related to the underlying concerns and values, in terms of which some definable functionings may be important and others quite trivial and negligible. The need for selection and discrimination is neither an embarrassment, nor a unique difficulty, for the conceptualization of functioning and capability.

3   *Value-objects and Evaluative Spaces*

In an evaluative exercise, we can distinguish between two different questions: (1) *What* are the objects of value? (2) *How valuable* are the respective objects? Even though *formally* the former question is an elementary aspect of the latter (in the sense that the objects of value are those that have positive weights), nevertheless the identification of the objects of value is *substantively* the primary exercise which makes it possible to pursue the second question.

Furthermore, the very identification of the set of value-objects, with positive weights, itself precipitates a 'dominance ranking' (x is at least as high as y if it yields at least as much of *each* of the valued objects). This dominance ranking, which can be shown to have standard regularity properties such as transitivity, can indeed take us some distance—often quite a long distance—in the evaluative exercise.[6]

The identification of the objects of value specifies what may be called an *evaluative space*. In standard utilitarian analysis, for example, the evaluative space consists of the individual utilities (defined in the usual terms of pleasures, happiness, or desire fulfilment). Indeed, a complete evaluative approach entails a class of 'informational constraints' in the form of ruling out *directly* evaluative use of various types of information, to wit, those that do not belong to the evaluative space.[7]

The capability approach is concerned primarily with the identification of value-objects, and sees the evaluative space in terms of functionings and capabilities to function. This is, of course, itself a deeply evaluative exercise, but

[5] Bernard Williams (1987) raises this issue in his comments on my Tanner Lectures on the standard of living (pp. 98–101); on which see also Sen. (1987b: 108–9). On the inescapable need for evaluation of different functioning and capabilities, see Sen (1985b: chs. 5–7). Just as the concentration on the commodity space in real-income analysis does not imply that every commodity must be taken to be equally valuable (or indeed valuable at all), similarly focusing on the space of functioning does not entail that each functioning must be taken to be equally valuable (or indeed valuable at all).

[6] On this and on other formulations and uses of dominance ranking, see Sen (1970: chs. 1*, 7*, 9*).

[7] On the crucial role of the informational basis, and on the formulation and use of informational constraints, see Sen (1970, 1977) and d'Aspremont and Gevers (1977).

answering question (1), on the identification of the objects of value, does not, on its own, yield a particular answer to question (2), regarding their relative values. The latter calls for a further evaluative exercise. Various substantive ways of evaluating functionings and capabilities can all belong to the general capability approach.

The selection of the evaluative space has a good deal of cutting power on its own, both because of what it *includes* as potentially valuable and because of what it *excludes*. For example, because of the nature of the evaluative space, the capability approach differs from utilitarian evaluation (more generally 'welfarist' evaluation[8]) in making room for a variety of human acts and states as important in themselves (not just *because* they may produce utility, nor just to the *extent* that they yield utility).[9] It also makes room for valuing various freedoms – in the form of capabilities. On the other side, the approach does not attach direct – as opposed to derivative – importance to the *means* of living or *means* of freedom (e.g. real income, wealth, opulence, primary goods, or resources), as some other approaches do. These variables are not part of the evaluative space, though they can indirectly influence the evaluation through their effects on variables included in that space.

4   *Capability and Freedom*

The freedom to lead different types of life is reflected in the person's capability set. The capability of a person depends on a variety of factors, including personal characteristics and social arrangements. A full accounting of individual freedom must, of course, go beyond the capabilities of personal living and pay attention to the person's other objectives (e.g. social goals not directly related to one's own life), but human capabilities constitute an important part of individual freedom.

Freedom, of course, is not an unproblematic concept. For example, if we do not have the courage to choose to live in a particular way, even though we *could* live that way if we so chose, can it be said that we do have the freedom to live that way, i.e. the corresponding capability? It is not my purpose here to brush under the carpet difficult questions of this – and other – types. In so far as there are genuine ambiguities in the concept of freedom, that should be reflected in corresponding ambiguities in the characterization of capability. This relates to a methodological point, which I have tried to defend elsewhere, that if an underlying idea has an essential ambiguity, a precise formulation of that idea

[8] Welfarism requires that a state of affairs must be judged by the individual utilities in that state. It is one of the basic components of utilitarianism (the others being 'sum-ranking' and 'consequentialism'); on the factorization, see Sen (1982a) and Sen and Williams (1982).

[9] Being happy and getting what one desires may be *inter alia* valued in the capability approach, but unlike in utilitarian traditions, they are not seen as the measure of all values.

must try to *capture* that ambiguity rather than hide or eliminate it.[10]

Comparisons of freedom raise interesting issues of evaluation. The claim is sometimes made that freedom must be valued independently of the values and preferences of the person whose freedom is being assessed, since it concerns the 'range' of choice a person has—*not* how she values the elements in that range or what she chooses from it. I do not believe for an instant that this claim is sustainable (despite some superficial plausibility), but had it been correct, it would have been a rather momentous conclusion, driving a wedge between the evaluation of *achievements* and that of *freedoms*. It would, in particular, be then possible to assess the freedom of a person independently of—or prior to —the assessment of the alternatives between which the person can choose.[11]

How can we judge the goodness of a 'range' of choice independently of—or prior to—considering the nature of the alternatives that constitute that range? Some comparisons can, of course, be made in terms of set inclusion, for example, that reducing the 'menu' from which one can choose will *not* increase one's freedom.[12] But whenever neither set is entirely included in the other, we have to go beyond such 'subset reasoning'.

One alternative is simply to *count* the number of elements in the set as reflecting the value of the range of choice.[13] But this number-counting procedure leads to a rather peculiar accounting of freedom. It is odd to conclude that the freedom of a person is no less when she has to choose between three alternatives which she sees respectively as 'bad', 'awful', and 'gruesome' than when she has the choice between three alternatives which she assesses as 'good', 'excellent', and

---

[10] On this, see Sen (1970, 1982a, 1987a). In many contexts, the mathematical representations should take the form of 'partial orderings' or 'fuzzy' relations. This is not, of course, a special problem with the capability approach, but applies generally to conceptual frameworks in social, economic, and political theory.

[11] The belief in this possibility seems to play a part in Robert Sugden's (1986) criticism of what he sees as my approach to capability evaluation, namely, a 'general strategy of trying to derive the value of a *set* of functioning vectors from prior ranking of the vectors themselves' (p. 821). He argues in favour of judging 'the value of being free to choose from a range of possible lives' *before* taking 'a view on what constitutes a valuable life'. This criticism is, in fact, based on a misunderstanding of the approach proposed, since it has been a part of my claim (on which more presently) that the judgement of the quality of life and the assessment of freedom have to be done *simultaneously* in an integrated way, and, in particular, that 'the quality of life a person enjoys is not merely a matter of what he or she achieves, but also of what options the person has had the opportunity to choose from' (Sen, 1985b: 69–70). But the point at issue in the present context is the possibility of judging a *range* of choice independently of the value characteristics of the *elements* in that range. It is this possibility that I am disputing.

[12] Even this can be questioned when an expanded menu causes confusion, or the necessity to choose between a larger set of alternatives is a nuisance. But such problems can be dealt with through *appropriate* characterization of all the choices one has or does not have. This must include the consideration of the overall choice of having *or* not having to choose among a whole lot of relatively trivial alternatives (e.g. the choice of telling the telephone company to shut out mechanically dialled calls from sales agents offering a plethora of purchasing options). The issues involved in this kind of complex evaluation, incorporating choices over choices, are discussed in Sen (1992).

[13] For an illuminating axiomatic derivation of the number-counting method of freedom evaluation, see Pattanaik and Xu (1990).

'superb'.[14] Further, it is always possible to add trivially to the number of options one has (e.g. tearing one's hair, cutting one's ears, slicing one's toes, or jumping through the window), and it would be amazing to see such additions as compensating for the loss of really valued options.[15] The assessment of the elements in a range of choice has to be linked to the evaluation of the freedom to choose among that range.[16]

5 Value-purposes and Distinct Exercises

While the identification of value-objects and the specification of an evaluative space involve norms, the nature of the norms must depend on precisely what the purpose of the evaluation is. Assessing well-being may take us in one direction; judging achievement in terms of the person's *overall* goals may take us in a somewhat different direction, since a person can have objectives other than the pursuit of his or her own well-being. Judging achievement of either kind may also differ from the evaluation of the *freedom* to achieve, since a person can be advantaged in having more freedom and still end up achieving less.

We can make a fourfold classification of points of evaluative interest in assessing human advantage, based on two different distinctions. One distinction is between (1.1) the promotion of the person's *well-being*, and (1.2) the pursuit of the person's overall *agency goals*. The latter encompasses the goals that a person has reasons to adopt, which can *inter alia* include goals other than the advancement of his or her own well-being. It can thus generate orderings different from that of well-being. The second distinction is between (2.1) *achievement*, and (2.2) the *freedom to achieve*. This contrast can be applied both to the perspective of well-being and to that of agency. The two distinctions together yield four different concepts of advantage, related to a person: (1) 'well-being achievement', (2) 'agency achievement', (3) 'well-being freedom', and (4) 'agency freedom'. These different notions, which I have tried to discuss more extensively elsewhere, are not, of course, unrelated to each other, but nor are they necessarily identical.[17]

---

[14] The unacceptability of this kind of number-counting evaluation of freedom is discussed in Sen (1985*b*). For an assessment of the axiomatic foundations of this and other methods of evaluation of freedom, see Sen (1991).

[15] This type of case also shows why the set-inclusion ranking is best seen as a 'weak' relation of 'no worse than' or 'at least as good as', rather than as the 'strict' relation of 'better than'. Adding the option of 'slicing one's toes' to the set of valued options a person already has may not *reduce* her freedom (since one can reject toe-slicing), but it is hard to take it to be a strict *increase* in that person's freedom.

[16] As was argued earlier, the relation is two-sided, and the evaluation of the freedom to lead a life and the assessment of the life led (including choosing freely) have to be done simultaneously, in a desegregated way.

[17] Since a person's agency objectives will typically include, *inter alia*, his or her own well-being, the two will to some extent go together (e.g. an increase in well-being, other things being equal, will involve a higher agency achievement). In addition, a failure to achieve one's *non*-well-being objectives

The assessment of each of these four types of benefit involves an evaluative exercise, but they are not the *same* evaluative exercise. They can also have very disparate bearings on matters to which the evaluation and comparison of individual advantages are relevant. For example, in determining whether a person is deprived in a way that calls for assistance from others or from the state, a person's well-being may be, arguably, more relevant than his agency success (e.g. the state may have better grounds for offering support to a person for overcoming hunger or illness than for helping him to build a monument to his hero, even if he himself attaches more importance to the monument than to the removal of his hunger or illness). Furthermore, for adult citizens, *well-being freedom* may be more relevant to state policy, in this context, than *well-being achievement* (e.g. the state may have reason to offer a person adequate opportunities to overcome hunger, but not to insist that he must take up that offer and cease to be hungry). Interpersonal comparisons can be of many distinct types, with possibly dissimilar evaluative interests. Despite the interdependences between the different value-purposes, they can generate quite distinct exercises with partly divergent concentration and relevance.

6   *Well-being, Agency, and Living Standards*

The well-being achievement of a person can be seen as an evaluation of the 'well-ness' of the person's state of being (rather than, say, the goodness of her contribution to the country, or her success in achieving her overall goals). The exercise, then, is that of assessing the constituent elements of the person's being seen from the perspective of her own personal welfare. The different functionings of the person will make up these constituent elements.

This does not, of course, imply that a person's well-being cannot be 'other-regarding'. Rather, the effect of 'other-regarding' concerns on one's well-being has to operate *through* some feature of the person's own being. Doing good may make a person contented or fulfilled, and these are functioning achievements of importance. In this approach, functionings are seen as central to the *nature* of well-being, even though the *sources* of well-being could easily be external to the person.

The functionings relevant for well-being vary from such elementary ones as escaping morbidity and mortality, being adequately nourished, having mobility, etc., to complex ones such as being happy, achieving self-respect, taking part in

---

may also cause frustration, thereby reducing one's well-being. These and other connections exist between well-being and agency, but they do not make the two concepts congruent—nor isomorphic in the sense of generating the same orderings. Similarly, more freedom (either to have well-being or to achieve one's agency goals) may lead one to end up achieving more (respectively, of well-being or of agency success), but it is also possible for freedom to go up while achievement goes down, and vice versa. We have here four *interdependent* but *non-identical* concepts. These distinctions and their inter-relations are discussed more fully in Sen (1985a, 1992).

the life of the community, appearing in public without shame (the last a functioning that was illuminatingly discussed by Adam Smith[18]). The claim is that the functionings make up a person's being, and the evaluation of a person's well-being has to take the form of an assessment of these constituent elements.

If the value-purpose is changed from checking the 'well-ness' of the person's being to assessing the person's success in the pursuit of all the objectives that he has reason to promote, then the exercise becomes one of evaluation of 'agency achievement', rather than of well-being achievement. For this exercise, the space of functionings may be rather restrictive, since the person's goals may well include other types of objective (going well beyond the person's own state of being). Also, the difference between agency achievement and well-being achievement is not only a matter of *space* (the former taking us beyond the person's own life and functionings), but also one of differential *weighting* of the shared elements (i.e. for the functionings that are pertinent both to one's well-being and to one's other objectives, possibly different weights may be attached in agency evaluation *vis-à-vis* well-being appraisal).

The assessment of agency success is a broader exercise than the evaluation of well-being. It is also possible to consider 'narrower' exercises than the appraisal of well-being. A particularly important one is that of evaluating a person's *standard of living*. This, too, may take the form of focusing on the person's functionings, but in this case we may have to concentrate only on those influences on well-being that come from the nature of his *own* life, rather than from 'other-regarding' objectives or impersonal concerns. For example, the happiness generated by a purely other-regarding achievement (e.g. the freeing of political prisoners in distant countries) may enhance the person's well-being without, in any obvious sense, raising his living standard.

In the ethical context, the explicit recognition that one's well-being may often be affected by the nature of other people's lives is not, of course, new. Even Emperor Asoka, in the third century BC, noted the distinction clearly in one of his famous 'rock edicts' in the process of defining what should count as an injury to a person: 'And, if misfortune befalls the friends, acquaintances, companions and relations of persons who are full of affection [towards the former], even though they are themselves well provided for, [this misfortune] is also an injury to their own selves.'[19] The inability to be happy, which will be widely recognized as a failure of an important functioning (even though not the *only* important one, except in the hedonist version of utilitarianism), may arise either from sources within one's own life (e.g. being ill, or undernourished, or otherwise deprived), or from sources outside it (e.g. the pain that comes from sympathizing with others' misery). While both types of factor affect one's well-being, the case

---

[18] See Adam Smith (1776: Vol. ii, Bk V, ch. 2 (section on 'Taxes upon Consumable Commodities')), in Campbell and Skinner (1976), 469–71.

[19] Rock Edicts XIII at Erragudi, statement VII. For a translation and discussion, see Sircar (1979: 34).

for excluding the latter from the assessment, specifically, of one's living standards would seem fairly reasonable, since the latter relates primarily to the lives of others, rather than one's own.[20]

7 Why Capability, not just Achievement?

The preceding discussion on the achievement of well-being and living standards has been related to functionings rather than to capabilities. This was done by design to introduce distinct problems in sequence, even though eventually an integrated view will have to be taken. In fact, the capability approach, as the terminology indicates, sees the capability set as the primary informational base. Why should we have to broaden our attention from functionings to capability?

We should first note that capabilities are defined derivatively from functionings. In the space of functionings any point, representing an n-tuple of functionings, reflects a combination of the person's doings and beings, relevant to the exercise. The capability is a *set* of such functioning n-tuples, representing the various alternative combinations of beings and doings any one (combination) of which the person can choose.[21] Capability is thus defined in the *space* of functionings. If a functioning achievement (in the form of an n-tuple of functionings) is a *point* in that space, capability is a *set* of such points (representing the alternative functioning n-tuples from which one n-tuple can be chosen).

Note further that the capability set contains information about the actual functioning n-tuple chosen, since it too is obviously among the feasible n-tuples. The evaluation of a capability set may be based on the assessment of the particular n-tuple chosen from that set. Evaluation according to the achieved functioning combination is thus a 'special case' of evaluation on the basis of the capability set as a whole. In this sense, well-being achievement can be assessed on the basis of the capability set, even when no freedom-type notion influences that achievement. In this case, in evaluating the capability set for the value-purpose of assessing well-being achievement, we would simply have to identify the value of the capability set with the value of the achieved functioning n-tuple in it. The procedure of equating the value of the capability set to the value of *one* of the elements of that set has been called 'elementary evaluation'.[22]

---

[20] This view may be disputed by considering a different way of drawing the line between well-being and living standards. One common approach is to relate the assessment of living standards only to real incomes and to 'economic' or 'material' causes. On this see A. C. Pigou (1920); and on the conceptual differences see Bernard Williams (1987). But the Pigovian view has problems of its own. For example, if one has a disability that makes one get very little out of material income or wealth, or if one's life is shattered by an inconvenient and incurable illness (e.g. kidney problems requiring extensive dialysis), it is hard to claim that one's standard of living is high just because one is well heeled. I have discussed this question and related matters in Sen (1987b: 26–9, 109–10).

[21] For formal characterizations, see Sen (1985b: chs. 2 and 7).

[22] On this see Sen (1985b: 60–1). The distinguished element can be the *achieved* one (as in this case), or more specifically the *chosen* one (if there is a choice exercise in determining what happens), or the *maximal* one (in terms of some criterion of goodness). The three will coincide if what is achieved is achieved through choice, and what is chosen is chosen through maximization according to that criterion of goodness.

Clearly, there is *at least* no informational loss in seeing well-being evaluation in terms of capabilities, rather than directly in terms of the achieved, or chosen, or maximal functioning n-tuple. While this indicates that the informational base of capability is at least as adequate as that of achieved functionings, the claim in favour of the capability perspective is, in fact, stronger. The advantages of the extension arise from two rather different types of consideration.

First, we may be interested not merely in examining 'well-being achievement', but also 'well-being freedom'. A person's actual freedom to live well and be well is of some interest in social as well as personal evaluation.[23] Even if we were to take the view, which will be disputed presently, that well-being achievement depends only on the achieved functionings, the 'well-being freedom' of a person will represent the freedom to enjoy the various possible well-beings associated with the different functioning n-tuples in the capability set.[24]

Second, freedom may have intrinsic importance for the person's well-being achievement. Acting freely and being able to choose may be directly conducive to well-being, not just because more freedom may make better alternatives available. This view is contrary to the one typically assumed in standard consumer theory, in which the contribution of a set of feasible choices is judged exclusively by the value of the best element available.[25] Even the removal of all the elements of a feasible set (e.g. of a 'budget set') other than the chosen best element is seen, in that theory, as no real loss, since the freedom to choose does not, in this view, matter in itself.

In contrast, if choosing is seen as a part of living (and 'doing x' is distinguished from 'choosing to do x and doing it'), then even 'well-being achievement' need not be independent of the freedom reflected in the capability set.[26] In that case, both 'well-being achievement' and 'well-being freedom' will have to be assessed in terms of capability sets. Both must then involve 'set evaluation' in a non-elementary way (i.e. without limiting the usable informational content of capability sets through elementary evaluation).

[23] As was argued earlier in dealing with responsible adults, it may be appropriate to see the claims of individuals on society in terms of the *freedom* to achieve well-being (and thus in terms of real opportunities) rather than in terms of *actual achievements*. If the social arrangements are such that a responsible adult is given no less freedom (in terms of set comparisons) than others, but he still 'muffs' the opportunities and ends up worse off than others, it is possible to argue that no particular injustice is involved. On this and related matters, see Sen (1985*a*).

[24] The same capability set can than be used for the evaluation of both 'well-being achievement' (through *elementary evaluation*, concentrating on the achieved element) and 'well-being freedom' (through *non-elementary set evaluation*).

[25] Thus, in standard consumer theory, set evaluation takes the form of elementary evaluation. For particular departures from that tradition, see Koopmans (1964) and Kreps (1979). In the Koopmans–Kreps approach, however, the motivation is not so much to see living freely as a thing of intrinsic importance, but to take note of uncertainty regarding one's own future preference by valuing—instrumentally—the advantage of having more options in the future. On the motivational contrasts, see Sen (1985*a*, 1985*b*).

[26] As was argued in an earlier paper, 'the "good life" is partly a life of genuine choice, and not one in which the person is forced into a particular life—however rich it might be in other respects' (Sen, 1985*b*: 69–70).

There are many formal problems involved in the evaluation of freedom and the relationship between freedom and achievement.[27] It is, in fact, possible to characterize functionings in a 'refined' way to take note of the 'counterfactual' opportunities, so that the characteristic of relating well-being achievement to functioning n-tuples could be retained without losing the substantive connection of well-being achievement to the freedom of choice enjoyed by the person. Corresponding to the functioning x, a 'refined' functioning (x/S) takes the form of 'having functioning x through choosing it from the set S'.[28]

Sometimes even our ordinary language presents functionings in a refined way. For example, fasting is not just starving, but starving through rejecting the option of eating. The distinction is obviously important in many social contexts: we may, for example, try to eliminate involuntary hunger, but not wish to forbid fasting. The importance of seeing functionings in a refined way relates to the relevance of choice in our lives. The role of the choice involved in a capability set has been discussed above in the context of well-being only, but similar arguments apply to the assessment of agency achievement and the standard of living.[29]

8 Basic Capability and Poverty

For some evaluative exercises, it may be useful to identify a subset of crucially important capabilities dealing with what have come to be known as 'basic needs'.[30] There tends to be a fair amount of agreement on the extreme urgency of a class of needs. Particular moral and political importance may well be attached to fulfilling well-recognized, urgent claims.[31]

It is possible to argue that equality in the fulfilment of certain 'basic capabilities' provides an especially plausible approach to egalitarianism in the

---

[27] See Sen (1985b, 1988a, 1991), Suppes (1987), Pattanaik and Xu (1990).

[28] The characteristics and relevance of 'refined functioning' have been discussed in Sen (1985a, 1988a).

[29] These issues are discussed in Sen (1985a, 1987b).

[30] The 'basic needs' literature is extensive. For a helpful introduction, see Streeten et al. (1981). In a substantial part of the literature, there is a tendency to define basic needs in the form of needs for commodities (e.g. for food, shelter, clothing, health care), and this may distract attention from the fact that these commodities are no more than the means to real ends (inputs for valuable functionings and capabilities). On this question, see Streeten (1984). The distinction is particularly important since the relationship between commodities and capabilities may vary greatly between individuals even in the same society (and of course between different societies). For example, even for the elementary functioning of being well nourished, the relation between food intake and nutritional achievements varies greatly with metabolic rates, body size, gender, pregnancy, age, climatic conditions, epidemiological characteristics, and other factors (on these and related matters, see Drèze and Sen, 1989). The capability approach can accommodate the real issues underlying the concern for basic needs, avoiding the pitfall of 'commodity fetishism'.

[31] The importance of socially recognized ideas of 'urgency' has been illuminatingly discussed by Thomas Scanlon (1975).

presence of elementary deprivation.[32] The term 'basic capabilities', used in Sen (1980), was intended to separate out the ability to satisfy certain crucially important functionings up to certain minimally adequate levels. The identification of minimally acceptable levels of certain basic capabilities (below which people count as being scandalously 'deprived') can provide a possible approach to poverty, and I shall comment on the relation of this strategy to more traditional income-focused analyses of poverty. But it is also important to recognize that the use of the capability approach is not confined to basic capabilities only.[33]

Turning to poverty analysis, identifying a minimal combination of basic capabilities can be a good way of setting up the problem of diagnosing and measuring poverty. It can lead to results quite different from those obtained by concentrating on inadequacy of income as the criterion of identifying the poor.[34] The conversion of income into basic capabilities may vary greatly between individuals and also between different societies, so that the ability to reach minimally acceptable levels of basic capabilities can go with varying levels of minimally adequate incomes. The income-centred view of poverty, based on specifying an interpersonally invariant 'poverty line' income, may be very misleading in the identification and evaluation of poverty.

However, the point is sometimes made that poverty must, in some sense, be a matter of inadequacy of income, rather than a failure of capabilities, and this might suggest that the capability approach to poverty is 'essentially wrongheaded'. This objection overlooks both the motivational underpinning of poverty analysis and the close correspondence between capability failure and income inadequacy when the latter is defined taking note of *parametric variations* in income–capability relations.

Since income is not desired for its own sake, any income-based notion of poverty must refer – directly or indirectly – to those basic ends which are promoted by income as means. Indeed, in poverty studies related to less developed countries, the 'poverty line' income is often derived explicitly with reference to nutritional norms. Once it is recognized that the relation between income and capabilities varies between communities and between people in the same community, the minimally adequate income level for reaching the same minimally acceptable capability levels will be seen as variable – depending on personal and social characteristics. However, as long as minimal capabilities can be achieved

---

[32] On this see Sen (1980). To avoid confusion, it should also be noted that the term 'basic capabilities' is sometimes used in quite a different sense from the one specified above, e.g. as a person's *potential* capabilities that *could* be developed, whether or not they are actually realized (this is the sense in which the term is used, for example, by Martha Nussbaum (1988)).

[33] While the notion of basic capabilities was used in Sen (1980, 1983c), in later papers the capability approach has been used without identifying certain capabilities as 'basic' and others as not so (see e.g. Sen, 1984, 1985a, 1985b). This point is relevant to G. A. Cohen's distinction between focusing on what he calls 'midfare' and on functioning and capabilities. There are more important distinctions to explore (to be taken up in Section 9), but the contrasts look artificially sharper if the capability approach is seen as being confined *only* to the analysis of basic capabilities.

[34] On this see Sen (1983c). See also Drèze and Sen (1989) and Hossain (1990).

by enhancing the income level (given the other personal and social characteristics on which capabilities depend), it will be possible (for the specified personal and social characteristics) to identify the minimally adequate income for reaching the minimally acceptable capability levels. Once this correspondence is established, it would not really matter whether poverty is defined in terms of a failure of basic capability or as a failure to have the *corresponding* minimally adequate income.[35]

Thus, the motivationally more accurate characterization of poverty as a failure of basic capabilities can also be seen in the more traditional format of an income inadequacy. The difference in formulation is unimportant. What is really important is to take note of the interpersonal and intersocial variations in the relation between incomes and capabilities. That is where the distinctive contribution of the capability approach to poverty analysis lies.

9 *Midfare, Functionings, and Capability*

In this paper, I have so far been primarily concerned with clarifying and integrating the basic features of the capability approach, though I have taken the opportunity to address, in passing, some criticisms that have been made of this approach. In this section and in the next, I discuss two different lines of criticism – presented respectively by G. A. Cohen and Martha Nussbaum – arguing for different ways of analysing and assessing the problems of well-being and quality of life.

In his paper in this volume, and elsewhere (Cohen, 1989, 1990), G. A Cohen has provided a critical assessment of my writings on capability (and also of the theories of others – utilitarians, John Rawls, Ronald Dworkin, Thomas Scanlon, *et al.*), at the same time presenting his own answer to the question 'equality of what?'. Cohen is generous in giving credit where he reasonably can, and his assessment is positive in many ways, but the criticisms he makes, if sustained, would indicate a major motivational confusion as well as a conceptual inadequacy underlying the capability approach as I have tried to present it.

Cohen's main thesis is that in my paper 'Equality of What?' (Sen, 1980), I 'brought two distinct aspects of a person's condition under that single name [capability] and that this unnoticed duality has persisted in [my] subsequent writings'. 'Both aspects, or dimensions of assessment, should attract egalitarian interest, but one of them is not felicitously described as "capability" ' (p. 17). One aspect is concerned with 'a person being able to do certain basic things'. The other is what Cohen calls 'midfare', because 'it is in a certain sense midway between goods and utility'. 'Midfare is constituted of states of the person

---

[35] Technically, what is being used in this analysis is the 'inverse function', taking us back from specified capability levels to necessary incomes, given the other influences on capability. This procedure will not be usable, in this form, if there are people who are so handicapped in terms of personal characteristics (e.g. being a 'basket case') that no level of income will get them to reach minimally acceptable basic capabilities; such people would then be invariably identified as poor.

produced by goods, states in virtue of which utility levels take the values they do' (p. 18).

Cohen finds the dimension of midfare important for normative understanding and he notes, rightly, that I had put some emphasis on the *state* of the person, distinguishing it both from the *commodities* that help to generate that state, and from the *utilities* generated by the state. 'We must look, for example, at her nutrition level, and not just, as Rawlsians do, at her food supply, or, as welfarists do, at the utility she gets out of eating food.' 'But', Cohen argues, 'this significant and illuminating reorientation is not equivalent to focusing on a person's capability.' 'Capability, and exercises of capability, form only one part of the intermediate midfare state' (p. 19); 'midfare, the product of goods which, in turn, generates utility, is not co-extensive with capability, and "capability" is therefore a bad name for midfare' (p. 20).

Is the distinction correct? I believe it is. The first thing to note is that Cohen's 'midfare' corresponds to what I have called a person's *functionings*, and not to *capability*. The two are related, but not meant to be the same. That distinction is, in fact, a basic part of the capability approach, and there is no embarrassment in acknowledging it. The real issue lies elsewhere, to wit, whether the capability set can have any relevance in analysing well-being, given the obvious connection between well-being and functionings (or midfare) – a connection that Cohen finds adequate for the analysis of well-being. This is an issue that was addressed in a less specific form earlier on in this paper (in Section 7). Cohen's preference for the perspective of midfare or functionings over that of capabilities relates to that substantive issue.

In Section 7, the relevance of the capability set for the analysis of well-being was defended on two different grounds, namely, (1) its connection with well-being *freedom* (even if well-being achievement depends only on the achieved functioning n-tuple), and (2) the possible importance of freedom (and thus of the capability set) for well-being *achievement* itself.

The second claim is the more controversial of the two. I believe it is correct, but I should also assert that even if it were incorrect, the capability approach would still be quite untarnished. As was discussed in Section 7, assessing well-being according to the achieved functioning n-tuple (or midfare) is a special case of the use of the capability perspective based on 'elementary evaluation' (focusing only on one distinguished element – the achieved functioning n-tuple – in the capability set). This point is obscured in Cohen's analysis by his conviction that 'the exercise of capability' must be a rather 'active' operation, and Cohen is misled by this diagnosis when he argues that he 'cannot accept . . . the associated athleticism, which comes when Sen adds that "the central feature of well-being is the ability to achieve valuable functionings" ' (p. 25). Cohen gives examples (e.g. small babies being well nourished and warm as a result of the activities of their parents) that clearly show that having midfare (or enjoying functionings) need not be a particularly athletic activity. I see no reason to object to this, since athleticism was never intended, despite the fact that Cohen has obviously been misled by my use of such words as 'capability' and 'achieving'.[36]

But let use move now from the minimalist defence to the claim that an active exercise of freedom might well be valuable for a person's quality of life and achieved well-being. Obviously, this consideration would be of no direct relevance in the case of babies (or the mentally disabled), who are not in a position to exercise reasoned freedom of choice (though babies *can* sometimes be amazingly cogent, choosy, and insistent). For people who are in a position to choose in a reasoned way and value that freedom to choose, it is hard to think that their well-being achievement would never be affected if the freedom to choose were denied, even though the (unrefined) functioning vector (or midfare) were guaranteed by the actions of others. Even in Cohen's analysis of midfare, I should have thought that room would have to be found to see it in choice-inclusive terms, in much the same way that the functionings can be redefined in 'refined' terms (as discussed in Section 7). And if this is done, that would be isomorphic to including substantive consideration of the capability set, going beyond focusing exclusively on the achieved – unrefined – functioning vector (as was also discussed in Section 7).

Freedom has many aspects. Being free to live the way one would like may be enormously helped by the choice of others, and it would be a mistake to think of achievements only in terms of active choice *by oneself*. A person's ability to achieve various valuable functionings may be greatly enhanced by public action and policy,[37] and these expansions of capability are not unimportant for freedom for that reason. Indeed, I have argued elsewhere that 'freedom from hunger' or 'being free from malaria' need not be taken to be just rhetoric (as they are sometimes described); there is a very real sense in which the freedom to live the way one would like is enhanced by public policy that transforms epidemiological and social environments.[38] But the fact that freedom has that aspect does not negate the relevance of active choice by the person herself as an important component of living freely. It is because of the *presence* of this element (rather than the *absence* of others), that the act of choosing between the elements of a capability set has a clear relevance to the quality of life and well-being of a person.

But suppose we were to accept (wrongly, I believe) that this element of freedom really has no direct impact on the well-being of a person. In that case, the capability perspective could still be used to relate well-being achievement to

---

[36] Perhaps the word 'capability' *is* misleading, but I am not sure that this should be the case. The pieces of *land* to which Capability Brown attributed 'capability' could not have been much more active in looking after themselves than babies are. The crucial Greek word used in this context (by Aristotle among others), namely *dunamin*, can be translated as 'capability of existing or acting', and presumably 'existing' need not be the result of some vigorous 'exercise of capability'. Nor do I have any great difficulty in saying that the babies in question *did achieve* the state of being nourished and warm. Perhaps something else in my inept prose misled Cohen.

[37] On this see Drèze and Sen (1989).

[38] These issues are extensively discussed in Sen (1992). On related matters, see also Sen (1982b, 1983a, 1983b).

achieved (unrefined) functionings (or midfare) through elementary evaluation. The need to relate well-being freedom to the capability set would also remain. That was indeed the first claim (in Section 7, pp. 38–9) in favour of the use of the capability set for analysing well-being (in this case, well-being freedom).

As was discussed earlier in this paper,[39] for many problems of individual behaviour and social policy, well-being freedom *is* a concept of relevance and importance. If achieved functionings (or midfare), defined in the 'unrefined' way, were all that mattered, we might be as worried about the rich person fasting as about the starving poor. If we are more concerned to eliminate the hunger of the latter, it is primarily because the former has the *capability* to be well nourished but chooses not to, whereas the latter lacks that capability and is forced into the state of starvation. Both may have the same midfare, but they differ in their capabilities. Capability does have importance in political and social analysis.

Motivationally, the focus on capability (in addition to achieved functionings) is, in fact, not altogether different from the concern that Cohen shows elsewhere for 'access to advantage'. Cohen notes that in his proposal

'advantage' is like Sen's 'functioning' in its wider construal, a heterogenous collection of desirable states of the person reducible neither to his resources bundle nor to his welfare level. And while 'access' includes what the term normally covers, I extend its meaning under a proviso that anything which a person actually has counts as something to which he has access, no matter how he came to have it, and, hence, even if his coming to have it involved no exploitation of access in the ordinary sense (nor, therefore, any exercise of capability). If, for example, one enjoys freedom from malaria because others have destroyed the malaria-causing insects, then, in my special sense, such freedom from malaria is something to which one has access (Cohen, p. 28).

I do not see any great difficulty in 'extending' the meaning of 'access' in this way. An 'access' I enjoy may not have been created by me. But exactly the same applies to freedom and capability as well. The fact that a person has the freedom to enjoy a malaria-free life (or, to put it slightly differently, that his choice of a malaria-free life is feasible) may be entirely due to the actions of others (e.g., medical researchers, epidemiologists, public health workers), but that does not compromise the fact that he can indeed have a malaria-free life and has the capability (thanks largely to others) to achieve such a life.[40]

I don't even see that much 'extension' of ordinary usage is involved in such use of the terms freedom and capability (even though this is not the central issue in any case).[41] Indeed, even the expression 'freedom from malaria', used also by Cohen, is a pointer to the fact that ordinary language takes a less narrow view of the use of the term freedom. Similarly, there is no underlying presumption that we have the capability to lead a malaria-free life only if we have

[39] For a more extensive discussion, see Sen (1985a).

[40] On this see also Drèze and Sen (1989) and Sen (1992).

[41] As was mentioned earlier (in footnote 2), in their well-known Greek–English lexicon, even Liddell and Scott (1977) had translated the Greek word *dunamin*, central to Aristotle's concept of human good, as 'capability of existing or acting' (p. 452).

ourselves gone around exterminating the malaria-causing insects.

Turning to a different issue also raised by Cohen, the really interesting question is not whether 'equality of access to advantage' coincides with 'capability' in general, since capability (as was discussed earlier) is a more versatile concept and its particular characterization has to be related to the 'evaluative purpose' of the exercise (e.g., whether 'agency' or 'well-being' is the focal concern in that exercise). But if advantage is seen specifically in terms of well-being (ignoring the agency aspect), then Cohen's 'equality of access to advantage' would indeed be very like equality of well-being freedom, defined in terms of evaluation of capability sets from that perspective.[42]

Cohen's analysis has brought out the distinctions between a number of different problems which are all addressed in the capability approach but which require separate treatment. While substantive differences may remain between his focus and mine (e.g. about the importance of *choosing* as a constitutive element in the quality of life), Cohen's analysis has greatly helped to pinpoint some focal issues and concerns, and the need to address them explicitly.

10   *The Aristotelian Connections and Contrasts*

In earlier writings I have commented on the connection of the capability approach with some arguments used by Adam Smith and Karl Marx.[43] However, the most powerful conceptual connections would appear to be with the Aristotelian view of the human good. Martha Nussbaum (1988, 1990) has discussed illuminatingly the Aristotelian analysis of 'political distribution', and its relation to the capability approach. The Aristotelian account of the human good is explicitly linked with the necessity to 'first ascertain the function of man' and it then proceeds to explore 'life in the sense of activity'.[44] The basis of a fair distribution of capability to function is given a central place in the Aristotelian theory of political distribution. In interpreting Aristotle's extensive writings on ethics and politics, it is possible to note some ambiguity and indeed to find some tension between different propositions presented by him, but his recognition of the crucial importance of a person's functionings and capabilities seems to emerge clearly enough, especially in the political context of distributive arrangements.

While the Aristotelian link is undoubtedly important, it should also be noted that there are some substantial differences between the way functionings and capabilities are used in what I have been calling the capability approach and the way they are dealt with in Aristotle's own analysis. Aristotle believes, as Nussbaum (1988) notes, 'that there is just one list of functionings (at least at a certain level of generality) that do in fact constitute human good living' (p. 152).

[42] Indeed, it is precisely as well-being freedom that 'advantage' was defined in Sen (1985*b*: 5–7, 59–71).

[43] See, particularly, Smith (1776) and Marx (1844). The connections are discussed in Sen (1984, 1985*a*, 1987*b*).

[44] See particularly *The Nicomachean Ethics*, Bk I, s. 7; in the translation by Ross (1980: 12–14).

That view would not be inconsistent with the capability approach presented here, but *not*, by any means, *required* by it.

The capability approach has indeed been used (for example, in Sen, 1983*c*, 1984) to argue that while the *commodity* requirements of such capabilities as 'being able to take part in the life of the community' or 'being able to appear in public without shame' vary greatly from one community to another (thereby giving the 'poverty line' a relativist character in the space of commodities), there is much less variation in the *capabilities* that are aimed at through the use of these commodities. This argument, suggesting less variability at a more intrinsic level, has clear links with Aristotle's identification of 'non-relative virtues', but the Aristotelian claims of uniqueness go much further.[45]

Martha Nussbaum, as an Aristotelian, notes this distinction, and also points to Aristotle's robust use of an objectivist framework based on a particular reading of human nature. She suggests the following:

It seems to me, then, that Sen needs to be more radical than he has been so far in his criticism of the utilitarian accounts of well-being, by introducing an objective normative account of human functioning and by describing a procedure of objective evaluation by which functionings can be assessed for their contribution to the good human life.[46]

I accept that this would indeed be a systematic way of eliminating the incompleteness of the capability approach. I certainly have no great objection to anyone going on that route. My difficulty with accepting that as the *only* route on which to travel arises partly from the concern that this view of human nature (with a unique list of functionings for a good human life) may be tremendously over-specified, and also from my inclination to argue about the nature and importance of the type of objectivity involved in this approach. But mostly my intransigence arises, in fact, from the consideration that the use of the capability approach as such does not require taking that route, and the deliberate incompleteness of the capability approach permits other routes to be taken which also have some plausibility. It is, in fact, the feasibility as well as the usefulness of a general approach (to be distinguished from a complete evaluative blueprint) that seems to me to provide good grounds for separating the general case for the capability approach (including, *inter alia*, the Aristotelian theory) from the special case for taking on *exclusively* this particular Aristotelian theory.

In fact, no matter whether we go the full Aristotelian way, which will also need a great deal of extension as a theory for practical evaluation, or take some other particular route, there is little doubt that the kind of *general* argument that Aristotle uses to motivate his approach does have a wider relevance than the defence of the particular form he gives to the nature of human good. This applies *inter alia* to Aristotle's rejection of opulence as a criterion of achievement (rejecting wealth and income as the standards), his analysis of *eudaimonia* in terms of valued activities (rather than relying on readings of mental states, as in some utilitarian procedures), and his assertion of the need to examine the

---

[45] On this see Nussbaum (1990).
[46] Nussbaum (1988: 176).

processes through which human activities are chosen (thereby pointing towards the importance of freedom as a part of living).

11 *Incompleteness and Substance*

The Aristotelian critique points towards a more general issue, namely, that of the 'incompleteness' of the capability approach – both in generating substantive judgements and in providing a comprehensive theory of valuation. Quite different specific theories of value may be consistent with the capability approach, and share the common feature of selecting value-objects from functionings and capabilities. Further, the capability approach can be used with different methods of determining relative weights and different mechanisms for actual evaluation. The approach, if seen as a theory of algorithmic evaluation, would be clearly incomplete.[47]

It may well be asked: why pause at outlining a general approach, with various bits to be filled in, rather than 'completing the task'? The motivation underlying the pause relates to the recognition that an agreement on the usability of the capability approach – an agreement on the nature of the 'space' of value-objects – need not *presuppose* an agreement on how the valuational exercise may be completed. It is possible to disagree both on the exact *grounds* underlying the determination of relative weights, and on the *actual* relative weights chosen,[48] even when there is reasoned agreement on the general nature of the value-objects (in this case, personal functionings and capabilities). If reasoned agreement is seen as an important foundational quality central to political and social ethics,[49] then the case for the pause is not so hard to understand. The fact that the capability approach is consistent and combinable with several different substantive theories need not be a source of embarrassment.

Interestingly enough, despite this incompleteness, the capability approach does have considerable 'cutting power'. In fact, the more challenging part of the claim in favour of the capability approach lies in what it denies. It differs from the standard utility-based approaches in not insisting that we must value *only happiness* (and sees, instead, the state of being happy as one among several objects of value), or *only desire fulfilment* (and takes, instead, desire as useful but imperfect evidence – frequently distorted – of what the person herself values).[50] It differs also from other – non-utilitarian – approaches in not placing among value-objects *primary goods as such* (accepting these Rawlsian-focus variables only derivatively and instrumentally and only to the extent that these goods promote capabilities), or *resources as such* (valuing this Dworkinian perspective only in terms of the impact of resources on functionings and capabilities), and so forth.[51]

---

[47] This relates to one part of the critique presented by Beitz (1986).

[48] On this see Sen (1985*b*: chs. 5–7).

[49] On this question, see Rawls (1971), Scanlon (1982), B. Williams (1985).

[50] For comparisons and contrasts between the capability approach and utilitarian views, see Sen (1984, 1985*a*).

[51] See Rawls (1971, 1988*a*, 1988*b*), Dworkin (1981), and Sen (1980, 1984, 1990*a*).

A general acceptance of the intrinsic relevance and centrality of the various functionings and capabilities that make up our lives does have substantial cutting power, but it need not be based on a prior agreement on the relative values of the different functionings or capabilities, or on a specific procedure for deciding on those relative values.

Indeed, it can be argued that it may be a mistake to move on relentlessly until one gets to exactly one mechanism for determining relative weights, or – to turn to a different aspect of the 'incompleteness' – until one arrives at exactly one interpretation of the metaphysics of value. There are substantive differences between different ethical theories at different levels, from the meta-ethical (involving such issues as objectivity) to the motivational, and it is not obvious that for substantive political and social philosophy it is sensible to insist that all these general issues be resolved *before* an agreement is reached on the choice of an evaluative space. Just as the utilization of actual weights in practical exercises may be based on the acceptance of a certain *range* of variability of weights (as I have tried to discuss in the context of the *use* of the capability approach[52]), even the general rationale for using such an approach may be consistent with some ranges of answers to foundational questions.

12 A Concluding Remark

In this paper I have tried to discuss the main features of the capability approach to evaluation: its claims, its uses, its rationale, its problems. I have also addressed some criticisms that have been made of the approach. I shall not try to summarize the main contentions of the paper, but before concluding, I would like to emphasize the plurality of purposes for which the capability approach can have relevance.

There are different evaluative problems, related to disparate value-purposes. Among the distinctions that are important is that between well-being and agency, and that between achievement and freedom. The four categories of intrapersonal assessment and interpersonal comparison that follow from these two distinctions (namely, well-being achievement, well-being freedom, agency achievement, and agency freedom) are related to each other, but are not identical. The capability approach can be used for each of these different types of evaluation, though not with equal reach. It is particularly relevant for the assessment of well-being – in the form of both achievement and freedom – and for the related problem of judging living standards.

As far as social judgements are concerned, the individual evaluations feed directly into social assessment. Even though the original motivation for using the capability approach was provided by an examination of the question 'equality of what?' (Sen, 1980), the use of the approach, if successful for equality, need not

---

[52] See Sen (1985b); on the general strategy of using 'intersection partial orders', see Sen (1970, 1977).

be confined to equality only.[53] The usability of the approach in egalitarian calculus depends on the plausibility of seeing individual advantages in terms of capabilities, and if that plausibility is accepted, then the same general perspective can be seen to be relevant for other types of social evaluation and aggregation.

The potentially wide relevance of the capability perspective should not come as a surprise, since the capability approach is concerned with showing the cogency of a particular *space* for the evaluation of individual opportunities and successes. In any social calculus in which individual advantages are constitutively important, that space is of potential significance.

[53] Corresponding to 'equality of what?', there is, in fact, also the question: 'efficiency of what?'

BIBLIOGRAPHY

ARISTOTLE (4th c. BC). *The Nicomachean Ethics*: see Ross (1980).

ARNESON, R. (1987). 'Equality and Equality of Opportunity for Welfare', *Philosophical Studies*, S4.

ASAHI, J. (1987). 'On Professor Sen's Capability Theory', mimeographed, Tokyo.

BASU, K. (1987). 'Achievements, Capabilities and the Concept of Well-being', *Social Choice and Welfare*, 4.

BEITZ, C.R. (1986). 'Amartya Sen's *Resources, Values and Development*', *Economics and Philosophy*, 2.

BRANNEN, J., and WILSON, G. (eds.) (1987). *Give and Take in Families*. London: Allen and Unwin.

BROOME, J. (1988). Review of On Ethics and Economics and *The Standard of Living* in *London Review of Books*.

CAMPBELL, R.H., and SKINNER, A.S. (eds.) (1976). Adam Smith, *An Inquiry into the Nature and Causes of the Wealth of Nations*. Oxford: Clarendon Press.

COHEN, G.A. (1989). 'On the Currency of Egalitarian Justice', *Ethics*, 99.

—— (1990). 'Equality of What? On Welfare, Goods and Capabilities', *Recherches Economiques de Louvain*, 56.

CULYER, A.J. (1985). 'The Scope and Limits of Health Economics', *Okonomie des Gesundheitswesens*.

DASGUPTA, P. (1986). 'Positive Freedom, Markets and the Welfare State', *Oxford Review of Economic Policy*, 2.

—— (1988). 'Lives and Well-being', *Social Choice and Welfare*, 5.

—— (1989). 'Power and Control in the Good Polity', in Hamlin and Pettit (1989).

D'ASPREMONT, C., and GEVERS, L. (1977). 'Equity and the Informational Basis of Collective Choice', *Review of Economic Studies*, 46.

DEBEUS, Jos (1986). 'Sen's Theory of Liberty and Institutional Vacuum', University of Amsterdam.

DEVOS, K., and HAGENAARS, ALDI J.M. (1988). 'A Comparison between the Poverty Concepts of Sen and Townsend', mimeographed, University of Leiden.

DEATON, A., and MUELLBAUER, J. (1980). *Economics and Consumer Behaviour*. Cambridge: Cambridge University Press.

DELBONO, F. (1987). Review article on *Commodities and Capabilities, Economic Notes*.

DRÈZE, J., and SEN, A. (1989). *Hunger and Public Action*. Oxford: Clarendon Press.

DWORKIN, R. (1981). 'What is Equality? Part 2: Equality of Resources', *Philosophy and Public Affairs*, 10.

ELSTER, J., and HYLLAND, A. (eds.) (1986). *Foundations of Social Choice Theory*. Cambridge: Cambridge University Press.

GAERTNER, W. (1988). Review of *Commodities and Capabilities* in *Zeitschriften fur National Okommnomia*, 48.

GOODIN, R.E. (1985). *Political Theory and Public Policy*. Chicago and London: University of Chicago Press.

—— (1988). *Reasons for Welfare: Political Theory of the Welfare State*. Princeton: Princeton University Press.

GRIFFIN, J. (1986). *Well-being*. Oxford: Clarendon Press.

GRIFFIN, K., and KNIGHT, J. (eds.) (1989a). 'Human Development in the 1980s and Beyond', special number, *Journal of Development Planning*, 19.

—— (1989b). 'Human Development: The Case for Renewed Emphasis', *Journal of Development Planning*, 19.

HAMLIN, A.P. (1986). *Ethics, Economics and the State*. Brighton: Wheatsheaf Books.

HAMLIN, A., and PETTIT, P. (eds.) (1989). *The Good Polity: Normative Analysis of the State*. Oxford: Blackwell.

HARE, R. (1981). *Moral Thinking*. Oxford: Clarendon Press.

HARRISON, R. (ed.) (1979). *Rational Action*. Cambridge: Cambridge University Press.

HAWTHORN, G. (1987). 'Introduction' in Sen (1987b).

HELM, D. (1986). 'The Assessment: The Economic Border of the State', *Oxford Review of Economic Policy*, 2.

HOSSAIN, I. (1990). *Poverty as Capability Failure*. Helsinki: Swedish School of Economics and Business Administration.

KAKWANI, N. (1986). *Analysing Redistribution Policies*. Cambridge: Cambridge University Press.

KANBUR, R. (1987). 'The Standard of Living: Uncertainty, Inequality and Opportunity', in Sen (1987b).

KOOHI-KAMALI, F. (1988). 'The Pattern of Female Mortality in Iran and some of its Causes', Applied Economics Discussion Paper 62, Oxford Institute of Economics and Statistics.

KOOPMANS, T.C. (1964). 'On Flexibility of Future Preference', in M.W. Shelly and G.L. Bryan (eds.), *Human Judgments and Optimality*. New York: Wiley.

KREPS, D. (1979). 'A Representation Theorem for Preference for Flexibility', *Econometrica*, 47.

KUMAR, B.G. (1987). Poverty and Public Policy: Government Intervention and Level in Kerala, India. D.Phil. dissertation, Oxford University.

KYNCH, J., and SEN, A. (1983). 'Indian Women: Well-being and Survival', *Cambridge Journal of Economics*, 7.

LIDDELL, H.G., and SCOTT, R. (1977). *A Greek–English Lexicon*, extended by H.S. Jones and R. McKenzie. Oxford: Clarendon Press.

LUKER, W. (1986). 'Welfare Economics, Positivist Idealism and Quasi-Experimental Methodology', mimeographed, University of Texas, Austin.

MARX, K. (1844). *Economic and Philosophic Manuscript*. English translation. London: Lawrence and Wishart, 1977.

McMURRIN, S.M. (ed.) (1980). *Tanner Lectures on Human Values*, i. Salt Lake City: University of Utah Press, and Cambridge: Cambridge University Press.

MUELLBAUER, J. (1987). 'Professor Sen on the Standard of Living', in Sen (1987*b*).

NUSSBAUM, M. (1988). 'Nature, Function, and Capability: Aristotle on Political Distribution', *Oxford Studies in Ancient Philosophy*, suppl. vol.

—— (1990). 'Non-Relative Virtues: An Aristotelian Approach', *Midwest Studies in Philosophy*, 13; revised version in this volume.

PATTANAIK, P.K., and XU, YONGSHENG (1990). 'On Ranking Opportunity Sets in Terms of Freedom of Choice', *Recherches Economiques de Louvain*, S6.

PIGOU, A.C. (1920). *The Economics of Welfare*. London: Macmillan.

RAWLS, J. (1971). *A Theory of Justice*. Cambridge, Mass.: Harvard University Press, and Oxford: Clarendon Press.

—— (1988*a*). 'Priority of Right and Ideas of the Good', *Philosophy and Public Affairs*, 17.

—— (1988*b*). 'Reply to Sen', mimeographed, Harvard University.

—— *et al.* (1987). *Liberty, Equality, and Law: Selected Tanner Lectures on Moral Philosophy*, ed. S. McMurrin. Cambridge: Cambridge University Press, and Salt Lake City: University of Utah Press.

RILEY, J. (1988). *Liberal Utilitarianism: Social Choice Theory and J.S. Mill's Philosophy*. Cambridge: Cambridge University Press.

RINGEN, J. (1987). *The Possibility of Politics: A Study of the Economy of the Welfare State*. Oxford: Clarendon Press.

ROEMER, J. (1982). *A General Theory of Exploitation and Class*. Cambridge, Mass.: Harvard University Press.

—— (1986). 'An Historical Materialist Alternative to Welfarism', in Elster and Hylland (1986).

ROSS, D. (1980). Aristotle, *The Nicomachean Ethics*. The World's Classics. Oxford: Oxford University Press.

SCANLON, T.M. (1979). 'Preference and Urgency', *Journal of Philosophy*, 72.

—— (1982). 'Contractualism and Utilitarianism', in Sen and Williams (1982).

SCHOKKAERT, E., and van Ootegem, L. (1990). 'Sen's Concept of the Living Standard Applied to the Belgian Unemployed', *Recherches Economiques de Louvain*, S6.

SEABRIGHT, P. (1989). 'Social Choice and Social Theories', *Philosophy and Public Affairs*, 18.

SEN, A.K. (1970). *Collective Choice and Social Welfare*. San Francisco: Holden-Day. Republished Amsterdam: North-Holland, 1979.

—— (1977). 'On Weights and Measures: Informational Constraints in Social Welfare Analysis', *Econometrica*, 45.

—— (1980). 'Equality of What?' (1979 Tanner Lecture at Stanford), in McMurrin (1980); repr. in Sen (1982*a*) and Rawls *et al.* (1987).

—— (1982*a*). *Choice, Welfare and Measurement*. Oxford: Blackwell, and Cambridge, Mass.: MIT Press.

—— (1982*b*). 'Rights and Agency', *Philosophy and Public Affairs*, 11.

—— (1983*a*). 'Liberty and Social Choice', *Journal of Philosophy*, 80.

—— (1983*b*). 'Development: Which Way Now?', *Economic Journal*, 93; repr. in Sen (1984).

—— (1983*c*). 'Poor, Relatively Speaking', *Oxford Economic Papers*, 35; repr. in Sen (1984).

—— (1984). *Resources, Values and Development*. Oxford: Blackwell, and Cambridge, Mass.: Harvard University Press.

—— (1985a). 'Well-being, Agency and Freedom: The Dewey Lectures 1984', *Journal of Philosophy*, 82.

—— (1985b). *Commodities and Capabilities*. Amsterdam: North-Holland.

—— (1985c). 'Women, Technology and Sexual Divisions', *Trade and Development*, 6.

—— (1987a). *On Ethics and Economics*. Oxford: Blackwell.

—— (1987b). *The Standard of Living* (1985 Tanner Lectures at Cambridge, with contributions by Keith Hart, Ravi Kanbur, John Muellbauer, and Bernard Williams, edited by G. Hawthorn). Cambridge: Cambridge University Press.

—— (1988a). 'Freedom of Choice: Concept and Content', *European Economic Review* 32.

—— (1988b). 'The Concept of Development', in H. Chenery and T. N. Srinivasan (eds.), *Handbook of Development Economics*. Amsterdam: North-Holland.

—— (1990a). 'Justice: Means versus Freedoms', *Philosophy and Public Affairs*, 19.

—— (1990b). 'Gender and Cooperative Conflicts', in Tinker (1990).

—— (1991). 'Preference, Freedom and Social Welfare', *Journal of Econometrics*, 50.

—— (1992). *Inequality Reexamined*. Oxford: Clarendon Press.

—— and WILLIAMS, B. (eds.) (1982). *Utilitarianism and Beyond*. Cambridge: Cambridge University Press.

SIRCAR, D. C. (1979). *Asokan Studies*. Calcutta: Indian Museum.

SMITH, ADAM (1776). *An Inquiry into the Nature of Causes of the Wealth of Nations*: see Campbell and Skinner (1976).

STEINER, H. (1986). 'Putting Rights in their Place: An Appraisal of Amartya Sen's Work on Rights', mimeographed, University of Manchester.

STEWART, F. (1988). 'Basic Needs Strategies, Human Rights and the Right to Development', mimeographed, Queen Elizabeth House.

STREETEN, P. (1984). 'Basic Needs: Some Unsettled Questions', *World Development*, 12.

STREETEN, P., et al. (1981). *First Things First: Meeting Basic Needs in Developing Countries*. New York: Oxford University Press.

SUGDEN, R. (1986). Review of *Commodities and Capabilities*, *Economic Journal*, 96.

SUPPES, P. (1987). 'Maximizing Freedom of Decision: An Axiomatic Analysis', in G. R. Feiwel (ed.), *Arrow and the Foundations of Economic Policy*. New York: New York University Press.

SUZUMURA, K. (1988). Introduction to the Japanese translation of *Commodities and Capabilities*. Tokyo: Iwanami.

TINKER, I. (ed.) (1990). *Persistent Inequalities*. New York: Oxford University Press.

WILLIAMS, A. (1985). 'Economics of Coronary Bypass Grafting', *British Medical Journal*, 291.

—— (1991). 'What is Health and Who Creates it?', in J. Hutton et al. (eds.), *Dependency to Enterprise*. London: Routledge.

WILLIAMS, B. (1985). *Ethics and the Limits of Philosophy*. London: Fontana, and Cambridge, MA: Harvard University Press.

—— (1987). 'The Standard of Living: Interests and Capabilities', in Sen (1987b).

WILSON, G. (1987). *Money in the Family*. Aldershot: Avebury.

ZAMAGNI, S. (1986). 'Introduzione', in A. Sen, *Scelta, Benessere, Equita*. Bologna: Il Mulino.

G.A. Cohen: Equality of What? On Welfare, Goods and Capabilities
Amartya Sen: Capability and Well-Being

Commentary by *Christine M. Korsgaard*

These two papers propose ways to understand and measure certain important aspects of the quality of life. Gerald Cohen is concerned specifically with equality: what it is people must have an equal amount of, in order for them to be equal in the sense egalitarians ought to care about. His paper criticizes the views of Rawls and Sen, and offers his own answer, which is that people should be equal in their *access to advantage*.[1] Both terms in this formula are meant to be eclectic. 'Advantage' includes both welfare and resources, and whatever else we might decide is a 'desirable state of the person'.[2] You have 'access' to things you have or can get or are given to you. To say that people should be equal in their access to advantage, according to Cohen, is to say that any involuntary disadvantage – any disadvantage which either was not chosen or cannot be voluntarily overcome – ought to be eliminated or compensated.

Amartya Sen's view is that the quality of a person's life should be assessed in terms of the person's capabilities. A capability is the ability or potential to do or be something – more technically, to achieve a certain functioning. Functionings are divided into four overlapping categories, which Sen calls well-being freedom, well-being achievement, agency freedom, and agency achievement. Our capabilities are our potentials for all of these things. Sen's view, like Cohen's, began as a thesis about the kind of value that egalitarians ought to be concerned about. People ought to be made equal in their capabilities, or at least in their *basic* capabilities. But Sen is now prepared to claim that his view provides a metric for other purposes as well.

We may assess any proposal about what constitutes the quality of life in various ways. First, we may assess it simply as a philosophical proposal about what a good life is. Second, we may assess it for its legitimacy as a *political* objective: whether it is the sort of thing we ought to bring about through political means. And third, we may assess it for its utility in determining actual political and economic policy – that is, whether it provides accurate enough measures to assess the effects of policy. Obviously, these three forms of assessment are not unrelated, and all are necessary. If capability and access to advantage were not at least important features of a good life, equalizing or maximizing them would not be politically desirable. If they were not legitimate political objectives, the fact that they enable us to make measurements, if it were one, would not carry any weight.

---

[1] Cohen defends his own view at greater length in his 'On the Currency of Egalitarian Justice', *Ethics*, 99 (July 1989), 906–44.

[2] Cohen, 'Equality of What? On Welfare, Resources, and Capabilities', in this volume, 9–29.

Nevertheless, the three forms of assessment are separate. And the question I will focus on, in considering both access to advantage and capability, is their legitimacy as political objectives.

In assessing the legitimacy of a political objective, we must keep in mind that the state uses coercion to achieve its aims, and that the use of coercion is in general wrong. Only the pursuit of certain kinds of aims, in special circumstances, can justify the use of coercion; only these, therefore, can be legitimate as political objectives. There are two familiar and related devices to which political philosophers appeal in order to alleviate the moral problem created by the coercive nature of government. One is the idea of the consent of the governed, either actual or hypothetical, to the general institution of government. I take it for granted that since actual consent has not in fact been given, hypothetical consent is the best we can hope for. That is, the best we can hope is to show that political institutions and their objectives are ones that it is reasonable for people to consent to. The other device is the mechanism of voting, as a way of approximating actual consent within society. Some philosophers believe that these two devices work together to dissipate the moral problem created by the use of state coercion. Each individual is supposed, hypothetically, to consent to submit to political decisions as long as she is allowed, actually, to contribute to those decisions by voting. But at least since Mill, few philosophers would say that voting is *sufficient* to justify the use of state coercion, for it leads to one version of what de Tocqueville called 'the tyranny of the the majority'.[3] Even in a democratic society, we must place limits on what may be achieved through political means. Political objectives must reflect the reasons people have for submitting to the coercive authority of the state in the first place.

The legitimacy of a political objective obviously depends on what sort of political philosophy one espouses, what one thinks the state is for. So I will begin by discussing the kinds of political objectives that have been thought legitimate, and sketching a view that I find plausible. I will then assess Sen's and Cohen's proposals in the light of that view. Following Rawls, I begin with the distinction between liberal and non-liberal political theories.[4] In a liberal theory, the purpose of the state is to allow each citizen to pursue his or her own conception of the good. In a non-liberal theory, some conception of the good is taken as philosophically established, and the goal of the state is to realize that conception. If a non-liberal theory is accepted, my first two forms of assessment are not after all separate: to show that something is a legitimate political objective, all we need do is show that it is indeed an established good. According to such theories, the state is in the business of bringing about the good. As Rawls points out, classical utilitarianism is strictly speaking a non-liberal theory, since it takes the goodness of the maximization of pleasure as both philosophically established and capable of justifying political policy.[5] An Aristotelian theory that takes the purpose of the state to be to educate the citizens for a virtuous life, or a Marxist theory aimed

---

[3] Mill, 1859: ch. 1.   [4] Rawls, 1982*b*: 159–85.   [5] Ibid., 160.

at rendering us truly human, would also be non-liberal. These theories take a certain conception of the good life to be both established and capable of justifying the use of state coercion.

Rawls defines a liberal theory, by contrast, as one that 'allow[s] for a plurality of different and opposing, and even incommensurable, conceptions of the good'.[6] But the phrase 'allows for' is unfortunately ambiguous. Accordingly, there are two kinds of liberal. One kind of liberal agrees with the non-liberal that the purpose of the state is to enable the citizens to achieve a good life, but disagrees that there is just one established conception of the good life. It is important that each person choose, construct, and pursue her own conception of the good. There are a number of different reasons why one might hold this view. They correspond roughly to the various reasons for religious tolerance, and, like those, they are held by many liberals in a rather jumbled way. One reason is *scepticism*: there is no best life, or anyway we cannot prove there is, so we have no solid ground for forcing people to lead one kind of life rather than another. Another reason is *ethical individualism*. According to this view, the goodness of a life essentially depends on its being chosen and constructed by the person who lives it. Your life, like your faith, must be your own spontaneous production if it is to be worth anything at all. A third reason, which lacks a theological analogue, is *epistemological individualism*, which consists of two propositions: first, there may be a best life for each person, but there is no one best life for everyone. Second, as a matter of fact, each person is best placed to *find out* for herself what the best life for her is. (It is by endorsing epistemological individualism that a utilitarian becomes a liberal.) What these views share is the idea that the direct realization of final goods, or best lives, is disqualified as a political goal. Either we do not know enough about final goods to use them in political justifications, or they are by their nature best left in the hands of individuals. The state can only be justified in controlling the distribution of instrumental or primary goods, the things that everyone pursuing a good life has reason to want. According to this view, the reason why people consent, or may be supposed hypothetically to consent, to political institutions, is because (i) they have a better life in society and (ii) the principles regulating society are such as they would have chosen. Because we must allow for a variety of conceptions of the good, however, the only legitimate way for the state to provide a better life is to increase and fairly distribute the stock of primary goods. For reasons that will become clear, I shall call this view 'the New Liberalism'.

There is another, older way to be a liberal which is a little different. According to Locke and Kant, the business of the state is to preserve and protect rights and freedom, *not* to facilitate the pursuit of a good life. These philosophers believed that it is of the nature of rights and freedom that their preservation justifies the use of coercion. Locke believed that you have natural rights which you are entitled to enforce: first, and innately, a right to your own labour, and

---

[6] Ibid.

second, by extension, a qualified right to what you mix your labour with.[7] Kant believed that everyone has an innate right to freedom, and, as a necessary extension of that right, to the acquisition of certain other rights, without which one cannot exercise one's freedom, and so which may be enforced.[8] Kant argued that rights may be coercively enforced this way: rights are a necessary extension of freedom, so anyone who tries to interfere with rights tries to interfere with freedom. A rights violator is a hindrance to freedom. But anything that hinders a hindrance to freedom is consistent with freedom. And anything that is consistent with freedom is legitimate. The coercive enforcement of rights, being consistent with freedom, is therefore legitimate.[9]

These views also ground state coercive authority in a social contract, but the effect of the contract is different. In the New Liberalism, the hypothetical social contract seems to give rise to the coercive authority of the state. The justification of the use of coercion lies in the fact that people may plausibly be supposed to consent to arrangements that they would have chosen and that give them a better life. In the Old Liberalism, coercive authority is thought to attach to rights and freedom by their very nature—all that the contract does is *transfer* this already existing coercive authority to the state.[10] Hypothetical consent is only allowed to determine *who* exercises coercive authority; it does not give rise to it.

A consequence is that, according to the Old Liberalism, state coercion can only be exercised in the protection and preservation of freedom. As in the New Liberalism, final goods are not legitimate political objectives, but there is a difference. In the New Liberalism, final goods are disqualified as political objectives because of their unknowability or variability. In the Old Liberalism, final goods are not so much disqualified as never qualified in the first place. I think the point is important because many people suppose that liberalism must be founded on philosophical scepticism about whether we can discover what the best life is. The Old Liberalism is consistent with the most thoroughgoing certainty about the best life. You can think, with Aristotle in book X of the *Nicomachean Ethics*, that you can prove that a contemplative life is best and still think that the state

---

[7] Locke, 1690: ch. 5, s. 27.

[8] Kant, 1797: 52; Prussian Academy page numbers (standard in most editions), 246. (Citations hereinafter given as e.g. 52/246.)

[9] Kant, 1797: 35–6/231.

[10] See e.g. Locke, 1690:ch. 7, s. 87. It follows that the goal of political society is the preservation of rights and property (ch. 9, s. 123). Locke, however, sometimes seems to give the government more extensive powers in acting 'for the good' of the citizens, so long as their property is not violated. But what licenses this, I believe, is that Locke believes that consent is actual (express or tacit), not hypothetical, and also that there is a real possibility of withdrawing it. Kant portrays government explicitly as arising from a hypothetical contract investing coercive authority in a state (1797: 76–7/312; 80–1/315–16). In this case, 'transfer' is not exactly the right word for the effect of the contract on coercive authority. Kant thinks that in order to be morally legitimate, the coercive enforcement of rights must be 'reciprocal' and therefore must be accomplished through the state (36–7/232; 64–5/255–6). In other words, the *only* legitimate way to enforce your rights is to join in a political state with the person whom you claim has attacked your rights and so to submit yourself as well as him to coercive enforcement (71–2/307–8).

has no business getting people to contemplate. Only the protection of free-dom, and not the achievement of the good, is grounds for the use of coercion.

There are two objections to the Old Liberalism, both of which the New Liberalism is designed partly to overcome. Both objections complain that the Old Liberalism is too conservative. First, according to the versions presented by Locke and Kant, extensive property rights are supposed to have existed in the state of nature, and the business of government is to protect those rights. This is objectionable both because it depends on a questionable premiss—that pro-perty rights exist independently of and prior to the state—and because it seems to saddle the government with an obligation to carry on and fortify inherited inequalities. I do not think this is essential to the view in its Kantian form. The only thing essential is that a right to freedom exist prior to the state, and that this be taken to be a natural human right. We can allow, with the New Liberal-ism, that we should determine what further rights will count as necessary exten-sions or realizations of freedom within the bounds of the state, by determining what people can reasonably agree to. But, the objection continues—and this is the second complaint—the Old Liberalism amounts to what some of us will regard as a dreary form of libertarianism. If the only thing that the state can guarantee is freedom, and not a good life, there will be no grounds for guarantee-ing things that seem clearly to be part of the good and not of freedom—food, medical care, an economic minimum, and so forth. This kind of theory makes it hard to be a welfare liberal.

There is also a way to overcome this objection. It is to insist both on the necessity of employing a rich positive conception of freedom, and on the idea that certain welfare conditions must be met in order to achieve what Rawls calls the 'worth of liberty', the real possibility of taking advantage of one's rights and opportunities.[11] Rawls himself declines to treat the conditions of the worth of liberty as part of, or essential to, being free. But in fact it does not matter much whether we talk of the worth of liberty or its reality. We cannot effectively guarantee liberty without guaranteeing its worth. The general idea behind this view, then, is that unless certain basic welfare conditions are met and resources and opportunities provided, we cannot seriously claim that society is preserving and protecting everyone's freedom. The poor, the jobless, the medically neg-lected, the unhoused, and the uneducated are not free no matter what rights they have been guaranteed by the constitution. There are two reasons for this. The first is their impaired capacity for formulating and pursuing a conception of the good. The second is just as important. A person who lacks these basic goods is subject to intimidation by the rich and powerful, especially if others depend on her. As unskilled woman labourer who puts up with a lower income, poor condi-tions, or even sexual harassment on the job because her only alternative is to let her children starve is not free. To fail to satisfy people's basic needs and provide

11 Rawls, 1971: s. 32, 204.

essential skills and opportunities is to leave people without recourse, and people without recourse are not free.[12]

I think that there are some important philosophical advantages in a welfarist version of the Old Liberalism. For if we must justify state coercion by appeal to the notion of hypothetical consent, we need some way to limit what sort of thing is a candidate for such consent. We cannot suppose that people hypothetically consent to coercion in the name of just anything society decides is good. The older, freedom-based theory allows the state to coerce people only for the sake of something for which they may legitimately be coerced anyway—the achievement of freedom for every person. It explains the priority of liberty over other goods, and yet at the same time its emphasis on positive freedom and the worth of liberty explains why the guarantee of basic welfare and opportunities is essential. The result of employing these notions is a very large coincidence in practice between the New Liberalism and the Old. But the justification is still different. In the Old Liberalism, primary goods are justified as essential to the worth, or the reality, of freedom in a positive sense, rather than as general means to various conceptions of the good.

Now I return to the proposals of Sen and Cohen. First, the view of legitimate political objectives that I have sketched leads immediately to a strong although qualified endorsement of Sen's proposal that we should distribute with an eye to capabilities. For Sen argues that the idea of capabilities gives us a way of understanding the idea of positive freedom, and I think that this is correct: to make people capable of effectively realizing their goals and pursuing their well-being is to make them positively free. The qualification is this. In his paper Sen considers whether and to what extent his view can be justified by the idea that human well-functioning, suitably defined, corresponds to some philosophical ideal of the final good: for instance that of Aristotle or Marx.[13] On the view I have sketched, this correspondence, if it were one, would play no role in justifying the distribution of capabilities as a political objective.

What I have to say about Cohen's paper is more complicated. First, I want to

---

[12] My way of portraying the situation may suggest that I think of Rawls as the exemplary New Liberal. On the whole this is correct, but I also think that there are elements in Rawls's later writings that suggest a shift in the direction of the welfarist version of Old Liberalism. A particular issue illustrates the point. In *A Theory of Justice*, Rawls treats liberties as items on the list of primary goods. In the general conception of justice, they may be traded off for other sorts of primary goods (s. 11, 62–3). Rawls then has to provide an explanation of the priority of liberty in the special conception of justice. That is, he has to explain why, in favourable conditions, the liberties come to acquire the special status of goods that citizens will not trade off for anything else (s. 82, 541–8). In his later writings, Rawls instead places more emphasis on the conception of the citizen as a moral person, one of whose highest-order interests is in the exercise of autonomy itself: not just achieving her conception of the good, but freely choosing and revising it. The citizen so understood views the state not only as a *locus* for pursuit of her determinate conception of the good, but also as a *locus* for the exercise of autonomy. See Rawls, 1980 and 1982*a*. This is a shift in the direction of the Old Liberalism, and among other things it makes the priority of liberty easier to explain. See esp. 1982*a*: 27 ff. This does not mean that the general conception of justice has disappeared from Rawls's account; rather, he has made it clearer why this conception is only acceptable when the worth of liberty cannot be established.

[13] Sen, 'Capability and Well-Being', in this volume, 30–53.

address Cohen's claim that 'midfare' is a legitimate political objective in its own right and his criticism of Sen's view on this point.[14] Cohen accuses Sen of 'athleticism', noticing places where Sen seems to say that the point of providing someone with, say, food is that they may *feed themselves* rather than just that they may *get fed*, whoever is the agent in the case. Cohen argues that it is important that people get fed, not just that they feed themselves, and supposes that Sen misses this point because he is focused too much on freedom and activity. But a person's getting fed may be justified politically by the contribution to his freedom that being well nourished makes. We do not have to choose between giving nourishment a political weight which is unrelated to freedom and the 'athleticism' of which Cohen accuses Sen. Feeding yourself is not the only free activity for which the provision of an adequate diet is essential.

Cohen's own proposal gives a different role to freedom from those of Sen and Rawls. Cohen believes that it is unjust that people should be disadvantaged in ways they do not freely choose. He thinks that this idea is what gives intuitive force to the 'expensive tastes' criticism of welfarism propounded by Rawls and others. Cohen accuses Rawls of switching back and forth between a deterministic and a libertarian view of human nature. When he attacks the political use of the notion of desert, Rawls uses deterministic arguments, saying that if someone is more diligent or ambitious than others, these virtues are most likely the product of a favourable upbringing. On the other hand, Rawls claims that people should be held responsible for their tastes, and should be regarded as the autonomous authors of their own conceptions of the good. What Rawls ought to say, according to Cohen, is just that it is difficult to *tell* to what extent people are responsible for either their efforts or their preferences.[15] But the fact that it is difficult to tell is no reason not to reward people to the extent that they *are* responsible for their efforts, and, more importantly to Cohen, no reason not to compensate them for disadvantageous preferences that they cannot help. Cohen acknowledges that his proposal requires assessment of the extent to which disadvantages are voluntary in individual cases, and that such judgements are not easy to make. But he says that 'there is no antecedent reason whatsoever for supposing that judgements of justice, at a fine grain degree of resolution, are easy'.[16]

There are several things wrong here. First, Cohen assumes that there is a single answer, in any given case, to the metaphysical question of the extent to which one's choice or effort was free. But this ignores a certain complication. Freedom of the will may *itself* be the result of a favourable upbringing and social conditions. We may believe that a human being is free, if ever, when she not only has a range of options but an education that enables her to recognize those options as such and the self-respect that makes her choice among them a real one. Ignorance, lack of imagination, and lack of self-respect are not just external constraints

---

[14] See Cohen, 'Equality of What?', 18 ff. 'Midfare' is Cohen's term for the effect of goods on the person.   [15] Ibid.   [16] Ibid.   [17] Rawls, 1971: ss 14, 48.

on the range of your options: they can cripple the power of choice itself. The possession of freedom of the will may itself be lucky.

If this is right, there is something better for the state to do than the acts of individual compensation Cohen proposes. We can set society up so that people's choices will be autonomous and free. And here it becomes important to insist, along with Rawls, that the subject of justice is the basic structure of society. Cohen envisions a world in which government officials make judgements about the extent to which people are responsible for their preferences. But part of the reason why Rawls thinks that we should focus on the basic structure is that this way we can avoid having to make moralizing judgements about individual cases. By setting up the basic structure of society as what Rawls calls a system of 'pure procedural justice', we avoid having to ask intractable questions about whether particular individuals deserve the positions in which they have landed.[17] In a similar way, we should avoid having to make particular metaphysical judgements about whether persons have formed their preferences autonomously or not. Society should be set up so that we can assume, as far as possible, that they have done so.

This is not just for the pragmatic reason that metaphysical judgements about free will are hard to make in particular cases. In the conceptions of Rawls and Sen, freedom is regarded as something society should bring about, not just as the occasion for judgements about what people deserve. And this leads me to a final point, which is that there is also a moral reason for working through the basic structure, and so avoiding particular judgements of the sort Cohen has in mind. Judgements about whether others have freely chosen their conceptions of the good are not only ones we cannot very easily make, they are ones we ought not to make. Such judgements are disrespectful. If one of our goals is to make it possible for the members of society to have decent *moral* relations with one another, this is an additional reason for making freedom appear instead as a *consequence* of justice; something that results, that is, from a just basic structure of society.

BIBLIOGRAPHY

KANT, IMMANUEL (1797). *The Metaphysical Elements of Justice*, trans. John Ladd (1965). Indianapolis: Bobbs-Merrill Library of Liberal Arts.

LOCKE, JOHN (1690). *Second Treatise of Government*. Indianapolis: Hackett Publishing.

MILL, JOHN STUART (1859). *On Liberty*. Indianapolis: Hackett Publishing.

RAWLS, JOHN (1971). *A Theory of Justice*. Cambridge, Mass.: Harvard University Press.

—— (1980). 'Kantian Constructivism in Moral Theory: The Dewey Lectures 1980', *Journal of Philosophy*, 77 (Sept. 1980).

—— (1982a). 'The Basic Liberties and Their Priority', in *Tanner Lectures on Human Values*, iii. Salt Lake City: University of Utah Press.

—— (1982b). 'Social Unity and Primary Goods', in *Utilitarianism and Beyond*, ed. Amartya Sen and Bernard Williams. Cambridge: Cambridge University Press.

Amartya Sen: Capability and Well-Being

Commentary by Wulf Gaertner

During the last three or four years the West German economy has witnessed an annual growth rate of GNP of between 3 and 4 per cent, while the number of persons out of work remained at roughly 2 million during the same period of time. Some people question this figure, others seem to get used to it. What is noteworthy is the fact that in spite of a thriving economy the unemployment rate seems to have got stuck at a rather high level (be it 2 million or only 1.5 million). In my opinion, the latter phenomenon should also be viewed from a somewhat different angle, namely the growing length of time many of these people have actually been jobless. It is being reported by doctors and psychologists that individuals who are out of work over a long period are suffering from this situation psychologically—and not only in terms of the obvious real income losses. They get isolated within society and start losing the capacity to do and initiate certain things, a capacity which they formerly possessed. This change is twofold. In Sen's terminology, their vector of functionings is altering, and at the same time their capability, namely, their ability to achieve 'various alternative combinations of beings and doings' is shrinking. This fact does not manifest itself in the official statistics, and quite often it remains unobserved in discussions about unemployment when growth and inflation rates, productivity changes, and other economic indicators are quoted.

It is still quite often the case that developing countries are only compared in terms of GNP per head. In his *Commodities and Capabilities* Sen has shown that India and China are close together in terms of GNP per head but quite far apart in terms of basic capabilities of survival and education, such as 'the ability to live long, the ability to avoid mortality during infancy and childhood, the ability to read and write, and the ability to benefit from sustained schooling' (p. 76).

These basic capabilities are certainly of great importance in an analysis of poverty. They are no longer of much interest in a comparison of highly developed countries, for the simple reason that most of the truly elementary functionings are achieved to a very high degree in those economies. It seems to me, however, that another set of basic functionings is more and more coming to the fore in highly industrialized countries, functionings we have forgotten to think about since everyone had accomplished them formerly. Some of these basic functionings are in danger of becoming unachievable (or only partially achievable), others appear to be out of reach for the time being. Let me just name a few: to drink tap-water, to take a swim in rivers or in the sea, to eat fish from the sea, to breathe clean air in a metropolitan area, to walk around at night without fear, to live without the danger of an accident in a nuclear power plant.

All these functionings are very basic though, admittedly, their aspect of 'basicness' is different from that in Sen's comparison between India and China. I find still another category of functionings worth mentioning, which seems to be closely correlated with the standard of living. Here, too, I want to mention only a few items: to receive further education, to be regularly employed, to take a holiday, to participate in social life. Some of these functionings are to some extent related to the notion of opulence. They have, however, a lot to do with a person's ability to choose between different ways of living, in other words, with a person's capability set.

The selection of a class of valuable functionings is obviously context-dependent. In some cases context should be interpreted in terms of the stage of development of the economies under investigation, in other cases it would be more appropriate to consider the cultural and historical development of a particular society. Sen writes that the choice of the class of functionings is intimately related to the selection of objects of value.

Is there something like a complete list of relevant functionings? In Sen's comparison between India and China, for example, which is very much in favour of China, should one perhaps include an item reflecting the historical fact that under Mao many people had to give up their proper occupation in order to work in agriculture or the coal-mines—a fact which severely limited the capability set of the Chinese intellectual at that time?

The following remark refers to the aspect of measurability within Sen's capability approach. Elementary functionings such as life expectancy, infant mortality, or adult literacy rate are relatively easy to measure, even on a cardinal scale. But how about more complex functionings such as achieving self-respect, taking part in social and or political life, being happy in one's job? It seems to me that for these items the measurability issue is quite difficult to resolve. Could it be solved indirectly, say, via commodities and prices? My first reaction is that such a proposal would introduce a profound inconsistency into Sen's analysis. In *Commodities and Capabilities* Sen argues convincingly against the opulence-focused approach and now, via the measurability issue, the perspective of commodity command would re-enter the scene. On the other hand, one should not forget that the availability of good-quality clothing at low prices, for example, makes it easier 'to appear in public without shame', a functioning mentioned by Adam Smith. Larger apartments provide the possibility of entertaining friends, and more leisure (i.e. fewer working hours) makes it easier to take part in the life of the community. Expenditure on leisure activities could, to some extent, serve as a proxy for the degree of social integration of a particular person or household.

In connection with the identification of the objects of value, Sen mentions the dominance ranking between vectors of functionings or capabilities. How far does the dominance relationship take us? This clearly depends on what is being compared to what.

It may be of some interest to report on a simple calculation which I have made on the basis of a vector of basis capabilities (namely, infant death rate, life expectancy, number of inhabitants per medical doctor, illiteracy rate, consumption of calories) and GNP per capita. I collected these data for about 130 countries and looked at the percentage of cases where a comparison between any two countries was possible via a simple vector dominance relationship (thereby avoiding the question of attaching appropriate weights).

I found out that for East European countries a simple vector dominance held in 16 per cent of the binary comparisons; for Western democratic countries (including Canada, Japan, and the USA), the percentage rate was 17; between elements of the first group and the second group, it was 21.4; among the first thirty countries in terms of GNP per head ('the richest'), it was 26; among the last thirty countries in terms of GNP per head ('the poorest'), it was 23; between elements of the richest group and the poorest group, vector dominance held in roughly 90 per cent of all binary comparisons. This shows that for some of the underlying issues, the simple dominance ranking cannot take us too far. Weighting therefore seems unavoidable, and this is clearly emphasized by Sen.

There are many schemes for choosing relative weights – strictly speaking, there is an infinite number of weighting schemes. As long as there is no agreed-on metatheory, any set of weights may be found arbitrary, except perhaps for an equal weighting system, which would satisfy an anonymity or neutrality condition. But neutrality itself is debatable. Maybe it is too much to ask for a metatheory since there are good reasons to argue that the construction of relative weights should depend on the proper context. Also, one should perhaps acquiesce in defining a certain range within which the relative weights could vary, a point mentioned by Sen. In an analysis and comparison of well-being among very poor countries, Dasgupta (1989) has established a ranking of these countries in terms of the classical Borda method. It has often been argued that this method, too, is arbitrary, but Dasgupta's findings are quite illuminating, particularly his results on the degree of correlation between elements of a vector of positive rights and elements of a vector of negative rights.

Let us return to capabilities. Sen argues that a capability set should not be evaluated according to the actual achievements of a person ('well-being achievement') but according to the set of real opportunities ('well-being freedom'). How can one define the set of real opportunities? This question is not an easy one. Is it true that well-being freedom increases whenever a particular person's range of choice increases? That depends. It depend on the particular items which have become additionally available. Do new products, for example, increase well-being freedom? This question was raised by Williams (1987) in response to Sen's 'standard of living' lectures (1987). The answer, I think, should be: not necessarily. A new washing powder normally does not create more freedom, since it does not represent a value-object. It provides some functionings which are more or less irrelevant. Things may, however, be different if the negative effects on the environment induced by the new detergent are less serious than those of the old product. It seems to me that for this kind of question the Gorman–Lancaster approach[1] of looking at characteristics could be of some help. An evaluation in terms of goods characteristics is probably a lot easier to perform than an evaluation in terms of extensions of a person's freedom. However, not every new characteristic which is created is valuable, nor is any increase in some particular characteristic.

The above issue is closely related to the question of set evaluation. Can the value of the capability set be equated to the value of one of its elements, the chosen element, for example? Sen calls this rather truncated procedure 'elementary evaluation'. Its merits are obvious, and if the selected element is chosen through maximization according to some intelligible criterion, then elementary evaluation may be satisfactory as a first approximation. The situation would, however, be quite different if the chosen element, that is, the achieved n-tuple of functionings, was picked at random or arbitrarily.

The foregoing argumentation shows how difficult it is to assess well-being freedom. A larger set of n-tuples of functionings is not necessarily tantamount to a preferable set (sometimes a smaller set could even be a better set when information gathering and processing become too costly). The evaluative problem may be less complicated when the rights aspect in well-being freedom is considered. It seems to me that there is a direct relationship between well-being freedom and a particular society's bill of rights or, formulated more cautiously, a society's list of guaranteed—that is, actually protected—fundamental human rights. Freedom of thought means freedom of expression, freedom of the press is tantamount to access to a huge amount of information, freedom to choose one's place of work increases one's flexibility, and so forth. In other words, civil and political liberties increase an individual's capability set and therefore his or her well-being freedom.

The situation again becomes more complicated when interdependencies are brought into the picture. My range of freedom, for example, is limited by your range of freedom, and vice versa. Also, capability sets do not seem to be given once and for all, that is, to be absolute and invariant. On the contrary, they vary over time due to cultural, economic, political, sociological, and technological changes (we have observed above that the choice of valuable functionings is context-dependent). All this adds to the degree of complexity of the evaluative exercise.

There have, of course, been attempts to deal with some of the points mentioned above. The issue of rights and liberty, for example, has been extensively discussed by many philosophers as well as economists. In economics, Hayek and his liberal school are well known for their investigation into the relationship between economic actions and systems of rights. In social choice theory,

---

[1] Both Gorman (1956) and Lancaster (1966) have developed an approach in which commodities are translated into characteristics.

many scholars have considered the exercise of individual rights within collective choice procedures. Concerning the enlargement of opportunity sets, Koopmans (1964) formulated axioms which, when followed by an individual, make him or her prefer the augmented set to the original one.

In my opinion, much more work has to be done on these and related issues. The various questions which I have raised in my discussion should not give the impression that I am sceptical about the merit of Sen's approach. On the contrary, I find the focus on functionings and capabilities within an analysis of well-being extremely significant and fruitful. Just to underline my conviction, I should like to refer again to the list of basic functionings mentioned at the beginning of my discussion, which apparently play an increasingly important role in highly industrialized countries—functionings, however, that are not adequately reflected in the official statistics many economists are used to working with. It would be misleading to think that Sen's approach to well-being and capability is primarily relevant to the analysis of poor nations, although his empirical studies in terms of the most elementary functionings have revealed an appalling degree of injustice in some of those countries. And the disclosure of this fact is, of course, highly significant, mostly for those who are suffering.

BIBLIOGRAPHY

DASGUPTA, P. (1989). 'Well-being: Foundations, and the Extent of its Realization in Poor Countries'. Discussion Paper, Stanford University, Stanford, Calif.

GORMAN, M. W. (1956). 'The Demand for Related Goods', Journal Paper J3/29, Iowa Experimental Station, Ames, Iowa.

KOOPMANS, T. C. (1964). 'On Flexibility of Future Preference', in M. W. Shelly, II and G. L. Bryan (eds.), *Human Judgments and Optimality*. New York: John Wiley.

LANCASTER, K. J. (1966). 'A New Approach to Consumer Theory', Journal of Political Economy, 74, 132–57.

SEN, A. (1985) *Commodities and Capabilities*. Amsterdam: North-Holland.

——— (1987). *The Standard of Living* (The Tanner Lectures) Cambridge: Cambridge University Press.

WILLIAMS, B. (1987). 'The Standard of Living: Interests and Capabilities', in Sen (1987).

Descriptions of Inequality: The Swedish Approach to Welfare Research

Robert Erikson

By the 1950s it had already become clear that, in spite of its widespread use, per capita GNP is an insufficient measure of the well-being of citizens. Thus, in 1954, an expert group within the United Nations suggested that we should not rely on monetary measures alone: the measurement of well-being should be based on several different components, together making up the level of living.[1] Partly influenced by the UN expert group, Johansson made level of living, seen as a set of components, the basic concept in the first Swedish Level of Living Survey conducted in 1968.[2] This survey has been followed by a number of similar studies, both in Sweden and in the other Nordic countries. To exemplify the Swedish approach to welfare research, I will here use the first survey from 1968 and its direct followers, conducted by the Swedish Institute for Social Research in 1974 and 1981. Apart from minor details, however, what I say also applies to what has been done by the Swedish Central Statistical Office as well as by other Scandinavian research organizations.[3]

The measurement and description of welfare implies a response to a series of questions. One concerns the basis of welfare measurement: should it be related to the needs or the resources of individuals? Another question is whether she herself or an outside observer should judge the individual's welfare. Furthermore, we must decide which types of indicator to use and how to use them, how relevant descriptions should be provided, and how we can give an overall picture of the individual's welfare. I will return to these questions later and discuss how they have been answered in the Swedish level of living surveys. Before doing so I will present some results from these surveys in the hope of making the issues clearer and more concrete.

1 The Level of Living Surveys

In 1965 the Swedish government set up a commission with the task of describing the conditions and problems of low income earners. The commission planned its task in three steps: (1) a study of the distribution of factor income, (2) a study of the distribution of disposable income, and (3) a study of the

I am indebted to Walter Korpi, Martha Nussbaum, and Michael Tåhlin for helpful comments on an earlier draft, and to Caroline Hartnell for improvement of my English.

[1] United Nations, 1954. See also United Nations, 1966.

[2] See Johansson, 1970.

[3] Thus, the subtitle of this paper could as well be 'The Scandinavian Approach to Welfare Research', which actually is the title of a paper by Hannu Uusitalo and myself (Erikson and Uusitalo, 1987).

distribution of welfare in non-monetary terms. This third study was carried out by a group of sociologists who communicated their results to the commission in a series of reports.

For the purpose of the third study, around 6,000 people in the 15–75 age range living in Sweden were interviewed in 1968. In 1974 and 1981 surviving people under 76 years of age still living in Sweden were interviewed again. At both these later interviews young people and recent immigrants were added to the sample in order to make it representative for the Swedish adult population. The interviewees were asked about their living conditions in nine different areas or components of life. A large number of indicators were used for most of the components. The components together with some typical indicators are shown in Table 1.

Table 1 Components and some Typical Indicators in the Swedish Level of Living Surveys*

Components	Indicators
1. Health and access to health care	Ability to walk 100 metres, various symptoms of illness, contacts with doctors and nurses
2. Employment and working conditions	Unemployment experiences, physical demands of work, possibilities to leave the place of work during work hours
3. Economic resources	Income and wealth, property, ability to cover unforeseen expenses of up to $1,000 within a week
4. Education and skills	Years of education, level of education reached
5. Family and social integration	Marital status, contacts with friends and relatives
6. Housing	Number of persons per room, amenities
7. Security of life and property	Exposure to violence and thefts
8. Recreation and culture	Leisure-time pursuits, vacation trips
9. Political resources	Voting in elections, membership of unions and political parties, ability to file complaints

* In the first survey in 1968 no questions were asked about security of life and property, whereas questions were included about diet and nutrition.

In a report on the three surveys which was published in 1984[4] the overriding aim was to answer three questions:

1. Had there been an average change in the level of living between 1968 and
   1981?
2. Were there any differences in level of living between different population
   groups, specifically between men and women, social classes, age groups,
   or regions?
3. Had there been any changes between 1968 and 1981 in differences in level
   of living between groups?

Our attempts to answer these questions followed several routes. Some examples will illustrate how the results were presented.

Three questions were asked about physical mobility: whether the respondent could walk 100 metres briskly without problems, whether he or she could
go up and down stairs without difficulty, and whether he or she could run
100 metres without difficulty. In Figure 1 we show results regarding the proportion saying that they had problems in at least two of these three respects,
which in nearly all cases included those who said that they had problems in
running and climbing stairs. The figure is a diagrammatic representation of
the outcome of a logarithmic regression analysis.[5]

The diagram is an attempt to present a complicated reality in a simple form,
though on the basis of a fairly sophisticated statistical technique. Technically,
the horizontal lines within each subfield represent regression coefficients and
their possible slopes give information on the interaction between the factor in
question (sex, age, community, and class) and year of investigation. The vertical
lines indicate the approximate length of 85 per cent confidence intervals. Our
hope, of course, is that the statistically untrained reader, through such diagrams,
will be able to get a grasp of the variations and changes in level of living.
The interpretation of Figure 1 would be as follows: the signs in the leftmost
field all appear on about the same level, thereby indicating that there has
been no overall change from 1968 to 1981 in the proportion of disabled people.
The next field to the right shows that women tend to be disabled more often
than men, when other factors are accounted for. That the horizontal lines
converge slightly (read from left to right) suggests that this difference has
decreased slightly during the period. The field thereafter indicates what we
could expect: that older people are disabled more often than younger, but
also that this difference has diminished between 1968 and 1981. The following
field shows that there are no clear differences in this respect between cities,
towns, and the countryside, and the rightmost field shows that members of
the working class (III) are disabled more often (having accounted for age, etc.)

---

[4] The report was published in Swedish in 1984. It was later published in English in a slightly
abridged version: Erikson and Åberg, 1987.
[5] The regression analysis and the diagrammatic technique are described in Selén, 1985 and
1987.

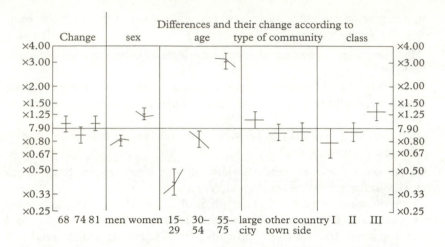

Figure 1 Regression Diagram of Proportions of Disabled People

than members of the upper middle class (I), with the lower middle class (II) in between.

In Figure 2 we show the corresponding results for political resources, in the sense of having taken part in opinion-forming activities.[6]

Figure 2 indicates that the proportion participating in opinion-forming activities has increased between 1968 and 1981, that men are more active than women but that this difference has diminished, that age differences have disappeared, that there are no differences between different types of communities, and that there are great and non-changing differences between the social classes.

Table 2 shows, in a more conventional fashion, the inequality in income from employment between different classes and occupational groups. The overall income inequality decreased over the period 1967–80. This decrease was partly the result of diminishing differences between occupational groups, but partly also of lessening inequality within classes. Wages in occupations mainly employing women increased considerably during the period.

In an attempt to get a more complete picture of variation and change in welfare problems at the individual level we counted the number of components, out of five, for which we had recorded problematic conditions for the individual respondent. The components were health, economic resources, political resources, social relations, and housing.[7] Figure 3 shows the variation and

---

[6] Opinion-forming activity is defined as having spoken at a meeting, written in a newspaper, or participated in a demonstration. See further Szulkin, 1987.

[7] The other components were not included because in some cases it was dubious to delimit a problematic state (education, leisure) or because the component was not included in all surveys (security). Employment and working conditions were treated in a separate analysis only including the labour force. The delimitation of problematic states for the five included components involved a large number of indicators. See further Erikson and Tåhlin, 1987.

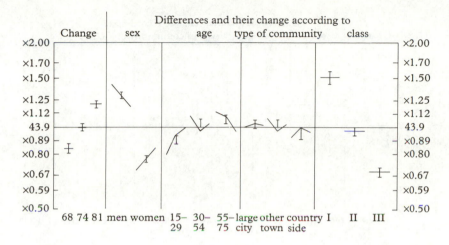

Figure 2 Regression Diagram of Proportions of People Participating in Opinion-forming Activities

Table 2 Earned Incomes for Full-time Year-round Workers in same Occupational Groups 1967, 1973, and 1980 (in SEK 1,000s computed to 1980 money values)

	Earned incomes			Percentage of average wage			Coefficients of variation		
	1967	1973	1980	1967	1973	1980	1967	1973	1980
All employees	74.6	87.8	89.6	100	100	100	49	41	37
Professionals executives in private employment	135.4	161.3	153.7	182	184	172	36	32	34
Professionals in public employment	140.7	141.2	131.7	189	161	147	32	34	32
Foremen	78.4	92.8	93.2	105	106	104	16	19	20
Private technical and clerical	65.0	82.9	90.7	87	94	101	31	27	24
Public salaried	68.5	79.3	84.4	92	90	94	30	19	17
Metal workers	59.4	71.7	70.1	78	82	78	25	16	15
Other manufacturing workers	55.9	67.3	68.8	75	77	77	25	20	20
Construction workers	63.8	73.9	79.7	86	84	89	37	15	18
Workers in local government	59.1	74.0	76.1	79	84	85	26	19	10
Workers in state government	63.9	74.7	78.0	86	85	87	18	13	9

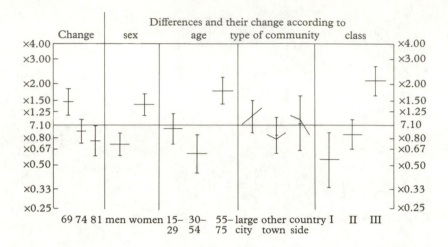

Figure 3 Regression Model for Proportions with Three or More Problems in the Population as a Whole

change in the proportion showing three or more of these problematic states.

Figure 3 shows that the proportion with many problems has decreased slightly over time, that women are more often exposed to many problems than men, that many problems are relatively common among old people, that there are small and unsystematic differences between different types of community, and that problems are more common in the working class than in other classes. Generally, the relative differences between groups seem to be stable over time.

Overall, a slight improvement in the average level of living seems to have taken place in the years 1968–81, especially in the areas of housing and education. Women's position relative to men improved considerably in most areas. The relative differences between age groups decreased slightly in terms of economic resources, as the positions of young and old people improved compared to those in the intermediate age groups. Differences between the social classes decreased slightly.

These are some examples of how variations and changes in the level of living in Sweden have been described. What, then, is the theoretical rationale behind this approach? I will first discuss the concept, then continue with some of the problems of operationalization, and finally consider some aspects of its presentation. In doing this I will return to the questions previously mentioned.

2   The Concept

'*The individual's command over resources* in the form of money, possessions, knowledge, mental and physical energy, social relations, security and so on,

through which the individual can control and consciously direct his living conditions.'
This was the definition of level of living given in the first discussion of the
concept in connection with the 1968 survey.[8] The central element is the
individual's 'command over resources', which was extracted from Richard
Titmuss's writings on welfare,[9] but a discussion of command over resources
can be found within economics as well.[10] The emphasis on several different
components of welfare was taken from the writings of the United Nations
expert group, referred to above. To judge the level of living of an individual
or a group, we have to know their resources and conditions in several respects,
which are not transferable between each other. To have knowledge about,
for example, economic conditions is thus not enough; we also have to know
about health, knowledge and skills, social relations, conditions of work, etc., in
order to determine the level of living. There is no common yardstick through
which the different dimensions could be compared or put on a par. No objective or impartial way exists by which it would be possible to decide which of
two men is better off if one of them has, for example, worse health but better
economic conditions than the other.

Welfare or level of living seems, at least in the European tradition, to be
based either on people's needs or on their resources.[11] If needs are made central,
then the concern is with 'the degree of need-satisfaction'.[12] If resources are
made central then the concern is rather with man's *capacity* to satisfy those
needs or, more generally, to 'control and consciously direct his living conditions'; the individual's level of living will thus be an expression of his 'scope
of action'.[13] Resources, as understood here, seem to be very close to Sen's
concept of capabilities. And, as Sen points out, well-being freedom, that is,
a capability to achieve satisfaction in many respects—or, as termed here, a
large scope of action—is not only a means to achieve a high level of satisfaction,
it is of value in itself.[14]

To base the concept of level of living on resources rather than on needs
has some advantages. We then look upon man as an active being who uses
his resources to pursue and satisfy his basic interests and needs. We do not
necessarily have to decide what these needs are, the individual is assumed to
use his resources in his best interests. On the other hand, we do have to decide
what the most important resources are and, in so doing, we have to consider
for what purpose they can be used. Thus, one way or another, we must take

---

[8] Johansson, 1970: 25. Italics in the original.
[9] See especially Titmuss, 1958.
[10] See Lebergott, 1968–72.
[11] In the discussion of quality of life, mainly of American provenance, happiness has also
been suggested as a central element, cf. Michalos, 1987, or Campbell *et al.*, 1976. There are,
however, a number of objections to making happiness a central element of level of living. See
Sen, 1985*a* and 1985*b*.
[12] Allardt, 1977. Compare also Drewnowski, 1974: 7.
[13] Erikson, 1974.
[14] Sen, 1985*a*: 201.

a stand on what the most central areas of human life are, the areas where it is most essential that the individual should be able to determine his living conditions.

However, it does not seem sufficient to restrict the concept of level of living to resources alone. Some conditions, especially good health, certainly are important resources, but this does not exhaust their significance. Their most important aspect may be as ends in themselves. Furthermore, some circumstances, such as the quality of the work environment or the amenities and space in the home, are important for the individual's well-being, but can only be regarded as resources in a very remote sense. Thus the level of living concept would be too restrictive if we based it on resources alone without adding essential conditions. Moreover, the same set of resources is not of equivalent value regardless of the context. A certain education, say in law, may be of high value on the labour market in the country where it was acquired, but of very limited value in another country. We must therefore consider the *arenas* in which the resources are to be used.[15] Individuals' resources and the characteristics of the arenas where they are to be used together determine the scope of individuals for directing their own lives.[16]

In essence, then, the position taken in Swedish welfare research is that the individual's resources, the arenas in which they are to be used, and his most essential living conditions, make up his level of living. This position, although independently arrived at, seems to be very close to Sen's as he writes that 'the central feature of well-being is the ability to achieve valuable functioning'.[17]

There is no universal theory which could guide us in deciding what the most important resources and conditions are. We therefore have to base our choice on mainly general considerations. The nine components referred to above (see Table 1) do not constitute a self-evident choice, but similar lists of the essential areas relevant to level of living look very much the same the world over (possibly to some extent because of communication and mutual influence). The list is to some extent influenced by the situation and culture of Sweden; in a developing country such a list would probably include, for example, access to food and nutrition. It is also obvious that such lists have a political character: they only include items which are at least in principle possible to influence. Thus, for instance, talent and climate are excluded in spite of being quite important for the individual's action potential. The components refer to conditions and problems which we all meet during our lives

[15] The arena concept was taken from Coleman, 1971, and was introduced to Scandinavian welfare research by the Norwegian level of living survey. See Hernes *et al.*, 1976. Compare also Erikson, 1974.

[16] The arena concept seems quite important in theory, but has never been much used in actual research. Often the outcome of the use of resources in an arena is taken as an indicator, e.g. inequality of the job rather than a particular skill in relation to the surrounding labour market.

[17] Sen, 1985*a*: 200.

and which are of such importance that there are collectively organized attempts to cope with them in all societies.[18]

One consequence of the multidimensionality of the level of living concept and of the incommensurability between dimensions is that no simple ordered indicator of level of living can be constructed, either on an individual or on an aggregate level. Differences and changes in the level of living must be described for each component. A total picture of variation and change will thus of necessity be rather complicated, and no satisfactory solution has yet been found to the problem of how to present such a picture. The indicator based on the number of components for which problems were registered, shown in Figure 3, was used as part of an attempt to describe the coexistence and accumulation of welfare problems. The total number of measured 'problems' is a crude indicator of the total situation of an individual, which gives each different type of problem an equal weight. This is of course quite problematic, and loads the indicator with implicit value judgements.

However, I do not believe that empirical research in this area is possible if we do not take such decisions, based on explicit or implicit value judgements.[19] Descriptions necessitate a choice of indicators, and parsimonious description often also necessitates the amalgamation of indicators into indices.[20] Such decisions already have to be taken at the component level. Within the health component we have to decide which symptoms we should consider and how they should be put together in constructing one or several indicators for health. We make similar judgements when we decide which aspects of a total work situation we should measure, and corresponding decisions must be made for the other components.

It then seems as if the question is not whether we should make value judgements or not but rather when we should make them and when we should leave them open. No general answer has been given to this question, but some principles have, overall, been followed. First of all, indicators relating to different components have not been merged into common indices—except for the single case in Figure 3 here. Within areas, indicators have in some cases been put together to create indices, but often only for subareas and in many cases only after some type of dimensionality test like factor analysis. On the whole, indicators relating to clearly different areas of the level of living have not been merged into summary measures but kept apart.

The drawback to this approach is that the total number of indices needed for a complete description of the level of living becomes quite large. It is thus difficult to get an overall picture of the level of living, although it is possible to see how the different components are related to one another. Can

[18] Johansson, 1979: 139.
[19] This should not be read as making any claim for the simple indicator used in Figure 3: that was a provisional solution which seemed to be feasible at the time.
[20] Compare Sen, 1980.

we then do nothing more than take our large number of indicators and present them one at a time?

I think that *within* components, we can in many cases order conditions in such a way that we get a small number of ordered scales, or in some cases even only one, which everybody, or nearly everybody, would accept. This would be especially likely if we were working with very broad classes of problems, or perhaps only with dichotomies, distinguishing problematic conditions from others.

But even so we will end up with a fairly large number of incommensurable indicators, say at best with a scale or dichotomy of problematic/not problematic conditions for each of the nine components mentioned before. It would still not be possible to construct a summary ordered measure of welfare, but it would be possible to distinguish between different types of total welfare and to find out how frequent these types are. Even if we cannot order all types in relation to each other, we can find orders within subsets of types. A type which includes all the problematic conditions of another type, but which also includes some additional ones, could clearly be regarded as more problematic than the other, according to a common Pareto criterion.

Of course we would still face quite serious problems. If we dichotomize each of nine components—which is in itself a questionable solution: we lose a lot of information by the dichotomization and will have to put very different conditions into the same category—we will get 512 possible combinations. Thus, we have by that operation not come very far towards a manageable empirical concept, which is feasible for purposes of analysis and presentation.

But it should be possible to reduce such the number of combinations into a smaller number of welfare types. Welfare components are correlated with each other so some combinations would probably be very rare indeed. In the Swedish level of living study we found, for example, a tendency for problems with health, few social contacts, and a lack of leisure activities to go together. These were problems which were especially common among older people. In a similar way economic problems and housing problems went together, especially within the working class and among the old and the young, and a low level of political activity, which is strongly related to educational level, appeared most common among women. Because of such correlations we could probably delimit a smaller number of types of welfare problems, and, furthermore, we would probably find that different types are differently located within the social and demographic structure.

3   A Descriptive or an Evaluative Approach?

The question about who should judge the level of living—the individual or the observer—is partly connected to that about needs or resources. If the concept of welfare (or well-being) is based on needs, it seems quite natural to measure its level by asking people whether they are satisfied or not, while this seems less obvious if the concept is based on resources. The problem with an approach based on people's own assessment of their degree of satisfaction is that it is partly determined by their level of aspiration, that is, by what they consider to be their rightful due.[21] This means that measuring how satisfied people are is to a large extent equivalent to measuring how well they have adapted to their present conditions. People who have experienced menial conditions for a long period may turn out to be more satisfied, and thus according to this definition to have a higher level of living, than a person who is used to a very high standard but who has recently experienced a minor lowering of it, an outcome which seems unacceptable. We therefore try to assess the individual's level of living in a way which makes it as little influenced as possible by the individual's evaluation of his own situation. This seems all the more natural as the individual's level of living is to a large extent based on his 'command over resources', resources which can be used for the ends which he himself finds most satisfactory.

The empirical question related to whether we should be looking at people's conditions or their satisfaction with these conditions is whether we should use 'objective' or 'subjective' indicators, a question which was much discussed within the so-called social indicators movement. Actually, the terms 'objective' and 'subjective' are slightly misleading, so it seems preferable to use the terms 'descriptive' and 'evaluative' indicators. With descriptive indicators, the individual is asked to describe his resources and conditions. 'How much do you receive as monthly salary?' and 'What temperature do you normally have indoors in the winter?' would be typical questions. When we use evaluative indicators the individual is asked to evaluate his conditions. 'Are you satisfied with your salary?' or 'How good is the heating in the winter?' would be typical questions used. The difference between the two types of indicator should not be exaggerated, however. Descriptive indicators certainly contain evaluative elements, and the indicators used by spokesmen for the different approaches are often quite similar.[22]

To put the emphasis on descriptive indicators does not mean that whether people are satisfied or not is judged to be of no interest. On the contrary, I would say that it is of very great interest to find out how people's resources influence their level of satisfaction *and*, of course, how this in turn influences their resources and conditions. But I suggest that welfare — or level of living — should be defined in terms of resources and conditions and is best measured by the use of descriptive indicators. And to the extent that welfare research is coupled to societal planning — which, in Scandinavia, is part of its historical

---

[21] For a more thorough discussion of these matters, see Tåhlin, 1989. See also Sen, 1985a, and Campbell et al., 1976.

[22] Compare the indicators used in the Swedish level of living surveys with those used by Allardt, 1975.

legacy but not necessarily of its future constraints—I find it quite essential that descriptive indicators should be used. The data for planning should refer to factual conditions and planning goals should be formulated in terms of such conditions. People's opinions and preferences should influence societal planning through their activities as citizens in the democratic political process, not through survey questions and opinion polls. That is, goals for planning should be set up in terms of factual conditions, not in terms of people's satisfaction with these conditions. It is the assumption that the planning and executive organs of the state act directly to influence people's satisfaction and happiness that is the basis for many of the futuristic hells suggested to us in literary works.

A high level of living, as conceptualized here, is not equivalent to enjoying all the good things in life. This is no drawback, as I see it. There are other good or bad aspects of life, and if we want to study them they must be conceptualized and measured in their own right. A concept which is meant to include everything desirable/undesirable would probably be of questionable value. Moreover, those who enjoy a high level of living are not necessarily satisfied and happy. It is well known that the association between conditions and satisfactions is rather weak.[23] Conditions and satisfactions are two different aspects of the good in life. A person who has better amenities at home than someone else is better off *in that respect* regardless of whether he is more or less satisfied with them. However, if his situation changed so that he had only the amenities of the other, he would probably become even less satisfied and *vice versa*. In a cross-sectional sample we would expect to get some association between conditions and satisfactions.[24] Over time, however, it is even questionable whether we should expect any relation at all on an aggregate level, at least not if basic needs for food and shelter are covered. People will not usually become more satisfied when the general level of living rises if their relative advantage is the aspect of their conditions that influences their satisfaction, and this seems to a large extent to be the case. Similarly, we cannot with certainty expect any association between conditions and satisfactions among different nations.[25]

4 *Presentation*

As described in the introduction, several indicators have been used to describe change over time and differences between various socio-demographic groups in their level of living. This has been partly the consequence of the indicators

[23] Compare Allardt, 1975, or Campbell *et al.*, 1976. This low association is actually one of the reasons why those who emphasize conditions do not want to use evaluative indicators and why those who put the emphasis on satisfaction do not want to use descriptive ones.
[24] Compare the association between income and general sense of well-being in Campbell *et al.*, 1976: 55ff. See also Easterlin, 1974.
[25] Compare Easterlin, 1974.

in most cases being on an ordinal level only – meaning that it is not possible to interpret an indicator value without making some form of comparison – but partly also the result of regarding inequality as a problematic societal condition and, thus, equality as an important political goal.

In these studies inequality has mostly been treated as the variation among socio-demographic groups rather than over the population at large and, accordingly, measured more through differences and relative rates than through, say, Gini indices or Lorenz curves. This is again a result of the ordinal indicators, but it is also based on the assumption that the socio-demographic groups are delimited in such a way that people will often be able to identify them in society, and that such a description of conditions in society will therefore be meaningful to a large part of the population. To tie the description of inequality to a recognized social structure, will make the description more pertinent to the political discussion. Moreover, it is a way to try to get round part of the problem of preferential choices in comparisons between individuals. If we compare two people and find that one goes on to higher education while the other does not, this could well be because the first one prefers a higher level of consumption later in life while the other is more interested in earning money immediately. Similarly, if we find that one person is unemployed while another, with the same education, etc., is not, the first may well prefer to work as little as possible and consequently to consume less while the other has different preferences. However, it is more difficult to make such an explanation plausible if we find that people of the same intellectual abilities but of different social origins systematically make different educational choices, or if we find systematic differences in unemployment between persons with similar human capital living in different regions. We cannot, of course, rule out the possibility that the differences in these cases are still due to different distributions of preferences, but those who claim so would have to make plausible their contention that such preferences vary with for example, social class and region.[26]

The study of inequality in non-distributable conditions – such as health or knowledge and skills, of which it is not possible to transfer units between persons – also becomes more meaningful when we study inequality between groups rather than between individuals. To study the distribution of handicap over the population at large is, for example, of rather limited interest; it could be supposed only to show some 'natural' variation in health. If, on the other hand, as in Figure 1, we show that physical mobility on average and net of age differences varies between social classes, more social explanations must be sought, explanations which in one way or another relate health to the conditions, experiences, and ways of life of people in different classes.

[26] This obviously does not mean that such explanations are impossible or not tried. An example is the well-known hypothesis that middle-class children accept deferred gratification to a greater extent than working-class children do.

5   *Poverty versus Inequality*

So far I have not discussed poverty. This is no oversight. As implied by the discussion above, inequality rather than poverty has been the important concept in Swedish welfare research. This follows partly from the emphasis on non-monetary aspects of welfare, given that poverty refers to economic resources.[27] But it is also partly the consequence of an interest in variation over the whole range of a condition and not only over a poverty line. On the other hand, Johansson, in his first discussion of the level of living concept, suggested a concentration on 'bad conditions',[28] and some indicators are just dichotomies, by which presumed bad conditions are delimited. Many other indicators, however, as mentioned, have the form of ordinal scales. Furthermore, for most dichotomous indicators the dividing line is too arbitrary to be given any other meaning than just being a dividing line. In constructing scales it is regarded as preferable to consider the whole distribution and not to restrict interest to a dichotomy. A desirable result of these considerations is that the intellectually rather empty discussion of whether the proverty line should be drawn here or there has been avoided.

I believe that there is also an ideological ground for this difference in emphasis in welfare research between Sweden and many of the other Western nations. I would suggest that poverty is the main welfare problem for social liberalism, while inequality is the main problem for social democracy. According to classical liberalism, the market is the 'natural' mechanism for distributing economic resources. To social liberalism, this is still true, but we have to correct the outcome of the market mechanism in one respect—we must for humanitarian reasons take care of those who end up destitute, that is to say, we must take the poor out of poverty. This can done through what Titmuss called the residual welfare model of social policy, the pursuit of which results in a marginal welfare state,[29] in which through governmental activities, the deficiencies of the market are corrected by money transfers to people below the poverty line. According to social democracy state activities are not merely a supplementary mechanism, but one on a par with the market. In an institutional welfare state a redistributive model of social policy should cover the basic needs of all citizens. The variation in essential conditions—between different groups in the population and over the life cycle—should thereby also be diminished. Various social provisions are seen as the rights of citizens in this perspective. The state should therefore, provide health care and education to all—the quality of these services should in principle be such that no demand for private hospitals or schools appears—and it should be possible to have a good standard of housing regardless of income and family size.

---

[27] Compare, however, Ringen, 1985.
[28] Johansson, 1970: 29f.
[29] Titmuss, 1974. Compare Wilensky and Lebaux, 1958, and also Korpi, 1983.

Those who can be expected to be in need should be given support as a matter of course. Child allowances and pensions should therefore, be provided to all.

In different political climates differently formulated questions appear most relevant. In this perspective it thus seems natural that poverty should become the central socio-political issue where social liberalism dominates the political climate whereas inequality becomes the main problem of welfare where social democracy is dominant.

6 *A Political Theory for Social Reporting*

In an attempt to formulate a political theory for social reporting, Johansson suggested that political decisions require answers to three questions.[30] They are: (1) What are the actual conditions? (2) What goals do we have? and (3) What means should be used? The second question can only be answered in political discussion, it has a purely normative character. The answer to the third question should involve the best expert knowledge: given the goal, what is the best way to get there? The first question is of yet another character. It cannot be answered in discussion—although this is often tried. Whether people's health, on average, is becoming better or worse, whether unemployment is going up or down, whether social selection in school is increasing or not, are questions on which people often have views and opinions, but reliable answers cannot be given on the basis of personal experience or found in the mass media, where they would be based on the methods of journalism and, moreover, probably influenced by the interests and expectations of editors and owners.[31] Unemployment or health problems may not necessarily be increasing even if more people in our neighbourhood are falling ill or becoming unemployed, and crime rates may not be rising even if newspapers do start to write more about crime. Reliable answers to such questions can only be found if people in different relevant conditions are counted with the help of established scientific methods. When we started to determine the rate of unemployment through counting the unemployed in representative samples of the population, political discussion could move from issues that cannot be resolved by it—how many are the unemployed?—to questions which, at least in principle, can be answered by it—what should we do about unemployment? To give answers to questions about levels and trends of welfare, about what conditions are like and how they are changing is, then, a task for social reporting. That a mechanism for answering the first question is not discussed in the theory of the democratic process can be seen as a lacuna in it, Johansson suggests.[32]

[30] Johansson, 1979: 112.
[31] When the results from the 1968 survey were published in 1970 and 1971, the standard reaction in the mass media was astonishment over the problems exposed. The general expectation was that most welfare problems had already been overcome.
[32] Johansson, 1979: 121.

Writing social reports seems to be a task for statistical offices rather than for social research institutes, and the major task of social reporting has in Sweden been given to the Central Bureau of Statistics. The task for welfare research is to develop theories, models, and methods in the field. This would include both developing a theory for social reporting and developing models of how the level of living components hang together, their determinants, casual connections, and interrelations. Welfare research in Sweden seems to have come quite a long way in developing ideas and methods for the description of individual welfare, but it has a long way to go in explaining its variations and changes.

BIBLIOGRAPHY

ALLARDT, ERIK (1975). *Att ha, att älska att vara* ('Having, Loving, Being'). Lund: Argos.
—— (1977). 'On the Relationship between Objective and Subjective Predicaments', University of Helsinki, Research Group for Comparative Sociology: Research Report 16.
CAMPBELL, ANGUS, CONVERSE, PHILIP E., and RODGERS, WILLARD L. (1976). *The Quality of American Life*. New York: Russel Sage.
COLEMAN, JAMES (1971). *Resources for Social Change*. New York: Wiley.
DREWNOWSKI, JAN (1974). *On Measuring and Planning the Quality of Life*. The Hague: Mouton.
EASTERLIN, RICHARD A. (1974). 'Does Economic Growth Improve the Human Lot? Some Empirical Evidence', in Paul A. David and Melvin W. Reder (eds.), *Nations and Households in Economic Growth*. New York: Academic Press.
ERIKSON, ROBERT (1974). 'Welfare as a Planning Goal', *Acta Sociologica*, 17.
—— and ÅBERG, RUNE (eds.) (1987). *Welfare in Transition*. Oxford: Clarendon Press.
—— and TÅHLIN, MICHAEL (1987). 'Coexistence of Welfare Problems', in Erikson and Åberg (1987).
—— and UUSITALO, HANNU (1987). 'The Scandinavian Approach to Welfare Research', in Robert Erikson, Erik Jørgen Hansen, Stein Ringen, and Hannu Uusitalo (eds.) *The Scandinavian Model: Welfare States and Welfare Research*. Armonck: M. E. Sharpe.
JOHANSSON, STEN (1970). *Om Levnadsnivåundersökningen* ('On the Level of Living Survey'). Stockholm: Allmänna Förlaget.
—— (1979). *Mot en teori for social rapportering* ('Towards a Theory of Social Reporting'). Stockholm: Institutet for social forskning.
KORPI, WALTER (1983). *The Democratic Class Struggle*. London: Routledge and Kegan Paul.
LEBERGOTT, STANLEY (1968–72). 'Income Distribution: Size', in David Sills, (ed.), *International Encyclopedia of the Social Sciences*. New York: Macmillan.
HERNES, GUDMUND, RØDSETH, TOR, AASE, ASBJØRN, and RINGEN, STEIN (1976).

Levekårsunderskelsen, Slutapport (The Level of Living Survey, Final Report'). Oslo: Universitets Porlager.

MICHALOS, ALEX (1987). 'What Makes People Happy: Social Indicators and Quality of Life', in *Levekårsforskning* ('Level of Living Research'). Oslo: Rådet for samfunnsviten-skaplig forskning.

RINGEN, STEIN (1985). 'Toward a Third Stage in the Measurement of Poverty', *Acta Sociologica*, 28.

SELÉN, JAN (1985). 'Multidimensional Descriptions of Social Indicators', *Social Indicators Research*, 17.

—— (1987). 'Regression as a Tool for Describing Level of Living', in Erikson and Åberg (1987).

SEN, AMARTYA (1980). 'Description as Choice', *Oxford Economic Papers*, 32.

—— (1985a). 'Well-Being, Agency and Freedom. The Dewey Lectures 1984', *Journal of Philosophy*, 82.

—— (1985b). *Commodities and Capabilities*. Amsterdam: North-Holland.

SZULKIN, RYSZARD (1987). 'Political Resources', in Erikson and Åberg (1987).

TÅHLIN, MICHAEL (1990). 'Politics, Dynamics and Individualism: The Swedish Approach to Level of Living Research', *Social Indicators Research*, 22.

TITMUSS, RICHARD M. (1958). *Essays on the Welfare State*. London: Unwin University Books.

—— (1974). *Social Policy*. London: George Allen and Unwin.

United Nations (1954). *International Definition and Measurement of Standards and Levels of Living*. New York: United Nations Publications.

—— (1966). *The Level of Living Index*. New York: United Nations Research Institute for Social Development.

WILENSKI, HAROLD, and LEBAUX, CLAUDE (1958). *Industrial Society and Social Welfare*. New York: Russel Sage Foundation.

Robert Erikson: Descriptions of Inequality
Commentary by Bengt-Christer Ysander

Erikson's paper presents both a survey method for measuring level of living and some empirical results from using the method on Swedish households. Both are interesting, but what I personally find most intriguing is what lies in between—the problems cropping up in implementing the theoretical concepts.

I will try to exemplify this by commenting on three broad implementation decisions, as they appear in the Swedish survey. They deal respectively with the choice of indicators, the choice of distribution space, and finally the choice of measure of distributional change.

Let me start with the choice of welfare indicators. As Erikson rightly stresses, this choice—always somewhat arbitrary—will reflect the concerns and interests of the investigator. This is certainly true in this case, where the Swedish government commissioned the survey. What the government wanted was not simply to know how to keep various voter groups happy in order to retain power, but a detailed description of living conditions, both as a background to planning distributive policies and to mobilize support for these policies. Hence the choice of detailed descriptive indicators instead of more general evaluative questions.

It is interesting to note that in searching for suitable indicators, the designer, Sten Johansson, had an ideal in mind, seemingly very close to Sen's concept of 'capability'. It is, of course, hard to be quite sure about what 'capability' rightly means. But it is here enough if we think of it as an opportunity set of actions, achievements, or functionings—a set which may of course forestall any question of choice by having just one member. 'Capability' thus simply becomes a measure of options.

What is even more interesting is the fact that in an overwhelming number of cases, the investigators failed to observe and measure anything which could, with the best will in the world, be called a capability. They had to make do with particular individual achievements, from which they could try to construct or estimate capabilities. This could, of course be due to lack of imagination and/or analytical flexibility on the part of the investigators. I rather suspect, however, that it also shows that capabilities are often rather elusive things to catch, that it is difficult to measure directly the counterfactual part which has to do with what a person might be or do—or might have been or have done. Economists may be confused here because they are used to dealing with one of the few aspects of life where the opportunity set can be reasonably well defined and measured.

If you try to look more closely at how capabilities are dealt with in the survey, you find that they usually seem to be implicitly defined in terms of some a priori behavioural model which spells out what the probability is that a certain capability or set of options will manifest itself in certain observable achievements. A certain degree of political capability, for example, means a certain probability that you will get politically organized, make speeches, and write to the newspapers. If you then observe the achievements of a specific individual, you can try a posteriori to estimate his capability. The reliability of the results will depend on how good or generally acceptable your a priori model is. It can be a risky business. If you are fond of marching in demonstrations or pestering your MP with phone calls, is this a sign of political capability **or the reverse**? Depending on prevailing political conditions, engaging in these activities may be a sign of political freedom—or frustration at finding all other channels of political influence blocked. In the Swedish survey these a priori models are very simple—and never made explicit. They deal mostly with dichotomies and usually seem to assign equal probability to all relevant achievements.

There are a number of conceptual problems involved here—apart from the unavoidable multidimensionality and the arbitrary division of options. One obvious problem has to do with the interdependence of individuals' choices in different areas. Whether or not you make use of your options for political action will, for example, depend on your capabilities in areas like education and income. The kind of a priori model you need should thus be formulated in terms of joint probabilities—a rather forbidding task.

A second difficulty arises when you try to use the indicators to measure differences in capabilities between different countries or different times. What options are implied by actual behaviour will always depend on the current social and institutional setting. Disposable income, for example, is a rather empty welfare concept if there is nothing to buy. The options indicated by observed actions can shrink drastically in the face of political regulations or social sanctions. You thus need a lot of complementary information on the institutional framework and the division of rights to draw any conclusions as to fundamental capabilities from the indicators used. Even within the comparatively stable and homogeneous Swedish society, Erikson runs into difficulties in making comparisons over a thirteen-year period. Achievements like having a secondary education or having seen a doctor mean different things in terms of job opportunities or physical capability after the big expansion in higher education and out-patient care during the 1970s.

Another connected conceptual problem has to do with social security. A high income, for example, has quite different welfare implications when it is reasonably secure from when it is part of a social lottery and can disappear at any time. You really need to measure not just present options but contingent future options. How well are your present options 'insured' against risks of various kinds? Even in the Swedish context, changes in the coverage of social insurance, etc., have been considerable, and if you extend the method to cover international comparisons the risk scenario would certainly have to be taken into account as a major component of welfare.

These various problems may raise some doubts about the possibility of making the capability concept operational for sophisticated welfare measurement. They may at least provide an argument for sticking to simple and basic capabilities.

Let me pass to the second kind of implementation decision: the choice of measure of welfare distribution.

When we discuss equality most of us probably think of welfare distribution among individuals. In the Swedish survey, however, what was studied was distribution for the three observation years among the fifty-four socio-economic groups, which result from combining sex, age, occupational class, and region. What this means is that it does not really deal with equality as such since it ignores all the differences between individuals which are the result of luck and choice. What it is concerned with is that part of welfare distribution which can be ascribed to social discrimination in the four given dimensions. You might of course question whether you can talk of discrimination in terms of occupation and region as being on a par with discrimination by sex and age, since the choice of occupation and region is at least in part voluntary.

More interesting and surprising is the fact that the distribution problems are here narrowed down to problems of discrimination, which seems to fit rather badly with the original political background of the study, as stressed by Erikson. It is hard to make this minimal conception of social justice compatible with the aim of equality pursued by the commissioning government.

Erikson's own explanation is that nothing more is possible, since the material is too shaky to allow anything but dichotomies into capable and non-capable. If taken at face value, this would mean that we would for ever abstain from investigating and discussing more general problems of equality in welfare. I do not think that is necessary even in dealing with this survey material. Admittedly, we will never get nice continuous indices of individual capabilities. But there is certainly room for sorting individuals into an ordered number of classes.

Let me finally deal with the third kind of implementation decision, which has to do with the choice of measure of distributional change.

What is done in the Swedish survey is simply to compare the distribution at different times. I would like to argue that this is seldom enough. In order to evaluate the change, understand it, and plan new policies, you must go a step further and study the change for the individuals making up the distribution.

We cannot really evaluate a distributional change without knowing, for example, if the formerly underprivileged have kept their place or if they have exchanged places with the privileged. We cannot hope to understand why a change occurs if we cannot trace how one position, or set of capabilities or lack of them, conditions the next. And this is what we need to know if we are to design a distributive strategy.

Now the survey material offers an unusual chance of looking into individual change, since for each subsequent observation year some 85 per cent of the respondents belong to a panel left over from the earlier survey. It does seem a pity to pass up this chance.

Problems do arise, however, when you try to apply concepts like capability or equality to the life careers of individuals. These concepts are usually defined within a static framework and are not unambiguous when applied to processes of change.

Every time an individual makes a choice or passes into a new state, he or she generally modifies his or her capabilities at the same time. If the change is the result of a conscious choice we can talk about this change of capabilities as investment or disinvestment. This means that every achievement is generally associated with two kinds of capability — before and after, opportunities forgone and opportunities anticipated.

Again, it is far from easy to know how to evaluate a change in the distribution of capabilities in terms of equality, when an unknown part of the change is due to voluntary acts of choice. You may avoid the problem by retreating to the study of some narrower concept — like non-discrimination. Otherwise, you will be faced with the impossible task of separating choice from luck over a historical sequence. I doubt whether there is any solution to that problem. If you want simply to give long-term insurance to cases without any moral hazard, it is better to abstain from insuring them at all. Or to insure them in certain basic respects and forget about the hazard.

We can learn a lot about Swedish welfare problems from the Swedish survey. At the same time it highlights the need for further work on defining and making operational the exact aim of the exercise. There is no such thing as a generally applicable measure of welfare.

Having, Loving, Being: An Alternative to the Swedish Model of Welfare Research

Erik Allardt

Nationwide surveys of the level of living and quality of life were conducted in all the Scandinavian countries in the 1970s. They were assumed to cover basic elements of human well-being in advanced, industrialized societies. It is to be noted that the word 'welfare' (in Swedish *välfärd*, in Danish *velfaerd*, in Norwegian *velferd*, and in Finnish *hyvinvointi*), in all the Scandinavian languages, also stands for well-being, and that it relates to both level of living and quality of life. The surveys were said to represent welfare research. They were based on interviews of national samples of the citizenry. As is the case with regard to institutionalization of the Scandinavian welfare state, Sweden also spearheaded the surveying of the level of welfare. The first nationwide national welfare study in the Scandinavian tradition was the Swedish Level of Living Survey conducted in 1968 (Johansson, 1970).

The second large-scale Scandinavian welfare study was a comparative one, conducted in 1972 by the Research Group for Comparative Sociology at the University of Helsinki, and supported by research councils in the Scandinavian countries. It was based on interviews of national probability samples of approximately 1,000 persons in each of Denmark, Finland, Norway, and Sweden (Allardt, 1975; Allardt, 1976: 227–40). The national samples in the comparative study were smaller than in the national studies focusing on one country only. The comparative approach contained many problems of measurement, and its measures did not, as a rule, have the same high degree of reliability as the Swedish Level of Living Survey. In retrospect the importance of the Comparative Scandinavian Welfare Study was that it offered a more comprehensive system of indicators for describing the level of living and the quality of life than the Swedish model. It is also a more open system, allowing for the introduction of new indicators and measures when society changes. On the other hand, the comparative study was clearly inspired by the Swedish Level of Living Survey. It was, however, felt that the Swedish model was too restrictive and narrowly conceived to convey a sociologically meaningful picture of the state of well-being in a society. In this paper the basic principles underlying the indicator system originated in the Comparative Scandinavian Welfare Study are briefly described. This is done by showing how it departs from the Swedish model, particularly as regards two basic assumptions and theoretical choices.

1 *Focus on the Level of Need Satisfaction rather than on Resources*

A strong assumption of the Swedish approach was that level of living surveys should mainly be concerned with gauging the resources by means of which individuals can master and control their lives. The level of living was in fact defined as 'the individual's command over resources in the form of money, possessions, knowledge, mental and physical energy, social relations, security, and so on, through which the individual controls and consciously directs his living conditions' (Erikson's paper in this volume). In planning for the comparative study, too, it was agreed that the resource aspect was an important one. Yet, it was felt that an emphasis on resources would be too restrictive and in practice lead to a one-sided focus on material conditions. In order to consider a fuller and richer range of conditions for human development, another approach would be needed. In the comparative study the indicator system was based on a basic needs approach developed by the Norwegian Johan Galtung (1980: 50–125).

The basic needs approach is both more complicated and more ambiguous than the resource approach. It allows, however, for a fuller consideration of the necessary conditions for human development. A basic needs approach focuses on conditions without which human beings are unable to survive, avoid misery, relate to other people, and avoid alienation. Having, Loving, and Being are catchwords for central necessary conditions of human development and existence. It is clearly assumed that there are both material and non-material basic human needs, and that both types of need have to be considered in indicator systems designed to gauge the actual level of welfare in a society.

Having refers to those material conditions which are necessary for survival and for avoidance of misery. It covers the needs for nutrition, air, water, for protection against climate, environment, diseases, etc. The material conditions may in the Scandinavian countries be measured by indicators denoting

— *economic resources*: income and wealth;
— *housing conditions*: measured both by space available and housing amenities;
— *employment*: usually described in terms of the occurrence or absence of unemployment;
— *working conditions*: noise and temperature at workplace, physical work routine, measures of stress;
— *health*: various symptoms (or their absence) of pain and illness, availability of medical aid, and
— *education*: years of formal education.

Indicators of this kind were used both in the Swedish Level of Living Survey and in the Comparative Scandinavian Welfare Study. It is to be noted that the indicators are designed to describe social conditions in the Scandinavian countries. In the Third World the indicators would be quite different and measure, for instance, sheer availability of food, water, and shelter.

The data gathered about the components listed can be used for constructing measures of different kinds. We are all familiar with the common technique of comparing countries by dividing the measures by the number of inhabitants. Thus we have GNP per capita, school enrolment per capita, the average number of household members per room, etc. Such aggregate measures and averages are often useful but they are clearly unsatisfactory in describing the national level of human welfare. They tell us, for instance, nothing about distribution and internal disparities. More important than dispersion measures, however, is the notion of a floor, a bottom level, below which no individual should be located (Galtung, 1975: 148). The average may, comparatively speaking, be impressively high, but if a large percentage of the population nevertheless remains below the floor, then the national level of human welfare can hardly be described as satisfactory.

The notion of a floor below which the values should not be permitted to fall is indeed a very natural idea when adding measures relating to the quality of the biological and physical environment to the list of indicators describing the material environment. The measures of the biological and physical environment designed to describe the level of human welfare in a society would in the first place have to reflect the degree and nature of polluting compounds in the air, the water, and the ground. Examples of conditions important to measure are:

– the degree of deposition of sulphur in the air;
– soil acidification (ph-values);
– lake acidification (pH-values);
– groundwater acidification (ph-values);
– nitrous acid concentration in the air;
– nitrous acid concentration in the sea and in the lakes;
– excess of algal production in the sea and in the lakes;
– heavy metal (lead) deposits in the soil and in the water;
– concentration of radon in the soil and in the water;
– sulphur content in pure needles of pine or spruce;
– concentration of mercury in fish (e.g. Alcomo *et al.*, 1987, 232–45).

Such measures are intended to describe predicaments in the biological and physical environments of individual citizens. It is to be noted that the research design for welfare survival imposes some restrictions on what environmental conditions can be included. The intention is to explain variations in human welfare among individual citizens, and the measures have therefore to reflect variations in the environment of individuals. Measures reflecting predicaments common to all humankind and to all citizens of a country would be of little use in this type of welfare survey.

Unfortunately a great deal of social science welfare research has continued in its traditional path without considering measures of the quality of the biological and physical environment. In a recent otherwise very well-edited and well-written book about the Scandinavian welfare model, welfare research is defined as 'research which in a systematic and explicit fashion conceptualizes good and bad conditions of man's life, and which aims at a comprehensive conception of his situation by including all crucial aspects of life' (Erikson *et al.*, 1987: 178). Nevertheless, measures of the quality of man's biological and physical environment are absent from the book.

Loving stands for the need to relate to other people and to form social identities. The level of need satisfaction can be assessed by measures denoting

- attachments and contacts in the local community;
- attachments to family and kin;
- active patterns of friendship;
- attachments and contacts with fellow members in association and organizations, and
- relationships with work-mates.

A general finding in the comparative study was that the amount and strength of social relations of companionship and solidarity were zero-correlated to the material level of living. In other words, in the Scandinavian countries social relations are equally rich in their contact and warmth in castles and huts. The zero-relationship between material level of living and the components measuring companionship and solidarity applies statistically to a normal Scandinavian population. As soon as material conditions become really bad solidarity and love relationships are also likely to suffer. Something similar might be expected when studying the relationship between the quality of the biological and physical environment and human companionship and solidarity. If the physical environment clearly deteriorates, people might lose some of their abilities for companionship, solidarity, and love.

Being stands for the need for integration into society and to live in harmony with nature. The positive side of Being may be characterized as personal growth, whereas the negative aspect stands for alienation. The indicators measure, for instance:

- to what extent a person can participate in decisions and activities influencing his life;
- political activities;
- opportunities for leisure-time activities (Doing);
- the opportunities for a meaningful work life, and
- opportunities to enjoy nature, either through contemplation or through activities such as walking, gardening, and fishing.

2   The Use of Both Objective and Subjective Indicators

The Comparative Scandinavian Welfare Study did not depart from the Swedish approach only as regards whether one should measure resources or the level of need satisfaction. Another difference had to do with whether one should use so-called objective or subjective indicators. A basic problem facing all construction of social indicators is whether, in assessing the level of human welfare, one should rely on objective measures of external conditions or on personal subjective evaluation by the citizens themselves. The former are simply designed by experts and researchers on the basis of what they think is either necessary or wanted by human beings. This was the option taken in the Swedish Level of Living Surveys. On the basis of what issues had been central in Swedish political debate, some areas of concern and components were singled out as particularly important to measure. In the comparative study the decision was to use both objective and subjective indicators.

The words 'objective' and 'subjective' are not entirely clear and unambiguous. As already said, objective refers here to reports of factual conditions and overt behaviour whereas subjective stands for measurement of attitudes. The distinction between objective and subjective has a certain resemblance to the philosophical distinction between needs and wants (Barry, 1965: 38–52). In using subjective indicators one is in fact studying people's wants. The objective indicators, however, sometimes refer to needs, sometimes to wants. The main point is that they are designed by experts who may think of both the needs and the wants of people in deciding what should be recorded about people's living conditions.

When objective indicators are being used respondents are not asked to evaluate whether their living conditions are good or bad, satisfactory or unsatisfactory. They are simply asked to report their living conditions or overt behaviour according to some given measures. The dilemma here is a very concrete one. In measuring housing standards, for instance, should one rely on objective measures of the space available and the number of household appliances in the family or should one ask whether or not the respondents are satisfied with their housing conditions? When assessing the quality of air should one rely simply on objective, external measures of the degree of pollution or should one also try to measure people's subjective satisfactions with the air they breathe? People may be aware of the fact that they live in risky environments but they may nevertheless judge the risks to be acceptable (Lowrance, 1976: 1–11). The issue may appear trivial but its solution is by no means self-evident in assessing human welfare. Superficially, as regards many socio-economic conditions, it may at least appear very democratic to base the indicators on people's own opinions and attitudes. It is well known, however, that there is great variation in the ability to articulate both satisfaction and discomfort, and that underprivileged people are usually less able to articulate their misgivings than others. To base the choice of welfare criteria entirely on people's subjective views is therefore likely to lead to an unfruitful conservatism. On the other hand, a complete disregard of what people themselves say in its turn allows for a dogmatism of experts. The dilemma would be easier to solve if strong empirical correlations existed between the outcomes of objective and subjective measures. In most studies, however, or rather in most settings studied, the relationship between the objective conditions and the subjective attitudes or perceptions seems surprisingly weak. In the comparative Scandinavian Welfare Study the issue was simply settled by including both objective and subjective indicators. This solution seemed to offer a practical solution in that it diminished the conservatism usually attached to the sole use of subjective indicators, while avoiding the undue dogmatism resulting from the use of objective indicators only. Yet the decision was by no means entirely an ideological one. As the objective and subjective indicators usually render different results, analyses of the relationships between them are likely to provide interesting information about social conditions and relationships.

3 *The Indicator System*

When the division into Having, Loving, and Being is cross-tabulated with the dichotomy of objective and subjective indicators, a six-field table is obtained. The cells denote different types of indicator to be used in analyses and evaluations of people's living conditions.

As indicated in Table 1, Having, Loving, and Being can all be studied by both objective and subjective indicators. The former are based on external observations and are usually applied by simply counting different activities. As it is possible to measure the space available per person in a house, one can simply ask the respondents to count the number of friends, observe the amount of political activity, and estimate the opportunities to enjoy nature, etc. Alternatively, people can be asked to express their own attitudes to their living conditions. When asking attitudinal questions about the physical environment it seems natural to phrase the questions in terms of dissatisfaction/satisfaction. When asking attitudinal questions about people's relations to other people, on the other hand, it seems appropriate to ask questions in terms of unhappiness/happiness. Again, when asking questions about people's relations to society and to nature the issue is whether a person experiences alienation or some form of personal growth. Dissatisfaction, unhappiness, and alienation are different and distinct social

Table 1 Use of Different Indicators for Research into Living Conditions

	Objective indicators	Subjective indicators
Having (material and impersonal needs)	1. Objective measures of the level of living and environmental conditions	4. Subjective feelings of dissatisfaction/satisfaction with living conditions
Loving (social needs)	2. Objective measures of relationships to other people	5. Unhappiness/happiness— subjective feelings about social relations
Being (needs for personal growth)	3. Objective measures of people's relation to (a) society, and (b) nature	6. Subjective feelings of alienation/personal growth

phenomena. This is also the empirical finding of the Comparative Scandinavian Welfare Study. Unhappiness with social relations is zero-correlated to both dissatisfaction and alienation, whereas there are positive correlations, although fairly weak ones, between dissatisfaction and alienation.

The indicator system described here is substantially different from the one used in the Swedish Level of Living Surveys. Yet it is clear that the construction of the indicator system was originally inspired by the Swedish model for welfare research.

BIBLIOGRAPHY

ALCOMO, JOSEPH, et al. (1987). 'Acidification in Europe: A Simulation Model for Evaluating Control Strategies', Ambio, 14, 232-51.

ALLARDT, ERIK (1975). Att ha, alska, att vara. Om valfard i Norden ('Having, Loving, Being. On Welfare in the Nordic Countries'). Borgholm: Argos.

—— (1976). 'Dimensions of Welfare in a Comparative Scandinavian Study', Acta Sociologica, 19, 227-40.

BARRY, BRIAN (1965). Political Argument. London: Routledge and Kegan Paul.

ERIKSON, ROBERT, et al. (eds.) (1987). The Scandinavian Model. Welfare States and Welfare Research. London: M. E. Sharpe.

GALTUNG, JOHAN (1975). 'Measuring World Development I', Alternatives, 1, 131-58.

—— (1980). 'The Basic Needs Approach', in Katrin Lederer (ed.), Human Needs. A Contribution to the Current Debate. Cambridge, Mass.: Oelgeschlager, Gunn and Hain.

JOHANSSON, STEN (1970). Om levnadsnivåundersökningen ('About the Level of Living Survey'). Stockholm: Allmanna forlaget.

LOWRANCE, WILLIAM W. (1976). Of Acceptable Risk. Science and the Determination of Safety. Los Altos, Calif.: William Kaufmann.

Quality of Life Measures in Health Care and Medical Ethics

Dan Brock

1 Introduction

There has been considerable philosophical work during the last two decades, especially in the United States but not limited to there, in a relatively new field called medical ethics. My aim in this paper is to explore what illumination that body of work might offer to our understanding of the quality of life. If one looks only to the medical ethics literature explicitly addressing the notion of the quality of life, there are few sustained analyses of it and of its role in various medical and health care contexts. Consequently, it is necessary to look more broadly to issues and areas of research that often do not explicitly address the quality of life, but that nevertheless have an important bearing on it. I believe there are two main areas of work in medical ethics that fit this criterion. The first is work on ethical frameworks for medical treatment decision-making in a clinical context, including accounts of informed consent and life-sustaining treatment decisions. The second is the development of valuational measures of outcomes of health care treatments and programmes; these outcome measures are designed to guide health policy and so must be able to be applied to substantial numbers of people, including across or even between whole societies. The two main parts of this paper will address these two main bodies of work. Before doing so, however, several preliminary issues need to be briefly addressed.

I have mentioned that the literature that I will be summarizing and drawing on often does not explicitly address the concept of the 'quality of life', but instead uses other notions that are either closely related or roughly equivalent in the context. Sometimes a notion of 'health' is employed, particularly in its broader interpretations, as exemplified in the World Health Organization definition of 'health' as a state of complete physical, mental, and social well-being.[1] The notion of patient 'well-being', independent of its use within a definition of health, is also often employed for evaluation of outcomes in health care. Another conceptual framework commonly employed for evaluating health care outcomes is the assessment of the benefits and burdens of that care for the patient (and sometimes for others as well). Still another common conceptual framework often employed looks to the effects of health care on patients' interests, with a best interests standard particularly prominent for patients whose preferences cannot be determined. These and other conceptual schemes are not fully interchangeable in health care, much less in broader contexts. Nevertheless, they all have in common their use in evaluating health care outcomes for patients and their

---

[1] Breslow, 1972: 347–55.

employment as at least part of a comprehensive account of a good life for persons. I shall freely draw here on each of these conceptual frameworks, and others, though indicating where differences between them become important.

The 'quality of life' can be given a number of more or less broad interpretations, depending on the scope of the evaluative factors concerning a person's life that it is taken to include. Medicine and health care often affect a person's life in only some limited areas or respects. Nevertheless, my concern will be with the broadest conception of, in Derek Parfit's words, 'what makes a life go best', and I shall try to show that medicine and health care may affect and illuminate more aspects of that question than might at first be thought.[2] No concept is entirely apt or widely accepted in either philosophical or common usage for this broad role, but I shall use the concept of a 'good life' to refer to the quality of life of persons in its broadest interpretation.

It is common in much philosophical work on theories of the good for persons or of a good life to distinguish three broad kinds of theory. While this classification misses some distinctions important for my purposes here, it provides a natural starting point. These three alternative theories I will call the hedonist, preference satisfaction, and ideal theories of a good life.[3] Much of the philosophical work on these theories has been in the service of developing an account of 'utility', broadly construed for employment in consequentialist moral theories.[4] What is common to hedonist theories, as I will understand them here, is that they take the ultimate good for persons to be the undergoing of certain kinds of conscious experience. The particular kinds of conscious experience are variously characterized as pleasure, happiness, or the satisfaction or enjoyment that typically accompanies the successful pursuit of our desires. Particular states of the person that do not make reference to conscious experience, such as having diseased or healthy lungs, and particular activities, such as studying philosophy or playing tennis, are part of a good life on this view only to the extent that they produce the valuable conscious experience.

Preference satisfaction theories take a good life to consist in the satisfaction of people's desires or preferences. I here understand desires or preferences as taking states of affairs as their objects: for example, my desire to be in Boston on Tuesday is satisfied just when the state of affairs of my being in Boston on Tuesday obtains. This is to be distinguished from any feelings of satisfaction, understood as a conscious experience of mine, that I may experience if I am in Boston on Tuesday. The difference is clearest in cases in which my desire is satisfied, but I either do not or could not know that it is and so receive no satisfaction from getting what I desire: for example, my desire that my children should have long and fulfilling lives, a state of affairs that will only fully obtain

---

[2] Parfit, 1984, cf. esp. app. I.

[3] See T. M. Scanlon's discussion in this volume of these alternative theories. What I call preference satisfaction and ideal theories he calls desire and substantive good theories.

[4] Some time ago I discussed these as alternative interpretations of utility (Brock, 1973). The most subtle and detailed recent discussion of these alternative theories is Griffin, 1986, chs. 1–4.

after my death. For preference satisfaction theories of a good life to be at all plausible, they must allow for some correcting or 'laundering' of a person's actual preferences.[5] The most obvious example is the need to correct for misinformed preferences: for example, my desire to eat the sandwich before me not knowing that its ingredients are bad and will make me ill. Other corrections of preferences have also been supported by proponents of the preference satisfaction theory that are compatible with its underlying idea that ultimately what is good for persons is that they should get what they most want or prefer.

The third kind of theory holds that at least part of a good life consists neither of any conscious experience of a broadly hedonist sort nor of the satisfaction of the person's corrected preferences or desires, but instead consists of the realization of specific, explicitly normative ideals.[6] For example, many have held that one component of a good life consists in being a self-determined or autonomous agent, and that this is part of a good life for a person even if he or she is no happier as a result and has no desire to be autonomous. Ideal theories will differ both in the specific ideals the theories endorse and in the place they give to happiness and preference satisfaction in their full account of the good for persons. There is a strong tendency in much of the philosophical literature to seek a simple, comprehensive theory, such as the hedonist or preference satisfaction theories: proponents of ideal theories commonly acknowledge a plurality of component ideals that place constraints on and/or supplement the extent to which happiness and/or preference satisfaction serves a person's good. The account I will develop of quality of life judgements in health care strongly suggests that it is a mistake to let the attractions of a simple, unified theory of a good life force a choice between the hedonist and preference satisfaction theories. Instead, these quality-of-life judgements suggest the importance of giving independent place to the considerations singled out by each of the three main alternative theories, as ideal theories do, in any adequate overall account of the quality of life or of a good life for persons. The quality of life judgements made in medicine and health care also help some to fill in the content of a theory of a good life.

A major issue concerning ethical judgements generally, and judgements concerning a good life in particular, is the sense and extent to which such judgements are objective or subjective. A number of different senses have been given to the notions of 'objectivity' and 'subjectivity' in these contexts, and other essays in this volume take up some of these general theoretical issues and will develop some of these alternative senses.[7] I will not attempt an extended analysis of

---

[5] Virtually all discussions of desire or preference satisfaction theories of the good contain some provision for correcting preferences. One of the better treatments, with extensive references to the literature, is Goodin, 1986: 75–101.

[6] What I call ideal theories are what Parfit (1984) calls 'objective list' theories. I prefer the label 'ideal theories', because what is usually distinctive about this kind of theory is its proposal of specific, normative ideals of the person.

[7] See the papers by H. Putnam, R. A. Putnam, and M. Walzer.

this general theoretical issue here. Nevertheless, one sense in which what constitutes a good life for a particular person is believed to be subjective or objective
mirrors the distinction between hedonist and preference satisfaction theories
on the one hand, and ideal theories on the other. Hedonist and preference
theories are both subjective in the sense that both hold that what is good for
a particular person depends on what in fact makes that person happy or what
that person in fact (with appropriate corrections) desires. (This is compatible,
of course, with acknowledging that what will make a particular person happy
or satisfy his or her preferences is an 'objective matter of fact', even if often an
extremely difficult one to determine.)

Ideal theories are objective, or at least contain objective components, in the
sense that they hold a good life for a person is, at least in part, objectively determined by the correct or justified ideals of the good life, and does not in those
respects depend either on what makes that person happy or on what that person's
(even corrected) preferences happen to be. The question of whether accounts
of a good life are objective or subjective is, then, an explicitly normative issue
about what is the correct or most justified substantive theory of a good life.
This sense of the objective–subjective dispute has been a central concern in the
debates in medical ethics and health care about the quality of life. Interestingly,
I believe that medicine and health care provide some of the most persuasive
instances for both the objective *and* the subjective components of a good life,
and so point the way towards a theory that incorporates hedonist, preference,
and ideal components.

Haavi Morreim has distinguished a different sense in which quality of life
judgements in medicine are either objective or subjective.[8] In her account,
objective quality of life judgements are made on the basis of intersubjectively
observable, material facts about a person (facts concerning his or her body,
mind, functional capabilities, and environment), together with a socially shared
evaluation of those facts, specifically of how those facts determine the person's
quality of life. Subjective quality of life judgements also appeal to material facts
about a person and his or her condition (though these may also include facts
about the person's private psychological states), together with *that person's* value
judgements about how those facts affect his or her quality of life. According to
this account, the essential issue that determines whether a quality of life judgement is objective or subjective is whether the evaluative judgements concerning
a particular individual's quality of life are and must be shared by some wider
group or are, instead, only the individual's own. Since there are many possible
wider social groups, one respect in which one could make sense of degrees of
this kind of objectivity is in terms of the size, breadth, or nature of the wider
social group; important variants include an individual's community or larger
society, and a maximally wide group might be all humans or rational agents.
It should be obvious that my and Morreim's senses of the objective–subjective

8 Morreim, 1986: 45–69.

distinction are independent: the individual whose quality of life is in question might hold any of the three substantive theories of the good for persons distinguished above, as might any wider social group.

A full conception of a good life for a person that does not reduce to a single property like happiness or preference satisfaction must assign a weight to the various components that contribute to that life's being good, though there may not be full comparability between different components and so in turn only partial comparability between different possible life courses for a person. Amartya Sen has suggested in several places the formal device of understanding these different components as independent vectors, each of which contributes to an overall assessment of the degree to which a person has a good life.[9] There are several benefits to an analysis of what constitutes a good life into a number of independent vectors. First, it allows us to accept part of what proponents of each of the three traditional theories of a good life have wanted to insist on, namely the theoretical independence of those components. The three components of happiness, preference satisfaction, and ideals of a good life can each be represented by their individual vectors, or subdivided further into distinct vectors within each component, having independent weight within an overall account of a good life. Second, the vector approach quite naturally yields the possibility of two senses of partial comparability of the quality of different lives. For a single individual, alternative possible lives may be only partially commensurable if one alternative life provides a greater value on one vector, but a lesser value on another vector, than another possible life. But for two different persons it is important that at least partial comparability between their lives may be possible, contrary to the dogma about the impossibility of interpersonal comparisons of utility, by comparing common vectors or by comparing different changes in common vectors making up a good life for each. Medicine and health care provide strong grounds for insisting on these independent vectors and, perhaps more important, also suggest a content and structure to the ideals along the lines proposed by Sen in his work on agency and capabilities, which drew on settings largely outside of health care.

We also need to distinguish between the relative importance of a particular feature or condition, say as represented by a specific vector, in its contribution to a person having a good life, compared with what I shall call its broader moral importance. A simple example will suffice. One condition that may plausibly contribute to a person's quality of life or good life is his or her physical mobility. It may be possible to specify roughly a normal level of physical mobility for persons of a similar age at a particular historical stage and in a particular society, and then to specify roughly levels of mobility say 25 per cent below and 25 per cent above the norm, such that the effect on a person's quality of life in moving

---

[9] Sen's main discussion of the 'vector view' applied to the notion of utility is in Sen, 1980. I am much indebted to Sen's subtle discussions in a number of places of distinctions of importance to conceptions of the quality of life and of a good life. Besides his essay in this volume, see esp. Sen, 1985a, 1985b, 1987.

from 25 per cent below the norm up to the norm is quantitatively roughly the same as moving from the norm to 25 per cent above it. While the degree or importance of the two changes in a person's quality of life or good life may be roughly the same, it can none the less be consistently held that these two comparable effects on the person's quality of life have different *moral* importance or priority. It might be held, for example, that on grounds of equality of opportunity bringing a person's mobility from 25 per cent below the norm up to the norm has greater moral priority than increasing his mobility from the norm to 25 per cent above it. The general point is that aspects of a person's quality of life may play a role not only in judgements about his quality of life or about how good a life he has, but also in other distinct moral and political judgements, or in the application of independent moral principles such as a principle of equal opportunity. This is, of course, a thoroughly familiar point in moral and political philosophy generally, and concerning consequentialist moralities in particular, against which it is often objected that they ignore the moral importance of whether the good is fairly or justly distributed. In the present context its importance is in reminding us to distinguish judgements concerning the improvement or reduction of people's quality of life from other independent moral evaluations of those same changes so as not to confuse needlessly the nature of quality of life judgements in health care.

2   *Ethical Frameworks for Health Care Treatment Decision-making*

The first broad area of work within medical ethics bearing on the concept of the quality of life concerns the aims of medicine and the account of medical treatment decision-making appropriate to those aims. It may be helpful to begin with a natural objection to thinking that these issues in medical ethics will illuminate any broad notion of the good life. On the contrary, as Leon Kass has argued, medicine's proper end is the much narrower one of health, or the healthy human being, and other goals such as happiness and gratifying patient desires are false goals for medicine.[10] Kass understands health to be a naturalistically defined property of individual biological organisms, organisms which must be understood as organic wholes, and whose parts

have specific functions that define their nature as parts: the bone marrow for making red blood cells; the lungs for exchange of oxygen and carbon dioxide; the heart for pumping the blood. Even at a biochemical level, every molecule can be characterized in terms of its function. The parts, both macroscopic and microscopic, contribute to the maintenance and functioning of the other parts, and make possible the maintenance and functioning of the whole.[11]

What constitutes well-functioning varies with the particular biological species in question, but Kass is at pains to argue that 'health is a natural standard or

---

[10] Kass, 1985.   [11] Ibid., 171.

norm – not a moral norm, not a "value" as opposed to a "fact", not an obligation – a state of being that reveals itself in activity as a standard of bodily excellence or fitness'.[12]

Kass's work constitutes one of the more ambitious attempts to justify two common-sense beliefs about the 'objectivity' of medicine: that the aim of medicine is and should be the patient's health, and that health is a biologically determined, objective matter of fact. If so, then physicians, with their impressive body of scientific knowledge concerning human biological functioning and the impact of therapeutic interventions on diseases and their natural courses, would seem to be the proper judges of whether we are healthy and, if we are not, what therapeutic interventions will be likely to make us more so. This hardly begins to do justice to the subtlety of Kass's view – though it is a view that I believe to be fundamentally mistaken – but it does bring out why one might think medicine, properly aimed only at human health defined in terms of biological functioning, has little to teach us regarding broader social issues about the quality of life. I believe it is fair to say that the main body of work in medical ethics within the last two decades has rejected Kass's view that the sole proper aim of medicine is health, defined in naturalistic, biological terms, and the ethical framework for medical treatment decision-making that it would seem to imply. We need to see how the alternative, broader view of the aims of medicine that should guide medical treatment decision-making bears on an understanding of the quality of life.

It has become a commonplace, at least in the developed countries, that medicine has achieved the capacity commonly to offer to patients suffering from particular diseases a number of alternative treatments, and to extend patients' lives in circumstances in which the benefit to the patient of doing so is increasingly problematic. In the United States this has led to patients pursuing various means of gaining control over decisions about their treatment. In the case of competent patients, a broad consensus has developed that such patients have the right to decide about their care in a process of shared decision-making with their physicians and to reject any preferred treatment. In the case of incompetent patients, an analogous consensus has been developing that an incompetent patient's surrogate, seeking to decide as the patient would have decided in the circumstances if competent, is likewise entitled to decide about the patient's care with the patient's physician and to reject any care the patient would not have wanted – though the consensus concerning incompetent patients is less broad and more ringed with qualifications. Each consensus is reflected in a large medical ethics literature, a growing body of legal decisions, legal mechanisms such as Living Wills and Durable Powers of Attorney for Health Care, whose purpose is to ensure patients' control over their care, pronouncements and

[12] Ibid., 173. For a more philosophically sophisticated analysis of the concept of health that also construes it in functional terms as a natural, biological norm not involving value judgements, see Boorse, 1975, 1977. One of the most useful collections of papers on concepts of health is Caplan, Engelhardt, and McCartney, 1981.

studies of authoritative bodies and commissions, policies of health care institutions, and the practice of health care professionals.[13]

The common view is now that health care decision-making should be a process of shared decision-making between patient (or the patient's surrogate in the case of an incompetent patient) and physician.[14] Each is seen as indispensable to sound decision-making. The physician brings his or her training, knowledge, and expertise to bear for the diagnosis of the patient's condition, the estimation of the patient's prognosis with different alternative treatments, including the alternative of no treatment, and a recommendation regarding treatment. The patient brings the knowledge of his or her aims, ends, and values that are likely to be affected by different courses of treatment, and this enables a comparative evaluation of different possible outcomes to be made. As alternative treatments have multiplied and become possible in circumstances promising increasingly marginal or questionable benefits, both physicians and patients are called upon to make increasingly difficult judgements about the effects of treatment on patients' quality of life. It is worth noting that proponents of shared decision-making need not reject the functional account of health as a biological norm defended by Kass and others. What they can reject is the claim that the only proper goal of medicine is health. Instead, medicine's goal should be to provide treatment that best enables patients to pursue successfully their overall aims and ends, or life plans. It is the relative value of health, and of different aspects of health, as compared with other ends, that varies for different persons and circumstances.

Most patients' decisions about life-sustaining treatment will be based on their judgement of the benefits and burdens of the proposed treatment and the life it sustains, though in some instances patients may give significant weight to other factors such as religious obligations, the emotional burdens and financial costs for their families, and so forth. Except for patients who hold a form of vitalism according to which human life should or must be sustained at all costs and whatever its quality, these decisions by competent patients must inevitably involve an assessment of their expected quality of life if life-sustaining treatment

[13] I make no attempt here to provide any more than a few representative references to this very large literature. Probably the single best source for the medical ethics literature in this area is the *Hastings Center Report*. In the medical literature, see Wanzer, 1984, and Ruark, 1988. For a good review of most of the principal legal decisions in the United States concerning life-sustaining treatment, see Annas and Glantz, 1986. The most influential treatment of these issues by a governmental body in the United States is the report of the President's Commission for the Study of Ethical Problems in Medicine and Biomedical and Behavioral Research (1983). See also the recent report by the Hastings Center (1987). For discussions of Living Wills and Durable Powers of Attorney see Steinbrook and Lo, 1984, and Schneiderman and Arras, 1985. An application to clinical practice of the consensus that patients should have rights to decide about their care is Jonsen, Siegler, and Winslade, 1982.

[14] An influential statement of the shared decision-making view is another report of the President's Commission for the Study of Ethical Problems in Medicine and Biomedical and Behavioral Research (1982). A sensitive discussion of the difficulties of achieving shared decision-making in clinical practice is Katz, 1984.

is employed, though, as I shall note shortly, of only a very restricted sort.

Some have rejected the acceptability of quality of life judgements in the case of incompetent patients unable to decide for themselves, for whom others must therefore make treatment decisions.[15] One version of the objection is that no one should decide for another whether that other's quality of life is such that it is not worth continuing it. More specifically, the objection is that it is unacceptable to judge that the quality of another person's life is so poor that it is not worth the cost and effort to others to sustain that person's life. This objection, however, is not to making quality of life judgements in this context generally, but only to concluding that a person's life is not worth sustaining because its poor quality makes it not of value, but instead a burden, to *others*. The sound point that this objection confusingly makes is that quality of life judgements concerning a particular person should address how the conditions of a person's life affect its quality or value to *that person*, and not its value to others. Moreover, persons might judge their quality of life to be low and nevertheless value their lives as precious. In economic and policy analysis one version of the so-called human capital method of valuing human life, which values a person's life at a given point in time by his or her expected future earnings minus personal consumption, in effect values a person's life in terms of its economic value to others.[16] But there is no reason to reject the soundness of any evaluation by one person of another's quality of life simply because some might draw a further unjustified conclusion that if its quality is sufficiently low to make it on balance a burden to others, it ought not to be sustained.

The quality of life judgement appropriate to life-sustaining treatment decisions, whether made by a competent patient or an incompetent patient's surrogate, should thus assess how the conditions of the patient's life affect the value of that life to that patient. Nevertheless, even properly focused in this way, the role of quality of life judgements in decisions about whether to withhold or withdraw life-sustaining treatment is extremely limited. This quality of life judgement focuses only on which side of a *single threshold* a person's quality of life lies. The threshold question is: 'Is the quality of the patient's life so poor that for that person continued life is worse than no further life at all?' Or, in the language of benefits and burdens commonly employed in this context: 'Is the patient's quality of life so poor that the use of life-sustaining treatment is unduly burdensome, that is, such that the burdens to the patient of the treatment and/or the life that it sustains are sufficiently great and the benefits to the patient of the life that is sustained sufficiently limited, to make continued life on balance no longer a benefit or good to the patient?'[17] The only discrimination in quality

[15] E.g. Ramsey, 1978: 206–7.

[16] I have discussed some of the ethical implications of different measures for valuing lives found in the economic and policy literatures (Brock, 1986).

[17] It has been argued that this is the proper understanding of the distinction between 'ordinary' and 'extraordinary' treatment. That is, extraordinary treatment is treatment that for the patient in question and in the circumstances that obtain is unduly burdensome. Cf. President's Commission, 1983: 82–9.

of life required here is whether the quality of the life is on balance sufficiently poor to make it worse than non-existence to the person whose life it is.

Some have objected that this judgement is incoherent since, though it is possible to compare the quality of two lives, or of a single person's life under different conditions, it is not possible to make the quality of life comparison needed here because one of the alternatives to be compared is non-existence. If a person no longer exists, there is no life that could possibly have any quality so as to enter into a comparison with the quality of the life sustained by treatment. This objection does correctly point out that the judgement in question cannot involve a comparison of the quality of two alternative periods of life, though it could compare two possible lives, one that ends at that time and another that continues longer. However, it does not follow that there is no sense to the question of whether the best life possible for a person with some form of life-sustaining treatment is of sufficiently poor quality, or sufficiently burdensome, to be worse for that person than no further life at all. Perhaps the most plausible example is the case of a patient suffering from an advanced stage of invariably fatal cancer, who is virtually certain to die within a matter of days whatever is done, and whose life will be filled in those remaining days with great and unrelievable pain and suffering. (With the appropriate use of presently available measures of pain relief, it is in fact only very rarely the case that great pain and suffering in such cases cannot be substantially relieved.) The burden of those remaining days may then be found by the patient to be virtually unbearable, while the life sustained provides nothing of value or benefit to the patient. This judgement addresses the quality of the life sustained and appears to be a sensible judgement. It is just the judgement that patients or their surrogates commonly understand themselves to be making when they decide whether to employ or continue life-sustaining treatment.

Alternatively, the objection to someone ever making such a judgement for another may not be based on any putative incoherence of such judgements, but may express instead a concern about the difficulty of ever reliably deciding how *another* would in such circumstances decide, due perhaps to the diversity and unpredictability of people's actual decisions for themselves. Moreover, if the difficulty of reliably making such judgements for others is in fact this great, then we might well have a related practical concern that the interests of others, which may be in conflict with those of the patient, may consciously or unconsciously infect judgements about what is best for the patient.

Despite these difficulties, there have been attempts to formulate some general substantive standards to determine when an incompetent patient's quality of life is so poor that withholding or withdrawing further life-sustaining treatment is justified. Nicholas Rango, for example, has proposed standards for nursing home patients with dementia.[18] He emphasizes the importance of being clear about the purposes for which care is provided and distinguishes three forms

---

[18] Rango, 1985.

of care: (1) palliative care aimed at relieving physical pain and psychological distress; (2) rehabilitative care aimed at identifying and treating 'excess disabilities, the gap between actual level of physical, psychological or social functioning and potential functioning capacity',[19] and (3) medical care aimed at reducing the risk of mortality or morbidity. He emphasizes the importance of therapeutic caution because a seriously demented patient will not be able to understand the purposes of painful or invasive interventions, and so presumably cannot choose to undergo and bear burdensome treatment for the sake of promised benefits.[20] Rango propose two conditions, either of which is sufficient to justify forgoing further treatment of a chronic medical condition or a superimposed acute illness: (a) when the patient is burdened by great suffering despite palliative and rehabilitative efforts; (b) when the dementia progresses 'to a stuporous state of consciousness in which the person lives with a negligible awareness of self, other, and the world'.[21] Even within the relatively narrow focus of life-sustaining treatment decisions for demented patients, Rango's proposal can be seen to include three different kinds of components of quality of life assessments. The first, covered by treatment aim (1) and patient conditions (a) and (b), concerns the quality of the patient's conscious experience. The second, covered especially by treatment aim (2) and patient condition (b), concerns the patient's broad functional capacities. The third, covered especially by patient condition (b) and by the patient's ability to understand the purpose of treatment and in turn to choose to undergo it, concerns the centrality to quality of life of the capacity to exercise choice in forming and pursuing an integrated and coherent life plan. I shall argue below that each of these three kinds of condition is an essential component of an adequate account of the quality of life.

At the other end of life, the debate in the United States about treatment for critically ill new-born infants has also focused on the role of quality of life considerations in determining when life-sustaining treatment is a benefit for the infant. One influential attempt to bring quality of life considerations into these decisions is the proposal of the moral theologian, Richard McCormick, that a new-born infant's life is a value that must be preserved only if the infant has the potential for a 'meaningful life'.[22] A meaningful life is one that contains some potential for human relationships: anencephalic new-borns, for example, wholly lack this potential, while those with Down's syndrome or spina bifida (to cite two of the most discussed kinds of case) normally do not. Nancy Rhoden has developed a more detailed proposal along similar lines regarding life-sustaining treatment for new-born infants:

aggressive treatment is not mandatory if an infant: (1) is in the process of dying; (2) will

---

[19] Ibid., 836, quoting E. M. Brody.
[20] The importance of this factor was stressed in a widely publicized legal decision concerning the use of painful chemotherapy for a man suffering from cancer who had been severely retarded from birth (*Superintendent of Belchertown State School* v. *Saikewicz*, 1977).
[21] Rango, 1985: 838.
[22] McCormack, 1974.

never be conscious; (3) will suffer unremitting pain; (4) can only live with major, highly restrictive technology which is not intended to be temporary (e.g., artificial ventilation); (5) cannot live past infancy (i.e., a few years); or (6) lacks potential for human interaction as a result of profound retardation.[23]

Rhoden's proposal is typical of those accepting the use of quality of life considerations in decisions about life-sustaining treatment for new-born infants in its focus on the infant's at least minimal capacity for positive conscious experience (conditions 2 and 3): the infant's capacities for physical, mental, and social functioning (conditions 2, 3, 4, and 6), and the infant's capacities to live far enough into childhood to begin a life that can be viewed and experienced 'from the inside' by the child as a life lived in a biographical, not biological, sense (conditions 1 and 4; I will say more about this special feature of infant 'life years' below in discussing the relevance of mortality data to good lives). However, the very limited, single-threshold character of the quality of life assessments required in decisions as to whether to forgo or to employ life-sustaining treatment, whether for adults or new-born infants, takes us only a little way in understanding quality of life assessments in health care treatment decision-making.

It is necessary, consequently, to broaden the focus from life-sustaining treatment decisions to medical treatment decisions generally. Here, as noted earlier, there is a widespread consensus that competent patients are entitled, in a process of shared decision-making with their physicians, to decide about their treatment and to refuse any proferred or recommended treatment. In the United States, the doctrine of informed consent, both in medical ethics and in the law, requires that treatment should not be given to a competent patient without that patient's informed and voluntary consent.[24] What does this doctrine, which lodges decision-making authority with the patient, imply about the nature of judgements concerning the patient's quality of life? An argument that it presupposes the normatively subjective, preference satisfaction account of a good life might, in rough outline, go as follows.

Each of the requirements of the informed consent doctrine can be understood as designed to provide reasonable assurance that the patient has chosen the treatment alternative most in accord with his or her own settled preferences and values. If the patient's decision is not informed—specifically, if the patient is not provided in understandable form with information regarding his or her diagnosis, the prognosis when different treatment alternatives (including the alternative of no treatment) are pursued, including the expected risks and benefits, with their attendant probabilities, of treatment alternatives—then the patient will lack the information needed to select the alternative most in accord with his or her settled preferences. If the patient's decision is not voluntary,

---

[23] Rhoden, 1985. Another sensitive discussion of the need for quality of life judgements in treatment decisions for imperilled new-born babies is Arras, 1984.

[24] The most comprehensive treatment of the informed consent doctrine is Faden and Bauchamp, 1986. See also President's Commission, 1982. The exceptions to the legal requirement of informed consent are discussed in Meisel, 1979.

but is instead forced, coerced, or manipulated by another, then it is likely not to be in accordance with the patient's settled preferences, but instead will forward another's interests, or another's view of what is best for the patient. If the patient is not competent to make the choice in question, then he or she will lack the ability to use the information provided to deliberate about the alternatives and to select the one most in accord with his or her settled preferences. When all three requirements are satisfied—the decision is informed and voluntary, and the patient competent—others can be reasonably assured that the patient's choice fits the patient's own conception of a good life, as reflected in his or her settled preferences.[25] Viewed in this way, the informed consent doctrine may appear to be grounded in a preference satisfaction account of the good or the quality of life, and so not to require any more complex vector account of the sort suggested earlier. Even in this very crude form, however, this argument can be seen to be unsound if one asks what values the informed consent doctrine and the account of shared decision-making in medicine are usually thought to promote, and what values support their acceptance.

The most natural and obvious first answer has already implicitly been given: the informed consent doctrine in health-care treatment decision-making is designed, when its three requirements are satisfied, to serve and promote the patient's well-being, as defined by the patient's settled, uncoerced, and informed preferences. If this were the only value at stake, or at least clearly the dominant value, then it would be plausible to argue that the informed consent doctrine rests, at least implicitly, on a preference satisfaction account of the good life. However, it is not the only value at stake. Usually regarded as at least of roughly commensurate importance is respecting the patient's self-determination or autonomy.[26] The interest in self-determination I understand to be the interest of persons, broadly stated, in forming, revising over time, and pursuing in their choices and actions their own conception of a good life; more narrowly stated for my specific purposes here, it is people's interest in making significant decisions affecting their lives, such as decisions about their medical care, for themselves and according to their own values. Sometimes this is formulated as the right to self-determination.

[25] When patients' settled preferences are not in accord with their values, then their informed and voluntary choices may not reflect their conception of their good. One of the clearest examples is the patient who is addicted to morphine, hates his addiction and tries unsuccessfully to resist it, but in the end is overpowered by his desire for the morphine and takes it. This in essence is Frankfurt's example in his classic paper (Frankfurt, 1971). Frankfurt's analysis is in terms of first- and second-order desires, but can also be put in terms of the desires a person in fact has as opposed to the desires the person values and wants to have. When these are in conflict his informed and voluntary choice may not reflect the values that define his own conception of his good. There is a sense in which his choice in these conditions is involuntary, so it would be possible to extend the informed consent doctrine's requirement of voluntariness to include this sense. Alternatively, it might be possible to interpret the requirement of competence in a way that makes the morphine addict incompetent to decide whether to continue using morphine.
[26] This account of the principal values underlying the informed consent doctrine as patient well-being and self-determination is common to many analyses of that doctrine; cf. President's Commission, 1982. I have employed it in Brock, 1987.

Whether interest or right, however, the greater the moral weight accorded
to individual self-determination as one of the values underlying and supporting
the informed consent doctrine, the weaker the basis for inferring that the doctrine
presupposes the normatively subjective, preference satisfaction account of the
good life. This is because the greater the moral weight accorded to individual
self-determination, the more self-determination can explain the requirement
of informed consent, even assuming the patient chooses in a manner sharply
contrary to his or her own well-being. Moreover, there is substantial reason
to suppose that the doctrine does in fact largely rest on respect for patients'
self-determination. In the celebrated 1914 legal case of *Schloendorff* v. *Society
of New York Hospitals*, usually cited as the first important enunciation of the
legal requirement of consent for medical care, Justice Cardozo held that: 'Every
human being of adult years and sound mind has a right to determine what shall
be done to his own body; and a surgeon who performs an operation without
his patient's consent commits an assault, for which he is liable in damages.'[27]
I shall make no attempt here to trace the development of the legal doctrine of
informed consent since *Schloendorff*, but it is probably fair to say that no other
subsequent case has been as influential or as often cited in that development.
And the later cases, in one form or another, repeatedly appeal to a right to
self-determination to support that developing doctrine.[28] Nearly half a century
later, for example, in the important 1960 case of *Natanson* v. *Kline* the Kansas
Supreme Court made an equally ringing appeal to self-determination:

Anglo-American law stars with the premise of thorough-going self-determination. It
follows that each man is considered to be master of his own body, and he may, if he be
of sound mind, expressly prohibit the performance of life-saving surgery, or other medical
treatment. A doctor might well believe that an operation or form of treatment is desirable
or necessary but the law does not permit him to substitute his own judgment for that
of the patient by any form of artifice or deception.[29]

The philosophical tradition regarding the problem of paternalism is equally
bound up in a commitment to the importance of individual self-determination
or autonomy. Here, the *locus classicus* is John Stuart Mill's renowned assertion
of the 'one very simple principle' that

the sole end for which mankind are warranted, individually or collectively, in interfering
with the liberty of action of any of their number is self-protection. That the only purpose
for which power can be rightfully exercised over any member of a civilized community,
against his will, is to prevent harm to others. His own good, either physical or moral,
is not a sufficient warrant. He cannot rightfully be compelled to do or forbear because
it will be better for him to do so, because it will make him happier, because, in the opinions
of others, to do so would be wise or even right.[30]

The voluminous subsequent philosophical literature on paternalism certainly
suggests that this principle is not as simple as Mill supposed, but it also makes

[27] *Schloendorf* v. *Society of New York Hospital*, 1914.   [28] Cf. Faden and Beauchamp, 1986: ch. 4.
[29] *Natanson* v. *Kline*, 1960.   [30] Mill, 1859: 13.

clear that, even for one like Mill who in other contexts was an avowed utilitarian, the case for non-interference with individual self-determination and liberty of action does not rest on any claim that doing so cannot be for a person's 'good', understood in a normatively subjective interpretation. Quite to the contrary, Mill and the many who have followed him have been at pains to insist that such interference is not justified even when it would truly be for the good of the one interfered with.[31] The result is that it is not possible to draw any firm conclusion from the doctrine of informed consent in medicine that patients' well-being or quality of life is understood according to a normatively subjective interpretation. Individual self-determination can serve as the foundation for the informed consent doctrine and can make that doctrine compatible with any of the three main alternative accounts of the good or quality of life that I have distinguished.

What is the relation between these two values of patient self-determination and well-being, commonly taken as underlying the informed consent doctrine, and the broad concept of a good life? The conventional view, I believe, is that the patient's well-being is roughly equivalent to the patient's good and that individual self-determination is a value independent of the patient's well-being or good. Respecting the patient's right to self-determination, then, at least sometimes justifies respecting treatment choices that are contrary to the patient's well-being or good.[32] Respecting self-determination is commonly held to be what is required by recognizing the individual as a person, capable of forming a conception of the good life for him or herself. If personal self-determination is a fundamental value—fundamental in that it is what is involved in respecting persons—however, then I suggest that our broadest conception of a good life should be capable of encompassing it rather than setting it off as separate from and in potential conflict with a person's well-being or good, as in the conventional account of informed consent. What we need is a distinction between a good life for a person in the broadest sense and a person's personal well-being, such that only personal well-being is independent of and potentially in conflict with individual self-determination.

We should think of being self-determined as central to—a central part of—having a good life in the broadest sense. It is in the exercise of self-determination that we maintain some control over, and take responsibility for, our lives and for what we will become. This is not to deny, of course, that there are always substantial limits and constraints within which we must exercise this judgement and choice. But it is to say that showing respect for people through respecting their self-determination acknowledges the fundamental place of

---

[31] The most detailed recent account of justified paternalism in the spirit of Mill's position is VanDeVeer, 1986. The most sophisticated development of a Millian position on paternalism in criminal law is Feinberg, 1986. I have explored some of the issues between rights-based and consequentialist accounts of paternalism in Brock, 1983 and 1988.

[32] This conventional view is reflected in the independent ethical principles of beneficence and autonomy in Beauchamp and Childress, 1979. This book has probably been the account of moral principles most influential with people in medicine and health care without philosophical training in ethics.

self-determination in a good life. I take this to be essentially what Rawls intends by his claim that people have a highest-order interest in autonomy and what Sen means by his notion of agency freedom.[33] We do not want this broad conception of a good life, however, to prevent our making sense of persons freely and knowingly choosing to sacrifice their own personal well-being for the sake of other persons. To cite an extreme case, a parent might knowingly and freely choose not to pursue expensive life-sustaining treatment such as a heart transplant in order to preserve financial resources for his children's education. Given his love and sense of responsibility for his children, he would judge his life to be worse if he had the transplant at the expense of his children's education, though certainly his health and his personal well-being would be improved. We might say here that he values his personal well-being in these circumstances less than the well-being of his children. In its requirement that such a choice be respected, the informed consent doctrine implicitly accepts that the best life for a person is a life of self-determination or choice, even if the exercise of that self-determination or choice results in a lessened state of personal well-being. Precisely how to make this distinction between the good life, as opposed to the personal well-being, of an individual raises difficulties that I cannot pursue here. The rough idea is that personal well-being makes essential reference to the states of consciousness, activities, and capacities for functioning of the person in question (I will pursue this further in Section 2 of this paper), and it is these that are worsened when the parent pursues his conception of a good life in sacrificing his personal well-being for that of his child.[34]

Medical treatment decisions must often be made for patients who are not

---

[33] Cf. Rawls, 1980, and Sen, 1985, esp. pp. 203–4.

[34] If personal well-being is understood in this way, it suggests that satisfaction of a person's non-personal desires that make no such reference to him do not increase the person's well-being. Consider a loyal fan of the Boston Red Sox baseball team, who wants the Red Sox to win the pennant. On the last day of the season, tied for first place with the New York Yankees, the Red Sox beat the Yankees and win the pennant. Suppose the fan is travelling in a remote area of Alaska on the day of the big game and a week later, before getting out of the wilderness area and learning of the Red Sox victory, he is killed by a rock slide. Was his personal well-being increased at all simply because the state of affairs he desired – the Red Sox victory – obtained? I believe the answer should be no.

The harder question is whether, in our broader sense of a good life, he had a better life even unbeknownst to him. And was the quality of his life any better? Certainly his life *as experienced by him* was no better and not of higher quality. Even in our broad sense of a good life, his life may seem not to have gone better, but perhaps that is only because this is a relatively unimportant desire. Suppose instead, to adapt an example of Parfit's (1984), a person devotes fifty years of his life to saving Venice and then, confident that it is safe, goes on vacation to the Alaskan wilderness. While he is there a flood destroys Venice, but, like the Red Sox fan, he never learns of it because a week after the flood and before getting out of the wilderness he is killed by a rock slide. Parfit notes that it is plausible to say of the destruction of Venice both that it has made the person's life go less well because he had invested his life in this goal and his life's work is now in vain, but also that it cannot lower the quality of his life if it does not affect the quality of his experience. This suggests a point where a broad notion of a good life may diverge from the notion of the quality of life. Since I believe that medicine and medical ethics have little illumination to offer on this point, I set it aside here and shall in the body of the paper continue to use the broad notion of a good life largely interchangeably with the quality of life.

themselves competent to make them. There has been considerable discussion both in medical ethics and in the law regarding appropriate ethical standards for such decisions.[35] Since quality of life considerations are virtually always relevant to these decisions, the ethical frameworks developed for these decisions must employ, either explicitly or implicitly, a conception of the quality of life of patients. There is considerable consensus that if the patient in question, while still competent, formulated and left an explicit advance directive clearly and unambiguously specifying his or her wishes regarding treatment in the circumstances now obtaining, then those wishes should be followed, at least within very broad limits, by those treating the patient. At the present time in the United States, most states have adopted legislation giving the force of law to one or another form of so-called Living Will, which allows people to give binding instructions about their treatment should they become incompetent and unable to decide for themselves. Several other states have more recently enacted legislation permitting people to draw up a Durable Power of Attorney for Health Care, which combines the giving of instructions about the person's wishes regarding treatment with the designation of who is to act as surrogate decision-maker, and so to interpret those instructions, should one become incompetent to make the decisions oneself.

In the usual case in which an incompetent patient has left no formal advance directive, two principles for the guidance of those who must decide about treatment for the patient have been supported – the *substituted judgement* principle and the *best interests* principle. The substituted judgement principle requires the surrogate to decide as the patient would have decided if competent and in the circumstances that currently obtain. The best interests principle requires the surrogate to make the treatment decision that best serves the patient's interests. This has the appearance of a dispute between what I earlier called normatively subjective and normatively objective accounts of a good life, since the only point of the best interests principle as an alternative to substituted judgement might seem to be that it employs a normatively objective standard of the person's good that does not depend on his or her particular subjective preferences and values. However, this appearance is misleading. These two principles of surrogate decision-making are properly understood, in my view, not as competing alternative principles to be used for the same cases, but instead as an ordered pair of principles to cover all cases of surrogate decision-making for incompetent patients in which an advance directive does not exist, with each of the two principles to apply in a different subset of these cases. (This is not to say that these two principles are always in fact understood in medical ethics, the law, or health care practice as applying to distinct groups of cases; the treatment of these two principles is rife with confusion.)

The two groups of cases are differentiated with regard to the information

---

[35] Allen Buchanan and I have discussed ethical issues in decision-making for incompetent persons in our paper (Buchanan and Brock, 1986: 17–94) and in our book (Buchanan and Brock, 1989).

available or obtainable concerning the patient's general preferences and values that has some bearing on the treatment choice at hand. The two principles are an ordered pair in the sense that when sufficient information is available about the relevant preferences and values of the patient to permit a reasonably well-grounded application of the substituted judgement principle, then surrogate decision-makers for the patient are to use that information and that principle to infer what the patient's decision would have been in the circumstances if he or she were competent.[36] In the absence of such information, and only then, surrogate decision-makers for the patient are to select the alternative that is in the best interests of the patient, which is usually interpreted to mean the alternative that most reasonable and informed persons would select in the circumstances. Thus, these two principles are not competing principles for application in the same cases, but alternative principles to be applied in different cases.

Nevertheless, it might seem that the best interests standard remains a normatively objective account when it is employed. However, this need not be so. If the best interests standard is understood as appealing to what most informed and reasonable persons would choose in the circumstances, it employs the normatively subjective preference standard. And it applies the choice of most persons to the patient in question because in the absence of any information to establish that the patient's relevant preferences and values are different than most people's, the most reasonable presumption is that the patient is like most others in the relevant respects and would choose like those others. Thus, the best interests standard, like the two other standards of choice for incompetent patients – the advance directive and substituted judgement standards – can be understood as requiring the selection of the alternative the patient would most likely have selected, with the variations in the standards suited to the different levels of information about the patient that is available. Just as with the informed consent doctrine that applies to competent patients, so these three principles – advance directives, substituted judgement, and best interests – guiding surrogate choice for incompetent patients can all be understood as supported and justified by the values of patient well-being *and* self-determination. Thus, each of these three principles implicitly employs an account of a good life that is a life of choice and self-determination concerning one's aims, values, and life plan.

Before leaving the ethical frameworks that have been developed in the medical ethics, legal, and medical literatures for treatment decision-making for competent and incompetent patients, I want to make explicit an indeterminacy in these frameworks concerning the nature of the ethical theory they presuppose. I have noted that it is common to base these ethical frameworks on two central values in a good life: patient well-being and self-determination. What is commonly left unclear, however, is the foundational status of the ethical value of

---

[36] Rebecca Dresser has developed a Parfitian challenge to the substituted judgement principle as well as to the authority of advance directives in cases in which the conditions creating the patient's incompetence also reduce or eliminate the psychological continuity and connectedness necessary for personal identity to be maintained. Cf. Dresser, 1986. Cf. also Buchanan, 1988.

individual self-determination in the underlying ethical theory supporting these decision-making frameworks. Self-determination might be held to have only derivative or instrumental value within a broadly consequentialist moral theory. Specifically, it might be held to be instrumentally valuable for the fundamental value of happiness or preference satisfaction within normatively subjective theories of a good life of a hedonist or preference satisfaction sort. If, as seems true at least for many social conditions and historical periods, most people have a relatively strong desire to make significant decisions about their lives for them-selves, then it is at least a plausible presumption that their doing so will generally promote their happiness or the satisfaction of their desires. If self-determination is only valuable at bottom in so far as it leads to happiness or preference satis-faction, then it will not be part of an ideal of the person that is objective in the sense of its value not being entirely dependent on happiness or satisfaction. Since on most plausible theories of the good, happiness and desire satisfaction are significant *part* of a good life, and since self-determination does commonly make a significant contribution to people's happiness or desire satisfaction, self-determination will commonly have significant instrumental value on any plausible theory of a good life.[37]

As a result, to single out self-determination as one of the two principal values underlying the informed consent doctrine in medical ethics as it applies both to competent and incompetent patients is not to make clear at a foundational level of ethical theory whether self-determination is held to have only instru-mental value, or also significant non-instrumental value as an important compo-nent of an objective ideal of the person. The vast majority of ethical discussions of informed consent and health care treatment decision-making simply do not either explicitly address this foundational question of ethical theory or even implicitly presuppose a particular position on it. From a practical perspective, this foundational indeterminacy has the value of allowing proponents of incom-patible ethical theories, for example consequentialists and rights-based theorists, to agree on the fundamental importance of self-determination and choice in a good life.

There is one final difficulty to be noted in attempting to infer the account of a good life at the level of basic ethical theory from the ethical frameworks for treatment decision-making advocated for and employed in medical practice. There is a general difficulty in inferring the underlying values or ethical prin-ciples that support social practices. A social practice like that of informed consent and shared decision-making in medicine must guide over time a very great number of treatment decisions carried out in a wide variety of circumstances by many and diverse patients, family members, and health care professionals. A well-structured practice must take account of and appropriately minimize the

---

[37] Scanlon argues in this volume that desire satisfaction is not itself a basic part of individual well-being, but is dependent on hedonistic or ideal (what he calls substantive good) reasons for its support.

potential in all involved parties for well-intentioned misuse or ill-intentioned abuse of their roles. Institutional constraints may thus be justified, though on some particular occasions they will produce undesirable results, because in the long run their overall results are better than those of any feasible alternatives. For example, even if we appeal only to the value of patient well-being and leave aside any independent value of self-determination, a strong right of patients to refuse any treatment might be justified if most of the time people are them-selves the best judges of what health care treatment will best promote their happiness or satisfy their enduring preferences and values. Alternatively, that same strong right to refuse treatment might be justified within a normatively objective ideal theory of a good life for persons because, though individuals can be mistaken about their own good when they pursue their happiness or seek to satisfy their desires, no reliable alternative social and legal practice is feasible that will produce better results in the long run, even judged by that ideal theory of a good life. The imperfections and limitations of people and institutions may lead supporters of quite different accounts of a good life to support roughly the same institutions in practice. In a more general form, this is a thoroughly familiar point in moral philosophy where defenders of fundamentally different moral theories, such as consequentialists and rights theorists, may converge on the institutions justified by their quite different theories. Without explicitly uncovering the justificatory rationales for specific social institutions accepted by particular persons, we cannot confidently infer the ethical principles or judgements, and specifically the conception of a good life, that they presuppose.

3 Health Policy Measures of the Quality of Life

I want now to shift attention from the account of the quality of life presupposed by ethical frameworks for medical treatment decision-making to more explicit measures used to assess health levels and the quality of life as it is affected by health and disease within larger population groups. Early measurement attempts focused on morbidity and mortality rates in different populations and societies. These yield only extremely crude comparisons, since they often employ only such statistics as life expectancy, infant mortality, and reported rates of specific diseases in a population. Nevertheless, they will show gross differences between countries, especially between economically developed and underdeveloped coun-tries, and between different historical periods, in both length and quality of life as it is affected by disease. Major changes in these measures during this century, as is well known, have been due principally to public health measures such as improved water supplies, sewage treatment, and other sanitation pro-grammes and to the effects of economic development in improving nutrition, housing, and education; improvements in the quality of and access to medical care have been less important. In recent decades, health policy researchers have developed a variety of measures that go substantially beyond crude morbidity and mortality measures. Before shifting our attention to them, however, it is worth underlining the importance of mortality measures to the broad concept of a good life.

When quality and quantity of life are distinguished, both are relevant to the degree to which a person has a good life. People whose lives are of high quality, by whatever measure of quality, but whose lives are cut short well before reaching the normal life span in their society, have had lives that have gone substantially less well, because of their premature death, than reasonably might have been expected. People typically develop, at least by adolescence, more or less articulated and detailed plans for their lives; commonly, the further into the future those plans stretch, the less detailed, more general, and more open-ended they are. Our life plans undergo continuous revision, both minor and substantial, over the course of our lives, but at any point in time within a life people's plans for their lives will be based in part on assumptions about what they can reasonably expect in the way of a normal life span.[38] When their lives are cut short prematurely by illness and disease they lose not just the experiences, happiness, and satisfactions that they would otherwise have had in those lost years, but they often lose as well the opportunity to complete long-term projects and to achieve and live out the full shape, coherence, and conclusion that they had planned for their lives. It is this rounding out and completion of a life plan and a life that helps enable many elderly people, when near death, to feel that they have lived a full and complete life and so to accept their approaching death with equanimity and dignity. The loss from premature death is thus not simply the loss of a unit of a good thing, so many desired and expected-to-be-happy life-years, but the cutting short of the as yet incompletely realized life plan that gave meaning and coherence to the person's life.

The importance of life plans for a good life suggests at least two other ways in which different mortality rates within societies affect the opportunites of their members to attain good lives. Citizens of economically underdeveloped countries typically have shorter life expectancies than do citizens of the developed countries. Thus, even those who reach a normal life span will have less time to develop and enjoy a richly complex and satisfying life than will those who reach a normal, but significantly longer, life span in the developed countries. Mortality data indicate that citizens of underdeveloped countries typically have less good lives as a result of inadequate health care *both* because of their shorter life expectancies *and* because of their increased risk of not living to even the normal life span in their own society.

One final relation between mortality data and the importance of life plans in a good life concerns infant and extremely early childhood mortality. It is common to view such early mortality as particularly tragic, both because of

---

[38] Two of the more important discussions of life plans and of how they can give structure and coherence to life are Fried, 1970: ch. 10, and Rawls, 1971: ch. 7.

the greater amount of expected life-years lost to the individual and because the life was cut short just as it was getting started. The loss is often deep for the parents, in part because of the hopes and plans for the infant's future that *they* had for the infant. But the death of an infant or extremely young child before he or she has developed the capacity to form desires, hopes, and plans for the future cuts that life short—'life' understood as a connected plan or unfolding biography with a beginning, middle, and end—before it has begun; the infant is alive, but does not yet have a life in this biographical sense.[39] From the perspective of this biographical sense of having a life as lived from the 'inside', premature death in later childhood, adolescence, or early adulthood commonly makes a life that has got started go badly, whereas infant death does not make a life go badly, but instead prevents it from getting started.

There is a voluminous medical and health policy literature focused on the evaluation of people's quality of life as it is affected by various disease states and/or treatments to ameliorate or cure those diseases.[40] The dominant conception of the appropriate aims of medicine focuses on medicine as an intervention aimed at preventing, ameliorating, or curing disease and its associated effects of suffering and disability, and thereby restoring, or preventing the loss of, normal function or of life. Whether the norm be that of the particular individual, or that typical in the particular society or species, the aim of raising people's function to *above* the norm is not commonly accepted as an aim of medicine of equal importance to restoring function *up to* the norm. Problematic though the distinction may be, quality of life measures in medicine and health care consequently tend to focus on individuals' or patients' *dysfunction* and its relation to some such norm. At a deep level, medicine views bodily parts and organs, individual human bodies, and people from a functional perspective. Both health policy analysts and other social scientists have done considerable work constructing and employing measures of health and quality of life for use with large and relatively diverse populations. Sometimes these measures explicitly address only part of an overall evaluation of people's quality of life, while in other instances they address something like overall quality of life as it is affected by disease. A closely related body of work focuses somewhat more narrowly on an evaluation of the effect on quality of life of specific modes of treatment for specific disease states. This research is more clinically oriented, though the breadth of impact on quality of life researchers seek to measure does vary to

[39] The notion of a biographical life is employed in the medical ethics literature by Rachels, 1986: 5–6, by Singer and Kuhse, 1985: 129–39, and by Callahan, 1987. It is also implicit in Tooley's (1983) account of the right to life.

[40] Among the useful papers consulted for this third section on health policy measures of quality of life, and not cited in other notes, are: Anderson 1986; Berg, 1986; Bergner, 1976; Calman, 1984; Cohen, 1982; Cribb, 1985; Editorial, 1986; Edlund and Tancredi, 1985; Flanagan, 1982; Gehrmann, 1978; Gillingham and Reece, 1980; Grogono, 1971; Guyatt, 1986; Hunt and EcEwen, 1980; Katz, 1963; Kornfeld, 1982; Klotkem, 1982; Liang, 1982; Najman and Levine, 1981; Pearlman and Speer, 1983; Presant, 1984; Report, 1984; Starr, 1986; Sullivan, 1966; Thomasma, 1984, 1986; Torrance, 1972, 1976a, 1976b.

some extent, depending often on the usual breadth of impact on the person of the disease being treated. Generally speaking, the population-wide measures tend to be less sensitive to individual differences as regards both the manner and the degree to which a particular factor affects people's quality of life. It will be helpful to have before us a few representative examples of the evaluative frameworks employed.[41]

The Sickness Impact Profile (SIP) was developed by Marilyn Bergner and colleagues to measure the impact of a wide variety of forms of ill health on the quality of people's lives.[42] Table 1 enumerates the items measured.

A second example of an evaluative framework is the Quality of Life Index (QLI) developed by Walter O. Spitzer and colleagues to measure the quality of life of cancer patients (see Table 2).[43]

A third prominent measure developed by Milton Chen, S. Fanshel and others is the Health Status Index (HSI), which measures levels of function along certain dimensions (see Table 3).[44]

It would be a mistake, of course, to attempt to infer precise and comprehensive philosophical theories of the quality of life or of a good life from measures such as these. The people who develop them are commonly social scientists and health care researchers who are often not philosophically sophisticated or concerned with the issues that divide competing philosophical accounts of a good life. The practical and theoretical difficulties in constructing valid measures that are feasible for large and varied populations require compromises with and simplifications of—or simply passing over—issues of philosophical importance. Nevertheless, several features of these measures are significant in showing the complexity of the quality of life measures employed in health care and, I believe, of any adequate account of the quality of life or of a good life.

First, the principal emphasis in each of the three measures of quality of life is on function, and functions of the 'whole person' as opposed to body parts and organ systems. In each case the functions are broadly characterized so as to be relevant not simply to a relatively limited and narrow class of life plans, but to virtually any life plan common in modern societies. Following the lead of Rawls's notion of 'primary goods', I shall call these 'primary functions'.[45] In the SIP, the categories of sleep and rest, and eating are necessary for biological function. The categories of work, home management, and recreation and pastimes are central activities common in virtually all lives, though the relative importance they have in a particular life can be adjusted for by making the measure relative to what had been the individual's normal level of activity in each of these areas prior to sickness. The two broad groups of functions, physical and psychosocial, are each broken down into several distinct components. For

---

[41] An example of a broad quality of life measure not focused on health care and disease can be found in the Swedish Level of Living Surveys discussed in the essay by Erikson in this volume.
[42] Bergner, 1981.   [43] Spitzer, 1981.
[44] Chen, Bush, and Patrick, 1975.   [45] Rawls, 1971: 62, 90–5.

Table 1 Sickness Impact Profile Categories and Selected Items

Dimension	Category	Items describing behaviour related to:	Selected items
Independent categories	SR	Sleep and rest	I sit during much of the day
			I sleep or nap during the day
	E	Eating	I am eating no food at all, nutrition is taken through tubes or intravenous fluids
			I am eating special or different food
	W	Work	I am not working at all
			I often act irritable towards my work associates
	HM	Home management	I am not doing any of the maintenance or repair work around the house that I usually do
			I am not doing heavy work around the house
	RP	Recreation and pastimes	I am going out for entertainment less
			I am not doing any of my usual physical recreation or activities
I. Physical	A	Ambulation	I walk shorter distances or stop to rest often
			I do not walk at all
	M	Mobility	I stay within one room
			I stay away from home only for brief periods of time
	BCM	Body care and movement	I do not bath myself at all, but am bathed by someone else
			I am very clumsy in my body movements
II. Psychosocial	SI	Social interaction	I am doing fewer social activities with groups of people
			I isolate myself as much as I can from the rest of the family
	AB	Alertness behaviour	I have difficulty reasoning and solving problems, e.g. making plans, making decisions, learning new things
			I sometimes behave as if I were confused or disoriented in place or time, e.g. where I am, who is around, directions, what day it is
	EB	Emotional behaviour	I laugh or cry suddenly
			I act irritable and impatient with myself, e.g. talk badly about myself, swear at myself, blame myself for things that happen
	C	Communication	I am having trouble writing or typing
			I do not speak clearly when I am under stress

each primary function, the SIP measures the impact of sickness by eliciting information concerning whether activities typical in the exercise of that function continue to be performed, or have become limited. Even for primary functions, about which it is plausible to claim that they have a place in virtually any life, the different functions can have a different *relative* value or importance within different lives, and the SIP makes no attempt to measure those differences. The QLI likewise addresses a person's levels of activity in daily living, specifically measuring the presence of related behaviours in the relevant areas. In measuring health and outlook, the primary concern is with subjective feeling states of the person, though here too there is concern with relevant behaviour. The category of support addresses both the social behaviour of the individual and the availability of people in the individual's environment to provide such relationships. This category illustrates the important point that most primary functional capacities require both behavioural capacities in the individual and relevant resources in the individual's external environment. The HSI addresses three broad categories of primary function—mobility, physical activity, and social activity—with evidence of current functional capacity found in current levels of activity. It is noteworthy that even this index, which focuses explicitly on the health status of individuals, does not measure the presence or absence of disease, as one might expect given common understandings of 'health' as the absence of disease; like the SIP and QLI, it too measures levels of very broad primary functions.

A second important feature of these measures shows up explicitly only in the first two—SIP and QLI—and is best displayed in the 'outlook' category of the QLI, though it is also at least partly captured in the 'emotional behaviour' category of the SIP. Both these categories can be understood as attempts to capture people's subjective response to their objective physical condition and level of function, or, in short, their level of happiness or satisfaction with their lives, though the actual measures are far too crude to measure happiness with much sensitivity. The important point is that the use of these categories represents a recognition that *part* of what makes a good life is that the person in question is happy or pleased with how it is going; that is, subjectively experiences it as going well, as fulfilling his or her major aims, and as satisfying. This subjective happiness component is not unrelated, of course, to how well the person's life is going as measured by the level of the other objective primary functions. How happy we are with our lives is significantly determined by how well our lives are in fact going in other objective respects. Nevertheless, medicine provides many examples that show it is a mistake to assume that the subjective happiness component correlates closely and invariably with other objective functional measures. In one study, for example, researchers found a substantial relation between different objective function variables and also between different subjective response or outlook variables, but only a very limited relation between objective and subjective variables.[46] These data reinforce the importance of

[46] Evans, 1985.

Table 2 Quality of Life Index: Formal of the Final Version Adopted

Study No _____

Age _____

See M_1 F_2 (Ring appropriate letter)

Primary Problem or Diagnosis _____

Secondary Problem or Diagnosis, or complication (if appropriate) _____

Scorer's Speciality _____

Scoring Form

Score each Reading 2, 1 or 0 according to your most recent assessment of the patient.

ACTIVITY

During the last week, the patient

- has been working or studying full time, or nearly so, in usual occupation; or managing own household, or participating in unpaid or voluntary activities, whether retired or not 2
- has been working or studying in usual occupation or managing own household or participating in unpaid or voluntary activities, but requiring major assistance or a significant reduction in hours worked or a sheltered situation or was on sick leave 1
- has not been working or studying in any capacity and not managing own household 0

DAILY LIVING

During the last week, the patient

- has been self-reliant in eating, washing, toileting, and dressing; using public transport or driving own car 2
- has been requiring assistance (another person or special equipment) for daily activities and transport but performing light tasks 1
- has not been managing personal care or light tasks and/or not leaving own home or institution at all 0

HEALTH

During the last week, the patient
- has been appearing to feel well or reporting feeling 'great' most of the time 2
- has been lacking energy or not feeling entirely 'up to par' more than just occasionally 1
- has been feeling very ill or 'lousy', seeming weak and washed out most of the time, or was unconscious 0

SUPPORT

During the last week
- the patient has been having good relationships with others and receiving strong support from at least one family member and/or friend 2
- support received or perceived has been limited from family and friends and/or by the patient's condition 1
- support from family and friends occurred infrequently or only when absolutely necessary or patient was unconscious 0

OUTLOOK

During the past week the patient
- has usually been appearing calm and positive in outlook, accepting and in control of personal circumstances, including surroundings 2
- has sometimes been troubled because not fully in control of personal circumstances or has been having periods of obvious anxiety or depression 1
- has been seriously confused or very frightened or consistently anxious and depressed or unconscious 0

QL INDEX TOTAL

How confident are you that your scoring of the preceding dimensions is accurate? Please ring the appropriate category.

Absolutely Confident	Very Confident	Quite Confident	Not Very Confident	Very Doubtful	Not at all Confident
1	2	3	4	5	6

Table 3 Scales and Definitions for the Classification of Function Levels

Scale	Step	Definition
		Mobility scale
5	Travelled freely	Used public transportation or drove alone. For below 6 age group, travelled as usual for age.
4	Travelled with difficulty	(a) Went outside alone, but had trouble getting around community freely, or (b) required assistance to use public transportation or automobile.
3	In house	(a) All day, because of illness or condition, or (b) needed human assistance to go outside.
2	In hospital	Not only general hospital, but also nursing home, extended care facility, sanatorium, or similar institution.
1	In special unit	For some part of the day in a restricted area of the hospital such as intensive care, operating room, recovery room, isolation ward, or similar unit.
0	Death	
		Physical activity scale
4	Walked freely	With no limitations of any kind.
3	Walked with limitations	(a) With cane, crutches, or mechanical aid, or (b) limited in lifting, stooping, or using stairs or inclines, or (c) limited in speed or distance by general physical condition.
2	Moved independently in wheelchair	Propelled self alone in wheelchair.
1	In bed or chair	For most or all of the day.
0	Death	
		Social activity scale
5	Performed major and other activities	*Major* means specifically: play for below 6, school for 6–17, and work or maintain household for adults. *Other* means all activities not classified as major, such as athletics, clubs, shopping, church, hobbies, civic projects, or games as appropriate for age.
4	Performed major but limited in other activities	Played, went to school, worked, or kept house but limited in other activities as defined above.
3	Performed major activity with limitation	Limited in the amount or kind of major activity performed, for instance, needed special rest periods, special school, or special working aids.
2	Did not perform major activity but performed self-care activities	Did not play, go to school, work or keep house, but dressed, bathed, and fed self.
1	Required assistance with self-care activities	Required human help with one or more of the following— dressing, bathing, or eating—and did not perform major or other activities. For below 6 age group, means assistance not usually required for age.
0	Death	

including both objective function and subjective response categories in a full conception of the quality of life, since neither is a reliable surrogate for the other. Given this at least partial independence between happiness and function variables, what is their relative weight in an overall assessment of a good life? Here, too, medicine brings out forcefully that there can be no uniform answer to this question. In the face of seriously debilitating injuries, one patient will adjust her aspirations and expectations to her newly limited functional capacities and place great value on achieving happiness despite these limitations. Faced with similar debilitating injuries, another patient will assign little value to adjusting to the disabilities in order to achieve happiness in spite of them, stating that she 'does not want to become the kind of person who is happy in that debilitated and dependent state'.[47]

There are other important qualifications of the generally positive relation between this happiness component of a good life and both the other primary function components and the overall assessment of how good a life it is. These qualifications are not all special to health care and the quality of life, but some are perhaps more evident and important in the area of health care than elsewhere. The first qualification concerns people's adjustments to limitations of the other primary functions. Sometimes the limitation in function, or potential limitation, is due to congenital abnormalities or other handicaps present from birth. For example, an American television programme recently reported on a follow-up of some of the children, now young adults, born to pregnant women who had taken the drug Thalidomide in the late 1950s.[48] The people reported on had suffered no brain damage but had been born with serious physical deformities, including lacking some or any arms and legs. While this placed many impairments in the way of carrying out primary functions such as eating, working, home management, physical mobility, and ambulation in the manner of normal adults, these people had made remarkable adjustments to compensate for their physical limitations: one was able to perform all the normal functions of eating using his foot in place of missing arms and hands; another made his living as an artist painting with a brush held between his teeth; another without legs was able to drive in a specially equipped car; and a mother of three without legs had adapted so as to be able to perform virtually all the normal tasks of managing a family and home.

These were cases where physical limitations that commonly restrict and impair people's primary functional capacities and overall quality of life had been so well compensated for as to enable them to perform the *same* primary functions, though in different ways, as well as normal, unimpaired persons do. While a few life plans possible for others remained impossible for them because of their limitations (for example, being professional athletes), their essentially

---

[47] The main character in the popular play and subsequent film *Whose Life is it Anyway?*, having become paralysed from the neck down, displayed this attitude of not wanting to become a person who had adjusted to his condition.

[48] *60 Minutes*, CBS television network programme, 21 February 1988.

unimpaired level of primary functions as a result of the compensations they had made left them with choice from among a sufficiently wide array of life plans that it is probably a mistake to believe that their quality of life had been lowered much or at all by their impairments. These cases illustrate that even serious physical limitations do not always lower quality of life if the disabled persons have been able or helped sufficiently to compensate for their disabilities so that their level of primary functional capacity remains essentially unimpaired; in such cases it becomes problematic even to characterize those affected as disabled.

In other cases, compensating for functional disabilities, particularly when they arise later in life, may require adjustments involving substantial changes in the kind of work performed, social and recreational activities pursued, and so forth. When these disabilities significantly restrict the activities that had been and would otherwise have been available to and pursued by the person, they will, all other things being equal, constitute reductions in the person's quality of life. If they do so, however, it will be because they significantly restrict the choices, or what Norman Daniels has called the normal opportunity range, available to the persons, and not because the compensating paths chosen need be, once entered on, any less desirable or satisfying.[49] The *opportunity for choice* from among a reasonable array of life plans is an important and independent component of quality of life: it is insufficient to measure only the quality of the life plan the disabled person now pursues and his or her satisfaction with it. Adjustments to impairments that leave primary functions undiminished or that redirect one's life plan into areas where function will be better—both central aims of rehabilitative medicine—can, however, enhance quality of life even in the face of a diminished opportunity range.

In his theory of just health care Daniels uses the notion of an *age-adjusted* normal opportunity range, which is important for the relation between opportunity and quality of life or a good life. Some impairments in primary functions occur as common features of even the normal aging process, for example, limitations in previous levels of physical activity. Choosing to adjust the nature and level of our planned activities to such impairments in function is usually considered a healthy adjustment to the aging process. This adjustment can substantially diminish the reduction in the person's quality of life from the limitations of normal aging. Nevertheless, even under the best of circumstances, the normal aging process (especially, say, beyond the age of 80), does produce limitations in primary functions that will reduce quality of life. Thus, while quality of life must always be measured against normal, primary functional capacities for humans, it can be diminished by reductions both in individual function below the age-adjusted norm and by reductions in normal function for humans as they age.

I have suggested above that adjustments in chosen pursuits as a result of

[49] Daniels, 1985: chs. 2 and 3.

impairments in primary, or previously pursued individual, functions can compensate substantially (fully, in the effects on happiness) for impaired function, but will often not compensate fully for significant reductions in the range of *opportunities* available for choice, and so will not leave quality of life undiminished. In some cases, however, a patient's response and adjustment to the limitations of illness or injury may be so complete, as regards his commitment to and happiness from the new chosen life path, that there is reason to hold that his quality of life is as high as before, particularly as he gets further away in time from the onset of the limiting illness or injury and as the new life becomes more securely and authentically the person's own. An undiminished or even increased level of happiness and satisfaction, together with an increased commitment to the new life, often seem the primary relevant factors when they are present. But we must also distinguish different *reasons* why the affective or subjective component of quality of life, which I have lumped under the notion of happiness, may remain undiminished, since this is important for an evaluation of the effect on quality of life.

A person's happiness is to some significant extent a function of the *degree* to which his or her major aims are being at least reasonably successfully pursued. Serious illness or injury resulting in serious functional impairment often requires a major revaluation of one's plan of life and its major aims and expectations. Over time, such revaluations can result in undiminished or even increased levels of happiness, despite decreased function, because the person's aspirations and expectations have likewise been revised and reduced. The common cases in medicine in which, following serious illness, people come to be satisfied with much less in the way of hopes and accomplishments illustrate clearly the incompleteness of happiness as a full account of the quality of life. To be satisfied or happy with getting much less from life, because one has come to expect much less, is still to get *less* from life or to have a less good life. (The converse of this effect is when rising levels of affluence and of other objective primary functions in periods of economic development lead to even more rapidly rising aspirations and expectations, and in turn to an *increasing gap* between accomplishments and expectations.) Moreover, whether the relation of the person's choices to his aspirations and expectations reflects his exercise of self-determination in response to changed circumstances is important in an overall assessment of his quality of life and shows another aspect of the importance of self-determination to quality of life.

Illness and injury resulting in serious limitations of primary functions often strike individuals without warning and seemingly at random, and are then seen by them and others as a piece of bad luck or misfortune. Every life is ended by death, and few people reach death after a normal life span without some serious illness and attendant decline in function. This is simply an inevitable part of the human condition. Individual character strengths and social support services enable people unfortunately impaired by disease or injury to adjust their aims and expectations realistically to their adversity, and then to get on with their lives, instead of responding to their misfortune with despair and self-pity. Circumstances beyond individuals' control may have dealt them a cruel blow, but they can retain dignity as self-determining agents capable of responsible choice in directing and retaining control over their lives within the limits that their new circumstances permit. We generally admire people who make the best of their lot in this way, and achieve happiness and accomplishment despite what seems a cruel fate. This reduction in aims and expectations, with its resultant reduction in the gap between accomplishments and aims, and the in turn resultant increase in happiness, is an outcome of the continued exercise of self-determination. It constitutes an increase in the happiness and self-determination components of quality of life though, of course, only in response to an earlier decrease in the person's level of primary functions.

Other ways of reducing this gap between accomplishments and expectations bypass the person's self-determination and are more problematic as regards their desirability and their effect on a person's quality of life. Jon Elster has written, for example, outside of the medical context, of different kinds of non-autonomous preferences and preference change.[50] Precisely characterizing the difference between what Elster calls non-autonomous preferences and what I have called the exercise of self-determination in adjusting to the impact of illness and injury raises deep and difficult issues that I cannot pursue here. Nevertheless, I believe that response to illness through the exercise of self-determined choice, in the service of protecting or restoring quality of life, is one of the most important practical examples of the significance for overall assessments of the quality of life of *how* to achieve the reasonable accord between aims and accomplishments that happiness requires.

4 Conclusion

Let us tie together some of the main themes in accounts of the quality of life or of a good life suggested by the literature in medical ethics and health policy. While that literature provides little in the way of well-developed, philosophically sophisticated accounts of the quality of life or of a good life, it is a rich body of analysis, data, and experience on which philosophical accounts of a good life can draw. I have presented here at least the main outlines of a general account of a good life suggested by that work. The account will be a complex one which, among the main philosophical theories distinguished earlier, probably most comfortably fits within ideal theories. I have suggested that we can employ Sen's construction of a plurality of independent vectors, each of which is an independent component of a full assessment of the degree to which a person has a good life.

The ethical frameworks for medical treatment decision-making bring out the centrality of a person's capacity as a valuing agent, or what I have called self-

---

[50] Elster, 1982.

determination, in a good life. The capacity for and exercise of self-determination can be taken to be a—or I believe *the*—fundamental ideal of the person within medical ethics. The exercise of self-determination in constructing a relatively full human life will require in an individual four broad types of primary functions: biological, including, for example, well-functioning organs; physical, including, for example, ambulation; social, including, for example, capacities to communicate; mental, including, for example, a variety of reasoning and emotional capabilities. There are no sharp boundaries between these broad types of primary function, and for different purposes they can be specified in more or less detail and in a variety of different bundles. The idea is to pick out human functions that are necessary for, or at least valuable in, the pursuit of nearly all relatively full and complete human life plans. These different functions can be represented on different vectors and they will be normatively objective components of a good life, though their relative weight within any particular life may be subjectively determined.

There are in turn what we can call agent-specific functions, again specifiable at varying levels of generality or detail, which are necessary for a person to pursue successfully the particular purposes and life plan he or she has chosen: examples are functional capacities to do highly abstract reasoning of the sort required in mathematics or philosophy and the physical dexterity needed for success as a musician, surgeon, or athlete. Once again, these functions can be represented on independent vectors, though their place in the good life for a particular person is determined on more normatively subjective grounds depending on the particular life plan chosen. The relative weight assigned to agent-specific functions and, to a substantially lesser degree, to primary functions, will ultimately be determined by the valuations of the self-determining agent, together with factual determinations of what functions are necessary in the pursuit of different specific life plans. The centrality of the valuing and choosing agent in this account of a good life gives both primary and, to a lesser extent, agent-specific functional capacities a central place in the good life because of their necessary role in making possible a significant range of opportunities and alternatives for choice.

At a more agent-specific level still are the particular desires pursued by people on particular occasions in the course of pursuing their valued aims and activities. Different desires and the degree to which they can be successfully satisfied can also be represented using the vector approach. It bears repeating that the level of a person's primary functional capacities, agent-specific functional capacities, and satisfaction of specific desires will all depend both on properties of the agent and on features of his or her environment that affect those functional capacities and desire pursuits. The inclusion of primary functions, agent-specific functions, and the satisfaction of specific desires all within an account of the good life allows us to recognize both its normatively objective and normatively subjective components. Analogously, these various components show why we can expect partial, but only partial, interpersonal comparability of the quality of life or of good lives—comparability will require interpersonal overlapping of similarly weighted primary functions, agent-specific functions, and specific desires. The importance of functional capacities at these different levels of generality reflects the centrality of personal choice in a good life and the necessity for a choice of alternatives and opportunities.

Finally, there will be the hedonic or happiness component of a good life, that aspect which represents a person's subjective, conscious response in terms of enjoyments and satisfactions to the life he or she has chosen and the activities and achievements it contains. These may be representable on a single vector or on a number of distinct vectors if the person has distinct and incommensurable satisfactions and enjoyments. Happiness will usually be only partially dependent on the person's relative success in satisfying his or her desires and broader aims and projects. Once again, it is the valuations of the specific person in question that will determine the relative weight the happiness vector receives in the overall account of a good life for that person.

Needless to say, in drawing together these features of an account of the quality of life or of a good life from the medical ethics and health policy literatures, I have done no more than sketch a few of the barest bones of a full account of a good life. However, even these few bones suggest the need for more complex accounts of the quality of life than are often employed in programmes designed to improve the quality of life of real people.

BIBLIOGRAPHY

ANDERSON, JOHN P., et al. (1986). 'Classifying Function for Health Outcome and Quality-of-Life Evaluation', Medical Care, 24, 454–71.

ANNAS, GEORGE, and GLANTZ, LEONARD (1986). 'The Right of Elderly Patients to Refuse Life-Sustaining Treatment', Milbank Quarterly, vol. 64, suppl. 2, 95–162.

ARRAS, JOHN (1984). 'Toward an Ethic of Ambiguity', Hastings Center Report, 14(Apr.), 25–33.

BEAUCHAMP, TOM L., and CHILDRESS, JAMES F. (1979). Principles of Biomedical Ethics. New York: Oxford University Press.

BERG, ROBERT L. (1986). 'Neglected Aspects of the Quality of Life', Health Services Research, 21, 391–5.

BERGNER, MARILYN, et al. (1976). 'The Sickness Impact Profile: Conceptual Formulation and Methodology for the Development of a Health Status Measure', International Journal of Health Services, 6, 393–415.

—— (1981). 'The Sickness Impact Profile: Development and Final Revision of a Health Status Measure', Medical Care, 19, 787–805.

BOORSE, CHRISTOPHER (1975). 'On the Distinction between Disease and Illness', Philosophy and Public Affairs, 5, 49–68.

—— (1977). 'Health as a Theoretical Concept', Philosophy of Science, 44.

BRESLOW, LESTER (1972). 'A Quantitative Approach to the World Health Organization

Definition of Health: Physical, Mental and Social Well-being', *International Journal of Epidemiology*, 1, 347–55.

BROCK, DAN W. (1973). 'Recent Work in Utilitarianism', *American Philosophical Quarterly*, 10, 241–76.

—— (1983). 'Paternalism and Promoting the Good', in Rolf Sartorius (ed.), *Paternalism*. Minneapolis: University of Minnesota Press.

—— (1986). 'The Value of Prolonging Human Life', *Philosophical Studies*, 50, 401–28.

—— (1987). 'Informed Consent', in Tom Regan and Donald VanDeVeer (eds.), *Health Care Ethics*. Philadelphia: Temple University Press.

—— (1988). 'Paternalism and Autonomy', *Ethics*, 98, 550–65.

BUCHANAN, Allen (1988). 'Advance Directives and the Personal Identity Problem', *Philosophy and Public Affairs* 17, 277–302.

—— and BROCK, DAN W. (1986). 'Deciding for Others', *Milbank Quarterly*, vol. 64, suppl. 2, 17–94.

—— —— (1989). *Deciding For Others*. Cambridge: Cambridge University Press.

CALLAHAN, DANIEL (1987). *Setting Limits*. New York: Simon and Schuster.

CALMAN, K.C. (1984). 'Quality of Life in Cancer Patients: An Hypothesis', *Journal of Medical Ethics*, 10, 124–7.

CAPLAN, ARTHUR L., *et al.* (1981). *Concepts of Health and Disease: Interdisciplinary Perspectives*. Reading, Mass.: Addison-Wesley.

CHEN, MILTON M., BUSH, J.W., and PATRICK, DONALD L. (1975). 'Social Indicators for Health Planning and Policy Analysis', *Policy Sciences*, 6, 71–89.

COHEN, CARL (1982). 'On the Quality of Life: Some Philosophical Reflections', *Circulation*, vol. 66 suppl. 3, 29–33.

CRIBB, ALAN (1985). 'Quality of Life: A Response to K.C. Calman', *Journal of Medical Ethics*, 11, 142–5.

DANIELS, NORMAN (1985). *Just Health Care*. Cambridge: Cambridge University Press.

DRESSER, REBECCA (1986). 'Life, Death, and Incompetent Patients: Conceptual Infirmities and Hidden Values in the Law', *Arizona Law Review*, 28, 373–405.

Editorial (1986). 'Assessment of Quality of Life in Clinical Trials', *Acta Medica Scandia*, 220, 1–3.

EDLUND, MATHEW, and TANCREDI, LAWRENCE (1985). 'Quality of Life: An Ideological Critique', *Perspectives in Biology and Medicine*, 28, 591–607.

ELSTER, JON (1982). 'Sour Grapes: Utilitarianism and the Genesis of Wants', in Amartya Sen and Bernard, Williams (eds.), *Utilitarianism and Beyond*. Cambridge: Cambridge University Press.

EVANS, ROGER W. (1985). 'The Quality of Life of Patients with End Stage Renal Disease', *New England Journal of Medicine*, 312, 553–9.

FADEN, RUTH R., and BEAUCHAMP, TOM L. (1986). *A History and Theory of Informed Consent*. New York: Oxford University Press.

FEINBERG, JOEL (1986). *Harm to Self*. New York: Oxford University Press.

FLANAGAN, JOHN C. (1982). 'Measurement of Quality of Life: Current State of the Art', *Archives of Physical Rehabilitation Medicine*, 63, 56–9.

FRANKFURT, HARRY (1971). 'Freedom of the Will and the Concept of a Person', *Journal of Philosophy*, 68, 5–20.

FRIED, CHARLES (1970). *An Anatomy of Values*. Cambridge, Mass.: Harvard University Press.

GEHRMANN, FRIEDHELM (1978). '"Valid" Empirical Measurement of Quality of Life', *Social Indicators Research*, 5, 73–109.

GILLINGHAM, ROBERT, and REECE, WILLIAM S. (1980). 'Analytical Problems in the Measurement of the Quality of Life', *Social Indicators Research*, 7, 91–101.

GOODIN, ROBERT (1986). 'Laundering Preferences', in Jon Elster and Aanund Hylland (eds.), *Foundations of Social Choice Theory*. Cambridge: Cambridge University Press.

GRIFFIN, JAMES (1986). *Well-Being*. Oxford: Oxford University Press.

GROGONO, A. W. (1971). 'Index for Measuring Health', *Lancet*, vol. 2 for 1971, 1024–6.

GUYATT, GORDON H., *et al.* (1986). 'Measuring Disease-Specific Quality of Life in Clinical Trials', *Canadian Medical Association Journal*, 134, 889–95.

Hastings Center (1987). *Guidelines on the Termination of Treatment and the Care of the Dying*. Briarcliff Manor, NY: The Hastings Center.

HUNT, SONYA, and MCEWEN, JAMES (1980). 'The Development of a Subjective Health Indicator', *Sociology of Health and Illness*, 2, 203–31.

JONSEN, ALBERT R., SIEGLER, MARK, and WINSLADE, WILLIAM J. (1982). *Clinical Ethics*. New York: Macmillan.

KASS, LEON (1985). *Toward a More Natural Science*. New York: Free Press.

KATZ, JAY (1984). *The Silent World of Doctor and Patient*. New York: Free Press.

KATZ, SIDNEY, *et al.* (1963). 'Studies of Illness in the Aged. The Index of ADL: A Standardized Measure of Biological and Psychosocial Function', *JAMA*, 185, 914–19.

KLOTKEM, FREDERIC J. (1982). 'Philosophic Considerations of Quality of Life for the Disabled', *Archives of Physical Rehabilitation Medicine*, 63, 59–63.

KORNFELD, DONALD S., *et al.* (1982). 'Psychological and Behavioral Responses After Coronary Artery Bypass Surgery', *Circulation*, vol. 66, suppl. 3, 24–8.

LIANG, MATHEW *et al.* (1982). 'In Search of a More Perfect Mousetrap (Health Status or Quality of Life Instrument)', *Journal of Rheumatology*, 9, 775–9.

MCCORMACK, S. J., RICHARD J. (1974). 'To Save or Let Die: The Dilemma of Modern Medicine', *JAMA*, 229, 172–6.

MEISEL, ALAN (1979). 'The "Exceptions" to the Informed Consent Doctrine: Striking a Balance Between Competing Values in Medical Decision-making', *Wisconsin Law Review*, 413–88.

MILL, J. S. (1859). *On Liberty*. Indiana/New York: Bobbs-Merrill, 1956.

MORREIM, E. HAAVI (1986). 'Computing the Quality of Life', in G. J. Agich and C. E. Begley (eds.), *The Price of Health*. Dordrecht: D. Reidel.

NAJMAN, JACKOB, and LEVINE, SOL (1981). 'Evaluating the Impact of Medical Care and Technologies on the Quality of Life: A Review and Critique', *Social Science and Medicine*, 15F, 107–15.

Natanson v. Kline (1960) 186 Kan. 393, 350 p. 2d 1093.

PARFIT, DEREK (1984). *Reason and Persons*. Oxford: Oxford University Press.

PEARLMAN, ROBERT, and SPEER, JAMES (1983). 'Quality of Life Considerations in Geriatric Care', *Journal of the American Geriatrics Society*, 31, 113–20.

PRESANT, CARY A. (1984). 'Quality of Life in Cancer Patients', *American Journal of Clinical Oncology*, 7, 571–3.

President's Commission for the Study of Ethical Problems in Medicine and Biomedical and Behavioral Research (1982). *Making Health Care Decisions*. Washington: US Government Printing Office.

—— (1983). *Deciding to Forgo Life-Sustaining Treatment*. Washington: US Government Printing Office.

RACHELS, JAMES (1986). *The End of Life*. Oxford: Oxford University Press.

RAMSEY, PAUL (1978). *Ethics at the Edge of Life*. New Haven, Conn.: Yale University Press.

RANGO, NICHOLAS (1985). 'The Nursing Home Resident with Dementia', *Annals of Internal Medicine*, 102,m 835–41.

RAWLS, JOHN (1971). *A Theory of Justice*. Cambridge, Mass.: Harvard University Press.

—— (1980). 'Kantian Constructivism in Moral Theory', *Journal of Philosophy*, 77, 515–72.

Report (1984). 'The 1984 Report of the Joint National Committee on Detection, Evaluation, and Treatment of High Blood Pressure', *Archives of Internal Medicine*, 144, 1045–57.

RHODEN, NANCY K. (1985). 'Treatment Dilemmas for Imperiled Newborns: Why Quality of Life Counts', *Southern California Law Review*, 58, 1283–347.

RUARK, JOHN E., *et al.* (1988). 'Initiating and Withdrawing Life Support', *New England Journal of Medicine* 318 (Jan.), 25–30.

Schloendorf v. *Society of New York Hospital* (1914). 211 N.Y. 125, 105 N.E. 92, 95.

SCHNEIDERMAN, LAWRENCE, and ARRAS, JOHN (1985). 'Counseling Patients to Counsel Physicians on Future Care in the Event of Patients Incompetence', *Annals of Internal Medicine*, 102, 693–8.

SEN, AMARTYA (1980). 'Plural Utility', *Proceedings of the Aristotelian Society*, 81, 193–218.

—— (1985a). *Commodities and Capabilities*. Amsterdam: Elsevier Science Publishers.

—— (1985b). 'Well-being, Agency and Freedom: The Dewey Lectures', *Journal of Philosophy*, 82, 169–221.

—— (1987). *The Standard of Living*. Cambridge: Cambridge University Press.

SINGER, PETER, and KUHSE, HELGA (1985). *Should This Baby Live?* Oxford: Oxford University Press.

SPITZER, WALTER O., *et al.* (1981). 'Measuring the Quality of Life of Cancer Patients: A Concise QL-Index for Use by Physicians', *Journal of Chronic Disease*, 34, 585–97.

STARR, T. JOLENE, *et al.* (1986). 'Quality of Life and Resuscitation Decisions in Elderly Patients', *Journal of General Internal Medicine*, 1, 373–9.

STEINBROOK, ROBERT, and LO, BERNARD (1984). 'Decision-making for Incompetent Patients by Designated Proxy: California's New Law', *New England Journal of Medicine*, 310, 1598–601.

SULLIVAN, DANIEL F. (1966). 'Conceptual Problems in Developing an Index of Health', *Vital and Health Statistics*, 2, 1–18.

Superintendant of Belchertown State School v. *Saikewicz* (1977). 370 N.E. 2d 417.

THOMASMA, DAVID C. (1984). 'Ethical Judgment of Quality of Life in the Care of the Aged', *Journal of the American Geriatrics Society*, 32, 525–7.

—— (1986). 'Quality of Life, Treatment Decisions, and Medical Ethics', *Clinics in Geriatric Medicine*, 2, 17–27.

TOOLEY, MICHAEL (1983). *Abortion and Infanticide*. Oxford: Oxford University Press.

TORRANCE, GEORGE W. (1972). 'Social Preferences for Health States: An Empirical Evaluation of Three Measurement Techniques', *Socio-Economic Planning Sciences*, 10, 129–36.

—— (1976) 'Toward A Utility Theory Foundation for Health Status Index Models', *Health Services Research*, 10, 129–36.

—— et al. (1972). 'A Utility Maximization Model for Evaluation of Health Care Programs', *Health Services Research*, 6, 118–33.

VANDEVEER, DONALD (1986). *Paternalistic Intervention*. Princeton, NJ: Princeton University Press.

WANZER, SIDNEY H., *et al.* (1984). 'The Physicians' Responsibility Toward Hopelessly Ill Patients', *New England Journal of Medicine*, 310 (Apr.), 955–9.

Dan Brock: Quality of Life Measures in Health Care and Medical Ethics

Commentary by James Griffin

Professor Brock asks, What does the literature of medical ethics have to tell us about the quality of life? He answers, Not much. That is not surprising. What makes up the quality of a life? It is a tough question. Doctors' dilemmas make it urgent, but not easier. And medical practice cannot do without settling at least a bit of theory. Medical administrators need to know to what extent the values that go to make up the quality of life are commensurable, and how commensuration in their case works, and how interpersonal comparisons work too.

Can these administrators get by with only a fairly narrow conception of well-being? Well, the aim of medicine is health, and it would be wrong, I think, to let the notion of 'health' swell to include everything that bears on the quality of life. Which patients should get scarce treatment? Should we do fewer expensive heart transplants and more inexpensive hip replacements? When should we pull the plug? Medical decisions—at any rate, decisions about when, and how far, and in what way, and for whom, to pursue health—need to use much wider normative notions than that of health alone. Brock says: 'my concern will be with the broadest conception of . . . "what makes a life go best"'. To my mind, he is right to be concerned with the broadest conception. But perhaps we should also be concerned with narrower conceptions. Perhaps the notion of the quality of life fragments into several notions appropriate to different sorts of social decision, even decisions about health. It is wrong of us, I think, to expect one notion of the quality of life to be up to answering all the questions that we try to answer with it. I shall come back to this shortly.

Brock thinks that we can extract from the literature on medical ethics 'the main outlines of a general account of a good life'. I think that the literature suggests his account no more than it suggests any one of many others. Still, his account is an interesting possibility. What I want to do is to express doubts about it.

Brock divides theories of a good life into three: (1) hedonist, (2) preference satisfaction or desire fulfilment, and (3) ideal. He does not think that we should force a choice between them but, rather, give independent place to items from each, as (he says) ideal theories can do. So Brock's is a kind of ideal theory. It can also be seen as a 'vector view' of the sort that Amartya Sen anatomized in his article 'Plural Utility'.[1] Brock goes on to identify four 'components' of a good life:

[1] Sen, 1980–1.

1. primary functions (such as mobility and communication, which are used in carrying out just about any life plan);
2. agent-specific functions (ones that are used in carrying out one agent's life plan in particular);
3. desire fulfilment, and
4. happiness.

Then, in a particularly fundamental place, there will be autonomy.

Now these items are very different in category. Happiness and autonomy *are* substantive prudential values. Functions, as Brock defines them, however, are not; they are characteristic means to realizing such values. And desire fulfilment, I should say, is not a substantive prudential value at all but rather a meta-ethical feature of those values. So, Brock's scheme does not touch rock bottom (that is, intrinsic prudential values), and I think, for reasons that I shall come to, that we ought to touch ground before taking off again.

Take desire fulfilment. Brock seems to me to treat it as a prudential value. At least, he speaks at one point of autonomy's being perhaps only instrumentally valuable, valuable because it leads either to happiness or to desire fulfilment. But I think that desire fulfilment is at some remove from prudential values. The desire fulfilment account of value, as Brock points out, has to be concerned with desires that are corrected in some way, because the fulfilment of actual desires comes nowhere near being a plausible candidate as a prudential value. But once we start talking about *corrected* desires, once we ask how stiff a demand 'corrected' represents, we move into territory where old maps do not help a lot. Now, how stiff a requirement should it represent? The rough idea of a corrected desire is one formed by an appropriate appreciation of the nature of its object, so it has to include whatever is necessary for that. 'Corrected' might be taken (as, for example, Richard Brandt takes it[2]) to require only that desires survive criticism by facts and logic, where it is meant to be a question of fact—largely of psychological fact—whether a desire is corrected. But a particularly irrational desire—say, one planted deep when one was young—might well survive criticism by facts and logic, and its mere persistence does not seem to guarantee that its fulfilment will make one better off. For instance, I might wish to hog the limelight on all occasions. I might have learned from long experience that succeeding does not work to my advantage, but still want to. I might not react appropriately, or strongly enough, to this important piece of self-knowledge. So 'corrected' cannot mean just 'formed while possessed of factual knowledge and correct logic'; it must mean something stronger such as 'formed in proper appreciation of the nature of the object'.

There are appropriate responses to certain pieces of knowledge, and 'appropriate' cannot here be just 'most common' because most of us sometimes go on wanting certain things—self-assertion, say—too much even when our desires

---

[2] Brandt, 1979: 10, but also chs. 2–7 *passim*.

are formed while possessed of factual knowledge and correct logic. 'Appropriate' has to mean something close to 'correct'. But this shifts importance away from the mere presence of a desire to the proper appreciation of its object. It gives us, I should say, some sort of ideal theory of prudential value. In that I agree with Brock. Where I disagree is with his regarding desire fulfilment as itself one of the values. Desire fulfilment seems to me best seen not as a substantive value, but as a formal notion of what it is for something to be prudentially valuable: it is for it to be (not entirely trivially) the object of a sufficiently well informed desire. A person can move from a desire's being unfulfilled to its being fulfilled and become a lot worse off as a result. He can make the same move, even with a fully enlightened desire, and be no better off. It is not the state of a desire's being fulfilled that is valuable. What are valuable are certain objects of desire. True, one can see various things that might make it *seem* that desire fulfilment is itself a prudential value — the frustration, for instance, that sometimes comes from non-fulfilment, the boost that can, although need not, come with fulfilment, and the autonomy that we respect in respecting the fulfilment of a person's *actual* (not *corrected*) desires. And frustrations, boosts, and autonomy all have to do with substantive values. Desire fulfilment counts towards the quality of life, not as such, but because when suitably corrected and restricted, desires are linked to objects subsumable under some desirability characteristic (autonomy, enjoyment, deep personal relations, accomplishing something with one's life, etc.). This, of course, changes the face of desire accounts a lot. But this is what they have to become for there to be a plausible link between fulfilment of desire and prudential value. I must apologize for whizzing through, and dogmatizing about, immensely difficult matters. I have, however, discussed much of this elsewhere.[3]

Take another item from Brock's list of the 'components' of a good life: functions. What Brock refers to as 'functions' are not, I take it, the same as what Sen calls 'functionings' or, as Sen also puts it, achievement of 'beings' and 'doings'.[4] Brock, I think, is interested in the *possession* of certain pretty *basic* abilities, while Sen, though his list includes those, wants to include much more besides — for example, the *exercise* of decidedly *non-basic* abilities. So Sen's category is so wide that it includes both means to substantive goods and the substantive goods themselves.

Now, what one includes in an account of a good life will, I think, depend upon what the notion of a good life is used for. We need a full notion in taking decisions about how we want to live our own lives, and a doctor probably needs the same full notion in taking decisions about what the best trade-offs are for a particular patient. It is, I think, a different, perhaps narrower, notion of a good life that comes into play in many of a government's decisions

---

[3] In Griffin, 1986: Part I; also, more recently, in Griffin, forthcoming *a*; Griffin, forthcoming *b*.
[4] See e.g. Sen, 1985, esp. chs. 2 and 4; Sen, 1987*a*, esp. ch. 2; Sen, 1987*b*, esp. lect. II.

about how it ought to allocate resources. And it is not a notion of a good life at all, but some accessible, tolerably reliable indicator of it, that we often have to fall back on. What Brock calls primary functions, for instance, are so central to most people's lives that it is entirely reasonable for them to feature in 'Sickness Impact Profiles' (Table 1). Even though they are just means to prudential values, they are accessible and measurable, and the link is close. So it makes sense to give them prominence in measures of quality of life that we must carry out in everyday settings. Still, they are at some remove from actual prudential values. The same handicap—say, the loss of a finger—can devastate some lives but have only minor cosmetic disadvantages in others. Medical decisions have often to be tailored to a particular patient; often it is only having seen the values at stake in *that* life that we can decide what to sacrifice for what. We have often got to get behind functions to the real prudential values that they are means to.

Suppose, then, we were to take not 'functions', as Brock uses the term, but the much more capacious class of 'functionings', as Sen uses the term. A large part of the interest in both functions and functionings stems from the belief that the value space cannot be identified with either material or social goods (e.g. Rawls's primary goods) or subjective responses to them (e.g. the classical utilitarians' utility), but is to be found somewhere between them. That seems to me right, but it is nothing new. Though classical utilitarians often wrote as if they saw utility in terms of mental states, at other times they suggested something quite different (recall Mill on qualitative differences in utility: the higher one is that to which '*all* or *almost all* who have experience of both give a decided *preference*';[5] and recall the example of the informed preference for Socrates dissatisfied—short on pleasures, in the ordinary sense of the term, and short on desire fulfilment—over the Fool satisfied; the values referred to here are far from subjective responses and close to, perhaps identical to, beings and doings). And certain preference utilitarians long ago moved utility into the realm of beings and doings.[6] With their notion of a 'rational' desire, they took the desire fulfilment account of utility well down the road towards, if

[5] Mill, 1863: ch. 2.

[6] This is obscured in Sen's writings by his generally construing 'utility' in quite a narrow way; he sees 'utility' as committed to a 'metric of happiness or desire-fulfilment', which (given his narrow interpretation of these two notions) he rightly says has obvious limitations as an explanation of human well-being (Sen, 1987a: 45). It is not that Sen is unaware of the great variety of possible, or actual past, uses of 'utility'—that 'versatile name', as he remarks (Sen, 1985: 17); far from it. But he thinks that happiness and desire fulfilment are 'the traditional meanings of utility' (Sen, 1985: 3), and he generally uses the term in that traditional sense. Still, his objections to utility as an interpretation of well-being show just how narrowly he uses 'happiness' and 'desire fulfilment'. People often become reconciled to deprivation, he rightly observes; they stop minding or hoping. So using either happiness or desire fulfilment as a metric may distort how well off a person actually is. That seems to me right and important, but the point I want to make here is that this works as an objection only if one uses especially narrow interpretations. Sen even seems to confine desires to *actual* desires, ignoring the tradition of corrected or rational or informed desires, and certainly ignoring any especially strong standard for a desire's being informed. See Sen, 1985: 20–2, 52–3; Sen, 1987a: 45–6; Sen 1987b: 7–12.

not quite all the way to, the list of prudential goods that seems to me the inevitable destination of a fully worked out desire account.[7] Then there was G.E. Moore's ideal version of utilitarianism as early as 1903. Prudential values can indeed be seen as beings and doings. Even 'happiness', in the sense most relevant to the quality of life, is probably best understood, for reasons that Aristotle gives, as falling into the category of *activity*, and so is caught by 'doings'. The talk of beings and doings leaves us well short of a delineation of value space, because those terms include vastly more than just values. We need a *differentia*. Without it, the job of locating the value space is virtually undone.

For Sen, nourishment and health are paradigmatic functionings.[8] But neither is itself a prudential value. It would make perfectly good sense to choose to be, at least for a while, undernourished through fasting, if one's spiritual life were thereby enhanced. And I do not think that it is just the presence of choice here that gives undernourishment through fasting a different moral status from undernourishment from starvation; to think so would be to overlook what makes sense of the choice. What makes sense of it is that fasting (and the discomforts of hunger that go with it) is to be seen as part of a process of reaching a larger good—say, spiritual growth. That is why the case of a child in a family that fasts who does not himself choose to fast is morally different from starvation too. Discomfort is small stuff compared to a spiritual life. We understand these cases best, I think, in terms of the various substantive values in play. It might also make good sense to accept some avoidable forms of ill health. It would make good sense not to spend long periods exercising one's legs to combat a wasting disease, if ease of walking had little relevance to the quality of one's particular life, while using the exercise time instead for one's work did have. Nourishment and health are both at some remove from prudential values. Unless we acknowledge that, we cannot explain the rationality of much prudential deliberation.

Why does this remoteness from real prudential values matter? Why does it matter whether we deliberate in terms of functions, desire fulfilment, and subjective reactions or in terms of what seem to me to be prudential values: enjoyment, accomplishment, deep personal relations, the elements of human dignity (autonomy, liberty), and so on? It seems to me to matter because we have to get a sense of the whole deliberative project that we are engaged in. We have to see how to compare one value with another, and one person's values with another's, and how far commensurability and comparability go. And we shall not find out—we shall not get even our crudest bearings—until we see what is prudentially valuable and what makes it valuable. Brock speaks of the vector view. But choosing vectors that are at some remove from actual prudential values does not allow us to get at how the vectoring actually works. For example, how important is *this* primary function (say, legs that work) to

[7] See e.g. Brandt, 1979, esp. ch. 6.   [8] See the list of functions in Sen, 1985: 46.

this person (say, Itzhak Perlman)? What is the significance of *this* person's contentment with a disability? Contentment with one's lot, as Brock notes, can variously be both a desirable constituent of the good life and an undesirable obstacle to a better. We cannot proceed, I think, until we have got the right materials to work with, and that means going deeper to the prudential values at stake.

This is not an objection to the vector view. On the contrary, as a view about the broad notion of the quality of life (as opposed to a moral view, which is an entirely different matter), some form of it must be right. There may be several irreducibly different prudential values. They may have different weights in different cases; they may vector into a single direction. But all of this just mentions possibilities. We need to see how it actually works. Well, suppose we use the vectors 'desire fulfilment' and 'subjective reaction'. Let me take an example of vectoring from Sen's paper 'Plural Utility'.[9] Suppose someone prefers bitter truth to comforting delusion but is palmed off with the latter. We feel sorry for him. Then later he learns that he was deceived. We feel sorrier for him. Sen says that bare desire fulfilment and experienced desire fulfilment (that is, subjective reaction) are both relevant, and that to insist on a choice between them seems 'arbitrary and uncalled for'.[10] But the trouble with leaving it at that is that at least sometimes we have to supply some weighting for various vectors, and the weighting ought to be neither arbitrary nor left to haphazard intuition. I doubt that the categories 'bare desire fulfilment' and 'experienced desire fulfilment' will help us get at the weightings that we are after. We are after a comparison of *values*, and neither 'bare desire fulfilment' not 'experienced desire fulfilment' even names a value.

Suppose, then, that we use instead actual prudential values as our vectors. One range of prudential values, I think (and shall have just to go on dogmatizing), comprises the elements of human dignity—that is, such things as our being able autonomously to choose a course through life and being at liberty to follow it. We also value pleasure and the avoidance of its opposites. With these in focus, with some understanding of their bounds and grounds, we can hope to make progress towards weightings. We value our liberty to carry out our plans, greatly in the case of our most central plans and less when the plans are more peripheral. Following these lines, we might hope eventually to explain how much weight to attach to the desire to live out the most central features of one's life plan, and how this weight compares with the upset and distress it might cause others. We can hope also to get an explanation of why liberty has different weights on different occasions—though the desire to carry out the central parts of our life plan generally outweigh our neighbours' huffiness over our doing so, the desire to swim nude, being not all that central, might not outweigh the upset *it* might cause.

In arguing for the need to identify actual prudential values, I am not claiming

---

⁹ Sen, 1980–1: 203–4.   ¹⁰ Ibid., 203.

that their identification is exclusively, or even supremely, important. We need the broad conception of the quality of life (that is, the list of prudential values) for our reasoning about how to make our own lives go best. Doctors need it for decisions about certain patients. But there are many reasons, both moral and practical, to work with a narrower conception of the quality of life in taking certain social decisions. And it may be (I strongly suspect it is) that we need several different conceptions of the quality of life for different sorts of social decision. That is, we need both the broad conception and also an understanding of the various considerations at work in generating narrower conceptions.

BIBLIOGRAPHY

BRANDT, R. B. (1979). *A Theory of the Good and the Right*. Oxford: Clarendon Press.
GRIFFIN, JAMES (1986). *Well-Being*. Oxford: Clarendon Press.
—— (forthcoming *a*). 'Against the Taste Model', in J. Elster and J. Roemer (eds.), *Interpersonal Comparisons of Well-Being*. Cambridge: Cambridge University Press.
—— (forthcoming *b*). 'Value: Reduction, Supervenience, and Explanation by Ascent', in K. Lennon and D. Charles (eds.), *Reduction, Explanation, and Realism*. Oxford: Clarendon Press.
MILL, J.S. (1863). *Utilitarianism*. London.
SEN, AMARTYA (1980–1). 'Plural Utility', *Proceedings of the Aristotelian Society*, 81.
—— (1985). *Commodities and Capabilities*. Amsterdam: North-Holland.
—— (1987*a*). *On Ethics and Economics*. Oxford: Blackwell.
—— (1987*b*). *The Standard of Living*. Cambridge: Cambridge University Press.

PART II
TRADITIONS, RELATIVISM, AND OBJECTIVITY

Objectivity and the Science–Ethics Distinction

Hilary Putnam

1 *The Fact–value Dichotomy: Background*

The Logical Positivists argued for a sharp fact–value dichotomy in a very simple way: scientific statements (outside of logic and pure mathematics), they said, are 'empirically verifiable' and value judgements are 'unverifiable'. This argument continues to have wide appeal to economists (not to say laymen), even though it has for some years been looked upon as naïve by philosophers. One reason that the argument is naïve is that it assumes that there is such a thing as 'the method of verification' of each isolated *scientifically meaningful* sentence. But this is very far from being the case. Newton's entire theory of gravity, for example, does not *in and of itself* (i.e. in the absence of suitable 'auxiliary hypotheses') imply any testable predictions whatsoever (cf. Putnam, 1974). As Quine has emphasized (Quine, 1951), reviving arguments earlier used by Duhem, scientific statements 'meet the test of experience as a corporate body'; the idea that each scientific sentence has its own range of confirming observations and its own range of disconfirming observations, independent of what other sentences it is conjoined to, is wrong. If a sentence that does not, in and of itself, by its very meaning, have a 'method of verification' is meaningless, then most of theoretical science turns out to be meaningless!

A second feature of the view that 'ethical sentences are cognitively meaningless because they have no method of verification' is that even if it had been correct, what it would have drawn would not have been a *fact–value* dichotomy. For, according to the positivists themselves, metaphysical sentences are cognitively meaningless for the same reason as ethical sentences: they are 'unverifiable in principle'. (So are poetic sentences, among others.) The positivist position is well summarized by Vivian Walsh (Walsh, 1987):

Consider the 'putative' proposition 'murder is wrong'. What empirical findings, the positivists would ask, tend to confirm or disconfirm this? If saying that murder is wrong is merely a misleading way of reporting what a given society believes, this is a perfectly good sociological fact, and the proposition is a respectable empirical one. But the person making a moral judgement will not accept this analysis. Positivists then wielded their absolute analytic/synthetic distinction: if 'murder is wrong' is not a synthetic (empirically testable) proposition it must be an analytic proposition, like (they believed) those of logic and mathematics—in effect, a tautology. The person who wished to make the moral judgement would not accept this, and was told that the disputed utterance was a 'pseudo-proposition' like those of poets, theologians and metaphysicians.

As Walsh goes on to explain, by the end of the fifties 'most of the theses necessary for this remarkable claim' had been abandoned. The positivist theory of 'cognitive significance' had fallen. The absolute analytic–synthetic distinction was seen to fail as an account of how scientific theories are actually put together. Writing in a volume honouring Carnap (Quine, 1963), Quine summed up its demise, writing, 'the lore of our fathers is black with fact and white with convention, but there are no *completely* white threads and no quite black ones.' Explaining the impact of all this, Walsh writes:

Another retreat, forced upon logical empiricism by the *needs* of pure science, opened the way for a further rehabilitation of moral philosophy. The old positivist attack on the status of moral judgements had required the claim that each *single* proposition must, at least in principle, be open to test. It became evident that many of the propositions of which the higher theory of pure science are composed could not survive this demand. Theoretical propositions, the logical empiricists decided, became 'indirectly' meaningful if part of a theory which possessed (supposed) observation statements which had empirical confirmation to some degree (never mind that the theoretical statement/ observation statement dichotomy itself broke down!); but the clear fact/value distinction of the early positivists depended upon being able to see if *each single* proposition passed muster. To borrow and adapt Quine's vivid image, if a theory may be black with fact and white with convention, it might well (as far as logical empiricism could tell) be red with values. Since for them confirmation *or* falsification had to be a property of a theory *as a whole*, they had no way of unraveling this whole cloth. Yet even today economists whose philosophical ancestry is logical empiricism still write as if the old positivist fact/value dichotomy were beyond challenge.

The collapse of the grounds on which the dichotomy was defended during the period Walsh is describing has not, however, led to a demise of the dichotomy, even among professional philosophers. What it has led to is a change in the nature of the *arguments* offered for the dichotomy. Today, it is defended more and more on metaphysical grounds. At the same time, even the defenders of the dichotomy concede that the old arguments for the dichotomy were bad arguments. For example, when I was a graduate student, a paradigmatic explanation and defence of the dichotomy would have been Charles Stevenson's. I attacked Stevenson's position at length in a book published some years ago (Putnam, 1981). When Bernard Williams's last book (Williams, 1985) appeared, I found that Williams gave virtually the same arguments against this position. Yet Williams still defends a sharp 'science–ethics' dichotomy; and he regards his science–ethics dichotomy as capturing something that was essentially right about the old 'fact–value' dichotomy.

Something else has accompanied this change in the way the dichotomy is defended. The old position, in its several versions—emotivism, voluntarism, prescriptivism—was usually referred to as 'non-cognitivism'. 'Non-cognitivism' was, so to speak, the generic name of the position, and the more specific labels were the proprietary names given the position by the various distributors. And the generic name was appropriate, because all the various slightly different formulations of the generic product had this essential ingredient in common:

ethical sentences were 'non-cognitive', that is to say, they were neither true nor false. Today, philosophers like Williams[1] do not deny that ethical sentences can be true or false; what they deny is that they can be true or false *non-perspectivally*. Thus, the position has been (appropriately) renamed: while the proprietary versions of the new improved drug still have various differences one from the other, they all accept the name Relativism. *Non-cognitivism has been rebaptized as Relativism.*

2 *The Entanglement of Fact and Value*

Just why and how non-cognitivism has given way to relativism is a complicated question, and it is not the purpose of this paper to explore it in detail. But one reason is surely an increased appreciation of what might be called the *entanglement* of fact and value. That entanglement was a constant theme in John Dewey's writing. But this aspect of pragmatism was neglected in Anglo-American philosophy after Dewey's death, in spite of Morton White's valiant effort to keep it alive (White, 1956), and it was, perhaps, Iris Murdoch who reopened the theme in a very different way.

Murdoch's three essays, published together in Murdoch, 1971, contain a large number of valuable insights and remarks: two have proved especially influential. Murdoch was the first to emphasize that languages have two very different sorts of ethical concepts: abstract ethical concepts (Williams calls them 'thin' ethical concepts), such as 'good', and 'right', and more descriptive, less abstract concepts (Williams calls them 'thick' ethical concepts) such as, for example, *cruel, pert, inconsiderate, chaste.* Murdoch (and later, and in a more spelled-out way, McDowell (1978 and 1979)) argued that there is no way of saying what the 'descriptive component' of the meaning of a word like 'cruel' or 'inconsiderate' is without using a word of the same kind; as McDowell put the argument, a word has to be connected to a certain set of 'evaluative interests' in order to function the way such a thick ethical word functions; and the speaker has to be aware of those interests and be able to identify imaginatively with them if he is to apply the word to novel cases or circumstances in the way a sophisticated speaker of the language would. The attempt of non-cognitivists to split such words into a 'descriptive meaning component' and a 'prescriptive meaning component' founders on the impossibility of saying what the 'descriptive meaning' of, say, 'cruel' is without using the word 'cruel' itself, or a synonym. Secondly, Murdoch emphasized that when we are actually confronted with situations requiring ethical evaluation, whether or not they also require some action on our part, the sorts of descriptions that we need— descriptions of the motives and character of human beings, above all—are

---

[1] The philosopher whose views are closest to Williams is, perhaps, David Wiggins (cf. Wiggins, 1987).

descriptions in the language of a 'sensitive novelist', not in scientistic or bureau-cratic jargon. When a situation or a person or a motive is appropriately described, the decision as to whether something is 'good' or 'bad' or 'right' or 'wrong' frequently follows automatically. For example, our evaluation of a person's moral stature may critically depend on whether we describe her as 'impertinent' or 'unstuffy'. Our Life-world, Murdoch is telling us, does not factor neatly into 'facts' and 'values'; we live in a messy human world in which seeing reality with all its nuances, seeing it as George Eliot, or Flaubert, or Henry James, or Murdoch herself can, to some extent, teach us to see it, and making appro-priate 'value judgments' are simply not separable abilities.

I confess that when I read *The Sovereignty of 'Good'* I thought that Murdoch gave a perceptive description of the sphere of private morality (which is, of course, the sphere with which a novelist has to deal), but that she too much ignored the public sphere, the sphere in which issues of social justice arise and must be worked out. But more recently I have come to think that a similar entanglement of the factual and the ethical applies to this sphere as well. It is all well and good to describe hypothetical cases in which two people 'agree on the facts and disagree about values', but in the world in which I grew up such cases are unreal. When and where did a Nazi and an anti-Nazi, a communist and a social democrat, a fundamentalist and a liberal, or even a Republican and a Democrat, agree on the facts? Even when it comes to one specific policy question, say, what to do about the decline of American education, or about unemployment, or about drugs, every argument I have ever heard has exem-plified the entanglement of the ethical and the factual. There is a weird discrepancy between the way philosophers who subscribe to a sharp fact–value distinction *make* ethical arguments sound and the way ethical arguments *actually* sound. (Stanley Cavell once remarked (Cavell, 1979) that Stevenson writes like someone who has *forgotten* what ethical discussion is like.)

3   Relativism and the Fact–value Dichotomy

According to Bernard Williams, a properly worked-out relativism can do justice to the way in which fact and value can be inseparable; do justice to the way in which some statements which are both descriptive and true ('Caligula was a mad tyrant') can also be value judgements. The idea is to replace the fact–value distinction by a very different distinction, the distinction between *truth* and *absoluteness*.

Although Williams does not explain what he understands truth to be very clearly, he seems to thinks truth is something like right assertability in the local language game; that is, if the practices and shared values of a culture determine an established use for a word like 'chaste' – a use which is sufficiently definite to permit speakers to come to agreement on someone's chastity or lack of chastity (or whatever the example of a 'thick ethical concept' may be) –

then it can be simply true that a person in the culture is 'chaste' (or 'cruel', or 'pious', or whatever). Of course, if I do not belong to the culture in question and do not share the relevant evaluative interests, then I will not describe the person in question as 'chaste', even if I know that that is a correct thing to say in that culture; I will be 'disbarred' from using the word, as Williams puts it. As he also puts it (with deliberate paradox), that so-and-so is chaste is possible *knowledge* for someone in the culture, but not possible knowledge for *me*.

If truth were the only dimension with respect to which we could evaluate the cognitive credentials of statements, then Williams would be committed to ethical realism or at least to the rejection of ethical *anti*-realism. For, on his view, 'Mary is chaste', 'Peter is cruel', 'George is a perfect knight', can be true in the very same sense in which 'Snow is white' is true, while still being ethical utterances. But there *is* an insight in non-cognitivism, these philosophers claim, even if non-cognitivism was mistaken in what it took to be its most essential thesis, the thesis that ethical sentences are not capable of truth (or, alternatively, the thesis that an ethical sentence has a distinct 'value component', and this 'value component' is not capable of truth). That thesis (or those theses) are rejected by Williams. As I said, he accepts the arguments of Murdoch and McDowell against the 'two components' theory; he recognizes the way in which fact and value are entangled in our concepts; and he agrees that ethical sentences can be true. How then can he maintain that there was an insight contained in non-cognitivism? What *was* the insight that the fact–value distinction tried to capture?

According to Williams, there are truths and truths. If I say that grass is green, for example, I certainly speak the truth; but I do not speak what he calls the *absolute* truth. I do not describe the world as it is 'anyway', independently of any and every '*perspective*'. The concept 'green' (and possibly the concept 'grass' as well) are not concepts that finished science would use to describe the properties that things have apart from any 'local perspective'. Martians or Alpha Centaurians, for example, might not have the sorts of eyes we have. They would not recognize any such property as 'green' (except as a 'secondary quality' of interest to human beings, a disposition to affect the sense organs of *homo sapiens* in a certain way), and 'grass' may be too unscientific a classification to appear in their finished science. Only concepts that would appear in the (final) description of the world that any species of determined natural researchers is destined to converge to can be regarded as telling us how the world is 'anyway' ('to the maximum degree independent of perspective'). Only such concepts can appear in statements which are 'absolute'. And the philosophically important point—or one of them, for there is something to be added—is that while value judgements containing thick ethical concepts can be true, they cannot be absolute. The world, as it is in itself, is *cold*. Values (like colours) are *projected* on to the world, not discovered in it.

What has to be added is that, on Williams's view, values are even *worse off*

than colours in this respect. For the discovery that green is a secondary quality
has not undermined our ability to use the word. We no longer think that
colours are non-dispositional properties of external things, but this in no way
affects the utility of colour classification. But the realization that value attributes,
even 'thick' ones ('chaste', 'cruel', 'holy'), are projections has a tendency to
cause us to lose our ability to use those terms. If we become reflective to too
great a degree, if we identify ourselves too much with the point of view of
the universe, we will no longer be able to employ our ethical concepts. The
realization that ethical concepts are projections places us in a ticklish position:
we cannot stop being reflective, but we cannot afford to be (very much of the
time) *too* reflective. We are in an unstable equilibrium.

The reason for this difference between ordinary secondary qualities like
green and thick ethical attributes like chastity, according to Williams, is that
the interests which colour classification subserves are universal among human
beings, whereas the interests that thick ethical concepts subserve are the
interests of one human community (one 'social world') or another. Even if
different cultures have somewhat different colour classifications, there is no
opposition between one culture's colour classifications and those of another
culture. But the interests which define one social world may be in conflict
with the interests which define a different social world. And realizing that
my ethical descriptions are in this way parochial (however 'true' they may
also be) is decentring.

Williams believes that coming to realize by just how far ethical description
misses describing the world as it is 'absolutely' not only does but *should* affect
our first-order ethical judgements. There are *moral* consequences to the 'truth
in relativism' (speaking, of course, from within *our* social world). The moral
consequence (and perhaps also the metaphysical consequence), according to
Williams, is that moral praise or condemnation of another way of life loses
all point when that other way of life is too distant from ours. (Too distant
in the sense that neither way of life is a live option for the other.) It makes
no sense to try to evaluate the way of life of the ancient Aztecs, for example,
or of the Samurai, or of a bronze age society. To ask whether their ways
of life were *right*, or their judgements *true*, is (or should be) impossible for
us; the question should lapse, once we understand the non-absoluteness of
ethical discourse. And the fact that the question lapses *constitutes* 'the truth in
relativism'.

4 *Absoluteness*

This dichotomy between what the world is like independent of any local
perspective and what is projected by us seems to me utterly indefensible. I
shall begin by examining the picture of science which guides Williams.

The picture of science is that science converges to a single true theory, a single explanatory picture of the universe. But one is hard put to know why one should believe this.

If we start at the level of common-sense objects, say stones, it suffices to notice that, in rational reconstruction, we can take a stone to be an aggregation — or as logicians say a 'mereological sum' of time-slices of particles (or, alternatively, of field-points — notice that these are incompatible but equally good choices!) — or we can take a stone to be an individual which consists of different particles in different possible worlds (and also occupies different locations in space in different possible worlds) while remaining self-identical. If a stone consists of *different* time-slices of particles in different possible worlds, then it cannot (as a matter of modal logic) be *identical* with an aggregation (mereological sum) of time-slices of particles[2], and obviously it makes no sense to say that a collection of space–time points could have occupied a different location than it did. So, if it is simply a matter of how we formalize our language whether we say (with Saul Kripke) that stones and animals and persons, etc., are *not* identical with mereological sums at all, or say (as suggested in Lewis, 1973) that they *are* mereological sums (and take care of Kripke's difficulty by claiming that when we say that 'the' stone consists of different particle slices in different possible worlds, then what that means is that the various modal 'counterparts' of the stone in different possible worlds consist of different particle slices, and not that the self-identical stone consists of different particle slices in different possible worlds — and to me this certainly looks like a mere choice of a formalism, and not a question of fact) we will be forced to admit that it is partly a matter of our conceptual choice which scientific object a given common-sense object — a stone or a person — is identified with.

Nor is the situation any better in theoretical physics. At the level of space-time geometry, there is the well-known fact that we can take points to be individuals *or* we can take them to be mere limits. States of a system can be taken to be quantum mechanical superpositions of particle interactions (*à la* Feynman) or quantum mechanical superpositions of field states. (This is the contemporary form of the wave–particle duality.) And there are many other examples.

Not only do single theories have a bewildering variety of alternative rational reconstructions (with quite different ontologies); but there is no evidence at all for the claim (which is essential to Williams's belief in an 'absolute conception of the world') that science converges to a *single* theory. I do not doubt that there is some convergence in scientific knowledge, and not just at the observational level. We know, for example, that certain *equations* are approximately correct descriptions of certain phenomena. Under certain conditions, the Poisson equation of Newtonian gravitational theory gives an approximately correct description of the gravitational field of a body. But the theoretical

---

[2] This argument is due to Kripke (in unpublished lectures).

picture of Newtonian mechanics has been utterly changed by General Relativity; and the theoretical picture of General Relativity may in turn be utterly replaced by Supergravitation theory, or by some theory not yet imagined. We simply do not have the evidence to justify speculation as to whether or not science is 'destined' to converge to some one definite theoretical picture. It could be, for example, that although we will discover more and more approximately correct and increasingly accurate equations, the *theoretical picture* which we use to explain those equations will continue to be upset by scientific revolutions. As long as our ability to predict, and to mathematize our predictions in attractive ways, continues to advance science will 'progress' quite satisfactorily; to say, as Williams sometimes does, that convergence to one big picture is required by the very concept of knowledge, is sheer dogmatism.

Yet, without the postulate that science 'converges' to a single definite theoretical picture with a unique ontology and a unique set of theoretical predicates, the whole notion of 'absoluteness' collapses. It is, indeed, the case that ethical knowledge cannot claim 'absoluteness'; but that is because the notion of 'absoluteness' is incoherent. Mathematics and physics, as well as ethics and history and politics, show our conceptual choices; the world is not going to impose a single language upon us, no matter what we choose to talk about.

5 *More about Absoluteness*

The notion of absoluteness has further properties that we should be clear about. According to Williams, what makes the truth of a statement 'absolute' is not the fact that scientists are destined to 'converge' on the truth of that statement, that is to say, admit it to the corpus of accepted scientific belief in the long run, but the *explanation* of the fact of convergence. We converge upon the statement that S is true, where S is a statement which figures in 'the absolute conception of the world', because 'that is the way things are' (independently of perspective). But what sort of an explanation is *this*?

The idea that some statements force themselves upon us because 'that is how things are' is taken with immense seriousness by Williams: indeed, it is the centre of his entire metaphysical picture. Sometimes when I don't want to give a reason for something I may shrug my shoulders and say, 'Well, that's just how things are'; but that is not what Williams is doing here. 'That is how things are' (independently of perspective) is supposed to be a *reason* (Williams calls it an 'explanation') not a refusal to give a reason.

The idea that some statements get recognized as true (if we investigate long enough and carefully enough) because they simply describe the world in a way which is independent of 'perspective' is just a new version of the old 'correspondence theory of truth'. As we have already seen, Williams does not claim that truth is correspondence—for him, truth is rather right assertability in the language game. But *some* truths—the 'absolute' ones—are rightly assertable in the language game *because* they correspond to the way things (mind-independently) are. Even if correspondence is not the definition of truth, it is the *explanation* of absolute truth. And I repeat my question: What sort of an explanation is this?

The idea of a statement's corresponding to the way things are, the idea of a term's having a correspondence to a language-independent class of things, and the idea of a predicate's having a correspondence to a language-independent attribute are ideas which have no metaphysical force at all unless the correspondence in question is thought of as a genuine relation between items independent of us and items in language, a correspondence which is imposed by the world, as it were, and not just a tautological feature of the way we talk about talk. What I have in mind by this perhaps puzzling-sounding remark is this: if you think it is just a *tautology* that 'snow' corresponds to snow, or that 'Snow is white' is true if and only if snow is white, then you regard the 'correspondence' between the word 'snow' and snow as a correspondence *within* language. Within our language we can talk about snow and we can talk about the word 'snow' and we can *say* they correspond. To this even a philosopher who rejects the very idea of a substantive notion of 'truth' or a substantive notion of reference can agree. But if, as Williams believes, the fact that we are 'fated' to accept the sentence 'Snow is white' is *explained* by something 'out there' and by the fact that the sentence corresponds to that something 'out there', then the correspondence too must be 'out there'. A *verbal* correspondence cannot play this kind of explanatory role. Williams's picture is that there is a *fixed* set of objects 'out there', the 'mind independent objects', and a fixed relation—a relation between words and sentences in *any* language in which 'absolute' truths can be expressed, any language in which science can be done, and those fixed mind-independent Reals—and that this relation *explains* the (alleged) fact that science converges. If this picture is unintelligible, then the notion of an 'absolute conception of the world' must also be rejected as unintelligible.

Now, I have argued for a number of years that this picture *is* unintelligible. First, I contend that there is not *one* notion of an 'object' but an open class of possible uses of the word 'object'—even of the technical logical notion of an object (value of a variable of quantification). The idea that reality itself fixes the use of the word 'object' (or the use of the word 'correspondence') is a hangover from pre-scientific metaphysics (Putnam, 1987). Secondly, the idea of the world 'singling out' a correspondence between objects and our words is incoherent. As a matter of model-theoretic fact, we know that even if we somehow fix the intended truth-values of our sentences, not just in the actual world but in all possible worlds, this does *not* determine a unique correspondence between words and items in the universe of discourse (Putnam, 1981). Thirdly, even if we require that words not merely 'correspond' to items in the universe of discourse but be causally connected to them in some way, the required notion of 'causal connection' is deeply *intentional*. When we say that a word and its referent must stand in a 'causal connection of the appropriate kind', then, even in cases where this is true, the notion of 'causal connection' being appealed to is fundamentally the notion of *explanation*. And explanation is a notion which lies in the same circle as reference and truth (Putnam, 1989).[3]

But why should this be a problem? Why should Williams and other metaphysical realists not just say, 'Very well, then. The ultimate description of the world—the world as it is in itself—requires intentional notions.' (In fact, Williams does not say this; Williams ends his book on Descartes (Williams, 1978) with an endorsement of Quine's criticism of intentional notions!) The answer, of course, is that a science of the intentional is a we-know-not-what. According to Williams, what gives the notion of an absolute conception of the world clout, what saves this notion from being a 'we-know-not-what', is that we have a good idea of what an absolute conception of the world would look like in *present-day physics*. But Williams does not expect present-day physics, or anything that looks like present-day physics, to yield an account of the intentional. He is thus caught in the following predicament: a correspondence theory of truth requires a substantive theory of reference. (And, I have argued, a belief in such a theory is hidden in Williams's talk of 'the way things are' *explaining* why we will come to believe 'the absolute conception of the world'.) If we say, 'Well, who knows, perhaps future science—we know not how—will come up with such a theory',—then we abandon the claim that we know the *form* of the 'absolute conception of the world' *now*. The absolute conception of the world becomes a 'we-know-not-what'. If we say, on the other hand, 'Reference can be reduced to physical parameters', then we commit ourselves to refuting the arguments (e.g. Putnam, 1988) against the possibility of a physicalist reduction of semantic notions. But Williams clearly does not wish to undertake any such commitment.

Instead, Williams's suggestion is that the intentional (or the 'semantic') is itself perspectival, and the absolute conception will some day explain why this kind of talk is useful (as it explains why talk of 'grass' and 'green' is useful, even though 'grass' and 'green' are not notions that figure in the absolute conception of the world). But here Williams shows a wobbly grasp of the logical structure of his own position. For the absolute conception of the world was *defined* in terms of the idea that some statements describe the world with a minimum of 'distortion', that they describe it 'as it is', that they describe it 'independently of perspective'—and what does any of this talk mean, unless something like a correspondence of truth is in place? Williams tacitly assumes a correspondence theory of truth when he defines the absolute conception, and then forgets that he did this when he suggests that we do not need to assume that such semantic notions as the 'content' of a sentence will turn out to figure in the absolute conception itself.

---

[3] Cf. my writings from 1978 to 1989, listed in the bibliography.

6 *Metaphysics and Entanglement*

What led Williams to defend this complicated metaphysical theory was the desire to assert a 'truth in relativism' while resisting relativism in science. But in the process of building up this intricate construction with its two kinds of truth (ordinary and 'absolute'), its perspectivalism about secondary qualities and ethics (and, oddly, also about the intentional) and its anti-perspectivalism about physics, he often ignores the entanglement of the factual and the ethical— although he himself stresses that entanglement at other points in his discussion. Consider, for example, the question as to whether we can condemn the Aztec way of life, or, more specifically, the human sacrifice that the Aztecs engaged in. On Williams's view, the Aztec belief that there were supernatural beings who would be angry with them if they did not perform the sacrifices was, as a matter of scientific fact, wrong. This belief we *can* evaluate. It is simply false; and the absolute conception of the world, to the extent we can now approximate it, tells us that it is false. But we cannot say that 'the Aztec way of life' was wrong. Yet, the feature of the Aztec way of life that troubles us (the massive human sacrifice) and the belief about the world that conflicts with science were interdependent. If we can say that the Aztec belief about the Gods was false, why can we not say that the practice to which it led was wrong (although, to be sure, understandable, given the false factual belief)? If we are not allowed to call the practice wrong, why are we allowed to call the belief false? The so-called 'absolute' and the ethical are just as entangled as the 'factual' and the ethical.

For a very different sort of example, consider the admiration we sometimes feel for the Amish (traditional Mennonite) way of life. Even atheists sometimes admire the community solidarity, the helpfulness, and the simplicity of the Amish way. If a sophisticated atheist who felt this way were asked why he or she admires the Amish, they might say something like this: 'I am not necessarily saying we should give up our individualism altogether. But the kind of individualism and competitiveness which has brought so much scientific and economic progress, also brings with it egotism, arrogance, selfishness, and downright cruelty. Even if the Amish way of life rests on what I regard as false beliefs, it does show some of the possibilities of a less competitive, less individualistic form of life; and perhaps we can learn about these possibilities from the Amish without adopting their religion.' Now, Williams does not deny that we can say things like this; that we can learn from cultures to which we stand in the relation he calls 'the relativity of distance', cultures which are not 'real options' for us. But how does this differ from saying, 'Some of the Amish beliefs are false, but other of their beliefs may be true?' Many of Williams's examples load the dice in favour of relativism by taking science to consist of individual judgements which may be called true or false, while taking 'cultures' to offer only 'take it as a whole or reject it as a whole' options.

The problem with the whole enterprise lies right here: Williams wants to acknowledge the entanglement of fact and value and hold on to the 'absolute' character of (ideal) scientific knowledge at the same time. But there is no way to do this. It cannot be the case that scientific knowledge (future fundamental physics) is absolute and nothing else is; for fundamental physics cannot explain the possibility of *referring to* or *stating* anything, including fundamental physics itself. So, if everything that is *not* physics is 'perspectival', then the notion of the 'absolute' is itself hopelessly perspectival! For that notion, as I have already pointed out, is explained (albeit in a disguised way) in terms of notions which belong to the theory of reference and truth, and not to physics. And the idea of a 'relativism of distance' which applies to ethics but not to science also fails, because ethics and science are as entangled as ethics and 'fact'. What we have in *Ethics and the Limits of Philosophy* is, in fact, *not* a serious argument for ethical relativism, but rather an expression of a mood. Reading *Ethics and the Limits of Philosophy*, one gets the feeling that one is being told that ethical relativism is the 'sophisticated' point of view, the 'modern' point of view, and that what is being offered is a *sophisticated reflection on the consequences of this presupposition*. But the presupposition itself does not stand up to any kind of examination—or at least, the way Williams defends the presupposition crumbles the moment one tries to subject it to any sort of careful examination.

7 *Entanglement and Positivism*

Relativism appeals to sophisticated people for different reasons. It appeals to Williams because the idea of ethical objectivity is metaphysically unacceptable. He does not see how we could *know* objective ethical truths if there were any. This metaphysical (or is it epistemological?) appeal is one I do not myself feel. It is not that I *do* know how I know that, for example, human dignity and freedom of speech are better than the alternatives, except in the sense of being able to offer the sorts of arguments that ordinary non-metaphysical people with liberal convictions can and do offer. If I am asked to explain how ethical knowledge is possible at all in 'absolute' terms, I have no answer. But there are all sorts of cases in which I have to say, 'I know this, but I don't know how I know it.' Certainly physics doesn't tell me how I know anything.

Another, very different, appeal is to those who fear that the alternative to cultural relativism is cultural imperialism. But recognizing that my judgements claim objective validity and recognizing that I am shaped by a particular culture and that I speak in a particular historical context are not incompatible. I agree with Williams that it would be silly to ask if the way of life of an eighteenth-century Samurai is 'right' or 'wrong'; but the reason this is a silly question isn't that we are too 'distant', or that becoming eighteenth-century Samurai isn't a 'real option' for us. In my view, it would be a silly question if we *were* eighteenth-century Samurai. Indeed, 'Is our own way of life right or wrong?' is a silly question, although it isn't silly to ask if this or that particular feature of our way of life is right or wrong, and 'Is our view of the world right or wrong?' is a silly question, although it isn't silly to ask if this or that particular belief is right or wrong. As Dewey and Peirce taught us, real questions require a context and a point. But this is as true of scientific questions as it is of ethical ones. Instead of trying once again to discover some deep truth contained in positivism—in the fact–value dichotomy, or in 'non-cognitivism', or in the verifiability theory of meaning—we should break the grip of positivism on our thinking once and for all.

The failure of the latest attempt to find some deep truths in positivism is no accident. Although Williams tries to do justice to the entanglement of fact and value, he fails do so, because positivism was fundamentally a denial of entanglement, an insistence on sharp dichotomies: science–ethics, science–metaphysics, analytic–synthetic. The science–ethics dichotomy that Williams wants to preserve presupposed the science–metaphysics and analytic–synthetic distinctions he rejects. This is why Williams's book-length attempt to spell out his position is either self-contradictory or hopelessly ambiguous at every crucial point.

Recognizing that the entanglement of fact and value, as well as of science and ethics, science and metaphysics, analytic and synthetic, is here to stay may also help us to see our way past another contemporary shibboleth: the supposed incompatibility of universalist (or 'enlightenment') and parochial values. Recently I was struck by something Israel Scheffler has written (Scheffler, 1987):

I have always supposed that the universal and the particular are compatible, that grounding in a particular historical and cultural matrix is inevitable and could not conceivably be in conflict with universal principles. I have thus belonged to both sides of a divide which separated most Jewish academics and intellectuals of my generation.

When we argue about the universal applicability of principles like freedom of speech or distributive justice we are not claiming to stand outside of our own tradition, let alone outside of space and time, as some fear; we are standing within a tradition, and trying simultaneously to learn what in that tradition we are prepared to recommend to other traditions *and* to see what in that tradition may be inferior—inferior either to what other traditions have to offer, or to the best we may be capable of. Williams is right when he says that this kind of reflection may destroy what we have taken to be ethical knowledge; it may certainly lead us to re-evaluate our beliefs, and to abandon *some* of them; but he is wrong when he fears that the most ultimate kind of reflective distance, the kind which is associated with the 'absolute conception of the world', will destroy *all* ethical knowledge. Here he is worrying about a distance which is wholly illusory. No conception of the world is 'absolute'.

Williams describes the 'absolute conception of the world' as something required by the very concept of knowledge. What this transcendental moment in Williams's argument shows is that, for him, there is no conceivable alternative to the idea of an absolute conception of the world—or no alternative save, perhaps, a scepticism as total as that of the ancient Greeks. But we are not forced to choose between scientism and scepticism in the way Williams thinks. The third possibility is to accept the position we are fated to occupy in any case, the position of beings who cannot have a view of the world that does not reflect our interests and values, but who are, for all that, committed to regarding some views of the world—and, for that matter, some interests and values—as better than others. This may be giving up a certain metaphysical picture of objectivity, but it is not giving up the idea that there are what Dewey called 'objective resolutions of problematical situations'—objective resolutions to problems which are *situated*, that is, in a place, at a time, as opposed to an 'absolute' answer to 'perspective-independent' questions. And that is objectivity enough.

BIBLIOGRAPHY

CAVELL, STANLEY (1979). *The Claim of Reason*. Oxford: Oxford University Press.
LEWIS, DAVID (1976). *Counterfactuals*. Cambridge, Mass.: Harvard University Press.
McDOWELL, JOHN (1978). 'Are Moral Requirements Hypothetical Imperatives?', *Proceedings of the Aristotelian Society*, suppl. vol. 52.
—— (1979). 'Virtue and Reason', *Monist*, 62.
MURDOCH, IRIS (1971). *The Sovereignty of 'Good'*. London: Routledge and Kegan Paul.
PUTNAM, HILARY (1974). 'The Corroboration of Theories', in P. A. Schilpp (ed.), *The Philosophy of Karl Popper*. LaSalle, Ill.: Open Court.
—— (1978). *Meaning and the Moral Sciences*. London: Routledge and Kegan Paul.
—— (1980). 'Models and Reality', *Journal of Symbolic Logic*, 45 (repr. in Putnam, 1983).
—— (1981). *Reason, Truth, and History*. Cambridge: Cambridge University Press.
—— (1983). *Realism and Reason* (vol. iii of my *Philosophical Papers*). Cambridge: Cambridge University Press.
—— (1986). 'Information and the Mental', in E. Lepore (ed.), *Truth and Interpretation*. Oxford: Oxford University Press.
—— (1987). *The Many Faces of Realism*. LaSalle, Ill.: Open Court.
—— (1988). *Representation and Reality*. Cambridge, Mass.: Bradford Books.
—— (1989). 'Model Theory and the Factuality of Semantics', in Alex George (ed.), *Reflections on Chomsky*. Oxford: Blackwell.
QUINE, WILLARD V. (1951). 'Two Dogmas of Empiricism', first published in *Philosophical Review*; repr. in *From a Logical Point of View* (revised edn., 1961). Cambridge, Mass.: Harvard University Press.
—— (1963). 'Carnap on Logical Truth', in P. A. Schilpp (ed.), *The Philosophy of Rudolf Carnap*. LaSalle, Ill.: Open Court.
SCHEFFLER, ISRAEL (1987). 'Teachers of My Youth' (unpublished). Copyright, I. Scheffler.)

WALSH, VIVIAN (1987). 'Philosophy and Economics', in J. Eatwell, M. Milgate, and P. Newman (eds.), *The New Palgrave: A Dictionary of Economics*, iii. London: Macmillan, and New York: Stockton Press.

WHITE, MORTON (1956). *Towards Reunion in Philosophy*. Cambridge, Mass.: Harvard University Press.

WIGGINS, DAVID (1987). *Needs, Values, Truth*. Oxford: Oxford University Press.

WILLIAMS, BERNARD (1978). *Descartes: The Project of Pure Enquiry*. Harmondsworth: Penguin Books.

—— (1985). *Ethics and the Limits of Philosophy*. Cambridge, Mass.: Harvard University Press.

Hilary Putnam: Objectivity and the Science–Ethics Distinction

Commentary by Lorenz Krüger

What I admire and appreciate very much about Putnam's paper on the science–ethics distinction – indeed about his more recent philosophical work (1981, 1987) in general – is the fresh and original attack on a key problem of the Western scientific–philosophical tradition: the problem of establishing a unified and coherent cognitive enterprise which comprises values and facts, decisions and insights, ethics and science alike. If he should succeed, we would – vis-à-vis the problem of quality of life – be in a very different situation, because we could settle disputes on values by co-operative *investigations* rather than controversial *negotiations*.

The commentator, it seems to me, must inevitably ask the following critical question: has Putnam succeeded in showing that unified concepts of objectivity and rationality can be developed for science *and* ethics? Indeed, is it even desirable or advisable to insist on the ideal of the unified scientific–ethical enterprise?

In pursuing these questions, I shall not adopt a strategy that might seem to be suggested, if not demanded, by the arrangement of Putnam's argument; that is, I shall *not* try to examine the possible defences of the opponents he attacks in his paper, notably Bernard Williams. I cannot do this, simply because I happen to accept Putnam's main argument against Williams. Like him, I think that the distinction between relative and absolute truth (in the sense he attributes to Williams) is untenable. But, unlike him, I see different reasons for this untenability; hence I am led to adopt different conclusions – conclusions that are at variance with the idea of a unified sphere of objectivity for science and ethics. Leaving other aspects of Putnam's paper aside, I turn immediately to the disputed distinction between the relative and the absolute.

Relative truths are such as will be accepted by some community or other of rational believers but remain dependent on certain limited cultural contexts. (What the limits of these contexts and of these cognitive communities are remains an open question to be explored for each case in its own right.) Absolute truths, however, are context-independent; and this they are said to be by virtue of their correspondence to the things 'out there', or, more precisely, by their corresponding to such features of reality as could invariantly and equivalently be expressed in any other sufficiently elaborate language.

Favoured candidates for the status of such features are, of course, suitably chosen objects as described by physics. Candidates for relative truths, on the other hand, are ordinary statements of everyday life such as 'the grass is green', 'our neighbour is a malicious person', or 'the tax laws are just'. What counts as 'grass' or 'green', let alone as a 'malicious character' or a 'just tax law', is hardly culturally invariant, though such statements may be recognized as true or false, once a cultural context is taken for granted.

Now Putnam opposes this view for at least two important reasons. First, he thinks that the conception of absolute truth is untenable, indeed unintelligible; second, he thinks that relative truth is less than we need and less than we can attain. I fully agree with both points.

My misgivings with Putnam's approach concern his views on the connection between his two critical points and the conclusions he derives from this connection. In my reading of his paper the connection is the following: If you grant the first point, that is, if you drop absolute truth and the correspondence between beliefs and things out there altogether, you are left with nothing but relative truths. Yet these—as far as their epistemic status is concerned—have already been granted to form a homogeneous field. That the neighbour is a malicious person is a truth, or a falsity, of the same kind and epistemological status as the assertion that the grass is green. Putnam, his opponents, and further authors (some cited in his paper, e.g. Iris Murdoch), have accumulated an impressive sample of statements that do not admit of an analysis into a 'factual' and an 'evaluative' component. The examples range from recognizing a person as pert or polite to condemning human sacrifice as utterly evil. All these cases display an inextricable 'entanglement of fact and value'. Nevertheless, they are all plausibly presented as acceptable candidates for the assignment of a truth-value, though Putnam does not deny that the actual ascription of either truth or falsity to such assertions about value-facts may depend on comprehensive ideologies and forms of life, for example, the Aztec religion, which demanded human sacrifice.

We can now see how the rejection of an admittedly ill-conceived and untenable partition of the set of truths combines with a positive characterization of those that fall on the relativistic side. As far as Putnam's present paper goes, it is this combination that leads on to further conclusions, conclusions which I believe to be unacceptable. The most important of these is the desired unity of our cognitive field. Another important conclusion (which, if true, would support the first) is the following: given that there is no absolute truth because there are no fixed objects 'out there', the notion of correspondence between statements or beliefs and transcendent 'facts' becomes an empty or even an unintelligible concept. It is replaced by rational acceptability.

Here are my objections. The first conclusion—the existence of a unified domain of rationally assertable truths—is an all-too-sweeping extrapolation of a correct observation: that of inextricable entanglements of fact and value in many life issues. This extrapolation in its turn is encouraged by the second conclusion, which is that truth can *never* consist in correspondence to external facts. To this I object that the inference from 'no correspondence to something fixed out there' to 'no correspondence at all' is a *non sequitur*. Now, if there were *some* kind of correspondence in some cases and no correspondence of *any* kind in some other cases, a new form of the fact–value distinction and of the ethics–science distinction might be established–a form that is freed from the metaphysical burden of absoluteness.

I take up the second point first, because it lies close to the centre of Putnam's theoretical philosophy, that is, his internal or pragmatic realism. To avoid misunderstandings, I want to stress that I second Putnam's criticism of external, absolute, or metaphysical realism, and that I am all for internal, knower-related, or pragmatic realism. Moreover, I share Putnam's hope of nevertheless resisting a sweeping cultural (let alone subjective or personal) relativism. I part company with him, however, on at least two issues. First, I do not believe that we can secure a non-relativistic realism without some notion of 'correspondence' to external reality. Second, I do not believe that all rationally acceptable propositions have the same epistemological status, rather that some are acceptable because of their correspondence, others for entirely different reasons. The first kind can be called 'true' (or 'false') in the standard meaning of the terms, the second kind cannot. If truth talk is applied to the second kind, this has to be done by tactful extension of, or on analogy with, the first type. But there are limits to these extensions or analogies, limits that are to be assessed in a rational analysis. In other words: I think that the field of rationality is much wider than that of truth, and that this circumstance is of vital importance for the survival of rationality.

What is correspondence if it is not to be absolute or metaphysical? It is a relationship between our statements or beliefs, on the one hand, and our perceptions and actions, on the other. Both relata are experiential and free from metaphysical suspicion. Take a simple example, for instance, the statement that there is now an even number of people in this room. If it should happen to be true, that would mean, among other things, that you could pair off all people present, so that no one is left alone. Here is an obvious correspondence between our verbal or mental representation and our material, that is, non-verbal and non-representational, contacts with a piece of reality.

Now, it may conceivably be the case that we could have a system of representations that lacks the conceptual distinction between 'odd' and 'even'. One may, therefore, argue–and this is quite in line with internal realism–that even my banal example illustrates the fact that our conceptual system (presumably together with our imaginative possibilities) irrevocably prejudges what can ever become an object for us. But it is equally clear from the example that it would be absurd to collapse the doubleness of representation and material contact.

So far everything seems trivial. But perhaps the next step is already less innocuous. We all believe that people come in countable integer units and that they cannot penetrate walls, so that it lies in the nature of things–that is, of our material contacts with the world–that there is actually no choice between alternative representational systems when it comes to the question of how many people have gathered in a closed room. Statements concerning such matters are simply true or false; and they are that, first, because of a certain correspondence with reality and, second, regardless of the cultural context, provided it is developed enough to discuss such matters at all.

Again, no more than a trivial point? Yes, as far as normal people's concerns go. But no, as soon as subtle philosophy is brought into play. What I am implying is no more, but also no less, than an assumption to the effect that the niceties of a logically refined ontology are completely irrelevant to our problem of correspondence. It is part of our material world contact that we do not encounter, and cannot count, time-slices of people, or experience them as portions of some stuff, of a kind of human mush. Nor do we have a choice between an individualistic ontology *à la* Carnap and a mereological ontology according to the Polish logicians (Putnam, 1987: 17–21) in this case. Brevity forces me to make an unduly perfunctory statement here: correspondence, and with it the reference of terms, does not suffer in the least from ontological relativity, at least not in our humdrum examples.

But how far do they carry us into more complex and more abstract matters? The lack of serious alternative descriptions smacks of absoluteness again. But here we must guard against the philosopher's professional disease, of turning universal experiences into conceptual necessities. I take the lack of serious alternative representations of simple matters to be no more but also no less than a contingent, if enduring, fact about those matters and about humans who take cognizance of them. Keeping this point in mind, let us now turn to a different example, for instance, the proposition that all the people in this room are independent and honest thinkers. There is—we will probably concede—some fact of the matter concerning this statement, that is, circumstances that justify its assertion or denial, as the case may be. But it is also clear that this statement is much less stable than the one about the even number, especially across time and across cultural boundaries. Now, I submit that the difference is not just one of precision or accessibility to examination or the like, but a difference in subject-matter and, by implication, in our relation to that subject-matter. (Here I find myself in partial, though not complete, agreement with Williams, as rendered by Putnam on pp. 146–56.)

What lies behind this apparent difference? It is not of our doing that humans—or shall I artificially say: instantiations of humanity—come in discrete physical units, whereas codes of intellectual independence, still more of honesty, are products of intentional and, within limits, free human life. True, they are far from arbitrary, and, as with everything historical, any single person will usually feel almost powerless to change them. But (*pace* Plato) numbers, whether in 'pure' mathematics or in experience, and honesty are worlds apart in kind. One may also express the contrast in a Kantian language, using a key term of his philosophy: with respect to some matters we are (or could and should be) *autonomous*, with respect to others we are not. This is what sharpens the point of the famous confrontation of the moral law in us with the starry sky above us. To be sure, we conceive of both *within the limits of our intellect and reason*, but we do not impose on ourselves, in Kant's terms, the laws of the intellect, whereas we do impose on ourselves the laws of our actions. In other words, what I want to say is that the distinction between facts and values can and should be reconstructed *within* the framework of internal realism.

In the spirit of the rejection of pre-scientific metaphysics—which I share with Putnam—I feel driven towards and into history for further instruction and examination of this claim. What I believe I see there is the following pattern (I hope the reader will forgive me for its crudeness, which I cannot avoid owing to lack of space and competence): to build the world of values and forms of life according to the order of the cosmos is a fundamental characteristic of our philosophical–scientific tradition—born with Pythagorean speculation, nourished by Plato (though not, or so it seems, by Socrates), pronounced the guideline of social order by the Stoics, surviving in the Christian idea of the participation of the rational human soul in the divine order of things, finally entering into the optimistic research programmes of the modern philosopher–scientists like Galileo, Descartes, Hobbes, and Hume. But precisely in its modern enlightened form the great programme has come to grief. We can only register, or so it seems to me, a deep disappointment with its outcome. The disillusionment is, first, that no scientific ethics, as projected by the philosopher–scientists of the New Age, has been established; second, that the same holds for a scientific insight into 'the laws' of history, if there are such at all. On the contrary, current and recurrent attempts at providing a specifically scientific basis for the responsible and rational investigation of history and ethics—sociobiology or certain orthodox versions of Marxism are examples—are at best helpless *vis-à-vis* our problems and at worst dangerously ideological.

My statement of the historical lesson is, of course, a sketch, no more. It lacks the elaboration and the defences it would need to stand up to scrutiny. But it may help to see what I am up to: in our age of science we cannot but connect even the most elementary statements with their actual or potential theoretical context. But if we try to do this with my two examples—the even number on the one hand and the intellectual independence and honesty on the other—we find ourselves confronted with two deeply different sorts of context: on the one side there is that growing web of scientific theories about that part of our experience that we cannot produce, change, or destroy. Let us call it 'non-human nature' (though it comprises, of course, a good part of our physical and mental apparatus). True, we can exploit this nature, but only, as Francis Bacon said, by obeying it. On the other side there is that part of our experience that we can change, one is tempted to say, that part of it that *is* us. And here obedience does not seem to be the right, perhaps not even a possible, attitude. We want to have, and to an impressive degree do have, disciplined research traditions and institutions that explore this domain of our experienced reality; but they would be ill advised, should they suppose as their object a human nature in any sense comparable to the non-human nature which is the supposed object of the natural sciences.

For easiness of reference, I may perhaps call the view I have just outlined 'historical realism'. I think of it as an elaboration, but also as a correction, of internal realism. The name is to remind us that we learn what is real in the course of our history. One lesson—the one I have mentioned—appears to be that self-conscious and potentially autonomous human beings are a peculiar reality of their own—a reality to which we do not react in the same way as that in which we react or respond to non-human nature, so that our beliefs or statements about this reality cannot correspond to their contents in a way in which our beliefs or statements about non-human nature can.

The significance of this lesson, if it is one, hardly needs to be pointed out. If we have a claim to autonomy, narrow as its bounds may be, it is important to recognize that, if for beliefs and statements belonging under its rule there is truth or falsity, then it is not truth or falsity that relates to 'correspondence' in the sense outlined above. I do not want to dispute anyone's use of 'true' or 'false'. We may find that all the people in this room *are* independent thinkers, and we may wish to say that a statement to this effect is *true*. But here 'true' will presumably mean something like 'rationally acceptable' or even 'not rationally rejectable'. Any attempt at ascertaining this kind of truth, however, will involve us in explications of what it is to be independent. These explications, in turn, will involve questions about what balance we want, or ought, to strike between individual originality and mutual social adjustment. In short, the answer to the question as to whether or not we are independent thinkers is not independent from the question as to what kind of people we want to be or what type of society we want to have.

For reasons like these, there can be no objectivity in the domain of autonomy, since there is no object. Instead, there is a world of subjects. Needless to say, I am not here denying the possibility of, indeed the urgent need for, intersubjectivity and rationality. What I claim is only that Putnam's renewed attempt at unifying human reason has not really advanced beyond Kant's great divide of theoretical and practical reason. But how could it have? And would that have been desirable? Besides the by now global unification of our substantial science plus its material technology, we will want to preserve cultural pluralism, an option I share with Putnam (see e.g. 1981: 147-9). It is true, he does not seem to fear that the continuity between science and ethics will work against pluralism. But I do fear that it would work against cultural pluralism, if only it were effectively realizable. And that would not be desirable.

Thus, I conclude that to reach reasonable agreement—or reasonable disagreement, wherever the circumstances leave room for it—is one thing; to claim objectivity or truth is another.

BIBLIOGRAPHY

PUTNAM, HILARY (1981). *Reason, Truth and History*. Cambridge: Cambridge University Press.
—— (1987). *The Many Faces of Realism*. La Salle, Ill.: Open Court.

Objectivity and Social Meaning

Michael Walzer

[1]

I probably do not have an objective view of objectivity. Having been accused
so often of disdaining it, I come to it now with some trepidation; I want to
make a cautious approach, repressing for a while the uneasy sense that the
conjunction in my title misrepresents the likely outcome of my argument. Let
me begin with a strong, simplistic, and usefully wrong definition of objectivity:
a given perception, recognition, or understanding can be called 'objective' if
its content is wholly or largely determined by its object—so that a range of
human subjects, differently placed, with different personalities and different,
even conflicting, interests, would agree on the same content so long as they
attended to the same object. The table determines the objective perception
of the table. What makes for objectivity is simply this: the object imposes
itself. The subject is passive and undiscriminating, a promiscuous consumer
of available 'data'.

For reasons philosophers have long understood, that cannot be right. Human
beings are active subjects. Our faculties of perception and cognition help to
determine whatever it is that we finally see or recognize or understand. But
we are still inclined to call the perception 'objective' so long as these faculties
are so widely shared as to constitute what we might call a normal subject.
Then perception is objective when it is jointly determined by the object and
the normal subject. If someone without depth perception reports on the existence of a table different from the one the rest of us see, his is the subjective
report. The table and the normal person looking at the table (who represents
'the rest of us') together determine what the table objectively is (looks like).
The object still imposes itself, but perception is conditioned by the character
of the receptive organism, and the idea of 'objectivity' incorporates the results
of this conditioning.

But that cannot be right either, and this time for reasons that have generated
a long series of complex, difficult, and sometimes high-flying philosophical
arguments. We do not come to the object with faculties alone but with interests
and ideas too. And what we see, recognize, and understand depends (with a
strong but not absolute dependency) on what we are looking for, our cognitive
concerns, and the ways we have of describing what we find, our conceptual
schemes. Given our concerns and our schemes, what opportunity is there now
for the object to impose itself? We seem armoured against imposition, shaping
the world to our own purposes.

But I do not mean to surrender objectivity so quickly—indeed, it is the
scientific perception of the world, driven by a strong purposefulness and

structured by elaborate and highly speculative schemes, that makes the most insistent claim these days to be called an objective perception. The claim takes many different forms, but in all its forms it must hold that if the object does not impose itself it is still recalcitrant to conceptual and purposive impositions. Scientific concepts must accommodate the object – not as the object appears, perhaps, but as it *really is*. I am not going to comment on that last assertion, except to say that for most of us, at least, appearance is an important aspect of reality. But I want to accept the claim that objectivity hangs (somehow) on the accommodation of the object by a knowing, inquiring subject. The knowing subject shapes the object, but he cannot shape it however he likes; he cannot just decide that a table, say, has a circular or a square shape without reference to the table. Similarly, someone self-confidently applying a conceptual scheme that divided the world into friends, enemies, reading matter, and edible plants would get the table wrong (objectively wrong), or he would miss the table entirely, and deny its reality, and that would be a merely idiosyncratic (subjective) denial.

This is still a very simple account of objectivity, a rough, commonsensical approach to philosophical difficulties that lie beyond my immediate cognitive concerns and possibly also beyond the conceptual schemes at my disposal. But the account works, more or less well, for simple objects-in-the-world. The question that I want to ask now is whether it works at all for objects to which we assign use and value, objects that carry 'social meanings'.[1] This term, borrowed from anthropology, seems to cast a cloud over all claims to objective knowledge. Social meanings are constructions of objects by sets of subjects, and once such constructions are, so to speak, in place, the understanding of the object has been and will continue to be determined by the subjects. New sets of subjects learn the construction and then respect or revise it with only a minimal accommodation of the object. The object may or may not limit the constructive work in which they are engaged. Obviously, the table cannot be constructed as an intercontinental ballistics missile. But it can become a desk, a workbench, a butcher's block, or an altar, and each of these can take on meanings to which the 'mere' table gives us no positive clue. Can perceptions of objects like these, objects-with-meanings, ever be called objective? It is easy enough to imagine situations in which one person's altar is another person's butcher's block. But we do accept reports on social constructions. Now objectivity (in the reports) hangs on an acknowledgement of the construction. Our shared understanding of what an altar is, what we have made it for, determines our perception of the table-that-is-an-altar. The holiness of the altar is similarly

---

[1] Are there any objects without social meaning? Perhaps the phrase 'simple objects-in-the-world' names a null set. But I am going to assume that there are such things, which we accommodate and shape directly, without any necessary reference to their sociological significance. Stones are, for my purposes, simple objects-in-the-world – until they are made into cornerstones, tombstones, grindstones, milestones, stepping stones, or doorsteps (or, more dramatically, until they are used for coronations or set up as markers for a sacred history). As for tables, see the argument below.

objective, since it is part of the same construction. All normal persons living within the system of social meanings would deliver similar reports on the objective reality of tables-that-are-altars-that-are-holy.

But this may go too far. Suppose that there are dissenting voices within the society where some tables are holy altars, people who deny the construction, who announce, 'There's nothing there but an old table.' That is also an objective report of a kind. Can we say that it is an incomplete report, that it misses something of real importance? Imagine a fuller report: 'Some people claim that it's an altar and treat it as if it were holy, but there's nothing there but an old table.' No incompleteness now, and now only the disagreement can be objectively reported: '*I think* there's nothing there but an old table.' Nothing in the nature of the table will lead us to say that it is or is not a holy altar. The altar is objectively there only for those who understand it to be objectively there. It is holy only for those who acknowledge its holiness. And what they will have to say, if they are to report objectively, is that it is holy *for them*.

Believers will want to say more than that. They will want to say that God has sanctified the table and made it into a holy altar; hence everyone who knows how things really are in the world will acknowledge its holiness. But I shall take it as given that altars and holiness are alike human creations. The believers are wrong, then, to take the holiness of their altar as a universally recognizable (objective) fact. The altar is holy only because and only in so far as they have made it so. With regard to such creations, the rest of us are not bound by majority rule; only the voice of the people as a whole resembles the voice of God. Social constructions must reflect a general agreement – or, better, since no vote is ever taken, there must be a consensus – if there is ever to be an unqualified objectivity, an objectivity without pronouns, in our reports about them. (Reports from outside observers will always need pronouns: 'their altars' or, in more extended form, 'these tables, which they use as altars'.) The more complex and specific the construction the more surprising it is when a consensus is actually reached. The social processes that make this possible are mixed processes, involving force and fraud, debate and consent, long periods of habituation; overall, they remain mysterious.

Compared to 'altar', 'table' is both uncomplicated and indeterminate; hence its meanings will rarely provoke significant or stirring dissent. Someone who says, 'That's not a table', while pointing to a flat piece of wood with a supporting structure of appropriate height, will probably lead us to talk about mistakes, not disagreements. (I will not stop here to imagine bizarre cases of table-like objects that are rarely not tables.) We would suspect some failure of normal understanding. A table is indeed a social construction, as well as a physical construction, but the socially constructive work is so rudimentary that we are unlikely to recognize much more in it than the assignment of a general name to the object. And then we expect people of normal understanding to remember the name. Nothing much follows from remembering it; the construction of the flat piece of wood, etc., as a table does not require us to use or to value the table in a certain way. More specific constructions, by contrast, have normative consequences.

Tables-that-are-altars-that-are-holy must be treated in accordance with certain principles and rules. I cannot use the altar, for example, as a desk on which to write profane essays on social meaning—not because the altar will resist the use or God strike me dead, but because it would be wrong to do that given what an altar is in my society (for me and my fellow members). Nor can I chop it up for firewood, even if the church is very cold; or trade it for personal profit—a new suit, say, or a season ticket to the opera, or a place on the Stock Exchange: it would be the wrong thing to do. But would it be objectively wrong? It seems to me that it is possible to ask questions like that too soon. Clearly the rules of use and value are not determined by the 'mere' table; nor are they jointly determined by the table and a normal person looking at the table; nor do they represent an accommodation of the table by a knowing subject or a scientific observer. The rules follow from the social construction of the table as a holy altar and they would seem to be objective rules only for those men and women who join in the construction or acknowledge its results. The other might be bound by some notion of 'decent respect' for the opinions of their fellows, but not by the idea of holiness.

But perhaps we can go a little further than this. If we think of the holiness of the altar not as an isolated construction but as one feature of a more complex whole, a cultural system or a way of life, then the force of the rules is considerably enhanced. Imagine the table-that-is-an-altar-that-is-holy within a set of connected constructions: socially meaningful occasions (holy days), spaces (churches), officials (priests and bishops), performances (religious services), texts (scriptures, prayers, homilies, catechisms), and beliefs (theologies or cosmologies), and the result is something from which individuals cannot so easily opt out. Some day there will be alternative occasions, spaces, officials, performances, texts, and beliefs, arising out of a long process of social change ('secularization', say); and then people will be able to explain to their fellows why the altar is not (really) holy. But now the refusal of some dissident or rebel to treat the altar in accordance with its rules of use and value is probably not a straightforward denial of its holiness but a specific act of desecration— literally, an effort to reverse the process through which this particular altar has been consecrated. And the religious rebel committed to desecration is likely to appeal, in much the same way as the early Protestants appealed, to other features of the existing cultural system or way of life, features that give him reasons, so he says, for what he does. The system as a whole still has objective value for him; he lives within the set of social constructions. Where else can he live?

[2]

We can still ask whether this is objectively the best place to live. But I want, again, to postpone that question in order to explore more fully the crucial implication of my argument thus far: that social construction is also moral legislation. The meanings with which we invest objects have normative consequences. I have been calling these norms 'rules of use and value'; they are also rules of distribution, that is, they regulate our relations not only with things but also with other people. Any number of philosophers have argued that morality is a human invention, writing mostly as if what we invent are the rules that govern a moral life. We leap to principles like equality before God or personal autonomy or the greatest happiness; and then we make lists, like the *Decalogue*. Maybe we do that, sometimes; but the thickness of the moral world and the density of our relationships suggest a radically different kind of invention. One of the ways we reach that thickness and density is through the social construction of objects (of all kinds). Social construction makes for a complex and rich world, many features of which will seem so obvious to us that we will not be prompted to ask whether they are, of all possible features of all possible worlds, objectively best. They will have a more immediate objectivity. So we will use and value objects in accordance with the meaning they have in our world, and we will exchange, share, and distribute them in accordance with their use and value. We will know what objects we owe to other people as soon as we understand what those objects (really) are and what they are for. And a great part of our conduct towards other people will be governed by these distributive entailments of social meanings.

At this point, it will be useful to take up another example, even though the difficulties of the table-that-is-an-altar-that-is-holy have by no means been exhausted. I want to consider the construction of a human life — not a biological but a social life, not a life span but a life course in a particular society, namely, our own. What we have constructed is a life-that-is-a-career-that-is-open-to-talents. Obviously, there is nothing in the nature of a human life that determines its construction as a career. Any given version of the life course is conditioned by the life span, so that youth, maturity, and age give rise to a pattern like training, professional practice, and retirement; but these latter three do not by themselves constitute a career. A career is an individual achievement; it is constituted by choice and qualification. Though career patterns may be collectively established and repetitively enacted, a career is none the less a projection of the self into a chosen and uncertain future. What makes this projection possible is the opening up of certain sorts of places and positions (professional or bureaucratic), which I will call 'offices'. Offices are the objects of careers. The social construction of the two goes hand in hand, like altars and offerings. If careers are open to talents, then offices must be distributed on meritocratic principles to qualified persons. If we imagine individual men and women planning careers-open-to-talents, we must also imagine competitions for office. If there are competitions, there must be rules protecting the competitors, not only against violence but also against discrimination, that is, against any refusal to attend honestly to their qualifications.

Once careers and offices are in place, nepotism becomes a wrongful practice. It would be wrong for me, the member of some search committee, say, to favour my brother over a more qualified candidate. It does not matter that I have a very strong, and to my mind overriding, belief in family loyalty; I am caught up in a complex set of social constructions that has normative entailments. Someone who fails to respect the table-that-is-an-altar-that-is-holy does no injury to the table, and in so far as the failure is private he does no injury (causes no offence) to other men and women either. His is one of the minor sins. But once constructions determine distributions, private refusals make for a more serious wrong. And when behaviour is in question, general agreement is no longer a necessary condition of rightness or wrongness; the rule against nepotism, for example, is binding even on individuals who argue that offices are family holdings and not objects of careers. There will not be many people, however, who will actually *argue* that offices are family holdings—except in the unlikely case that a strong familial idealism is part of the same set of social constructions as the career-open-to-talents, and then we might well recognize the public nepotist as a conscientious objector. Acts of refusal and opposition commonly have a basis of this sort, in the coexistence of contradictory constructions. Then people have to choose, guided only by their best understanding of the complex social world they inhabit.

I want to stress that it would not be objectively wrong to adopt the argument for offices-as-family-holdings. Majority rule does not govern arguments about social meaning; it only governs behaviour. The rules of behaviour, then, are objectively right relative to the prevailing meanings, but the prevailing meanings are not objectively right (or wrong). They are only objectively *there*, the objects, that is, of more or less accurate reports. The life-that-is-a-career could, over time, be constructed in an entirely different way, and offices could be reconstructed to match the difference, and no wrong would have been done. It would not be the case that lives or offices had somehow been misunderstood; nor would the men and women leading lives and holding (or not holding) offices under the new dispensation have been treated unjustly.

It is not my claim that the whole of morality is objectively relative (relatively objective?) in this way, only whatever part of it is entailed by the social construction of objects. Even here we might plausibly ask whether there are cases where construction is jointly determined by its objects and its human agents in such a way that the same normative entailments appear again and again, in all or almost all human societies. Then the same behaviour would be wrongful for the same reasons in all human societies; morality would lose its particularist character without ceasing to be relative to social construction. The easiest case has to do with the things we call 'food': given the human body, the construction of edible objects is not an entirely free construction—though people in different cultures do choose different things to eat and not eat, edibility itself is (in part) socially determined. In any case, the experience or expectation of hunger and the possibility of eating certain things work together to turn some of those things into human provisions, and it would seem to follow from this that provisions should be provided for those in need;

food belongs to the hungry. (Who should do the providing and at whose expense are questions not so easily answered.) More complex and specific constructions will still be culturally relative: we save certain food for festive occasions or we burn it before the gods or we waste it at extravagant banquets. But the original construction of things-that-are-food-for-the-hungry entails certain distributive rules that have, I suspect (this could be checked), always been recognized. Hoarders in time of famine act wrongly, for example, given what food is for.

I shall assume that reiterated social construction rather than diffusion from an authoritative centre is the preferred explanation for the appearance of identical or similar used and valued objects in different societies. There is no authoritative centre, no Jerusalem from which meanings go forth. The list of similarly constructed uses and values, then, constitutes what we might think of as a universal and objective morality—relative to social construction where construction repetitively takes the same form, relative to the prevailing argument where the same argument always prevails. We could go on to further explanations: if certain things-in-the-world are constructed in the same way again and again, presumably there is something in the nature of the things and/or something in the nature of the human agents that accounts for the construction. As the example of food suggests, the account is likely to be a naturalistic one. But I doubt that the list of similar constructions would be very long; nor would it include the complex and specific constructions that make for the thickness of moral life: food for eating would get on the list, not food for offerings. This is what it means to say that complexity is free: the more complex the construction the more room there is for cultural difference. Complex constructions do not turn up again and again, and they do not have plausible or satisfying naturalistic explanations.

There is no universal model for social construction, and the range of difference among actual outcomes is very wide. It might be argued, however, that this is so only because the constructive work takes place under a great variety of adverse and advantageous (mostly adverse) conditions. Only a common necessity, like the need for nourishment, makes for sameness. But if we imagine social construction in ideal conditions (and if ideal conditions are a single set of conditions), then we will get a model outcome, that is, a free construction that is at the same time the best construction. I am afraid that this is an impossible dream. For we can replace actual with hypothetical social construction only if we know, and not hypothetically, what conditions are ideal. And if we know that, then we already know the model outcome. We simply pull into our account of the imagined (ideal, original, natural) conditions all those materials, and only those materials, out of which we want society constructed. We might as well draw a blueprint of the good society and give up the idea that construction is free.

[3]

But if we do not have a model outcome, how can we ever criticize actual outcomes? This question is motivated, I think, by a misunderstanding of what an actual outcome is. Social construction is first of all conceptual in character. Holy altars and careers-open-to-talents are ideas, and the distributive norms that follow from them are also ideas. These ideas are never more than partially instantiated in the world; holiness and openness are more often than not honoured in the breach. What social critics commonly do is to hold the idea, or some more or less elaborated interpretation of the idea, over against the instance of the idea. Or, just as commonly, they hold some other idea or complex set of ideas, also the product of social construction, over against this idea and its instances. They say, if careers are open to talents, then why are they not open to the talents of Jews, or blacks, or women? Or, if our society is a union of families or a democratic and co-operative community of citizens, how can we tolerate the intense competitiveness generated by careers-open-to-talents?

Criticism of this sort depends on objective values, where objectivity is a true report on social meaning. The criticism itself, however, is not objectively true or false, for it also depends on an interpretation of social meaning, and interpretations are (except at the margins) only more or less persuasive and illuminating. But surely there are times when we want to say something stronger than this. We want to say that though the report is objectively true, the meaning is wrong (and not just *wrong for us*). Or we want to say that that is not the way we ought to think about altars or careers or whatever. Or even, that is not what an altar or a career *really is*.

Is it possible for a whole society to get things wrong in this fundamental way? This is the question that I have been postponing, and it is time now to try to deal with it. I want to make sure, though, that we understand exactly what the question is. Clearly, it is possible for individuals within a society to get things wrong, even fundamentally wrong, and it is also possible for groups of individuals to do the same thing. We should think of the Nazi case in these terms. It would strain the imagination to describe a fully elaborated world of complex meanings of a Nazi sort; in any case, no such world has ever existed. Within German or European or Western culture, the Nazis were an aberration, and in so far as we can make out their distributive principles – air for Aryans, gas for Jews – we can readily say that these are objectively wrong, immoral, monstrous. All the resources necessary for a judgement of this sort are already available, the products of a long history of social construction. It is a great mistake to make of the Nazis a hard case. The hard case comes when we begin to think that a long history of social construction has somehow gone awry.

Consider, then, those societies where women (all women) seem to have been socially constructed as objects of exchange and where rules of exchange follow from the construction. I will not attempt an internal account of the exchanges that actually take place or of the meanings attached to them. Perhaps our understanding of an 'object' and even of an 'exchange' is not available to the participants. All I will say about the social construction at this point is that women are transferred among households, from one patriarchal jurisdiction to another, as if they were objects of exchange. What should we think of that? Are exchanges conducted in accordance with the rules objectively just?

There are a number of possibilities here: either women have or have not played a part in the constructive work; either they agree or they do not agree to its outcomes. Or, in a language less marked by our own conceptions of moral agency and lives-as-careers, they acquiesce or do not acquiesce, go along or do not go along with the outcomes. If they have played no part and do not go along, then the exchanges cannot be described as just. We can only report on the disagreement. Or perhaps we can say, as I would be inclined to say, that the exchanges are unjust, because in this case the objects are also human subjects, capable (as tables and lives are not) of going along or not, and the resistance of the constructed object nullifies the construction. It does not matter if the resistance is inarticulate, passive, hidden, or private. So long as we can in one way or another discover it, so long as we have probable cause to believe in its reality, the social construction fails.

The women involved may or may not be able to describe themselves as persons-engaged-in-social-construction; the vocabulary that I have deployed here is presumably not their own vocabulary. But we can see how their resistance 'works' in the world and why the construction fails. The unanimity or consensus principle plays a part in explaining this failure, but something more is involved. Constructions of persons are not free—and not only in the obvious sense that we cannot make women or men into intercontinental ballistics missiles. The theory of social construction implies (some sort of) human agency and requires the recognition of women and men as agents (of some sort). We might say, looking at the idea itself as something we have made, that the construction of social-construction-with-human-agents has certain moral entailments. Among these is the right of subjective nullification, the right of the agents to refuse any given object status—as commodities, 'hands', slaves, or whatever.[2]

But what if women, for whatever reasons, actually agree that they are objects of exchange and live willingly by the rules of exchange? The phrase 'for

---

[2] A friend writes in criticism of this 'right' that some participants in *any* social system 'will resist or resent or reject the position or identity they are given . . . Not all resistance nullifies.' So we have to decide in each case whether the resistance is legitimate or not, and this requires standards that are extrinsic to the business of social construction. Yes, we will have to decide whether the resistance is just a way of avoiding particular obligations incurred by particular men or women. Agency itself cannot be denied, and promises made by agents are not subject to unilateral repudiation. But the denial of agency can always be repudiated, with the consequences described further on in the text. The right of nullification is simply the agent's right to claim her agency against any social process of objectification—and it does follow, I think, from the view of objectification as the work of human agents.

whatever reasons' conceals a problem here, which philosophers who are quick with hypothetical examples are prone to ignore. What reasons could these women possibly have? We can easily see the reasons they might have for concealing disagreement, for stifling anger, for expressing resentment only in private or only in the company of other women. But if the experience of being treated as an object of exchange is the sort of experience we think it is, and if the women being exchanged are beings like us, what reasons could they have for agreeing? If, on the other hand, the experience does not match our understanding of it, and if these hypothetical women are beings of a different sort, then what is the philosophical issue here? What can we say, why should we want to say anything at all, about experiences and beings of which we are entirely ignorant?

Still, let us accept the hypothesis in its strongest form: here is a society in which women really do agree to the construction of themselves as objects of exchange. They do not agree because they have been brainwashed, because some chemical process or some hitherto unknown social process has turned them into moral robots or made servitude a reflex—for then, whatever they did or said, it would not constitute *agreeing*. Nor do they agree because they have no choice or because they are physically coerced or because they find themselves in desperate difficulties from which agreement is the only escape—like the women who sells herself into slavery in order to feed her children. For their agreement in these circumstances would not count as the construction of themselves as objects of exchange; it would represent only a reluctant and resentful acceptance of a pretence, a role that they could not refuse or escape. We must imagine reasons of a different sort: that the exchange of women brings some benefits to at least some women (even if the benefits are much greater for men); that it is only one part of a larger pattern of relationship, fitted to a system of beliefs, symbolically represented, ritually enacted and confirmed, handed down from mothers to daughters over many generations. So women accept the construction, even participate in it. What normative consequences follow?

One possible response is that no consequences follow, for agency is inalienable. This is Rousseau's argument, not applied by him to the self-subordination of women but obviously applicable: 'To renounce liberty is to renounce being a man, to surrender the rights of humanity and even its duties . . . Such a renunciation is incompatible with man's nature; to remove all liberty from his will is to remove all morality from his acts.'[3] Since human beings are agents by nature, and necessarily responsible for the worlds they make, the surrender of agency simply does not count; it is a gesture without effect. The argument from social construction is harder than this since it cannot refer to a universal and unconditioned *moral* agency. Now agents are socially produced, themselves involved in the production. It is still true that we (with our per-

---

[3] Jean Jacques Rousseau, *The Social Contract*, trans. G. D. H. Cole (London: Dent), 9.

ceptions, understandings, theories) can recognize the-woman-who-is-an-object-of-exchange as a social construction with moral entailments only if we also recognize the same woman as a moral agent capable of agreeing (or not) to the construction. She can only be (morally) an object if she is simultaneously a subject confirming her object status. She is constituted by a contradiction—in so far as her subordinate status depends (morally) on her own agreement or acquiescence and is therefore inconsistent with subordination itself—and therein lies her freedom. She can never become just an object of exchange; the proof of this is that if she ever repudiates her object status, she is immediately and wholly a subject; the rules of exchange instantly lose their force. But so long as she confirms them (and even if her confirmation takes, as it commonly will, some other form than explicit agreement), they retain their force: she is partly an object.[4] There is nothing in the nature of a woman, or a man, that rules out contradictions of this sort. (The case is somewhat similar, I think, to Kant's means–ends polarity. We do not have to treat every person we meet, on every occasion, as an end-in-himself, for persons can agree to be means, like good civil servants who make themselves into the instruments of their fellow citizens, even surrendering some of their civil rights. But they can always resign from instrumentality.)

So long as the woman-who-is-an-object-of-exchange confirms her object status, the contradiction in her being is an objective contradiction. We can give a true account of it. Someone who claims that she is wholly an object is wrong. But so is someone who claims that she is wholly a subject (this would be roughly analogous to insisting that we must always, on every occasion, treat the civil servant as an end-in-himself). This last turn of the argument may well seem to many readers too relativistic, a surrender to what Marxists call 'false consciousness'. But once we have ruled out brainwashing and coercion, I see no morally acceptable way of denying the woman-who-is-an-object-of-exchange her own reasons and her own place in a valued way of life. That does not mean that we cannot argue with her, offering what we take to be better reasons for the repudiation of (what we take to be) object status. It does mean that, once the argument begins, she has to choose what *she* thinks are the better reasons, without any certainty as to which ones are objectively best. But we can say, and this seems to me all that we should want to say, that the choice is truly hers.

Is this not a plausible account of social construction seemingly gone awry? If nature provided a blueprint for construction, the process would not go awry as often as it does (seems to do). If something like gender equality were

---

[4] I do not mean to say more than this. I do not mean that the construction is right because the woman confirms it, only that it is effective and consequential in the moral world. Her agreement (or acquiescence) had evidentiary, not legitimizing, force. Agreement makes for rightness only within moral systems where it is understood to do that, and in such systems it is commonly hedged with qualifications as to the freedom of subjects, the knowledge available to them, and so on. Hence women-who-are-objects-of-exchange can be exchanged justly or unjustly; but the objectification itself is not justified by their agreement.

a simple entailment of the constructive process and every internal contradiction were ruled out a priori, then arguments for equality would be much easier than they are. When we encounter a complex set of social meanings, we enter a moral world, and it is no tribute to the creators of that world to deny its reality. Social meanings are constructed, accepted, and revised for reasons, and we have to engage those reasons. When we engage them from the outside, as in the case of women-who-are-objects-of-exchange, we are like missionaries preaching a new way of life to the natives, and we would do best, morally and politically, to try to work out what they find valuable or satisfying in their old way of life. More often, and more importantly, criticism of the old ways comes from within, as the result of long processes of social change. For the construction of objects-with-meanings and thus of moral worlds goes on and on; it is a continuous process in which we are all engaged. Conservatives try to freeze the process, but that effort is only one more instance of constructive activity (it has its reasons), one more expression of human agency. Criticism is no different in form.

Consider, for example, the construction of lives-that-are-careers-that-are-open-to-talents in a society where women are still objects of exchange. Over a period of time, institutions and practices take shape that make it possible (or necessary) for some members of the society, mostly men, to plan their lives — and, over the same period, lives of this sort are discussed, argued about, rendered meaningful. In the course of this process women will find that they have a new reason to repudiate their object status, for only by doing so can they undertake careers of their own. Some of them will seize upon this reason, and then more and more of them; at some point women-who-are-objects-of-exchange will be relics, sad memories, their agreement to subordination hard to understand. If a few people try to act out the rules of exchange, they will appear quixotic, not so much defenders of old ways as fools of time. In similar fashion, an archaeological guide might say to us: 'These were the holy altars of Xanadu, in the days when holiness reigned in the city.'

[4]

I come back at last to my initial reservations. The kind of objectivity that I have attached to social meanings is probably not the kind that philosophers seeking objectivity are interested in. They are in search of things as they really are or as they must be. But I know very little about things as they really are, social construction apart. It is true (we can give objective reports) that particular constructions are reiterated in one social setting after another. The extent of the reiteration and the reasons for it — these are empirical matters. Exactly what evidence would lead us to say that such and such a construction could not or should never be otherwise, I do not know; in any case, that sort of evidence will not often be available. Interesting objects, all the more complex constructions, can always be otherwise. Tables need not be altars; lives need not be careers.

But is it not objectively true that meanings are always constructed? Men and women who claimed to have discovered meaning in nature, say, would surely be misreporting (misconstructing) their own activity—as if they were telling us that it was not Adam but God who named the animals. Even if no particular meaning were objectively true or right or necessary, it would still be the case that the construction of meaning is a real process. Men and women really have made tables into holy altars and lives into careers. This has been the presupposition of my argument, and I have even pointed to its possible moral entailments; I do not want to run away from it now. But it is a strange 'objectivity' that leaves us adrift in a world we can only make and remake and never finish making or make correctly.

Note: In this paper I have tried to sketch an account of 'social meaning' that might underpin and uphold the theory of distributive justice presented a few years ago in my book *Spheres of Justice* (New York: Basic Books, 1983). My views on objectivity have been guided, stimulated, and provoked by recent philosophical and anthropological work that I can only acknowledge in a general way by listing a few crucial books: Hilary Putnam, *Reason, Truth and History* (Cambridge: Cambridge University Press, 1981) and *The Many Faces of Realism* (La Salle, IU.: Open Court, 1988); Nelson Goodman, *Ways of Worldmaking* (Indianapolis: Hackett, 1978); Thomas Nagel, *The View from Nowhere* (Oxford: Oxford University Press, 1986); Clifford Geertz, *Local Knowledge* (New York: Basic Books, 1986); and the essays collected in *Rationality and Relativism*, ed. Martin Hollis and Steven Lukes (Cambridge, Mass.: MIT Press, 1982) and in *Objectivity and Cultural Divergence*, ed. S.C. Brown (Cambridge: Cambridge University Press, 1984). I am grateful to Ruth Anna Putnam, Alan Wertheimer, John Goldberg, and Thomas Nagel, who read the paper in an earlier version and told me what was wrong with it. Martha Nussbaum suggested that I write the paper and provided its title, but she is responsible only for its existence, not for its argument.

Michael Walzer: Objectivity and Social Meaning

Commentary by Ruth Anna Putnam

That social meanings lack objectivity, that we are 'adrift' in the world, matters
to Michael Walzer because it threatens to deprive us of any foundation from
which to criticize injustice in cultures other than our own. So Walzer uses
the theory of the social construction of meanings (values) itself to provide
a new foundation for intercultural social criticism. I do not think that that
attempt is successful; nor do I think it is needed. I shall modify Walzer's initial
account of objectivity, I shall argue that the modified notion is the only notion
of objectivity we need, and I shall conclude that we are not adrift in the world
although we do keep making and remaking it.

Walzer's first sense of 'objective' is this: 'objectivity hangs (somehow) on the
accommodation of the object by a knowing, inquiring subject.' What is involved
here is a double accommodation. First, the conceptual scheme itself must
accommodate the world: someone using the scheme 'friends, enemies, reading
matter, and edible plants' is said to 'get the table wrong (objectively wrong),
or he would miss the table entirely, and deny its reality, and that would be
a merely idiosyncratic (subjective) denial'. In contrast, 'the scientific perception
of the world . . . makes the most insistent claim these days to be called an
objective perception'. Second, given the framework, we cannot just decide
how things are, our beliefs must accommodate the object.

The second point is, of course, correct. Given a conceptual scheme which
allows for the distinction, we can distinguish between objective beliefs and
all sorts of other things: imaginative constructions, illusions and hallucinations,
neurotic fantasies, etc. In so far as these can be communicated at all, they
depend on the shared conceptual scheme relative to which they fail to be
objectively true.

But what is objectively true relative to one scheme may be objectively
false relative to another—relative to the common-sense scheme this table
is solid, relative to some scientific scheme it consists mainly of empty
space. We, not individually but as communities, make and modify conceptual schemes; we do so in response to concerns which we have. So we have to
specify the concerns relative to which a particular scheme accommodates the
world. And we should remember that we never stand outside all conceptual
schemes.

Standing within the common-sense scheme, we see that objective truth
relative to it is most likely to be achieved by disinterested inquiry. That does
not mean that the scientific schemes with which we replace the common-sense
scheme as a result of these inquiries are more objective *sans phrase*. We can
say only that given certain cognitive concerns, one or another scientific scheme

is best; but none of these schemes can be called 'the scientific perception of the world'.

So I shall rephrase Walzer's first account of objectivity as follows: A belief (perception, recognition, understanding) is objective relative to a conceptual framework, if its truth or falsehood relative to that framework depends on how the world is rather than on what the knower thinks it is.

Walzer holds that his first concept of objectivity 'works, more or less well, for simple objects-in-the-world' but wonders whether 'it works at all for objects to which we assign use and value, objects that carry "social meanings"'. In contrast, I shall argue that this notion (at least as I have reformulated it) is the only notion of objectivity he needs. I am inclined to reject any dichotomy between objects-that-carry-social-meaning and simple-objects-in-the-world, or between objects that entail moral legislation and objects than do not. There is a difference between trees and tables: human beings make tables out of trees, human beings do not, in that sense of 'make', make trees; there is no comparable difference between tables and altars. We recognize trees as trees — we have the concept 'tree' — because they are important to us, important as resources and, sometimes, as obstacles. Trees answer many of our needs, including the needs which we meet by making tables. We make and recognize tables because we need objects with flat surfaces to put things on, to work on, to consecrate as altars. Finally, trees, tables, and altars entail moral legislation: trees are to be protected from various kinds of blight, tables are not to be chopped up for firewood, altars are not to be used as desks, etc.

Walzer points out that some social constructions (e.g. food) are reiterated in culture after culture and encourages us to think of the list of reiterated constructions 'as a universal and objective morality', not, to be sure, objective absolutely but 'relative to social construction where construction repetitively takes the same form'. Such universal constructions can be, he thinks, explained naturalistically; they respond to deep and pervasive human needs and give rise to a (to be sure, rebuttable) presumption that they best meet these needs. Conversely, objects/meanings which exist in only one, or a few, cultures may not be necessary for human life. So universal values, although socially constructed, appear to Walzer to be more like simple objects-in-the-world, for they accommodate the world that includes our needs, while the social constructions that are peculiar to a single culture are 'free'. And so universality of construction appears to him as a new sort of objectivity.

From my perspective, no new sense of objectivity is required. To say that interculturally shared values — food, for example — are objective while those peculiar to one culture — altar-to-the-Virgin or freedom-of-the-press — are not is to say that most reports about something being food are objectively true or false relative to the intersection of most communities' conceptual schemes while reports about altars-to-the-Virgin or freedom-of-the-press are not simply because these concepts are not found in that intersection. But then objectivity is still the same old thing; why should the extent of agreement, or the extent of the possibility of agreement, change the ontological or epistemological status of a thing?

Interculturality is a form of intersubjectivity. Intersubjectivity is a familiar criterion of objectivity. A perception or judgement can be more or less widely shared; the more widely it is shared, the more objective it is said to be. We suspect perceptions and judgements that are tainted by interests, fears, and other subjective influences, we distrust what is seen from one point of view only. Beliefs so formed, we think, accommodate the knower more than the object. But in opting for intersubjectivity we are the losers. Intersubjectivity is not achieved by superposition of subjective views: that results in cubist paintings but is not a way in which we can manage to see the world, so why should it be an objective picture? Intersubjectivity can also be achieved by eliminating whatever fails to agree with all the subjective perceptions; that results in a thin and transparent rather than a thick and dense moral world; it results in the cold, clean world of science rather than the warm, messy world of everyday life. Does that really accommodate the object (the world and us, us-in-the-world) best?

The thickness and complexity of our moral world are given us by constructions that are peculiar to a given culture. Walzer's paper is essentially a search for an objectivity suitable to these. The question he asks is, I think, this: take a set of concepts that are peculiar to a given culture—a particular notion of the divine, of altars holy to a divine being, of worship required by that divinity, of behaviour that consecrates tables into altars, and of behaviour that would reverse that transformation. When we now say that a certain table is objectively an altar, are we 'accommodating the object'? Since there is nothing about tables that requires some of them to become altars, how could 'altar' accommodate or fail to accommodate a particular table? I would like to suggest that that is the wrong question; 'altar' accommodates the object table-which-has-undergone-the-prescribed-consecration-rites. That is why for both the members of the culture in question, and the anthropologist who studies them, the thing is objectively an altar. For the members of the culture, the complex I have described is part of their common-sense world; for the anthropologist that same complex is part of the culture under investigation.

Still, there are such things as religious strife. Because of that possibility, Walzer says that 'Social constructions must reflect a . . . consensus if there is ever to be an unqualified objectivity in our reports about them'. Why so? Dissension in the culture is no obstacle to objectivity in the reports of 'outsiders', of anthropologists; they can describe divided opinions as easily, as objectively, as unanimity. Dissension casts a shadow over the reports of 'insiders' only. Recognizing a particular table as an altar, treating it as altars in that culture are to be treated, will be a matter of course only if there exists some kind of religious consensus in that culture, a consensus which may range from everyone worshipping the same deity or deities in the same way to everyone respecting each other's different worship of different deities. But what happens when conflicting faith communities exist within one society in which there is no mutual respect? The members of each faith community will say of their altars that they are objectively altars, and of those of other communities perhaps that they are mere tables, perhaps (therein lie the roots of religious strife) that they are abominations. The members of each group maintain that their perspective somehow accommodates the world while that of their opponents does not. Walzer maintains, in effect, that the claims of both groups are subjective. I want to take issue with that claim.

To be sure, there is nothing in the nature of a table that necessitates its becoming an altar; but there is something in our nature that gives rise to a sense of awe and that in turn frequently gives rise to the construction of altars. So one can ask whether altars (of religions in general, or of a particular religion) and the ways of life in which they are embedded accommodate the sense of awe and the need to give it expression. More radically, one can ask whether the sense of awe and all it brings in its train is a good thing in human lives or whether our children would be better off were we to raise them so as to be immune to it. Of course, those living within and affirming a religious tradition will not ask these questions; but my point here is simply that just as some conceptual schemes are worse than others because they frustrate our cognitive needs—they misclassify tables or deny their existence—so some sets of social meanings are worse than others because they frustrate other human needs—they misclassify not only objects but human beings, their needs, their emotions, etc., or they deny the existence or legitimacy of these. Social meanings are deeply embedded in our conceptual schemes—even scientific schemes involve the notions of relevance, warrant, truth, etc.—and value judgements are not neatly separable from descriptions. One has to know facts to know whether something is an altar, whether a certain type of behaviour is nepotism; but saying that something is an altar or nepotism is at the same time to evaluate and to prescribe. Walzer is exactly right when he says that these objects carry social meaning; he is wrong when he fears that that deprives them of a sort of objectivity that other things have.

Let me then return briefly to the contending groups, Protestants and Catholics, or, more dramatically, Christians and Aztecs. How could the Christians say (how can we say) that it was wrong for the Aztecs to practise human sacrifice unless they (we) recognize their practice as sacrifice? For if they say, simply, that the Aztecs committed murder, they have obviously failed to understand the Aztec practice. (Notice that even a pacifist does not say, simply, that soldiers are murderers, though he holds that taking a human life while fighting as a soldier is just as heinous, just as sinful, as ordinary murder, perhaps even more so.) But if they recognize the practice as sacrifice, on what basis may they criticize it? This raises the issue of the possibility of social criticism.

There is no puzzle concerning the possibility of social criticism from within, though I am puzzled by Walzer's claim that it depends on objective values but is not itself objective. I shall let that pass. There is a puzzle concerning criticism from without. Since there is no Archimedean point from which to raise such a critique, we can only offer it from within our own culture. But we are wary of cultural imperialism, of attempting to impose our way of life on others who are doing very well by their own lights; and, in some cases and in some sense, even by ours—I am thinking of the Amish that Hilary Putnam mentioned. There is also the sheer fact that often we do not understand one another; William James talks about that in his wonderful little essay 'On a Certain Blindness in Human Beings' (James, 1983). There is, finally, the fact that some things done in another culture strike us as so wrong that we would be doing wrong were we not to criticize it, where criticism is the least we can do and a precondition of doing anything more.

It is this last that prompts Walzer to develop his arguments against the practices of the patriarchal society, the society which passes women from one male jurisdiction to another and does not recognize women as agents. There are two possibilities: either the women accept the construction or they do not. If they do not, then the resources for internal criticism are at hand; but in both cases Walzer is prepared to offer critical arguments from 'outside', from his, and that means our, perspective. I want to look at these arguments.

In the case where the women do not accept their construction as objects, Walzer says, 'The theory of social construction implies (some sort of) human agency and requires the recognition of women and men as agents (of some sort) . . . the construction of social-construction-with-human-agents has certain moral entailments. Among these is . . . the right of the agents to refuse any given object status.' I find this argument puzzling. Of course, if one construes morality as a social construction, then one construes human beings as agents, although I do not see how it follows that one construes *all* human beings as agents; but I shall put that concern aside. Instead I wish to inquire after the point of the argument. How is this argument supposed to enable us to take sides *inter*culturally with the women in their *intra*cultural struggle? How is it supposed to enable us to rebut charges of cultural imperialism and to claim a transcultural objectivity for our view?

Walzer would reply, I think, that the claim that meanings are socially constructed is objectively true, that is, part of the scientific world view. If it follows from this that human beings are agents, then that claim too is objectively true in this strong sense of objective. And if it follows from this that they are not to be construed as mere objects, then that too will be objective, as objective as anything can be. But if, as I have argued, the scientific perspective does not carry with it a particularly robust objectivity—and here we deal not even with the hard sciences but with quite speculative explanations of very complex social phenomena—then Walzer's argument is simply one more liberal argument against patriarchy and the charge of cultural imperialism remains undefeated if the argument is to be exported to other cultures. But, of course, better a little cultural imperialism than a lot of oppression.

When Walzer considers a society in which women accept themselves as objects of exchange, his argument becomes more complicated and I become more puzzled. In this situation the woman is said to be constituted by a contradiction: on the one hand, she is (objectively) an object of exchange, on the other hand, the construction succeeds only if she is (objectively) a moral agent capable of consenting (or not) to the construction. But there is no contradiction here: she is an object of exchange relative to the world view of her society, which she shares. She is a moral agent relative to Michael Walzer's world view, which she does not share. There is no more contradiction here than in saying that this table is solid (in the common-sense view) and that it is mostly empty space (from the viewpoint of quantum physics).

Perhaps I am obtuse. Perhaps the 'objective contradiction' in this woman's being, which exists as long as she affirms her object status, consists in this: the woman cannot simultaneously think of herself as an object and as someone who agrees to/disagrees with anything. But if she cannot do that, neither can Walzer. And if he cannot do it, how can he say: 'I see no morally acceptable way of denying the-woman-who-is-an-object-of-exchange her own reasons and her own place in a valued way of life'? How can he say that 'the choice is (truly) hers'? I am genuinely puzzled. This seems a far too complicated way of saying that before we preach a new way of life to the natives 'we would do best, morally and politically, to try to work out what they find valuable or satisfying in their old way of life'. If we regard human beings as free and equal moral agents, then for us it follows that we are to respect them, that we are not to impose our morality on them but rather to reason with them. In every society some human beings are regarded as more than mere objects; that seems to me to be a basis from which one might begin to argue 'from inside' against patriarchy and other forms of oppression and enslavement. This is the sense in which intercultural meanings are important: they enable us to engage in intercultural criticism, to structure it as internal criticism. Or so it would be if ways of life were always based on consensus. When they are not, when there is oppression, when the dictator, or the oppressing group, is not amenable to reason, we face a different problem: the problem of how to deal with evil. Nothing is gained by calling it 'objective evil', and there is no single answer.

Recognizing that there is only one kind of objectivity, that all criticism is internal but that the resources for such criticism are greater than they would be if there were a dichotomy of simple-objects-in-the-world and objects-which-carry-social-meanings, should alleviate the feeling of being 'adrift in a world we can only make and remake and never finish making or make correctly'. We are not adrift, we are anchored by the world, by our needs, by how we have understood and made the world until now.

I want to conclude by saying briefly how all this connects with the concerns of this volume, that is, with the quality of life. Certain needs are universal, and one can establish 'scientifically' what will satisfy these needs—for example, the quantity and kind of food that will keep a person not just alive but healthy.

As soon as we go beyond this, disagreements arise. What is seen as a necessity in one society—universal education up to a fairly advanced level, for example—is regarded as a luxury in another; what is valued highly here is perceived as a threat to a valued way of life there—pluralism, for instance. Measures that seem absolutely essential if the quality of life is to improve, such as limiting family size, may run counter to fundamental values. I take it that Michael Walzer and I agree that these are matters about which we should reason together; but because I believe that one cannot separate facts and values, cognitive and other concerns, because I believe that our descriptions and our evaluations of features of the world are inextricably intertwined, I am more optimistic than he concerning the possibilities of cross-cultural agreement. We live in one world not only because of the extensive interdependence of our economies, not only because all of us together may become victims of ecological or nuclear disasters; we live in one world because to a large extent we share our understanding of that world, and on the basis of that shared understanding we can come to further agreements.

BIBLIOGRAPHY

JAMES , WILLIAM (1983). *Talks to Teachers on Psychology and to Students on Some of Life's Ideals*. Cambridge, Mass.: Harvard University Press.

Value, Desire, and Quality of Life

Thomas Scanlon

The subject of this volume, the quality of life, suffers from an embarrassing richness of possibilities. First, there are a number of related but distinct questions with which this notion might be associated. What kinds of circumstances provide good conditions under which to live? What makes a life a good one for the person who lives it? What makes a life a valuable one (a good thing, as Sidgwick put it, 'from the point of view of the universe')? Second, each of these questions admits of different interpretations and a number of possible answers. Finally, there are a number of different standpoints from which the question of what makes a person's life better, in any one of these senses, might be asked. It might be asked from the point of view of that person herself, who is trying to decide how to live. It might be asked from the point of view of a benevolent third party, a friend or parent, who wants to make the person's life better. It might be asked, in a more general sense, from the point of view of a conscientious administrator, whose duty it is to act in the interest of some group of people. It might be asked, again in this more general sense, by a conscientious voter who is trying to decide which policy to vote for and defend in public debate and wants to support the policy which will improve the quality of life in her society. Finally, the question of what makes a person's life better also arises in the course of moral argument about what our duties and obligations are, since these duties and obligations are surely determined, at least to some extent, by what is needed to make people's lives better or, at least, to prevent them from being made worse.

It is important to keep in mind not only the question we are asking but also the point of view from which it is being asked, since the plausibility of various answers can be strongly influenced by the point of view of the question, and unnoticed shifts in point of view can drive us back and forth between different answers. I assume that in discussing the quality of life our main concern is with the second question listed above, 'What makes a life a good one for the person who lives it?' and perhaps with the closely related question 'What circumstances constitute good conditions under which to live?' These questions have priority in so far as we see improvement in the quality of people's lives as morally and politically important because of the benefit it brings *to them*.

I have mentioned the third question, the question of value, primarily to distinguish it from these two, with the intention of then leaving it aside. This question admits of several interpretations, each of which is somewhat tangential to what I take to be our present concern. One might be moved to improve the quality of a person's life by the thought that one would thereby make it more valuable—

that the world containing this life would become a better world. But this aim seems, to me at least, to depart from the concern with what we owe *to the person* which lies at the heart of morality and justice. An individual might try to make her own life more valuable, in a slightly different sense, by making herself a morally better person or by aiming at other things that she takes to be worthwhile. This is certainly a laudable aim, but making people's lives more valuable in this sense does not seem to me to be part of the concern with others which lies behind our inquiry into the quality of life. (That it is not is a consequence of the point of view from which the question is normally asked, a matter I will discuss in Section 2.)

Several answers—or, rather, several types of answer—to the question of what makes a life good for the person who lives it have become established in the literature as the standard alternatives to be considered. Derek Parfit,[1] for example, distinguishes hedonistic theories, desire theories, and objective list theories. The defining mark of hedonistic theories is what James Griffin[2] has called the 'experience requirement', that is, the thesis that nothing can affect the quality of a life except by affecting the experience of living that life. A hedonistic theory needs to be filled out by specifying how the quality of this experience is to be judged. This has normally been done by specifying certain states (such as pleasure or happiness, understood in a particular way) as the ones which make a life better or worse. An alternative is to adopt the view that the experience of living a life is made better by the presence in it of those mental states, whatever they may be, which the person living the life wants to have, and is made worse by containing those states which that person would prefer to avoid. Parfit calls this alternative view 'preference hedonism'.

Desire theories reject the experience requirement and allow that a person's life can be made better and worse not only by changes in that person's states of consciousness but also by occurrences elsewhere in the world which fulfil that person's preferences. The most general view of this kind—it might be called the 'unrestricted actual desire theory'—holds that the quality of a person's life at a given time[3] is measured by the degree to which the preferences which he or she has at that time are fulfilled. Since a person can in principle have preferences about anything whatever—about the number of moons the planet Uranus has, about the colour of Frank Sinatra's eyes, or about the sexual mores of people whom they will never see—this theory makes the determinants of the quality of a person's life very wide indeed. Other forms of desire theory restrict the range of these determinants. Sometimes this is done by restricting the objects

I am grateful to Sissela Bok and James Griffin for their helpful comments on the version of this paper presented at the Helsinki conference.

[1] Parfit, 1984: app. I.

[2] Griffin, 1986: 13.

[3] I set aside here the problem of how this view can be extended into an account of the quality of a person's life as a whole which allows for the fact that preferences change over time. The difficulty of making this extension has been emphasized by Richard Brandt. See Brandt, 1979: ch. 13.

which the relevant preferences can have. What Parfit calls the 'success theory', for example, counts only preferences which are, intuitively, 'about the person's own life'.[4] Other forms of desire theory restrict attention to preferences which have a certain sort of basis. Harsanyi,[5] for example, excludes preferences based on a person's moral beliefs, as well as what he calls 'anti-social' preferences, and Griffin proposes what he calls an 'informed desire theory', which would make the quality of people's lives depend only on the fulfilment of those desires that they would have if they 'appreciated the true nature' of the objects of those desires.[6]

What is the rationale for these departures from the unrestricted actual desire theory? Parfit's success theory might be proposed simply as a way of bringing the desire theory closer to the ordinary meaning of the phrase 'quality of a person's life'. It sounds odd to say that if I happen to have a desire that Uranus should have six moons, then my life will be better if it turns out that this is in fact the case. (Assuming, of course, that I am not an astronomer and have not invested any effort in trying to determine how many moons Uranus has or in developing cosmological theories which would be confirmed or disconfirmed by such a fact.)

A second reason for such restrictions is provided by the aim of describing a concept of well-being which preserves the idea that any improvement in a person's well-being has positive ethical value. The unrestricted actual desire theory fails to preserve this idea, since there are many preferences whose fulfilment appears to have no weight in determining what others should do. If, for example, I were to have a strong preference about how people quite remote from me in time and space lead their personal lives, this preference would give rise to no reason at all—not even a reason which is outweighed by other considerations—why they should behave in the way that I prefer. So the unrestricted actual desire theory must be scaled back if the direct ethical significance of well-being is to be preserved, and I believe that most modifications of the desire theory are motivated by similar ethical concerns.[7]

The appeal of desire theories also derives in large part from ethical ideas. Harsanyi, for example, bases his preference utilitarianism on what he calls the 'principle of preference autonomy', 'the principle that, in deciding what is good and what is bad for a given individual, the ultimate criterion can only be his own wants and his own preferences'.[8] Some of the modified desire theories mentioned above involve departures from this principle, however. The exclusion of preferences based on moral beliefs may not be such a departure: since a person who wants a certain thing to happen because he considers it morally right is

[4] Parfit, 1984: 494. For a similar proposal see Griffin, 1986: 13.
[5] See Harsanyi, 1977: 56.
[6] Griffin, 1986: 11.
[7] I argue elsewhere that this is true of the modifications which Harsanyi proposes. See Scanlon, 1991.
[8] Harsanyi, 1977: 55.

unlikely to take its happening as a benefit *to him*, the preferences excluded by this restriction may not represent a person's view about 'what is good and bad for him'. The same may be true of the preferences excluded by the success theory. But the informed desire theory is in stronger tension with the principle of preference autonomy, since it allows us to say that some of a person's firmly held preferences about his life are simply mistaken. For this reason and some others, I believe that the informed desire theory should probably not be counted as a form of desire theory at all but assigned instead to Parfit's third category, which he calls objective list theories. I will return to this question after I have discussed that category in more detail.

Of the three categories listed by Parfit, the category of objective list theories is least closely tied to a specific and well-known view of what makes a life go better. (There is no familiar theory of which it is the generalization in the way that the category of mental state theories is a generalization of hedonism.) None the less, this category seems to me to contain all the most plausible candidates for an account of what makes a life better. The name, 'objective list theory', is doubly unfortunate. The term 'list' suggests a kind of arbitrariness (just what its critics would charge), and 'objective' suggests a kind of rigidity (as if the same things must be valuable for everyone), as well as inviting a host of difficult questions about the various forms of objectivity and the possibility of values being objective in any of these senses. One might think the name had been coined by opponents of views of this kind.[9]

But while its name may seem to imply a controversial claim to objectivity, this is not what is essential to the category as I understand it. What is essential is that these are theories according to which an assessment of a person's well-being involves a substantive judgement about what things make life better, a judgement which may conflict with that of the person whose well-being is in question. This is in contrast to the central idea of desire theories, according to which substantive questions about which things are actually good are (at least within limits) deferred to the judgement of the person whose well-being is being assessed. According to the unrestricted actual desire theory, for example, if a person cares as much about A as about B then A contributes as much to that person's well-being as B does, and if a person cares more about A than about B then A contributes more to that person's well-being. Other desire theories depart from this principle in some cases, but it remains the central touchstone of theories of this type. Since this seems to amount to the claim that standards of well-being are subjective, it is tempting to apply the contrasting term 'objective' to any view which rejects this principle. But this now seems to me a mistake.[10] I am not sure what the best label is for theories in Parfit's third

---

[9] Though Parfit is not such an opponent, and I myself bear some responsibility here since I have also used the term 'objective' in arguing for the necessity of a view of this kind. See Scanlon, 1975.

[10] In Scanlon 1975: 658, I wrote, 'By an objective criterion I mean a criterion which provides a basis for appraisal of a person's well-being which is independent of that person's tastes and interests.'

category, but I suggest that we call them 'substantive good theories' since, unlike desire theories, they are based on substantive claims about what goods, conditions, and opportunities make life better.

Hedonism in its classical form,[11] according to which pleasure is the only thing which contributes to the quality of a life, counts as a substantive good theory on the definition I have offered. This may seem odd. Hedonism may seem more akin to desire theories because it bases well-being in certain mental states and because it introduces an important element of subjectivity into the determination of well-being since different people receive pleasure from, and are made happy by, different things. But both of these reasons for associating the two views with one another are mistaken. Both views involve 'mental states', but they do so in very different ways. Hedonism takes certain mental states to be the only things of ultimate value. Desire theories count things as valuable if they are the objects of the appropriate 'mental states' or attitudes, but the things valued need not be mental states and the attitudes which confer value need not themselves be valuable.

The mistake underlying the second reason for linking hedonism and desire theories is, for present purposes, more important. What Parfit calls objective list theories of well-being, and I am calling substantive good theories, have often been accused of excessive rigidity, as if they had to prescribe the same goods for everyone without regard for individual differences. Griffin, for example, cites 'flexibility' as an important advantage of his informed desire theory, and as his main reason for classifying it as a form of *desire* theory:

The informed-desire account can allow that the values on the list (enjoyment, accomplishment, autonomy, etc.) are values for everyone, but it also allows that there may be very special persons for whom any value on the list (say, accomplishment), though valuable for them as for everybody, conflicts enough with another value (say, freedom from anxiety) for it not, all things considered, to be valuable for them to have.[12]

As Griffin goes on to acknowledge, however, substantive good theories can also allow for this kind of variation. They can count various kinds of enjoyment among those things that can make a life better, and can also recognize that different people experience these forms of enjoyment under different

---

This formulation now seems unfortunate in several respects. As I have said, the term 'objective' was not apt. In addition, I should have made it clearer that by 'independent of' I meant 'not wholly dependent on'. I did not mean to suggest that a criterion of the kind I had in mind would always ignore differences in individual tastes and interests, but only that it did not have to be governed by them.

[11] 'Preference hedonism' may seem a different case since, while it retains the experience requirement, it leaves the qualities of experience which make life better to be determined by each individual's own preferences. It could thus be classed as a restricted desire theory. But the restriction in question — excluding everything other than the quality of a person's experience — is sufficiently strong that I would count preference hedonism too as a substantive good theory. Note that it could be arrived at from the informed desire theory only by adding a strong claim about what it is in fact rational to desire.

[12] Griffin, 1986: 33.

circumstances, and are capable of experiencing them to different degrees and at different costs. Consequently, a substantive good theory can allow for the fact that the best lives for different people may contain quite different ingredients. Griffin observes that a substantive good theory of this kind becomes 'very hard to distinguish from the informed-desire approach'.[13] As he also suggests, a decision about how to classify the resulting theory is apt to turn on the question of priority between value and desire. As I see it, according to a desire theory, when something makes life better this is always because that thing satisfies some desire. Substantive good theories can allow for the fact that this is sometimes the case— it is sometimes a good thing simply to be getting what you want—but according to these theories being an object of desire is not in general what makes things valuable.

Someone who accepts a substantive good theory, according to which certain goods make a life better, will no doubt also believe that these goods are the objects of informed desire—that they would be desired by people who fully appreciated their nature and the nature of life. But the order of explanation here is likely to be from the belief that these things are genuine goods to the conclusion that people will, if informed, come to desire them. The fact that certain things are the object of desires which are, as far as we can tell, informed desires, can be a reason for believing these things to be goods. But 'reason' here is a matter of evidence—of reason for believing—not a ground of value of the sort which the original desire theory was, I am assuming, supposed to supply.

This assumption raises a general question about what a philosophical theory of well-being is supposed to do. One objective of such a theory is to describe a class of things which make lives better, perhaps also offering some account of the kind of case that can be made for the claim that a thing belongs to this class. A second, more ambitious objective is to give a general account of the ground of this kind of value—a general account of what it is that makes a life a good life. I take it that classical hedonism was supposed to do both of these things, and I have been assuming that the unrestricted actual desire theory also aimed at the second of these objectives at least as much as the first; that is, that it sought to explain what makes things valuable at least as much as to identify any particular group of things as desirable.

If I am right about this then the introduction of the adjective 'informed', which looks like a small qualification, in fact represents a significant departure. Informed desires are desires which are responsive to the relevant features of their objects. By acknowledging the importance of these features in making the objects good (and making the desires for them appropriate rather than mistaken), this theory parts company sharply with the unrestricted actual desire theory, according to which it was the *satisfaction of desire* which made things good.[14]

---

13 Ibid.
14 Compare Gilbert Harman's observation about the tendency of emotivism to evolve into ideal observer theory in Harman, 1977:ch. 4.

A substantive good theory could have both of the theoretical objectives mentioned above, but the most plausible theories of this kind aim only at the first. Such a theory claims that certain diverse goods make a life better, and it will be prepared to defend this claim by offering reasons (possibly different in each case) about why these things are desirable. But it may offer no unified account of what makes things good. It seems to me unlikely that there is any such account to be had, since it is unlikely that there are any good-making properties which are common to all good things. If this is correct, then there will be no general theory of goodness in between, on the one hand, a purely formal analysis of 'good' such as 'answers to certain interests' or 'has the properties it is rational to want in a thing of that kind'[15] and, on the other hand, diverse arguments about why various properties of particular objects make those objects good.

[2]

Let me turn now to a consideration of the various points of view which I have distinguished above. I have long been sceptical about desire theories as an account of well-being appropriate for moral theory, but I have supposed that there is more to be said for them as an account appropriate for individual decision-making. This seems to me to be a mistake, and I now believe that desire theories should also be rejected as accounts of well-being appropriate to the first-person point of view. I will argue against such theories in the following way. The fact that an outcome would improve a person's well-being ('make his or her life go better') provides that person with a reason (other things being equal) for wanting that outcome to occur. If a desire theory were correct as an account of well-being, then, the fact that a certain outcome would fulfil a person's desire would be a basic reason for that person to want that thing to come about. But desires do not provide basic reasons of this sort, at least not in non-trivial cases. The fact that we prefer a certain outcome can provide us with a serious reason for bringing it about 'for our own sake'. But when it does, this reason is either a reason of the sort described by a mental state view such as hedonism or a reason based on some other notion of substantive good rather than a reason grounded simply in the fact of desire, in the way that desire theories would require. To see this we need to consider each of these cases in a little more detail.

In many cases, the fact that I desire a certain outcome provides me with a reason for trying to bring it about because the presence of that desire indicates that the outcome will be pleasant or enjoyable for me. I can have reasons of this kind, for example, for ordering fish rather than tortellini, for climbing to the top of a hill, or for wearing a particular necktie. The end sought in these cases is the experience or mental state which the object or activity in question

---

[15] Analyses such as those offered in Ziff, 1960: ch. 6; and Rawls, 1971: ch. 7.

is expected to produce, and the desire is an indication that this state is likely to be forthcoming (as well as, perhaps, a factor in producing it).

In other cases, my desire that a certain state of affairs should obtain reflects my judgement that that state of affairs is desirable for some reason other than the mere fact that I prefer it: it may reflect, for example, my judgement that state of affairs is morally good, or that it is in my overall interest, or that it is a good thing of its kind. This represents, I believe, the most common kind of case in which preferences are cited as reasons for action; the fact that I prefer a certain outcome *is* a reason for action in such a case, but not a fundamental one. My preferences are not the source of reasons but reflect conclusions based on reasons of other kinds. There are, of course, other cases in which I might say that the only reason I have for doing or choosing something is simply that 'I prefer it'. But these cases are trivial ones rather than examples of the typical form of rational decision-making.

My conclusion, then, is that when statements of preference or desire represent serious reasons for action they can be understood in one of the two ways just described: either as stating reasons which are at base hedonistic or as stating judgements of desirability reached on other grounds. What convinces me of this conclusion is chiefly the fact that I am unable to think of any clear cases in which preferences provide non-trivial reasons for action which are not of these two kinds.

Additional support for this conclusion is provided by its ability to explain the familiar fact, emphasized by Richard Brandt, that past desires do not in general provide reasons for action and that their fulfilment does not in itself contribute to a person's well-being. Brandt[16] gives the example of a man who, as a child, desired intensely that he go for a roller-coaster ride on his fiftieth birthday. As the date approaches, however, the man finds that he no longer enjoys roller-coaster rides and that there are many other things he would rather do to celebrate his birthday. Surely, Brandt claims, the fact that he once had this desire gives the man no reason to take a roller coaster ride which he will not enjoy, nor would taking the ride contribute towards making his life better on the whole just because it is something which he once desired.

Brandt's conclusion is that the desire theory should be rejected as an account of what makes a person's life go better, and that a mental state theory should be adopted instead. But these examples provide no reason to move to a mental state theory rather than a substantive good theory, particularly when we bear in mind the fact that any plausible substantive good theory will count agreeable mental states among the things which can make a life better. If some such theory is correct, then the conclusion arrived at above—namely that the reason-giving force of preferences always depends either on the pleasure which their fulfilment will bring or on the truth of the substantive judgements of desirability which they reflect—provides a systematic explanation of the phenomenon which Brandt describes.

[16] Brandt, 1979: ch. 13.

On the one hand, the fulfilment of desires that are no longer held brings no pleasure or satisfaction. On the other, in so far as the reason-giving force of past preferences depends on substantive judgements of desirability, they obviously lose this force when those judgements are rejected. That is to say, the agent will no longer regard these preferences as providing reasons for action. Of course it may be that the agent's original judgement of desirability was correct, and he or she is therefore wrong to reject it. In that case the fulfilment of the original preference might indeed make the agent's life better and so, in a sense, he or she may have reason to seek its fulfilment. But the force of that reason, if it is one, has nothing to do with the fact that the agent once had this preference.

Similar remarks apply to future preferences. When one agrees with the judgement of desirability that a future preference will express, one will believe that one has reason now to promote the fulfilment of that preference. So, for example, a person who believes that in ten years she will have children for whom she will want to provide a good education, and who believes now that educating one's children is very important, will believe that she now has a reason to promote that future goal. But the future preference itself is doing little work in such cases; what matters is the underlying judgement of desirability. The cases in which the fact of future preference is itself most clearly fundamental fit the hedonistic (or, more broadly, experiential) model: our concern in these cases is to bring ourselves the pleasant experience of having these preferences fulfilled or to spare ourselves the unpleasant experience of having them frustrated. For example, a 19-year-old who cares nothing for old family photographs but believes that in thirty years he will feel quite different about such things has reason to save them simply in order to bring himself pleasure, and avoid sadness, in the future.

It is difficult to come up with a plausible example in which future preferences which one does not now have none the less provide one with direct reasons for action that are independent of experiential or other indirect effects and independent of the merits of the judgements on which those preferences are based. My belief is that if such an example were offered, it would turn out on examination to be better understood as an instance of a quasi-moral obligation to respect the autonomy of one's future self rather than as a case of regard for one's overall well-being (identified with one's level of preference satisfaction). For it is hard to see how a concern for one's *well-being* could be the motive for promoting the fulfilment of a future preference if one regards that preference as mistaken (i.e. believes that its object is inferior to other alternatives) and if one's concern is not with the quality of one's future experience.

Nothing that I have said here in criticizing the desire theory as an account of an individual's view of his or her own well-being is incompatible with the thesis that it is rational to act in such a way as to maximize one's expected utility. This thesis does not assert that people should take utility maximization to be their most basic reason for action. It is not a thesis about the reasons people have for acting but rather a thesis about the structure which the preferences of a rational individual will have (whatever the content or ground of these preferences may be). The thesis asserts that the preferences of a rational person will satisfy certain axioms and that when this is the case there will be a mathematical measure of expected preference satisfaction such that the individual will always prefer the alternative to which this measure assigns the greater number. In short, it asserts that a rational individual will choose in such a way as to maximize utility, but does not claim that utility is a quantity which (like pleasure) supplies the reasons for these choices.[17]

Let me turn now to consider the point of view of a benevolent third party, such as a friend or parent, who wants to promote a person's well-being. What concept of well-being is appropriate here? Harsanyi has suggested that the relevant notion is fulfilment of the preferences of the intended beneficiary, and he points out that this is what we aim at when we are selecting a gift for a friend.[18] Brandt, on the other hand, has argued, citing psychological evidence, that what benevolent individuals in fact aim at is the happiness of their intended beneficiaries rather than the fulfilment of their desires, and he defends this aim as rational.[19] It seems to me that Brandt offers the correct account of Harsanyi's examples. Preferences are important when we are selecting a gift, baking a birthday cake, or deciding where to take a friend to dinner because what we are aiming at in such cases is a person's happiness. What we want is to please them, and preferences play a double role here. First, they indicate what gift is likely to bring pleasure. In addition, a person can be pleased simply by the fact that we have taken care to discern what his preferences are and to find a gift that fulfils them. But, contrary to Brandt's suggestion, it is not clear that pleasure is what we should always aim at *qua* benefactors. Surely there are cases in which a true benefactor will aim at a person's overall good at the expense of what would be pleasing (or will at least be torn between these two objectives). If this is correct, then a benefactor's conception of well-being must include a notion of the substantive good of the beneficiary which can diverge from the idea of what the beneficiary will find pleasing. But in so far as the idea of pure desire satisfaction diverges from these two it seems to play little role in the thinking of a rational benefactor.

This idea gets greater weight, however, when we shift from the role of benefactor to that of agent or representative. A person who is acting for a friend (or son or daughter) may be constrained by that person's preferences, in so far as these are known, in a way that a benefactor is not. (Certainly this is the view that my own children take!) Whatever view children may take, however,

---

[17] It should also be noted that the most plausible version of the utility maximization thesis is one in which the relevant notion of utility is based on *all* of a person's preferences, no matter what the objects of these preferences may be. For the reasons noted in the previous section, the breadth of this notion of utility makes it an implausible account of well-being, whatever merits it may have as a description of what a rational individual would aim at.

[18] Harsanyi, 1975: 600–1.

[19] Brandt, 1979: 147–8.

the role of parents is not merely to be the *agents* of their children. They are not bound always to take their children's preferences as definitive of their good, and need to be able to form an independent judgement about that good. But it is when we focus on people whose role is solely that of agents for other adults that the desire theory has its greatest plausibility. That view owes much of its influence to its wide acceptance among economists, and it seems likely that this acceptance is in turn based on the idea that officials who must choose social policies for a society should think of themselves as agents of the members of that society, and therefore as bound to promote the fulfilment of the members' preferences.

It is no objection here that from the point of view of the members themselves the reason-giving force of these preferences depends on other factors, in the way I have argued above. These preferences can count as ultimate sources of reasons from the point of view of the decision-maker whatever their standing may be for the individuals whose preferences they are. Official responsibility can be defined in many different ways, but it is natural to suppose that an official could be conceived both to be acting for the good of a group and to be bound to accept the expressed judgement of members of that group as to where that good lies. Here, then, is a natural home for desire theories.

What makes such theories seem appropriate to questions of social policy is not the nature of the questions at issue. If the same policy questions were to be decided by referendum then each individual voter would be free to consider what he or she thinks would be best, and not bound to take the idea of what is 'best' as defined by the expressed preferences of all the members of society. The appeal of desire theories arises rather from the constraints which we have taken to apply to the decision-maker, and the point to be made is that these constraints, which may in context be quite appealing, are also quite special. The question is how broadly they apply. Do they, for example, apply to each of us when we adopt the attitude of impartiality which is appropriate to moral argument? I will turn next to that question.

[3]

Any discussion of the role of well-being in moral argument takes place against the background of utilitarianism, which assigns this concept such a fundamental role. Even in non-utilitarian theories, however, the justification of rights and principles must refer at least in part to the importance of the interests which they promote and protect, and any such theory must therefore face the questions of how these interests are to be characterized and how their claims to moral importance are to be justified.

Answers to these questions depend on a view of the nature of moral judgement and moral argument. I will discuss the answers which seem to me to be supported by my own contractualist moral theory.[20] According to this theory, the basic motive behind morality is the desire to be able to justify one's actions to others on grounds that they have reason to accept if they are also concerned with mutual justification. The theory holds that when we address a question of right and wrong the question we are addressing is whether the proposed action would be allowed by principles of conduct which people moved by this desire could not reasonably reject.

When can a principle be reasonably rejected by someone who is motivated in this way? This is a difficult question which I cannot answer fully, but I think that at least the following is true. A person can reasonably reject a principle if (1) general acceptance of that principle in a world like the one we are familiar with would cause that person serious hardship, and (2) there are alternative principles, the general acceptance of which would not entail comparable burdens for anyone. In order, then, to decide whether a given principle can reasonably be rejected we will need some interpretation of the terms 'serious hardship' and 'comparable burden'. This is how the notion of individual well-being makes its fundamental appearance in contractualist moral argument.

Note that the context of moral argument as contractualism describes it differs in two important respects from the situation of the social decision-maker discussed at the end of the preceding section. First, that decision-maker was assumed to be dealing with a given set of specific individuals whose preferences had been expressed. But when we are trying to work out what is right we are concerned with the choice of general principles of action, which will apply to an indefinite range of individuals whose particular preferences there is no way of knowing in detail (though we do know general facts about the kinds of preference most people have.) Second, while the task of the official is to reach a decision by amalgamating the stated preferences of the members of the group, a person considering a moral question is (according to contractualism) trying to work out the terms of a hypothetical agreement among these people. The imagined role of the members of the group is thus quite different in the two cases: in one case all they are taken to have done is to submit their personal preferences, while in the other they are thought of, hypothetically, as reacting to one another, trying to find principles that they can all accept. These two features, the generality of moral argument and the central place within it of the aim of agreement, are important in determining the relevant notions of individual benefit and burden.

I argued above that individuals' choices, and their conceptions of their own well-being, are guided by their ideas of substantive good, which typically include but are not limited to the experiential goods of various 'desirable states of consciousness'. Such a conception of substantive goods will provide an individual with a basis for deciding what a good life is, but it may also go beyond that, since the things which an individual recognizes as substantive goods may include

---

[20] As outlined in Scanlon, 1982.

some which lie outside his or her 'life' in the ordinary sense.

An individual will thus have *a* reason for wanting to reject a principle if the results of its general acceptance would be very bad from the point of view of that person's conception of substantive good. Suppose, however, that the person is moved to find and act on principles which no one could reasonably reject. How could his or her rejection of this principle be shown to be reasonable? What the person must do to show this is to put the reasons for that rejection in terms that others must recognize as important, terms that they would want to employ themselves to reject principles which burden them and that they are therefore prepared to recognize as generally compelling.

It is easiest to claim this status for substantive bads which everyone recognizes as serious: such things as loss of life, intense physical pain, and mental or physical disability. In general, losses of what Sen[21] calls 'functionings' will be good candidates for this list. But the things that are important to an individual will go beyond these basic functionings, and there will normally be less agreement about the nature and relative value of these further goods. Different individuals may enjoy different pursuits, follow different religions, and find different aims worth pursuing.

There are several ways to find agreement despite this diversity. First, there may be agreement on the importance of those goods and opportunities which are the main means to these diverse ends. Rawlsian 'primary social goods' such as income, wealth, and socially protected opportunities for self-expression would be examples of such means. The value that we can agree to assign to these resources need not be 'fetishistic' in the sense criticized by Sen[22] as long as it is acknowledged that their moral importance depends on their strategic role in the pursuit of diverse individual aims. Even if they are of only instrumental value, however, it might be claimed that these resources are none the less *morally* basic measures of well-being because their importance to life can be the object of the kind of consensus required to confer moral status, whereas there may be no consensus on the value of the particular pursuits to which they are the means (no agreement, for example, on the value of the particular forms of expression which various individuals want to engage in).

It is unlikely, however, that particular resources will be morally basic in this sense.[23] Lying behind such primary goods will be broad categories of good and harm which carry specific weight in moral argument. People can agree, for example, on the importance of having opportunities for self-expression (the exact form of these opportunities being as yet unspecified) even though they disagree sharply over the merits of particular speeches, plays, demonstrations,

[21] In, for example, Sen, 1984: 197 ff.

[22] See Sen, 1980: 366.

[23] This is not an objection to Rawls since he does not present 'primary social goods' as the most fundamental moral measures of well-being but rather as an index of distributive shares to be used for the purposes of assessing the justice of basic economic and political institutions. Their adequacy for this more specialized purpose is a separate question from the one I am discussing.

etc. Similarly, people who hold very different and conflicting beliefs may still be able to agree that 'being able to follow one's religion' is (for those who have one) an important part of life, and consequently a personal value which must be given significant weight in moral argument. The formulation of such abstract categories of good and harm is one of the main means through which a common set of moral values is developed. Moral argument clearly requires values of this kind which are intermediate between specific resources on the one hand and particular individual aims on the other, since the adequacy of specific resources, such as specific legally defined rights of freedom of expression or freedom of religion, can always be questioned, and these rights may need to be redefined as conditions change. In order to argue about such matters we need a moral vocabulary in which we can express the moral importance of the underlying individual interests.

What emerges, then, as a basis for arguing about the acceptability or unacceptability of particular moral principles is a heterogeneous collection of conditions, goods, and categories of activity[24] to which certain moral weights are assigned. Let me call this a system of moral goods and bads. The process of thought through which one arrives at such a system includes a mixture of 'fact' and 'value' elements. One begins with one's own view of the substantive goods which, in general, make life better and with a knowledge of how other individuals differ in their circumstances and in their views about what is substantively good.[25] The pressure to formulate a system of common values is then provided by the moral aim of finding a way of evaluating principles of action which all these individuals could accept despite their differences.

I argued in Section 2 that individuals themselves, and benevolent third parties, assess well-being in terms of substantive goods rather than in terms of the satisfaction of desires. In moral thinking as well, what we should (and, I believe, normally do) appeal to is our best estimate of what is important to making our lives and the lives of others good (recognizing that, in view of our differences, this will not always be the same). But the aim of finding a mode of argument that others could not reasonably refuse to accept forces us to consider not only what *we* take to be important goods for other people (what we think they would recognize as good if they were fully informed and rational) but also what it would be unreasonable of them, under normal conditions, not to recognize as important goods. The aim then is to develop a set of goods and bads which we all, in so far as we are trying to find a common vocabulary of justification, have reason to accept as covering the most important ways in which life can be made better or worse.

The system of moral goods and bads which emerges from such a search for common standards of evaluation may include some elements, such as the importance of avoiding physical pain and bodily harm, which are common to almost

---

24 Sen's notion of 'functionings' may be broad enough to encompass all of these.
25 See Griffin, 1986: 114, for an excellent statement of this starting point.

every individual's list of substantive goods. But because it must be the object of a consensus, the system of moral goods and bads may not assign these goods and bads the same relative values which they receive in some individual outlooks. In addition, it may contain some elements which have no analogous role in individuals' views of the good. The category of religion can be seen as an example of this. For a believer, the abstract category of religion may be of little interest since it groups her own most important beliefs together with other systems of thought which may strike her as, at best, objects of curiosity. The importance of this category lies either in sociological reflection or, more relevant for present purposes, in liberal morality. In the former, it groups together disparate practices and systems of belief in virtue of similarities in the role they play in the lives of different groups of people. In the latter, it serves to express a willingness to equate, *for the purposes of moral argument,* beliefs and practices which have a similar importance in the lives of different people but which are, from the point of view of any one such person, of very different value. The moral aim of finding forms of justification which others can also accept pushes us to develop such categories and to give them a central role in our thinking.

In so far as a system of moral goods and bads differs in these ways from individual conceptions of well-being, it could be said to be 'not subjective', that is, not an expression of any individual's preferences. As I mentioned earlier in this paper, however, it does not follow that such a system is 'objective'. For one thing, there is the question of the objectivity of the judgement that a particular system of values of this kind represents a standard which it is reasonable to employ, given the existing diversity of individual points of view. Second, the process I have described, through which such a system is arrived at and defended, can be expected to yield different outcomes in different social settings, since the activities and pursuits which are important to individual lives will vary from society to society. Even the relative importance of various physical and mental capacities will vary depending on the kind of life that people have the opportunity to live. Whether these considerations undermine the 'objectivity' of a system of moral goods and bads, and how, if at all, that matters, are difficult questions which it seems best to leave aside for the present.

For the purposes of argument about which principles it is reasonable to reject, a system of moral goods and bads does not need to provide a very complete ordering of levels of well-being. It is enough to distinguish between those 'very severe' losses which count as grounds for reasonable rejection and those gains and losses which are not of comparable severity. If we were to accept a principle requiring the equalization of well-being (as defined by such a system of moral goods and bads) then the level of completeness demanded would be much stronger. My own view is that such a global principle of equality is not very plausible: the ideas of equality which are most significant and morally compelling deal with a narrower range of goods. But that is larger issue which I will leave for another occasion.

BIBLIOGRAPHY

BRANDT, RICHARD (1979). *A Theory of the Good and the Right*. Oxford: Oxford University Press.

GRIFFIN, JAMES (1986). *Well Being*. Oxford: Oxford University Press.

HARMAN, GILBERT (1977). *The Nature of Morality*. New York: Oxford University Press.

HARSANYI, JOHN C. (1975). 'Can the Maximin Principle Serve as a Basis for Morality? A Critique of John Rawls's Theory', *American Political Science Review*, 69, 594–606.

—— (1977). 'Morality and the Theory of Rational Behaviour', *Social Research*, 44. Repr. in Sen and Williams, 1982: 39–62. (Page references in text are to the reprinted version.)

PARFIT, DEREK (1984). *Reasons and Persons*. Oxford: Oxford University Press.

RAWLS, JOHN (1971). *A Theory of Justice*. Cambridge, Mass.: Harvard University Press.

SCANLON, T.M. (1975). 'Preference and Urgency', *Journal of Philosophy*, 72, 655–69.

—— (1982). 'Contractualism and Utilitarianism', in Sen and Williams, 1982: 103–28.

—— (1991). 'The Moral Basis of Interpersonal Comparisons', in Jon Elster and John Roemer (eds.), *Interpersonal Comparisons of Well-Being*. Cambridge: Cambridge University Press.

SEN, AMARTYA K. (1980). 'Equality of What?' in S.M. McMarrin (ed.), *The Tanner Lectures on Human Values*, I. Salt Lake City: University of Utah Press, and Cambridge, Cambridge University Press. Repr. in Sen, *Choice, Welfare and Measurement*. Cambridge, Mass.: MIT Press. (Page references in text are to reprinted version.)

—— (1984). 'Well-being, Agency and Freedom', *Journal of Philosophy*, 82, 169–221.

—— and WILLIAMS, BERNARD (eds.) (1982). *Utilitarianism and Beyond*. Cambridge: Cambridge University Press.

ZIFF, PAUL (1960). *Semantic Analysis*. Ithaca: Cornell University Press.

Thomas Scanlon: Value, Desire, and Quality of Life

Commentary by Sissela Bok

In this paper, Scanlon continues and refines the analysis of the issues of preference and choice that he has carried out in previous writings. He sheds new light, in so doing, on the relation of these issues to different questions about the quality of life and in turn to his own conception of contractualism. This approach is of special significance from the point of view of economic and social development; for among the factors that impede efforts at such development, and that often injure rather than enhance the quality of life for the intended beneficiaries, a faulty understanding of human needs plays a prominent role. The ignorance, miscalculations, and assorted biases that skew so many well-meant projects from the outset do so the more easily to the extent that policy-makers ignore the deeper issues concerning the quality of life that Scanlon raises in this paper:

— What are the central questions about helping individuals and societies achieve a better quality of life?
— What types of answer address these questions?
— Does the standpoint of those answering affect the appropriateness of the type of answer given?
— What is the role of moral argument with respect to such questions, such answers, and such standpoints?

Because these issues are so often bypassed, the development debate displays a curious discrepancy: it addresses human problems of the highest significance, yet it peters out, too often, into triviality—either through improbable dogmatic assertions about what enhances or damages the quality of life or else through equally improbable doubts as to whether anything can be said that goes beyond sheer subjectivity. By analysing these issues more closely, Scanlon helps open them to reasoned debate in a practical context.

To begin with, Scanlon lists three questions that might be associated with the topic of the quality of life: 'What kinds of circumstances provide good conditions under which to live? What makes a life a good one for the person who lives it? What makes a life a valuable one (a good thing, as Sidgwick put it, "from the point of view of the universe")?' Scanlon suggests that the second of the three questions should be central for the discussion of the quality of life, with the possible addition of the closely related first question. He expressly sets aside the third question, having to do with value. The various efforts to make lives more valuable through improving their quality seem to him 'to depart from the concern with what we owe to the person which lies at the heart of morality and justice'.

Leaving this third question out of the paper on such grounds is understand-able. There is little agreement about where to locate 'the point of view of the universe'. And even if the question were simplified so as simply to ask, as so many thinkers have, what makes lives more valuable, it would call for lengthier exploration than the paper allows – the more so because distinctions between human lives on the basis of their value are used to buttress innumerable abuses in practice. But precisely for that reason, the question must not be dismissed from the larger debate about the quality of life in social and economic develop-ment. Valuations on the basis of race, religion, or nationality affect development efforts everywhere, intertwining with valuations based on wealth, gender, health, and status. Measures that alter the sense of felt worth or worthlessness of some category of individuals affect the quality of their lives, even their chances of survival. In villages in Bangladesh, for example, where around 30 per cent more girls die during infancy and childhood than boys, that difference has been wiped out by projects in which village women are encouraged to do something that raises their value in their own eyes as well as in those of their husbands or fathers: contributing to the family economy, for instance, by raising chickens and selling eggs.

Even apart from differential values ascribed to different categories of indi-viduals, troubling questions of value remain central to the development debate. Many practices involved in distribution and policy-making regarding, say, mater-nal health, AIDS, or earthquake relief rely on implicit or explicit quantitative assumptions about the value of lives. So long as these assumptions remain implicit, there is room for every form of bias and miscalculation. But setting them forth explicitly often reveals egregiously shallow criteria of value and appears disrespectful in exactly the sense Scanlon indicated. The practical dangers of either response call for taking the third question as seriously as the first two and for including it among those that require analysis.

Having chosen to focus on the question of what makes a life good for the person who lives it, Scanlon takes up three standard types of answer, set forth by Derek Parfit and discussed by Brandt and others. They are hedonistic theories, which hold that nothing can affect the quality of a life except by affecting the experience of living that life; desire theories, according to which a person's life can also be. made better by occurrences elsewhere in the world which fulfill that person's preferences; and objective list theories, for which an assessment of a person's well-being involves a substantive judgement about what things make life better – one that may conflict with the judgement of the person whose well-being is in question.

Scanlon opts for the third type of theory. But he suggests calling such theories, instead, 'substantive good theories', since they are based on substantive claims about what goods, conditions, and opportunities – or, as he sometimes calls them, 'ingredients' – make life better. Rawls's 'primary goods' are central ones for Scanlon as well; and he sees Sen's 'functionings' as capable of being incorporated into such a list without much difficulty, just as their loss can be part of a list of 'bads'. He mentions as especially compelling those 'substantive bads which everyone recognizes as serious, such as the loss of life, intense physical pain, and mental or physical disabilities'.

Although Scanlon admits that the term 'list' suggests 'a kind of arbitrariness', he takes such an interpretation to be erroneous, given the agreement about many of the 'ingredients' on people's lists and the process of debate and efforts at persuasion that he suggests for including still further items. His paper continues to refer to such lists; but the likelihood that the term will be misinterpreted is one of the reasons he offers for calling the theory he prefers a substantive good theory rather than an objective list theory.

But simply renaming the theory while continuing the practice of referring to lists will not satisfy those who seek more coherent criteria for what should go on the lists in question: some underlying conception of what it is that helps make human lives better. Exploring such conceptions is what much of moral philosophy has traditionally been all about. In response, Scanlon shifts the discussion from the goods or things that make lives better to what makes these things good. He argues that it is unlikely that any 'unified account' of 'what makes things good' is to be had, 'since it is unlikely that there are any good-making properties which are common to all good things'.

People who hold unified accounts may argue, in response, that human lives are good precisely to the extent that they acknowledge such an account: to the extent, perhaps, that they are lived in accordance with certain secular or religious ideals; or in so far as they further the life of the mind, the well-being of a particular community, or global survival; or, more generally, in so far as they are part of some larger meaning or contribute to some greater good. Others might question Scanlon's narrowing of the choice regarding unified accounts to one between only two alternatives: holding an account in which all good things possess the same good-making properties and rejecting all unified accounts. They might argue that what matters is not so much a unified as a coherent account. It need not hold that all good things share identical good-making properties but rather that these properties relate to one another and enhance one another, much as do the virtues and other factors that contribute to *eudaimonia* for Aristotle.

Can Scanlon's contractualist theory help resolve differences of opinion about such accounts? Can it, in particular, help evaluate the different preferences of the holders of unified or coherent accounts, as well as the differences between them and those who, for differing reasons, reject such accounts? The contractualist theory, as set forth in the last part of his paper, aims to facilitate the working out in imagination of 'the terms of a hypothetical agreement' among an indefinite range of individuals who have different or only partially overlapping lists of goods, and thereby to produce a weighted 'system of moral goods and bads'.

The contractualist process of working out an agreement is envisaged purely as a thought experiment. As such it could prove instructive at many levels. But could it arrive at specific items on a shared list? It might help, in order to answer this question, to consider it in the light of actual debates about the quality of life. Doing so might reveal difficulties less easily perceived in carrying out the thought experiment at a more general level.

One difficulty is that of achieving compromises between people's views of what makes life good or valuable. The religious beliefs of some, for instance, lead them to insist that the point of human existence is to suffer for the sake of expiation of sins and for benefits in a future life; those sharing such a faith tend to downplay most development efforts in our present, earthly existence. For them, there is little incentive to take part in a process of accommodation with groups holding diverging beliefs. Holders of millenarian beliefs may be even more resistant. They may be willing to sacrifice not only their own present quality of life but that of countless others for the sake of the higher quality of life they expect to achieve in the new existence that they anticipate. The Anabaptists, who believed that the millennium would come in 1534, or the seventeenth-century Jews who were convinced by Sabbatai Sevi that the messianic kingdom was near, were no more interested in their earthly quality of life than the twentieth-century American groups preparing for an imminent Second Coming.[1] Many Marxists have advocated working to counteract reformist development efforts, holding that human welfare is best served by increasing chaos and misery wherever doing so can speed the revolution that is bound to come.

Scanlon specifically includes the capacity to follow one's religion (and, presumably, belief systems more generally) as one of the values to be weighed with others in a list of substantive goods. But with divergences among belief systems such as those I have noted, the problems of accommodating diametrically opposed views on the part of policy-makers or beneficiaries of aid become acute. In addition, what is often at issue in practical contexts is more than respect for the beliefs of others. It is a question of the degree to which those aiming to improve the quality of life in a community or region take seriously the recipients' own view of what makes life good or worth living. Even when efforts to provide them with what most people would place on a 'list of substantive goods' are utterly well intentioned, any approach that does not take into consideration precisely the recipients' own unified account about what makes lives good, better, or more valuable, can be destructive.

A second set of difficulties that might arise in a practical application of Scanlon's contractualist procedure has to do with assigning weights to the goods that should go on the list that the different parties debate. What are the 'moral weights' that he suggests will be assigned to a 'heterogeneous collection of conditions, goods, and categories of activity'? Who assigns them? What kind of 'system of moral goods and bads' is it that emerges from this process? Will it be a closed system to replace the heterogeneous collection with which the con-

---

[1] See S. Bok, *Secrets: On the Ethics of Concealment and Revelation* (New York: Pantheon Books, 1982), 232–4, for a discussion of studies of millenarian societies.

tractualist effort at persuasion would normally begin? Or, if it is an open-ended system, how will diverging preferences count within it? And is there, once such preferences are taken into account, a risk of collapsing back from Scanlon's substantive good theory into a preference theory?

These questions about how the contractual approach relates to practical social choice are linked to a more general inquiry. Is this approach meant to be of universal scope? Is it, in particular, intended to encompass non-contractual circumstances outside of the Western democratic societies that have traditionally been regarded as contractualism's home territory? John Rawls has stated his hesitation about extending the reach of the conception of 'justice as fairness' beyond such societies. He has held that he is not 'trying to find a conception of justice suitable for all societies regardless of their particular social or historical circumstances'. Rather, he hopes that a common desire for agreement along with a 'sufficient sharing of certain underlying notions and implicitly held principles' will offer some foothold to the effort to reach an understanding.[2]

In 'Contractualism and Utilitarianism', on the other hand, Scanlon has indicated that he does not envisage his version of contractualism as thus bounded. Rather, it applies to all beings for whom things can be said to go better or worse and with respect to whom the idea of trusteeship consequently makes sense.[3] But does his procedure not itself presuppose some agreement about shared liberal values? The very notion of arriving at decisions through efforts at reasonable persuasion aiming at achieving agreement, so central to the proper functioning of democracies, is far from universally accepted. The same is true for the conceptions of what is reasonable and unreasonable, rational and irrational. Thus Scanlon proposes 'finding a mode of argument that others could not reasonably refuse' and suggests that participants, in evaluating goods, must consider what they would recognize as good 'if they were fully informed and rational'. But how does one incorporate into the hypothetical negotiating process the differing views of what constitutes informed and rational assessment of items on different lists?

Caution is needed in envisaging how such a process might function between individuals, organizations, and societies that do not share the 'underlying notions and implicitly held principles' of which Rawls speaks in his article on Kantian constructivism. Shaping a contractualist approach to ethical issues between (and presumably across) societies remains, as he suggests in the same article, 'immensely difficult'.[4]

One factor that may encourage moral theorists to explore new approaches to international ethics is a greater sense of urgency. Nations now face two overriding threats: the possibility that vast numbers of human lives may be destroyed in an escalating world-spanning war, nuclear or 'conventional'; and the

---

[2] John Rawls, 'Kantian Constructivism in Moral Theory', *Journal of Philosophy*, 67, (1980), 518.

[3] T. M. Scanlon, 'Contractualism and Utilitarianism', in Amartya Sen and Bernard Williams (eds.), *Utilitarianism and Beyond* (Cambridge: Cambridge University Press, 1982).

[4] Rawls, 'Kantian Constructivism', 524.

slower-acting but equally deadly risk of accelerating environmental deterioration, exacerbated by increasing poverty and population levels. These threats call for co-ordinated social choice beyond anything that governments, organizations, and individuals have ever mustered in the past. It will help parties trying to attain such levels of co-ordination if they can trust one another to take seriously certain fundamental moral principles. Among them, the constraints on violence and on deceit are foremost, since they are the two ways in which human beings do deliberate harm to whatever others value in their lives. These constraints are basic to a great many moral, religious, and political traditions, including, but not limited to, democratic ones. They can therefore serve in a coherent framework of fundamental principles shared by widely diverging moral theories and cutting across national, professional, and disciplinary boundaries.[5]

The debate over the Universal Declaration of Human Rights illustrates how such agreement on fundamentals might be achieved, much as Scanlon's contractualist debate proceeds on the basis of 'substantive bads which everybody recognizes as serious: such things as loss of life, intense physical pain, and mental or physical disabilities'. The provisions of the Declaration range from the right not to be enslaved or tortured to the right to adequate food, clothing, housing, and medical care.[6] Each one represents a good that signatories have agreed, at least in principle, to consider as so essential to human well-being that it should count as a right. Yet the numerous violations of these rights have been defended in quite different ways. There is relative consensus, once again at least in principle, regarding extreme uses of violence such as torture. No state legalizes torture in its constitution or penal code.[7] As Henry J. Steiner has pointed out, even governments engaged in massive repression

do not advance legal justifications for their murder and torture, as they might to defend against certain charges of group discrimination or censorship. Rather, they try to shield their conduct from the public eye, or accuse their critics of distortion, or attribute responsibility to non-governmental terrorists, or simply bear the label of outlaw as they ignore foreign censure. Even if governments claim moral justification for such conduct because of temporary exigent circumstances, they do not dispute what a full realization of the right [not to be arbitrarily deprived of life or subjected to torture] would entail.[8]

At least such fundamental rights, then, can form the basis for moral agreement among widely differing groups. Many other rights are increasingly accepted as preferable, however wide the gulf is between acceptance and implementation. In a number of nations, moreover, that gulf is narrowing. This is in part because pressures are mounting for governments to abolish practices violating human

[5] For a discussion of the role of such fundamental moral principles in personal, national, and international ethics, see S. Bok, *A Strategy for Peace* (New York: Pantheon Books, 1989).

[6] *Universal Declaration of Human Rights*, 1948 (United Nations, Department of Public Information).

[7] Amnesty International, *Torture in the Eighties* (London: Amnesty International, 1984), 4.

[8] See Henry J. Steiner, 'Political Participation as a Human Right', *Harvard Human Rights Yearbook*, 1 (Spring 1988), 82.

rights—pressures from the international community, armed with legal provisions not previously available, from domestic political parties, and from human rights organizations. These pressures cannot by themselves bring about a respect for the social and economic rights included in the Declaration of Human Rights, but they are increasingly helping to structure development efforts. Over the past four decades, they have shaped, not so much a system as a network of partially coherent, partially weighted, partially agreed upon, and partially implemented values affecting the quality of human lives.

Explanation and Practical Reason

Charles Taylor

[1]

Our modern conceptions of practical reason are shaped – I might say distorted – by the weight of moral scepticism. Even conceptions which intend to give no ground to scepticism have frequently taken form in order best to resist it, or to offer the least possible purchase to it. In this practical reason falls into line with a pervasive feature of modern intellectual culture, which one could call the primacy of the epistemological: the tendency to think out the question of what something *is* in terms of the question of how it is *known*.

The place of what I call scepticism in our culture is evident. By this I do not mean just a disbelief in morality, or a global challenge to its claims – though the seriousness with which a thinker like Nietzsche is regarded shows that this is no marginal position. I am also thinking of the widespread belief that moral positions cannot be argued, that moral differences cannot be arbitrated by reason, that when it comes to moral values, we all just ultimately have to plump for the ones which feel/seem best to us. This is the climate of thought which Alasdair MacIntyre calls (perhaps a bit harshly) 'emotivist',[1] which at least ought to be called in some sense 'subjectivist'. Ask any undergraduate class of beginners in philosophy, and the majority will claim to adhere to some form of subjectivism. This may not correspond to deeply felt convictions. It does seem to reflect, however, what these students regard as the intellectually respectable option.

What underpins this climate? Some fairly deep metaphysical assumptions, when one gets down to it. But certainly, on the immediate level, it is fostered by the actual experience of moral diversity. On an issue like abortion, for instance, it does not seem to be possible for either side to convince the other. Protagonists of each side tend to think that their position is grounded in something self-evident. For some it just seems clear that the foetus is not a person, and that it is absurd to ruin the life of some being who undeniably has this status in order to preserve it. For others it is absolutely clear that the foetus is both a life and human, and so terminating it cannot be right unless murder is. Neither side can be budged from these initial intuitions, and once one accepts either one the corresponding moral injunctions seem to follow.

If the seeming helplessness of reason tells us something about its real limits, then a worrying thought arises: what if some people came along who just failed to share our most basic and crucial moral intuitions? Suppose some people thought that innocent human beings could be killed in order to achieve some advantage for the others, to make the world more aesthetically pleasing, or some-

---

[1] Alasdair MacIntyre, *After Virtue* (University of Notre Dame Press, 1981) ch. 2.

thing of the sort? And have we not actually experienced people who stepped way outside the bounds of our core morality: the Nazis, for instance? Is reason as powerless before such people as it seems to be to arbitrate the dispute about abortion? Is there no way to show them they are wrong?

This is where our implicit model of practical reason begins to play an important role. If 'showing them' means presenting facts or principles which they cannot but accept, and which are sufficient to disprove their position, then we are indeed incapable of doing this. But one could argue that this is a totally wrong view of practical reason. Faced with an opponent who is *unconfusedly* and *undividedly* convinced of his position, one can indeed only hope to move him rationally by arguing from the ground up, digging down to the basic premises we differ on, and showing him to be wrong there. But is this really our predicament? Do we really face people who quite lucidly reject the very principle of the inviolability of human life?

In fact, this does not seem to be the case. Intellectual positions put forward to justify behaviour like that of the Nazis—to the extent that any of their ravings justify this appellation at all—never attack the ban on murder of conspecifics frontally. They are always full of special pleadings: for example, that their targets are not really of the same species, or that they have committed truly terrible crimes which call for retaliation, or that they represent a mortal danger to others, and so on. This kind of stuff is usually so absurd and irrational that it comes closer to raving than to reason. And, of course, with people like this reason is in fact ineffective as a defence. But this is not to say that reason is powerless to show them they are wrong. Quite the contrary. The fact that these terrible negations of civilized morality depend so much on special pleading, and of a particularly mad and irrational sort, rather suggests that there are limits beyond which *rational* challenges to morality have great trouble going.

This might indicate a quite different predicament of, and hence task for, practical reasoning. Its predicament would be defined by the fact that there are limits to what people can unconfusedly and undividedly espouse; so that, for instance, in order to embrace large-scale murder and mayhem, they have to talk themselves into some special plea of the sort mentioned above, which purports to square their policies with some recognized version of the prohibition against killing. But these pleas are vulnerable to reason, and in fact barely stand up to the cold light of untroubled thought.

The task of reasoning, then, is not to disprove some radically opposed first premiss (e.g. killing people is no problem), but rather to show how the policy is unconscionable on premisses which both sides accept, and cannot but accept. In this case, its job is to show up the special pleas.

On this model—to offer here at any rate a first approximation—practical argument starts off on the basis that my opponent already shares at least some of the fundamental dispositions towards good and right which guide me. The error comes from confusion, unclarity, or an unwillingness to face some of what he cannot lucidly repudiate; and reasoning aims to show up this error. Changing someone's moral view by reasoning is always at the same time increasing his self-clarity and self-understanding.

There are two quite different models of practical reason, let us call them the apodeictic and the *ad hominem*, respectively. I think that John Stuart Mill was making use of a distinction of this kind, and opting for the second, in his famous (perhaps notorious) remarks in *Utilitarianism*. 'Questions of ultimate ends are not amenable to direct proof', he avers, and yet 'considerations may be presented capable of determining the intellect either to give or to withhold its assent to the doctrine [namely, of utility]; and this is the equivalent to proof'.[2] This may sound like someone trying to squirm his way out of a contradiction, but the distinction is quite clear and sound. You cannot argue someone into accepting an ultimate end, utility or any other, if he really rejects it. But in fact, the whole case of utilitarians is that people do *not* reject it, that they all really operate by it, albeit in a confused and therefore self-defeating fashion. And this is why there may be 'considerations . . . capable of determining the intellect'. In fact, Mill shows us what he thinks these are in chapter 4, where he goes on to argue that what people in fact desire is happiness.[3] The appeal is to what the opponent already seeks, a clear view of which has to be rescued from the confusions of intuitionism.

But, it might be thought, this invocation of Mill is enough to discredit the *ad hominem* model irremediably. Is this not exactly where Mill commits the notorious naturalistic fallacy, arguing from the fact that men desire happiness to its desirability, on a glaringly false analogy with the inference from the fact that men see an object to its visibility?[4] Derisive hoots have echoed through philosophy classes since G.E. Moore, as first-year students cut their teeth on this textbook example of a primitive logical error.

There is no doubt that this argument is not convincing as it stands. But the mistake is not quite so simple as Moore claimed. The central point that the Moorean objection indicates is the special nature of moral goals. This is a phenomenon which I have tried to describe with the term 'strong evaluation'.[5] Something is a moral goal of ours not just in virtue of the fact that we are *de facto* committed to it. It must have this stronger status, that we see it as demanding, requiring, or calling for this commitment. While some goals would have no more claim on us if we ceased desiring them, for example, my present aim of having a strawberry ice cream after lunch, a strongly evaluated goal is one such that, were we to cease desiring it, *we* would be shown up as insensitive or brutish or morally perverse.

That is the root of our dissatisfaction with Mill's argument here. We feel that just showing that we always desire something, even that we cannot help

---

[2] *Utilitarianism* (Indianapolis: Hackett Edition, 1979), 4–5, 34.
[3] *Ibid.*, 34.
[4] Ibid.
[5] Cf. e.g. 'What is Human Agency?' in *Human Agency and Language* (Cambridge University Press, 1985).

desiring it, by itself does nothing to show that we *ought* to desire it, that it is a moral goal. Supposing I were irremediably addicted to smoking. Would that prove that I ought to smoke? Clearly not. We understand smoking from the beginning as a weakly evaluated end. We have to distinguish between showing of some end that we cannot help desiring it, and showing that all our strong evaluations presuppose it, or involve it, once we overcome our confusions about them. In the second case, we would have demonstrated that we cannot be lucid about ourselves without acknowledging that we value this end. This is the sense in which it is inescapable, not after the fashion of some *de facto* addiction. Whereas addictions are rightly declared irrelevant to moral argument, except perhaps negatively, the proof of inescapable commitment is of the very essence of the second, *ad hominem* mode of practical reasoning, and is central to the whole enterprise of moral clarification.

Mill plainly had some intuition to this effect when he deployed the argument in *Utilitarianism*. One of the things he was trying to show is that everyone else's commitment collapses into his. But the argument is botched because of a crucial weakness of the doctrine of utility itself, which is based on the muddled and self-defeating attempt to do away with the whole distinction between strong and weak evaluation. The incoherence of Mill's defence of the 'higher' pleasures, on the grounds of mere *de facto* preference by the 'only competent judges',[6] is also a testimony to the muddles and contradictions which this basically confused theory gives rise to.

But this does point to one of the most important roots of modern scepticism. We can already see that people will tend to despair of practical reason to the extent that they identify its mode of argument as apodeictic. This clearly sets an impossible task for it. But this will be accepted to the degree that the alternative, *ad hominen* mode of argument appears inadequate or irrelevant. And this it is bound to do, as long as the distinction between strong and weak evaluation is muddled over or lost from sight. This confusion can only breed bad arguments *à la* Bentham and Mill, and these, once denounced, discredit the whole enterprise.

But utilitarianism does not come from nowhere. The whole naturalist bent of modern intellectual culture tends to discredit the idea of strong evaluation. The model for all explanation and understanding is the natural science which emerges out of the seventeenth-century revolution. But this offers us a neutral universe: it has no place for intrinsic worth, or goals which make a claim on us. Utilitarianism was partly motivated by the aspiration to build an ethic which was compatible with this scientific vision. But to the extent that this outlook has a hold on the modern imagination, even beyond the ranks of utilitarianism, it militates in favour of accepting the apodeictic model, and hence of a quasi-despairing acquiescence in subjectivism.

The link between naturalism and subjectivism is even clearer when looked

---

[6] *Utilitarianism*, 8–11.

at from another angle. The seventeenth-century scientific revolution destroyed the Platonic-Aristotelian conception of the universe as the instantiation of Forms, which defined the standards by which things were to be judged. The only plausible alternative construal of such standards in naturalist thought was as projections of subjects. They were not part of the fabric of things, but rather reflected the way subjects react to things, the pro- or con-attitudes they adopt. Now perhaps it is a fact that people's attitudes tend to coincide – a happy fact, if true; but this does nothing to show that this point of coincidence is more right than any other possible one.[7]

The opposition to this naturalist reduction has come from a philosophical stance which might in a broad sense be called 'phenomenological'. By that I mean a focus on our actual practices of moral deliberation, debate, and understanding. The attempt is to show, in one way or another, that the vocabularies we need to explain human thought, action, and feeling, or to explicate, analyse, and justify ourselves or each other, or to deliberate on what to do, all inescapably rely on strong evaluation. Or, to put it negatively, that the attempt to separate out a language of neutral description, which combined with commitments or pro/con-attitudes might recapture and make sense of our actual explanations, analysis, deliberations, etc., leads to failure and will always lead to failure. It seems to me that this case has been convincingly made out, in a host of places.[8]

This kind of argument is, of course, not only a justification of the very foundation of the *ad hominem* mode of reasoning, but an example of it. It tries to show us that in all lucidity we cannot understand ourselves, or each other, cannot make sense of our lives or determine what to do, without accepting a richer ontology than naturalism allows, without thinking in terms of strong evaluation. This might be thought to beg the question, establishing the validity of a mode of argument through a use of it. But the presumption behind this objection ought to be challenged: what in fact ought to trump the ontology implicit in our best attempts to understand or explain ourselves? Should the epistemology derived from natural science be allowed to do so, so that its metaphysical bias in favour of a neutral universe overrules our most lucid self-understandings in strongly evaluative terms? But does this not rather beg the crucial question, namely, whether and to what extent human life is to be explained in terms modelled on natural science? And what better way to answer this question than by seeing what explanations actually wash?

---

[7] See J. L. Mackie, *Ethics* (Penguin Books, 1977), for an excellent example of the consequences of uncompromisingly naturalist thinking.

[8] Cf. e.g. John McDowell, 'Virtue and Reason', *The Monist*, 62 (1979), 331–50; and also MacIntyre, *After Virtue*. Bernard Williams makes the case very persuasively in his *Ethics and the Limits of Philosophy* (Harvard University Press, 1985), ch. 8. See also my 'Neutrality in Political Science', in *Philosophy and the Human Sciences* (Cambridge University Press, 1985).

[2]

Enough has been said in the above, I hope, to show that one of the strongest roots of modern scepticism and subjectivism in regard to ethics is the naturalist temper of modern thought. This tends to discredit in advance the *ad hominem* mode of argument, which actually might hold out the hope of settling certain moral issues by reason, and leaves only the apodeictic model in the field, which clearly sets an impossible standard. Within a human situation inescapably characterized in strongly evaluative terms, we can see how argument aimed at self-clarification might in principle at least bring agreement. In a neutral universe, what agreement there is between attitudes seems merely a brute fact, irrelevant to morals, and disagreement seems utterly inarbitrable by reason, bridgeable only by propaganda, arm-twisting, or emotional manipulation.

But this analysis brings to mind another source of modern scepticism, constituted by the independent attractions of the apodeictic model itself. This is where we really measure the tremendous hold of epistemology over modern culture.

This model emerges *pari passu* with and in response to the rise of modern physical science. As we see it coming to be in Descartes and then Locke, it is a foundationalist model. Our knowledge claims are to be checked, to be assessed as fully and responsibly as they can be, by breaking them down and identifying their ultimate foundations, as distinct from the chain of inferences which build from these towards our original unreflecting beliefs. This foundationalist model can easily come to be identified with reason itself. Modern reason tends to be understood no longer substantively but procedurally, and the procedures of foundationalism can easily be portrayed as central to it. But from the foundationalist perspective, only the apodeictic mode of reasoning is really satisfactory; the appeal to shared fundamental commitment seems simply a recourse to common prejudices. The very Enlightenment notion of prejudice encapsulates this negative judgement.

This brings us to another aspect. Foundationalist reasoning is meant to shake us loose from our parochial perspective. In the context of seventeenth-century natural science this involved in particular detaching us from the peculiarly human perspective on things. The condemnation of secondary qualities is the most striking example of this move to describe reality no longer in anthropocentric but in 'absolute' terms.[9]

But if the canonical model of reasoning involves breaking us free from our perspective as much as possible, then the *ad hominem* mode cannot but appear inferior, since by definition it starts from what the interlocutor is already committed to. And here a particularly important consideration comes into play. Starting from where your interlocutor is not only seems an inferior mode of

[9] I borrow the term from the interesting discussion in Bernard Williams's *Descartes* (Penguin Books, 1978), 66–7. See also Thomas Nagel, *The View from Nowhere* (Oxford University Press, 1986). I have discussed this issue in my 'Self-interpreting Animals', in *Human Agency and Language*.

reasoning in general, but it can be presented as a peculiarly bad, and indeed vicious, form of practical reason. For all those whose instinct tells them that the true demands of morality require radical change in the way things are, and the way people have been trained to react to them, starting from the interlocutor's standpoint seems a formula for conservatism, for stifling at the start all radical criticism, and foreclosing all the really important ethical issues.

This has always been one of the strongest appeals of utilitarianism, and one of the greatest sources of self-congratulation on the part of partisans of utility. It is not only that their theory seems to them the only one consonant with science and reason, but also that they alone permit of reform. J.S. Mill argues against views based on mere 'intuition' that they freeze our *axiomata media* for ever, as it were, and make it impossible to revise them, as mankind progresses and our enlightenment increases. 'The corrolaries from the principle of utility, . . . admit of indefinite improvement, and, in a progressive state of the human mind, their improvement is perpetually going on.'[10]

Here, then, is a source of modern scepticism and subjectivism which is as powerful as naturalism, and tends to operate closely in tandem with it, namely, the belief that a critical morality, by its very nature, rules out the *ad hominem* mode of practical reasoning. Naturalism and the critical temper together tend to force us to recognize the apodeictic mode as the only game in town. The obvious severe limitations of this mode in the face of ethical disagreement then push us towards a half-despairing, half-complacent embracing of an equivocal ethical subjectivism.

I have tried to show elsewhere that this identification of the demands of critical morality with a procedural understanding of reason and the apodeictic mode is deeply mistaken.[11] But erroneous or not, it has clearly been immensely influential in our intellectual culture. One can see this in the way people unreflectingly argue in terms of this model.

Discuss the question of arbitrating moral disputes with any class, graduate or undergraduate, and very soon someone will ask for 'criteria'. What is aimed at by this term is a set of considerations such that, for two explicitly defined, rival positions X and Y, (1) people who unconfusedly and undividedly espouse both rival positions X and Y have to acknowledge them, and (2) they are sufficient to show that Y is right and X is wrong, or vice versa. It is then driven home, against those who take an upbeat view of practical reason, that for any important moral dispute, no considerations have both a and b. If the rift is deep enough, things which are b must fail of a, and vice versa.

The problem lies with the whole unreflecting assumption that criteria in this sense are what the argument needs. We shall see, as we explore this further, that this assumption, as it is usually understood in the context of foundationalism, amounts to ruling out the most important and fruitful forms of the *ad hominem* mode.

10 *Utilitarianism*, 24.
11 'Justice after Virtue', unpublished MS.

But this whole assumption that rational arbitration of differences needs criteria has become very problematic, not only for practical reasons. It is a notorious source of puzzlement and sceptical challenges in the history of science as well. It is some underlying assumption of this kind that has driven so many people to draw sceptical conclusions from the brilliant work of Thomas Kuhn (conclusions to which Kuhn himself has sometimes been drawn, without ever succumbing to them). For what Kuhn persuasively argued was the 'incommensurability' of different scientific outlooks which have succeeded each other in history. That is, their concepts are non-intertranslatable, and—what is even more unsettling—they differ as to what features or considerations provide the test of their truth. The considerations each recognizes as having *b* are diverse. There are no criteria. And so the radical inference of a Feyerabend has seemed widely plausible: 'anything goes'.

But, as Alasdair MacIntyre has argued in another work,[12] it is clear that what needs revision here is our metatheory of scientific reasoning, rather than, for example, our firmly established conviction that Galileo made an important step forward relative to Aristotelian physics. The blind acceptance of a foundationalist, apodeictic model of reasoning is perhaps just as damaging here as in ethics. Calling to mind how inadequate the model is here can both help to weaken its hold on us in general, and allow us to see more exactly what is truly peculiar to practical reason.

MacIntyre argues very convincingly that the superiority of one scientific conception over another can be rationally demonstrated, even in the absence of what are normally understood as criteria. These are usually seen as providing some externally defined standard, against which each theory is to be weighted independently. But what may be decisive is that we are able to show that the *passage* from one to the other represents a gain in understanding. In other words, we can give a convincing narrative account of the passage from the first to the second as an advance in knowledge, a step from a less good to a better understanding of the phenomena in question. This establishes an asymmetrical relation between them: a similarly plausible narrative of a possible transition from the second to the first could not be constructed. Or, to put it in terms of a real historical transition, portraying it as a *loss* in understanding is not on.[13]

What I want to take from this is the notion that one can sometimes arbitrate between positions by portraying *transitions* as gains or losses, even where what we normally understand as decision through criteria—*qua* externally defined standards—is impossible. I should like to sketch here three argument forms, in ascending order of radical departure from the canonical, foundationalist mode.

1. The first takes advantage of the fact that we are concerned with transitions,

---

[12] 'Epistemological Crises, Dramatic Narrative, and the Philosophy of Science', *The Monist*, 60 (1977), 453–72.

[13] For a parallel notion of the asymmetrical possibilities of transition, this time applied to practical reason, see Ernst Tugendhat's notion of a possible *Erfahrungsweg* from one position to another, in *Selbstbewusstsein und Selbstbestimmung* (Frankfurt, 1979), 275.

that the issue here is a comparative judgement. On the standard, unreflecting assumptions of foundationalism, comparative judgements are usually secondary to absolute ones. Rival positions X and Y are checked against the facts, and one is shown to be superior to the other because it predicts or explains certain facts which the other does not. The comparative judgement between the two is based on absolute judgements concerning their respective performance in the face of reality, just as in a football game, the comparative verdict: team X won, is founded on two absolute assessments: team X scored three goals, and team Y scored two. The role of criteria here is taken by facts, observations, protocols, or perhaps by standards to be applied to explanations of facts—such as elegance or simplicity. The most popular theory of scientific reasoning with this traditional structure, Popper's, does indeed resemble the eliminative rounds in a championship. Each theory plays the facts, until it suffers defeated, and is then relegated.

But, as MacIntyre shows, comparative reasoning can draw on more resources than this. What may convince us that a given transition from X to Y is a gain is not only or even so much how X and Y deal with the facts, but how they deal with each other. It may be that from the standpoint of Y, not just the phenomena in dispute, but also the history of X, and its particular pattern of anomalies, difficulties, makeshifts, and breakdowns, can be greatly illuminated. In adopting Y, we make better sense not just of the world, but of our history of trying to explain the world, part of which has been played out in terms of X.

The striking example, which MacIntyre alludes to, is the move from Renaissance sub-Aristotelian to Galilean theories of motion. The Aristotelian conception of motion, which entrenched the principle: no motion without a mover, ran into tremendous difficulty in accounting for 'violent' motion, for example, the motion of a projectile after it leaves the hand, or the cannon mouth. The Paduan philosophers and others looked in vain for factors which could play the continuing role of movers in pushing the projectile forward. What we now see as the solution did not come until theories based on inertia altered the entire presumption of what needs explaining: continued rectilinear (or for Galileo circular) motion is not an explanandum.

What convinces us still today that Galileo was right can perhaps be put in terms of the higher 'score' of inertial theories over Aristotelian ones in dealing with the phenomena of motion. After all this time, the successes of the former are only too evident. But what was and is also an important factor—and which obviously bulked relatively larger at the time—is the ability of inertial theories to make sense of the whole pattern of difficulties which had beset the Aristotelians. The superiority is registered here not simply in terms of their respective 'scores' in playing 'the facts', but also by the ability of each to make sense of itself and the other explaining these facts. Something more emerges in their stories about each other than is evident in a mere comparison of their several performances. This show an asymmetrical relation between them: you can move from Aristotle to Galileo realizing a gain in understanding, but not vice versa.

2. This is still not a radical departure from the foundational model. True, decisive criteria are not drawn from the realm of facts, or of universally accepted principles of explanation. But the crucial considerations are still accessible to both sides. Thus the pre-Galileans were not unaware of the fact that they had a puzzling problem with violent motion. To speak Kuhnian language, this was an 'anomaly' for them, as their intellectual perplexity and the desperate expedients they resorted to testify. The decisive arguments are transitional – they concern what each theory has to say about the other, and about the passage from its rival to itself – and this takes us beyond the traditional way of conceiving validation, both positivist and Popperian. But in the strict sense of our definition above, there are still criteria here, for the decisive considerations are such that both sides must recognize their validity.

But, it can be argued, if we look at the seventeenth-century revolution from a broader perspective, this ceases to be so. Thus if we stand back and compare the dominant models of science before and after the break, we can see that different demands were made on explanation. The notion of a science of nature, as it came down from Plato, and especially from Aristotle, made explanation in terms of Forms (*eidē* or species) central, and beyond that posited an order of Forms, whose structure could be understood teleologically, in terms of some notion of the good, or of what ought to be. Principles like that of plenitude, which Lovejoy identifies and traces, make sense on that understanding: we can know beforehand, as it were, that the universe will be so ordered as to realize the maximum richness.[14] Similarly, explanations in terms of correspondences are possible, since it follows from the basic conception that the same constellation of ideas will be manifested in all the different domains.

Now if science consists of a grasp of order of this kind, then the activity of explaining why things are as they are (what we think of as science) is intrinsically linked to the activity of determining what the good is, and in particular how human beings should live through attuning themselves to this order. The notion that explanation can be distinct from practical reason, that the attempt to grasp what the world is like can be made independent of the determination of how we should stand in it, that the goal of understanding the cosmos can be uncoupled from our attunement to it, made no sense to the pre-modern understanding.

But notoriously the seventeenth-century revolution brought about an uncoupling of just this kind. The turn to mechanism offered a view of the universe as neutral; within it cause–effect relations could be exploited to serve more than one purpose. Galileo and his successors, we might say, turned towards an utterly different paradigm of explanation. If scientific explanation can always be roughly understood as in some sense rendering the puzzling comprehensible by showing how the phenomenon to be explained flows from mechanisms or

---

[14] Arthur Lovejoy, *The Great Chain of Being* (Harper Torchbook Edition, 1960).

modes of operation which we understand, then the seventeenth century sees a massive shift in the kind of understanding which serves as the basic reference point.

There is certainly one readily available mode of human understanding which the Platonic-Aristotelian tradition drew on. We are all capable of understanding things in terms of their place in a meaningful order. These are the terms in which we explain the at first puzzling behaviour of others, or social practices which at first seem strange, or some of the at first odd-seeming details of a new work of art, or the like. In another quite different sense of 'understanding', we understand an environment when we can make our way about in it, get things done in it, effect our purposes in it. This is the kind of understanding a garage mechanic has, and I unfortunately lack, of the environment under the hood of my car.

One of the ways of describing the seventeenth-century revolution in science is to say that one of these paradigms of understanding came to take the place of the other as the basic reference point for scientific explanation of nature.[15] But this has as an ineluctable consequence the distinction of explanation from practical reason I mentioned above. Only the first type of understanding lends itself to a marriage of the two.

But once we describe it in this way, the scientific revolution can be made to seem not fully rationally motivated. Of course, we all accept today that Galileo was right. But can we *justify* that preference in reason? Was the earlier outlook shown to be inferior, or did its protagonists just die off? If you ask the ordinary person today for a quick statement of why he holds modern science to be superior to the pre-modern, he will probably point to the truly spectacular technological pay-off that has accrued to Galilean science. But this is where the sceptic can enter. Technological pay-off, or the greater ability to predict and manipulate things, is certainly a good criterion of scientific success on the post-Galilean paradigm of understanding. If understanding is knowing your way about, then modern technological success is a sure sign of progress in knowledge. But how is this meant to convince a pre-Galilean? He will be operating with a quite different paradigm of understanding, to which manipulative capacity is irrelevant, which rather proves itself through a different ability, that of discovering our proper place in the cosmos, and finding attunement with it. And, it could be argued, modern technological civilization is a spectacular failure at *this*, as ecological critics and green parties never tire of reminding us.

Is the argument then to be considered a stand-off between the two, judged at the bar of reason? Here the sceptical spin-off from Kuhn's work makes itself felt. Once one overcomes anachronism and comes to appreciate how different earlier theories were, how great the breaks are in the history of knowledge – and this has been one of the great contributions of Kuhn's work – then it can appear that no

---

[15] I am borrowing here from Max Scheler's analysis in his essays 'Soziologie des Wissens' and 'Erkenntnis und Arbeit'.

rational justification of the transitions is possible. For the considerations that each side takes into account diverge. Each theory carries with it its own built-in criteria of success—moral vision and attunement in one case, manipulative power in the other—and is therefore invulnerable to the other's attack. In the end, we all seem to have gone for manipulative power, but this has to be for some extra-epistemic consideration, that is, not because this mode of science has been shown superior as *knowledge*. Presumably, we just like that pay-off better. In terms of my earlier discussion, what we lack here are 'criteria': there are no decisive considerations which *both* sides must accept.

Some people are driven by their epistemological position to accept some account of this kind.[16] But this seems to me preposterous. Once more, the account can appear plausible only because it fails to consider the transition between the two views. It sees each as assessing a theory's performance in face of reality by its own canons. It does not go further and demand of each that it give an account of the existence of the other: that is, not just explain the world, but explain also how this other, rival (and presumably erroneous) way of explaining the world could arise.

Once one makes this demand, one can appreciate the weakness of pre-Galilean science. There is a mode of understanding which consists of knowing one's way about. This is universally recognized. In making another mode a paradigm for scientific explanation, pre-Galilean science drew on a set of assumptions which entailed that this manipulative understanding would never have a very big place in human life. It always allowed for a lower form of inquiry, the domain of 'empirics', who scramble around to discover how to achieve certain effects. But the very nature of the material embodiment of Forms, as varying, approximate, never integral, ensured that no important discoveries could be made here, and certainly not an exact and universal body of findings. Consequently, the very existence of such a body of truths, and the consequent spectacular manipulative success, represents a critical challenge for pre-modern science. Indeed, it is difficult to see how it could meet this challenge. On its basic assumptions, modern science should not have got off the empiric's bench, emerged from the dark and smelly alchemist's study to the steel-and-glass research institutes that design our lives.

So the problem is not some explanatory failure on its own terms, not some nagging, continuing anomaly, as in the narrower issue above of theories of motion; it is not that pre-Galilean science did not perform well enough by its own standards, or that it did not have grounds within itself to downgrade the standards of its rivals. If we imagine the debate between the two theories being carried on timelessly on Olympus, before any actual results are obtained by one or the other, then it is indeed a stand-off. But what the earlier science cannot

---

[16] For instance, this seems to be implicit in Mary Hesse's view: see her 'Theory and Value in the Social Sciences', in C. Hookway and P. Pettit (eds.), *Action and Interpretation* (Cambridge University Press, 1979). She speaks there of prediction and control as 'pragmatic' criteria of scientific success (p. 2).

explain is the very success of the later *on the later's own terms*. Beyond a certain point, you just cannot pretend any longer that manipulation and control are not relevant criteria of scientific success. Pre-Galilean science died of its inability to explain or assimilate the actual success of post-Galilean science, where there was no corresponding symmetrical problem. And this death was quite rationally motivated. On Olympus the grounds would have been insufficient; but, faced with the actual transition, you are ultimately forced to read it as a gain. Once again, what looks like a stand-off when two independent, closed theories are confronted with the facts, turns out to be conclusively arbitrable in reason when you consider the transition.[17]

I have been arguing in the above that the canonical, foundationalist notion of arbitrating disputes through criteria generates scepticism about reason, which disappears once we see that we are often arguing about transitions. And we have seen that this scepticism affects some of the more important transitions of science just as much as it does the disputes of morality, and for the same reason, namely, the seeming lack of common criteria. In particular, it tends to make the history of science seem less rational than it has in fact been.

The second case is in a sense a more radical departure from the canonical model than the first. For the defeat does not come from any self-recognized anomaly in the vanquished theory. Nevertheless, there was *something* which the losing theory had to recognize outside the scope of its original standards, namely, that the very success of mechanistic science posed a problem. If we ask why this is so, we are led to recognize a human constant, namely, a mode of understanding of a given domain, *D*, which consists in our ability to make our way about and effect our purposes in *D*. We might borrow a term from Heidegger, and call this understanding as we originally have it prior to explicitation or scientific discovery 'pre-understanding'. One of the directions of increasing knowledge of which we are capable consists in making this pre-understanding explicit, and then in extending our grasp of the connections which underlie our ability to deal with the world as we do. Knowledge of this kind is intrinsically linked with increased ability to effect our purposes, with the acquisition of potential recipes for more effective practice. In some cases, it is virtually impossible to extend such knowledge without making new recipes available; and an extension of our practical capacities is therefore a reliable criterion of increasing knowledge.

Because of these links between understanding and practical ability, we cannot deny whatever increases our capacities its title as a gain in knowledge in some sense. We can seek to belittle its significance, or deem it to be by nature limited, disjointed, and lacunary, as Plato did. But then we have to sit up and take notice when it manages to burst the bounds we set for it—and this is what has rendered the transition to Galilean science a rational one.

---

[17] I have discussed this point at somewhat greater length in my 'Rationality', in M. Hollis and S. Lukes (eds.), *Rationality and Relativism* (Cambridge, Mass., 1982), reprinted in my *Philosophy and the Human Sciences* (Cambridge University Press, 1985).

The mediating element is something deeply embedded in the human life form, of which we are all implicitly aware, and which we have to recognize when made explicit: the link between understanding (of a certain kind) and practical capacity. But then is not the predicament of reason here coming to look analogous to the description I offered above of moral disputes? The task is not to convince someone who is undividedly and unconfusedly attached to one first principle that he ought to shift to an entirely different one. So described, it is impossible; rather, we are always trying to show that, granted what our interlocutor already accepts, he cannot but attribute to the acts or policies in dispute the significance we are urging on him.

Now here it has been a question of altering the first principles of science – the paradigms of understanding underlying it and the standards of success. And we can see a rational path from one to the other, but only because in virtue of what the pre-Galilean already accepts he cannot but recognize the significance of Galilean science's massive leap forward. No more in one case than in the other is it a question of radical conversion from one ultimate premiss to the other. That would indeed be irrational. Rather we show that the pre-Galilean could not undividedly and unconfusedly repudiate the deliverance of post-Galilean science as irrelevant to the issue that divides them.

Perhaps, then, those ultimate breakpoints we speak of as 'scientific revolutions' share some logical features with moral disputes. They are both rendered irrational and seemingly inarbitrable by an influential but erroneous model of foundationalist reasoning. To understand what reason can do in both contexts, we have to see the argument as being about transitions. And, as the second case makes plain, we have to see it as appealing to our implicit understanding of our form of life.

This brings to the fore one of the preconceptions which has bedevilled our understanding here and fostered scepticism. On the standard foundationalist view, the protagonists are seen as closed explicit systems. Once one has articulated their major premisses, it is assumed that all possible routes of appeal to them have been defined. So the pre-Galilean model, with its fixed standards of success, is seen as impervious to the new standards of prediction and control. But the real positions held in history do not correspond to these water-tight deductive systems, and that is why rational transitions are in fact possible.

We could argue that there are also moral transitions which could be defended in a way very analogous to the scientific one just described. When one reads the opening pages of Foucault's *Surveiller et Punir*,[18] with its riveting description of the torture and execution of a parricide in the mid-eighteenth century, one is struck by the cultural change we have gone through in post-Enlightenment Western civilization. We are much more concerned about pain and suffering than

---

[18] Paris, 1975.

our forebears, and we shrink from the infliction of gratuitous suffering. It would be hard to imagine people taking their children to such a spectacle in a modern Western society, at least openly and without some sense of unease and shame.

What has changed? It is not that we have embraced an entirely new principle, that our ancestors would have thought the level of pain irrelevant, providing no reason at all to desist from some course of action involving torture or wounds. It is rather that this negative significance of pain was subordinated to other weightier considerations. If it is important that punishment in a sense undo the evil of the crime, restore the balance—what is implicit in the whole notion of the criminal making 'amende honorable'—then the very horror of parricide calls for a particularly gruesome punishment. It calls for a kind of theatre of the horrible as the medium in which the undoing can take place. In this context, pain takes on a different significance: there has to be lots of it to do the trick. The principle of minimizing pain is trumped.

But then it is possible to see how the transition might be assessed rationally. If the whole outlook which justifies trumping the principle of minimizing suffering—which involves seeing the cosmos as a meaningful order in which human society is embedded as a microcosm or mirror—comes to be set aside, then it is rational to be concerned above all to reduce suffering. Of course, our ultimate judgement will depend on whether we see the change in cosmology as rational; and that is, of course, the issue I have just been arguing in connection with the scientific revolution. If I am right there, then here too the transition can perhaps be justified.

Of course, I am not claiming that all that has been involved in this important change has been the decline of the earlier cosmology. There are other, independent grounds in modern culture which have made us more reluctant to inflict pain. Some of them may have sinister aspects, if we believe Foucault himself. I have not got space to go into all this here.[19] But surely we must recognize the decline of the older notion of cosmic/social order as *one* consideration which lends a rational grounding to modern humanitarianism. This change would not only be linked to that in scientific theory, it would also be analogous to it in rational structure: to something which has always been recognized, although formerly in a subordinate place (the link between understanding and practice, the good of reducing pain), we are now constrained to give a more central significance because of changes which have taken place.

But the analogy I have been trying to draw between the justification of some scientific and moral revolutions cannot hide the fact that a great many moral disputes are much more difficult to arbitrate. To the extent that one can call on human constants, these are much more difficult to establish. And the suspicion dawns that in many cases such constants are of no avail. The differences between some cultures may be too great to make any *ad hominem* form of argument valid

---

[19] I have discussed this at greater length in my 'Foucault on Freedom and Truth', in *Philosophy and the Human Sciences*.

between them. Disputes of this kind would be inarbitrable.

3. But this form of argument, from the constants implicitly accepted by the interlocutor, does not exhaust the repertoire of practical reason. There is one more form, which is also an argument about transitions, but an even more striking departure from the canonical model. In both the above two forms the winner has appealed to some consideration which the loser had to acknowledge: his own anomalies, or some implicit constant. In the light of this consideration it was possible to show that the transition from X to Y could be seen as a gain, but not the reverse. So there is still something like a criterion operating here.

But we can imagine a form or argument in which no such consideration is invoked. The transition from X to Y is not shown to be a gain because this is the only way to make sense of the key consideration: rather it is shown to be a gain directly, because it can plausibly be described as mediated by some error-reducing move. This third mode of argument can be said to reverse the direction of argument. The canonical, foundationalist form can only show that the transition from X to Y is a gain in knowledge by showing that, say, X is false and Y true, or X has probability n, and Y has $2n$. The two forms we have been considering focus on the transition, but they too only show that the move from X to Y is a gain because we can make sense of this transition from Y's perspective but not of the reverse move from X's perspective. We still ground our ultimate judgement in the differential performance of X and Y.

But consider the possibility that we might identify the transition directly as the overcoming of an error. Say we know that it consisted in the removing of a contradiction, or the overcoming of a confusion, or the recognition of a hitherto ignored relevant factor. In this case, the order of justifying argument would be reversed. Instead of concluding that Y is a gain over X because of the superior performance of Y, we would be confident of the superior performance of Y because we know that Y is a gain over X.

But are we ever in a position to argue in this direction? In fact, examples abound in everyday life. First take a simple case of perception. I walk into a room, and see, or seem to see, something very surprising. I pause, shake my head, rub my eyes, and observe carefully. Yes, there really is a pink elephant with yellow polka dots in the class. I guess someone must be playing a practical joke.

What has gone on here? In fact, I am confident that my second perception is more trustworthy, but not because it scores better than the first on some measure of likelihood. On the contrary, if what I got from the first look was something like: 'maybe a pink elephant, maybe not', and from the second: 'definitely a pink elephant with yellow polka dots', there is no doubt that the first must be given greater antecedent probability. It is after all a disjunction, one of whose arms is overwhelmingly likely in these circumstances. But in fact I trust my second perception, because I have gone through an ameliorating transition. This is something I know how to bring off, it is part of my know-how as a perceiver. And that is what I in fact bring off by shaking my head (to clear the dreams), rubbing my eyes (to get the rheum out of them), and setting myself to observe with attention. It is my direct sense of the transition as an error-reducing one which grounds my confidence that my perceptual performance will improve.

Something similar exists in more serious biographical transitions. Joe was previously uncertain whether he loved Anne or not, because he also resents her, and in a confused way he was assuming that love is incompatible with resentment. But now he sees that these two are distinct and compatible emotions, and the latter is no longer getting in the way of his recognizing the strength of the former. Joe is confident that his present self-reading (I certainly love Anne) is superior to his former self-reading (I'm not sure whether I love Anne), because he knows that he passed from one to the other via the clarification of a confusion, that is, by a move which is in its very nature error-reducing.

Some of our gains in moral insight prove themselves to us in just this way. Pete was behaving impossibly at home, screaming at his parents, acting arrogantly with his younger siblings; he felt constantly resentful and very unhappy. He felt a constant sense of being cheated of his rights, or at least that is how it was formulated by his parents to the social worker. Now things are much better. Pete himself now applies this description to his former feelings. In a confused way, he felt that something more was owed to him as the eldest, and he resented not getting it. But he never would have subscribed to any such principle, and he clearly wants to repudiate it now. He thinks his previous behaviour was unjustified, and that one should not behave that way towards people. In other words, he has gone through a moral change: his views of what people owe each other in the family have altered. He is confident that this change represents moral growth, because it came about through dissipating a confused, largely unconsciously held belief, one which could not survive his recognizing its real nature.

These three cases are all examples of my third form of argument. They are, of course, all biographical. They deal with transitions of a single subject, whereas the standard disputes I have been discussing occur between people. And they are often (in the first case, always) cases of inarticulate, intuitive confidence, and hence arguably have nothing to do with practical *reason* at all, if this is understood as a matter of forms of *argument*.

These two points are well taken. I have chosen the biographical context, because this is where this order of justification occurs at its clearest. But the same form can be and is adapted to the situation of interpersonal argument. Imagine I am a parent, or the social worker, reasoning with Pete before the change. Or say I am a friend of Joe's talking out his confused and painful feelings about Anne. In either case, I shall be trying to offer them as an interpretation of themselves which identifies these confused feelings as confused, and which thus, if accepted, will bring about the self-justifying transition.

This is, I believe, the commonest form of practical reasoning in our lives, where we propose to our interlocutors transitions mediated by such error-reducing moves—the identification of contradiction, the dissipation of confusion, or rescuing from (usually motivated) neglect a consideration whose significance they cannot contest. But this is a form of argument where the appeal to criteria, or even to the differential performance of the rival views in relation to some decisive consideration, is quite beside the point. The transition is justified by the very nature of the move which effects it. Here the *ad hominem* mode of argument is at its most intense, and its most fruitful.

[3]

I would like in conclusion to try to draw together the threads of this perhaps too rambling discussion. I argued at the outset that practical arguments are in an important sense *ad hominem*. As a first approximation, I described these as arguments which appeal to what the opponent is already committed to, or at the least cannot lucidly repudiate. The notion that we might have to convince someone of an ultimate value premiss which he undividedly and unconfusedly rejects is indeed a ground for despair. Such radical gaps may exist, particularly between people from very different cultures; and in this case, practical reason is certainly powerless.

The discussion in the second part allows us to extend our notion of this kind of argument. It is not just cases where we can explicitly identify the common premiss from the outset that allow of rational debate. This was in fact the case with my opening example. Both the Nazi and I accept some version of the principle 'Thou shalt not kill', together with a different set of exclusions. Rational argument can turn on why he can permit himself the exclusions he does, and in fact, this historic position does not stand up long to rational scrutiny. It was really mob hysteria masquerading as thought.

But our discussion of transitions shows how debate can be rationally conducted even where there is no such explicit common ground at the outset. Now these arguments, to the effect that some transition from X to Y is a gain, are also *ad hominem*, in two related ways. First, they are specifically directed to the holders of X, in a way that apodeictic arguments never are. A foundational argument to the effect that Y is the correct thesis shows its superiority over the incompatible thesis X only incidentally. The proof also shows Y's superiority over all rivals. It establishes an absolute, not just a comparative claim. If I establish that the correct value for the law of attraction is the inverse square and not the inverse cube of the distance, this also rules out the simple inverse, the inverse of the fourth power, etc.

It is crucial to transition arguments that they make a more modest claim. They are inherently comparative. The claim is not that Y is correct *simpliciter*, but simply that, whatever is 'ultimately' true, Y is better than X. It is, one might say, less false. The argument is thus specifically addressed to the holders of X. Its message is: whatever else turns out to be true, you can improve your epistemic position by moving from X to Y; this step is a gain. But nothing need follow from this for the holders of a third, independent position. Above all, there is no claim to the effect that Y is the ultimate resting point of inquiry. The transition claim here is perfectly compatible with a further one which in turn supersedes Y. As MacIntyre puts it:

we are never in a position to claim that now we possess the truth or now we are fully rational. The most that we can claim is that this is the best account which anyone has been able to give so far, and that our beliefs about what the marks of 'a best account so far' are will themselves change in what are at present unpredictable ways.[20]

Second, these arguments all make their case by bringing to light something the interlocutor cannot repudiate. Either they make better sense of his inner difficulties than he can himself (case 1); or they present him with a development which he cannot explain on his own terms (case 2); or they show that the transition to Y comes about through a move which is intrinsically error-reducing (case 3). In relation to the original example of arguing with a Nazi, these greatly extend the range of rational debate. For what they appeal to in the interlocutor's own commitments is not explicit at the outset, but has to be brought to light. The pattern of anomalies and contradictions only becomes clear, and stands out as such, from the new position (case 1); the full significance of a hitherto marginalized form of understanding only becomes evident when the new position develops it (case 2); the fact that my present stance reposes on contradiction, confusion, and screening out the relevant only emerges as I make the transition — indeed, in this case, making the transition is just coming to recognize this error (case 3).

The range of rational argument is greatly extended, in other words, once we see that not all disputes are between fully explicated positions. Here the canonical, foundationalist model is likely to lead us astray. As we saw above with the second case, pre-Galilean science is indeed impregnable if we think only of its explicit standards of success: it has no cause to give any heed to technological pay-off. But in fact this pay-off constitutes a devastating argument, which one can only do justice to by articulating implicit understandings which have hitherto been given only marginal importance. Now I would argue that a great deal of moral argument involves the articulation of the implicit, and this extends the range of the *ad hominem* argument far beyond the easy cases where the opponent offers us purchase in one of his explicit premises.

Naturally none of the above shows that all practical disputes are arbitrable in reason. Above all, it does not show that the most worrying cases, those which divide people of very different cultures, can be so arbitrated. Relativism still has something going for it, in the very diversity and mutual incomprehensibility of human moralities. Except in a dim way, which does more to disturb than enlighten us, we have almost no understanding at all of the place of human sacrifice, for instance, in the life of the Aztecs. Cortés simply thought that these people worshipped the devil, and only our commitment to a sophisticated plural-

[20] Cf. my 'Epistemological Crisis', 455.

ism stops us making a similar lapidary judgement.

And yet, I want to argue that the considerations above show that we should not give up on reason too early. We do not need to be so intimidated by distance and incomprehensibility that we take them as sufficient grounds to adopt relativism. There are resources in argument. These have to be tried in each case, because nothing assures us a priori that relativism is false either. We have to try and see.

Two such resources are relevant to this kind of difference. First, there is the effect of working out and developing an insight which is marginally present in all cultures. In its developed form, this will make new demands, ones which upset the moral codes of previous cultures. And yet the insight in its developed form may carry conviction; that is, once articulated, it may be hard to gainsay. This is analogous to case 2 above, where the spectacular development of technology makes post-Galilean science hard to reject.

Second, the practices of previous cultures which are so challenged will often make sense against the background of a certain cosmology, or of semi-articulate beliefs about the way things have to be. These can be successfully challenged, and shown to be inadequate. Something of the kind was at stake in the discussion above of our changed attitude to suffering. Indeed, that case seems to show both these factors at work: we have developed new intuitions about the value and importance of ordinary life,[21] and, at the same time, we have fatally wounded the cosmology which made sense of the earlier gruesome punishments. These two together work to feed our convictions about the evil of unnecessary suffering.

Perhaps something similar can make sense of and justify our rejection of human sacrifice, or – to take a less exotic example – of certain practices involving the subordination of women. In this latter case, the positive factor – the developed moral insight – is that of the worth of each human being, the injunction that humans must be treated as ends, which we often formulate in a doctrine of universal rights. There is something very powerful in this insight, just because it builds on a basic human reaction, which seems to be present in some form everywhere: that humans are especially important, and demand special treatment. (I apologize for the vagueness in this formulation, but I am gesturing at something which occurs in a vast variety of different cultural forms.)

In many cultures, this sense of the special importance of the human is encapsulated in religious and cosmological outlooks, and connected views of human social life, which turn it in directions antithetical to modern rights doctrines. Part of what is special about humans can be that they are proper food for the gods, or that they embody cosmic principles differentially between men and women, which in fact imposes certain roles on each sex.

The rights doctrine presents human importance in a radical form, one that is hard to gainsay. This latter affirmation can be taken on several levels. Just

---

[21] I have discussed this new affirmation of ordinary life as one of the important constituents of Western modernity in *Sources of the Self* (Cambridge University Press, 1989), 3.

empirically there seems to be something to it, although establishing this is not just a matter of counting heads, but of making a plausible interpretation of human history. One that seems plausible to me goes something like this: recurrently in history new doctrines have been propounded which called on their adherents to move towards a relatively greater respect for human beings, one by one, at the expense of previously recognized forms of social encapsulation. This has been generally true of what people refer to as the 'higher' religions. And, of course, it has been the case with modern secular ideologies like liberalism and socialism. Where these have appeared, they have exercised a powerful attraction for human beings. Sometimes their spread can be explained by conquest, for example, Islam in the Middle East, liberalism in the colonial world, but frequently this is not the case, for example, Buddhism in India, Christianity in the Mediterranean world, Islam in Indonesia. Disencapsulated respect for the human seems to say something to us humans.

But, of course, this is a remark from the 'external' perspective, and does not by itself say anything about the place of reason. Can we perspicuously reconstruct these transitions in terms of *arguments*? This is hazardous, of course, and what follows could only at best be a crude approximation. But I think it might be seen this way. Disencapsulated respect draws us, because it articulates in a striking and far-reaching form what we already acknowledge in the sense I vaguely indicate with the term 'human importance'. Once you can grasp this possibility, it cannot help but seem prima-facie right. A demand is 'prima-facie right', when it is such as to command our moral allegiance, if only some other more weighty considerations do not stand in our way. Probably most of us feel like this about the ideal anarchic communist society; we'd certainly go for it, if only . . .

But, of course, the condition I mentioned: 'if you can grasp the possibility', is no pro forma one. For many societies and cultures, a disencapsulated view is literally unimaginable. The prescriptions of general respect just seem like perverse violations of the order of things.

Once one is over this hump, however, and can imagine disencapsulation, a field of potential argument is established. Universal respect now seems a conceivable goal, and one that is prima-facie right, if only. . . . The argument now turns on whatever fits into this latter clause. Yes, women are human beings, and there is a case therefore for giving them the same status as men, but unfortunately the order of things requires that they adopt roles incompatible with this equality, or they are crucially weaker or less endowed, and so cannot hack it at men's level, etc.

Here reason can get a purchase. These special pleadings can be addressed, and many of them found wanting, by rational argument. Considerations about the order of things can be undermined by the advance of our cosmological understanding. Arguments from unequal endowment are proved wrong by trying it out. Inequalities in capacity which seem utterly solid in one cultural setting just dissolve when one leaves this context. No one would claim that argument alone has produced the revolution in the status of women over the last centuries and decades in the West. But it all had something to do with the fact that the opponents of these changes were thrown on to a kind of strategic defensive; that they had to argue about the 'if onlys' and 'but unfortunatelys'. They had a position which was harder and harder to defend in reason.

But, one might argue, this is exactly where one is in danger of falling into ethnocentrism. The plight of, say, nineteenth-century opponents of women's franchise is utterly different from that of, say, certain Berber tribesmen today. On one account, the Berbers see the chastity of their womenfolk as central to the family honour, to the point where there can be a recognized obligation even to kill a kinswoman who has 'lost' her honour. Try telling them about Kant's *Critique of Practical Reason* or the works of John Stuart Mill, and you will get a different reaction from that of mainstream politicians in nineteenth-century Europe.

The gap can seem unbridgeable; there is this claim about honour, and what can you say to that? Honour has to do with avoiding shame, and can you argue with people about what they find shameful? Well, yes and no. If honour and shame are taken as ultimates, and if the fact that they are differently defined in different societies is ignored or discounted as just showing the depravity of the foreigner, then no argument is possible. But if one takes seriously the variety of definitions, and at the same time acknowledges that there are other moral or religious demands with which honour must be squared, then questions can arise about what really should be a matter of honour, what is true honour, and the like. The thought can arise: maybe some other people have a better conception of honour, because theirs can be squared with the demands of God, say, or those of greater military efficacy, or control over fate.

The watershed between these two attitudes is more or less the one I mentioned above, whereby one becomes capable of conceiving of disencapsulated conditions, or at least of seeing one's society as one among many possible ones. This is undoubtedly among the most difficult and painful intellectual transitions for human beings. In fact, it may be virtually impossible, and certainly hazardous, to try to *argue* with people over it. But what does this say about the limitations of reason? Nothing, I would argue. The fact that a stance is hard to get to does not in any way show that it is not a more rational stance. In fact, each of our cultures is one possibility among many. People can and do live human lives in all of them. To be able to understand this sympathetically—or at least to understand some small subset of the range of cultures, and realize that one ought ideally to understand more—is to have a truer grasp of the human condition than that of people for whom alternative ways are utterly inconceivable. Getting people over this hump may require more than argument, but there is no doubt that the step is an epistemic gain. People may be unhappier as a result, and may lose something valuable that only unreflecting encapsulation gives you, but none of that would make this encapsulation any the less blind.

Even the most exotic differences do not therefore put paid to a role for reason.

Of course, no one can show in advance that the 'if onlys' or 'but unfortunatelys' which stand in the way of universal rights can be rationally answered. It is just conceivable that some will arise which will themselves prove superior, more likely that there will be some where reason cannot arbitrate, and almost certain that we pay a price for our universalism in the loss of some goods which were bound up with earlier, more encapsulated forms of life. But none of this gives us cause a priori to take refuge in an agnostic relativism.

Unless, that is, we have already bought the faulty meta-ethic I have been attacking here. I want to end with the basic claim with which I started, and which underlies this whole exploration: and that is that modern philosophy, and to some extent modern culture, has lost its grip on the proper patterns of practical reason. Moral argument is understood according to inappropriate models, and this naturally leads to scepticism and despair, which in turn has an effect on our conception of morality, gives it a new shape (or misshapes it). We are now in a better position to see some of the motivations behind this misunderstanding.

I believe that we can identify in the above discussion three orders of motivation which combine to blind us. First, the naturalist outlook, with its hostility to the very notion of strong evaluation, tends to make the *ad hominem* argument seem irrelevant to ethical dispute. To show that your interlocutor is really committed to some good proves nothing about what he ought to do. To think it does is to commit the 'naturalistic fallacy'.

Second, naturalism together with the critical outlook have tended to brand *ad hominem* arguments as illegitimate. Reason should be as disengaged as possible from our implicit commitments and understandings, as it is in natural science, and as it must be if we are not to be victims of the status quo with all its imperfections and injustices. But once we neutralize our implicit understandings, by far the most important field of moral argument becomes closed and opaque to us. We lose sight altogether of the articulating function of reason.

This distorts our picture not only of practical reason, but also of much scientific argument. And this brings us to the third motive: the ascendancy of the foundationalist model of reasoning, which comes to us from the epistemological tradition. This understands rational justification as (a) effected on the basis of criteria, (b) judging between fully explicit positions, and (c) yielding in the first instance absolute judgements of adequacy or inadequacy, and comparative assessments only mediately from these. But we have just seen what an important role in our reasoning is played by irreducibly comparative judgements — judgements about transitions — in articulating the implicit, and in the direct characterization of transitional moves which make no appeal to criteria at all. To block all this from view through an apodeictic model of reasoning is to make most moral discussion incomprehensible. Nor does it leave unimpaired our understanding of science and its history, as we have amply seen. The connections between scientific explanation and practical reason are in fact close: to lose sight of the one is to fall into confusion about the other.

BIBLIOGRAPHY

FOUCAULT, MICHEL (1975). *Surveillir et punir: naissance de la prison.* Paris: Gallimard.

HESSE, MARY (1978). 'Theory and Value in the Social Sciences', in C. Hookway and P. Pettit (eds.), *Action and Interpretation. Studies in the Philosophy of the Social Sciences.* Cambridge: Cambridge University Press, 1979.

LOVEJOY, ARTHUR O. (1942). *The Great Chain of Being: A Study of the History of an Idea.* Cambridge, Mass.: Harvard University Press.

MACINTYRE, ALASDAIR C. (1981). *After Virtue: A Study in Moral Theory.* Notre Dame, Ind.: University of Notre Dame Press.

MACKIE, J. L. (1977). *Ethics: Inventing Right and Wrong.* Harmondsworth: Penguin Books.

MCDOWELL, JOHN (1979). 'Virtue and Reason'. *The Monist,* 62, 331–50.

MILL, JOHN STUART (1863). *Utilitarianism.* Edited with introduction by G. Sher. Indianapolis: Hackett.

SCHELER, MAX (1926a). 'Erkenntnis und Arbeit', in *Die Wissensformen und die Gesellschaft.* Leipzig: Der Neue Geist Verlag, 233–486.

—— (1926b). 'Die Soziologie des Wissens', in ibid., 47–229.

TAYLOR, CHARLES (1977). 'Epistemological Crisis, Dramatic Narrative, and the Philosophy of Science'. *The Monist,* 60, 453–72.

—— (1985a). *Human Agency and Language. Philosophical Papers I.* Cambridge: Cambridge University Press.

—— (1985b). *Philosophy and the Human Sciences. Philosophical Papers II.* Cambridge: Cambridge University Press.

—— (1989). *Sources of the Self: The Making of Modern Identity.* Cambridge, Mass., and London: Harvard University Press.

—— 'Justice after Virtue' (unpublished MS).

TUGENDHAT, ERNST (1979). *Selbstbewusstein und Selbstbestimmung: Sprachanalytische Interpretatinen.* Frankfurt am Main: Suhrkamp Verlag.

WILLIAMS, BERNARD A. O. (1978). *Descartes: The Project of Pure Inquiry.* Atlantic Highlands, NJ: Humanities Press.

Charles Taylor: Explanation and Practical Reason

Commentary by Martha Nussbaum

[1]

Charles Taylor's argument is, I believe, both convincing and important. And it is especially important for this project, since it shows an illuminating way of looking at the difficult evaluative disputes we encounter in thinking about the development of societies that are both different from one another and also (in most cases) internally heterogeneous. Development is itself an evaluative concept: it implies a progression from one situation to another that is (allegedly) in some ways better or more complete. Sometimes this issue of evaluation is ignored. Sometimes policy-makers and social scientists proceed as if it were perfectly clear to everyone what the values involved in development are – or even as if there were no evaluative question involved at all, but only certain facts which are alleged to be measurable independently of evaluation. Several of the papers in this volume, notably Hilary Putnam's, but also, in a very different way, Robert Erikson's, convincingly show the incoherence and barrenness of that way of thinking.[1]

But if we do accept the fact that we are grappling with a difficult evaluative question here, we then need to know how to reflect about such questions. We need to have a clear conception of what it is to ask and answer them, how to argue about them where there is disagreement, and what sort and degree of success to expect from reason and rational argument. Providing a powerful account of rational ethical argument seems to me to be one of the central challenges for a practical philosophy, a philosophy that will really help people to make progress on troublesome human problems. The need for such an account in connection with development problems was certainly one of the primary motivations for bringing philosophers together with economists and other social scientists in this project. And Taylor's account seems to me among the most powerful of those currently before us in philosophy, so his participation in the project is especially valuable. I do not find much to criticize in the paper: I am in sympathy with most of what Taylor says. So in commenting I want simply, first, to say a little more about why I think Taylor's work in general, and this paper in particular, is significant for the concerns and projects of development studies. Then I shall briefly add two points to Taylor's analysis: one about the history of science, one about moral psychology.

---

[1] See also the papers in this volume by Brock, Scanlon, and Sen, and the comments by Griffin (on Brock) and Sen (on Bliss). For related philosophical discussion, see Sen and Williams (1982), Sen (1980, 1985, 1987), Williams (1973, 1985), and Wiggins (1987).

[2]

A person who studies the history of philosophical approaches to the social sciences over the past several decades in search of a model for the analysis of development would be likely to conclude that she is faced with just two alternatives, each in its own way unpalatable. On the one hand, she would find an approach that conceives of social science as a kind of natural science,[2] and of the reasoned understanding of human beings that is the goal of social science as an understanding detached from the commitments and self-understandings that are characteristic of human beings in their daily lives. Such approaches usually involve some sort of reduction of qualitative distinctions to quantitative distinctions; and they attach a great deal of importance to the simplified mathematical representation of complex human matters. This approach, which has had enormous influence in shaping economic approaches to development, seems to have the advantage of promising truly rational solutions to difficult problems of choice. But it may, in the end, seem unacceptable because of the way in which it obscures or denies the richness and plurality of human values and commitments (both across societies and within each single society), and because of its reductive understanding of what human beings and communities are.

On the other hand, she would find a reaction against this approach, a reaction by now itself well entrenched in the social sciences. The alternative approach insists on restoring human self-interpretations to the sphere of social analysis in all their richness and variety. But its proponents frequently give up on practical reason, holding that there is no way in which reason can really resolve evaluative disputes. It is held that once we understand that the points of view of the participants in the dispute, to be correctly represented, must be represented from within the participants' own perspectives on the world, and once we understand, in addition, that cultural value schemes are highly various and largely incommensurable with one another, we will realize that practical reason has no effective part to play in such disputes. If it tries to take up a position of neutrality, detaching itself from all the competing conceptions, it will be unable to do so coherently, since no such external standpoint is available. If, on the other hand, it remains within the perspective of one of the parties, it seems that it must prove unfair and insensitive to the concerns of the other party, and be, really, nothing more than an attempt to dominate the other party. At the bottom of all so-called reasoning, then, is nothing but power. The work of Michel Foucault is frequently invoked in defence of this pattern of reasoning – although I believe that this is in some ways a misleading oversimplification of Foucault's contribution.[3]

This alternative approach has been highly influential, especially in anthro-

---

[2] Notice, however, that the conception of natural science employed here is not above reproach: see below, and Putnam's paper in this volume; also Putnam (1981).

[3] See, for example, Foucault (1984), discussed in my paper in this volume.

pology, literary theory, and discussions of legal interpretation. It has an obvious appeal, where development studies are concerned, since it restores to the field of analysis so much of human life that the other approach omits.[4] And yet it may well seem in the end as unpalatable as the other, since it tells us that we cannot succeed in establishing by practical reasoning any conclusions critical of things we might like to criticize in societies whose traditions we are examining. To use Taylor's example, it tells us that any attempt we might make to criticize another society's treatment of women, or to hold that real development for that society must include some changes in women's position, is and can be nothing more than a kind of cultural imperialism.

For the past twenty-five years, Charles Taylor has been developing a distinctive position in this dispute, one that combines, I believe, the best features of the two approaches, and also reinterprets their disagreement with one another in an illuminating way.[5] Beginning with *The Explanation of Behaviour* in 1964,[6] Taylor has consistently offered arguments of very high quality against a reductive natural science approach to the study of human beings and human action, insisting that any human science worthy of being taken seriously must include, and indeed base itself upon, the sense of value and the commitments that human beings actually display as they live and try to understand themselves. On the other hand, he has also consistently argued, as he does here, that this does not leave practical reason nowhere to go. In a series of papers on anthropological understanding of different cultures, he has shown that it is possible to take very seriously the data of cultural anthropology and of history, and the differences between conceptual schemes, and yet to hold that, in certain ways and under certain circumstances, practical reason can legitimately criticize traditions.[7] The combination of anthropological sensitivity with philosophical precision in these papers gives them a more or less unique place in the debate, and they are certainly an invaluable guide to anyone working on development issues.[8]

The present paper is, I think, of special interest in Taylor's defence of practical reason. According to Taylor's own account, in order to argue successfully against an opponent he needs to be able, among other things, to give a plausible account of the opponent's error. And in this paper he does just that. First, he argues effectively against the opponent of practical reason, presenting forms of unmistakably

---

[4] For a variant of this approach in literary theory, see Derrida (1976, 1979), Fish (1980, 1985); in legal studies, see Fish (1982), and many others. In the development context, a related approach is powerfully presented in Marglin and Marglin (1990). A number of these writers have been influenced by R. Rorty (1979, 1982).

[5] Views with which Taylor's might be fruitfully compared include those of Putnam (1981, 1987), Davidson (1984), and, in literary theory, Wayne Booth (1988). For a related discussion of the law, which makes a powerful case for a richer descriptive language, see White (1989); the implications of Booth's work for legal studies are discussed in Nussbaum (1988), repr. in Nussbaum (1990).

[6] Taylor (1964).

[7] Taylor (1985a, 1985b).

[8] See also Taylor (1989), a major philosophical account of the development of modern conceptions of the self.

rational argument that do not depend on the starting points that this opponent has held, plausibly, to be unavailable. Then he goes on to tell us where the opponent went wrong, and in a very interesting way. For the error of the sceptical opponent of practical reason consists in remaining too much in the grip of the very picture of rational argument that is allegedly being criticized. While objecting to the hegemony of the natural sciences over the human sciences, and while seeking to restore to the human sciences their own rich humanistic character, the opponent has, presumably without full awareness, imported into her analysis one very central part of the natural science model, namely, its understanding of what constitutes a rational argument. For she seems to assume that rational argument requires neutrality, and deduction from premises that are external to all historical perspectives. If this is not available, then we can say goodbye to reason itself. It is only because of this residual commitment to the rejected model, and her consequent neglect of other forms of rational arguing, that the opponent has been able so quickly to conclude that, the ethical domain being what it is, there are no good rational arguments to be found in it.

This, I think, is a profound diagnosis. In various forms this problem is present in many contemporary positions that end up embracing some form of subjectivism or scepticism about practical reason: in Foucault's work, at least sometimes; in the work of Jacques Derrida, who seems to argue that without unmediated access to the world as it is in itself we have no arguments, nothing but the free play of interpretations; in other ways, in the work of numerous others who have influenced recent thinking in the human sciences.[9] What Taylor does is, first of all, to point out the opponent's reliance on a model of arguing drawn from natural science; second, to argue from the history of science that this is not even a very persuasive picture of the way scientific argument goes, especially in times of scientific change; and, third, to offer several models of reasoning that both explain the recalcitrant scientific cases and offer examples of ethical rationality. Like Hilary Putnam, Taylor shows that a really good account of science and scientific progress will not yield as hard a distinction between the scientific and the ethical as has been defended by some philosophers. And he shows that in both areas progress can be achieved by a complex and patient type of self-clarification, by patterns of argument in which implicit commitments are brought to light. Such arguments might well be said to be as old as Socratic cross-examination, and to have as their goal something like the self-understanding sought by Socrates.[10]

Several morals for development studies might be drawn from this analysis. First, that we ought to reject disengaged pseudoscientific understandings of the human being, in favour of conceptions that give a larger role to people's own commitments and self-understandings. Second that when we do so we need not and should not give up on rational argument. But we must not expect the rational

[9] See, for example, my criticism of Fish in Nussbaum (1985), repr. in Nussbaum (1990).
[10] See the illuminating account of Socratic procedure in Vlastos (1983).

arguments we use to be like those we associate with a certain view of natural science. They are likely to be piecemeal rather than global; they will be very much rooted in the particularities of people's historical situations; and frequently, as Taylor has said, they will be biographical rather than abstract. They will describe progress in a way that may seem to lack neatness and simplicity. For they will be, as he says, inherently comparative in their understandings of development, rather than absolute. And since they are attempts to bring to light what is deep and incompletely perceived in the thought of the person or group in question, they will be, frequently, both highly concrete and somewhat indirect. They may, for example, tell stories, appeal to the imagination and the emotions – tapping, through a very non-scientific use of language, people's intuitions about what matters most.[11] All of this I find exemplified in a striking way in Robert Erikson's account of a sociological approach that is both humanistic and committed to practical reason; and I think that Erikson should perhaps be less defensive than he is about the apparent messiness and complexity of his descriptions. There is precision in the lucid depiction of a highly complex and indeterminate situation; there is evasion and vagueness in the simple schematic description of a multi-faceted concrete case.

Finally, Taylor points out that the process of rational argument is frequently associated with raising the level of discontent and unhappiness in the people who are doing the arguing. People who, as a result of arguments such as those he describes, become aware of the variety of human societies and lose the isolation of what Taylor calls their 'encapsulated' condition frequently feel pain: both the pain of a new dissatisfaction with current arrangements and the pain of reflection itself. It seems to me that this is an important observation, and one that arises in development in significant ways. If one is committed to measuring development in terms of utility – construed either as happiness (pleasure) or as the satisfaction of current desires and preferences – one will be bound to judge that self-understanding is inimical to development, in such cases. Taylor seems to me to be right that self-understanding has a value of its own, apart from any utility (so construed) it brings. And his example of the changing position of women shows us one case where the pain of discontent has had a definite positive link with development. This connection is also supported by Amartya Sen's data on women's changing perceptions of their health situation.[12]

[3]

My one quarrel with the picture of scientific change presented by Taylor is that the picture he opposes is actually much *less* plausible, even initially, than his

---

[11] The case for such language in the law is powerfully made in White (1989), a critical review of Posner (1988); White contrasts the language of literature with the language characteristic of much of economics. The case for the use of literary language in moral reflection is made in Nussbaum (1990); see also Nussbaum and Sen (1989).

[12] See Sen (1985: app. B).

account makes it seem. Taylor's final answer to the alleged conceptual discontinuity between ancient Greek science and Galilean science is, I think, the right one: that there were all along interests in practical control and being able to lead a flourishing life that motivated all parties to the dispute, interests in terms of which partisans of the new science could show its superiority, in a way that the old-time Aristotelian could not deny. My objection is only that the fact that ancient science did have an interest in practical control is unmistakably clear; the opponent's account of the alleged conceptual discontinuity has simply obscured it by describing the ancient picture in too narrow and monolithic a way.

In fact, if one looks not only at Plato, but also at the people who were actually doing science in the ancient world—above all at the development of Greek medicine—one finds ubiquitous reference to practical manipulation and control, and one finds that this is one of the primary hallmarks of the scientific. Doctors regularly defend their procedures on the grounds that they work, and oppose rival medical procedures on the grounds that they are too abstract and schematic to be useful.[13] Even mathematics is repeatedly presented as a discipline whose primary point and motivation is its practical usefulness, in measuring and navigation and so forth. Prometheus, in Aeschylus' *Prometheus Bound*, calls it 'chief of all the clever stratagems'.[14] Even if the later Aristotelians of Taylor's story played down this aspect of science, they could hardly have been ignorant of it, since Aristotle himself gives it prominence.[15] So it seems to me that the opponent's story does not really get off the ground; the alleged rupture is just bad history.

Why is this worth mentioning here? It is worth mentioning because so much of the historiography on which contemporary debates about conceptual discontinuity are based is bad in exactly this way. So many alleged discontinuities look like discontinuities because the historian in question has made a highly selective use of texts, or has stuck to theoretical work, neglecting the history of popular thought. Much of Foucault's work is flawed in this way,[16] although I still believe it to be important work. My experience is that if one studies any single society in sufficient depth one finds in it a rich plurality of views and conceptions, frequently in active debate with one another; and frequently these debates themselves are very important in explaining such large-scale conceptual shifts as do take place. This is essential to any good history of the later reception of ancient Greek ideas. Amartya Sen and I have argued that it is also essential to good work on India, where the existence of debate and internal criticism needs emphasis.[17] If I have any slight criticism of Taylor's historiography in several of his papers,

---

[13] See especially the treatises 'On the Art' and 'On Ancient Medicine'; some of the relevant issues are discussed in Nussbaum (1986; ch. 4).

[14] Aeschylus, *Prometheus Bound*, line 459.

[15] Cf. Aristotle, *Metaphysics*, I. 1.

[16] The *History of Sexuality*, for example, relies above all on Plato and Xenophon—both philosophers and both from wealthy oligarchic backgrounds. Both are extremely unrepresentative of popular thought.

[17] See Nussbaum and Sen (1989).

it is that things sometimes look simpler and more monolithic than in fact they were. Appreciating their complexity gives us new ways of understanding how practical reason can function in social argument, and reinforces the general picture Taylor presents here.[18]

[4]

Now I want to make a point about psychology. Despair about the efficacy of practical reason, in the recent philosophical literature, frequently takes a form slightly different from the form that Taylor criticizes here (the form of despair that seeks scientific neutrality, even while it holds it to be unavailable). Frequently the problem of practical reason is put in terms of an alleged gap between reason and motivation. The argument imagines some bad or immoral person, and then says, 'All right. Even supposing that we can show to *our* satisfaction that this person is engaging in bad reasoning, even if we can convince ourselves *about* her by an argument that moves *us*, isn't there something troublesome about the fact that the argument doesn't do anything *for that person*? Have we really given that person reasons for action, if they are not reasons that have some force with that person, in the sense that they arouse desires and emotions of the appropriate motivational type?' The point is often made by saying that the only reasons we should care about are 'internal' reasons, reasons that are (or could become) part of the system of desires and motivations of the person involved. If that does not happen in our case, there is something peculiar about calling these reasons for that person at all, or saying that a rational argument has established something that this person ought to believe or to do.[19] But the question of what reasons can become 'internal' for a person seems to depend very much on what desires and emotions that person happens to have. And this seems to be something that rational argument can do little or nothing about. Even if the argument should convince our person to *believe* its conclusion (this argument says), it is hard to see how it could reform her desires. But unless this happens, nothing much has been accomplished.

This is a deep and complex issue in philosophy, and, indeed, in life. I cannot even fully state it here, much less resolve it, but what I want to suggest, as my second friendly amendment to Taylor's account, is that I think he needs to supplement his account of reason with a picture of the connection between argument and motivation, between reason and passion. And I suspect that if one probes this issue, one will find that the sceptic about reason is in the grip, here too, of a picture of reason that is the outcome of a relatively recent naturalistic understanding of the human being, a picture that could not withstand the scrutiny of our deepest beliefs concerning who we are.

[18] Taylor (1989) is therefore especially to be welcomed, since its dense and complex historical account lays out the issues with a fullness impossible in the shorter papers.
[19] See Williams (1981) for one forceful argument along these lines.

There has been a tendency in philosophy—ever since Descartes analysed the passions in connection with his view of the mind–body split, dissociating them strongly from beliefs—to think of passions as brute feelings, more or less impervious to reasoning, coming from altogether different parts of our nature. Most philosophers have long since given up the Cartesian picture of the mind–body split; but many still retain the associated picture of emotions as feelings that are distinct from and relatively impervious to reasoning. If one looks back to the correspondence of Descartes with Princess Elizabeth, that very astute and sceptical philosophical mind, one finds in her challenges (and in their mutual references to Stoic ideas) an older and also, I believe, more adequate view of the passions, one that was the dominant picture in the thought of most of the ancient Greek philosophers, and one that was extremely important to their picture of the ways in which philosophy can be practical, changing people and societies for the better.

This picture (which one can find in different forms in Aristotle and in the Epicureans, but above all in the Stoics) insists that emotions or passions[20] are highly discriminating evaluative responses, very closely connected to beliefs about what is valuable and what is not. Grief, for example, is intimately linked to the belief that some object or person, now lost, has profound importance; it is a recognition of that importance. Anger involves and rests upon a belief that one has been wronged in a more than trivial way. And so forth. What follows from this view is that a rational argument can powerfully influence a person's passions and motivations. If rational argument can show either that the supposed bad event (the death or insult or whatever) did not take place, or that the purported occasion for grief or anger is really not the sort of thing one ought to care very much about, then one can actually change a person's psychology in a more than intellectual way. The Stoics and Epicureans took on this task in many ways, showing people, for example, that the worldly goods and goods of reputation that are commonly the bases of anger should not be valued as people value them. Such arguments do not just operate on the surface of the mind. They conduct a searching scrutiny of the whole of the person's mental and emotional life. And this is so because emotions are not just animal urges, but fully human parts of our outlook on the world.[21]

On this basis the Hellenistic philosophers built up a powerful picture of a practical philosophy, showing how good arguments about topics like death and the reasons for anger could really change the heart, and, through that, people's personal and social lives. They compared the philosopher to the doctor: through reasoning he or she treats and heals the soul. It seems to me that such an account of motivational change through argument would be an attractive and important addition to Taylor's picture. I believe that an account like this can be defended

---

[20] I am using 'emotions' and 'passions' interchangeably; both words are historically well entrenched, and both have, for many centuries, been used more or less interchangeably to designate a species of which the most important members are anger, fear, grief, pity, love and joy.

[21] See Nussbaum (1987, 1989a, 1989b).

today,[22] and that the defence will make a powerful contribution to the defence of practical reason.

If Taylor chooses to develop his picture of practical reasoning along these lines, he will need to move even further than he has already from the scientific model of reasoning. For good 'therapeutic' argument may wish to make use of techniques like story-telling and vivid exemplification – techniques that lie far indeed from the scientific model – in order to bring to light hidden judgements of importance and to give a compelling picture of a life in which such judgements are absent. All this would fit in well with Taylor's emphasis in his paper on the 'biographical' nature of argument, and its function of bringing hidden things to light. Such further developments would yield arguments that could, I believe, be defended as Taylor defends his examples here: as examples of rational argument and epistemic progress.

BIBLIOGRAPHY

BOOTH , W. (1988). *The Company We Keep: An Ethics of Fiction*. Berkeley and Los Angeles: University of California Press.

DAVIDSON, D. (1984). *Inquiries into Truth and Interpretation*. Oxford: Clarendon Press.

DERRIDA, J. (1976). *Of Grammatology*, trans. G. C. Spivak. Baltimore: Johns Hopkins University Press.

—— (1979). *Spurs: Nietzsche's Styles*, trans. B. Harlow. Chicago: University of Chicago Press.

de SOUSA, R. (1987). *The Rationality of Emotions*. Cambridge, Mass.: MIT Press.

FISH, S. (1980). *Is There a Text in this Class? The Authority of Interpretive Communities*. Cambridge, Mass.: Harvard University Press.

—— (1982). 'Working on the Chain Gang: Interpretation in Law and Literature', *Texas Law Review*, 551.

—— (1985). 'Anti-Professionalism', *New Literary History*, 17.

FOUCAULT, M. (1984). *The Use of Pleasure. History of Sexuality*, ii, trans. R. Hurley. New York: Pantheon.

LUTZ, C. (1988). *Unnatural Emotions*. Chicago: University of Chicago Press.

MARGLIN, F. A., and MARGLIN, S. (1990). *Dominating Knowledge: Development, Culture, and Resistance*. Oxford: Clarendon Press.

NUSSBAUM, M. (1985). 'Sophistry about Conventions: A Reply to Stanley Fish', *New Literary History*, 17. Reprinted in Nussbaum (1990).

—— (1986). *The Fragility of Goodness: Luck and Ethics in Greek Tragedy and Philosophy*. Cambridge: Cambridge University Press.

—— (1987). 'The Stoics on the Extirpation of the Passions', *Apeiron*, 20, 129–77.

---

[22] Aspects of it are being powerfully defended in several fields, including philosophy, cognitive psychology, anthropology, psychoanalysis, and legal studies: see Nussbaum (1990) for discussion and references, and see especially Lutz (1988), A. Rorty (1980, 1988), and de Sousa (1987).

—— (1988). 'Reading for Life', a review of Booth (1988), *Yale Journal of Law and the Humanities*, 1. Reprinted in Nussbaum (1990).

—— (1989*a*). 'Beyond Obsession and Disgust: Lucretius' Genealogy of Love', *Apeiron*, 22, 1–59.

—— (1989*b*). 'Mortal Immortals: Lucretius on Death and the Voice of Nature', *Philosophy and Phenomenological Research*, 50, 305–51.

—— (1990). *Love's Knowledge: Essays on Philosophy and Literature*. Oxford and New York: Clarendon Press and Oxford University Press.

—— and SEN, A. (1989). 'Internal Criticism and Indian Rationalist Traditions', in M. Krausz (ed.), *Relativism: Interpretation and Confrontation*. Notre Dame: University of Notre Dame Press.

POSNER, R. A. (1988). *Law and Literature: A Misunderstood Relation*. Cambridge, Mass.: Harvard University Press.

PUTNAM, H. (1981). *Reason, Truth and History*. Cambridge: Cambridge University Press.

—— (1987). *The Many Faces of Realism*. La Salle, Ill.: Open Court.

RORTY, A. (ed.) (1980). *Explaining Emotions*. Berkeley: University of California Press.

—— (1988). *Mind in Action. Essays in the Philosophy of Mind*. Boston: Beacon Press.

RORTY, R. (1979). *Philosophy and the Mirror of Nature*. Princeton: Princeton University Press.

—— (1982). *Consequences of Pragmatism: Essays*, 1972–1980. Minneapolis: University of Minnesota Press.

SEN, A. (1980). 'Plural Utility', *Proceedings of the Aristotelian Society*, 80.

—— (1985). *Commodities and Capabilities*. Amsterdam: North-Holland.

—— (1987). *The Standard of Living. Tanner Lectures on Human Values 1985*, ed. G. Hawthorn. Cambridge: Cambridge University Press.

—— and WILLIAMS, B. (1987). *Utilitarianism and Beyond*. Cambridge: Cambridge University Press.

TAYLOR, C. (1964). *The Explanation of Behaviour*. London: Routledge and Kegan Paul.

—— (1985*a*). *Human Agency and Language. Philosophical Papers I*. Cambridge: Cambridge University Press.

—— (1985*b*). *Philosophy and the Human Sciences. Philosophical Papers II*. Cambridge: Cambridge University Press.

—— (1989). *Sources of the Self: The Making of Modern Identity*. Cambridge, Mass., and London: Harvard University Press.

VLASTOS, G. (1983). 'The Socratic Elenchus', *Oxford Studies in Ancient Philosophy*, i. Oxford and New York: Oxford University Press.

WHITE, J. B. (1989). 'What Can a Lawyer Learn from Literature?', *Harvard Law Review*, 102, 2014–47.

WIGGINS, D. (1987). *Needs, Values, Truth: Essays in the Philosophy of Value*. Oxford and New York: Basil Blackwell.

WILLIAMS, B. (1973). 'A Critique of Utilitarianism', in J. C. Smart and B. Williams, *Ultilitarianism For and Against*. Cambridge: Cambridge University Press.

—— (1981). 'Internal and External Reasons', in *Moral Luck: Philosophical Papers*, 1973–1980. Cambridge: Cambridge University Press.

—— (1985). *Ethics and the Limits of Philosophy*. Cambridge, Mass.: Harvard University Press.

Non-Relative Virtues:
An Aristotelian Approach

Martha Nussbaum

All Greeks used to go around armed with swords.

Thucydides, *History of the Peloponnesian War*

The customs of former times might be said to be too simple and barbaric. For Greeks used to go around armed with swords; and they used to buy wives from one another; and there are surely other ancient customs that are extremely stupid. (For example, in Cyme there is a law about homicide, that if a man prosecuting a charge can produce a certain number of witnesses from among his own relations, the defendant will automatically be convicted of murder.) In general, all human beings seek not the way of their ancestors, but the good.

Aristotle, *Politics*, 1268a39 ff.

One may also observe in one's travels to distant countries the feelings of recognition and affiliation that link every human being to every other human being.

Aristotle, *Nicomachean Ethics*, 1155a21–2

[1]

The virtues are attracting increasing interest in contemporary philosophical debate. From many different sides one hears of a dissatisfaction with ethical theories that are remote from concrete human experience. Whether this remoteness results from the utilitarian's interest in arriving at a universal calculus of satisfactions or from a Kantian concern with universal principles of broad generality, in which the names of particular contexts, histories, and persons do not occur, remoteness is now being seen by an increasing number of moral philosophers as a defect in an approach to ethical questions. In the search for an alternative approach, the concept of virtue is playing a prominent role. So, too, is the work of Aristotle, the greatest defender of an ethical approach based on the concept of virtue. For Aristotle's work seems, appealingly, to combine rigour with concreteness, theoretical power with sensitivity to the actual circumstances

This paper was originally motivated by questions discussed at the WIDER Conference on Value and Technology, summer 1986, Helsinki. I would like to thank Steve and Frédérique Marglin for provoking some of these arguments, with hardly any of which they will agree. I would also like to thank Dan Brock for his helpful comments, Amartya Sen for many discussions of the issues, and the participants in the WIDER conference for their helpful questions and comments. Earlier versions of the paper were presented at the University of New Hampshire and at Villanova University; I am grateful to the audiences on those occasions for stimulating discussion. An earlier version of the paper was published in *Midwest Studies in Philosophy*, 1988.

of human life and choice in all their multiplicity, variety, and mutability.

But on one central point there is a striking divergence between Aristotle and contemporary virtue theory. To many current defenders of an ethical approach based on the virtues, the return to the virtues is connected with a turn towards relativism—towards, that is, the view that the only appropriate criteria of ethical goodness are local ones, internal to the traditions and practices of each local society or group that asks itself questions about the good. The rejection of general algorithms and abstract rules in favour of an account of the good life based on specific modes of virtuous action is taken, by writers as otherwise diverse as Alasdair MacIntyre, Bernard Williams, and Philippa Foot,[1] to be connected with the abandonment of the project of rationally justifying a single norm of flourishing life for all human beings and a reliance, instead, on norms that are local both in origin and in application.

The position of all these writers, where relativism is concerned, is complex; none unequivocally endorses a relativist view. But all connect virtue ethics with a relativist denial that ethics, correctly understood, offers any transcultural norms, justifiable by reference to reasons of universal human validity, by reference to which we may appropriately criticize different local conceptions of the good. And all suggest that the insights we gain by pursuing ethical questions in the Aristotelian virtue-based way lend support to relativism.

For this reason it is easy for those who are interested in supporting the rational criticism of local traditions and in articulating an idea of ethical progress to feel that the ethics of virtue can give them little help. If the position of women, as established by local traditions in many parts of the world, is to be improved, if traditions of slave-holding and racial inequality, religious intolerance, aggressive and warlike conceptions of manliness, and unequal norms of material distribution are to be criticized in the name of practical reason, this criticizing (one might easily suppose) will have to be done from a Kantian or utilitarian viewpoint, not through the Aristotelian approach.

This is an odd result, as far as Aristotle is concerned. For it is obvious that he was not only the defender of an ethical theory based on the virtues, but also the defender of a single objective account of the human good, or human flourishing. This account is supposed to be objective in the sense that it is justifiable by reference to reasons that do not derive merely from local traditions and practices, but rather from features of humanness that lie beneath all local traditions and are there to be seen whether or not they are in fact recognized in local traditions. And one of Aristotle's most obvious concerns was the criticism of existing moral traditions, in his own city and in others, as unjust or repressive, or in other ways incompatible with human flourishing. He uses his account of the virtues as a basis for this criticism of local traditions: prominently, for example, in Book II of the *Politics*, where he frequently argues against existing social forms by

---

[1] See MacIntyre (1981), and by contrast MacIntyre (1988); Foot (1978); Williams (1984, 1985); Walzer (1983, 1987).

pointing to ways in which they neglect or hinder the development at some important human virtue.[2] Aristotle evidently believed that there is no incompatibility
between basing an ethical theory on the virtues and defending the singleness and
objectivity of the human good. Indeed, he seems to have believed that these two
aims are mutually supportive.

Now the fact that Aristotle believed something does not make it true (though
I have sometimes been accused of holding that position!). But it does, on the
whole, make that something a plausible *candidate* for the truth, one deserving our
most serious scrutiny. In this case, it would be odd indeed if he had connected
two elements in ethical thought that are self-evidently incompatible, or in favour
of whose connectedness and compatibility there is nothing interesting to be said.
The purpose of this paper is to establish that Aristotle did indeed have an
interesting way of connecting the virtues with a search for ethical objectivity and
with the criticism of existing local norms, a way that deserves our serious consideration as we work on these questions. Having described the general shape of
the Aristotelian approach, we can then begin to understand some of the objections that might be brought against such a non-relative account of the virtues,
and to imagine how the Aristotelian could respond to those objections.

[2]

The relativist, looking at different societies, is impressed by the variety and the
apparent non-comparability in the lists of virtues she encounters. Examining the
different lists, and observing the complex connections between each list and a
concrete form of life and a concrete history, she may well feel that any list of
virtues must be simply a reflection of local traditions and values, and that, virtues
being (unlike Kantian principles or utilitarian algorithms) concrete and closely
tied to forms of life, there can in fact be no list of virtues that will serve as
normative for all these varied societies. It is not only that the specific forms of
behaviour recommended in connection with the virtues differ greatly over time
and place, it is also that the very areas that are singled out as spheres of virtue,
and the manner in which they are individuated from other areas, vary so
greatly. For someone who thinks this way, it is easy to feel that Aristotle's own
list, despite its pretensions to universality and objectivity, must be similarly
restricted, merely a reflection of one particular society's perceptions of salience
and ways of distinguishing. At this point, relativist writers are likely to quote
Aristotle's description of the 'great-souled' person, the *megalopsuchos*, which
certainly contains many concrete local features and sounds very much like the
portrait of a certain sort of Greek gentleman, in order to show that Aristotle's list
is just as culture-bound as any other.[3]

But if we probe further into the way in which Aristotle in fact enumerates and

---

[2] For examples of this, see Nussbaum (1988*a*).
[3] See, for example, Williams (1985: 34–6); Hampshire (1983: 150ff.).

individuates the virtues, we begin to notice things that cast doubt upon the suggestion that he simply described what was admired in his own society. First of
all, we notice that a rather large number of virtues and vices (vices especially)
are nameless, and that, among the ones that are not nameless, a good many are
given, by Aristotle's own account, names that are somewhat arbitrarily chosen
by Aristotle, and do not perfectly fit the behaviour he is trying to describe.[4] Of
such modes of conduct he writes, 'Most of these are nameless, but we must try
. . . to give them names in order to make our account clear and easy to follow'
(*EN* 1108a 6–19). This does not sound like the procedure of someone who is
simply studying local traditions and singling out the virtue-names that figure
most prominently in those traditions.

What *is* going on becomes clearer when we examine the way in which he does,
in fact, introduce his list. For he does so, in the *Nicomachean Ethics*,[5] by a
device whose very straight-forwardness and simplicity has caused it to escape the
notice of most writers on this topic. What he does, in each case, is to isolate a
sphere of human experience that figures in more or less any human life, and in
which more or less any human being will have to make *some* choices rather than
others, and act in *some* way rather than some other. The introductory chapter
enumerating the virtues and vices begins with an enumeration of these spheres
(*EN* II. 7); and each chapter on a virtue in the more detailed account that follows
begins with 'Concerning X . . .', or words to this effect, where X names a sphere
of life with which all human beings regularly and more or less necessarily have
dealings.[6] Aristotle then asks, what is it to choose and respond well within that
sphere? And what is it to choose defectively? The 'thin account' of each virtue
is that it is whatever being stably disposed to act appropriately in that sphere consists in. There may be, and usually are, various competing specifications of what
acting well, in each case, in fact comes to. Aristotle goes on to defend in each
case some concrete specification, producing, at the end, a full or 'thick' definition
of the virtue.

Here are the most important spheres of experience recognized by Aristotle,
along with the names of their corresponding virtues:[7]

---

[4] For 'nameless' virtues and vice, see *EN* (*Nicomachean Ethics*) 1107b1–2, 1107b7–8, 1107b30–1,
1108a17, 1119a10–11, 1126b20, 1127a12, 1127a14; for recognition of the unsatisfactoriness of
names given, see 1107b8, 1108a5–6, 1108a20 ff. The two categories are largely overlapping, on
account of the general principle enunciated at 1108a16–19, that where there is no name a name should
be given, satisfactory or not.

[5] It should be noted that this emphasis on spheres of experience is not present in the *Eudemian
Ethics*, which begins its discussion with a list of virtues and vices. This seems to me a sign that
that treatise expresses a more primitive stage of Aristotle's thought on the virtues—whether earlier
or not.

[6] For statements with *peri* ('concerning') connecting virtues with spheres of life, see *EN*
1115a6–7, 1117a29–30, 1117b25 and 27, 1119b23, 1122a19, 1122b34, 1125b26, 1126b13—and
EN II. 7 throughout. See also the related usages at 1126b11, 1127b32.

[7] My list here inserts justice in a place of prominence. (In the *EN* it is treated separately,
after all the other virtues, and the introductory list defers it for that later examination.) I have
also added at the end of the list categories corresponding to the various intellectual virtues discussed

Sphere	Virtue
1. Fear of important damages, esp. death	Courage
2. Bodily appetites and their pleasures	Moderation
3. Distribution of limited resources	Justice
4. Management of one's personal property, where others are concerned	Generosity
5. Management of personal property, where hospitality is concerned	Expansive hospitality
6. Attitudes and actions with respect to one's own worth	Greatness of soul
7. Attitude to slights and damages	Mildness of temper
8. 'Association and living together and the fellowship of words and actions'	
a. Truthfulness in speech	Truthfulness
b. Social association of a playful kind	Easy grace (contrasted with coarseness, rudeness, insensitivity)
c. Social association more generally	Nameless, but a kind of friendliness (contrasted with irritability and grumpiness)
9. Attitude to the good and ill fortune of others	Proper judgement (contrasted with enviousness, spitefulness, etc.)
10. Intellectual life	The various intellectual virtues, such as perceptiveness, knowledge, etc.
11. The planning of one's life and conduct	Practical wisdom

There is, of course, much more to be said about this list, its specific members, and the names Aristotle chose for the virtue in each case, some of which are indeed culture-bound. What I want to insist on here, however, is the care with which Aristotle articulates his general approach, beginning from a characterization of a sphere of universal experience and choice, and introducing the virtue-name as the name (as yet undefined) of whatever it is to choose appropriately in

---

in *EN* VI, and also to *phronesis*, or practical wisdom, discussed in *EN* VI as well. Otherwise the order and wording of my list closely follows II. 7, which gives the programme for the more detailed analyses from III. 5 to IV.

that area of experience. On this approach, it does not seem possible to say, as the relativist wishes to, that a given society does not contain anything that corresponds to a given virtue. Nor does it seem to be an open question, in the case of a particular agent, whether a certain virtue should or should not be included in his or her life—except in the sense that she can always choose to pursue the corresponding deficiency instead. The point is that everyone makes some choices and acts somehow or other in these spheres: if not properly, then improperly. Everyone has *some* attitude, and corresponding behaviour, towards her own death; her bodily appetites and their management; her property and its use; the distribution of social goods; telling the truth; being kind to others; cultivating a sense of play and delight, and so on. No matter where one lives one cannot escape these questions, so long as one is living a human life. But then this means that one's behaviour falls, willy-nilly, within the sphere of the Aristotelian virtue, in each case. If it is not appropriate, it is inappropriate; it cannot be off the map altogether. People will of course disagree about what the appropriate ways of acting and reacting in fact *are*. But in that case, as Aristotle has set things up, they are arguing about the same thing, and advancing competing specifications of the same virtue. The reference of the virtue term in each case is fixed by the sphere of experience—by what we shall from now on call the 'grounding experiences'. The thin or 'nominal' definition of the virtue will be, in each case, that it is whatever being disposed to choose and respond well consists in, in that sphere. The job of ethical theory will be to search for the best further specification corresponding to this nominal definition, and to produce a full definition.

[3]

We have begun to introduce considerations from the philosophy of language. We can now make the direction of the Aristotelian account clearer by considering his own account of linguistic indicating (referring) and defining, which guides his treatment of both scientific and ethical terms, and of the idea of progress in both areas.[8]

Aristotle's general picture is as follows. We begin with some experiences—not necessarily our own, but those of members of our linguistic community, broadly construed.[9] On the basis of these experiences, a word enters the language of the group, indicating (referring to) whatever it is that is the content of those experiences. Aristotle gives the example of thunder.[10] People hear a noise in the clouds, and they then refer to it, using the word 'thunder'. At this point, it may be that nobody has any concrete account of the noise or any idea about what it really is. But the experience fixes a subject for further inquiry. From now on,

---

[8] For a longer account of this, with references to the literature and to related philosophical discussions, see Nussbaum (1986a: ch. 8).

[9] Aristotle does not worry about questions of translation in articulating this idea; for some worries about this, and an Aristotelian response, see below, sections 4 and 6.

[10] *Posterior Analytics* II. 8, 93a21ff.; see Nussbaum (1986a: ch. 8).

we can refer to thunder, ask 'What is thunder?', and advance and assess competing theories. The thin or, we might say, 'nominal' definition of thunder is 'That noise in the clouds, whatever it is'. The competing explanatory theories are rival candidates for correct full or thick definition. So the explanatory story citing Zeus' activities in the clouds is a false account of the very same thing of which the best scientific explanation is a true account. There is just one debate here, with a single subject.

So too, Aristotle suggests, with our ethical terms. Heraclitus, long before him, already had the essential idea, saying, 'They would not have known the name of justice, if these things did not take place.'[11] 'These things', our source for the fragment informs us, are experiences of injustice – presumably of harm, deprivation, inequality. These experiences fix the reference of the corresponding virtue word. Aristotle proceeds along similar lines. In the *Politics* he insists that only human beings, and not either animals or gods, will have our basic ethical terms and concepts (such as just and unjust, noble and base, good and bad), because the beasts are unable to form the concepts, and the gods lack the experiences of limit and finitude that give a concept such as justice its points.[12] In the enumeration of the virtues in the *Nicomachean Ethics*, he carries the line of thought further, suggesting that the reference of the virtue terms is fixed by spheres of choice, frequently connected with our finitude and limitation, that we encounter in virtue of shared conditions of human existence.[13] The question about virtue usually arises in areas in which human choice is both non-optional and somewhat problematic. (Thus, he stresses, there is no virtue involving the regulation of listening to attractive sounds, or seeing pleasing sights.) Each family of virtue and vice or deficiency words attaches to some such sphere. And we can understand progress in ethics, like progress in scientific understanding, to be progress in finding the correct fuller specification of a virtue, isolated by its thin or nominal definition. This progress is aided by a perspicuous mapping of the sphere of the grounding experiences. When we understand more precisely what problems human beings encounter in their lives with one another, what circumstances they face in which choice of some sort is required, we will have a way of assessing competing responses to those problems, and we will begin to understand what it might be to act well in the face of them.

Aristotle's ethical and political writings provide many examples of how such progress (or, more generally, such a rational debate) might go. We find argument against Platonic asceticism, as the proper specification of moderation (appro-

---

[11] Heraclitus, fragment Diels-Kranz B23; see Nussbaum (1972).
[12] See *Politics* I. 2, 1253a1–18; that discussion does not explicitly deny virtues to the gods, but this denial is explicit in *EN* 1145a25–7 and 1178b10ff.
[13] Aristotle does not make the connection with his account of language explicit, but his project is one of defining the virtues, and we would expect him to keep his general view of defining in mind in this context. A similar idea about the virtues, and about the way in which a certain sort of experience can serve as a plausible basis for a non-relative account, is developed (without reference to Aristotle) in Sturgeon (1984).

priate choice and response *vis à vis* the bodily appetites), and in favour of a more generous role for appetitive activity in human life. We find argument against the intense concern for public status and reputation, and the consequent proneness to anger over slights, that was prevalent in Greek ideals of maleness and in Greek behaviour, together with a defence of a more limited and controlled expression of anger, as the proper specification of the virtue that Aristotle calls 'mildness of temper'. (Here Aristotle evinces some discomfort with the virtue term he has chosen, and he is right to do so, since it certainly loads the dice heavily in favour of his concrete specification and against the traditional one.[14]) And so on for all the virtues.

In an important section of *Politics* II, part of which forms one of the epigraphs to this paper, Aristotle defends the proposition that laws should be revisable and not fixed, by pointing to evidence that there is progress towards greater correctness in our ethical conceptions, as also in the arts and sciences. Greeks used to think that courage was a matter of waving swords around; now they have (the *Ethics* informs us) a more inward and a more civic and communally attuned understanding of proper behaviour towards the possibility of death. Women used to be regarded as property, to be bought and sold; now this would be thought barbaric. And in the case of justice as well we have, the *Politics* passage claims, advanced towards a more adequate understanding of what is fair and appropriate. Aristotle gives the example of an existing homicide law that convicts the defendant automatically on the evidence of the prosecutor's relatives (whether they actually witnessed anything or not, apparently). This, Aristotle says, is clearly a stupid and unjust law; and yet it once seemed appropriate – and, to a tradition-bound community, must still be so. To hold tradition fixed is then to prevent ethical progress. What human beings want and seek is not conformity with the past, it is the good. So our systems of law should make it possible for them to progress beyond the past, when they have agreed that a change is good. (They should not, however, make change too easy, since it is no easy matter to see one's way to the good, and tradition is frequently a sounder guide than current fashion.)

In keeping with these ideas, the *Politics* as a whole presents the beliefs of the many different societies it investigates not as unrelated local norms, but as competing answers to questions about justice and courage (and so on) with which all societies are (being human) concerned, and in response to which they all try to find what is good. Aristotle's analysis of the virtues gives him an appropriate framework for these comparisons, which seem perfectly appropriate inquiries into the ways in which different societies have solved common human problems.

In the Aristotelian approach it is obviously of the first importance to distinguish two stages of the inquiry: the initial demarcation of the sphere of choice,

---

[14] See *EN* 1107a5, where Aristotle says that the virtues and the corresponding person are 'pretty much nameless', and says, 'Let us call ... ' when he introduces the names. See also 1125b29, 1126a3–4.

of the 'grounding experiences' that fix the reference of the virtue term; and the ensuing more concrete inquiry into what the appropriate choice, in that sphere, *is*. Aristotle does not always do this carefully; and the language he has to work with is often not helpful to him. We do not have much difficulty with terms like 'moderation' and 'justice' and even 'courage', which seem vaguely normative, but relatively empty, so far, of concrete moral content. As the approach requires, they can serve as extension-fixing labels under which many competing specifications may be investigated. But we have already noticed the problem with 'mildness of temper', which seems to rule out by fiat a prominent contender for the appropriate disposition concerning anger. And much the same thing certainly seems to be true of the relativists' favourite target, *megalopsuchia*, which implies in its very name an attitude to one's own worth that is more Greek than universal. (A Christian, for example, will feel that the proper attitude to one's own worth requires an understanding of one's lowness, frailty, and sinfulness. The virtue of humility requires considering oneself *small*, not great.) What we ought to get at this point in the inquiry is a word for the proper attitude towards anger and offence, and for the proper attitude towards one's worth, that are more truly neutral among the competing specifications, referring only to the sphere of experience within which we wish to determine what is appropriate. Then we could regard the competing conceptions as rival accounts of one and the same thing, so that, for example, Christian humility would be a rival specification of the same virtue whose Greek specification is given in Aristotle's account of *megalopsuchia*, namely, the proper attitude towards the question of one's own worth.

In fact, oddly enough, if one examines the evolution in the use of this word from Aristotle through the Stoics to the Christian fathers, one can see that this is more or less what happened, as 'greatness of soul' became associated, first, with the Stoic emphasis on the supremacy of virtue and the worthlessness of externals, including the body, and, through this, with the Christian denial of the body and of the worth of earthly life.[15] So even in this apparently unpromising case, history shows that the Aristotelian approach not only provided the materials for a single debate but actually succeeded in organizing such a debate, across enormous differences of both place and time.

Here, then, is a sketch for an objective human morality based upon the idea of virtuous action—that is, of appropriate functioning in each human sphere. The Aristotelian claim is that, further developed, it will retain the grounding in actual human experiences that is the strong point of virtue ethics, while gaining the ability to criticize local and traditional moralities in the name of a more inclusive account of the circumstances of human life, and of the needs for human functioning that these circumstances call forth.

[15] See Procope (forthcoming).

[4]

The proposal will encounter many objections. The concluding sections of this paper will present three of the most serious and will sketch the lines along which the Aristotelian might proceed in formulating a reply. To a great extent these objections were not imagined or confronted by Aristotle himself, but his position seems capable of confronting them.

The first objection concerns the relationship between singleness of problem and singleness of solution. Let us grant for the moment that the Aristotelian approach has succeeded in coherently isolating and describing areas of human experience and choice that form, so to speak, the *terrain* of the virtues, and in giving thin definitions of each of the virtues as whatever it is that choosing and responding well within that sphere consists in. Let us suppose that the approach succeeds in doing this in a way that embraces many times and places, bringing disparate cultures together into a single debate about the good human being and the good human life. Different cultural accounts of good choice within the sphere in question in each case are now seen not as untranslatably different, but as competing answers to a single general question about a set of shared human experiences. Still, it might be argued, what has been achieved is, at best, a single discourse or debate about virtue. It has not been shown that this debate will have, as Aristotle believes, a single answer. Indeed, it has not even been shown that the discourse we have set up will have the form of a *debate* at all—rather than a plurality of culturally specific narratives, each giving the thick definition of a virtue that corresponds to the experience and traditions of a particular group. There is an important disanalogy with the case of thunder, on which the Aristotelian so much relies in arguing that our questions will have a single answer. For in that case what is given in experience is the definiendum itself, so that experience establishes a rough extension, to which any good definition must respond. In the case of the virtues, things are more indirect. What is given in experience across groups is only the *ground* of virtuous action, the circumstances of life to which virtuous action is an appropriate response. Even if these grounding experiences are shared, that does not tell us that there will be a shared appropriate response.

In the case of thunder, furthermore, the conflicting theories are clearly put forward as competing candidates for the truth; the behaviour of those involved in the discourse about virtue suggests that they are indeed, as Aristotle says, searching 'not for the way of their ancestors, but for the good'. And it seems reasonable in that case for them to do so. It is far less clear, where the virtues are concerned (the objector continues), that a unified practical solution is either sought by the actual participants or a desideratum for them. The Aristotelian proposal makes it possible to conceive of a way in which the virtues might be non-relative. It does not, by itself, answer the question of relativism.

The second objection goes deeper. For it questions the notion of spheres of shared human experience that lies at the heart of the Aristotelian approach. The approach, says this objector, seems to treat the experiences that ground the virtues as in some way primitive, given, and free from the cultural variation that we find in the plurality of normative conceptions of virtue. Ideas of proper courage may vary, but the fear of death is shared by all human beings. Ideas of moderation may vary, but the experiences of hunger, thirst, and sexual desire are (so the Aristotelian seems to claim) invariant. Normative conceptions introduce an element of cultural interpretation that is not present in the grounding experiences, which are, for that very reason, the Aristotelian's starting point.

But, the objector continues, such assumptions are naïve. They will not stand up either to our best account of experience or to a close examination of the ways in which these so-called grounding experiences are in fact differently constructed by different cultures. In general, first of all, our best accounts of the nature of experience, even perceptual experience, inform us that there is no such thing as an 'innocent eye' that receives an uninterpreted 'given'. Even sense-perception is interpretative, heavily influenced by belief, teaching, language, and in general by social and contextual features. There is a very real sense in which members of different societies do not see the same sun and stars, encounter the same plants and animals, hear the same thunder.

But if this seems to be true of human experience of nature, which was the allegedly unproblematic starting point for Aristotle's account of naming, it is all the more plainly true, the objector claims, in the area of the human good. Here it is only a very naïve and historically insensitive moral philosopher who would say that the experience of the fear of death, or of bodily appetites, is a human constant. Recent anthropological work on the social construction of the emotions,[16] for example, has shown to what extent the experience of fear has learned and culturally variant elements. When we add that the object of the fear in which the Aristotelian takes an interest is death, which has been so variously interpreted and understood by human beings at different times and in different places the conclusion that the 'grounding experience' is an irreducible plurality of experiences, highly various and in each case deeply infused with cultural interpretation, becomes even more inescapable.

Nor is the case different with the apparently less complicated experience of the bodily appetites. Most philosophers who have written about the appetites have treated hunger, thirst, and sexual desire as human universals, stemming from our shared animal nature. Aristotle himself was already more sophisticated, since he insisted that the object of appetite is 'the apparent good' and that appetite is therefore something interpretative and selective, a kind of intentional awareness.[17] But he does not seem to have reflected much about the ways in which historical and cultural differences could shape that awareness. The Hellenistic philosophers who immediately followed him did so reflect, arguing that the experience

---

16 See, for example, Harré (1986); Lutz (1988).
17 See Nussbaum (1978: notes on ch. 6), and Nussbaum (1986a: ch. 9).

of sexual desire and of many forms of the desire for food and drink are, at least in part, social constructs, built up over time on the basis of a social teaching about value; this is external to start with, but it enters so deeply into the perceptions of the individual that it actually forms and transforms the experience of desire.[18] Let us take two Epicurean examples. People are taught that to be well fed they require luxurious fish and meat, that a simple vegetarian diet is not enough. Over time, the combination of teaching with habit produces an appetite for meat, shaping the individual's perceptions of the objects before him. Again, people are taught that what sexual relations are all about is a romantic union or fusion with an object who is seen as exalted in value, or even as perfect. Over time, this teaching shapes sexual behaviour and the experience of desire, so that sexual arousal itself responds to this culturally learned scenario.[19]

This work of social criticism has recently been carried further by Michel Foucault, in his *History of Sexuality*.[20] This work has certain gaps as a history of Greek thought on this topic, but it does succeed in establishing that the Greeks saw the problem of the appetites and their management in an extremely different way from that of twentieth-century Westerners. To summarize two salient conclusions of his complex argument: first, the Greeks did not single out the sexual appetite for special treatment; they treated it alongside hunger and thirst, as a drive that needed to be mastered and kept within bounds. Their central concern was with self-mastery, and they saw the appetites in the light of this concern. Furthermore, where the sexual appetite is concerned, they did not regard the gender of the partner as particularly important in assessing the moral value of the act. Nor did they treat as morally salient a stable disposition to prefer partners of one sex rather than the other. Instead, they focused on the general issue of activity and passivity, connecting it in complex ways with the issue of self-mastery.

Work like Foucault's—and there is a lot of it in various areas, some of it very good—shows very convincingly that the experience of bodily desire, and of the body itself, has elements that vary with cultural and historical change. The names that people call their desires and themselves as subjects of desire, the fabric of belief and discourse into which they integrate their ideas of desiring: all this influences, it is clear, not only their reflection about desire, but also their experience of desire itself. Thus, for example, it is naïve to treat our modern debates about homosexuality as continuations of the very same debate about sexual activity that went on in the Greek world.[21] In a very real sense there was no 'homosexual experience' in a culture that did not contain our emphasis on the gender of the partner, the subjectivity of inclination, and the permanence of

[18] A detailed study of the treatment of these ideas in the three major Hellenistic schools is presented in Nussbaum (forthcoming *b*); portions are published in Nussbaum (1986*b*, 1987*a*, 1989, 1990*a*); see also Nussbaum (1988*b*).

[19] The relevant texts are discussed in Nussbaum (forthcoming *b*); see also Nussbaum (1986*b*, 1989, 1990*a*).

[20] Foucault (1984).

[21] See also Halperin (1990); Winkler (1990); Halperin, Winkler, and Zeitlin (1990).

appetitive disposition, nor our particular ways of problematizing certain forms of behaviour.

If we suppose that we can get underneath this variety and this constructive power of social discourse in at least one case – namely, with the universal experience of bodily pain as a bad thing – even here we find subtle arguments against us. For the experience of pain seems to be embedded in a cultural discourse as surely as the closely related experiences of the appetites, and significant variations can be alleged here as well. The Stoics had already made this claim against the Aristotelian virtues. In order to establish that bodily pain is not bad by its very nature, but only by cultural tradition, the Stoics had to provide some explanation for the ubiquity of the belief that pain is bad and of the tendency to shun it. This explanation would have to show that the reaction is learned rather than natural, and to explain why, in the light of this fact, it is learned so widely. This they did by pointing to certain features in the very early treatment of infants. As soon as an infant is born, it cries. Adults, assuming that the crying is a response to its pain at the unaccustomed coldness and harshness of the place where it finds itself, hasten to comfort it. This behaviour, often repeated, teaches the infant to regard its pain as a bad thing – or, better, teaches it the concept of pain, which includes the notion of badness, and teaches it the forms of life its society shares concerning pain. It is all social teaching, they claimed, though this usually escapes our notice because of the early and non-linguistic nature of the teaching.[22]

These and related arguments, the objector concludes, show that the Aristotelian idea that there can be a single, non-relative discourse about human experiences such as mortality or desire is a naïve one. There is no such bedrock of shared experience, and thus no single sphere of choice within which the virtue is the disposition to choose well. So the Aristotelian project cannot even get off the ground.

Now the Aristotelian confronts a third objector, who attacks from a rather different direction. Like the second, she charges that the Aristotelian has taken for a universal and necessary feature of human life an experience that is contingent on certain non-necessary historical conditions. Like the second, she argues that human experience is much more profoundly shaped by non-necessary social features than the Aristotelian has allowed. But her purpose is not simply, like the second objector's, to point to the great variety of ways in which the 'grounding experiences' corresponding to the virtues are actually understood and lived by human beings. It is more radical still. It is to point out that we could imagine a form of human life that does not contain these experiences – or some of them – at all, in any form. Thus the virtue that consists in acting well in that sphere need not be included in an account of the human good. In some cases, the experience may even be a sign of *bad* human life, and the corresponding virtue therefore no

---

[22] The evidence for this part of the Stoic view is discussed in Nussbaum (forthcoming *b*); for a general account of the Stoic account of the passions, see Nussbaum (1987*a*).

better than a form of non-ideal adaptation to a bad state of affairs. The really good human life, in such a case, would contain neither the grounding deficiency nor the remedial virtue.

This point is forcefully raised by some of Aristotle's own remarks about the virtue of generosity. One of his arguments against societies that eliminate private ownership is that they thereby do away with the opportunity for generous action, which requires having possessions of one's own to give to others.[23] This sort of remark is tailor-made for the objector, who will immediately say that generosity, if it really rests upon the experience of private possession, is a dubious candidate indeed for inclusion in a purportedly non-relative account of the human virtues. If it rests upon a grounding experience that is non-necessary and is capable of being evaluated in different ways, and of being either included or eliminated in accordance with that evaluation, then it is not the universal the Aristotelian said it was.

Some objectors of the third kind will stop at this point, or use such observations to support the second objector's relativism. But in another prominent form this argument takes a non-relativist direction. It asks us to assess the grounding experiences against an account of human flourishing, produced in some independent manner. If we do so, the objector urges, we will discover that some of the experiences are remediable deficiencies. The objection to Aristotelian virtue ethics will then be that it limits our social aspirations, encouraging us to regard as permanent and necessary what we might in fact improve to the benefit of all human life. This is the direction in which the third objection to the virtues was pressed by Karl Marx, its most famous proponent.[24] According to Marx's argument, a number of the leading bourgeois virtues are responses to defective relations of production. Bourgeois justice, generosity, etc., presuppose conditions and structures that are not ideal and that will be eliminated when communism is achieved. And it is not only the current *specification* of these virtues that will be superseded with the removal of the deficiency. It is the virtues themselves. It is in this sense that communism leads human beings beyond ethics.

The Aristotelian is thus urged to inquire into the basic structures of human life with the daring of a radical political imagination. It is claimed that when she does so she will see that human life contains more possibilities than are dreamed of in her list of virtues.

[5]

Each of these objections is profound. To answer any one of them adequately would require a treatise. But we can still do something at this point to map out

---

[23] *Politics* 1263b11ff.

[24] For discussion of the relevant passages in Marx, see Lukes (1987). For an acute discussion of these issues I am indebted to an exchange between Alan Ryan and Stephen Lukes at the Oxford Philosophical Society, March 1987.

an Aristotelian response to each one, pointing the direction in which a fuller reply might go.

The first objector is right to insist on the distinction between singleness of framework and singleness of answer, and right, again, to stress that in constructing a debate about the virtues based on the demarcation of certain spheres of experience we have not yet answered any of the 'What is X?' questions that this debate will confront. We have not even said much about the structure of the debate itself, beyond its beginnings – about how it will both use and criticize traditional beliefs, how it will deal with conflicting beliefs, how it will move critically from the 'way of one's ancestors' to the 'good' – in short, about whose judgements it will trust. I have addressed some of these issues, again with reference to Aristotle, in two other papers;[25] but much more remains to be done. At this point, however, we can make four observations to indicate how the Aristotelian might deal with some of the objector's concerns here. First, the Aristotelian position that I wish to defend need not insist, in every case, on a single answer to the request for a specification of a virtue. The answer might well turn out to be a disjunction. The process of comparative and critical debate will, I imagine, eliminate numerous contenders – for example, the view of justice that prevailed in Cyme. But what remains might well be a (probably small) plurality of acceptable accounts. These accounts may or may not be capable of being subsumed under a single account of greater generality. Success in the eliminative task will still be no trivial accomplishment. If we should succeed in ruling out conceptions of the proper attitude to one's own human worth that are based on a notion of original sin, for example, this would be moral work of enormous significance, even if we got no further than that in specifying the positive account.

Second, the general answer to a 'What is X?' question in any sphere may well be susceptible of several or even of many concrete specifications, in connection with other local practices and local conditions. The normative account where friendship and hospitality are concerned, for example, is likely to be extremely general, admitting of many concrete 'fillings'. Friends in England will have different customs, where regular social visiting is concerned, from friends in ancient Athens. Yet both sets of customs can count as further specifications of a general account of friendship that mentions, for example, the Aristotelian criteria of mutual benefit and well-wishing, mutual enjoyment, mutual awareness, a shared conception of the good, and some form of 'living together'.[26] Sometimes we may want to view such concrete accounts as optional alternative specifications, to be chosen by a society on the basis of reasons of ease and convenience. Sometimes, on the other hand, we may want to insist that a particular account gives the only legitimate specification of the virtue in question for that concrete context; in that case, the concrete account could be viewed as a part of a longer or fuller version

---

[25] Nussbaum (1986a; ch. 8), and Nussbaum and Sen (1989).
[26] See Nussbaum (1986a: ch. 12).

of the single normative account. The decision between these two ways of regarding it will depend upon our assessment of its degree of non-arbitrariness for its context (both physical and historical), its relationship to other non-arbitrary features of the moral conception of that context, and so forth.

Third, whether we have one or several general accounts of a virtue, and whether this/these accounts do or do not admit of more concrete specifications relative to ongoing cultural contexts, the particular choices that the virtuous person, under this conception, makes will always be a matter of being keenly responsive to the local features of his or her concrete context. So in this respect, again, the instructions the Aristotelian will give to the person of virtue do not differ from part of what a relativist would recommend. The Aristotelian virtues involve a delicate balancing between general rules and a keen awareness of particulars, in which process, as Aristotle stresses, the perception of the particular takes priority. It takes priority in the sense that a good rule is a good summary of wise particular choices, and not a court of last resort. Like rules in medicine and navigation, ethical rules should be held open to modification in the light of new circumstances; and the good agent must therefore cultivate the ability to perceive and correctly describe his or her situation finely and truly, including in this perceptual grasp even those features of the situation that are not covered under the existing rule.

I have written a good deal elsewhere on this idea of the 'priority of the particular', exactly what it does and does not imply, in exactly what ways that particular perception is and is not prior to the general rule. Those who want clarification on this central topic will have to turn to those writings.[27]

What I want to stress here is that Aristotelian particularism is fully compatible with Aristotelian objectivity. The fact that a good and virtuous decision is context-sensitive does not imply that it is right only *relative to*, or *inside*, a limited context, any more than the fact that a good navigational judgement is sensitive to particular weather conditions shows that it is correct only in a local or relational sense. It is right absolutely, objectively, anywhere in the human world, to attend to the particular features of one's context; and the person who so attends and who chooses accordingly is making, according to Aristotle, the humanly correct decision, period. If another situation should ever arise with all the same ethically relevant features, including contextual features, the same decision would again be absolutely right.[28]

It should be stressed that the value of contextual responsiveness and the value of getting it right are seen by the Aristotelian as mutually supportive here, rather than in tension. For the claim is that only when we have duly responded to the complexities of the context, seeing it for the very historical situation it is, will

---

[27] Nussbaum (1986*a*: ch. 10); Nussbaum (1985, 1987*b*).
[28] I believe, however, that some morally relevant features, in the Aristotelian view, may be features that are not, even in principle, replicable in another context. See Nussbaum (1986*a*: ch. 10) and Nussbaum (1985, 1990*b*).

we have any hope of making the right decision. Short of that, the importation of plausible general values, however well intentioned, may do no good at all, and may actually make things worse. Nor, the Aristotelian argues, have we been sufficiently responsive to the context before us if we do not see the humanity in it: do not, that is, respond to the claims of human need, the strivings towards the good, the frustrations of human capability, that this situation displays to the reflective person. To study it with detached scientific interest, as an interesting set of local traditions, is not to respond sufficiently to the concrete situation it is; for whatever it is, it is concretely human.

An example from the development context will illustrate this mutual support. In *A Quiet Revolution*, an eloquent study of women's education in rural Bangladesh,[29] Martha Chen describes the efforts of a government development group, the Bangladesh Rural Advancement Committee, to increase the rate of female literacy in certain rural areas. The project began from a conviction that literacy is an important ingredient in the development of these women towards greater capability to live well. It was seen as closely linked with other important values, such as economic flourishing, autonomy, and self-respect. This conviction did not derive from the local traditions of the villages, where women had in fact little autonomy and no experience of education; it derived from the experiences and reflections of the development workers, who were themselves from many different backgrounds and two nationalities. (Chen herself is an American with a Ph.D. in Sanskrit.) The group as a whole lacked experience of the concrete ways of life of rural women, and thus had, as Chen says, 'no specific concepts or strategies'[30] for working with them. In the first phase of the programme, then, the development workers went directly to the rural villages with their ideas of literacy and its importance, offering adult literacy materials borrowed from another national programme, and trying to motivate the women of the communities they entered to take them on.

But their lack of contextual knowledge made it impossible for them to succeed, in this first phase. Women found the borrowed literacy materials boring and irrelevant to their lives. They did not see how literacy would help them; even the accompanying vocational training was resisted, since it focused on skills for which there was little demand in that area. Thus failure led the agency to rethink their approach. On the one hand, they never abandoned their basic conviction that literacy was important for these women; their conclusion, based on wide experience and on their picture of what the women's lives might be, still seemed sound. On the other hand, they recognized that far more attention to the lives and thoughts of the women involved would be necessary if they were going to come up with an understanding of what literacy might do and be for them. They began to substitute for the old approach a more participatory one, in which local co-operative groups brought together development workers with local women,

[29] Chen (1986).
[30] Chen (1986: p. ix).

whose experience and sense of life were regarded as crucial. This concept of the co-operative group led to a much more complex understanding of the situation, as the development workers grasped the network of relationships within which the women had to function and the specific dimensions of their poverty and constraints, and as the women grasped the alternative possibilities and began to define for themselves a set of aspirations for change. The result, which continues, has been a slow and complex evolution in the role of women in the villages. A visiting journalist wrote, some years later:

I saw the seeds of the quiet revolution starting in village women's lives. At the meeting houses BRAC has built, the wives, young and old, are learning to read and write. Forbidden from doing marketing, they now at least can keep the accounts . . . In one fishing village, the women have even become the bankers, saving over $2000 and lending it to their men to buy better equipment. It started in the simplest way—they collected a handful of rice a week from each family, stored it, and sold it in the market. About 50 villages from each area have thriving women's cooperatives, investing in new power-pumps or seed, and winning respect for their members.[31]

This is how the Aristotelian approach works—hanging on to a general (and open-ended) picture of human life, its needs and possibilities, but at every stage immersing itself in the concrete circumstances of history and culture. Chen's detailed narrative—which in its very style manifests a combination of Aristotelian commitment to the human good and Aristotelian contextual sensitivity—shows that the two elements go, and must go, together. If the development workers had approached these women as alien beings whose ways could not be compared with others and considered with a view to the human good, no change would have taken place—and the narrative convinces the reader that these changes have been good. On the other hand, general talk of education and self-respect did nothing at all until it came from within a concrete historical reality. Immersion made it possible to get the choice that was humanly right.

Thus the Aristotelian virtue-based morality can capture a great deal of what the relativist is after, and still make a claim to objectivity, in the sense we have described. In fact, we might say that the Aristotelian virtues do better than the relativist virtues in explaining what people are actually doing when they scrutinize the features of their context carefully, looking at both the shared and the non-shared features with an eye to what is best. For, as Aristotle says, people who do this are usually searching for the good, not just for the way of their ancestors. They are prepared to defend their decisions as good or right, and to think of those who advocate a different course as disagreeing about what is right, not just narrating a different tradition.

Finally, we should point out that the Aristotelian virtues, and the deliberations they guide, unlike some systems of moral rules, remain always open to revision

[31] Cited in Chen (1986: 4–5). Chen stresses that one important factor in this later success was that the group had no dogmatic adherence to an abstract theory of development, but had a flexible and situation-guided approach.

in the light of new circumstances and new evidence. In this way, again, they contain the flexibility to local conditions that the relativist would desire – but, again, without sacrificing objectivity. Sometimes the new circumstances may simply give rise to a new concrete specification of the virtue as previously defined; in some cases it may cause us to change our view about what the virtue itself is. All general accounts are held provisionally, as summaries of correct decisions and as guides to new ones. This flexibility, built into the Aristotelian procedure, will again help the Aristotelian account to answer the questions of the relativist, without relativism.

[6]

We must now turn to the second objection. Here, I believe, is the really serious threat to the Aristotelian position. Past writers on virtue, including Aristotle himself, have lacked sensitivity to the ways in which different traditions of discourse, different conceptual schemes, articulate the world, and also to the profound connections between the structure of discourse and the structure of experience itself. Any contemporary defence of the Aristotelian position must display this sensitivity, responding somehow to the data that the relativist historian or anthropologist brings forward.

The Aristotelian should begin, it seems to me, by granting that with respect to any complex matter of deep human importance there is no 'innocent eye', no way of seeing the world that is entirely neutral and free of cultural shaping. The work of philosophers such as Putnam, Goodman, and Davidson[32] – following, one must point out, from the arguments of Kant and, I believe, from those of Aristotle himself[33] – have shown convincingly that even where sense-perception is concerned, the human mind is an active and interpretative instrument, and that its interpretations are a function of its history and its concepts, as well as of its innate structure. The Aristotelian should also grant, it seems to me, that the nature of human world interpretations is holistic and that the criticism of them must, equally, be holistic. Conceptual schemes, like languages, hang together as whole structures, and we should realize, too, that a change in any single element is likely to have implications for the system as a whole.

But these two facts do not imply, as some relativists in literary theory and in anthropology tend to assume, that all world interpretations are equally valid and altogether non-comparable, that there are no good standards of assessment and 'anything goes'. The rejection of the idea of ethical truth as correspondence to an altogether uninterpreted reality does not imply that the whole idea of searching for the truth is an old-fashioned error. Certain ways in which people see the world can still be criticized exactly as Aristotle

[32] See Putnam (1979, 1981, 1988); Goodman (1968, 1978); Davidson (1984).

[33] On his debt to Kant, see Putnam (1988); on Aristotle's relationship to 'internal realism', see Nussbaum (1986a: ch. 8).

criticized them: as stupid, pernicious, and false. The standards used in such criticisms must come from inside human life. (Frequently they will come from the society in question itself, from its own rationalist and critical traditions.) And the inquirer must attempt, prior to criticism, to develop an inclusive understanding of the conceptual scheme being criticized, seeing what motivates each of its parts and how they hang together. But there is so far no reason to think that the critic will not be able to reject the institution of slavery, or the homicide law of Cyme, as out of line with the conception of virtue that emerges from reflection on the variety of different ways in which human cultures have had the experiences that ground the virtues.

The grounding experiences will not, the Aristotelian should concede, provide precisely a single, language-neutral bedrock on which an account of virtue can be straightforwardly and unproblematically based. The description and assessment of the ways in which different cultures have constructed these experiences will become one of the central tasks of Aristotelian philosophical criticism. But the relativist has, so far, shown no reason why we could not, at the end of the day, say that certain ways of conceptualizing death are more in keeping with the totality of our evidence and the totality of our wishes for flourishing life than others; that certain ways of experiencing appetitive desire are for similar reasons more promising than others.

Relativists tend, furthermore, to understate the amount of attunement, recognition, and overlap that actually obtains across cultures, particularly in the areas of the grounding experiences. The Aristotelian, in developing her conception in a culturally sensitive way, should insist, as Aristotle himself does, upon the evidence of such attunement and recognition. Despite the evident differences in the specific cultural shaping of the grounding experiences, we do recognize the experiences of people in other cultures as similar to our own. We do converse with them about matters of deep importance, understand them, allow ourselves to be moved by them. When we read Sophocles' *Antigone*, we see a good deal that seems strange to us; and we have not read the play well if we do not notice how far its conceptions of death, womanhood, and so on differ from our own. But it is still possible for us to be moved by the drama, to care about its people, to regard their debates as reflections upon virtue that speak to our own experience, and their choices as choices in spheres of conduct in which we too must choose. Again, when one sits down at a table with people from other parts of the world and debates with them concerning hunger, or just distribution, or in general the quality of human life, one does find, in spite of evident conceptual differences, that it is possible to proceed as if we were all talking about the same human problem; and it is usually only in a context in which one or more of the parties is intellectually committed to a theoretical relativist position that this discourse proves impossible to sustain. This sense of community and overlap seems to be especially strong in the areas that we have called the areas of the grounding experiences. And this, it seems, supports the Aristotelian claim that those experiences can be a good starting point for ethical debate.

Furthermore, it is necessary to stress that hardly any cultural group today is as focused upon its own internal traditions and as isolated from other cultures as the relativist argument presupposes. Cross-cultural communication and debate are ubiquitous facts of contemporary life, and our experience of cultural interaction indicates that in general the inhabitants of different conceptual schemes do tend to view their interaction in the Aristotelian and not the relativist way. A traditional society, confronted with new technologies and sciences, and the conceptions that go with them, does not in fact simply fail to understand them, or regard them as totally alien incursions upon a hermetically sealed way of life. Instead, it assesses the new item as a possible contributor to flourishing life, making it comprehensible to itself, and incorporating elements that promise to solve problems of flourishing. Examples of such assimilation, and the debate that surrounds it,[34] suggest that the parties do in fact recognize common problems and that the traditional society is perfectly capable of viewing an external innovation as a device to solve a problem that it shares with the innovating society. The village woman of Chen's narrative, for example, did not insist on remaining illiterate because they had always been so. Instead, they willingly entered into dialogue with the international group, viewing co-operative discussion as a resource towards a better life. The parties do in fact search for the good, not the way of their ancestors; only traditionalist anthropologists insist, nostalgically, on the absolute preservation of the ancestral.

And this is so even when cross-cultural discourse reveals a difference at the level of the conceptualization of the grounding experiences. Frequently the effect of work like Foucault's, which reminds us of the non-necessary and non-universal character of one's own ways of seeing in some such area, is precisely to prompt a critical debate in search of the human good. It is difficult, for example, to read Foucault's observations about the history of our sexual ideas without coming to feel that certain ways in which the Western contemporary debate on these matters has been organized, as a result of some combination of Christian moralism with nineteenth-century pseudoscience, are especially silly, arbitrary, and limiting, inimical to a human search for flourishing. Foucault's moving account of Greek culture, as he himself insists in a preface,[35] provides not only a sign that someone once thought differently, but also evidence that it is possible for *us* to think differently. (Indeed, this was the whole purpose of genealogy as Nietzsche, Foucault's precursor here, introduced it: to destroy idols once deemed necessary, and to clear the way for new possibilities of creation.) Foucault announced that the purpose of his book was to 'free thought' so that it could think differently, imagining new and more fruitful possibilities. And close analysis of spheres of cultural

---

[34] Abeysekera (1986).
[35] Foucault (1984: ii, preface).

discourse, which stresses cultural differences in the spheres of the grounding experiences, is being combined, increasingly, in current debates about sexuality and related matters, with a critique of existing social arrangements and attitudes, and an elaboration of new norms of human flourishing. There is no reason to think this combination incoherent.[36]

As we pursue these possibilities, the basic spheres of experience identified in the Aristotelian approach will no longer, we have said, be seen as spheres of *uninterpreted* experience. But we have also insisted that there is much family relatedness and much overlap among societies. And certain areas of relatively greater universality can be specified here, on which we should insist as we proceed to areas that are more varied in their cultural expression. Not without a sensitive awareness that we are speaking of something that is experienced differently in different contexts, we can none the less identify certain features of our common humanity, closely related to Aristotle's original list, from which our debate might proceed.

1. *Mortality.* No matter how death is understood, all human beings face it and (after a certain age) know that they face it. This fact shapes every aspect of more or less every human life.

2. *The body.* Prior to any concrete cultural shaping, we are born with human bodies, whose possibilities and vulnerabilities do not as such belong to any culture rather than any other. Any given human being might have belonged to any culture. The experience of the body is culturally influenced; but the body itself, prior to such experience, provides limits and parameters that ensure a great deal of overlap in what is going to be experienced, where hunger, thirst, desire, and the five senses are concerned. It is all very well to point to the cultural component in these experiences. But when one spends time considering issues of hunger and scarcity, and in general of human misery, such differences appear relatively small and refined, and one cannot fail to acknowledge that 'there are no known ethnic differences in human physiology with respect to metabolism of nutrients. Africans and Asians do not burn their dietary calories or use their dietary protein any differently from Europeans and Americans. It follows then that dietary requirements cannot vary widely as between different races.'[37] This and similar facts should surely be focal points for debate about appropriate human behaviour in this sphere. And by beginning with the body, rather than with the subjective experience of desire, we get, furthermore, an opportunity to criticize the situation of people who are so persistently deprived that their *desire* for good things has actually decreased. This is a further advantage of the Aristotelian approach, when contrasted

---

[36] This paragraph expands remarks made in a commentary on papers by D. Halperin and J. Winkler at the conference on 'Homosexuality in History and Culture' at Brown University, February 1987; Halperin's paper is now in Halperin (1990) and Winkler's in Halperin, Winkler, and Zeitlin (1990). The proposed combination of historically sensitive analysis with cultural criticism was forcefully developed, at the same conference, by Abelove (1987).

[37] Gopalan (forthcoming).

with approaches to choice that stop with subjective expressions of preference.

3. *Pleasure and pain*. In every culture, there is a conception of pain; and these conceptions, which overlap very largely with one another, can plausibly be seen as grounded in universal and pre-cultural experience. The Stoic story of infant development is highly implausible; the negative response to bodily pain is surely primitive and universal, rather than learned and optional, however much its specific 'grammar' may be shaped by later learning.

4. *Cognitive capability*. Aristotle's famous claim that 'all human beings by nature reach out for understanding'[38] seems to stand up to the most refined anthropological analysis. It points to an element in our common humanity that is plausibly seen, again, as grounded independently of particular acculturation, however much it is later shaped by acculturation.

5. *Practical reason*. All human beings, whatever their culture, participate (or try to) in the planning and managing of their lives, asking and answering questions about how one should live and act. This capability expresses itself differently in different societies, but a being who altogether lacked it would not be likely to be acknowledged as a human being, in any culture.[39]

6. *Early infant development*. Prior to the greater part of specific cultural shaping, though perhaps not free from all shaping, are certain areas of human experience and development that are broadly shared and of great importance for the Aristotelian virtues: experiences of desire, pleasure, loss, one's own finitude, perhaps also of envy, grief, and gratitude. One may argue about the merits of one or another psychoanalytical account of infancy. But it seems difficult to deny that the work of Freud on infant desire and of Klein on grief, loss, and other more complex emotional attitudes has identified spheres of human experience that are to a large extent common to all humans, regardless of their particular society. All humans begin as hungry babies, perceiving their own helplessness, their alternating closeness to and distance from those on whom they depend, and so forth. Melanie Klein records a conversation with an anthropologist in which an event that at first looked (to Western eyes) bizarre was interpreted by Klein as the expression of a universal pattern of mourning. The anthropologist accepted her interpretation.[40]

7. *Affiliation*. Aristotle's claim that human beings as such feel a sense of fellowship with other human beings, and that we are by nature social animals, is an empirical claim; but it seems to be a sound one. However varied our specific conceptions of friendship and love are, there is a great point in seeing them as overlapping expressions of the same family of shared human needs and desires.

8. *Humour*. There is nothing more culturally varied than humour; and yet, as Aristotle insists, some space for humour and play seems to be a need of

---

[38] *Metaphysics* I. 1.
[39] See Nussbaum (1988), where this Aristotelian view is compared with Marx's views on truly human functioning.
[40] Klein (1984): 247–63.

any human life. The human being is not called the 'laughing animal' for nothing; it is certainly one of our salient differences from almost all other animals, and (in some form or other) a shared feature, I somewhat boldly assert, of any life that is going to be counted as fully human.

This is just a list of suggestions, closely related to Aristotle's list of common experiences. One could subtract some of these items and/or add others.[41] But it seems plausible to claim that in all these areas we have a basis for further work on the human good. We do not have a bedrock of completely uninterpreted 'given' data, but we do have nuclei of experience around which the constructions of different societies proceed. There is no Archimedean point here, no pure access to unsullied 'nature'—even, here, human nature—as it is in and of itself. There is just human life as it is lived. But in life as it is lived, we do find a family of experiences, clustering around certain focuses, which can provide reasonable starting points for cross-cultural reflection.

This paper forms part of a larger project. The role of the preliminary list proposed in this section can be better understood if I briefly set it in the context of this more comprehensive enterprise, showing its links with other arguments. In a paper entitled 'Nature, Function, and Capability: Aristotle on Political Distribution',[42] I discuss an Aristotelian conception of the proper function of government, according to which its task is to make available to each and every member of the community the basic necessary conditions of the capability to choose and live a fully good human life, with respect to each of the major human functions included in that fully good life. I examine sympathetically Aristotle's argument that, for this reason, the task of government cannot be well performed, or its aims well understood, without an understanding of these functionings. A closely connected study, 'Aristotelian Social Democracy',[43] shows a way of moving from a general understanding of the circumstances and abilities of human beings (such as this list provides) to an account of the most important human functions that it will be government's job to make possible. It shows how this understanding of the human being and the political task can yield a conception of social democracy that is a plausible alternative to liberal conceptions.

Meanwhile, in a third paper, 'Aristotle on Human Nature and the Foundations of Ethics',[44] I focus on the special role of two of the human capabilities

---

[41] See Nussbaum (1990c) for a slightly longer list, including discussion of our relationship to other species and to the world of nature. It is very interesting to notice that three other lists in this volume, prepared independently, contain almost the same items as this one: Dan Brock's list of basic human functions used in quality of life measures in medical ethics; Erik Allardt's enumeration of the functions observed by Finnish social scientists; and Robert Erikson's list of functions measured by the Swedish group. Only the last two may show mutual influence. So much independent convergence testifies to the ubiquity of these concerns and to their importance.

[42] Nussbaum (1988a).

[43] Nussbaum (1990c).

[44] Nussbaum (forthcoming a).

recognized in this list: affiliation (or sociability) and practical reason. I argue that these two play an architectonic role in human life, suffusing and also organizing all the other functions—which will count as truly human functions only in so far as they are done with some degree of guidance from both of these. Most of the paper is devoted to an examination of Aristotle's arguments for saying that these two elements are parts of 'human nature'. I argue that this is not an attempt to base human ethics on a neutral bedrock of scientific fact outside of human experience and interpretation. I claim that Aristotle seeks, instead, to discover, among the experiences of groups in many times and places, certain elements that are especially broadly and deeply shared. And I argue that the arguments justifying the claims of these two to be broad and deep in this way have a self-validating structure: that is, anyone who participates in the first place in the inquiry that supports them affirms, by that very fact, her own recognition of their salience. This is an important continuation of the project undertaken in this paper, since it shows exactly how Aristotle's 'foundation' for ethics can remain inside human history and self-interpretation, and yet still claim to be a foundation.

[7]

The third objection raises, at bottom, a profound conceptual question: What is it to inquire about the *human* good? What circumstances of existence go to define what it is to live the life of a *human being*, and not some other life? Aristotle likes to point out that an inquiry into the human good cannot, on pain of incoherence, end up describing the good of some other being, say a god—a good that, on account of our circumstances, it is impossible for us to attain.[45] What circumstances then? The virtues are defined relatively to certain problems and limitations, and also to certain endowments. Which ones are sufficiently central that their removal would make us into different beings, and open up a wholly new and different debate about the good? This question is itself part of the ethical debate we propose. For there is no way to answer it but to ask ourselves which elements of our experience seem to us so important that they count, for us, as part of who we are. I discuss Aristotle's attitude to this question elsewhere, and I shall simply summarize here.[46] It seems clear, first of all, that our mortality is an essential feature of our circumstances as human beings. An immortal being would have such a different form of life, and such different values and virtues, that it does not seem to make sense to regard that being as part of the same search for good. Essential, too, will be our dependence upon the world outside us: some sort of need for food, drink, the help of others. On the side of abilities, we would want to include cognitive

---

45 Cf. *EN* 1159a 10–12, 1166a 18–23.
46 Nussbaum (forthcoming *a*).

functioning and the activity of practical reasoning as elements of any life that we would regard as human. Aristotle argues, plausibly, that we would want to include sociability as well, some sensitivity to the needs of and pleasure in the company of other beings similar to ourselves.

But it seems to me that the Marxist question remains, as a deep question about human forms of life and the search for the human good. For one certainly can imagine forms of human life that do not contain the holding of private property—nor, therefore, those virtues that have to do with its proper management. And this means that it remains an open question whether these virtues ought to be regarded as virtues, and kept upon our list. Marx wished to go much further, arguing that communism would remove the need for justice, courage, and most of the bourgeois virtues. I think we might be sceptical here. Aristotle's general attitude to such transformations of life is to suggest that they usually have a tragic dimension. If we remove one sort of problem—say, by removing private property—we frequently do so by introducing another— say, the absence of a certain sort of freedom of choice, the freedom that makes it possible to do fine and generous actions for others. If things are complex even in the case of generosity, where we can easily imagine the transformation that removes the virtue, they are surely far more so in the cases of justice and courage. And we would need a far more detailed description than Marx ever gives us of the form of life under communism, before we could even begin to see whether it would in fact transform things where these virtues are concerned, and whether it would or would not introduce new problems and limitations in their place.

In general it seems that all forms of life, including the imagined life of a god, contain boundaries and limits.[47] All structures, even that of putative limitlessness, are closed to something, cut off from something—say, in that case, from the specific value and beauty inherent in the struggle against limitation. Thus it does not appear that we will so easily get beyond the virtues. Nor does it seem to be so clearly a good thing for human life that we should.

[8]

The best conclusion to this sketch of an Aristotelian programme for virtue ethics was written by Aristotle himself, at the end of his discussion of human nature in *Nicomachean Ethics* I:

So much for our outline sketch for the good. For it looks as if we have to draw an outline first, and fill it in later. It would seem to be open to anyone to take things further and to articulate the good parts of the sketch. And time is a good discoverer or ally in such things. That's how the sciences have progressed as well: it is open to anyone to supply what is lacking. (*EN* 1098a20–6)

[47] See Nussbaum (1986*b*: ch. 11).

BIBLIOGRAPHY

ABELOVE, H. (1987). 'Is Gay History Possible?' Paper (unpublished) delivered at the Conference on Homosexuality in History and Culture, Brown University, Feb. 1987.

ABEYSEKERA, C. (1986). Address (unpublished) to the WIDER Conference on Value and Technology, summer 1986.

CHEN, M. (1986). *A Quiet Revolution: Women in Transition in Rural Bangladesh.* Cambridge, Mass.: Schenkman Publishing Company.

DAVIDSON, D. (1984). *Inquiries into Truth and Interpretation.* Oxford: Clarendon Press.

FOOT, P. (1978). *Virtues and Vices.* Berkeley: University of California Press.

FOUCAULT, M. (1984). *Histoire de la sexualité,* ii, iii. Paris: Les Belles Lettres.

GOODMAN, N. (1968). *Languages of Art.* Indianapolis: Hackett.

—— (1978). *Ways of World-Making.* Indianapolis: Hackett.

GOPALAN, C. (1992). 'Undernutrition: Measurement and Implications', In S. Osmani (ed.), *Nutrition and Poverty.* Oxford: Clarendon Press.

HALPERIN, D. (1990). *One Hundred Years of Homosexuality and Other Essays on Greek Love.* New York: Routledge, Chapman, and Hall.

——, WINKLER, J., and ZEITLIN, F. (1990). *Before Sexuality.* Princeton: Princeton University Press.

HAMPSHIRE, S. (1983). *Morality and Conflict.* Cambridge, Mass.: Harvard University Press.

HARRÉ, R. (ed.) (1986). *The Social Construction of the Emotions.* Oxford: Basil Blackwell.

KLEIN, M. (1984). 'Our Adult World and its Roots in Infancy', in *Envy, Gratitude and Other Works 1946–1963.* London: Hogarth Press, 247–63.

LUKES, S. (1987). *Marxism and Morality.* Oxford: Clarendon Press.

LUTZ, C. (1988). *Unnatural Emotions.* Chicago: University of Chicago Press.

MACINTYRE, A. (1981). *After Virtue.* Notre Dame: Notre Dame University Press.

—— (1988). *Whose Justice? Which Rationality?* Notre Dame: Notre Dame University Press.

NUSSBAUM, M. (1972). '*Psuche* in Heraclitus', *Phronesis,* 17, 1–17, 153–70.

—— (1978). *Aristotle's De Motu Animalium.* Princeton: Princeton University Press.

—— (1985). 'The Discernment of Perception: An Aristotelian Model of Public and Private Rationality', *Proceedings of the Boston Area Colloquium for Ancient Philosophy,* 1, 151–201. Also in Nussbaum (1990).

—— (1986a). *The Fragility of Goodness: Luck and Ethics in Greek Tragedy and Philosophy.* Cambridge: Cambridge University Press.

—— (1986b). 'Therapeutic Arguments: Epicurus and Aristotle', in M. Schofield and G. Striker (eds.), *The Norms of Nature.* Cambridge: Cambridge University Press, 31–74.

—— (1987a). 'The Stoics on the Extirpation of the Passions', *Apeiron,* 20, 129–77.

—— (1987b). '"Finely Aware and Richly Responsible": Literature and the Moral Imagination', in A. Cascardi (ed.), *Literature and the Question of Philosophy.* Baltimore: Johns Hopkins University Press, 169–91.

—— (1988a). 'Nature, Function, and Capability: Aristotle on Political Distribution', *Oxford Studies in Ancient Philosophy,* suppl. vol., 145–84.

—— (1988b). 'Narrative Emotions: Beckett's Genealogy of Love', *Ethics,* 98, 225–54.

—— (1989). 'Beyond Obsession and Disgust: Lucretius' Genealogy of Love', *Apeiron*, 22, 1–59.

—— (1990*a*). 'Mortal Immortals: Lucretius on Death and the Voice of Nature', *Philosophy and Phenomenological Research*, 50, 305–51.

—— (1990*b*). *Love's Knowledge: Essays on Philosophy and Literature*. Oxford: Oxford University Press.

—— (1990*c*). 'Aristotelian Social Democracy', in R.B. Douglass, G. Mara, and H. Richardson (eds.). *Liberalism and the Good*. New York: Routledge, 203–52.

—— (forthcoming *a*). 'Aristotle on Human Nature and the Foundations of Ethics', in a volume on the philosophy of Bernard Williams, ed. J. Altham and R. Harrison. Cambridge: Cambridge University Press.

—— (forthcoming *b*). *The Therapy of Desire: Theory and Practice in Hellenistic Ethics*. The Martin Classical Lectures, 1986.

—— and SEN, A. (1989). 'Internal Criticism and Indian Rationalist Traditions', in M. Krausz (ed.), *Relativism*. Notre Dame: Notre Dame University Press.

PROCOPE, J. (forthcoming). 'Hochherzigkeit', *Reallexikon für Antike und Christentum*, 14.

PUTNAM, H. (1979). *Meaning and the Moral Sciences*. London: Routledge and Kegan Paul.

—— (1981). *Reason, Truth, and History*. Cambridge: Cambridge University Press.

—— (1988). *The Many Faces of Realism: The Carus Lectures*. La Salle, Ill. Open Court.

STURGEON, N. (1984). Review of Foot, *Journal of Philosophy*, 81, 326–33.

WALZER, M. (1983). *Spheres of Justice*. Oxford: Basil Blackwell.

—— (1987). *Interpretation and Social Criticism*. Cambridge, Mass.: Harvard University Press.

WILLIAMS, B. (1984). 'Philosophy', in *The Legacy of Greece*, ed. M.I. Finley. Oxford: Oxford University Press.

—— (1985). *Ethics and the Limits of Philosophy*. Cambridge, Mass.: Harvard University Press.

WINKLER, J. (1990). *The Constraints of Desire*. New York: Routledge, Chapman, and Hall.

Martha Nussbaum: Non-Relative Virtues: An Aristotelian Approach

Commentary by Susan Hurley

Does appeal to forms of life underwrite or undermine claims to objectivity? The question arises in various contexts and forms. The forms of life appealed to may be linguistic or other practices, or aspects of experience or thought. Objectivity may seem threatened in various ways: by relativism, given the variety of forms of life; by idealism, if a claim about the way things are is made to depend on forms of life that are ultimately down to us, not the world; by verificationism, if it is suggested that necessary conditions for our practices of determining something to be true are necessary conditions of its *being* true. On the other hand, some, such as Wittgenstein, have thought that the appeal to practices keeps such threats from arising, by engaging one's mind immediately with the world and other minds: if we are able to do certain things well, together, there is no further real issue as to how our private intentions can ever match up. Martha Nussbaum's paper considers whether appeal to the varying forms of life that ground talk of specific virtues tends to support relativism, and argues that it does not. She sketches forms of life that are distinctive of human beings, hedged in as we are in some sense between the gods and the beasts. In contrast with the gods, we have essentially in common certain basic reference-fixing experiences of the conditions of limited, mortal human (as opposed to godlike) life, which allow us to address the same question—how should one act with respect to *that* sort of situation?—even though we may disagree about the best answer. In contrast with the beasts, we also have essentially in common certain distinctive capacities, for sociality and practical reason, our valued exercises of which may be appealed to in the course of ethical disagreement. Correctly understood, she argues, the role of these specific and distinctively human forms of life in ethics, and in Aristotelian ethics in particular, does not support relativism and does support objectivism.

I am in substantial accord with her conclusion, and indeed have myself offered different arguments for related conclusions, which I will not repeat here.[1] Her responses to the first objection she considers to her position, concerning singleness of solution, seem to me correct. The second objection she considers concerns the lack of culturally neutral, uninterpreted common starting points in experience or practice; while I have certain reservations about her formulation of a response to this objection in terms of different conceptual schemes, I shall pass over those issues here. What I will focus on are certain issues arising out of suggestions she makes in responding to the third objection, concerning the possibility of human life that simply lacks

---

[1] See my *Natural Reasons* (1989), esp. Part I.

certain forms of life altogether. These issues concern another way in which arguments that appeal to forms of life may seem to undermine claims to objectivity.

Nussbaum suggests that a particular kind of self-validating argument is available in discussions of the value to be placed on certain of the features of our common humanity that she lists, such as sociality and practical reason. This is a kind of argument that gets its force not from any logical inconsistency in the position it argues against, but rather from a pragmatic inconsistency: some aspect of the form of life, the activity, practice, or mentality, of the sceptic has implications inconsistent with the content of his view. As we shall see below, such pragmatic inconsistencies often play a role in transcendental arguments—arguments concerning how certain forms of life are possible, what the necessary conditions for them are. Nussbaum suggests an example of what I am calling pragmatic inconsistency: the sceptic's very participation in discussion of the value of practical reason in the course of expressing his sceptical view about it in some sense affirms its value, and so is at odds with the sceptical content of his view. She further suggests that there may be cases in which the essential properties as a human being of the person holding a sceptical view would be negated by the living out of that view, so that such a life—say, the life of a god, or of a beast—could not be a life for that person.

I want to consider two questions about these suggestions. (1) What is the significance with respect to issues about objectivity of the fact that certain expressions of some propositions presuppose other inconsistent propositions? (2) How is our capacity for self-determination related to the way in which we may be constrained in the evaluative views we can defend by what we essentially are as human beings, our essential limitations and aspirations?

The first question arises in the debate about whether transcendental arguments undermine objectivity. They may seem to involve some kind of idealism or relativism or verificationism, by deriving conclusions about the world and/or other possible minds from features of our forms of life, so cutting the world and/or other minds down to the size of our minds.[2] Ross Harrison has offered a rebuttal of the view that transcendental arguments must involve idealism. He points out that such arguments are of the valid inferential form: p, necessarily if p then q; therefore q. The minor premiss p is often established pragmatically, by immersion in certain forms of life: experience, language, thought. Various celebrated if problematic arguments, which are not my focus here, support the conditional premisses of such inferences: arguments made by Kant, Strawson, Davidson, etc., concerning the necessary conditions of experience, language, content, thought. But we should notice, Harrison says, that for such inferences to be valid the minor premiss 'f' need not be necessary. There might not, for example, have been any minds, or any language, at all. Far from being mind-dependent, the world might have been mindless,

---

[2] See Nagel (1986: ch. 6); Williams (1981).

hence not the object of judgement or thought at all. Such an admission is hardly idealist in implication, nor does it tend to undermine a view of the world as objective.

While there is clearly something right about it, Harrison's argument does not seem to go to the heart of the intuition that transcendental arguments somehow tend to undermine objectivity. To this end, we should distinguish between two ways in which the minor premiss of a transcendental argment gets established, even if not established as necessary. This is the premiss for which support may be pragmatic, conceded by something the sceptic does or is, his form of life. Such pragmatic support can take at least two forms. It can be either presuppositional, or demonstrative.

Presuppositional support derives from our presupposing that p in many of our activities and from the fact that forgoing such activities would be terribly costly. Consider, for example, the argument that the contents of the reactive attitudes presupposed by many of our relationships and practices imply, under certain conditions, blame and guilt, and that such attitudes, presupposed as they are in many of our valued ways of living, would be terribly costly to forgo. We have no good reason to forgo them, when we consider what the consequences would be in terms of the impoverishment of our lives.[3] Consider also the argument, suggested by Nussbaum, that participation in philosophical discussion of the value of practical reason presupposes that there is reason to go in for such discussion, which implies the value of practical reason. Or the argument put forward by Putnam that successful reference by someone to vats in asserting that he might be a brain in a vat presupposes that he is in the right sort of a causal connection with vats — not, that is, merely a generic causal connection to artificial skull — in which case he is not a brain in a vat.[4]

Harrison's point, applied to such arguments, would be that there is no necessity that we go in for reactive attitudes, or for philosophical discussion of the value of practical reason; nor does any necessity attach to reference to vats. We could simply cut ourselves off from other people, refrain from deliberation, or language, or thought about vats, and nothing would be presupposed; in some cases, the price of pragmatically consistent scepticism is silence, isolation, perhaps ever denaturing ourselves, and it may very well not be worth paying, but nevertheless we could pay it. If we were to, nothing could be demonstrated about blame, or the value of practical reason, or whether we are brains in vats. (Nussbaum seems to agree on this when she stresses, in another paper, that there is no hard external obstacle, only internal appeal to what we already value, to block certain sceptical views.[5])

But it seems to me that this point is not enough to keep the threat to objectivity at bay. The worry that persists can be expressed thus: there is a problem about the relationship between the form of life and the truth of the proposition it presupposes. How can whether we choose to pay the terrible costs of for-

[3] See Strawson (1974).   [4] Putnam (1979, 1981).   [5] Nussbaum (forthcoming).

going our presuppositions tell us anything about whether the sceptic is wrong? Surely, the objectivist will say, whether he is wrong cannot depend on what forms of life we go in for and hence on what we presuppose; such dependence would itself undermine objectivity. Of course, our withholding our presuppositions does not make the sceptic right; but how can we regard our presuppositions as making him wrong, without giving up objectivity? An objective world is not obliged to conform to our presuppositions. As Stroud points out with respect to conditional necessities to the effect that 'such-and-such is necessary if we are to think and speak as we now do', no theoretical justification is thereby given of our acceptance of the propositions at issue, since we could give up our present ways of thinking and speaking and adopt others – however unattractive a prospect that might be.[6]

This leads me to the second, stronger kind of pragmatic support for the minor premiss '*p*' – *demonstrative support*. Perhaps it is only really here that transcendental arguments completely avoid the threat to objectivity. If so, it would be important to distinguish weaker, presuppositional varieties of transcendental argument from stronger, demonstrative ones. An indication of demonstrative support is that the heroic sceptical move of forgoing the form of life that supports the minor premiss is utterly pointless, self-defeating.[7] Suppose, for example, we have a sceptic about the existence of language. We point out to him that his expressions of his scepticism are self-defeating; his expression demonstrates the existence of a particular meaningful sentence, which necessarily implies that language exists. It would be utterly pointless for him now heroically to renounce language; indeed, it would be self-defeating in somewhat the same way that it would be self-defeating for a sceptic about other minds to proceed in trying to win his argument by systematically killing off his fellows. There would be no point in renouncing language unless one had already conceded implicitly the existence of language; the whole point of renouncing it is to avoid having one's sceptical thesis refuted by it. In this sense, the sceptic's expression of his thesis does not merely presuppose something inconsistent with his thesis; it actually demonstrates the falsity of it. Harrison's point still holds: there is no necessity that there should have been language; the world might have been languageless. Nevertheless, the threat to objectivity involved when the world is held to conform to our presuppositions is absent. In these cases, our forms of life do not merely presuppose something inconsistent with the scepticism in question; rather, our forms of life demonstrate the truth of something inconsistent with scepticism. Other examples of the demonstrative variety of pragmatic support might be arguments that involve appeal to the existence of experience, or thought, as necessarily implying the existence of embodied, or world-situated, persons. Again, if the conditional premiss, 'necessarily if *p* then *q*', holds (which I am not discussing at all here),

---

[6] Stroud (1982: 126).
[7] Compare Stroud's 'privileged class', in Stroud (1982: 127).

no pragmatic retreat route from the minor premiss '*p*' is available: refraining from experience, or thought—that is, deliberately doing away with it by, say, suicide—would be self-defeating as well as heroic on the part of a sceptic in a way that refraining from personal relationships, practical reason, or attempted reference to vats would not be. Even though it is perfectly possible that there might not have been any experience, or thought, in the universe, doing away with one's own experience or thought concedes its existence; by contrast, refraining from the latter activities makes no concession about the reasons for going in for them or their success.

Now I return to the second question: I will try to apply the above points to arguments which appeal for pragmatic support to human nature, to what we essentially are. Suppose that there are various distinctive features, both negative and positive, limitations and capacities, that are essential to us as human beings. If so, then those that Nussbaum highlights in her reply to the third objection—for example, limitations owing to mortality and physiological requirements, the capacity for practical rationality, and sociality—may plausibly be claimed to be among the strongest candidates for such essential features. Certain kinds of lives, then, could not be lives for us as human beings, given our nature; they would rather be lives for gods, or asocial anthromorphs, or grazing animals, or shellfish.[8] Towards the end of 'Non-Relative Virtues', Nussbaum asks 'What circumstances of existence go to define what it is to live the life of a human being, and not some other life?' and comments: 'Aristotle likes to point out that an inquiry into the human good cannot, on pain of incoherence, end up describing the good of some other being, say a god, a good, that on account of our circumstances, it is impossible for us to obtain.' If someone is tempted to ask the question: But is it best, after all, to live the life of a human being, rather than one of these other kinds of life? The response cannot be simply that it is impossible for human beings to decide to live lives that lack these characteristics. If that were true, the discussion would lose much of its point. As Nussbaum emphasizes,[9] there is no hard external obstacle to or knock-down argument against a human being's deciding to live the life of a grazing animal or an asocial anthromorph, even though the cost of doing so would be a radical impoverishment of life. Nevertheless, as she suggests, the very raising of the question for thought or discussion reveals the committed participation of the person who raises it in practical reason, which is pragmatically inconsistent with denying there is reason to go in for it.

What kind of pragmatic inconsistency is there between participating in practical reason and denying its value? If someone were just to keep quiet, empty his mind, and graze, nothing would have been shown. By thus declining to participate in practical reason, he does not covertly participate in it or affirm its value; there is no self-defeatingness about such a heroic response. So, as I

8 I am drawing here also on Nussbaum (forthcoming).   9 Ibid.

suggested earlier, this pragmatic inconsistency seems to provide presuppositional rather than demonstrative support for the importance of practical reason. Is the presuppositional rather than demonstrative force of this pragmatic inconsistency a consequence of the particular context, namely, theories of human nature and scepticism about value? Or can we find a way to run a pragmatic argument in this context that provides the stronger, demonstrative kind of support? This would strengthen the claim that appeal to forms of life underwrites rather then undermines objectivity in this context.

I suggest we consider the idea put forward by various philosophers, that a distinctive property of persons is their capacity for higher-order attitudes. To have attitudes about one's own and others' attitudes is to be an interpreter, and in particular a self-interpreter; and self-interpretation that takes the form of working out one's own higher-order desires, for example, in the face of conflicting values, can be regarded as a kind of self-determination.[10] Consider the view, then, that a cluster of tightly related capacities—for higher-order attitudes, self-interpretation, and self-determination—is essential to persons; we are pragmatically committed to there being reason to exercise them, and hence to their value, through our regular exercise of them. Consider now the position of a sceptic about the value of these capacities and their exercise. Is it open to him to avoid the force of the pragmatic inconsistency of his position by opting out? I suggest not: the desire or intention not to have higher-order attitudes, even if successful (e.g. one deliberately undergoes brain surgery), is itself a higher-order attitude; a belief that one does not have higher-order beliefs (as opposed to a mere lack of higher-order beliefs) is self-defeating. The desire not to be a person, in these respects is itself the characteristic mark of a person, an exercise of the capacity of persons for self-determination, even if it results in lobotomy or suicide, or deliberate affirmation of or submersion of oneself in a culture that represses one's status as a person, say, because one is a member of some racial group, or religion, or because one is female. We find the kind of self-defeatingness here characteristic of the stronger, demonstrative kind of pragmatic argument. However, we do not seem to get all the way to full demonstrative support, even so: the sceptic's attempt to opt out of these forms of life does not demonstrate the truth of the premiss that he is sceptical about, namely, that there is reason to exercise the capacities in question, merely his practical commitment to it, which could still be unjustified. Perhaps in the evaluative realm this kind of middle ground between the presuppositional and demonstrative cases is the strongest kind of pragmatic support we can hope for; at any rate, I have not been able to think of an evaluative example of fully demonstrative support. Nevertheless, we can get something stronger than mere presuppositional support.

Perhaps not all human beings have these capacities. But, if so, this fact can be accommodated in appropriate cases by saying that some human beings

---

[10] I elaborate a view of this kind in Hurley (1989).

are not persons, rather than that they are not really human.[11] This slippage from talk of what is essential to us as human beings to talk of what is essential to us as persons has advantages; there is less of a strain in regarding some lacks as impugning someone's personhood than in regarding them as impugning his humanity. And this slippage allows more scope for that characteristic human activity of misguided efforts at self-determination, for example, emulation of the beasts, or the gods.

In conclusion: I have sketched the way Nussbaum's view about the relationship between relativism and the practices that ground the virtues, and especially her response to the third objection she considers, raise a more general issue, about the relationship between appeal to forms of life and objectivity. And I have pursued her suggestion of a certain pragmatic form of argument, from participation in forms of life to value, in order to consider further senses in which the appeal to forms of life may or may not threaten objectivity.

BIBLIOGRAPHY

DAVIDSON, D. (1984). *Inquiries into Truth and Interpretation*. Oxford: Clarendon Press.
FRANKFURT, H. (1971). 'Freedom of the Will and the Concept of a Person', in G. Watson (ed.), *Free Will*. Oxford: Oxford University Press.
HARRISON, R. (1982). 'Transcendental Arguments and Idealism', in G. Vesey (ed.), *Idealism Past and Present*, Royal Institute of Philosophy Lecture Series 13. Cambridge: Cambridge University Press.
HURLEY, S.L. (1989). *Natural Reasons: Personality and Polity*. New York: Oxford University Press.
NAGEL, T. (1986). *The View from Nowhere*. Oxford: Oxford University Press.
NUSSBAUM, M. (forthcoming). 'Aristotle on Human Nature and the Foundations of Ethics', in a volume on the philosophy of Bernard Williams, ed. J. Altham and R. Harrison. Cambridge: Cambridge University Press.
PUTNAM, H. (1979). *Meaning and the Moral Sciences*. London: Routledge and Kegan Paul.
—— (1981). *Reason, Truth and History*. Cambridge: Cambridge University Press.
STRAWSON, P.F. (1959). *Individuals*. London: Methuen.
—— (1966). *The Bounds of Sense*. London: Methuen.
—— (1974). 'Freedom and Resentment', in *Freedom and Resentment and Other Essays*. London: Methuen.
STROUD, B. (1982). 'Transcendental Arguments', in R. Walker (ed.), *Kant on Pure Reason*. Oxford: Oxford University Press.
WILLIAMS, B. (1981). 'Wittgenstein and Idealism', in *Moral Luck*. Cambridge: Cambridge University Press.

---

[11] See Frankfurt (1971) on the use of the term 'wanton' here, to contrast with 'person'.

PART III
WOMEN'S LIVES AND GENDER JUSTICE

Women and the Quality of Life:
Two Norms or One?

Julia Annas

[1]

Questions about the quality of life are questions about the lives of individuals in society. But, apart from the complication that individuals come already grouped into families,[1] there is the crucial complication that individuals come divided into two sexes. The biological sex differences between men and women bring with them, in all known societies, enormous cultural divisions. To a greater or lesser extent, the shape of men's lives is in all societies different from that of women's. And not only do social institutions and attitudes everywhere divide up kinds of activity between the sexes, but women and men see their own lives, from the inside, very differently.

Even casual reflection on the details of everyday life shows that these differences are deep and wide. It is, I think, fair to say that there is no society in which there is not, in some degree, sexual division of activity; and so, for any individual, the fact of being a man or a woman to some extent determines both what that individual's options are for undertaking various kinds of activity and how that individual sees his or her own life. There are everywhere *two actual norms* for human life: in no society is it indifferent to the shape of your life and what you can make of it, whether you are a man or a woman. Your sex may close some options to you entirely, or merely make them more difficult; it always makes a difference to what your options are over your life as a whole.[2]

Societies all lie on a spectrum from what I shall call traditional societies at

I am very grateful for helpful comments to Ann Levey, David Owen, Patricia Scaltsas, and Holly Smith. Allen Buchanan enormously improved the early stages of this paper with comments and discussion. The discussion at WIDER was wide-ranging and helpful; I would like to thank especially my commentator, Margarita Valdés, and also Christine Korsgaard, Hilary Putnam, Paul Seabright, Tim Scanlon, and Michael Walzer. I would also like to thank Martha Nussbaum for useful comments at more than one stage, and for her role in getting me to explore the actual usefulness as well as the historical roles of the notion of human nature.

[1] Cf. Elizabeth Wolgast, *Equality and the Rights of Women* (Ithaca, NY: Cornell University Press, 1980), ch. 6, esp. p. 143; if society is viewed straightforwardly as a collection of individuals, children come out as anomalies. Cf. A. Sen, 'Economics and the Family', in *Resources, Values and Development*, (Oxford: Blackwell, 1984), 369–85.

[2] There are of course other divisions that we find salient in everyday life which tend to cut across sexual division of activity: wealth and poverty, for example. (I am grateful to Paul Seabright for pressing this point.) But present and past experience shows that sexually divided norms of activity do present themselves to people as particularly salient even before explicit reflection on the topic, perhaps even more vividly because of the importance of the distinctions that cut across them.

one end to what I shall call liberal societies at the other. A society is traditional if the fact of having two norms for the lives of men and women produces a strongly enforced actual division of activities and ways of living; it is liberal if this division of actual activities is weakly enforced. This gives us a way of contrasting societies which cuts across other differences in values, and makes it possible to say that women in otherwise very different societies face the same problem, without overdramatizing what the problem is.[3]

We are used to living with the two norms, and often cease to notice them. But they generate deep problems when we ask about the quality of individuals' lives.

Let us make the point more vividly by setting up a situation where we are on the outside. Consider a society which is more traditional than ours, say one in which the man is the family's main provider and the woman has total charge of bringing up the children. In this society men are educated to make as much as they can of their talents and to achieve as much as they can; but women are not, because they do not use their talents outside the domestic area. We do not need to suppose that there are actual laws forbidding women to hold certain jobs; custom will suffice, for example by making parents reluctant to 'waste' resources on educating daughters.[4] Nor do we have to imagine that the women are not educated at all; suppose them to be educated to the level needed for them to be companions to the appropriate men.[5] But now we know that educational opportunities in this society are distributed unfairly; regardless of ability, men will take more than they should.

There are two obvious retorts, of course. The first is that in this society women do not *want* education; they want to be home-makers. And even if some of them *do* want it, it will still be said that in this society women have less *need* for these opportunities, for they lack the opportunity to put them to use. If it is unthinkable for a woman to have a career, or a least one equal to her husband's, then opportunities equal to his will be wasted on her. So the opportunities are in fact, given the two actual norms, being distributed in accordance with a principle of need.

But it is clear that we cannot justify the distribution by pointing out that it answers to a pattern of need created by the differences between the two norms. Rather, it is because we can clearly appreciate that the distribution is unjust that we come to criticize the two norms and the different patterns of

---

[3] For 'traditional' and 'liberal' see below. 'Traditional' carries no implications about economic or cultural development; thus America in the 1950s is on my account a highly traditional society.

[4] We can suppose that there are some women who do get educated, and aim for a career; but they have to *choose* between the man's role (career) and the woman's role (domesticity). This does not affect the roles: the fact that a few women can become 'honorary men' has no effect on the existence of two norms. (In most societies class cuts across sex, and there are some élite women who are as advantaged as most men, but this makes no impact on the different roles and kinds of life for the two sexes. See below.)

[5] A situation which was far from dead when I was an undergraduate at Oxford. The recent past of one's own society will often provide a good example of a traditional society.

need that they create. It is, of course, easier to appreciate the injustices that the norms of a society give rise to if we do not have to live with the norms ourselves. It is much harder to stand back from, and criticize, the injustices arising from the differentiated norms that are part of our own society's current ways of thinking.[6] None the less, as soon as we do position ourselves with regard to a more traditional society it is obvious that injustice results from the existence of two norms.

This is not just an 'intuition', if that means a judgement which we happen to make but might not have, and cannot defend. Rather we have here a systematic *pattern* of judgements; whatever the adequacy of our view of our own society, when faced by a society more traditional than ours, we conclude that the two norms for men and women produce injustice. This holds, I think, whoever 'we' are; even a traditional society will find fault with an even more traditional society in this area. The Greeks in Aristotle's time formed a very traditional society; yet Aristotle records the feeling that they had *progressed* in not buying and selling women for wives as their ancestors had done.[7] So we do not just *happen* to feel that these women are being wronged; this is a judgement that people *systematically* come to when they see things from a less traditional viewpoint than the situation being considered. It is an empirical fact that people tend to judge in this way; but it is also an important and, as we shall see, revealing fact. Of course I am not claiming that it will be easy to isolate people's judgements about the position of women from their judgements about other matters in the more traditional society (about inheritance, for example). And of course societies can consciously revert to more traditional ways. (Though it is a moot point how successfully one can *go back* to these ways, as opposed to imposing them on people.) But this does not affect the point that, when we look from the outside at a society which is more traditional than our own, we systematically perceive injustice in the ways in which the two norms impose different kinds of life on men and women.

Can we locate more precisely the nature and source of the injustice? A popular approach is that the injustice arises from the frustration of well-being in some form. If we pass over obviously inadequate accounts of this in terms

[6] Thus we should not be too surprised or shocked that it has generally been found easier, by both women and men, to acquiesce in injustices arising from sexually differentiated norms, than to focus on the injustices and think about the norms. It is, after all, often perfectly acceptable to acquiesce in one's society's ways of thinking; moral theories are suspect which put us at odds with them right at the start. Serious moral thinking about the sexes is very difficult just because of this fact, that it requires us not just to reflect on but to stand aside from some everyday habits of thought.

[7] *Politics* 1268b38–41. The passage is discussed in Martha Nussbaum's paper in this volume, 'Non-Relative Virtues: An Aristotelian Approach'. At *Politics* 1252a34–b6 Aristotle also criticizes non-Greeks for treating women like slaves, not recognizing the natural difference between them. He regards his own society as less traditional than other societies, and than its own past.

of pleasure or happiness,[8] the most promising approach is in terms of the frustration of desires. But attempts to locate the source of the injustice in the frustration of women's desires are doomed to failure for familiar reasons. For people's desires can be in large part formed by the circumstances and options that they perceive as being open to them. (The point holds across different conceptions of what a desire is.) In societies in which the options open to them are fewer than those open to men, it has always been a common adaptive strategy for women to adjust their desires to what they can realistically expect. So examining the actual desires of women may lead us to the conclusion that women on the whole get what they want. But it is clear that desires which owe their nature even in part to the agent's reduced circumstances cannot adequately adjudicate questions of justice. This approach would lead us to conclude that it is women in the most traditional societies—those where in every area of living activity is divided by sex in the most marked and rigid way—who are most satisfied. For women in these societies, where alternatives are hardest even to conceive, are most likely to have adjusted their desires successfully to achieve a measure of content with their lot.[9] But it cannot, of course, be right that the happiest women should turn out to be those whose horizons are so limited that they cannot even conceive of alternatives. And even apart from this issue, we have only to look at the way that women's desires have expanded with the expansion of the alternatives open to them to see that women's actual desires cannot settle this issue for us.

We might appeal to 'informed' desires: the women in the traditional society, with their domestic futures, do not desire education (at least, not the kind their husbands get). But, it could be argued, their desires are superficial, resting on an unreflective view of their circumstances. If their desires were to be fully informed—if they were the desires which they would form given full knowledge of all aspects of their situation—then they would form desires for the kind of education their husbands have.

Often the appeal to informed desires is fruitful, but in this case it is hard to see how it could be adequate. Giving these women information in the ordinary sense cannot produce what we need. The more facts the women acquire, not only about men's and women's abilities but about their situation, the explanation for it, the historical background, the patterns of needs it generates, and so on, the *less* likely they are to develop the relevant desire. For in this situation, and in many involving differentiated activity between the sexes, the more you know about the situation, the more *hopeless* it seems

---

[8] Happiness, that is, on a modern subjective view of what it is, which has prevailed in most ethical discussions: whether someone is happy is settled by what they think, happiness can be momentary, temporary, etc. I think that the notion of happiness as a satisfactory and well-lived life, an objective notion well worked out in ancient ethics, has more footing in our ethical thinking than most ethical discussion allows, but I shall not pursue the point here.

[9] See J. Elster, 'Sour Grapes', in A. Sen and B. Williams (eds.), *Utilitarianism and Beyond* (Cambridge: Cambridge University Press, 1982).

to develop the relevant desire; the more clearly you see why that desire cannot be fulfilled, given the existing two norms, the more motivation you have to adjust to things the way they are to avoid frustration. Perhaps, then, 'informed' means more than just having more information: if these women *understood* their situation fully they would find in themselves desires for education like their husbands have. But any notion of understanding that could produce this result would be an unsatisfactorily expansive one. The women would have to grasp that they had no reason not to desire what they were being unjustly denied; and that is rather a lot to demand of a notion of understanding. No concept of informed desire can on this issue avoid the Scylla of inadequacy and the Charybdis of begging the question.

We might appeal to considerations more abstract than happiness and the fulfilment of desires. We might just point to unequal possession of goods on the part of men and women in a given society. Suppose that we aggregate the amounts of a certain good possessed by men and by women, and compare. And suppose, not too implausibly, that the men have more money, education, etc.; surely this is what gives rise to an unjust situation, unless we can show that the inequality rests on some basis other than the sheer fact of difference between the sexes.

But apart from familiar objections to this kind of procedure, there are special reasons why it will not work in this case, so that we do not need to work out sophisticated versions of it. It provides no answer to the person who claims that the inequality does answer to unequal needs, given the two norms. And it could well give the wrong answers, given the complication that class always cuts across sex. In nearly every society there will be a small number of élite women, wives and daughters of the socially most prominent and powerful men, who have large amounts of the desirable goods that most women are lacking in. So when we are looking at the amount of a certain good possessed by women in total, the results will be most misleading about the position of all but a few women.[10] Moreover, in many cases the great wealth possessed by a few élite women in a society makes no impact on the ability even of these women to live in a way different from that imposed on them by the two norms. Until fairly recently, for example, rich women could spend money to influence votes and politicians, but could not themselves vote or hold political office. No approach in terms of what men and women *have* can get to the heart of the problem, which is what men and women *do*.

---

[10] Two frivolous examples: Aggregate the personal wealth of British women, and add that of the Queen. Or: aggregate the personal political power of British women, and add that of Mrs Thatcher. The totals will be impressive, but not a good guide to the wealth and power of British women in general. (Of course this is only a crude approach. The Queen and Mrs Thatcher raise the average for women, but we would realistically focus on something more fine-grained, e.g. average of personal property, or average of property held by women compared with that for men. The more realistic our approach, the less likely we are to reach results that are misleading with respect to the position of women in a society. This point thus has limited force when compared with the following one.)

Many prefer at this point to find the source of the injustice that we discern in terms of the violation of rights, or principles of equality, or the wrongness of denying autonomy to people in imposing sex roles on them. I do not think that these approaches have been conspicuously successful. In this area there is no consensus as to what the basic rights are that we would appeal to, nor as to the principles of equality that we would have to use, nor as to the justifiability of appealing to autonomy when this would involve overriding people's actual considered judgements. Further, it is hard to feel that these approaches go deep enough. Why is it important for men and women to have equal rights and not to have distinct norms for living their lives imposed on them? Some further answer is needed, and I suspect that it will have to be in terms of something like the importance of their capacities for living a flourishing human life.[11] However, nothing in this paper hinges on these other approaches having been ruled out, and I offer no arguments against them here. What I would like to do instead is simply to defend the most intuitive way that we actually think about these matters, and to clear away some misconceptions about it. Defending it fully against all alternatives, and working out its relation to them, particularly to the rights approach, is clearly a much larger task.

We grasp that what is done in the more traditional society is unjust. What could be the basis for this, if not the frustration of desires or the violation of rights? The key seems to lie, as hinted above, not in what people want, or in what they possess, but in what they do. In the traditional society the women's activities, and hence the ways they shape and give meaning to their lives, are limited by the different norms of life and activity for the two sexes, in a way that bears no relation to, and can frustrate, their abilities, and the ways they could act and shape their lives if the norms were not distinct. Men and women can benefit equally from education, can learn skills and develop their intellectual capacities equally; and this does not depend on whether they desire to do these things.

The appeal seems to be to a general and indeterminate shared notion of human nature—human nature, that is, as shared by men and women. And, of course, though we are most likely to come to the thought of it by noticing injustices to women, the point applies equally to men. In the case of either sex, we discern injustice when relevantly similar groups of people are treated differently. In this case the thought that these groups of people are in fact relevantly similar rests, I have claimed, not on thoughts about similarity of desires or of rights, but on similarity in the way they are, their human nature.

Serious objections have been made to such an appeal to human nature, but before turning to them I want to expand on the idea and make it clearer what is involved. We see that what is done about, for example, education in the traditional society is unjust because what people make of their lives is restricted

---

[11] To avoid misunderstanding: of course there are many areas where appeal to rights or autonomy need involve nothing like this; I am simply claiming that on this issue it seems to.

by norms that do not answer to differences in their natures, differences of actual ability. But is this not far too general a claim, and one that will end up being far too strong? Many social norms can, or could, rest on differences that are conventional, answering to no natural differences of ability. Such norms can be mutually advantageous, and it seems no objection to them that they answer to no natural differentiation. So the objection to sex roles, and the distinct norms they spring from, on the grounds that they do not answer to natural distinctions between the sexes, would seem to imply, absurdly, objections to any conventionally based social norms, whether or not they are mutually advantageous and acceptable on other grounds. If not, there must be some demonstrable differences as regards sex roles and distinct norms of life for the sexes which makes it plausible that they create injustice in ways that other conventionally based norms may not.

There is such a difference, I think, but we find it not by argument but by considering history. In the course of recorded history people have objected to distinct sexually based norms for life in ways that they have not objected to other norms which do not seem to be based on differences in people's natures. We are back with the point that people do systematically, from a certain perspective, discern injustice in the operation of sex roles. There could be worlds in which enforced sexual division of activity did not produce injustice, but ours is not one of them, as history shows us.[12]

In appealing to the way that people have objected to sex roles, are we not back to some version of the subjective approach in terms of people's desires? No. The objections have taken the form of claims that the imposition of sex roles is *unjust*, and I have suggested that behind this lies the claim that they do not answer to real differences in the natures of men and women. In fact, I think that if we take seriously the claim that this is the basis of the objections, we can better understand why it is that our judgements about the injustice of sex roles are typically made from the perspective of a less traditional society than the one being criticized.

In any society reasons will be given for having distinct norms for the lives and activity of men and women. (In a very unreflective society the members will perhaps feel no need to give these reasons to one another, and so they will remain implicit, discernible only by a more reflective outsider.) And these reasons typically come down to various assertions of relevant differences

---

[12] Several writers have seen the point that there must be something special about sex roles and norms for them to create injustice when other conventionally based roles and norms need not. But they tend at this point to appeal straight away to some *theory* to explain what it is about sex roles in particular that produces injustice: e.g. 'the problem is not that sex roles restrict freedom but that sex roles and the sexual division of labour are used in patriarchal societies to oppress women' (Francine Rainone and Janice Moulton, 'Sex Roles and the Sexual Division of Labor', in M. Vetterling-Braggin (ed.), *'Femininity', 'Masculinity' and 'Androgyny'* (Totowa, NJ: Rowman and Littlefield, 1982), 222). I want to avoid this approach and to pay more attention to the question of what thoughts we actually have, what we are in fact appealing to, when we perceive injustice flowing from sexually divided norms but not from other norms.

between men's and women's natures. Thus it has been held, for example, that women may justly be kept from participation in public life because they are more self-centred and less capable of impartial thought than men. In any given society these reasons may well be accepted. It is only from the perspective of a less traditional society, in which men and women are no longer restricted by this division of activity, that people can clearly see that the reasons given for the restriction were not good reasons but mere rationalizations. The backward-looking nature of our discernment of the injustice of sex roles is grounded in this point: it is those no longer bound by a sexual division of activities who can see that the reasons offered for it when it was in force were not good ones; for they are the ones who can see that there is in fact no such natural division of abilities as the one the division of activities was supposed to rest on.[13]

Aristotle, as I mentioned, congratulated his society on being less traditional than their ancestors, and non-Greeks, on the position of women. We do not have to assume that he was aware of the level of frustration of women's desires, or that he had even a faint grasp of the principle of equality of rights for women and men. Rather, living in a society where women were not treated as property, he could see that the reasons offered in the past and by non-Greeks for treating women as property were not good ones, and did not answer to a relevant natural similarity. It is easy to see how this could coexist with a massive failure to see what was wrong with the reasons offered by Aristotle himself for having two norms of life for women and men; nor is it hard to explain this failure, since Aristotle was living within the norms in question. And this case illustrates what I have claimed is a systematic pattern. It is in societies more traditional than our own that we discern the injustice of sex roles; this is the perspective from which we can see that there is no natural basis for these roles.

The backward-looking perspective on this issue can throw light on two other points also. One is the striking non-reversibility of attitudes to the division of sex roles. For while societies can become more reactionary, they cannot reinstate past attitudes to sex-divided norms. This is most plausibly explained as the straightforward cognitive difficulty in coming to regard as a reason something that you have seen to be a mere rationalization.[14] The other is the acceleration of liberalization on this issue in societies where discussion and questioning of the reasons behind various socially marked divisions is prominent. Societies which are traditional in the sense I introduced of strongly enforcing sex-divided norms are also likely to be traditional in the more common

<hr />

[13] This phenomenon is often clearest on a small scale. It was very obvious, for example, in Oxford during the period when single-sex colleges were becoming coeducational, and colleges stood to one another as more to less traditional societies.

[14] Past attitudes can of course be recreated indirectly: if the government restricts opportunities for discussion and public reflection, destroys evidence of the liberal past, etc., for long enough people may be returned to their previous cognitive state.

sense of discouraging public reflection on the basis of those norms. And societies that are liberal in the sense of enforcing sex-divided norms only weakly are likely to be liberal also in encouraging public rational reflection on just this kind of issue.[15]

[2]

We should now face the principled objections to the idea that it is in terms of human nature that we understand, and have to reflect on, the injustice of sex-divided norms.

Why might one be reluctant to adopt this approach? One reason might be a reluctance to accept objectivism in ethics, at least until all else fails. Now would not be the time to defend objectivism in ethics in a general way; but it should be pointed out that it is really very difficult to avoid in this case. For, as I have noted, we cannot doubt that having two norms for the lives of men and women produces injustices; this is clear as soon as we turn to a society more traditional than our own. And we cannot understand why that is so as long as we do not go deeper than the desires people have. I have argued that this is so because the desires in question are infected by the norms in question. But there seems in this case to be another reason also. For once we come to the conclusion about injustice there are large implications. The injustices in question are not minor ones; if we take them seriously then we are committed to serious criticism of the social institutions and attitudes that help to create and sustain them. How could we be entitled to do that on the basis of people's desires? However information-enriched, how could desires ever have that authority? A large-scale criticism of a fundamental and pervasive fact of social life can only be solidly based if it is founded on *the way people actually are*, and makes a claim that social life is failing to answer to the way people actually are.[16]

An interesting objection enters at this point. We might reject informed desire accounts without accepting that notion of human nature.[17] For we might accept that objectively there are important goods for people, but be unwilling to accept the further, more restrictive notion of human nature. This objection, I think, comes from seeing the ethical employment of human

[15] One could develop this point to show why liberal societies can justifiably claim to be advancing our conception of what is natural, even though the traditionalist may claim that changes in a liberal direction are unnatural. Public rational reflection, rather than traditional acquiescence, is more likely to produce an understanding of, and an explanation for, both what is rejected and what is accepted about human nature. I am grateful to Michael Walzer for stressing the point that a theory of human nature must be explanatory and not just critical of what it replaces.

[16] It could, of course, be based on moral concern, for example at the violation of rights. But, as suggested above, I think that in this case this is not what is fundamental; such concern rests ultimately on beliefs about what people's natures are.

[17] This point was raised by Tim Scanlon and by several others; I have learned much on this issue from Scanlon's paper in this volume and the comments by James Griffin.

nature as being in a tradition that is committed to things like essentialist thinking, which can independently be seen to be dubious or controversial; it can thus seem best to steer clear of this tradition altogether. I have not taken this option because I believe that the human nature tradition is more complex than often thought, and that when properly understood it is not open to familiar objections. While this project can obviously not be undertaken here, I believe there to be good reasons for not resting content with notions less robust than that of human nature.

Someone might accept what has been said so far and still not proceed further because of a feeling of futility in the face of the problem. Every known society has upheld different norms for the lives of men and women. No more basic social fact can be imagined. Further, it has entered in many ways into every less basic social fact. What makes us think that we have any chance of going behind the lives of men and women as they have developed and asking what they could be like if human activities were not divided by sex? This objector will claim that it is theoretically futile to try to establish what people are 'really' like here: even if we could in some areas, we surely cannot in this one, where people's conception of their lives is moulded by the basic division of life activities produced by different norms for the sexes. And this is matched by the practical futility of trying to do anything about the situation. We might hope to rectify injustices of a more tractable nature. But when we are considering injustices on this scale, it is romantic to think that we might make any difference.

It is this feeling of futility which explains, I think, why so many people ignore or acquiesce in these injustices in their own society. But the difficulty is surely exaggerated on both fronts. Recognizing the practical difficulties here should lead us neither to complacency nor to an unrealistic overestimation of what we personally can achieve. The claims of theoretical difficulty are more serious, however.

One familiar objection is that there is no such thing as the notion of human nature that we think we are appealing to. There is no bedrock of natural fact about humans, facts true of anyone regardless of culturally produced perspective. For our own culture affects the way we consider ourselves and others so deeply that it is useless to try to produce an objective theory of human nature; all we succeed in doing is to project our own parochial concerns on to a wider screen. It is worth noting that this type of objection has been rather popular with feminist writers, who, far from basing any feminist arguments on an appeal to human nature, tend to regard it as discredited. Indeed it is easy to produce examples of appeals to human nature in past writers, particularly political philosophers, which are rather discreditable. Women have been presented as defective in terms of theories of human nature which are manifestly biased towards men. (Rousseau is perhaps the most flagrantly un-self-critical example of this.) The response to this by many feminists has been to relativize one's theory of human nature to one's political theory. Thus past male political thinkers have a theory of human nature to support their theories, feminists have their own, and so forth. In a recent book Alison Jaggar openly sets out different theories (liberal feminism, radical feminism, and so on), each with its associated theory of human nature. You choose between the theories on several grounds, of which the plausibility of the associated theory of human nature is one. But it is assumed throughout that there are no facts about human nature to which one could appeal to *decide* between theories.[18]

But as a response to past theories of human nature this is surely faulty. Of course Aristotle, and some more recent thinkers, have put forward 'factual' claims about the inferiority of women that manifestly spring from other preconceptions, and what they say about human nature to back this up is a transparent rationalization. But then they are wrong; they are doing something badly and in a biased way which might be done better and in a less biased way. To the extent that we disagree, as we do, with people like Aristotle and Rousseau on what women are like, the remedy is to improve on what they do, not to retreat to the position that we can do no better.[19] Feminists have been unwise to accept relativism so readily on this issue, and to withdraw from discussion about human nature rather than continuing it.[20] Consistent relativism here, for example, weakens the feminist case for social reform as well as blunting criticisms of past thinkers.

Secondly, I have argued that we need the notion of human nature here, to take the issue seriously. Just as we cannot stay at the level of people's desires, because these can be infected by the norms in question, so we cannot stay at the level of a theory of human nature which answers to and depends on a particular political theory or outlook. If I accept a theory of human nature but recognize that this depends on my position as, say, a liberal feminist, then I am accepting that my position on human nature is but one of many alternatives among which I choose. My choice depends on a number of factors, of course, and can be made on rational grounds and not on whim, but it is still a matter of choice. But then we are not talking about human nature, but about something else; human nature is *the way we are*, and we cannot

[18] Alison Jaggar, *Feminist Politics and Human Nature* (Totowa, NJ: Rowman and Allanheld, 1983). Cf. p. 170: 'The values that identify each group of feminists are connected conceptually with their characteristic view of human nature.' According to Jaggar an individual's political values and conception of human nature hang together in a holistic way.

[19] Jaggar (*Feminist Politics*, 22) says that feminist critiques of male political philosophy 'will necessitate a reconstruction not only of political philosophy, but of all the human sciences and perhaps of the physical sciences as well'. But talk of reconstruction suggests an engagement with, rather than a repudiation of, the past tradition, and this is incompatible with a thoroughgoing relativism. Jean Grimshaw, (*Feminist Philosophers* (Brighton: Harvester Press, 1986), ch. 3) makes some pertinent criticisms on this point.

[20] Some feminists argue at this point that the notion of objectivity in any science is a product of male thinking; women must do their own science and cannot appeal to any of the sciences in our tradition as a neutral point. This way of thinking puts women outside any current or past debate and leaves them to a discussion among themselves not bound by any current methodological rules. It is then not clear why any current thinking should take this seriously.

choose the way we are.[21] And on this issue what we need to appeal to is nothing less than the way we are. When we judge that there is injustice in the society more traditional than our own, we are judging that the social arrangements are out of kilter with the way these people are—not that they are out of kilter with what these people want, or would want given certain information, nor that they are out of kilter with the way that we (liberal feminists, for example) judge people to be. The crucial thought is that there is something wrong, and that this wrongness does not depend on what these people happen to want, or think, or on what alternative theories we have decided to hold about them. We do not, of course, always have to have this thought when judging some state of affairs to be unjust, but in this case it is hard to avoid.

We need to appeal, then, to something which could decide between various moral and political theories, not something which is itself a product of the one we happen to hold. It does not follow, of course, that what we are appealing to is an account of humans which is 'value-free' or 'value-neutral', or in the domain of the 'hard' sciences. One reason why feminists have been eager to relativize theories of human nature to specific moral and political theories is that they have conceived the alternative to be a theory which is 'purely factual' and scientific. And there are major problems with *this* view.

We know, just from looking at the attempts, that it is very difficult to produce a scientific, value-neutral view of the lives of our own species in a way that is independent of cultural factors. Biology can tell us about an individual's heart or liver, but we find no clear way to resolve the dispute as to the social and sexual patterns of the species *homo sapiens*, independently of cultural values, nor to improve its terms. We are primates, but primates have developed completely opposed social patterns of life, so biology seems to leave the dispute as to whether we are naturally monogamous, promiscuous, etc., no further on than what we can learn from an Updike novel. Of course there are facts here; but it is grotesque to think that we can appeal to the present state of what we know about these facts to learn about our present encultured state.[22]

What we need, then, is a notion of human nature which tells us about ourselves—not just biology but something on which ethics can build. Human nature, as I understand it, is not 'value-free'; we find out about it empirically, but by examining human life and the values it contains, not by doing science. But neither is it already moralized; it gives us a basis for our moral judgements, but it is not itself a moral notion.[23] This conception of human nature

---

[21] More accurately: we cannot choose the total way we are, although this certainly includes aspects about which we can do nothing and aspects which we can develop or manipulate.

[22] Though this is a pseudo-exercise many like to do; cf. the popularity of reductive forms of sociobiology. Since these are usually crudely unaware of the sexist values they are reading into biology, they have unfairly discredited serious attempts to take biology seriously in ethics. See M. Midgley, *Beast and Man* (Brighton: Harvester Press, 1979).

[23] Hilary Putnam, in the closing remarks of his paper in this volume, remarks that human nature can figure as very different kinds of notion. As I use it, it is an *empirical* notion: what we find out about ourselves and refine in an ongoing way as we learn more about various forms of

has recently become more respectable in ethics; it is no longer automatically ruled out as a confusion of 'fact' and 'value'. But putting it to serious work is another matter, and several objections are commonly still thought to stand against this. It has commonly been argued that we have no reason to think that there could be such a conception unless we are committed to a teleological view of the world and the functions of humans within it; and that if such a view were correct it would preclude our ethical options in an unacceptable way. I have argued elsewhere that these objections are unsuccessful.[24] Appeal to human nature in ethics has nothing to do with teleology (it turns up in ancient ethics in conjunction with a variety of views on teleology, including its complete denial). Nor is it dependent on any background theory of a metaphysical kind. As we have seen, it emerges in a quite straightforward way from ethical reflection. It is simply an appeal to the way people are, grounded in a refusal to take the level of people's expressed desires as the deepest we can go.

[3]

But even if we accept this there remains a serious problem: we may think that if the appeal to human nature is not to be uselessly vague, an appeal to a merely edifying ideal, then it must deliver to us a fairly specific pattern for the course of a human life. But if we think this, then in the present context of the roles of the sexes we run into a striking problem.

A judgement about the injustice done to women in the traditional society turned out to be a case of a more general pattern: when we criticize the two actual norms in a given society, it is on the grounds that they ignore the fact that men and women are actually similar in the relevant respect. And if this is grounded in human nature, it looks as though what we are doing is appealing beyond the two actual norms to a *single ideal norm*, an 'androgynous' or unisex one. And since there are no obvious limits set in advance to the ways in which more traditional societies than our own give us material for criticism, we seem to get an argument applicable in principle to all sex roles. If we continue with this argument we reach the conclusion that all sex roles are to be rejected

---

social life. It is to be distinguished from human nature as a *conceptual* notion: what is shared and obvious and can be appealed to in a distinctively human form of life – and also from human nature as a *moral* notion: a normative idea playing a determinate role in an ethical theory.

[24] I have examined the appeal to human nature in ancient ethics, and modern understandings (and misunderstandings) of this, in 'Naturalism in Greek Ethics', *Proceedings of the Boston Area Colloquium in Ancient Philosophy*, 4 (1988). Cf. also Martha Nussbaum, 'Aristotle on Human Nature and the Foundations of Ethics' (forthcoming), and 'Non-Relative Virtues' (in this volume); also the work of Christopher Gill in 'The Human Being as an Ethical Norm', in C. Gill (ed.), *The Person and the Human Mind* (Oxford: Oxford University Press, 1990). From different directions we have converged upon a criticism of certain assumptions, articulated most powerfully in Bernard Williams's *Ethics and the Limits of Philosophy* (London: Fontana, 1985), ch. 3.

because they falsify and distort the nature that we share. There is a single ideal of human life as far as our nature goes; all actual division of activity by sex is the creation of social norms.

It is not hard to find statements of this view in feminist writers, for example: 'male/female roles are neither inevitable results of "natural" biological differences between the sexes, nor socially desirable ways of socializing children in contemporary societies.'[25] From Mill on, these writers are ready to admit that we have little idea in advance what the details of this unisex ideal will turn out to be, but they have no doubt that sexual differentiation of activity is imposed on our nature, not part of it.

But more recent writers, also feminist, have queried this whole way of proceeding. Thus Elizabeth Wolgast claims that not all aspects of sex roles and imposed on us: a unisex society, free of sex roles, finds no resonance in our nature, she says, and talks of the respect we owe to our nature to recognize essential differences based on but not limited to biological differences.[26] We should note that this is a dispute among people all of whom accept the appeal to objective human nature as a basis for criticism of the two actual norms in our society. But they give different answers to the question, What is the ideal form of life that answers just to human nature? Some feminists argue that this ideal is unisex: sex roles are learned and could be learned differently. Others argue that we should have two ideal norms and not one; that the biological differences between men and women bring with them differences in instinct, need, and way of seeing one's life, and that to deny this is to flout biology. We are one species among others; in all other species biological differences bring with them different social patterns. Further, distinct social patterns may well give rise to different kinds of virtues in men and in women;

---

[25] Ann Ferguson, 'Androgyny as an Ideal for Human Development', in M. Vetterling-Braggin *et al.* (eds.), *Feminism and Philosophy* (Totowa, NJ: Littlefield, Adams, 1977), 45. Cf. also p. 56, where Ferguson claims that, compared with any 'static universal theory of what the "natural relationship" of man to woman should be', 'it seems more plausible to assume that human nature is plastic and moldable, and that women and men develop their sexual identities, their sense of self, and their motivations through responding to the social expectations placed upon them'. On pp. 61–2 she claims, 'There is good evidence that human babies are bisexual, and only *learn* a specific male or female identity by imitating and identifying with adult models . . . on this analysis, if the sexual division of labor were destroyed, the mechanism that trains boys and girls to develop heterosexual sexual identities would also be destroyed.' On 'androgyny' as an ideal, see further Joyce Trebilcot, 'Two Forms of Androgynism', in Vetterling-Braggin *et al.*, *Feminism and Philosophy*, 70–8, and in Vetterling-Braggin, *'Femininity'*, 161–9; also M. A. Warren, 'Is Androgyny the Answer to Sexual Stereotyping?' in Vetterling-Braggin, *'Femininity'*, 170–86.

[26] Wolgast, *Equality*, 108: 'an arrangement [where the roles of men and women will be indistinguishable] may not find answering resonance in our nature—on the contrary, our nature may constitute an obstacle', and p. 110: 'when we come to deal with sex roles and their justice, we should try to understand the respect we owe our nature.' Cf. Mary Midgley and Judith Hughes, *Women's Choices* (London: Weidenfeld and Nicholson, 1983), 185, where they talk of 'The extraordinary assumption that everything physical (the whole 'genetic and morphological structure') could be different and yet everything mental could remain the same'. Midgley and Hughes are, however, cautious in inferring from pervasiveness of sexual difference to legitimacy of sexual roles.

if women's role as mothers leads them, for example, to excel in caring and nurturing qualities, then why not value this alongside the different qualities that men have? A single specific ideal for both sexes disregards what is characteristically different and valuable about women's perspectives.[27]

This debate about our nature looks depressingly insoluble. Both sides can recognize the biological evidence, for what it is worth; but they give it a different significance. Both can recognize that as things are the sex roles in our society (and even more in more traditional societies) render many people's lives unfairly stunted; but one side will claim that we should get rid of sex roles altogether, the other that we should adjust them. It looks as though it is hard to find any consideration which will be decisive as to whether human nature provides us with one ideal norm or two for human lives.[28] We find thoughtful opinion divided between the single unisex ideal norm and two ideal norms. They have very different implications for practice. A unisex ideal norm would base no differential treatment merely on difference of sex; activities and roles would be divided as little as possible by sex. A proponent of two ideal norms would condone and strengthen some sex roles, for example, mothers caring for children, and would insist on differential treatment for women on the grounds of different needs. Human nature seems compatible with two conflicting ideals for humans; but if we choose on other grounds between the conflicting ideals we seem to have lost the whole advantage of appealing to human nature in the first place.

The problem here comes from expecting the notion of human nature itself to provide us with a specific ideal for human life. I have argued elsewhere[29] that we misconceive the role of human nature in ethics if we expect it to produce a specific ideal form of life. Human nature does not impose on us a specific set of things to do and way of living; rather it functions in a more unspecific and negative way, as a constraint on proposed forms of life and ethical rules. In the case of this issue the point comes out with especial clarity. We appeal to human nature deeper than the level of actual desires; but if we expect this to lead us to a specific ideal we find that all the unresolved problems about the importance of biology for our conception of human nature

---

[27] I am indebted to Martha Nussbaum for stressing the importance of this point in the argument.

[28] We might try to find such a consideration in a specific case where it makes a difference to one's decision which side one takes. A central role has been taken in this debate by the Supreme Court case *Geduldig* v. *Aiello* (cf. Wolgast, *Equality*, 88–90; Midgley and Hughes, *Women's Choices*, 160–1), in which the court decided that there was no wrongful discrimination against women in an insurance programme that did not cover pregnancy; it simply excluded pregnant *persons*, and would equally exclude pregnant men, were there any. Supporters of the two-ideal-norms view conclude that this is what happens if one goes for a unisex ideal. Since only women get pregnant, they have different needs which should be allowed for in a distinct ideal for female life. Even this is hardly decisive, though; the other side could say that in this case what has gone wrong is that the ideal in question is not unisex at all, but just the traditional old male one; allowing that women have special needs, e.g. in pregnancy, is just the kind of thing needed to make the ideal unisex, rather than traditionally male.

[29] In the article referred to in n. 24 above.

reappear within the notion of human nature itself. Are we essentially a two-sexed species, as Wolgast claims? Or is this a fact about us that does not have to have specific moral consequences? As long as we look for a specific ideal, we shall find the situation dear to the hearts of ancient sceptics: there is dispute, it is unresolvable, and the person who thinks about the matter tends to end up in suspension of judgement. (And since she has to act, she will act in accordance with her own view, but having no rational confidence in that view.)

But why should we expect our notion of human nature to be capable of delivering to us a specific norm or two specific norms for human life? We know that we cannot derive a single specific way of life or set of virtues from the notion of human nature alone. The difficulties here come from the common problem of trying to overwork the notion of human nature, to get from it what could not possibly be in it. And in the present case it is particularly obvious that we do not know what precise conclusion we should draw for human life from primate social behaviour and other facts of biology; how could the intervening notion of human nature magically solve the problems for us?

We should reject the two actual social norms that divide activities by sex without aiming at any specific ideal norm at all. We know enough about human nature to know that even if we had a complete account of it, it would not determine in detail what kinds of life we should lead. So the fact that we must appeal to it here is not undercut by the fact that we know depressingly little about it. We can work towards an ideal norm without being committed in advance to the form it will take. The actual argument I have concentrated on involves rejecting actual discrimination about education on the grounds that men and women are similar in the relevant respect. The best course would be to proceed entirely in this way, talking always about particular abilities. An advantage of a piecemeal approach like this is that it relates the claims we do make about human nature fairly directly to particular claims about the injustices in actual society. This is just the backward-looking perspective that I have stressed. Thus, it is because we can see the injustice of discriminating in educational opportunities on the basis of sex (at least in more traditional societies than our own) that we can see that human nature supports equal opportunities for education for men and women, for there is no relevant basis for denying it. This claim is not based on a prior commitment to a specific ideal unisex way of life for men and women, and so is not disturbed by claims that might be made in other areas to the effect that men and women have distinct needs.

Thus we expand our knowledge of human nature and our natural needs and wants on the basis of our recognition of what goes wrong when society imposes two actual norms for male and female lives. This is our only route to discovering human nature, and our only hope of disentangling, to the extent that we can, very general facts about our nature from their specific, culturally differentiated appearances. Why should we think that there is a quicker and better route to this knowledge, that we can know *now* either that there is an ideal, natural, unisex form of life, with all sexual division of roles and activity on the culturally imposed side, or that biology pervades culture and gives us two ineliminably different norms of life for men and women? Indeed, progress in serious consideration of particular capabilities in men and women has often been blocked by prior commitment to one or other of these pictures. I have argued that our judgements about injustice where sex roles are concerned are systematically backward-looking: we are often confused or uncertain about our own society, but able to discern more clearly the wrongs in a society more traditional than our own. And there is a good reason for this: it is those who no longer have to live with a particular sex-linked restriction who can rationally reject the claim that it was needed to answer to a natural difference.

[4]

This stress on the backward-looking perspective eliminates familiar problems, but does it then give us too exiguous a basis to make judgements about injustice in our own society?[30] If we can clearly discern the injustice only of practices that we no longer suffer from, will we not always be one stage behind, unable rationally to criticize the injustice of practices that we do still suffer from? This is an important and difficult issue; in fleeing premature dogmatizing we do not want to end up excessively sceptical. Our best route to avoiding both lies, I think, in stressing the *piecemeal* nature of what we gain from the backward-looking perspective. Rather than having a complete perspective on gender justice at a given time, we have a variety of views, at different levels and of different institutions. Our grasp of the injustice of a sex-divided norm that we live with is built up from the insights we have as to the injustice of various other norms we no longer live with, together with our usual capacities to make inferences, generalizations, and so on. And it is, I think, bound to be less secure than our grasp of past injustice. But it need not lead us to an over-sceptical view if we give due account to the different sources and levels of past injustice and our ability to reason about these.

The appeal to human nature has become discredited through its association with authoritarian traditions, and with claims to produce specific patterns of human life that give us answers to difficult questions right at the start. I have argued that once we clear misconceptions away, the appeal appears more modest, and also gives us the basis for progress and advance. This is a distinct advantage over alternative approaches in terms of rights, for example – though I emphasize that I have not here argued against these approaches.[31] We start from the unspecific notion that we have of human nature, arrived at negatively

---

30 As is lucidly argued by Margarita Valdés in her reply to this paper.
31 Onora O'Neill's lucid and forceful paper in this volume presents an excellent example of a different, more Kantian approach.

through our recognition of various injustices arising as a result of imposed sex roles. We make it more specific as we consider the various capabilities and the kinds of life that they can coexist in. For a consideration of history gives us reason to think that the problem of ideal unisex versus sex-divided norms is unlikely to be solved in just the terms we now conceive it in. It is more likely to dissolve into many smaller and more tractable problems about the various capacities of men and women. And progress here will, I suspect, for a long time reflect the fact that our best route to discovering human nature is reflection on the mistakes and rationalizations of those who got it wrong.

BIBLIOGRAPHY

ELSTER, J. (1982). 'Sour Grapes', in A. Sen and B. Williams (eds.), *Utilitarianism and Beyond*. Cambridge: Cambridge University Press.

FERGUSON, ANN (1977). 'Androgyny as an Ideal for Human Development', in Vetterling-Braggin *et al.* (1987).

GILL, CHRISTOPHER (1990). 'The Human Being as an Ethical Norm', in C. Gill (ed.), *The Person and the Human Mind*. Oxford: Oxford University Press.

GRIMSHAW, JEAN (1986). *Feminist Philosophers*. Brighton: Harvester Press, ch. 3.

JAGGAR, ALISON (1980). *Feminist Politics and Human Nature*. Totowa, NJ: Rowman and Allanheld.

MIDGLEY, MARY (1979). *Beast and Man*. Brighton: Harvester Press.

—— and HUGHES, JUDITH (1983). *Women's Choices*. London: Weidenfeld and Nicholson.

NUSSBAUM, MARTHA (forthcoming). 'Aristotle on Human Nature and the Foundations of Ethics', in a volume on the philosophy of Bernard Williams, ed. J. Altham and R. Harrison. Cambridge: Cambridge University Press.

RAINONE, FRANCINE, and MOULTON, JANICE (1982). 'Sex Roles and the Sexual Division of Labor', in Vetterling-Braggin (1982).

SEN, A. (1984). 'Economics and the Family', in *Resources, Values and Development*. Oxford: Blackwell.

TREBILCOT, JOYCE (1982). 'Two Forms of Androgynism', in Vetterling-Braggin (1982).

VETTERLING-BRAGGIN (ed.) (1982). *'Femininity', 'Masculinity' and 'Androgyny'*. Totowa, NJ: Rowman and Littlefield.

—— *et al.* (eds.) (1977). *Feminism and Philosophy*. Totowa, NJ: Littlefield, Adams.

WARREN, M.A. (1982). 'Is Androgyny the Answer to Sexual Stereotyping?', in Vetterling-Braggin (1982).

WILLIAMS, Bernard (1985). *Ethics and the Limits of Philosophy*. London: Fontana.

WOLGAST, Elizabeth (1980). *Equality and the Rights of Women*. Ithaca, NY: Cornell University Press.

Julia Annas: Women and the Quality of Life: Two Norms or One?

Commentary by Margarita M. Valdés

First of all I would like to congratulate Julia Annas on her interesting paper. I must say that basically I agree with her analysis of injustice to women and the way it affects women's quality of life. I am also as convinced as she is that one has to appeal to some notion of human nature if one is going to explain why there is injustice in the sexual division of activity and in the way opportunities are distributed between men and women.

The paper touches upon many problems. I will concentrate mainly on two of them: first, the epistemological problem concerning how we come to detect injustice to women within our own society; second, the problem of whether the notion of human nature, as introduced by Annas in her paper in order to explain injustice to women, might provide us with one ideal norm or two for human lives.

All through the paper Annas emphasizes the fact that it is easy to detect injustice arising from the fact of having two separate norms for men and women when we *look back* at societies more traditional than ours. It seems, indeed, an empirical fact that when looking from the outside at a society where sexual division of activity is more strongly enforced than in our own society, we tend to perceive injustice in the ways in which the two norms impose different kinds of life on men and women. The explanation Annas gives of this fact is that when we perceive in another society a sexual division of activity, or an inequality in opportunities for men and women, which no longer exists in our own society, we have the best evidence for concluding that the two norms for men and women are unjust, given that they are not grounded in any relevant natural difference between the two sexes. In this way, any attempt to explain the sexual division of activity in the traditional society by appealing to some presumed natural difference between men and women can be exposed as mere rationalization or ideological justification. So far, so good. But in the case of injustice arising from a double standard in our own society, how do we discover that there is such a thing? How can we come to know that there is injustice to women in our own society arising from the two actual norms? A society twenty years from now will most probably realize that there were injustices to women in out present two-norms system. But the fact that we can explain how *they* will know is of little help to the problem of explaining how *we* can know. Notice that it is important to explain how we can know that there is injustice to women within our own society, or from the inside of our own moral system, for if we cannot give an explanation of this we do not even allow for the possibility of a rational change from a traditional society to a more liberal one.

In several passages in her paper Annas acknowledges the difficulty involved in criticizing injustice to women arising from the two norms when they form part of our own society's way of thinking, for, she says, 'it requires us not only to reflect on, but to stand aside from some everyday habits of thought' (n. 6). In other passages she suggests that despite the difficulty involved in such a task it is not an impossible thing to do, given that in judging a certain situation (for example, the present one) we could adopt a less traditional viewpoint than that of the situation being considered. So it would seem that injustice to women in our own social system can be detected, after all, in a way similar to that used when we come to recognize injustice to women in societies more traditional than ours. We just have to adopt a more liberal point of view than that of our own society. Apart from the difficulties concerning the possibility of adopting a less traditional viewpoint than that of the society in which we are immersed, I see some problem with Annas's suggested strategy, that is to say, with her attempt to explain how we can acquire knowledge of injustice to women in our own society by analogy with the way we acquire such knowledge when we consider more traditional societies. For we must keep in mind that it is essential to her explanation of our knowledge in the latter case that out judgement is made from a society where the sexual division of activity under criticism no longer exists. In other words, according to Annas, our ground for judging that a certain sexual division of activity in a society more traditional than ours is unjust refers precisely to the fact that that division of activities no longer exists in our own society, but that kind of ground is exactly what we cannot have when we consider the imposed sex roles in our own society to be unjust.

Annas not only holds that it is an empirical fact that our judgements concerning injustice to women are systematically backward-looking, but also stresses the point that these judgements are themselves empirical in the sense that they are backed by the empirical evidence that the division of activities we are criticizing as unjust no longer exists in our own society. Now, if our judgements about injustice to women were always to be empirical in this way, then it would be difficult, if not impossible, to make such judgements with respect to our own society where the injustice still exists. And if that is so, then, as I mentioned above, it would be difficult to explain, within Annas's view, the possibility of a rational change from a traditional society to a more liberal one.

Judgements concerning injustice to women are not only presented as empirical in character, but also as contingent. In this vein, Annas writes the following: 'there could be worlds in which enforced sexual division of activity did not produce injustice, but ours is not one of them'. This is tantamount to asserting that sexual division of activity by itself does not produce injustice and that the fact that it does in our actual world is no more than a contingent fact. I wonder whether that is really so. On the one hand, a world seems 'conceivable' in which, for example, women are naturally more gifted than men (or the other way round), and so sexual division of activity is not unjust. On the other hand, in order to conceive such a possible world we *have to specify* that in such a world men and women are *not equally gifted*; so, even in a world where sexual division of activities is not in fact unjust, what justifies the division of activities is not the difference of sex but the difference in capabilities. In other words, given that the difference of sex does not entail any difference in relevant capabilities, and given that the only rational justification for enforced division of activities would be a difference in capabilities, it seems that any division of activities on the basis of sex alone would pick out the wrong kind of criterion to establish a *fair* division of activities, and so would tend to produce injustice. It would be a matter of chance or of luck if it did not. So, the connection between enforced division of activity on the basis of sex alone and injustice seems to be stronger than that suggested by Annas. It would be as irrational or unjust to impose a division of activities on a purely sexual basis as it would be to do it on the basis of race, colour, or any other inborn status or characteristic.[1]

Coming back to the question about the possibility of rational internal criticism concerning injustice to women, one gets the impression from Annas's paper that it is almost impossible to make such criticism. On page 295, for example, she asserts: 'judgements about injustice where sex roles are concerned are *systematically* backward-looking: we are often confused or uncertain about our own society', and the reason for this, she says, is that 'it is those who no longer have to live with a particular sex-linked restriction who can *rationally* reject the claim that it was needed to answer to a natural difference' (italics added). If the only people who can rationally reject as unjust a particular sex-linked restriction are people living outside that restriction, then rational internal criticism on this matter seems impossible and, once more, it is the impossible for an autonomous, rational, liberal change to come from within an unjust society. All this seems very important, for if we believe that there is injustice to women in our own society and that that injustice affects women's quality of life, then we have to explain how we can rationally come to have such a belief. Otherwise any struggle tending to eliminate injustice to women in our own society would seem an irrational enterprise.

I think that we find this rather sceptical attitude towards rational change from a traditional society to a more liberal one in some other parts of the paper. For example, in discussing what it would be for oppressed women to have 'informed desires', Annas says: 'The more facts the women acquire . . . about their situation, the explanation for it, . . . the patterns of need it generates, and so on, the *less* likely they are to develop the relevant desire. For in this situation, . . . the more you know about [it] . . . the more motivation you have to adjust to things the way they are to avoid frustration'.[2] Annas seems to assume that a very strong motivation in the desire-forming process in oppressed women is the avoidance of frustration through the suppression of the relevant desire: the more they learn about their oppression, the less likely they are to

---

[1] Cf. John Rawls, 1971: 149.   [2] We find a similar view in Okin, 1987: 59.

form the desire to do what they know has unjustly been forbidden to them. Admittedly there must be cases of 'adaptive desires', but not all the desires of traditional or oppressed women have to be of this sort. I agree that the desire approach to the problem of injustice to women is not the best one, and Annas gives very good reasons for that in her paper, but the rejection of such an approach need not involve scepticism about the possibility of oppressed women forming the adequate desires once they realize how unjust their situation is. As Amartya Sen has pointed out, 'the lack of perception of personal welfare . . . is neither immutable nor particularly resistant to social development'.[3] Education and politicization may take the form of making women face the possibilities of an increase in their objective well-being and consider the ways of achieving such an increase. If it were the case that oppressed women could only or mostly form adaptive desires, then education on the matter would seem pointless. And we would have to accept that only those who are not oppressed—to wit, men, or people from a more liberal society—could rationally change a traditional society into a more liberal one. So we would come to an unacceptable paternalistic view of the matter.

Returning to the problem of how we can know whether there is injustice to women arising from the two actual norms in our own society, I think that our knowledge of past situations in which we have seen that enforced sexual roles produced injustice to women gives us a strong reason to believe that all present or future cases of enforced sexual division of activity are highly likely to turn out to be the same. Our backward-looking judgements about injustice to women provide us with a knowledge that can be used in judging present similar cases. For we must remember that in making our backward-looking judgements we have appealed to the notion of human nature, and that same notion is perhaps just what is needed to explain our recognition of present injustice to women in our own social system. This takes us to the last topic I would like to touch upon: whether the notion of human nature introduced to explain injustice to women might lend support to one or two ideal forms of life.

As we have seen, Annas's argument to explain injustice to women turns on the idea that men and women share a common human nature, that is to say, the idea that they have similar capacities to live a flourishing human life. However, when she comes to discuss whether this notion provides the basis for one ideal natural form of life, with all sexual division of roles falling on the culturally imposed side, or whether biology pervades culture and produces two ineliminably different norms of life for men and women, she reaches the conclusion that there is no way of deciding this question now, that things may turn out one way or the other. So, even if we appeal to the notion of human nature we can end up having two different norms.

---

[3] Sen, 1987: 7.

I wonder whether this conclusion might not undermine her argument for explaining injustice to women. That is to say, if the explanation relies on the fact that men and women share a common human nature, while at the same time we have to admit the possibility that human nature might give a grounding, after all, to two ideal norms for the lives of men and women, then it is difficult to see how the alleged explanation could possibly work. This seems especially clear if we try to explain cases of injustice to women that we seem to perceive in our own society and which are different from other cases encountered in the past. Take the case of women who want to become priests in the Catholic Church and who are not allowed to on the ground that they do not have the same 'spiritual capacities' that men do. According to Annas, the notion of human nature to which we have to appeal to explain injustice in this new case is a notion built upon past experience. But this notion will tell us nothing about the new capacity which is in question, it will not be sufficient to answer the question of whether women have the same capacity as men to become spiritual or religious leaders. Perhaps this example does not strike us as very important, for, after all, it only affects a very small group of women within a religious community; but we must realize that the same kind of problem could arise, and in fact does arise, in more traditional societies where the question of whether women have certain very basic capabilities has to be answered. In other words, Annas's empirical notion of human nature is insufficient to explain why the sexual division of activity that we perceive in our own society is unjust: for it could always be the case that the particular aspect in which we seem to discover injustice to women could turn out to be precisely one of the aspects in which men and women happen to be naturally different.

I am afraid that if we want to have a notion of human nature that could serve to explain injustice to women in our own two-norms system, we have to appeal to a much 'thicker' notion than that introduced by Annas. In rejecting the dichotomy between fact and value, or between descriptive and evaluative notions, we come to realize that our notion of human nature is loaded with moral meaning. Concepts such as 'dignity', 'equality', autonomy', and 'freedom' seem to be inseparable from our notion of human nature. This notion, of course, will not deliver any 'fairly specific pattern for the course of a human life', but it will be enough for the exhibition and explanation of injustice to women arising from enforced sexual division of activity. As we have heard repeatedly in this conference, a person's well-being, and with this her quality of life, seems to increase with any increase in her functionings, in Amartya Sen's words, and in her capabilities or freedom to chose between different ways of living. A two-norms system for the lives of men and women, far from increasing the functionings or widening the capabilities of both men and women, would seem to reduce them for all.

BIBLIOGRAPHY

OKIN, SUSAN MOLLER (1987). 'Justice and Gender', *Philosophy and Public Affairs*, 16, (Winter 1987), 42–72.

RAWLS, JOHN (1971). *A Theory of Justice*. Cambridge, Mass.: Harvard University Press.

SEN, AMARTYA (1987). 'Gender and Cooperative Conflicts', WIDER Working Paper. Helsinki: World Institute for Development Economics Research.

Justice, Gender, and International Boundaries

Onora O'Neill

1 *Justice for impoverished providers*

Questions about justice to women and about international justice are often raised in discussions of development. Yet the most influential theories of justice have difficulty in handling either topic. I shall first compare some theoretical difficulties that have arisen in these two domains, and then sketch an account of justice that may be better suited to handling questions of gender and international justice.

I begin by distinguishing *idealized* from *relativized* theories of justice. Idealized accounts of justice stress the need to abstract from the particularities of persons. They paint justice as blind to gender and nationality. Its principles are those that would regulate the action of idealized 'abstract individuals'. They take no account of differences between men and women; they transcend international boundaries. Relativized accounts of justice acknowledge the variety and differences among humankind; they ground principles of justice in the discourse and traditions of actual communities. Since nearly all of these relegate (varying portions of) women's lives to a 'private' sphere, within which the political virtue of justice has no place, and see national boundaries as the limits of justice, appeals to actual traditions tend both to endorse institutions that exclude women from the 'public' sphere, where justice is properly an issue, and to insulate one 'public' sphere from another.

Both idealized and relativized accounts of justice look inadequate from the perspective of those whom they marginalize. Women, in particular poor women, will find that neither approach takes account of the reality of performing both reproductive and productive tasks, while having relatively little control over the circumstances of one's life. Women's lives are not well conceived just as those of abstract individuals. A world of abstract individuals assumes away relations of dependence and interdependence; yet these are central to most lives actually available to women. Nor are women's lives well conceived solely in terms of traditions that relegate them to a 'private' sphere. The productive contributions and the cognitive and practical independence of actual women are too extensive, evident, and economically significant to be eclipsed by ideologies of total domesticity and dependence.

The awkward fit of theory to actuality is most vivid for poor women in poor economies. These women may depend on others, but lack the supposed securities

I would particularly like to thank Deborah Fitzmaurice, James Griffin, Barbara Harriss, Martha Nussbaum, and Sara Ruddick for help with various problems that arose in writing this paper.

of dependence. They are impoverished, but are often providers. They are power-less, yet others who are yet more vulnerable depend on them for protection.[1] Their vulnerability reflects heavy demands as much as slender resources. They may find that they are relegated to and subordinated within a domestic sphere, whose separate and distinctive existence is legitimated not by appeals to justice but by entrenched views of family life and honour. They may also find that this domestic sphere is embedded in an economy that is subordinate to distant and richer economies. They not only raise children in poverty; they raise crops and do ill-paid and insecure work whose rewards fluctuate to the beat of distant economic forces. This second subordination, too, is legitimated in varied dis-courses which endorse an internationalized economic order but only national regimes of taxation and welfare. A serious account of justice cannot gloss over the predicaments of impoverished providers in marginalized and developing economies.

2   *Preview: Abstraction and Contextualization*

Both idealized and relativized approaches to justice make seemingly legitimate demands. Idealized approaches insist that justice must *abstract* from the particu-larities of persons. Blindness to difference is a traditional image of justice and guarantees impartiality. Yet principles of justice that are supposedly blind to differences of power and resources often seem to endorse practices and policies that suit the privileged. Hence a demand that justice take account of *context* can seem equally reasonable. Justice, it is argued, needs more than abstract principles: it must guide judgements that take account of actual contexts and predicaments and of the differences among human beings. Relativized principles of justice meet this demand: but since they are rooted in history, tradition, or local context, they will endorse traditional sexism or nationalism. Any relativism tends to prejudice the position of the weak, whose weakness is mirrored and partly constituted by their marginalization in received ways of thought and by their subordination and oppression in established orders. Yet idealizing approaches do no better. Where relativist approaches are uncritical of established privilege, idealized approaches are uncritical of the privileges from which they abstract.

If idealized and relativized accounts of justice were the only possibilities we would have to choose between demands for abstraction from difference and for sensitivity to difference. If there are other possibilities, an account of justice may be able to meet demands both for abstract principles and for contextualized judgements. I shall try to sketch a third possibility, which gives both abstraction

---

[1] Cf. Ruddick (1989). Her account of women's predicament stresses that it reflects heavy demands as much as meagre resources. To be preferred, I think, because it does not take for granted that the lack of resources is significant because 'public' while the press of others' demands is less so because merely 'private'.

and contextualization their due – but only their due. This can be done by meeting the demands for abstract and contextual reasoning in two distinct, successive moves.

The first move is to argue for abstract principles of universal scope, while rejecting the supposed link between abstraction and positions that not merely abstract but (in a sense to be explained) idealize. Much contemporary moral reasoning, and in particular 'abstract liberalism' (whether 'deontological' or utilitarian), handles issues of gender and international justice badly not because it abstracts (e.g. from sex, race, nationality), but because it almost always idealizes specific conceptions of the human agent and of national sovereignty which are often more admired and more (nearly) feasible for developed rather than developing societies and in men rather than in women. Genuine abstraction, without idealization, is, however, the route rather than the obstacle to broad scope and is unobjectionable in *principles* of justice.

The second move answers demands that we take account of the context and particularities of lives and societies, but does not endorse established ideals of gender and of national sovereignty. Abstract principles of justice are not rejected, but viewed as intrinsically incomplete and indeterminate, a guide rather than an algorithm for judging cases. The second move insists that justice can take account of *certain* differences by applying abstract principles to determinate cases without either tacitly reintroducing restricted ideals (e.g. by privileging certain views of gender and sovereignty) or relativizing principles of justice to accepted beliefs, traditions, or practices. Abstract principles can guide contextualized judgements without lapsing into relativism.

3   *Feminist Critiques of Abstract Justice*

Discussions of gender justice have been structured by disagreements over the extent and import of differences between men and women. For liberals who defend abstract principles of justice it has been embarrassing that the Rights of Man were taken for so long and by so many of their predecessors as the rights of men, and that liberal practice failed for so long to end male privilege.[2] (Socialist feminists suffer analogous embarrassments.) Starting with Wollstonecraft and J. S. Mill, liberal feminists argued against the different treatment of women, and claimed that women's rationality entitled them to equal rights.

Later liberal feminists noted that even when women had equal political and legal rights, their political participation and economic rewards remained less than those of men – and less than those of men whose qualifications and labour force participation women matched. Supposedly gender-neutral and neutralizing institutions, such as democratic political structures and markets, turned out

---

2. Okin (1979); Charvet (1982); Pateman (1988); Jaggar (1983).

to be remarkably bad at reducing gender differentials.[3] Approximations to political and legal justice in various domains of life evidently will not close the radical gap between men's and women's paths and prospects.[4]

In response many liberal feminists argued that justice demands more thorough equal treatment. It may, for example, require forms of affirmative action and reverse discrimination in education and employment, as well as welfare rights to social support for the poor and those with heavy family responsibilities. *Some* differences are to be acknowledged in principles of justice. This move has two difficulties. First, many liberals deny that justice demands compensatory redistribution, especially of positional goods. They think these should be allocated by competitive and meritocratic procedures. This debate is of particular importance in the developed world.

The second problem arises even where the goods to be distributed are not positional, and is particularly significant in the Third World. Where resources are scarce, non-positional goods such as basic health care, income support, children's allowances, or unemployment insurance will not be fundable out of a slender national tax base. If social justice demands basic welfare provision, justice has to reach across boundaries. An account of gender justice would then have to be linked to one of international distributive justice.[5]

This liberal debate continues, but its terms have been increasingly questioned by feminists in the last decade, many of whom claim that, despite its aspirations, gender bias is integral to liberal justice.[6] Their suspicions focus on the very abstraction from difference and diversity which is central to liberal justice. Some feminist critics of abstract liberalism have highlighted respects in which particular supposedly gender-neutral theories covertly assume or endorse gendered accounts of the human subject and of rationality. Many aspects of this critique are convincing.

However, the most fundamental feminist challenge to abstract liberalism impugns reliance on abstraction itself. Gilligan's influential work claims that an emphasis on justice excludes and marginalizes the 'other voice' of ethical thought. 'Abstract liberalism' simply and unacceptably devalues care and concern for particular others, which are the core of women's moral life and thought, seeing them as moral immaturity.[7] The voice of justice is intrinsically 'male'

---

[3] Scott (1986).

[4] The differences run the gamut of social indicators. Most dramatically in some Third World countries women and girls do worse on a constellation of very basic social indicators: they die earlier, have worse health, eat less than other family members, earn less, and go to school less. See Sen (1987); Harriss (1988 and 1991).

[5] The problem is not merely one of resources. Where funds have been adequate for publicly funded welfare provision, this too has been inadequate to eliminate the differences between the economic and political prospects of men and of women. Many women in the formerly socialist countries, for example, find that they have secured greater equality in productive labour with no reduction in reproductive tasks. This is a reason for doubting that arguments establishing welfare rights – e.g. a right to food – take a broad enough view of disparities between men's and women's prospects.

[6] E.g. Pateman (1988); Okin (1987).

[7] Gilligan (1982); Kittay and Meyers (1987); Lloyd (1984); MacMillan (1982); Ruddick (1987); Noddings (1984); Chodorow (1978).

in its refusal to grasp the actualities of human difference, in its supposed agnosticism about the good for man, and in its resulting disregard of the virtues, and specifically of love and care. On this account the problem is not to secure like treatment for women, but to secure differentiated treatment for all.

In locating the distinction between justice and care (and other virtues) in a disagreement over the legitimacy of relying on abstract principles, some feminist critics of abstract liberalism construe concern for care as opposing concern for justice. They can end up endorsing rather than challenging social and economic structures that marginalize women and confine them to a private sphere. Separatism at the level of ethical theory can march with acceptance of the powers and traditions that be. The cost of a stress on caring and relationships to the exclusion of abstract justice may be relegation to the nursery and the kitchen, to purdah and to poverty. In rejecting 'abstract liberalism' such feminists converge with traditions that exclude and marginalize women. Even when they appeal to 'women's experience', rather than to established traditions and discourses, as the clue to understanding the other 'voice', they agree that differences are taken seriously only when actual differences are endorsed.[8]

The disputes that divide liberal feminists and their contextualist critics pose an unwelcome dilemma about gender justice. If we adopt an abstract account of justice, which is blind to differences between people—and so to the ways in which women's lives in the developed and in the undeveloped world differ from men's lives—we commit ourselves (it is said) to uniform treatment regardless of difference. If we acknowledge the ethical importance of differences, we are likely to endorse traditional social forms that sustain those differences, including those that subordinate and oppress women.

4   The Communitarian Critique of Abstract Justice

This dilemma recurs in certain discussions of international justice. Abstract liberalism proclaims the Rights of Man. As Burke was quick to complain, this is quite a different matter from proclaiming the rights of Englishmen, or of Frenchmen, or of any coherent group. Abstraction was the price to be paid for ethical discourse that could cross the boundaries of states and nations and have universal appeal; and Burke found the price unacceptable. The internationalist, cosmopolitan commitments that were implicit in the ideals of liberalism have repeatedly been targets of conservative and communitarian criticism.

Liberal practice has, however, once again been embarrassingly different. It

---

[8] Many of those who urge respect for the 'other' voice insist that they do not reject the demands of justice, and that they see the two 'voices' as complementary rather than alternative. The positions taken by different writers, and by the same writers at different times, vary. The protests must be taken in context: those who appeal to 'women's experience' or 'women's thinking' appeal to a source that mirrors the traditional relegation of women to a 'private' sphere, and cannot readily shed those commitments. It is important to remember that those who care have traditionally been thought to have many cares.

has not been universalistic, but clearly subordinated to the boundaries and demands of nation states. This is evident in relations between rich and poor states. Like treatment for like cases is partially secured by laws and practices within many democratic states; only a few enthusiasts argue for world government, or think that rights of residence, work, and welfare, as well as burdens of taxation, should be global. Such enthusiasm is often dismissed by practical people who hold that a plurality of national jurisdictions provides the framework within which liberal ideals can be pursued. Liberals may not be generally willing to take differences seriously; but they have taken differences between sovereign states remarkably seriously.

Their communitarian critics take differences and boundaries seriously in theory as well as in practice.[9] When boundaries are taken wholly seriously, however, international justice is not just played down, but wiped off the ethical map. Walzer's work is a good case in point. He holds that the largest sphere of justice is the political community and that the only issues not internal to such communities are about membership in them and conflicts between them. The issues of membership concern the admission of individual aliens; rights and duties do not go beyond borders.[10] A commitment to community is a commitment to the historical boundaries of political communities, whatever these happen to be and whatever injustices their constitution and their preservation entail. Communitarians cannot easily take any wider view of ethical boundaries since their critique of abstraction is in part a demand for ethical discourse that takes 'our' language, 'our' culture, and 'our' traditions seriously.[11]

Like current debates on gender justice, discussions of international justice apparently pose an unwelcome choice. Either we can abstract from the reality of boundaries, and think about principles of justice that assume an ideal cosmopolitan world, in which justice and human rights do not stop at the boundaries of states. Or we can acknowledge the reality of boundaries and construe the principles of justice as subordinate to those of national sovereignty. Cosmopolitan ideals are evident in the discourse of much of the human rights movement; but recent liberal theorists have shifted towards the relativism of their communitarian critics, and even come to regard liberal principles of justice as no more than the principles of liberal societies. Rawls in particular now[12]

---

[9] Such approaches can be found in Walzer (1983); Sandel (1982); MacIntyre (1981 and 1984); Williams (1985), and, perhaps most surprisingly, Rawls (1985). For some discussion of the implications of these works for international justice see O'Neill (1988b).

[10] Walzer acknowledges that this means that he can 'only begin to address the problems raised by mass poverty in many parts of the globe' (1983: 30). Critics may think that his approach in fact pre-empts answers to questions of global justice.

[11] Communitarians can, however, take lesser loyalties seriously: where a state is divided into distinct national and ethical communities, those distinct traditions may in fact be the widest boundaries within which issues of justice can be debated and determined. They could argue for secession from a multinational state; but they cannot say anything about what goes on beyond the boundaries of 'our' community. Cf. Walzer (1983: 319).

[12] Rawls (1985).

hinges his theory of justice not on an abstract and idealized construction of an original position but on the actual ideals of citizens of liberal democratic societies. Here we see a surprising and perhaps unstable convergence between abstract liberal theorists and their communitarian critics.

5   Abstraction with and without Idealization

Debates about gender and international justice are not merely similar in that each is structured by a confrontation between advocates of abstract and of contextualized justice. In each debate many advocates of supposedly abstract approaches to justice go far beyond abstraction. What these debates term 'abstraction' is often a set of specific, unargued *idealizations* of human agency, rationality, and life, and of the sovereignty and independence of states. And in each debate what is said to be attention to actual situations and contexts in judging is in fact *relativism* about principles. These conflations are avoidable.

Abstraction, taken strictly, is simply a matter of detaching certain claims from others. Abstract reasoning hinges nothing on the satisfaction or non-satisfaction of predicates from which it abstracts. All uses of language must abstract more or less: the most detailed describing cannot dent the indeterminacy of language. Indeed it is not obvious that there is anything to object to in very abstract principles of justice. Highly abstract ways of reasoning are often admired (mathematics, physics), and frequently well paid (accountancy, law). What is different about abstract ethical reasoning? When we look at objections to 'abstract' ethical principles and reasoning in detail, it appears that they are often objections not to detachment from certain predicates, but to the inclusion of predicates that are false of the objects of the domain to which a theory is then applied. Reasoning that abstracts from some predicate makes claims that do not hinge on the objects to which the reasoning is applied satisfying that predicate. Reasoning that idealizes does make claims that hinge on the objects to which it is applied satisfying certain predicates. Where those predicates are unsatisfied the reasoning simply does not apply.

The principles and theories of justice to which the critics of 'abstract liberalism' object are indeed abstract. They take no account of many features of agents and societies. However, these principles and theories not only abstract but idealize. They assume, for example, accounts of rational choice whose claims about information, coherence, capacities to calculate, and the like are not merely not satisfied by some deficient or backward agents, but are actually satisfied by no human agents (perhaps they are approximated, or at least admired, in restricted shopping and gambling contexts!). They also assume idealized accounts of the mutual independence of persons and their opportunities to pursue their individual 'conceptions of the good'; and of the sovereignty and independence of states, that are false of all human beings and all states. Such idealizations no doubt have theoretical advantages: above all they allow us to construct models that can readily be manipulated. However, they fail to apply to most, if not all, practical problems of human choice and foreign policy.

If idealized descriptions are not abstracted from those that are true of actual agents, they are not innocuous ways of extending the scope of reasoning. Each idealization posits 'enhanced' versions of the objects of the domain to which the model is applied. They may privilege certain sorts of human agent and life and certain sorts of society by covertly presenting (enhanced versions of) their specific characteristics as the ideal for all human action and life. In this way covert gender chauvinism and exaggerated respect for state power can be combined with liberal principles. Idealization masquerading as abstraction produces theories that appear to apply widely, but which covertly exclude those who do not match a certain ideal, or match it less well than others. Those who are excluded are then seen as defective or inadequate. A review of the debates about gender and international justice shows that the feminist and communitarian critique of liberal justice can legitimately attack spurious idealizations without impugning abstraction that eschews idealization.

6   Gender and Idealized Agents

Liberal discussions of justice ostensibly hinge nothing on gender differences. They apply to individuals, considered in abstraction from specific identities, commitments, and circumstances. Recent critics insist that liberal theories of justice are far from being as gender-blind as their advocates claim. An instructive example is Rawls's *A Theory of Justice*. Rawls was particularly concerned not to rely on an extravagant model of rational choice. His principles of justice are those that would be chosen by agents in an 'original position' in which they know *less* rather than *more* than actual human agents. He conceives his work as carrying the social contract tradition to 'a higher level of abstraction'. In particular, agents in the original position do not know their social and economic position, their natural assets, or their conceptions of the good.[13] The original position operationalizes the image of justice as blind to difference.

However, Rawls has at a certain point to introduce grounds for those in the original position to care about their successors. He suggests that we may think of them as heads or at other times as representatives of families, 'as being so to speak deputies for an everlasting moral agent or institution'[14] and that some form of family would be just. Yet in doing so he pre-empts the question of intrafamilial justice. He pre-empts the question not by crude insistence that heads of families must be men, but by taking it as read that there is some just form of family which allows the interests of some to be justly represented by others. The shift from individuals to heads of families as agents of construction is not an innocent abstraction; it *assumes* a family structure which secures iden-

---

[13] Rawls (1970: 11–12).   [14] Rawls (1970: 128).

tity of interests between distinct individuals. It takes for granted that there is some just 'sexual contract',[15] that justice can presuppose a legitimate separation of 'private' from 'public' domains. This is idealization indeed: it buries the question of gender justice rather than resolving it. Rawls's text leaves it surprisingly obscure whether women are to be relegated to a 'private' sphere and represented by men in the construction of justice, whether both 'public' and 'private' realms are to be shared by all on equal terms, or whether women alone are to carry the burdens of both spheres.[16]

The more radical feminist critique of abstract liberalism rejects not merely the suppressed gendering of the subject which Pateman and Okin detect in classical and contemporary liberal writers, but abstraction itself. In advocating an ethic of care these critics, we have seen, come close both to traditional misogynist positions and to ethical relativism. When the 'voices' of justice and of care are presented as alternatives between which we must choose, each is viewed as a complete approach to moral issues. However, the two in fact focus on different aspects of life. Justice is concerned with institutions, care and other virtues with character, which is vital in unmediated relationships with particular others. The central difference between the 'voices' of justice and care is not that they reason in different ways. Justice requires judgements about cases as well as abstract principles; care is principled as well as responsive to differences. Justice matters for impoverished providers because their predicament is one of institutionally structured poverty which cannot be banished by idealizing an ethic of care.

7 Idealized Boundaries

A comparable slide from abstraction to idealization can be found in discussions of international justice. Discussions of global economic and political issues often take it for granted that the principal actors are states. Traditionally the main divide in these discussions has been between realists, who contend that states, although agents, are exempt from moral obligations and criticism, and idealists, who insist that states are not merely agents but accountable agents who must meet the demands of justice.[17]

In discussions of distributive justice, however, the salient issue has not been the conflict between idealists and realists, but their agreement that state

[15] Cf. Pateman (1988); Nicholson (1987).

[16] See Okin (1987: 46–7). She considers whether the original position abstracts from knowledge of one's sex. Even if she is right in thinking that Rawls relies on a covertly gendered account of the subject, this idealization may have little effect on his theory of justice if the thought experiment of the original position has so relentlessly suppressed difference that the supposed plurality of voices is a fiction. In that case we should read the work as taking an idealized rather than a merely abstract view of rational choice from the very start, and as appealing to a single ideally informed and dispassionate figure as the generator of the principles of justice.

[17] See Beitz (1979) for an account of debates between realists and idealists.

boundaries define the main actors in international affairs. These shared terms of debate endorse an exaggerated, idealized view of the agency and mutual independence of sovereign states, which is now often criticized as obsolete. The common ground on which realists and idealists traditionally debated international relations is being eroded as other actors, including international agencies, regional associations, and above all transnational corporations, play a more and more significant role in world affairs.[18] A world that is partitioned into discrete and mutually impervious sovereign states is not an abstraction from our world, but an idealized version of it, or perhaps an idealized version of what it once was. Realists as well as idealists idealize the sovereignty of states.

Idealized conceptions both of state sovereignty and of state boundaries limit discussions of international distributive justice. Although long subject to theoretical questioning from advocates of human rights, who deny that states can be sovereign in determining the fates of individuals, many liberals are coy about criticizing rights violations elsewhere. They limit criticism to violations of liberty rights, and offer little account of the agency or responsibilities of institutions; they find it hard to see how justice could require that state boundaries be breached to reduce the poverty that lies beyond them. Even those liberals who defend welfare rights are often concerned with welfare in one (rich) country. It is commonplace to view economic development of poorer regions as optional 'aid', not obligatory justice. Those who have tried to argue for global welfare rights within a liberal framework have to show who bears the obligations that correspond to these rights, and this has proved uphill work.[19] Meanwhile liberals, like communitarians, confine justice within national boundaries. Liberals do so self-consciously and provisionally; communitarians on principle and unapologetically; others tacitly and without discussion.

8. *Abstraction without Idealization*

The only way to find theories that have wide scope is to abstract from the particularities of agents; but when abstraction is displaced by idealization we are not led to theories with wide scope, but to theories that apply only to idealized agents.

This suggests that if we are interested in international or gender justice we should resist the temptation to rely on idealizing models of human agency or national sovereignty. We should instead consider what sort of theory of justice we would have if we abstracted but refused to idealize any one conception of rationality or independence, and so avoided marginalizing or excluding those who do not live up to specific ideals of rationality or of independence from others. Abstraction without idealization may allow us to consider a wide range of human

---

[18] Keohane and Nye (1970); Luper-Foy (1988).

[19] See Shue (1980, 1984); Alston and Tomasevski (1984); Brown and Shue (1977); Gewirth (1982); Luper-Foy (1988); O'Neill (1986).

agents and institutional arrangements without hinging anything on the specific features of agents' traditions, ideologies, and capacities to act. If we could do this we might avoid idealized accounts of agency and sovereignty without following feminist and communitarian critics of abstract liberalism into relativism.

Recent discussions may simply have been mistaken in treating appeals to idealized and relativized standards of rationality and agency as the only options. There are other possibilities. We do not have to hinge liberal arguments for rights or for the limits of government power either on the *hypothetical* consent of those who meet some *ideal* standard of rationality and mutual independence, or on the *actual* acceptance of an outlook and its categories that *relativizes* consent to an established order. We could instead begin simply by abstracting from existing social orders. We could consider what principles of action must be adopted by agents who are numerous, diverse, and *neither* ideally rational *nor* ideally independent of one another, and yet avoid specific assumptions about these agents. We can bracket both idealizations and the status quo. The issue then becomes: how powerful and convincing an account of justice can we offer if we appeal neither to fictions of ideal rationality and independence nor to the contingencies of actual agents and institutions? What happens if we abstract without idealizing?

9   Plurality and Justice: Who Counts?

Let us begin with the thought of a plurality of potentially interacting and diverse agents. This rules out two cases. First, it rules out the case where justice is not a problem because there is no plurality, or no genuine plurality, of agents, hence no potential for conflict between agents. (The action of agents in such a degenerate plurality would be automatically or necessarily co-ordinated, e.g. by instinct or by a pre-established harmony.) Second, it rules out hinging an account of justice on an assumed, contingent, and determinate limit to the diversity of its members, which provides a common ground between them and permits a contingent, socially guaranteed convergence and co-ordination. The two cases that are ruled out are once again those which would base principles of justice on an assumed ideal convergence or an assumed actual historical or social convergence.

What does justice require of such a plurality? At least we can claim that their most basic principles must be ones that *could* be adopted by all. If they were not, at least some agents would have to be excluded from the plurality for whom the principles can hold, whose boundaries would have to be drawn more narrowly.

Such a redrawing of boundaries is, of course, the very move often used to exclude women and foreigners, let alone foreign women, from the domain of justice. Those who exclude simply refuse to count certain others as members of a plurality of potentially interacting agents. An account of justice which hinges on the sharability of principles can be pre-empted by excluding some from the domain of justice without argument. So it is important to see the move for what it is. This can best be done by asking *who* makes the move.

The move is not made by idealized genderless theorists who live outside state and society. It is made by people who generally expect women to interact with them, to follow language and reason, to understand and take part in elaborate traditions and institutions, perhaps even to love, honour, and obey. It is made by people who expect ordinary processes of translation, trade, and negotiation to work with foreigners. To deny the agency of others with whom we plan to interact in complex ways reeks of bad faith. Bad faith can be avoided only by counting as members of the plurality for whom principles of justice are to hold *anybody* with whom interaction is to be attempted or held possible. The question then becomes: are there any principles which must be adopted by all members of a plurality of potentially interacting agents? We cannot simply stipulate that such principles are irrelevant for interactions with certain others on whose (no doubt imperfect) capacities to reason and (no doubt limited) abilities to act independently we know we depend.

If women were all transported to Betelgeuse, and so beyond all interaction with the remaining men on Earth, neither men nor women would have to see the other as falling within the domain of justice. Less fancifully, since the ancient inhabitants of the Andes and their contemporaries in Anglo-Saxon England could not and did not interact, neither would have acted in bad faith if they had excluded the other from the domain of justice. Neither could practise either justice or injustice towards the other. Things are different for the actual men and women who inhabit the earth now: the potential for interaction cannot be assumed away, and others cannot be arbitrarily excluded from the domain of justice. We rely on global economic and political processes, so cannot consistently insist that justice (conveniently for the developed world) stops at state frontiers, any more than we can rely on women's rationality and their productive contribution and then argue that justice (conveniently for some men) stops at the edge of a supposed 'private' sphere, whose existence and demarcation is in fact presupposed in defining a 'public' sphere.

10   *Plurality and Justice: What Principles?*

Justice is then in the first place a matter of keeping to principles that can be adopted by any plurality of potentially interacting beings. But if we eschew both idealization and relativism, and rely on mere abstraction, will we have strong enough premisses to identify those principles? Does a universalizability test cut any ice? Granted that universalizability is not uniformity (as some critics of abstract liberalism suppose), is it not too weak a demand to ground an account of justice? In particular, will not any internally coherent principle for individual action be a universalizable principle?[20]

---

[20] This is the hoary problem of formalism in Kantian ethics. For recent discussions of aspects of the problem see Bittner (1974); Höffe (1977); O'Neill (1989: Part II).

We have, however, to remember that we are considering the case of a plurality of *potentially interacting* beings, that is of beings who share a world. Any principle of action that is adopted by all members of such pluralities alters the world that they share and becomes a background condition of their action. This is why certain principles of action which can coherently be held by some cannot be coherently held by all. Examples of non-universalizable principles can illustrate the point. A principle of deception, which undermines trust, would, if universally adopted, make all trusting, hence all projects of deception, incoherent. Selective deception is on the cards: universal deception is impossible. Since a principle of deception cannot be a fundamental one for any plurality, justice requires that it be rejected. Equally, a policy of coercion which seeks to destroy or undercut the agency and independence of at least some others for at least some time cannot be universally held. Those who are victims of coercion cannot (while victims) also act on the principles on which their coercers act.[21] Equally, a principle of violence which damages the agency of some others cannot be universally acted on. Put quite generally, principles of action that hinge on victimizing some, so on destroying, paralysing, or undercutting their capacities for action for at least some time and in some ways, can be adopted by some but cannot be adopted as fundamental principles by any plurality.[22]

To keep matters under control, let us imagine only that justice demands (at least) that action and institutions should not be based on principles of deception and victimization. (There may be other principles of justice.) We are still far from showing just what justice demands, since we do not know what refusing to deceive or to coerce may demand in specific circumstances. These guidelines are highly indeterminate. We seem to have paid the classic price of abstraction. Highly abstract principles do not tell us what to do in a specific context.

Abstract principles are only part of practical, or specifically of ethical, reasoning, however. Principles never determine their own applications; even the culturally specific principles that relativists favour do not determine their own applications. All practical reasoning requires judgement and deliberation by which principles are applied to particular cases. An account of gender and international justice is no exception. We need in particular to be able to judge what specific institutions and action are needed if poor women in poor economies are to be accorded justice.

11 *Plurality and Justice: Deliberation without Relativism*

Two background issues must be dealt with summarily before considering moves from abstract basic principles to determinate judgements. First, we have no

---

[21] It does not follow that every coercive act is unjust; some coercion, e.g. the use of sanctions to enforce law, may be the condition of any reliable space for uncoerced action. In such cases the appropriate expression of an underlying principle of rejecting coercion is, surprisingly, and crucially for political argument, one that, taken out of context, might express an underlying principle of coercion.

[22] I have put these matters briefly. For more extended treatment see the references given in n. 20 and O'Neill (1988a).

reason to expect that principles of justice will provide any algorithm of rational choice. Nor do we need any algorithm for principles to be important. Even principles that provide only a set of side constraints on action may exert a powerful influence. Second, we have no reason to think that principles of justice are relevant only to the action of individuals. A full account of the agency of institutions would be a complex matter. I shall not go into it here, but will assume that it can be given and that institutions and practices, like individuals, must meet the demands of justice.

These moves, however, are preliminary to the main task of giving a more determinate account of what may be required if principles of deception or victimization are rejected. How, for example, can we judge whether specific types of family or economic activity are based on deception or victimization? Are all forms of hierarchy and subordination coercive? If not, how do we discern the boundaries of deceit and coercion in actual contexts? It is not hard to see that certain categories of individual action—for example, fraud or wife burning or battering—deceive or victimize, but other cases of deception and coercion by individuals are hard to adjudicate. It may also be hard to judge whether social traditions that isolate or exclude women, or economic and familial arrangements that ensure their acute economic vulnerability, amount to modes of deceit and coercion.

In this paper the task cannot be to reach determinate judgements about particular cases, but only to see that reasoned moves from very abstract principles towards more specific principles, whose relevance and application to particular cases may be easier to assess, may be possible. It will not be enough to lean on the received criteria by which 'our' tradition or nation picks out ethically significant 'cases' or 'options' for approaching them. We beg questions if we assume that categories of thought that have been hospitable to male dominance and imperialism can be decisive for discerning or judging justice to those whose problems have been marginalized and whose agency and capacities have been formed, perhaps deformed, by unjust institutions. We cannot rely uncritically on the categories of established discourse, including the discourse of social scientists and the 'helping' professions, to pick out the significant problems. These categories are themselves matters for ethical concern and criticism.[23] We have, after all, no more reason to trust relativized discussions of justice, gender, or boundaries than to trust idealized approaches unequivocally. Those discussions are no more free of theory and ideology than are idealized discussions of justice. Their ways of individuating typical problem cases may be familiar; but familiarity may mask contentious and unjust delimitations. If the received views of a society or tradition are taken as defining the domain of problems to which abstract principles of justice are applied, unvindicated ideals will be introduced and privileged, just as they are in idealized approaches to justice.

Some confirmation of the ways in which received descriptions of social rela-

---

[23] Edelman (1984).

tions reflect larger and disputed ideals is suggestive. Consider, for example, how issues of gender are passed over as if invisible. We find an enormous amount of shifting around in the choice of basic units of social analysis. In the shifts between descriptions that focus on individuals, wage-earners, and heads of families, there is enough flexibility for the blunt facts of economic and other subordination of women to be veiled. Women's low wages can seem unworrying if they are wives for whom others provide; their dependence on husbands and fathers can seem acceptable if they are after all wage-earning individuals, so not invidiously dependent. Reproductive labour may (with convenient ambiguity!) be thought of as priceless.[24] Wage-earning women's low pay can be seen as fitting their low skills and vindicating their domestic subordination to wage-earning men, who as 'heads of families' are entitled to discretionary expenditure and leisure which wage-earning women must do without because they (unlike men!) have family commitments. The gloomy evidence of social structures that classify women's contributions as less valuable even when more onerous or more skilled is evident enough. We continually find ourselves 'thinking about men as individuals who direct households and about women as family members'.[25]

There are equally serious reasons to mistrust the move from abstract principles to determinate judgements in discussions of individual motivation. These too are shaped by received views, and in milieux which are strongly individualist are easily diverted into attempts to pin blame for injustices on individuals. Women, after all, commonly acquiesce in their social and economic subordination. Are they then to be blamed for servility? Or are men to be blamed for oppressing or exploiting women?[26] Or do these individualist approaches to assigning blame lead no further than the higher bickering? It can seem that we have reasons to mistrust not only relativist approaches to gender justice but even the attempt to apply an abstract, non-idealized principle of justice. But we do not inhabit an ideal world. Idealized conceptions of justice simply do not apply to international relations, social relations, or individual acts in a world in which states, men, and women *always* lack the capacities and the opportunities of idealized agents. States are not really sovereign—even superpowers have limited powers; and men and women are always more or less vulnerable, ignorant, insecure, lacking in confidence or means to challenge or oppose the status quo. In a world of agents with finite capacities and opportunities, poor women in poor economies differ not in kind but in degree in their dependence on others and in others' demands on them.

12 *Just Deliberation in a World of Vulnerable Agents*

If we are to apply principles of justice that are neither idealized, nor merely relative to actual societies, to vulnerable lives and their predicaments, we must

---

[24] Nicholson (1987).
[25] Stiehm (1983); Scott (1986); Sen (1987).
[26] Postow (1978–9); Hill (1979); Pfeffer (1985); Sen (1987).

see how to move towards determinate judgements about actual cases. The principles of justice for which I have argued take us in this direction because they focus neither on the arrangements to which ideally rational and mutually independent beings would consent, nor on the arrangements to which others in possibly oppressive situations do consent. Rather they ask which arrangements a plurality of interacting agents with finite capacities *could* consent to. I have suggested, provisionally, that this non-idealizing construction identifies the rejection of deception, coercion, and other ways of victimizing others as principles of justice.

But principles are not enough. Non-idealizing abstraction avoids some problems, but not others. If we are to move from abstract principles to determinate judgements we need to operationalize the idea of avoiding acting on unsharable principles, without subordinating it to the categories and views of the status quo. One reasonable way of doing so might be to ask to what extent the arrangements that structure vulnerable lives are ones that *could have been refused or renegotiated by those whom they actually constrain.* If those affected by a given set of arrangements could have refused or renegotiated them, their consent is no mere formality, but genuine, legitimating consent. If they could not but 'accept' those institutions, their 'consent' will not legitimate. The point of this way of operationalizing the notion of possible consent is that it neither ascribes ideal reasoning capacities and ideal independence from others nor hinges legitimation on an actual 'consent' that may reflect injustice. On this account justice requires that institutions, like acts, allow those on the receiving end, even if frail and dependent, to refuse or renegotiate the roles and tasks assigned to them.

Dissent becomes harder when capacities to act are less developed and more vulnerable, and when opportunities for independent action are restricted. Capacities to act are constrained both by lack of abilities and by commitments to others. Institutional arrangements can disable agency both by limiting capacities to reason and act independently and by increasing the demands to meet the needs and satisfy the desires of others. Apparent consent to such arrangements does not show that they are just. Whenever 'consent' reflects lack of capacity or opportunity to do anything else, it does not legitimate. Thinking in this way about justice, we can see that *it demands more, not less, to be just to the vulnerable.* The vulnerable are much easier to deceive and to victimize than the strong. If we are to judge proposals for action by seeing whether they involve serious deception or victimization (coercion or violence), *more* will be demanded when others are vulnerable than when they are secure, and most when they are most vulnerable.[27] By contrast both idealized and relativized accounts of justice tend to conceal the fact that justice to the weak demands more than justice to the

---

[27] I focus here on the obligations of the strong rather than the rights of the weak. This is not to deny that agitation and resistance by the weak can help remind and persuade the strong of their obligations and make it more difficult for them to repudiate them. However, to focus primarily on rights falsifies the predicament of the weak, who are in no position to ensure that others meet their obligations.

strong. Idealized accounts of justice tend to ignore vulnerability and relativized accounts to legitimate it.

13 *Achieving Justice for Impoverished Providers*

The lives of poor women in poor economies illustrate these points well. Consider, for example, daily commercial transactions and practices. Their justice, it is usually said, lies in the fact that arrangements are mutually agreed. But where there are great disparities of knowledge and vulnerability between agents, the 'agreement' of the weak may be spurious. They may have been duped by offers they did not understand or overwhelmed by 'offers' they dared not refuse. Within national jurisdictions these facts are well recognized, and commercial practice is regulated to prevent pressure and fraud. Contracts can be voided for fraud; there are 'truth in lending' provisions; debt and bankruptcy lead not to loss of liberty but to loss of property; those with dependants can rely on a safety net of welfare rights. International economic transactions take place in a far less regulated space, yet link agents with far greater disparities in power and resources. The weak can suffer both from particular others who take advantage of their ignorance and vulnerability, and because nothing informs them about or shields them from the intended or unintended consequences either of distant or of local economic forces. The poor, and above all women who are impoverished providers, cannot refuse or renegotiate economic structures or transactions which hurt them. They are vulnerable not only to low wages, low standards of industrial safety, endemic debt, and disadvantageous dependence on those who provide credit, but also to disadvantageous patterns of entitlement within the family. Debtors who need further loans for survival, for example, cannot make much fuss about the terms creditors offer for purchasing their crops.[28] Market 'imperfections' are neither avoidable nor trivial for vulnerable agents with many dependants; equally, 'perfect' markets can magnify vulnerability to distant economic forces.

Idealized pictures of justice have tended to overlook the import of economic power: by idealizing the capacities and the mutual independence of those involved in market transactions they obscure the reasons why the weak may be unable to dissent from arrangements proposed by the strong. They also tend to distinguish sharply between intended and unintended consequences, and to view the latter as unavoidable 'forces'. Yet these forces are themselves the outcome of institutional arrangements and could be changed or modified, as they have been within many jurisdictions. The problem of shielding the weak from these forces has nothing to do with 'natural' processes, and everything to do with the weakness of the voices that call for change. This is hardly surprising. Market institutions magnify the security and so the voices of the haves. Formal democracy provides only slender and partial redress for the weak, and is often lacking.

[28] Shue (1984); Harriss (1987 and 1991).

Typical family structures illustrate the gulf between ideally independent agents (whom 'ideal' market structures might suit) and actual powerlessness. These structures often draw a boundary between 'public' and 'private' domains, assign women (wives and daughters) to the 'private' domain, and leave them with slender control of resources, but heavy commitments to meet others' needs. They may lack adequate economic entitlements, effective enfranchisement, or access to sources of information or debate by which to check or challenge the proposals and plans of the more powerful. Women in this predicament lack security, and must meet the demands of others (often fathers and husbands) who dominate them. Family structures can enable, even impose, forms of deception and domination. Where women are isolated, secluded, barred from education or wage earning, or have access to information only via the filter of more powerful family members, their judgement is weakened, and their independence stunted. Often this vulnerability may be shielded by matching concern and restraint; often it will not. A rhetoric of familial concern and protective paternalism can easily camouflage a callous lack of concern and legitimate deceptive acts and practices.

Similar points can be made about victimization. A principle of non-coercion, for example, basically demands that action should not undercut others' agency. If agents were all ideally independent of one another, they might find little difficulty in dissenting from many forms of attempted domination. However, family structures always limit independence, and usually limit women's independence more. A woman who has no adequate entitlements of her own, and insecure rights to a share in family property or income, will not always be coerced, but is always vulnerable to coercion.[29] When her independence is also restricted by family responsibilities she will be even easier to coerce. In these circumstances ostensible consent reveals little; it certainly does not legitimate forms of domination and subordination. Relations of dependence are not always or overtly coercive; but they provide structures of subordination within which it is all too easy to silence or trivialize the articulation of dissent. To guarantee that action is not based on principles which others cannot share, it is necessary to ensure that proposals that affect others are ones from which *they* can dissent. Institutionalized dependence tends to make dissent hard or impossible. Those who cannot secure economic independence or who cannot rely on others to take a share in caring for genuine dependants (children, the elderly) cannot easily say 'no' or set their own terms. They must go along with the proposals of the more powerful.

Genuine, legitimating consent is undermined by the very institutions which most readily secure an appearance of consent. Institutionalized dependence may ensure that the weak provide a spurious 'consent' to the action of the strong, while remaining at their mercy. If the strong reliably show restraint, there may *in*

---

[29] See Sen (1987) for a fuller account of entitlements. While I have chosen to stress *vulnerabilities* that must not be exploited, rather than *capabilities* that ought to be secured, I believe this account of justice to the powerless is fully compatible with Sen's.

fact be no injustice within relationships which institutionalize dependence; but institutions that rely too heavily on the self-restraint of the stronger cannot reliably avoid injustice. Whether the proposals of the strong are economic or sexual, whether they rely on the ignorance and isolation of the weak to deceive them, or on their diminished opportunities for independent action, or on the habits of deference and appeasement which become second nature for the weak, they ride on unjust social practices. *The weak risk recurrent injustice unless institutions are structured to secure the option of refusal or renegotiation for those whose capacities and opportunities are limited.*

A woman who has no entitlements of her own lives at the discretion of other family members who have them, so is likely to have to go along even with proposals she greatly dislikes or judges imprudent. If she were an ideally independent agent, or even had the ordinary independence and opportunities of those who have entitlements adequate for themselves and their dependants, she could risk dissent from or at least renegotiate proposals put by those who control her means of life. Being powerless and vulnerable she cannot readily do either. Hence any consent that she offers is compromised and does not legitimate others' proposals. Just as we would find it absurd to hinge legitimating consent to medical treatment on procedures geared to the cognitive capacities and independence of a notional 'ideal rational patient', so we should find it absurd to hinge legitimating consent to others' plans on the cognitive capacities and independence of a notional ideal rational impoverished provider for others.

This is not to say that impoverished providers are irrational or wholly dependent or cannot consent. It is, however, a matter of taking seriously the ways in which their capacities and opportunities for action constrain their possibilities for refusal and negotiation. If they are to be treated with justice, others who interact with them must not rely on these reduced capacities and opportunities to impose their will. Those who do so rely on unjust institutional structures that enable deceit, coercion, and forms of victimization.

In applying abstract, non-idealizing principles we have to take account not indeed of the actual beliefs, ideals, or categories of others, which may reflect unjust traditions, but of others' actual *capacities* and *opportunities* to act — and their incapacities and lack of opportunities. This move does not lead back to relativism: no principle is endorsed because it is actually accepted. Put in general terms we can use modal notions to identify principles, but indicative ones to apply them. The principles of justice can be determined for any possible plurality: for they demand only the rejection of principles that cannot be shared by all members of a plurality. Judgements about the justice of actual situations are regulated but not entailed by these principles. The most significant features of actual situations that must be taken into account in judgements about justice are the security or vulnerability that allow actual others to dissent from and to seek change in the arrangements which structure their lives.

BIBLIOGRAPHY

ALSTON, P. (1984). 'International Law and the Human Right to Food', in P. Alston and K. Tomasevski (eds.), *The Right to Food*. Dordrecht: Nijhoff.

—— and TOMASEVSKI, K. (eds.) (1984). *The Right to Food*. Dordrecht: Nijhoff.

BEITZ, CHARLES (1979). *Political Theory and International Relations*. Princeton, NJ: Princeton University Press.

BITTNER, RÜDIGER (1974). 'Maximen', in G. Funke (ed.), *Akten des 4. Internationalen Kant-Kongresses*. Berlin: De Gruyter.

BROWN, PETER, and SHUE, HENRY (eds.) (1981). *Boundaries: National Autonomy and its Limits*. New Jersey: Rowman & Littlefield.

CHARVET, JOHN (1982). *Feminism*. London: Dent.

CHODOROW, NANCY (1978). *The Reproduction of Mothering*. Berkeley, Calif.: University of California Press.

EDELMAN, MURRAY (1984). 'The Political Language of the Helping Professions', in Michael J. Shapiro (ed.), *Language and Politics*. New York: NYU Press.

GEWIRTH, ALAN (1982). 'Starvation and Human Rights', in his *Human Rights: Essays on Justification and Applications*. Chicago: Chicago University Press.

GILLIGAN, CAROL (1982). *In a Different Voice: Psychological Theory and Women's Dependence*. Cambridge, Mass.: Harvard University Press.

HARRISS, BARBARA (1987). 'Merchants and Markets of Grain in South Asia', in Teodor Shanin (ed.), *Peasants and Peasant Societies*. Oxford: Blackwell.

—— (1988). *Differential Female Mortality and Health Care in South Asia*, Working Paper 13. Oxford: Queen Elizabeth House, and *Journal of Social Studies*, 41, Dhaka University.

—— (1991). 'Intrafamily Distribution of Hunger in South Asia', in J. Drèze and A. K. Sen (eds.), *The Political Economy of Hunger*, i. Oxford: Clarendon Press.

HILL, THOMAS (1973). 'Servility and Self Respect', *Monist*, 57, 87–104.

HÖFFE, OTFRIED (1977). 'Kants kategorischer Imperativ als Kriterium des Sittlichen', *Zeitschrift für Philosophische Forschung*, 31, 354–84.

HOFFMAN, STANLEY (1981). *Duties Beyond Borders: On the Limits and Possibilities of Ethical International Politics*. Syracuse, New York: Syracuse University Press.

JAGGAR, ALISON M. (1983). *Feminist Politics and Human Nature*. Brighton: Harvester Press.

KEOHANE, ROBERT O., and NYE, JOSEPH S. (eds.) (1970). *Transnational Relations and World Politics*. Cambridge, Mass.: Harvard University Press.

KITTAY, EVA FEDERS, and MEYERS, DIANE T. (eds.) (1987). *Women and Moral Theory*. New York: Rowman and Littlefield.

LLOYD, GENEVIEVE (1984). *The Man of Reason: 'Male' and 'Female' in Western Philosophy*. London: Methuen.

LUPER-FOY, STEPHEN (ed.) (1988). *Problems of International Justice*. Boulder and London: Westview Press.

MACINTYRE, ALASDAIR (1981). *After Virtue*. London: Duckworth.

—— (1984). *Is Patriotism a Virtue?* University of Kansas, Lawrence: Philosophy Department.

MACMILLAN, CAROL (1982). *Women, Reason and Nature*. Oxford: Blackwell.

NICHOLSON, LINDA (1987). 'Feminism and Marx: Integrating Kinship with the

Economic', in Seyla Benhabib and Drucilla Cornell (eds.), *Feminism as Critique*. Cambridge: Polity Press.

NODDINGS, NELL (1984). *Caring*. Berkeley, Calif.: University of California Press.

OKIN, SUSAN MILLER (1979). *Women in Political Thought*. Princeton, NJ: Princeton University Press.

—— (1987). 'Justice and Gender', *Philosophy and Public Affairs*, 16, 42–72.

O'NEILL, ONORA (1986). *Faces of Hunger: An Essay on Poverty, Justice and Development*. London: George Allen and Unwin.

—— (1988a). 'Children's Rights and Children's Lives', *Ethics*, 98, 445–63.

—— (1988b). 'Ethical Reasoning and Ideological Pluralism', *Ethics*, 98, 705–22.

—— (1989). *Constructions of Reason: Explorations of Kant's Practical Philosophy*. Cambridge: Cambridge University Press.

PATEMAN, CAROLE (1988). *The Sexual Contract*. Cambridge: Polity Press.

PFEFFER, RAYMOND, (1985). 'The Responsibility of Men for the Oppression of Women', Journal of Applied Philosophy, 2, 217–29.

POSTOW, B.C. (1978–9). 'Economic Dependence and Self-respect', *Philosophical Forum*, 10, 181–201.

RAWLS, JOHN (1970). *A Theory of Justice*. Cambridge, Mass.: Harvard University Press.

—— (1985) 'Justice as Fairness: Political not Metaphysical', *Philosophy and Public Affairs*, 14, 223–51.

RUDDICK, SARA (1987). 'Remarks on the Sexual Politics of Reason', in Kittay and Meyers (1987).

—— (1989). 'Maternal Thinking', in her *Maternal Thinking: Towards a Politics of Peace*. Boston, Mass: Beacon Press.

SANDEL, MICHAEL (1982). *Liberalism and the Limits of Justice*. Cambridge: Cambridge University Press.

SCOTT, ALISON MACEWEN (1986). 'Industrialization, Gender Segregation and Stratification Theory', in Rosemary Crompton and Michael Mann (eds.), *Gender and Stratification*. Cambridge: Polity Press.

SEN, AMARTYA K. (1981). *Poverty and Famines: An Essay on Entitlement and Deprivation*. Oxford: Clarendon Press.

—— (1987). *Gender and Cooperative Conflicts*. WIDER Working Paper. Helsinki: World Institute for Development Economics Research.

SHUE, HENRY (1980). *Basic Rights: Subsistence, Affluence and U.S. Foreign Policy*. Princeton, NJ: Princeton University Press.

—— (1981). 'Exporting Hazards', in Brown and Shue (1991).

—— (1984). 'The Interdependence of Duties', in Alston and Tomasevski (1984).

SINGER, PETER (1972). 'Famine, Affluence and Morality', *Philosophy and Public Affairs*, 3, 229–43.

STIEHM, JUDITH HICKS (1983). 'The Unit of Political Analysis: Our Aristotelian Hangover', in Sandra Harding and Merrill B. Hintikka (eds.), *Discovering Reality: Feminist Perspectives on Epistemology, Metaphysics, Methodology and Philosophy of Science*. Dordrecht: Reidel.

WALZER, MICHAEL (1983). *Spheres of Justice: A Defence of Pluralism and Equality*. Oxford: Martin Robertson.

WILLIAMS, BERNARD (1985). *Ethics and the Limits of Philosophy*. London: Fontana.

Onora O'Neill: Justice, Gender, and International Boundaries

Commentary by Martha Nussbaum

[1]

In commenting on O'Neill's rich and penetrating account of justice to the vulnerable, I shall focus on the situation of women. O'Neill has performed a valuable service for the project as a whole by showing how many of the most urgent problems faced by women are cases of more general difficulties of the weak, the marginalized, the exploited. I find the argument for these links convincing; and I shall accept them, in what follows, as successfully established. But since issues concerning women were always central in the motivation and planning of this project, I want to focus these comments on that portion of O'Neill's discussion. First, I shall briefly describe the role of women's issues in the project as a whole. Then I shall comment on O'Neill's general Kantian approach to issues of gender, contrasting it with another available approach, one based upon Aristotle and other related ancient Greek discussions, that makes use of a concept of the human being and human functioning. Finally, I shall introduce an issue not explicitly raised by O'Neill, but intrinsic to the consideration of norms for women and men: the issue of conflict of values, one common approach to which has traditionally been thought to yield the conclusion that we need separate and distinct norms of quality of life for the lives of women and men.

[2]

Reflection on the situation of women in developing countries brings to the fore, with special vividness and urgency, certain more general philosophical problems. It was to investigate these problems—especially with a view to women's concerns—that we decide to arrange a meeting to promote foundational dialogue between philosophers and economists. First of all, the situation of women provides a particularly clear example of the defectiveness of views of development that construe development's aim in terms of utility—whether construed as happiness or as the satisfaction of desires and preferences. For, as Amartya Sen has documented, women who have lived their entire lives in situations of deprivation frequently do not feel dissatisfied with the way things are with them, even at the level of physical health.[1] Since one necessary condition of much desiring seems to be the ability to imagine the object of desire, it is easy to see why severe limitations of experience, in the case of many of the world's women, should lead, as well, to limitations of desire. It is especially striking that

---

[1] See Sen (1985: app. B).

women who have been persistently taught that they should eat less than other members of their households will frequently report that their nutritional status and physical health are good, even when they can be shown to be suffering from physical ailments associated with malnutrition. If this is the case even with physical health, the situation must surely be far worse where education and many other capabilities are concerned. For example, women frequently report when polled that they do not desire more education. But how should we regard such answers? When such replies are given in situations in which it is clear that the women in question have little experience of education, little incentive (indeed, often a strong disincentive) from the society around them to pursue their education, and no clear paradigms of women's lives that have been transformed by education, it seems clear that their announced contentment with the uneducated life means relatively little.[2] Desires adjust to deprivation; and the awareness of new possibilities frequently brings an increase in discomfort and dissatisfaction.[3] Such facts should make us suspicious that utility, as a measure of quality of life, will be biased in the direction of maintaining the status quo, however defective; they should motivate the search for a more adequate measure.

Problems concerning women also motivated us to undertake, in this project, a detailed assessment of cultural relativism. I find it very interesting indeed that both Michael Walzer's qualified defence of a limited relativism and Charles Taylor's defence of a historically sensitive objectivism focus, as they do, on the example of women's position in society—Taylor claiming as a strength of his account that it can show the rationality of women's demand for equality, Walzer trying to assure us, up to a point, that his relativism does not have all the disturbing consequences for the position of women that one might have imagined. O'Neill seems to me to be plainly correct when she writes, 'Any relativism tends to prejudice the position of the weak, whose weakness is mirrored and partly constituted by their marginalization in received ways of thought and by their subordination and oppression in established orders.' It was with this worry in mind that we thought it important to investigate the whole issue of relativism, asking whether there was a coherent and satisfactory way of responding to the relativist's demand for concreteness and historical sensitivity while maintaining a more objective position that might be the basis for a convincing criticism of local traditions; asking, as well, whether there were forms of relativism that did not have negative and somewhat reactionary consequences. I believe that we have learned a lot from the project about how argument on this issue might go, and that we have a lot more to learn.[4] It is good, as we pursue the issues further, to have O'Neill's powerful reminder of some of the motivating problems before us.

---

[2] See Sen (1985, 1987a, 1987b, MS); for a related discussion, see Chen (1987).

[3] See the discussion of this point in Charles Taylor's paper in this volume.

[4] This issue, in relation to women's issues, is currently being pursued in another WIDER project, whose participants include Marty Chen, Martha Nussbaum, Hilary Putnam, Ruth Anna Putnam, and Amartya Sen.

[3]

Now I want to make some remarks about O'Neill's approach to the question of gender justice.[5] O'Neill seems to me very convincing when she says that what we require is a methodology that is able, on the one hand, to abstract, in seeking a normative account, from certain contingent features of women's situations — features that may be defective and productive of deficiency in judgement and desire — and, on the other, to remain down to earth, rather than ideal, in what it does take into account. Her distinction between idealization and abstraction is an important one. Her criticisms of several different sorts of idealization of the human being, in both philosophy and economics, seem entirely just; such understandings have certainly impeded both professions in their approach to women's issues. So if I have some doubts about the particular procedure she proposes, it is against the background of a large measure of agreement with the general constraints she sets forth.[6]

Within these constraints, at least two different general accounts of gender justice seem to be available: an account based, as is O'Neill's, on the test of universalizability of principles, and the question about the consistency of the imagined result; and the approach that Julia Annas, Hilary Putnam, Amartya Sen, and I have in different ways described,[7] an approach based on the concept of human functioning and an idea of the human being. (I think that as I understand this latter approach it is very closely affiliated to Charles Taylor's approach via the notion of strong evaluation; see my comment on his paper.)

O'Neill's Kantian approach asks us to abstract more or less totally from the content of the lives of the individuals we are asked to imagine, and then to think what universally sharable principles would have to govern their lives with one another, given that they are 'numerous, diverse, and *neither* ideally rational *nor* ideally independent of one another'. By applying the test of universalizability, O'Neill, following Kant, is able to rule out principles that could not consistently be held by all of a plurality of potentially interacting beings. Among these will be various forms of deception and victimization. And if we then look at the actual lives of women in many societies, we will discover, O'Neill argues, that these lives exhibit the bad effects of these non-universalizable principles.

I think that O'Neill puts the case for the Kantian approach as well as it can be put; and she does well in showing how a certain amount of very important ethical content can be generated out of the formal interest in consistency and universalizability. I am impressed by her discussions of exploitation and

---

[5] This paper is related in complex ways to O'Neill's other work in moral philosophy: see O'Neill (1975, 1986, 1990).

[6] Related discussion of similar constraints can be found in Nussbaum (1988a, 1988b, 1990b, forthcoming).

[7] See our papers in this volume — and also Putnam (1987); Sen (1984, 1985, 1987a, MS). There are differences, clearly, among the approaches; for example, it is not clear that the material Annas discusses uses the concept of the human being as an evaluative notion — not consistently, at any rate.

deception. But I have doubts in the end about how far we can go in moral argument on this issue through an approach so thin on content. (An approach that discourages us from asking some of our most basic and ordinary questions, such as 'Who *are* these people? What are they trying to do? What general abilities and circumstances do they have?') These doubts will perhaps be clearer when I have described the other approach, as I understand it.

The approach through an idea of the human being and human functioning urges the parties involved in the argument to ask themselves what aspects of living they consider so fundamental that they could not regard a life as a fully human one without them. Put this way, it is not a request for a matter of metaphysical or biological fact, but a request for a particularly deep and searching kind of evaluative inquiry.[8] This inquiry does abstract, certainly, from many concrete features of actual lives, for it asks us to consider what are the most important things that must turn up in any life that we will be willing to recognize as human. Asking this requires us to abstract from many local features of our lives that are more dispensable, and to explore those areas of life, those functions, that are the basis for our sense of recognition and affiliation, for our judgements of humanness, when we meet other humans from ways of life that are in many respects very different. Frequently this inquiry will be carried on (as I have argued elsewhere[9]) by myth-making and story-telling, in which we imagine beings who are like us in some ways and not in others, asking whether they count for us as human; or in which we imagine transformations, and ask whether the life in question is still a human life or some other sort of life. Several remarks can now be made about the differences between this approach and the Kantian approach.

1. Here, in contrast to the Kantian's focus on the formal characteristics of principles, we are all along talking about content, and the actual living of lives— though at a very general level. This inquiry is, in fact, continuous with a more general inquiry into the quality of life, or what the ancient Greeks (who did much to develop this approach) would have called the question of human flourishing, or the good life for a human being. It provides some parameters for such an inquiry, by showing us which lives fall altogether beyond the pale of humanness.

2. In this inquiry, much of the important moral work is done by the imagination, and by our deepest emotions about what our imagination produces; in the Kantian approach, by contrast, the work is supposed to be done by the formal notion of consistency, a notion the consideration of which involves the intellect, far more than the imagination or emotions. Kant himself was certainly rather hostile to the role played by emotions in practical judgement; although this may

---

[8] Here the close connection between this approach and the one described in Charles Taylor's paper becomes clear. See also Sen (MS: ch. 4) on the evaluation of functionings. The case for finding such an approach in Aristotle is discussed in Nussbaum (1990*b*, 1990*c*).

[9] See Nussbaum (1990*a*, 1990*b*, forthcoming).

not be a necessary feature of the Kantian approach, it has certainly had a great deal of influence on many modern Kantians.[10]

3. In the approach through the idea of human functioning, we are learning about how we understand ourselves, about our deepest attachments and commitments and the reasons for them. In the Kantian approach, by contrast, we are learning certain things about what rational consistency requires of all rational beings, but (deliberately) not much about the specific sort of rational being we are, or about why we care about what we do care about, consistency included.

4. The approach through human functioning makes it very easy to apprehend the fact that lives may contain conflicting obligations or values. For the stories of human life on which such an approach frequently relies show us how progress in one area of life can bring tensions, and even deficiencies, in other areas — and in general how full the world is of things we care about and ought to honour in action. They lead us, then, to expect that in the course of living well we will face some difficult dilemmas. The Kantian insistence on ethical consistency avoids, and even denies, this. I shall later return to this question.

But so far I have said little about how I think an approach in terms of human functioning would handle the question of women. For many believers in some such approach have been far from feminist. Indeed, they frequently just left women out, claiming that they were not fully-fledged human beings and did not have the capacity for fully human functioning. How, then, does my version of the approach propose to deal with that problem?

I believe that by directing us, first, to look at what is deepest and also most broadly shared in human life in many times and places, and, second, by urging us to do so by using our imaginations, the human functioning approach provides valuable resources for the defender of women's equality. In order to make this clearer I want to offer two examples of such arguments, taken from ancient Greek thought. The two are really, I think, complementary parts of what would be a single process of argument, the one part being more schematic, the other involving a fuller and more concrete exercise of imagination. The examples are an argument from the Stoic treatise, 'Should Women Too Do Philosophy?', written by Musonius Rufus at Rome in the first century AD; and Aristophanes' great comic play *Lysistrata*, written at Athens in the fifth century BC. It is important to mention at the start that both are radical arguments, in that their conclusions go enormously beyond and dramatically against the norms that were actually recognized by their societies.

The Musonius argument is marvellously simple. It goes like this. Women (he asserts) have, as anyone can see, exactly the same basic faculties as men. Let's go through the list, he now says. Women, as you cannot deny, can see, hear, taste, smell, feel. Furthermore, they can also reason. And on top of this they plainly

---

[10] This is especially clear in Rawls (1971), where a conception of 'considered judgement' is employed that rules out judgements made under emotional influence. For discussion and criticism of this, see Nussbaum (1990*a*); Richardson (forthcoming).

display a sensitivity to ethical distinctions. So: if you believe that getting a 'higher education' that includes some training in philosophical reflection is a good thing for someone with those basic human abilities, then, if you are consistent, you must grant that it is a good thing for women. Musonius now imagines the male interlocutor raising various objections about the consequences of this educational proposal: – for example, that it will lead women to sit around talking philosophy rather than getting the housework done. He dismisses such points as special pleading. Nobody, he says, should neglect practical duties for philosophical conversation; but this applies as much to men as to women, and cannot therefore be used as the basis for an educational difference.

What this argument does is to get the unreflective interlocutor to look closely at various features of his daily dealings with women, and to admit that he implicitly recognizes, in those dealings, the presence of the list of basic abilities that he believes to be both necessary and sufficient for humanness. He talks to his wife as a reasoning being, and a being sensitive to ethical norms; so how can he consistently deny her what would be good for a reasoning being? By looking at the actual content of her life, with imagination and responsive feeling – and at a rather general level – he comes to recognize what he himself values. Notice that this approach relies on an interest in consistency too, but in a different place: for it asks the interlocutor to examine himself – his statements, his actions, his relations with others – for consistency, thus treating consistency as a regulative part of a larger inquiry into content.[11]

The *Lysistrata* performs a similar job, I think, far more concretely. In Aristophanes' famous comedy about how women end the Peloponnesian War by refusing sex to their husbands,[12] the first thing that happens to the male member of the audience is that he is taken inside the women's quarters of the house, somewhere that might have seemed to him altogether alien and different. (Athenian women rarely left the house, so there were relatively few opportunities for the type of interaction that would have prompted the recognition of female rationality.) What he now finds is that here inside the house, far from the market-place and the assembly with which he would tend to associate the (male) world of reason, practical reasoning is going on, including reasoning about central public issues. This reasoning is carried on with much spirit, and in a morally resourceful way. By the end of the play, it is difficult to see how a sincere member of the audience can have failed to accept the remarkable heroine as a reasoning political being similar to himself, and to grant that such a being has a substantial role to play in the city's political life. The charm and verbal resourcefulness of the drama play a large part in luring the audience in, so that they will recognize

---

[11] For further discussion of Musonius, see Nussbaum (1987a); the treatise is not generally available in translation. For further discussion of Stoic views of women, see Foucault (1984) and de Sainte Croix (1981). On the relationship of arguments of this type of the Socratic elenchus, see my comment on Charles Taylor, with references.

[12] For an authoritative discussion of the play, see Henderson (1987); on the position of women in ancient Athens, see Pomeroy (1975), Lefkowitz and Fant (1982).

what the drama wants them to recognize. As with Musonius, this argument focuses on some very general features of human life, depicting the rest in a fanciful way: it gets us to abstract from other contingencies of current arrangements. Thus it leads us to ask which features are the most essential, to focus on those features, and to realize that women share them.

Of course, like any other sort of moral argument, this sort might not work. This one plainly did not, as any rate not on a large scale, since Athenian women went on living as they had lived, and the war went on as well, with disastrous results. But the failure of a single argument to overcome entrenched resistance does not seem to me to count against it. And on the whole I am inclined to believe that arguments of this sort will get us further, where women are concerned, than formal arguments of the Kantian type. I believe that, with respect to the four differences I have mentioned, the human function arguments probably come out ahead, both in terms of efficacy and in terms of philosophical power.

First, it seems essential to focus on *content* as these arguments do—because the actual doings and beings of people seem to be what we have to talk about here, not just what traffic rules will police their doings and beings. Indeed, it seem hard to say anything meaningful about traffic rules until we know who the parties are and what they are doing. Second, we need to rely upon the faculties on which these arguments rely—for the imagination of ways of life seems to be a faculty absolutely indispensable for the full and fully rational investigation of these and other questions concerning deprived people. Both imagination and emotions are necessary to the full recognition of what, in the end, we need to recognize in these cases: that this is a human life before me, and not merely a thing.[13] Third, it seems vital to promote self-understanding as these arguments do. At the conclusion of this sort of argument, we understand more than we do at the conclusion of a formal argument, for we understand why certain things matter to us, how much they matter, how this grounds our relations with others, and so forth. Finally, this approach, and not the other, prepares us for a just appreciation of the problem of conflict among values.

But before I turn to that problem, I want to mention that I think O'Neill herself actually uses what I would call a human function argument at certain crucial points in her paper: for example, when she asks us to recognize our mutual interdependence, our vulnerability, and our general situation as beings 'whose agency and capacities have been formed, perhaps deformed, by unjust institutions'. Much of the force in her application of principles to situations comes from such rich though general description of features of human life; and I doubt that the paper would have had the power it does without them. In fact, at one point

---

[13] In this connection, Seneca (Moral Epistle 108) makes a spirited defence of literature as an essential source of ethical reflection. He argues that literary language and the structures of dramatic plots make ethical meanings more vivid and forceful, so that they appeal to the imagination, producing moral progress through self-recognition. (Note that like most Stoic thinkers Seneca, with great plausibility, thinks of the emotions as cognitive and selective, not merely animal urges. For discussion and defence of this view, see Nussbaum (1987*b*, 1990*a*).)

she insists that one *must* take account of capacities and forms of life in this very general way: 'In applying abstract, non-idealizing principles we have to take account not indeed of the actual beliefs, ideals, or categories of others, which may reflect unjust traditions, but of others' actual *capacities* and *opportunities* to act — and their incapacities and lack of opportunities.' She suggests that this sort of reflection is necessary only in applying principles and not in formulating them. But in some of her concrete arguments it seems an important part of her scrutiny of principles. So I conclude that her approach is actually a mixed approach, which, as such, may be able to surmount many of the difficulties I have raised here for the Kantian approach.

[4]

In concluding, I want to discuss what I have called the problem of conflicting values. But since there are several different problems that might be called by this name, I need to be more precise about what I mean. I am not talking about conflicts among different complete conceptions of the good human life; I am also not talking about conflicts of *interest* that arise within a society as people differently positioned try to realize their various conceptions. These are important issues; they clearly require discussion in the overall pursuit of questions about the quality of life. The problem I want to raise here arises within a single conception of the good, and within the life of a single agent. It concerns the fact that a single conception may contain values that are difficult to combine in a single life — and that this will, inevitably, produce painful tensions and conflicts for individuals. Before I go into greater detail, let me connect this problem with the concerns of women.

When we planned for discussion, in this project, of the question, 'Women and Men: Two Norms or One?', one of the things we had in mind was the critical scrutiny of a venerable part of the philosophical tradition. This tradition holds that women and men must have discrete norms, since otherwise there would be too many difficult conflicts for individuals in realizing everything that, in a good and complete society, ought to be realized. We divide up the functions, so to speak. There are, in turn, two different forms of this argument; these can be called the *direct conflict* view and the *contingent conflict* view. The direct conflict view holds that any good society must contain certain valuable activities or ways of being that cannot, on account of their very nature, be coherently combined in a single person. In a very mundane version, this is an argument frequently made by opponents of military service for women. Society (the argument goes) needs both aggressiveness and gentleness. If we train women to be aggressive they will no longer be gentle. So we should leave the aggressiveness to the men, the gentleness to the women, and exempt women from military service. In a much more sophisticated form, this sort of argument seems to be made by Jean-Jacques Rousseau, in his contrasting portraits of Emile and Sophie. His argument seems to be that citizenly autonomy and the qualities of a good homemaker cannot go together; they are produced by incompatible modes of education, and require incompatible modes of life. They would simply undercut one another if we tried to combine them in a single person.

I am not really convinced by this type of argument. In every instance I have so far encountered, it seems to me that either one of the allegedly conflicting elements is not really valuable—as I think is the case with military aggressiveness[14]—or the alleged conflict is not convincingly established. The latter position has been powerfully argued against Rousseau in Jane Roland Martin's excellent book on philosophical views of women's education.[15] She claims, plausibly, that even in Rousseau's text itself there are signs that citizens who lack the concerns that bind the family together will be defective citizens; homemakers who have not learned to take charge of their own reasoning will be bad homemakers. The two parts of life are actually necessary for one another, if we want to develop each in the best way possible. In the light of good arguments like these, I feel that we are entitled to go on thinking (until further notice) that the most valuable human functionings, at least in their basic and general nature, are, on the whole, mutually supportive, and do not require the postulation of two discrete norms.[16]

Contingent conflict in particular circumstances is, however, another story. For it seems plain that when you value a plurality of different goods, all of which are taken to make a non-homogeneous contribution to the goodness of a life, then you will discover, either more or less often, depending on how you live, that you are faced with a situation in which you cannot satisfy the demands of all the things to which you are committed. This is not just a women's problem, of course; but it is a problem that has been recognized and felt more prominently, on the whole (in certain areas of life at least), by women than by men.

There seem to be two reasons for this. First, women frequently try to combine a plurality of commitments—especially commitments to both work and family—that men less frequently try to combine. If we put the problem that way, it is, I think, a plus for women. For if you believe, as I do, that caring for your family and/or children and doing some form of valued work are both important func-

---

[14] Notice that this does not as yet say anything about the question of military *functioning*. For, as Seneca argues powerfully in *On Anger*, appropriate military activity does not require, and may even be impeded by, military aggressiveness and fierceness.

[15] See Martin (1985) and Nussbaum (1986b).

[16] The work of Carol Gilligan, esp. Gilligan (1982), requires comment here. For she has claimed that the perspective of justice—frequently associated, in contemporary America, with the moral reasoning of men—is incompatible with the perspective of care and affiliation—more frequently found in the moral reasoning of women. Although she believes that the two perspectives should be combined in a complete human life, she believes that the combination will always involve a good deal of tension, and the need to oscillate between two very different ways of thinking. I am not myself convinced that the tension is as severe as she makes out. For if one adopts a conception of justice based upon the Aristotelian ideas of equity and the perception of particularity, rather than on universal principles of broad generality (as in Gilligan's rather Kantian framework), the two perspectives will actually support one another, and indeed be continuous with one another. And I think it can be argued that the Aristotelian framework gives a more satisfactory account of justice—see Nussbaum (1990a).

tions in most human lives, male and female, then it is better to recognize that fact and to feel the associated conflicts than to deny the fact (for example, by simply neglecting your children) and to have an apparently conflict-free existence (one that avoids recognition of the conflicts).

The second reason such conflicts are an especially acute problem for women is, however, a negative one: societies have, on the whole, given women relatively little help in managing the conflicts they face, and men far more help. A good system of public child care would simply eliminate some, though not all, of the conflicts women face in this sphere. (And of course this would also be a great advantage for *men* who face those conflicts.) While I do think that some level of conflict, or at any rate the permanent risk of conflict, is an inevitable concomitant of any human life that is plainly rich in value,[17] there is no reason why society should not alleviate this situation by arranging things so that conflict-producing situations arise more rarely.

A serious difficulty I have with O'Neill's Kantian approach is that it gives us no direction as to how to face such conflicts. Kant himself famously, or infamously, invoked his own idea of practical consistency in order to deny that there are any such conflicts.[18] O'Neill is far too sensitive, and sensible, to do this. But to test the acceptability of an arrangement as she does, by testing for consistency, does raise a problem. What sort of consistency are we looking for, and what guidance do we get about what sort is the right sort, and how much enough? I think the human function approach does far better, by instructing us to imagine the various components of a life, both singly and in various combinations, so that we will naturally come to understand how richness of life brings dilemmas and tensions, how the distinctness of each valuable thing imports a possibility of disharmony.

One of the most important things that many of the papers in this project have stressed is the multifacetedness of the concept of quality of life. Living well as a human being has a plurality of distinct components, none of them reducible to the others—a fact that any approach in terms of a single quantitative scale simply obscures from view. This aspect of human life is well represented in the polytheism of ancient Greek religion. For this religion tells us, in effect, that there are many spheres of human living that claim our commitment, and commitment to which makes us the beings we are; we ought to honour all of those spheres—including political life, the arts, love, reasoning, the earth on which we live. And it tells us, as well, that these gods, so to speak, do not always agree; that frequently a devotion to one will risk offence against another, so we are faced with many difficult choices.[19] That, none the less, the quality of any individual life, and also of any city of country's life, will be measured by and on all of these distinct dimensions, so that we can neither simply leave some out nor treat them as commensurable by some single quantitative scale.

---

[17] See Nussbaum (1986a: chs. 2–3; 1989).
[18] Kant's views are presented in the Introduction to the *Metaphysics of Morals*: see Kant (1797).
[19] See Nussbaum (1986a: chs. 2–3).

This is a human problem, not just a women's problem. But right now it is in most societies particularly a women's problem, both because of the institutional neglect of which I have spoken, and also because women have been insisting that there are, for human life, more 'gods', so to speak, than anyone might have thought—affiliation as well as autonomy, the care of the family as well as independent work. My own view is that the resulting conception, while more prone to conflict, is a richer and more adequate conception of the quality of life. Richer because the components are more numerous and more diverse; richer, too, because, while the diverse component activities sometimes get in one another's way, they equally or more often provide mutual illumination and enhancement—as the love of individuals in the family gives citizenship a new depth of understanding, as personally satisfying work gives new vitality to the care of the family. In this way, the experience of women should be viewed not simply as a source of many bad examples of social injustice and difficult problems of social arrangement—though of course we must continue to stress that aspect— but also as a source of certain sorts of insight and aspiration, as we try to arrive at an adequate conception of the quality of life.

BIBLIOGRAPHY

CHEN, M. (1987). *A Quiet Revolution: Women in Transition in Rural Bangladesh* (Dhaka: BRAC).

DE SAINTE CROIX, G.E.M. (1981). *The Class Struggle in the Ancient Greek World*. London: Duckworth.

FOUCAULT, M. (1984). *The History of Sexuality*, iii, trans. R. Hurley. New York: Pantheon.

GILLIGAN, C. (1982). *In a Different Voice: Psychological Theory and Women's Dependence*. Cambridge, Mass.: Harvard University Press.

HENDERSON, J. (1987). *Aristophanes: Lysistrata* (edition and commentary). Oxford: Clarendon Press.

KANT, IMMANUEL. (1797). *The Metaphysical Elements of Justice*. Part I of *The Metaphysics of Morals*, trans. J. Ladd. Indianapolis: Bobbs Merrill, 1965.

LEFKOWITZ, M., and FANT, M. (eds.) (1982). *Women's Life in Greece and Rome*. Baltimore, Md.: Johns Hopkins University Press.

MARTIN, JANE ROLAND (1985). *Reclaiming a Conversation*. New Haven: Yale University Press.

NUSSBAUM, M. (1986a). *The Fragility of Goodness: Luck and Ethics in Greek Tragedy and Philosophy*. Cambridge: Cambridge University Press.

—— (1986b). Review of Martin (1985). *New York Review of Books*, 30 Jan.

—— (1987a). 'Undemocratic Vistas'. Review of Allan Bloom, *The Closing of the American Mind. New York Review of Books*, 5 Nov.

—— (1987b). 'The Stoics on the Extirpation of the Passions', *Apeiron*, 20, 129–77.

—— (1988*a*). 'Nature, Function, and Capability: Aristotle on Political Distribution', *Oxford Studies in Ancient Philosophy*, suppl. vol., 145–84.

—— (1988*b*). 'Non-Relative Virtues: An Aristotelian Approach', *Midwest Studies in Philosophy*, 13. A revised and expanded version appears in this volume.

—— (1989). 'Tragic Dilemmas', *Radcliffe Quarterly* (Mar.).

—— (1990*a*). *Love's Knowledge: Essays on Philosophy and Literature*. New York and Oxford: Oxford University Press.

—— (1990*b*). 'Aristotelian Social Democracy', in G. Mara and H. Richardson (eds.), *Liberalism and the Good*. New York: Routledge, Chapman, and Hall, 203–52.

—— (forthcoming). 'Aristotle on Human Nature and the Foundations of Ethics', in a volume in honour of Bernard Williams, ed. J. Altham and P. Harrison Cambridge: Cambridge University Press.

O'NEILL, O. (Onora Nell) (1975). *Acting on Principle: An Essay on Kantian Ethics*. New York: Columbia University Press.

—— (1986). *Faces of Hunger: An Essay on Poverty, Justice, and Development*. London: George Allen and Unwin.

—— (1990). *Collected Essays on Moral Philosophy*. Cambridge: Cambridge University Press.

POMEROY, S. (1975). *Goddesses, Whores, Wives, and Slaves: Women in Classical Antiquity*. New York: Schocken Books.

PUTNAM, H. (1987). *The Many Faces of Realism*. LaSalle, Ill.: Open Court.

RAWLS, J. (1971). *A Theory of Justice*. Cambridge, Mass.: Harvard University Press.

RICHARDSON, H. (forthcoming). 'The Emotions of Reflective Equilibrium'.

SEN, A. (1980). 'Equality of What?' in S. McMurrin (ed.), *Tanner Lectures on Human Values*, i. Cambridge: Cambridge University Press. Repr. in Sen (1982).

—— (1982). *Choice, Welfare, and Measurement*. Oxford: Basil Blackwell.

—— (1984). *Resources, Value, and Development*. Oxford: Basil Blackwell.

—— (1985). *Commodities and Capabilities*. Amsterdam: North-Holland.

—— (1987*a*). *The Standard of Living*. Tanner Lectures on Human Values 1985, ed. G. Hawthorne. Cambridge: Cambridge University Press.

—— (1987*b*). 'Gender and Cooperative Conflicts'. WIDER Working Paper. Helsinki: World Institute for Development Economics Research; published in I. Tinker, ed., *Women and World Development* (Oxford 1990).

—— (1992). *Inequality Reexamined*. Oxford, Cambridge, MA, and New York: Clarendon Press, Harvard University Press, and Russell Sage Foundation.

SENECA, L. A. *On Anger* (*De Ira*), in *L. A. Senecae Dialogorum Libri Duodecim*, ed. L. D. Reynolds. Oxford: Clarendon Press.

—— *Moral Epistles* (*Epistulae Morales*), ed. L. D. Reynolds. Oxford: Clarendon Press.

PART IV

POLICY ASSESSMENT AND WELFARE ECONOMICS

Distributing Health: The Allocation of Resources by an International Agency

John E. Roemer

1 The Problem

An agency of the United Nations has at its disposal an endowment of resources that it will distribute to various countries, with the aim of lowering their rates of infant mortality. The rate of infant survival, abbreviated RIS (one minus the rate of infant mortality), is taken to be an important indicator of the general level of physical well-being of a population, for a high rate is only achieved by good nutrition for women of child-bearing age, clean water supplies, and programmes providing ante-natal care to women. If infant mortality is low, the factors responsible have an impact upon others (than infants and mothers) in the population generally. The level of a population's physical well-being is, of course, an essential ingredient of its quality of life.

When the UN agency looks at the various countries, the data that are most important to it are the rates of infant survival in each country, and the 'technology' that the country will use to convert the resources it is granted into a higher RIS. Technology must be broadly interpreted. One country may be particularly efficient at using such resources because it already has a well-organized network of rural clinics in place. Another country might make less effective use of resources granted, not because it has a less adequate distribution system for bringing the resources to the population, but because the regime in power channels too large a fraction of the resources, from the agency's point of view, to the urban middle class, who comprise a small fraction of the population. The agency is powerless to affect this kind of political decision, in part because it is an international and not a supranational agency.

The technology for increasing the RIS, from the agency's viewpoint, is a function $u(\mathbf{x})$, where $\mathbf{x}$ is the vector of resources per capita that the agency grants to the country, and $u(\mathbf{x})$ is the consequent RIS achieved. Thus $u(\mathbf{0})$ is the RIS before UN intervention. I take $u(\mathbf{x})$ to have the usual features of a production function: it is non-decreasing in each component of $\mathbf{x}$, it is continuous and concave. If, for example, a country siphons off, and uses for another purpose, some of the resources that it is allocated to increase its RIS, then '$\mathbf{x}$' in $u(\mathbf{x})$ stands for the vector of resources per capita allocated by the agency, not the vector of resources actually used effectively by the country. The UN has no control

I am indebted to the following officers at the World Health Organization, Geneva, for their assistance: Dr J. Cohen, Mr A. Creese, Dr T. Fülöp, Dr J. Keja, Dr F. Partow, Mr C. G. Sandstrom, and Dr E. Tarimo. Research was funded by the World Institute for Development Economics Research (WIDER), and the US National Science Foundation.

of the siphoning: this is what it means to say that u is the technology from the UN's viewpoint.

A first attempt at formulating the resource allocation problem that the agency faces is to represent the relevant information by an ordered set $E = \langle M, n, \Omega,$ $(u^1, N^1), (u^2, N^2), \ldots, (u^r, N^r) \rangle$, where M is the budget of the agency, n is the number of resources the agency decides are relevant, Ω is the set of all n-dimensional vectors of resources that the agency can purchase, at going prices, with budget M, u^i is the technology the ith country uses, from the agency's viewpoint, to increase its RIS, and N^i is the population of country i. Each u^i is a function of the n resources, and it expresses the country's RIS as a function of the resources per capita allocated to it by the agency. There are r countries, the ith one of which has a pre-intervention RIS of $u^i(\mathbf{0})$.

Other information may, however, be relevant to the allocation decision. Perhaps the agency will take into consideration the various endowments of the countries, which affect their RIS, although they are not specifically represented in E: their climates, their population densities, the degree of organization of their health services. These things appear in E only implicitly, as they affect the technologies u^i. Perhaps the agency should make use of its knowledge of this information directly. For example, suppose two countries have the same technologies $u(\mathbf{x})$ (in particular, they have the same pre-intervention RIS, $u(\mathbf{0})$), and the same population size. In the first country, there is a good water supply, a favourable climate, and a corrupt government, which siphons resources away from their intended use. In the second, there is an unfavourable climate and dirty water, but a conscientious bureaucracy, which uses the resources allocated effectively. The upshot is that the two countries have the same effective technology u. Should the UN allocate the same bundle of resources to both countries? If not, then one believes it should make use of this other information.

The ancillary information, for a country i, can be represented by a set Φ^i, which summarizes all kinds of political, social, geographical, and cultural information about a country, which may be relevant to decisions involving resource allocation for the purpose of raising the RIS. Ancillary information is taken to include only facts that are known to the agency. (One such fact might be that, for a certain country, the agency knows that it has very little ancillary information.) A more complete representation of the problem the agency faces is $E = \langle M, n, \Omega, (u^1, N^1, \Phi^1), (u^2, N^2, \Phi^2), \ldots, (u^r, N^r, \Phi^r) \rangle$.

I have argued that the information summarized in E should suffice for the agency to decide how resources should be allocated among countries to achieve its goal. How might the agency proceed? Given the problem E, what distribution of resources $(\mathbf{x}^1, \mathbf{x}^2, \ldots, \mathbf{x}^r)$ of some feasible resource bundle $\bar{\mathbf{x}} \, \epsilon \, \Omega$ should the agency choose, where $\mathbf{x}^i$ is the vector of resources allocated to country i, $\Sigma \mathbf{x}^i = \bar{\mathbf{x}}$, and $\bar{\mathbf{x}} \, \epsilon \, \Omega$?

2 Necessary Conditions for Resource Allocation

What the agency must discuss is the *budget allocation rule*, which will associate with every reasonable problem E that the agency might face, an allocation of resources that the agency should implement. The rule, F, thus far unknown, can be viewed as a function that maps possible problems E into feasible allocations for those problems: using the above notation, $F(E) = (\mathbf{x}^1, \mathbf{x}^2, \ldots, \mathbf{x}^r)$. In fact, we can dispense with the information on the agency's budget, and consider problems of the type $\xi = \langle n, \Omega, (u^1, N^1, \Phi^1), \ldots, (u^r, N^r, \Phi^r) \rangle$. The feasible set upon which the agency concentrates is the set Ω of possible resource bundles that it can purchase with its budget. The budget is only needed to determine the set Ω. From now on, it is only necessary to consider problems of the form ξ.

I will propose that the agency proceed by discussing general principles that should or must apply to any resource allocation rule that it might adopt. This is a piecemeal approach, less ambitious than trying to come up with a complete allocation rule all at once. Deciding upon these principles can considerably narrow down the class of acceptable rules. I will consider five general principles, and particular axioms that follow from these principles. The perhaps surprising conclusion is that, having adopted restrictions on the class of acceptable allocation rules that are required by the five principles, the problem of choosing an allocation rule will have been completely solved.

Let $F(\xi) = (\mathbf{x}^1, \ldots, \mathbf{x}^r)$ specify the allocation rule; define $F^i(\xi) = \mathbf{x}^i$. Thus $u^i(F^i(\xi)/N^i) = u^i(\mathbf{x}^i/N^i)$ is the RIS in country i after it receives and puts into use the resources it has been allocated.[1] The notation $u[F(\xi)/N]$ is the r-vector whose i[th] component is $u^i(F^i(\xi)/N^i)$.

1. *Efficiency.* The allocation of resources should be efficient in the sense of *Pareto optimality* (PO). That is, no other allocation of any vector of resources in Ω can raise the RIS of some countries above what it is at $F(\xi)$ without lowering the RIS of some other country. This will be called axiom PO. Pareto optimality is probably not a contentious principle, in the context of a resource allocation problem.

2. *Fairness.* Suppose that two problems ξ^1 and ξ^2 differ only in that, in the first, the agency faces a feasible set of resources Ω^1 which includes the set of resources Ω^2, available in the second. The principle of *monotonicity* (MON) states that every country in the first problem should end up, after the allocation, with at least as high an RIS as in the second. Formally, let $\xi^1 = \langle n, \Omega^1, (u^1, N^1, \Phi^1), \ldots, (u^r, N^r, \Phi^r) \rangle$ and $\xi = \langle n, \Omega^2, (u^1, N^1, \Phi^1), \ldots, (u^r, N^r, \Phi^r) \rangle$ be possible worlds with $\Omega^1 \supset \Omega^2$. Then $u(F(\xi^1)/N) \geq u'F(\xi^2)/N)$.

In particular, MON implies that if the budget increases, but nothing else changes, then each country should end up at least as well off (in terms of its RIS).

---

[1] It is more realistic to think of $u^i(\mathbf{x}^i/N^i)$ as the RIS that the agency *expects* to attain after the country uses the resources $\mathbf{x}^i$.

Monotonicity certainly does not summarize all aspects of fairness that may be of import, but it is arguably a necessary condition of a fair allocation rule. Note that MON is a weaker principle than one that would require each country to receive more of every resource as the agency's resource bundle increases. It says that no country should suffer in terms of its RIS as resources become collectively more abundant. It also requires that if the agency's budget is reduced, each country should (weakly) share in the decrease of aggregate RIS that must ensue.

MON is not a principle that is patently required for ethical reasons. For instance, if the agency were only concerned with increasing the world's aggregate RIS, taken as the population-weighted sum of the countries' individual rates, then it should not adopt MON as a principle. Population-weighted utilitarianism, the allocation rule that allocates resources in that way which maximizes the weighted sum of the countries' rates of infant survival, violates MON.[2] MON is adopted only if the agency views its charge as reducing the rate of infant mortality in *each* country, not simply the rate of infant mortality internationally. This kind of principle might be adopted, for instance, if all countries contributed to the budget of the UN. If the allocation rule violated MON, some country could have reason to reduce its allocation to the UN, in order to increase thereby its effective allocation from the agency.

A second principle of fairness is *symmetry* (S): if all the countries happen to be identical, with respect to both their technologies for processing resources and their sets of ancillary information, then the resources should be distributed in proportion to their populations. Formally, if $\xi = \langle n, \Omega, (u, N^1, \Phi), (u, N^2, \Phi), \ldots, (u, N^r, \Phi)\rangle$, then $F^i(\xi) = (N^i/N)\bar{\mathbf{x}}$, for some $\bar{\mathbf{x}} \in \Omega$, for all i.

3. *Neutrality.* For a problem $\xi = \langle n, \Omega, (u^1, N^1, \Phi^1), \ldots, (u^r, N^r, \Phi^r)\rangle$, the distribution of resources should depend only on the technological information $u^1, \ldots, u^r$, the populations N^i, and the resource availabilities Ω. I call this the *irrelevance of ancillary information* (IAI); it is formally stated as follows. Let ξ be as above, and let $\xi^* = \langle n, \Omega, (u^1, N^1, \Phi^{*1}), \ldots, (u^r, N^r, \Phi^{*r})\rangle$ be another problem with technologies, populations, and resource data exactly as in ξ, but in which the vectors of ancillary information (may) differ. Then $F(\xi) = F(\xi^*)$: resource allocation should be the same for the two problems.

IAI may be a contentious principle, as can be seen from the examples given in Section 1. The reason behind it may be motivated by noting that the agency is directed by the General Assembly[3] of the UN to distribute its endowment in a neutral fashion, that is, without regard to the internal politics and culture of the countries. Its task is one of engineering—given the present state of resource-

---

[2] That is, there are problems ξ having the property that, should resources increase, the international RIS (i.e. the population-weighted average of the country RISs) is increased by transferring some resources from a low RIS country to a high RIS country.

[3] If the World Health Organization (WHO) is the agency, then the question is decided by its own general assembly. WHO operates as an independent affiliate of the UN.

processing technologies as summarized in the u^i, to allocate resources in a fair manner in order to reduce infant mortality.

Because the independence of ancillary information is assumed throughout, we may delete the symbols Φ^i and from now on represent a problem as $\xi = \langle n, \Omega, (u^1, N^1), \ldots, (u^r, N^r) \rangle$.

4. *Consistency*. There are many versions of consistency conditions in resource allocation problems. Generally, consistency means that if two problems are related in a certain natural way, then their solutions should be related in a similarly natural way. I consider two consistency axioms.

Suppose the agency faces a problem in which there are $n + m$ resources to distribute: $\xi = \langle n + m; \Omega; (u^1, N^1), \ldots, (u^r, N^r) \rangle$, where the set of feasible resources Ω is of dimension $n + m$. The technologies are defined as functions of all the resources, $u(\mathbf{x}, \mathbf{y})$, where $\mathbf{x}$ represents the first n resources per capita and $\mathbf{y}$ the last m resources per capita. Under the allocation rule F, the distribution of resources is $F(\xi) = (\mathbf{x}^1, \mathbf{y}^1), \ldots, (\mathbf{x}^r, \mathbf{y}^r))$, where $(\mathbf{x}^i, \mathbf{y}^i)$ is the allocation to country i. Suppose the $\mathbf{y}$-resources are distributed first, as planned: $(\mathbf{y}^1, \mathbf{y}^2, \ldots, \mathbf{y}^r)$. The agency can now be viewed as facing, temporarily, a new problem, as the countries are 'consuming' the $\mathbf{y}$-resources. The technologies of the countries with the $\mathbf{y}$-resources fixed are now $u^{*1}(\mathbf{x}) = u^{*1}(\mathbf{x}, \mathbf{y}^1/N^1), \ldots, u^{*r}(\mathbf{x}) = u^r(\mathbf{x}, \mathbf{y}^r/N^r)$, and there are n $\mathbf{x}$-resources left to distribute. The new problem is $\xi^* = \langle n, \Omega^*, (u^{*1}, N^1), \ldots, (u^{*r}, N^r) \rangle$, where Ω^* describes the possible allocations of the $\mathbf{x}$-resources (it is the projection of Ω on to the n-dimensional subspace of $\mathbf{x}$-resources at the point $(\mathbf{y}^1, \mathbf{y}^2, \ldots, \mathbf{y}^r)$). The principle of *consistent resource allocation across dimension* (CONRAD) states that the solution to ξ^* must be $(\mathbf{x}^1, \ldots, \mathbf{x}^r)$: that is, F must allocate the $\mathbf{x}$-resources in ξ^* just as it allocated them in ξ.

Formally, CONRAD says that, for any problem ξ as described above, if $F(\xi) = [(\mathbf{x}^1, \mathbf{y}^1), (\mathbf{x}^2, \mathbf{y}^2), \ldots, (\mathbf{x}^r, \mathbf{y}^r)]$, and if ξ^* is defined as above with respect to $(\mathbf{y}^1, \ldots, \mathbf{y}^r)$, then $F(\xi^*) = (\mathbf{x}^1, \ldots, \mathbf{x}^r)$. If this principle of consistency holds, then, having decided upon the allocation of all the resources, the agency can distribute resources to countries as they become available, and it will never be faced with a need to revise its plan.[4]

The second consistency axiom is called the *deletion of irrelevant countries* (DIC). Suppose there is a problem $\xi = \langle n, \Omega, (u^1, N^1), \ldots, (u^r, N^r) \rangle$, and $F^1(\xi) = 0$: the first country is allocated no resources. Consider the same problem, but

---

[4] Indeed, the dimension of time is fabricated for this example, and may make CONRAD a less appealing axiom than it actually is. The axiom states that if the agency faces two problems that are related to each other in the manner of ξ and ξ^*, then it must allocate the $\mathbf{x}$-goods in the same way in both problems—there is no presumption that the agency faces ξ^* after it faces ξ. It should also be pointed out that the version of CONRAD stated here is stronger than what is actually required below for Theorem 1. CONRAD need only apply when the $\mathbf{y}$-goods have a special property: that they are completely country-specific in their use, that is, that each $\mathbf{y}$-good, $j = n + 1, m + n$, is useful to only one country. Because these kinds of good hardly ever exist in practical problems, the CONRAD axiom can be viewed as a weak restriction on the behaviour of resource allocation. For further discussion of CONRAD, see Roemer (1986, 1987).

without the first country: $\xi^* = \langle n, \Omega, (u^2, N^2), \ldots, (u^r, N^r) \rangle$. Then $F^i(\xi^*) = F^i(\xi)$, for $i = 2, \ldots, r$. That is, if a country that is allocated nothing withdraws from the problem, the allocation of resources to the other countries should not change.[5]

5. *Scope*. The agency must adopt an allocation rule that will be applicable for a variety of problems it may encounter. It may, over the course of years, face many different budgets, many different prices that change the resource availabilities, and variations in the number of resources, their identities as well as their quantities. It can be expected that the technologies of the countries will change, and their rates of infant survival too. The *domain* (D) axiom states that the resource allocation rule the agency adopts should be capable of application to any possible problem ξ specified by arbitrary choice of n, for any convex set Ω in R_+^n, for any concave, monotonic, continuous functions $u^1, u^2, \ldots, u^r$ defined on R^n, and any distribution $N^1, \ldots, N^r$ of populations. The agency must also be able to solve problems for all r, such that $2 \leq r \leq \bar{r}$, for some integer $\bar{r}$.

Formally, let Δ be the domain of possible worlds on which the allocation rule is defined. Then for all $\{n, \Omega, (u^1, N^1), \ldots, (u^r, N^r)\}$ as specified, there exist $\Phi^1, \Phi^2, \ldots, \Phi^r$ such that $\xi \in \Delta$, where $\xi = \langle n, \Omega, (u^1, N^1, \Phi^1), \ldots, (u^r, N^r, \Phi^r) \rangle$.[6] This is a large class of possible worlds, but it consists of technologically reasonable ones. Some realism is imposed by requiring that the technologies be concave, monotonic functions of **x**.

I should emphasize that the principles discussed in this section are not ethically mandatory, but rather ones that a sensible agency may impose upon itself. The monotonicity axiom, for example, may be justified on purely pragmatic grounds: if all countries contribute to the budget, it may not be politically feasible, in a democratic organization of countries, to reduce the allocation to some countries when the budget increases.

3 Acceptable Allocation Rules

A resource allocation rule F ia a function mapping any element ξ in the domain Δ into a feasible allocation. It is remarkable that the seven axioms discussed above suffice to determine a *unique resource allocation mechanism* on one domain $\tilde{\Delta}$, a sub-domain of problems of Δ defined precisely in the appendix, of Roemer (1989).

Theorem 1: Let a resource allocation rule, F, be defined on $\tilde{\Delta}$, and satisfy axioms PO, MON, S, IAI, CONRAD, DIC, and D. Then F must choose, for every problem ξ in $\tilde{\Delta}$, the distribution of resources that realizes the

---

[5] This axiom is a very weak version of an axiom called stability in bargaining theory, introduced by Lensberg (1987).

[6] The domain is more precisely defined in the unpublished appendix (available from the author), in which the theorem is proved, where the admissible technologies are discussed.

lexicographic egalitarian distribution of the rates of infant survival; that is, F is the leximin allocation rule.[7]

Resources are allocated in the following way under the leximin rule. First, resources are allocated to the country with the lowest RIS until its RIS is raised to the RIS of the second lowest country. Then resources are used to raise the RISs of these two countries, until they become equal to the RIS of the third lowest country, etc. More generally, no resources are devoted to raising the RIS of a country until all countries with lower RISs have been raised either to its level, or, if that is impossible, as high as they can be.

In a sense, the axioms S, MON, CONRAD, and DIC appear to be weak restrictions on the behaviour of the allocation mechanism, because they are all concerned with situations that hardly ever occur. How often must the agency deal with a problem in which all the countries are identical, as postulated by S? How often must it deal with a pair of problems that are identical in their technological descriptions, except that there are more resources in one problem than in the other (MON)? (One might take the problems in consecutive years to be of this form, if the budget has increased, but, to be precise, this is not exactly the case, because the technology functions change at least slightly from year to year.) And how much of a restriction is DIC, since it hardly ever occurs that the agency faces a problem in which some country will be allocated no resources? Similarly, CONRAD refers to only a very small class of pairs of problems, which bear a certain intimate relation to each other.

It would appear that the axioms can be seen as either quite weak, in the sense of the above paragraph, or are quite reasonable, or both. The domain axiom (D) is, however, strong, for it requires the agency to have a solution to problems that will never come up. The theorem claims to answer definitively the policy problem of the international agency. In the remainder of the paper, I discuss how salient this model and theorem are to the practice of one international agency.

4 The World Health Organization (WHO)

WHO is an international organization with 166 member countries, which is affiliated to the United Nations, although it is a juridically separate organization. Its own World Health Assembly, which meets annually, is the supreme decision-making body. The budget of WHO comes from two sources, the first of which is the assessment of member countries. The United States, for example, is committed to supplying 25 per cent of the biennial budget of the organization.[8] The planned income from member assessments in 1986–7 was $543 million. Secondly, WHO relies on 'extra-budgetary sources', contributions from private

---

[7] The proof is available in the appendix of Roemer (1989).

[8] At the time of writing (1988), the Reagan administration is delinquent with its payments.

philanthropic organizations in various countries, and other national governmental sources, which contribute money to specific programmes. These sources for the same budget period are estimated at $520 million. Thus, WHO operates on a biennial budget of approximately $1 billion.

WHO has a sequence of plans nested in time, which guide its operations. The World Health Assembly adopted a long-term strategy in 1981 for the 'attainment of health for all by the year 2000'.[9] The measures of health are defined with various degrees of precision by the organization. The most aggregate measures consist of twelve indicators, each defined as the number of countries in WHO that have achieved a certain degree of success with respect to a particular health indicator. For example, one such indicator is the number of countries in which at least 90 per cent of new-born infants have a birth weight of at least 2,500 grams. Others are: the number of countries in which the infant mortality rate is below 50 per 1,000 live births; in which life expectancy is over sixty years; in which the adult literacy rate for men and women exceeds 70 per cent; in which the GNP per capita exceeds $500; in which safe water is available within fifteen minutes' walking distance; in which there is complete immunization against diphtheria; tetanus, whooping cough, measles, polio, and tuberculosis: and so on.[10] The next level of planning consists of a six-year plan. Finally, there are the biennial plans, which are specifically budgeted in the biennial budgets.

It is, therefore, a great oversimplification to model the problem of WHO as seeking to improve one indicator, such as the rate of infant mortality. Indeed, there are some fifty-four programmes in WHO, administered under twenty divisions of the organization.[11] There is no attempt to form a single objective function to aggregate the many indicators, which measure success, into one welfare measure.

As well as the programme or function dimension, there is an area dimension along which the operations and budget of WHO are disaggregated. The world is divided into six regions (Africa, the Americas, South-east Asia, Europe, the Eastern Mediterranean, and the Western Pacific), as well as a Global and Interregional category, which handles interregional programmes. Each region has a regional director (RD), appointed by the executive board in consultation with a regional committee. For each country, there is a WHO representative (WR), who represents the concerns of headquarters. Very briefly, the budget is nego-

---

[9] The twenty-year strategy is summarized in World Health Organization (1981*a*).

[10] These indicators may seem to be quite precise, but they are in fact quite broad. An example of a more precise health indicator, taken from a list of over a hundred such, is: the percentage of children in a country whose upper-arm circumference is no less than the value corresponding to the fifth percentile of the frequency distribution for well-nourished children. This physical measurement is apparently a sensitive indicator of malnutrition.

[11] There are divisions of environmental health, epidemiology, health education, communicable diseases, vector biology and control, mental health, health manpower development, non-communicable diseases, and so on. There are programmes in malaria control, parasitic diseases, immunization, diarrhoeal disease control, biomedical information, and so on.

tiated as follows. First, only the regular budget—the budget from country assessments—is officially negotiated and allocated in this process. The secretariat proposes a division of the budget among the six regions and a global and inter-regional category. As will be seen below, this division is highly constrained by history. When the regular budget is virtually constant in real terms, as it has been during the 1980s, there is not much room for altering the division of the budget among regions from year to year. The regional allocation is followed by discussions between the regional committees of WHO and the governments in each region concerning the allocation of the regional budget among countries and among programmes. Each region compiles a regional budget. Officially, the regions have control of these decisions. Countries must request specific programmes. The important point is that, from an accounting point of view, the interregional division of the budget takes place first, in a centralized way, and the interprogramme division is secondary and decentralized to the regional level.

In terms of our model, it is clear that the relevant units are not countries, but regions of the world: this is the level of disaggregation that is relevant for budget decision-making at WHO headquarters.

WHO has had surprisingly little discussion of the general principles that should guide budget allocation.[12] There is, however, a clearly enunciated principle of monotonicity: 'the Director-General has sought to effect necessary reallocations by means of selective application of increases in available resources, without reducing the current level of allocation to any one region' (World Health Organization, 1979). In the same document, the question is raised whether it is possible objectively to quantify health needs, and, if so, whether or to what extent the allocation of WHO resources between regions should be guided by these factors. 'The definition of need is itself a subjective process, and it is not at all clear that criteria applicable to one population apply with equal force to all populations. The answer of the modern public health planner to the problem of allocation of resources would be to set up a mathematical model, using as objective, quantitative criteria as possible, but agreement on the parameters of such a model would be hard to reach.' It is admitted, however, that 'in view of the complexity of the matter and the great number of largely unquantifiable factors involved, it has been a matter of "feeling one's way" over the years in arriving at the allocations of WHO resources between regions' (p. 7).

In Table 1, the regular budget allocation among regions is presented for each biennial budget, beginning in 1978-9, calculated both in current prices and deflated prices, this last to make a real comparison with the previous biennial budget possible. It is important to note that only the regular budget is subject to this careful process, and the regularities that I discuss are observed only

---

[12] Officers of WHO whom I interviewed knew of only one document in which these principles were discussed, summarizing a meeting of the executive board held in 1979. The statements that follow are taken from that document.

Table 1 WHO Regular Budget Allocations by Region by Year

	Africa	Americas	SE Asia	Europe	E. Med.	W. Pacific	Global and Interregional	Total
1988–9 (p = 86)*	98.9	57.9	68.8	33.6†	62.2	50.8	170.5	542.7
1986–7 (p = 86)	98.9	57.9	68.9	32.2†	62.2	50.8	172.4	543.3
1986–7 (p = 84)	90.1†	51.3	62.9	35.3	55.1	47.1	178.3	520.1
1984–5 (p = 84)	94.3†	50.8	61.3	35.2	53.8	46.1	178.5	520.1
1984–5 (p = 82)	82.9†	40.4	53.1†	32.6†	47.5†	38.3	172.6	467.4
1982–3 (p = 82)	81.3	44.0	52.9	32.3	46.6	39.1	172.8	468.9
1982–3 (p = 80)	70.7	37.6	46.8	24.0	41.1	34.4	182.3	436.9
1980–1 (p = 80)	68.1	37.5	45.0	23.8	39.7	33.0	180.2	427.3
1980–1 (p = 78)	61.3	31.7	40.3	21.2	35.3	29.8	141.9†	361.5
1978–9 (p = 78)	55.4	30.3	36.2	20.2	32.4	26.6	153.2†	354.3

* (p = 86) means in 1986 prices.
† Violation of monotonicity.
‡ Decreasing allocation to the secretariat, due to 1978 WHO resolution.
Source: Compiled from *Proposed Programme Budgets* (WHO, Geneva). Biennial budgets 1980–1 to 1988–9.

with respect to it. Note that the last period in which the regular budget increased in real terms was 1982–3. In the budgets of that and previous periods, there is monotonicity with respect to regions. The only deviation from monotonicity is in the treatment of the global and interregional budget, from 1978–9 to 1980–81, when this allocation fell from $153 million to $142 million in real terms. This fall was the consequence of a World Health Assembly decision in 1978 to cut back on the operations at headquarters, and to direct a larger fraction of resources to country programmes.

Beginning in 1984–5, the budget stagnated in real terms. In that period, when the real regular budget fell by $1.5 million, there were indeed violations of monotonicity. All regions should suffer a cutback, according to the monotonicity axiom, when the total budget is cut back;[13] but only the Western Pacific and the Americas region suffered, with the brunt being borne by the Americas. Upon further investigation, however, the apparent *large* fall in the Americas budget is due to an accounting procedure.[14] Nevertheless, some real fall must have been absorbed by the Americas region, since the total budget fell. The fall in the African real budget in 1986–7 is due to the same accounting practice. The only other violation of monotonicity occurs in 1988–9, when the European region is budgeted for a real increase, while other regions either experience no change or a slight decrease in their budgets, due to a small fall in the total real budget. But this turns out to be due to a reclassification of some global and interregional programmes to the European region.

Thus, the only clear violation of the monotonicity principle in these years is in the 1984–5 budget. Why does WHO seem to follow budget monotonicity in such strict fashion? From discussions with planners in the organization, it appears that this process is politically rather than ethically motivated. It would be difficult to cut the budget of any region, in an organization in which each region has political representation, and in which all regions contribute to the budget.

Although the motivation for budget monotonicity seems to be pragmatic, it is perhaps not coincidental that in many documents WHO expresses an egalitarian philosophy with regard to its project. 'At present, health resources are not shared equally by all the people: significant gaps still exist in many countries and health is the privilege of the few. Indicators should reflect progress toward correcting this imbalance and closing the gap between those who "have health" and those

[13] In fact, MON states that the *RIS* of no country should rise when the budget falls; throughout this discussion, however, I am taking the *budget allocation* to a region as the magnitude whose monotonicity is relevant. It is, of course, possible that the budget allocation to a region fall, while its RIS rises.

[14] Each region is asked to estimate the mark-up on its previous biennial allocation which is required due to changes in exchange rates alone. For the 1984–5 period, the Americas estimated a bigger mark-up than the secretariat was willing to grant. It would grant the mark-up only on the condition that the real budget allocation to the region would be proportionately reduced. Hence, the *nominal* allocation to the Americas was the same as it would have been with a slight increase in its real budget, had it not overestimated the mark-up, from the secretariat's point of view.

who do not' (World Health Organization, 1981*b*:12). To be sure, this statement refers to inequality within a country, but the same egalitarian sentiment is expressed to apply across countries. As we have seen, monotonicity is closely linked with an egalitarian outcome, so the practice of monotonicity, if not ethically motivated, is serendipitous.

While monotonicity is observed at the regional level, it does not hold at the country level. There are many violations at the country level of disaggregation, which are mainly due to the lumpiness of programmes. When an immunization programme ends, for example, the allocation to the country may fall in the next period. These indivisibilities are not seen at the regional level, because there are, on average, twenty-eight countries per region.

How does the WHO budget allocation process conform to the other axioms? It is impossible to test for Pareto optimality, because we lack precise formulations of the functions which characterize the 'technologies' for the various countries. (Indeed, calculating such functions is not simply an engineering problem; it also involves deciding upon a social welfare function that appropriately aggregates the many different measures of health achievement.) It also seems impossible to test the symmetry axiom and the deletion of irrelevant countries axiom, because the situations described in the hypotheses of these axioms do not occur in practice. But it seems uncontroversial to claim that the planners would follow these axioms if the occasion arose.

With regard to the irrelevance of ancillary information, there is some evidence. Among the most important of considerations for planning a programme in a country is the 'probability of achieving successful and useful results, . . . a reasonable assurance from the government that the programme will be continued' (World Health Organization, 1979: 11). Whether a country will, with reasonable assurance, continue a programme is a characteristic not summarized in the technological information that describes it—although the function $u(\mathbf{x})$ does summarize how effectively the country uses resources. This must therefore count as a violation of IAI, although not, perhaps, an important one. I do not know how often this criterion comes into play in deciding upon the allocation of resources among countries, or how well correlated the 'reasonable assurance' trait is with the effectiveness of the technology u.

An apparent violation of IAI by WHO is that the Assembly voted, in 1947, to apply sanctions to South Africa, preventing it from voting in the World Health Assembly and from receiving assistance from WHO. This is tantamount *de facto* to excluding South Africa from membership in WHO; there is, however, no provision for explicit exclusion in the WHO constitution. Here is a case where a country is refused assistance because of aspects of its society that are not clearly reflected in its technology—that is, because of ancillary information. It is noteworthy that this is, in fact, no violation of IAI, because South Africa does not enter the specification of the budget allocation problem.[15] *Among its*

---

[15] I thank Joshua Cohen of the Massachusetts Institute of Technology for this fine point.

effective members, WHO claims to make budget decisions using only the 'technological' and resource information about a country.

The allocation process conforms to the model in the respect that services and resources, not grants, are distributed to countries. Whether, however, resource allocation satisfies the consistency axiom (CONRAD) is difficult to judge – again, because it is difficult to imagine situations in which the axiom might actually act as a constraint on behaviour. Suppose the agency decides to allocate resources to regions in a certain way, given a problem with ten resources. Someone asks: if the agency faced a problem where the first five resources had already been allocated as the agency had decided they should be in the ten-resource problem, should it reconsider how the remaining resources are to be allocated? If the answer is 'no', then resource allocation is consistent in the sense that CONRAD requires.[16] I do not claim that CONRAD must be observed. It is certainly not a requirement of 'rational' budget planning, although planning will be 'inconsistent' without it.[17]

Let us suppose that there is some technology function for each region that, although unknown to the secretariat, is being maximized subject to the resources made available to the region. That is to say, although the planners are not able to articulate the functions $u^i(\mathbf{x})$, it is as if the problems they face are described in the form $\xi = \langle n, \Omega, (u^1, N^1), \ldots, (u^r, N^r) \rangle$. I have argued that it is reasonable to suppose that the axioms PO, S, MON, DIC, CONRAD, and IAI are being followed. Yet it is clear that the allocation rule is not the lexicographic egalitarian rule: even when there is a small increase in the total real budget, the resources allocated to all the areas are increased, while according to leximin, all the resources should be assigned to the region with the worst health status – this is perhaps Africa – until its health indicators are brought up to the level of the next worst region, perhaps South-east Asia. We can say this without knowledge of the particular technologies.

What may account for this apparent contradiction of the theorem is the domain axiom, which states that the allocation mechanism must be defined for 'all' possible problems. The WHO planners only have to produce an allocation every two years. In the period of a generation, they will face only twelve 'problems'. It is not difficult to allocate budgets, for twelve problems, which obey the six 'substantive' axioms listed above, but fail to conform to the leximin allocation

---

[16] Recall the caveat that the CONRAD axiom does not actually have a time dimension. This is for heuristic purposes only.

[17] An example of an allocation rule that does not obey CONRAD is 'equal division Walrasian equilibrium'. Divide the available resources among countries as they would be allocated according to the Walrasian equilibrium from equal initial endowments of the resources, where countries are assumed to take their technologies as utility functions. While it would be difficult to claim this allocation mechanism is irrational, it is inconsistent. Suppose, for example, we begin with a problem with two resources, and we compute the equal division Walrasian equilibrium allocation. We now fix the first resource as it has been allocated, and ask, in the new one-resource problem, how will the equal division Walrasian equilibrium mechanism allocate the remaining resource? In general, the allocation will not be the same as in the original two-resource problem.

rule. What we *can* say is that it is impossible to extend the budget rule that WHO has been using to the class of all possible problems it might face, while not violating some of the six substantive axioms. But this objection may seem pedantic, for the probability is almost zero that the organization will ever be forced into a violation of an axiom in any finite number of years. Discussion of this point is pursued in Section 5.3.

5 Further Evaluation

Three questions will be discussed: (1) the tension between egalitarianism and utilitarianism in WHO; (2) the appropriateness of the specification of the technologies in the model; (3) the domain assumption of the model.

5.1. Egalitarianism versus Utilitarianism

A prominent competitor of the leximin allocation rule is the population-weighted utilitarian rule, which distributes resources among countries in that way that maximizes the population-weighted sum of the regional (or country) rates of infant survival. Indeed, it can be verified that the utilitarian rule satisfies all the axioms of Theorem 1, except MON, and because of this our concentration on the observance of MON in the above discussion was not entirely innocent.[18] Note that population-weighted utilitarianism would, when faced with an allocation decision between two countries of the same population, assign the larger fraction of resources to the country whose health-status would gain the most. In particular, it is well known that utilitarianism is insensitive to the initial statuses, $u^i(\mathbf{0})$; it takes into account only the rates at which the health indicators would improve under resource allocation.

While in modern ethical theory utilitarianism, as applied to the allocation of goods among persons, is the subject of much criticism,[19] in the present context of health status among nations it is arguably quite an attractive alternative to leximin. To maximize the population-weighted sum of the country rates of infant survival is equivalent to *maximizing the total number of infant lives saved internationally*.[20] The difference between utilitarianism applied to persons and countries is this. Utilitarianism among persons treats each individual as a vessel for utility, but pays no attention to the boundaries, or rights, of the individual; utilitarianism with regard to countries treats each country as a vessel for health, but pays no particular attention to national boundaries, or

[18] The population-weighted symmetry axiom S is satisfied by population-weighted utilitarianism. If unweighted utilitarianism were the rule, the appropriate symmetry axiom would have to be unweighted symmetry, which is blind to the populations of countries. This is an indefensible axiom.

[19] For example, see the essays in Sen and Williams (1982).

[20] Actually, this is only strictly true if the intervention of WHO does not affect the total number of births. If, for example, education about and distribution of contraceptives is one programme for reducing the rate of infant mortality, this will not necessarily be the case.

the rights of countries. What in the first case violates conceptions that some of us hold about individual rights—about the ethically relevant boundaries between individuals—in the second ignores what some of us consider to be ethically irrelevant national boundaries.

The tension between population-weighted utilitarianism and lexicographic egalitarianism is observable in WHO. The stated goal of allocating resources to countries in which they will be most effectively used is utilitarian; the stated concern with egalitarianism suggests the leximin rule. In evaluating the achievement of various of the health indicators, stated in terms of the number of *countries* which have achieved certain levels, there is often a companion statement referring to the fraction of the world *population* that has achieved health: 'It will be seen that 98 countries, representing 62 per cent of the world population, have achieved a life expectancy of 60 years or more. . . . On the other hand, more than a quarter of [the countries], representing 29 per cent of the world population, still have rates [of infant mortality] above the level of 100 per 1000 live births' (World Health Organization, 1987: 70, 73).

The indicators that WHO has adopted, phrased in terms of the number of countries that have achieved specific levels of health status, are neither population-weighted utilitarian nor leximin. It will count more to lower the rates of infant mortality of several small countries over the threshold of 50 infant deaths per 1000 births than to lower the infant mortality rate of India from 100 to 80, although the second could save vastly more lives. By the same token, these indicators are not faithful to implementing leximin either. According to that objective, perhaps all the resources in the infant mortality programme should go to Sierra Leone, whose rate of infant mortality is the highest in the world.

To maximize the number of countries whose rate of infant mortality is less than 50 per 1000, which is WHO's success indicator, one should proceed as follows. For each country i, calculate the cost, C_i, of bringing its RIS up to 950 per 1,000. Arrange the countries in order of these costs, so that C_1 is the lowest cost. Let M be the budget and let j be the largest integer such that $\Sigma_1^j C_i \leq M$. Then the budget should be spent entirely on countries 1 through j, to bring their rates of infant survival up to 950 per 1,000. This procedure, in particular, would usually mean not giving any resources to the worst off countries, so it is antithetical to leximin. On the other hand, it will tend to discriminate against large countries, because, other things being equal, they will require more resources to raise them up to the required rate—so it is quite antithetical to population-weighted utilitarianism. It is closest to an 'unweighted country utilitarianism', in the following sense. Define a new welfare indicator for each country, v^i. Let $v^i(\mathbf{x}) = 1$ if, with resources $\mathbf{x}$, country i has a rate of infant mortality of 50 or less, and $v^i(\mathbf{x}) = 0$ otherwise. Then maximizing the number of countries whose rates of infant mortality are 50 or less is equivalent to distributing resources to maximize $\Sigma v^i(\mathbf{x}^i)$. I will therefore call the policy that follows from this procedure 'modified unweighted country utilitarianism'.

I asked planners at WHO to what extent the secretariat was guided by trying to maximize the 'numbers of countries' indicators, and was told that these were rules of thumb, but were not observed when their maximization clearly involved ignoring the severe problems of large countries. I was told that the indices were 'indicators', not 'objectives'. Still, in a large and complex organization, where workers at the lower levels may take seriously the precise indicators of performance set by higher authorities, it may be the case that such indicators guide policy more literally than is intended.

There have been some examples in the recent history of WHO where resource allocation has been guided by unmodified unweighted country utilitarianism, but these examples seem to be isolated cases. Several years ago, it was decided to allocate a larger than usual amount of resources to certain countries—one was Sri Lanka—which were judged to be capable of showing fast and dramatic results. This move was a political one, whose intent was to demonstrate the potential impact of WHO programmes. Apparently, the policy was quickly discontinued.[21]

It is probably impossible to attain the WHO objective of Health for All by the Year 2000, by its own definitions of what constitutes health. Indeed, the slogan is put forth as a 'strategy'. That the organization follows in some cases a modified unweighted country utilitarian objective, sometimes a country egalitarian one, and sometimes a population-weighted utilitarian one is in part due to political considerations (in the World Health Assembly, each of 166 countries has one vote), and in part due to having no clearly enunciated second-best policy. The most general policy statements from the Director General tend to propose objectives which are impossible (such as health for all); their flavour, however, is decidely egalitarian across people. For example: '*All* people in *all* countries should have a level of health that will permit them to lead a socially and economically productive life . . . It [the policy] does mean that there will be an even distribution among the population of whatever resources for health are available' (World Health Organization, 1981a: 31–2). If one tries to implement this policy by concentrating on the worst-off country first, one gets leximin; if one tries to maximize the number of people who approach the goal, one gets population-weighted utilitarianism. If one tries to set a particularly simple indicator, which can be measured with some precision, and which can be easily communicated to and understood by politicians, potential donors, and the public at large, one has a modified, unweighted country utilitarian policy.

5.2. *Specification of the Technologies in the Model*

WHO distinguishes itself from the United Nations International Children's Emergency Fund (UNICEF) in that UNICEF provides materials and WHO

---

[21] I learned of this episode from Dr Joshua Cohen of WHO.

provides technical assistance. (According to the organization, it 'engages in technical cooperation with its Member states'.) WHO intends to build up countries' technical expertise and health infrastructure, rather than to supply them with materials. In an immunization campaign, for example, WHO is concerned with building up local clinics and educating health personnel so that immunizations will take place every year. UNICEF supplies the vaccines. Although the WHO allocation is just a tiny fraction of the health budget for each country, its importance is understated by this figure, because of the organizational nature of the service that it provides.

This suggests that the model I have studied may be misspecified. It may be more accurate to model the WHO problem as the allocation of resources to *change* most effectively the technologies that the countries possess. Let U be the class of all possible technologies. We can represent the technology of technical change by a mapping $T: U \times R_+ \to U$, where R_+ is the set of positive real numbers, interpreted as follows: $T(u, y) = v$ means that expending y dollars can transform technology u into technology v. Suppose that 'conventional' resources, such as vaccines, are available in amount $\mathbf{x}$. Then the provision of 'technical assistance' in amount y by WHO has the effect of changing the RIS from $u(\mathbf{x})$ to $T(u, y)(\mathbf{x}) = v(\mathbf{x})$. If we fix u, as it is fixed in a country, and recall that the set of available resources is Ω, then $T(u, y)(\mathbf{x})$ can be viewed as a mapping t_u from $\Omega \times R_+$ into R_+: $T(u, y)(\mathbf{x}) = t_u(\mathbf{x}, y)$. It may be appropriate to assume that t_u is *convex* and increasing in y and concave and increasing in $\mathbf{x}$.[22] The convexity in y follows from the fact that investment in the development of infrastructure is best viewed as one of increasing returns to scale. The better the infrastructure is, the less costly it is to improve the 'technology' for transforming resources into a rate of infant survival. The function t_u is concave in $\mathbf{x}$, for with fixed y, t_u is just a normal 'technology'.

Suppose that the conventional resources to which a country has access are given—from the viewpoint of WHO. The conventional resource distribution among countries is $(\mathbf{x}^1, \mathbf{x}^2, \ldots, \mathbf{x}^r)$. WHO has budget M. The technical change transformation T is given, and the technologies $u^1, u^2, \ldots, u^r$ are given. Define, for any positive scalar y, $T(u^i, y)(\mathbf{x}^i) \equiv w^i(y)$. By our assumptions, v^i is a convex, increasing function of y. WHO's problem would then be summarized as $\epsilon = \langle M, (w^1, N^1), \ldots, (w^r, N^r) \rangle$: that is, how to distribute a budget M as $M = \Sigma y^i$ among the countries. Instead of the resource allocation problem with concave functions studied in Sections 1–3, we face a budget allocation problem with convex functions.

The analysis of problems of the type ϵ will not be carried out here. Is the criticism against the concave model, in regard to the specification of the WHO problem, apt? I am not sure. The technical assistance that WHO provides to a country takes the form of supporting specific programmes. Within a

---

[22] By increasing in y, I mean that if $T(u, y) = v$ and $T(u, y') = v'$, for $y' > y$, then for all $\mathbf{x}$, $v'(\mathbf{x}) \geq v(\mathbf{x})$.

programme, the technology may be properly characterized as one of decreasing returns to scale (concave). If we take the case of the rate of infant survival, for example, it is surely the case that at some level the functions u^i become concave: for a doubling of resources will not forever bring a doubling of the RIS.

5.3. The Domain Assumption

Even if the other axioms are followed by WHO in its resource allocation procedure, the domain axiom is not compelling, in the sense that the organization need only worry about efficiency, fairness, consistency, and so on, for a very small number of problems. Theorem 1 tells us that it is impossible to extend the resource allocation decisions that WHO has made over the past decade to a procedure which would be defined for every possible problem in the domain Δ, without violating at least one of the six substantive axioms. But is this not a foolish consistency to ask for?

The theory of resource allocation that I have presented depends, as does much of social choice theory and bargaining theory more generally, on the requirement that the allocation rule be defined for a large domain of possible problems. This axiom, in many circumstances, is justified not by the claim that, in the application at hand, all possible problems in the domain will eventually be encountered, but rather by the fact that one *does not know beforehand* which problems will be encountered, and so the allocation rule must be specified for all problems. But in WHO, and doubtless in most organizations, the allocation rule is not written down; the agency has the freedom to choose the allocation *after the problem has been specified*. With a history of a finite number of solved problems, it is almost always the case that when a new problem is introduced, the agency will have a great deal of latitude in proposing a solution for it, while not violating the substantive axioms that embody the agency's principles of resource allocation, within the set of problems that comprises recent history.

It is this difference in procedure, I think, that renders the formal theory of allocation mechanisms largely irrelevant for the study of practical policy. The domain axiom of the theory is most easily justified by the requirement—an unstated axiom—that the choice of mechanism must precede the specification of problems that are to be solved. In the real world, organizations have the freedom to specify the allocation after the problems are encountered. The use of mechanism theory to describe what resource-allocating agencies do must therefore be severely circumscribed.

My ambivalent thoughts are best phrased as a pair of questions: If WHO decides that it either should (e.g. consistency) or must (e.g. monotonicity) follow the substantive axioms, then, knowing that it will only encounter a small number of 'problems', should it nevertheless follow a leximin policy? (Alternatively, an axiomatic characterization of population-weighted utilitarianism could be derived, and a similar question posed.) Or should the planners feel that they are following the spirit of the general principles, even if the leximin rule is not followed, knowing that they can in all likelihood avoid any overt axiom violation for the foreseeable future? As a normative tool, at least, I think the axiomatic analysis is useful. Planners can perhaps gain insight about contrasting policies by understanding the axioms (such as monotonicity) that distinguish between them.

BIBLIOGRAPHY

LENSBERG, TERJE (1987). 'Stability and Collective Rationally', *Econometrica*, 55, 935–62.

ROEMER, JOHN (1986). 'Equality of Resources Implies Equality of Welfare', *Quarterly Journal of Economics*, 101, 751–84.

—— (1987). 'Egalitarianism, Information, and Responsibility', *Economics and Philosophy*, 3, 215–44.

—— (1989). 'Distributing Health: The Allocation of Resources by an International Agency', WIDER Working Paper No. 71, Helsinki.

SEN, AMARTYA, and WILLIAMS, BERNARD (1982). *Utilitarianism and Beyond*, Cambridge: Cambridge University Press.

World Health Organization (1979–80 to 1988–9). *Proposed Programme Budgets*. Geneva.

—— (1979). *Allocation of Resources between Regions*, Doc. EB61/INF.DOC./No. 4. Geneva.

—— (1981a). *Global Strategy for Health for All by the Year 2000*. Geneva.

—— (1981b). *Development of Indicators for Monitoring Progress Towards Health for All by the Year 2000*. Geneva.

—— (1987). *Evaluation of the Strategy for Health for All by the Year 2000*. Geneva.

John Roemer: Distributing Health: The Allocation of Resources by an International Agency

Commentary by Paul Seabright

It is rare for contributors to the literature on social choice theory to discuss how a social choice rule might be implemented in a practical policy-making context. It is rarer still for them to examine the practice of political institutions to see how these measure up to the standards prescribed by theory. In his paper John Roemer offers us the pioneering combination of an axiomatic argument in social choice and a practical study of the allocation of resources by the World Health Organization (WHO). He discusses a set of criteria that he believes a satisfactory resource allocation rule for such an agency may be constrained to satisfy; he then shows that only one rule satisfies all the criteria. He argues that the practice of the WHO diverges from the rule; and he leaves us guessing whether to conclude that the agency's practice should be adapted to fit the rule better, or our criteria for a rule adapted to match the constraints of practice. It is a stimulating paper whose example I hope will be widely emulated. I shall confine my comments to two issues: first, it is harder than he implies to compare theory with practice when technologies are changing over time; second, and more important, while I support the enterprise of developing normative rules and using them to assess the practice of policy-makers, I wish that he had discussed a more persuasive rule than the leximin allocation rule, some of whose unattractive features deserve a more conspicuous exposure than he gives them.

Roemer begins by imposing restrictions on the kinds of budget allocation rule that can be judged acceptable. There are seven axioms: Pareto optimality, the independence of ancillary information, monotonicity, symmetry, consistency of resource allocation across dimension, the deletion of irrelevant countries, and the domain condition. It is worth noting straight away that the domain condition is less demanding than it appears, because of the restriction that the technologies $u^i(.)$ be represented by concave functions. Roemer's defence of this assumption for the WHO's programmes is not very convincing: of course the functions $u^i(.)$ become concave at some level, but they may well contain convex segments, and actual resource allocation problems may find countries on these convex segments. Given the importance of infrastructural investment (which typically displays increasing returns) in reducing infant mortality, the relevance of Theorem 1 to real-world problems is not quite clear.

Several of the seven axioms raise important issues, but here I shall concentrate on monotonicity (I disagree that 'the axioms can be seen as either quite weak . . .

or quite reasonable, or both', but have no space to pursue the point here). Monotonicity is the only axiom that appears to have been violated by the practice of the WHO to date, according to the evidence in Roemer's Table 1. Even here he argues that some apparent violations of monotonicity are really due to changes in accounting procedures. The sole clear case of violation, he contends, was in 1984–5, where in spite of a fall in the total budget the budgets for some regions increased. Now one of the regions whose real allocation increased was Africa. The continent at this time was going through considerable turmoil: the world had only recently become aware of the importance of Africa's AIDS epidemic, there were threats to food supplies from poor harvests and civil disturbance in a number of areas, and falling commodity prices had delivered a major blow to many countries' economic prospects. In terms of Roemer's economic environments, this means that their technologies had changed (alternatively, one could say that their country-specific resources had been cut back). Either way, we cannot judge, from the rise in their real budget allocation at a time when the total WHO budget was falling, that the monotonicity axiom was violated. Roemer does not, in any case, attach great significance to this (he argues that the spirit of monotonicity pervades much of the agency's practice). My point is merely that even if we can establish clearly whether or not the agency is following a particular rule (WHO clearly does not follow leximin), diagnosing axiom violation on the basis of the evidence realistically available may be much harder than Roemer makes it appear. His enterprise, though important, is also difficult.

The points I have made so far are largely matters of emphasis. But the shortcomings of the leximin rule are a more serious matter. Roemer discusses an attractive alternative to leximin, namely population-weighted utilitarianism. It should be noted that this is not actually utilitarianism, but rather a rule for allocating resources that has some structural features that are similar to utilitarianism properly so called. Instead of maximizing total utility this rule recommends maximizing the total number of infant lives saved. As Roemer points out, the shortcomings of utilitarianism (its indifference to the boundaries between persons, for instance) are not obviously applicable here: saving infant lives would seem to be valuable irrespective of where the infants are situated, and the boundaries between nations morally irrelevant to that end. He provides no further argument against population-weighted utilitarianism, so presumably he considers its failure to satisfy the monotonicity axiom the most likely reason for its failure to find favour with the WHO. This would be a satisfactory outcome only if our intuitions in favour of the monotonicity axiom were more compelling than our intuitions in favour of maximizing the number of infant lives saved. Are they?

To see whether they are we can do no better than to examine an example in which population-weighted utilitarianism violates monotonicity. Consider two countries: in the first, infant mortality is neither very high nor very low, and its causes are a familiar mixture of poor sanitation, low nutrition, shortages of primary health care, and low educational levels. Most of the obvious infra-structural investments in lowering infant mortality have already been made, however, and significant extra resources would be required to lower it significantly further. In the second country, infant mortality is considerably higher: in addition to the familiar causes (the state of poverty and infrastructure is roughly the same in the two countries), the second country also suffers from a serious endemic water-borne disease. Since the country is criss-crossed by rivers, lakes, and canals the cost of eradicating the disease by destroying its habitat would far exceed the total available resources in both countries. There is an alternative cure using genetic engineering to eradicate the parasite that breeds in the water, but initially the cost of this technology is prohibitively high. At a certain date, however, there is a significant fall in the price of the genetic engineering technology. This corresponds with an increase in the total resources available to the two countries. It also means that investing resources in the second country produces dramatically greater reductions in infant mortality than before. Provided both countries had previously been recipients of WHO aid, population-weighted utilitarianism would prescribe that some resources be diverted from existing programmes in both countries towards the programme of parasite eradication. A consequence of this would be that the resources allocated to the first country would decline, in spite of the increase in total resources. This would be an entirely reasonable outcome, since that increase in total resources had made possible the assault on a pressing problem that could not be effectively tackled before.

The monotonicity axiom would rule out this reasonable response. Worse still, the leximin principle would have meant that the first country received no resources at all from the WHO. If the second country had a higher infant mortality rate than the first, the leximin principle would have prescribed that the second country should receive all the available resources so long as the returns, however small, were not precisely zero. So expensive and wasteful programmes of eradicating waterways in the second country might have saved a few hundred infants per year while hundreds of thousands died in the first country through lack of a programme to spread information about oral rehydration therapy. The leximin principle is inexorable. If Liechtenstein (say) were to be afflicted with an AIDS epidemic that lowered its infant mortality rate below that of China or India, then so long as expensive nursing care, by prolonging the lives of AIDS-infected infants, could make marginal reductions in their mortality rate, WHO aid to China and India would be diverted in its entirety to Liechtenstein (I an assuming that Liechtenstein is a member of the WHO). Leximin can be described as favouring heroic and almost futile programmes over effective and productive ones, so long as the former are not absolutely futile and so long as they occur in sufficiently blighted countries. In turn this makes the boundaries between countries of crucial importance: epidemics may ravage infant lives in regions of China without provoking the tiniest reallocation of resources, but a similar outbreak in Mauritius could have major effects on the budget. Nothing could be better calculated to provoke secessionist movements in Bombay, Bangkok, or even (who knows?) the Bronx.

In the end it is unclear how much force an axiomatic argument of this kind should have. Roemer's introductory discussion of the monotonicity axiom, for example, suggests that it is justified not on ethical but on pragmatic grounds, due to the fact that countries contribute as countries to the budget of the WHO. On the other hand, he later discusses the way in which population-weighted utilitarianism has exerted an influence on the decision-making of the WHO, albeit in tension with other principles. This might be taken to imply that the monotonicity axiom is not an inscrutable given of the political situation, in which case its ethical shortcomings are of relevance after all. One thing this shows is that using social choice theory to illuminate policy-making is fraught with uncertainty: to what degree must theorists take themselves to be articulating the preferences of policy-makers, and to what extent may they legitimately seek to influence those preferences? An instructive contrast is with Roemer's own justly influential article 'Equality of Resources Implies Equality of Welfare',[1] whose formal argument has a very similar structure to the present one. That article (apart from bringing insights from bargaining theory powerfully to bear on a problem in social choice) draws out the consequences of a particular form of egalitarian social theory. It shows that egalitarianism with respect to resources implies egalitarianism with respect to welfare, provided resources are interpreted sufficiently broadly to enable differences in utility functions between agents to be ascribed to different endowments of 'internal' resources. Egalitarianism with respect to welfare has itself some disturbing consequences (the presence of a single severely disabled person would justify diverting enormous resources to that person so long as the marginal welfare benefit of doing so were not quite zero). But it is clear what Roemer's argument establishes: one theory (already articulated by others, notably Ronald Dworkin) implies another, and those who espouse the first should espouse the second if they also accept the auxiliary assumptions. Here, however, it is less clear what the argument of this paper establishes: a set of axioms, which may or may not characterize the principles guiding resource allocation in an international agency, implies an allocation rule that does not characterize the agency's actions—and probably should not, in any case. Should we reform the agency or the principles? The answer is probably that we should reform both. At any rate, the theorem's claim 'to answer definitively the policy problem of the international agency' is untenable as long as its conclusion favours leximin. The question of what policy should replace leximin remains very much an open one.

---

[1] *Quarterly Journal of Economics*, 101 (1986), 751–82.

The Relativity of the Welfare Concept

B. M. S. van Praag

1 Introduction

In most sciences there are phenomena that are understood only partially or not at all. Nevertheless, if we take the basic phenomenon for granted it is frequently possible to build a theory on them explaining more complicated phenomena. The basic phenomena are called the *primitive* concepts of that science. When science progresses we do not only see an outward movement trying to explain and understand newly observed phenomena but also an inward movement where an attempt is made to explain phenomena hitherto taken as primitive concepts. Unavoidably this leads to the definition of more basic concepts as the primitive concepts of the theory. Nowadays two outstanding examples of this scientific evolution are seen in the developments in physics, where the atom is no longer the primitive concept, it having become possible to dissect the atom into ever smaller particles, and in medicine and biology, where we are discovering the secrets of genetics.

In economics we have the same problem: some basic concepts are needed to build a theory on, but those concepts themselves are not well understood or even not measurable for the time being. A prime example is the *welfare* or *utility* concept. It is taken to be a primitive concept. As the concept is also used in sociology and psychology as a basic concept, the understanding of that concept may be seen as a common task of the social sciences. The main objective of this paper will be to make a contribution to that understanding of the welfare concept.

Section 2 sketches the mainstream approach in economic literature. In Section 3 we consider the measurability problem and suggest a measurement method. Some results are reported, which suggest measurability in a certain sense. In Section 4 we consider the differences between respondents and try to explain those differences by relatively simple regression equations. Section 5 introduces some more complex models, which include past and future expectations as co-determinants. In Section 6 we consider the social filter model, which incorporates the social reference group. In Section 7 we study a cardinal utility framework. Section 8 is the conclusion.

The nature of this presentation is non-mathematical, following the general style of this volume. Hence, some matters will not be exactly defined or described. The references, where the reader may find a more exact presentation, are given in the text.

The main message of this paper is, then, that from attitude questions an

I am grateful to Dr Siddiq R. Osmani for his constructive critique which led to some revisions in this paper.

ordinal but interpersonally comparable individual welfare concept may be constructed which is 'operationally meaningful' in the sense of Samuelson (1947). At the end of the paper we suggest an attractive cardinalization of this utility index. We do *not* touch on the problem of whether and how we can define a social welfare function using as a building stone the *individual* welfare concept described.

2   *The Economic Mainstream Approach to Utility*

The attitude of economics towards utility has always been ambiguous. On the one hand, the concept was absolutely needed in order to develop a positive and a normative theory of economic behaviour. On the other hand, economists have felt very uneasy with the concept as its measurability is doubtful. As such it does not seem to be an operational concept (Samuelson, 1947). How can a science be based on non-measurable concepts?

At a non-scientific level welfare or well-being is a well-known concept. It is an evaluation by the individual of his situation. We know from introspection and observation that it is fairly possible to evaluate situations in terms of feeling 'well' or feeling 'badly'. It follows that an intrapersonal comparison of situations is possible. Now this evaluation is done in terms of verbal labels, which is not a good point of departure for the formation of a quantitative theory. It has, however, been demonstrated that many esoteric things may be evaluated on a numerical scale: for example, the quality of wine, a musical performance, commodity testing, etc. The evaluation of school results is frequently done in terms of a scale from 0 to 10, where the numbers are explicitly translated as 10 standing for 'excellent', 9 standing for 'very good', 8 standing for 'good' and so forth. When we are first confronted with such numerical evaluations they look strange and unfamiliar. When we have got some experience with this type of rating, they become ingrained in our value pattern and we begin to think in those numerical terms. Hence, we do not reject the idea that more general situations may be evaluated by human beings in terms of numbers on a numerical scale just as well as in terms of verbal labels on a verbal scale. This may apply for the welfare concept as well.

This was also the position of the classical economists like Edgeworth (1881) and Cohen Stuart (1889). Edgeworth assumed that welfare positions could be described by the consumption levels $x_1, \ldots, x_n$ of n commodities $X_1, \ldots, X_n$, shortly denoted by the vector $\mathbf{x}$. Then he assumed that an individual was able to evaluate each situation $\mathbf{x}$ by a number $U(\mathbf{x})$ called the *utility* attached to that situation. Consumer behaviour was then basically a search for the welfare position $\mathbf{x}$ with the highest utility, given the constraint that total expenditures $p_1 \mathbf{x}_1 + \ldots + p_n \mathbf{x}_n$ will not exceed a given income y, where p_1, $\ldots, p_n$ stand for the prices of the different commodities. In this way demand for goods could be described as a function of prices and income. In this analysis utility is just a tool of analysis. The fact that individuals try to improve or even to optimize their behaviour according to some criterion is more or less a tautology. If this were not the case, we could expect purely random behaviour, which is not observed in practice. As a result of this analysis we can also evaluate income levels y by assigning to them the utility value U corresponding to the optimal consumption pattern that can be reached at given prices p and income y. That value U depends on y and p and it is nowadays called the indirect utility function $V(y, p)$. If prices are taken fixed we denote it by $V(y)$ and it is then also called the *utility function of income*.

This brings the second problem to the fore. Cohen Stuart was looking for a tool to construct a just taxation model, as he realized that, although there is a case for taxing all citizens by an equal amount as they get the same services in the public sector, in some way the *pain* caused by taxation is not the same for everyone. It is easier for a millionaire to pay $1,000 than for someone with an annual income of $10,000. This points to progressive taxation. Then $V(y)$ is a measuring rod by which the tax pain may be equalized. Let us assume that we tax someone with $10,000 by $500, then the pain inflicted will be $V(10,000) - V(9,500) = A$. If we like to inflict the same pain on someone with $20,000 to begin with we have to tax him by T with $V(20,000) - V(20,000 - T) = A$. There are two problems that are rather basic in this approach.

The first problem is whether equal *differences* in the value of the utility function imply equal pain differences for the individual. If we return to the evaluation by verbal labels this question may be translated into the question whether the fall from 'very good' to 'good' is equivalent to the fall from 'good' to 'amply sufficient', being the usual translations in Dutch schools of the grades 9,8, and 7. We cannot solve this problem. We cannot say that the differences imply equal utility jumps, but neither can we say that they do not. The reason for this is that we lack a measuring rod to measure utility itself, say, by a 'utility meter' (see also Suppes and Winet, 1954). All we can do is observe correlates, which we assume to be strongly related to the latent non-cognitive concept *utility*.

The second problem arises if we accept that equal utility differences imply equal pain differences. Then we still have to answer the problem whether *two* individuals have the same utility function of income and whether the fact that two individuals attach the same utility value to the same income implies that they *feel equally satisfied* with their income. Again in terms of verbal labels: does the fact that two individuals call the same income level 'good' imply that they feel equally satisfied or dissatisfied about their welfare position? Here too we have to confess our *agnostic* position. It follows that the utility function approach cannot be applied for intra- or interpersonal welfare comparisons without a reasonable measurement method and/or the willingness to accept some unproven assumptions as a matter of working convention. You may call it an 'act of faith'. But such acts are performed by all individuals, mostly unconsciously. There is an infinity of social conventions that serve to replace metaphysical notions by observed correlates. It would be hard to imagine how any being or society could function without such conventions. Obviously the convention is just a working assumption, which is invalidated when its consequences do not conform to our expectations of real phenomena.

The measurability problem was recognized by Pareto (1904). It led him to the conclusion that the assumption of utility maximization is a useful device to explain consumer behaviour but that a utility function in the context of the description of consumer demand is actually only needed to describe indifference curves in commodity space, indicating that people are indifferent between various consumption patterns and prefer more to less. He did not regard it as necessary for the explanation of the consumer problem to assume that utility differences are comparable, or, more technically, no cardinal utility had to be assumed. Pareto did not state that the idea of cardinal utility was nonsense, only that the assumption of cardinal utility was superfluous for dealing with the consumer problem. Robbins (1932), a man of tremendous influence in English and American literature, went much further in denying the existence of a measurable cardinal utility function and proclaiming henceforth the impossibility of measuring such a concept. Mainstream economics accepted this verdict for a long time.

This position had a significant impact on the state of the art in economics. All welfare comparisons were forbidden, except for the assumption that, if an individual A has not less of anything than an individual B, he cannot be worse off than B. It follows, then, that a social allocation of goods over individuals can be improved if nobody gets less and at least someone gets more in the new allocation.

Clearly this denied any foundation to normative economics, which has to be based on the evaluation of individual situations and the evaluation of the state of society as a whole by an aggregate of some sort of individual welfare evaluations. It is nevertheless widely felt that it is one of the basic tasks of economists to measure inequality and to advise on methods to reduce social inequality. In this light it is untenable to maintain the position that welfare situations cannot be compared by some kind of utility function. In fact, economists have developed economic theories on inequality (Atkinson, 1970; Sen, 1973), taxation, uncertainty (Arrow, 1964), and economic growth that are either implicitly or explicitly based on a cardinal utility concept, including intra- and interpersonal utility comparisons. At the same time colleagues— or even these economists themselves—have professed their refusal to accept cardinality of some sort. Those studies are based on a postulate of the type: 'Let us assume that individuals have a common utility function $U(.)$ and that there is a social welfare function of the type $W = W(U_1, \ldots, U_m)$', where m is the number of individuals in society. This being postulated one proceeds without further discussion or doubts on this basic postulate. This leads to a rather schizophrenic situation in economics as some authors, while on the one hand painstakingly ordinal, in normative studies accept cardinality in the way pictured above if the need arises. The only interpretation of this behaviour is that a theory is constructed which is applicable under the proviso that the basic postulate has been verified or taken for granted as a primitive concept. In a sense it is building the first floor when the foundations are not yet laid. It may also be seen as accepting the reality of scientific method that one has to accept some primitive concepts and assumptions in order to get anywhere. The more one is willing to accept, the more specific will be the resulting theory. Nevertheless, it would be very nice if we could find some credible method of getting evidence on utility.

3   A Measurement Method

Individuals evaluate their situation in terms of 'good' and 'bad'. This idea actually involves three elements. Situations have to be described by means of observable variables $X_1, \ldots, X_k$, *which assume values* $x_1, \ldots, x_k$ on a domain **X**. The situation has to be evaluated by a welfare (or utility) function assigning a welfare value U to the situation described by the k-vector **x**; the welfare values are then elements of an evaluation set **U**. The first question is how we would like to characterize our situations. What is the choice of variables $X_1, \ldots, X_k$ that are required to describe our welfare position? Obviously an exact description would require an infinite set of variables like income, consumption bundle, number of working hours, family life, the weather, and even the political system. In our analysis, however, we shall confine ourselves to one variable to begin with, namely, family income denoted by y. It does not imply that we believe that this *provides a perfect characterization* but we use it as a start. We take it that y varies from 0 to ∞, that is, **X** is the positive semi-axis. Which values $U(y)$ can assume is a much more problematic question. As we argued before, it does not seem obvious that welfare positions are evaluated by numbers on a numerical scale. Theoretically it may be possible, but individuals do not think in numerical values. They think in verbal labels like 'good' or 'bad'. It follows that it is more natural to assume that the welfare function $U(.)$ assumes values on the set of verbal labels. That set is denoted by **U**.

A question which is now crucial is whether different people assign the same emotional value to the same verbal label. The verbal labels are after all assumed to reflect emotional values, which are described in verbal language. The reason we are not sure is that emotions cannot be measured in an exact way. There are, however, experiments where individuals have been asked to translate such verbal labels into figures on a 0–10 scale or to draw lines of a specific length, where the convention was that 'very bad' corresponded to zero length and 'excellent' to, say, 8 centimetres. A consistent response pattern was found which suggests that those verbal labels have roughly the same connotation for most individuals. These experiments are described in Saris (1988) (see especially van Doorn and van Praag; see also Van Praag, 1989).

Another argument, which is of a more philosophical nature, is the following. Human language is a transmitter of information between members of the language community. Hence, words are symbols of concepts and things that must have about the same meaning for two individuals who communicate in that language. Obviously we cannot prove beyond all doubt that the word 'table' has the same meaning for all English people, but on the other hand it does not seem far-fetched to assume that this is roughly the case. Otherwise, language would be no means of communication, and it is precisely that which is the *raison d'être* of a language.

This is also in line with Sen's (1982: 9) statement on empirical economic methodology, where he refers to the predilection among economists for observable behaviour.

One reason for the tendency in economics to concentrate only on 'revealed preference' relations is a methodological suspicion regarding introspective concepts. Choice is seen as solid information, whereas introspection is not open to observation ... Even as behaviorism this is peculiarly limited since *verbal* behavior (or *writing* behavior, including response to questionnaires) should not lie outside the scope of the behaviorist approach.

A third indication that it is not odd to assume that verbal labels in **U** do approximately mean the same for all members of the language community can be constructed by posing the so-called *income evaluation question* (IEQ), which runs as follows:

Please try to indicate what you consider to be an appropriate amount for each of the following cases. Under my/our conditions I would call a net household income per week/month/year of:

about . . . . very bad
about . . . . bad
about . . . . insufficient
about . . . . sufficient
about . . . . good
about . . . . very good

Please enter an answer on each line, and underline the period you refer to.

At first sight this attitude question, developed by myself (van Praag, 1971) looks somewhat awkward. It would have seemed more natural to specify income levels first and to ask the respondents for their corresponding verbal evaluations. The problem with that is that different respondents have different incomes, one being a millionaire and one being a poor man. The evaluation of an income sequence of $10,000, $20,000, etc., would therefore yield *different* evaluations when offered to a poor man and a millionaire, to whom those income levels would make *no* difference. He would not be able to distinguish a real difference between such petty amounts. A typical response, quoted from a British respondent in 1979 for this IEQ, is the following:

about £25 . . . . very bad
about £35 . . . . bad
about £45 . . . . insufficient
about £70 . . . . sufficient
about £120 . . . . . . good
about £160 . . . . . . very good

*(Figures are for household income per week.)

Let us denote such a response sequence for respondent n by the vector $c_n = (c_{1n}, .., c_{6n})$. We call those amounts the *income standards* of the individual concerned. The dimension of this vector – that is, the number of levels supplied as stimuli to the respondent – could vary. In practice six levels works rather well in the sense that people are willing and able to answer, but that limitation is only suggested by practice. Similarly the monotonic ordering of the levels is useful to calibrate the answers and to make the answers comparable between respondents, but any other ordering of the stimuli is also conceivable. As already hinted at, the responses vary between individuals. It follows that there is no one uniform opinion on what is a 'good' income, etc. This does not indicate, however, that the verbal labels represent different things to different people. Let us denote the mean of the six levels by m_n, so that

$$m_n = \sum_{i=1}^{6} c_{in}$$

It may then be expected that the mean response will vary between individuals. However, if the proportional deviation pattern were constant, say 'good' always corresponds to 20 per cent above the mean and 'bad' to 20 per cent below the mean, then this regularity would strongly suggest that people translate the verbal labels on the same emotional scale. As always when studying income, it is advisable to study relative income differences rather than absolute differences. Relative differences are studied most easily by looking at the logarithm of the answers. This implies that all responses are translated on a logarithmic scale and that we shall consider the vector $\ln(c) = [\ln(c_1), \ldots, \ln(c_6)]$. It follows then that equal log-differences stand for equal income proportions. The hypothesis that the difference $\ln(c_i) - \ln(c_j)$ is equal over respondents, that is, that the verbal labels i and j give rise to the same proportional response has to be rejected as well. However, let μ stand for the mean of the logarithmic answers and σ for the standard deviation of the log-answers about their mean μ, then we find that the *standardized response* $u_{in} = [\ln(c_{in}) - \mu_n)]/\sigma_n$ is practically constant. (van der Sar, van Praag, and Dubnoff, 1988). Table 1 refers to a sample of about 500 American respondents. We see that u_1 has an average value of -1.291 and that the sample dispersion over individuals about that value is 0.236. This table is very interesting. First, although there is variation among respondents it could not be explained by personal characteristics of the respondents, in other words, the observed variation is purely random.

Table 1 Average u-levels and Sample Deviations

Label	u_i	$\sigma(u_i)$
1	-1.291	0.236
2	-0.778	0.190
3	-0.260	0.241
4	0.259	0.239
5	0.760	0.190
6	1.311	0.229

Second, the dispersion is roughly the same at each level. This implies that the response variation is not level-specific. Third, and this is the most interesting aspect, the values are nearly symmetrical about zero. All this seems to imply that, for given μ and σ the values u_i roughly predictable except for a random disturbance. It follows that for given μ_n and σ_n also $\ln(c_{in}) = \mu_n + u_i \sigma_n$ is predictable. This predictability is evidence that the emotional content of the set of stimuli is about the same for all respondents. It follows that we feel justified in treating the individual responses as meaningful.

In the following sections we shall try to explain (in a statistical sense) the differences in the values of μ and σ by personal variables. If we succeed in that explanation we will actually be able to identify the determinants of why people derive different welfare from a fixed amount of income.

But before doing so, let us pose the question whether the values $u_1, \ldots, u_6$ may be considered as the numerical welfare levels assigned to the amounts $c_1, \ldots, c_6$ by the respondent. Or, phrased differently, are the values u the numerical translations of the verbal labels 'bad', 'good', etc.? The answer is yes *and* no.

The answer is *yes* as we find statistically that log-standardization of the response yields always roughly the same u-values. So it makes sense to connect the label 'sufficient' with 0.259 in Table 1. Obviously that value has no *emotional connotation* unless we use this scaling frequently. Think of the academic grading A–E in Britain or the grading on a 0–20 scale usual in Belgian universities. Those gradings are also completely arbitrary, but they have an emotional connotation for people who are used to them. Another example is temperature measurement in Celsius or Fahrenheit degrees.

The answer is *no*, as the log-standardization used above is an arbitrary procedure. We may continue by taking the exponential of u and we find a new scale defined on the positive semi-axis. Hence there are more value schemes, which may serve as a translation of the verbal labels. However, the primary step of log-standardization seems essential, as we thereby discard any effect of personal respondent characteristics. Here again there is no mathematical certainty that another transformation could not be made that would have statistically the same effect of discarding the respondent's personal characteristics, but I can only report that we were unable to find such an alternative.

Hence, the basis of our method is the idea that the individual is able to evaluate income levels in terms of *verbal labels* like 'bad' or 'good' and so on. A question that is now crucial is whether different people assign the same emotional value to the same verbal label. This assumption is crucial for the method and it has not been tested. Even stronger, the assumption is *untestable per se*. It is a *primitive assumption*, like many others in science, for example, in physics. It is maintained as long as it does not run counter to empirical evidence. In this section we give strong empirical and philosophical evidence that this assumption should not be rejected, but we do not claim in the paper (nor elsewhere) that we have *shown its truth*.

Actually, the problem of whether words have the same meaning to people in the same language community is fundamental to the significance of language outside any specific context. Take the words 'red' and 'blue'. Two members of a language community will not disagree whether an object is 'red' or 'blue'; however, this is not evidence that both individuals have the same physical sensation or internal perception of the two colours. It may well be that person A has the same internal sensation corresponding to 'red' as person B experiences when he is seeing 'blue'. In other words, there are two elements involved, namely, internal sensations on the one hand and verbal labels on the other. Obviously, *aspects* of internal sensations can frequently be observed by means of external signs like heart-beat frequency or electrical activity in the brain, but even then we cannot say that we have measured the internal sensation itself. We can only assume that there is a measurable phenomenon which 'stands for' or is 'correlated with' the sensation. The sensation itself is unmeasurable, unless we agree by convention that the measurable phenomenon completely describes the sensation. Equating the metaphysical concept to the measurable outcome of an experiment is always a convention. We have to accept primitive assumptions of this kind in science everywhere, and one of the basic assumptions concerning a language community – or even the *definition* of a language community – is that verbal labels have roughly the same (emotional) meaning, that is, a *common* interpretation, to all members of the language community. This is not 'an act of faith' but just a working assumption, towards which I feel morally neutral. Without making such assumptions we are doomed to sterile solipsism. I am inclined to maintain this assumption, until credible counter-evidence is presented.

4 *Interpersonal Differences Explained: Virtual and True Standards*

In the previous section we reported that the answers to the IEQ, that is, the income standards of the individual, are pretty much constant over individuals, if we standardize for the μ and σ.

Our next task will thus be either to discover a systematic relationship between

μ and σ and some objectively measurable characteristics of the individual or to look directly for a relationship between the income standards and those individual characteristics. By 'systematic' we mean that differences may be explained by intuitively understandable models, preferably of a simple type. In this paper we shall follow the second road and concentrate on the explanation of the standards themselves, although we shall consider the value of σ, that is, the spread in the levels, in Section 6.

Our problem is now to find out what factors determine the money values of the standards. On the one hand we have our intuition, on the other hand we have a host of samples with Dutch and other data on which we may test the hypothesized relationships. We shall now report in a non-technical way on a number of such results, which have been described elsewhere in great detail (see bibliography).

The first factor that will influence the response is clearly the *current* income of the respondent or the respondent's household. Let current income be denoted by y_c, then the idea would be that $c = c(y_c)$. The expectation would be that people with a higher income will also regard higher income levels as being 'good', 'bad', etc., than respondents with a low income. That would imply that the standards reported would be increasing functions of current income. The functional relationship between c_i and y_c is sketched in Figure 1 where both variables are measured on a logarithmic scale. Empirically it is found that the relationship is then approximately linear. Actually, the relationship can be sketched for each level $i = 1, \ldots, 6$ separately. In Figure 1 the lines corresponding to two levels are sketched.

A special case is that where the lines are horizontal. In that case there is uniformity of opinion between respondents with different incomes about the income standard. Then it is a generally accepted standard.

We said above that the respondent's current income would *clearly* be the

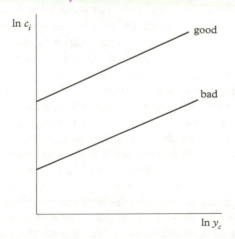

Figure 1 Current Income and Virtual Income Standards

first factor to think of in respect of influencing the response. But is that so clear after all? There seem to be two strands of opinion. The first is that of the traditional economist. In economics the assumption of a common preference structure and a unique utility function of income is the basic point of departure. This would imply that there can be no individual variation on what a 'good' income is. The second is that of the psychologist or rather the psychophysicist (Helson, 1964; Stevens, 1975). It is well known from measurement experiments on the individual perception of the brightness of light or the volume of sound that perceptions as to what is a 'lot' and what is not are heavily influenced by the environment before the experiment. Respondents refer to the situation they have presently in mind as their 'anchor'-situation. If we assume that the income evaluation question is a similar psychophysical experiment with 'income' as its subject-matter, it is fairly natural to assume that respondents are heavily influenced by their own current income, which plays the role of an anchor in this case. However, let statistical analysis enlighten us as to the value of either assumption. It is possible to estimate the slope of the lines in Figure 1 empirically. If the lines are horizontal we are in the position of the traditional economist.

A second extreme position would be that where the slope of the lines corresponds to 45 degrees. In that case 10 per cent increase in income would cause an increase of the standard by the same ratio. It would then be impossible to make the individual better off by an increase in current income. His standards would increase *pari passu*. In the latter situation we may call standards purely relative.

In reality the slope coefficient is estimated to be about 0.6. Hence, income standards are neither purely absolute nor purely relative. (See also Hagenaars and van Praag, 1985).

The fact that the slope coefficient is estimated at 0.6 indicates that people with different incomes have different standards with respect to what level represents a 'good' income. In other words, contra to what is frequently assumed, there is not *one* social norm with respect to income; rather, each individual has his or her own standards. This obviously presents a major difficulty when we try to evaluate the welfare situation of individuals or of society as a whole. The problem is: according to *whose* standards we have to evaluate? The poor citizen believes that nearly everybody is fairly rich, while the rich man believes that nearly everyone is poor (according to his standards).

The phenomenon of people shifting their norms with their income I have called (1971) *preference drift* and the value of the slope coefficient the *preference drift ratio*. The existence of preference drift is a disturbing factor for social policy. First, the top of society may have a different view on social distribution than the majority of the population, the rank and file. Second, we may expect a difference in the evaluation *ex ante* and *ex post* of social changes. *Ex ante* a wage increase may look marvellous, but *ex post* the standard has shifted upwards and people evaluate their wage increase as being relatively minor.

Such a phenomenon will obviously create frustration.

We call the standards used by different individuals *virtual* standards. They are called virtual, because the individual's evaluation of all incomes, especially other incomes than his current income, will change when his current income changes. Is it possible to find out how people evaluate their own current income?

Let us look back at Figure 1. We draw it again in Figure 2, where we add the 45-degree line. Consider the line corresponding to the verbal label 'bad' and its point of intersection A with the 45-degree line. To the left of A people evaluate their own current income as worse than 'bad'. To the right of A they evaluate it as better than 'bad'. It follows that people with an income equal to the projection of A on the horizontal axis evaluate their own income as being 'bad'. We call that income level the *true* income standard corresponding to the verbal label 'bad', say y^*_{bad}. Similarly the point of intersection B with the 'good' line determines the true standard y^*_{good}. We notice that we would not find one true standard if there were no point of intersection, or more than one.

5 Compensating Equivalence Scales

The previous results have been found for a sample of respondents that are not differentiated with respect to personal characteristics except for their current income y_c. In this section we consider the question whether people with different personal characteristics and/or living in a different environment will have different virtual and true standards. If so—and intuition suggests that this is not improbable—we are interested in the quantitative relationship

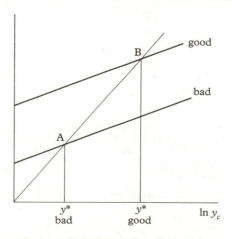

Figure 2 Virtual and True Standards

between these differences and the resulting differences in income standards. If people need different amounts to feel equally happy in terms of their own income evaluation, this will lead automatically to the derivation of compensating equivalence scales. We shall consider two example: (*a*) the welfare implications of differences in *family size*, (*b*) the welfare implications of differences in *climate*.

It is generally recognized that it makes a difference whether one has to support a small or a large family from a fixed amount of income. Let us characterize *family size* quite simply by the number of household members to be supported out of household income. That number is denoted by *fs*. It is obvious that we may think of more elaborate definitions that take into account the ages as well, but that is outside the scope of this article (see e.g. Kapteyn and van Praag, 1976).

Again the way in which we can try to discover the empirical relationship between *fs* and the response on the IEQ is to estimate the line in Figure 1 for various values of *fs*. In Figure 3 we sketch the 'good' line for households with $fs = 2$ and $fs = 4$. Not unexpectedly, the line for households with four members is situated at a higher level than that for two-person households. The difference between $y^*_{good}(fs = 2)$ and $y^*_{good}(fs = 4)$ is just the income difference needed to get the two households to the same welfare level. It has generally been found (see e.g. Kapteyn and van Praag, 1976) that a 10 per cent increase in household size has to be compensated by an income increase of 2.5 per cent. *Family size elasticity* thus equals 2.5/10, or 25 per cent. Several observations are appropriate at this point. First, we notice that the compensation rule does not depend on the specific income level at the point of departure; neither is the rule utility-specific: the compensation factor does not depend on the welfare level considered. The log-linear specification, as depicted in Figure 1, was not dictated by a theory, but was simply the best-fitting specifi-

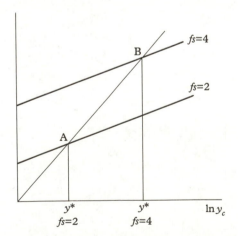

Figure 3 True Standards for a three-person and four-person household

cation within a class of non-complex functional specifications. So we do not exclude the possibility of there being better-fitting specifications which yield utility- or income-specific compensation factors. Second, we found for a number of roughly comparable societies (see van Praag and van der Sar, 1988) values of roughly the same order of magnitude, although the elasticity value of 25 per cent is certainly not an empirical law. We may think of rural societies where children are primarily a production instead of a consumption good for the household. In such societies we would expect a lower value for family size elasticity; it might even be *negative*. Indeed, in a recent Pakistani sample we find that self-employed people feel better off with more children than with less.

Looking back on this analysis, we see that the result is twofold. First, it gives an empirical insight into the welfare differences corresponding to differences in family size; this is a *positive* result. Second, it yields a compensation factor according to which welfare differences due to differences in family size may be compensated by income changes. This is a *normative* result.

Now we shall consider an analogous analysis dealing with the influence of *climatic differences* on welfare (see van Praag, (1988). The naïve approach would be to define a variable called *climate* denoted by C and to hypothesize a relationship between climate C and the income standards.

We have to create a sample of households that exhibits not only variation with respect to current income and family size, but also with respect to climate. It will then be possible to estimate that relation. Once this has been estimated, we can define climate elasticity in a similar way as we defined family size elasticity. The only problem here is the definition of the climate variable C. What we need is a climate index. There is more than one relevant variable. First, we have temperature, either measured as an annual average or as a maximum or minimum per year. But the hours of sunshine may also matter. And anybody who knows a dry climate like California will be aware of the fact that rain, measured in centimetres per year, is also a relevant variable, as is air humidity. Finally, altitude, windiness, and especially the chilliness of the wind, may be important as well. In short, climate is a multi-dimensional phenomenon. The problem is then how to define C.

A practical start was to experiment with some alternative selections of climate variables and to end up with a best-fitting and intuitively interpretable estimated equation. We used a sample of about 10,000 European households, surveyed among the 'old' members of the European Community. This guaranteed a climatic variation from Berlin to the Channel Islands and from the north of Denmark to the south of Italy. We ended up with *three* variables that seemed relevant for the description of a climate in this context.

Those three climatic variables are *TEMP*, standing for the average annual temperature, *HUM*, standing for average humidity, and *PREC*, standing for

Table 2 Climate Compensation Factors for some European sites

Paris	1.00	Rome	0.95
Berlin	1.11	Sicily	0.94
Copenhagen	1.10	Nice	0.91
London	1.08	Channel Isl.	0.87
Amsterdam	0.99		

precipitation. The composite climate index C is then estimated by

$$\ln(C) = -[0.15 \ln(TEMP) + 0.40 \ln(HUM) + 0.10 \ln(PREC)]$$

In Table 2 we give the resulting climate compensation factors for some European sites, having set the climate index of Paris at 100. Using our estimate of the climate influence on income standards we see from Table 2 that one needs 11 per cent more income in Berlin than in Paris to reach the same income standard.

We notice that this exercise has brought us two results. First, we have estimated the climate effect on income evaluation. It follows that we are able to work out the effect of a change in temperature, humidity, or precipitation on the evaluation of income, a *positive* result. Second, we have found a *normative* result, namely, what compensation factor would be needed in terms of income to neutralize for a climate change. Moreover, we have come more or less unexpectedly to the definition of a climate index which is an aggregate of three dimensions of climate.

In this section we used a relatively simple method to estimate the effects of differences in personal conditions on income evaluation. In the first instance, we estimated the effect of differences in family size. The method is rather unorthodox, as it uses responses to attitude questions as the basic observations. The effect itself is intuitively fairly obvious, and it is investigated elsewhere in the economic literature by observing consumer behavior under the hypothesis that equal purchasing behavior implies an equal preference structure, and hence—although this is not necessarily true—that people with the same consumption pattern evaluate their welfare situation equally.

The second example deals with a much more esoteric case. Climate is not an individual variable but rather a public good. It is part of the environment, like public health, safety in the street, etc. In the second analysis we analysed its effect, while simultaneously constructing an aggregate index which best reflects climate differences in the framework of this problem. Obviously there is no reason why the same method should not be viable to estimate the money value to individuals of changes in the *environment, health,* or *public goods.*

In the scope of this paper we have found that there are traceable welfare differences between individuals, which are caused by specific external factors. It should be remembered that we consider here a narrow welfare concept, as it refers only to that part of welfare which is related to money income.

In the following section we shall consider a more difficult model, where we consider the influence of past and anticipated income on the evaluation of *present* income.

6 The Impact of the Past and the Future on Present Income Evaluation[1]

In the previous models we stressed the dependency of income standards on the concept of an 'anchor income', which we defined to be (net) *current* income. Although the empirical results are intuitively plausible and statistically of good quality, we have to admit that the choice of current income is a rather rough one, dictated by the circumstances. It is well known that income fluctuates a great deal even for regular employees, and that apart from these more or less random fluctuations, income over life is not constant but will follow a first rising and then falling profile, with a maximum somewhere near the age of 40 – although this obviously depends on the job and schooling of the individual. This relation between income and age is frequently called an earnings profile (see Mincer, 1958).

It follows that we may doubt whether the income level of a specific individual at a specific moment in time is the best operationalization of the anchor-income. Are we not looking for a sort of 'permanent income' in the sense of Friedman (1957) to use as an anchor? Let us denote that concept by y_π. Let us assume we know the earning profile of an individual; it is the sequence . . . y_{-1}, y_0, y_1, y_2 . . . where the moment zero is located at present. Then we assume that the permanent income must be a weighted average of the individual's earning profile. For instance, assuming only three periods of interest: the *past* with income y_p, the *present* with income y_o and the *future* with income y_f, we may define the permanent income concept by taking a weighted average of the log-incomes where the weights W_p, W_o, W_f, adding up to one, reflect the relative impact of the past, the present, and future expectations on the formation of the permanent income concept. More specifically, we assume

$$\ln (y_\pi) = W_p \ln (y_p) + W_o \ln (y_o) + W_F \ln (y_F)$$

The weight W_p may be called the *memory* weight and W_f the *anticipation* weight. It is evident that this concept may be refined by the distinction of more than three periods. In fact we may consider time as a continuous variable; then the weight distribution is described by a continuous density function over the time axis.

We estimated this weight pattern by explaining the observed income standards not by current income alone, as done before, but by a weighted average of past, present, and future income levels, where the past and future incomes have been calculated by applying the previously estimated earnings profile. We specified a specific weight pattern in such a way that it depends also on

---

[1] This section is based on van Praag and van Weeren, 1988.

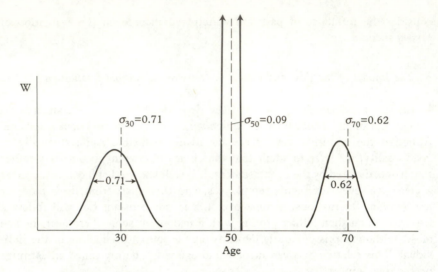

Figure 4 Time-Discounting Density Functions for Various Ages

the *age* of the individual, so as to reflect the intuitive fact that people's time horizon, both backwards and forwards, varies with age. It turned out that the weight pattern could be estimated. It is depicted graphically for three typical ages in Figure 4.

We see two remarkable things. First, the distribution is not symmetrical about the present. Second, the top at μ_τ is for young and old people situated in the past and for people in midlife in the near future. The shape of the density also varies with age, becoming very peaked at midlife. Table 3 (van Praag and van Weeren, 1988) shows the values of μ_τ, W_p, W_o, and W_f for various ages.

We notice explicitly that the weights estimated refer only to the formation of the permanent income concept. The weight of the past might well turn out much greater if we were studying the formation of other standards, say, strength of religious attitudes; similarly, the weight of the past might be much less important (than for income) if we were studying standards regarding

Table 3 Values of μ_τ, W_p, W_o, W_f for various ages

Age	μ_τ	W_p	W_o	W_f
20	−1.32280	0.71557	0.18098	0.10345
30	−0.31780	0.39848	0.47742	0.12409
40	0.27360	0.00135	0.80874	0.18992
50	0.45140	0.00000	0.69937	0.30063
60	0.21560	0.00041	0.90787	0.09172
70	−0.43380	0.45750	0.47642	0.06608

the length of girls' skirts. The weight distribution estimated has to be considered as specific for the phenemenon studied, in this case income standards. In this paper we cannot dwell on the methodological problems posed by the psychological interpretation of these results. We do, however, get the result that the weights are *age*-dependent. It follows that income standards increase if past income increases. This implies that people have higher standards if their past earnings were higher. Likewise standards rise if expectations for the future increase. Moreover, one sees that a specific change in an individual's earnings has a different impact on his standards depending on his age and consequently his distribution of memory and anticipation weights.

This implies that young populations and old populations will have different income standards, given the same distribution of present incomes. It also implies that the same distribution is differently perceived in terms of welfare, according to whether one arrives at that distribution from 'below', in a situation of steady growth, or from 'above' in a situation of steady decline. We may observe again that the analysis yields a *positive* and a *normative* result. First, it describes the impact of income changes over time on income standards. Second, it becomes possible to find equivalent income profiles which yield either momentarily or permanently the same welfare. Finally, we found as a by-product an interesting quantification of the memory and anticipation process, in so far as it concerns income perception and evaluation. This is properly speaking a product of experimental psychology, which sheds light on the perception of time by individuals at different stages of life. We shall resist the temptation to look into it any further at this point.

7 *The Social Reference Process*

At this point it will be sufficiently clear that the evaluation of income varies a lot among individuals and that that variation may be explained to a considerable extent by observable variables related to the respondent. We saw that the main determinants were own current income, family size, climate, and income history and expectations about future income. Up to now all explanations referred to separate response levels, and we have not considered the standard deviation of the log-response, denoted by σ. In this section we will take the whole response pattern into consideration.

Apart from the individual determinants already considered, it is frequently thought that the question as to whether an income is *good* cannot be decided outside of a context. The context is then the incomes of other individuals in the individual's social reference group. If I know practically no one with an income of more than $50,000, then I will consider that income extremely good. On the other hand, if all my social peers earn more than that amount, I will consider the same amount a very bad income. This suggests that the verbal labels will correspond to quantiles in the income distribution of the respondent's social reference group. The label 'good', for instance, will correspond to the 80 per cent quantile. The fact that different social reference groups with different respondents give different answers will then reflect the fact that different people have different income distributions in mind. The response pattern will then be a discrete image of the income distribution of the respondent's social reference group. Let us be more specific now. Let us denote the density function of the income distribution in the population by $f(y)$ and the income distribution in the social reference group of individual n by $f_n(y)$. We then define the *social filter function* $\phi_n(y)$ by the relation $f_n(y) = \phi_n(y)f(y)$. If we interpret the value $f(y)$ as the *fraction* of the income bracket y in the population and $f_n(y)$ as the corresponding fraction in the individual's social reference group, the factor ϕ gets an interesting interpretation. If ϕ equals one, the bracket y has equal importance in the social reference group and in the objective income distribution. If ϕ is larger than one, the individual assigns more than proportionate weight to that bracket, and if ϕ is smaller than one that bracket is less weighted in the social reference group than corresponds with its share in the objective income distribution.

Using this idea I estimated this social filter function. It is depicted in Figure 5, together with the objective income distribution. We call the income level where the filter function reaches its top the *focal point* of the filter. If the filter is very peaked, the individual looking through that filter suffers from social myopia to a large extent. If the filter is flat, there is no social myopia. In that case the individual's social reference group is just society as a whole.

The social filter function differs between individuals. These differences may be partly attributed to objectively observable differences in individual characteristics. These effects have been estimated on the basis of a sample of

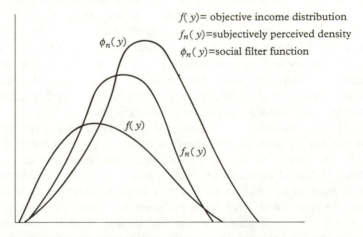

$f(y)$= objective income distribution
$f_n(y)$=subjectively perceived density
$\phi_n(y)$=social filter function

Figure 5 The Objective Income Density and the Social Filter Function

more than 500 American respondents and they give insight into the width of the social reference group, or, to put it differently, the situation of the social focal point and the myopia of different individuals. The main results were that

1. social myopia becomes less if people are better educated;
2. social myopia increases with experience, where we have to be aware that experience and age are strongly correlated;
3. the social focal point varies positively with the income of the respondent;
4. in general the social focal point is situated at a higher income than one's own: people are looking upwards.

Sociologists will not be very surprised by these results. Nevertheless, there are some points to be made. The first is that the definition of a social reference group is not given a priori in terms of who belongs to it and who does not, but the group itself is *estimated* from the data. Second, we observe that in most literature each member of the social reference group gets the same weight in influencing the individual, that is, zero or one, while in this model the weight varies continuously according to the social filter mechanism.[2]

Unfortunately we do not have the space to dwell on the technicalities of the estimation procedure, for which we refer to van Praag (1981), van Praag and Spit (1982), or van der Sar and van Praag (1988).

8   Cardinality or Not?

Up to now our analysis has been cast in ordinal welfare terms. We observed that individuals assign different verbal labels to the same income levels depending on their personal circumstances and outlook on society. Or, to put it differently, there are differences between what people call a *good* income and those differences may be quantitatively explained and predicted. The mechanisms discovered conform pretty well with our intuitive feelings and with other findings in the social sciences. The fundamental question of normative welfare economics is whether we can compare the welfare positions of different individuals in society in the sense that we can evaluate trade-offs. One person gets less and another gets more: what is the net result for society? Does the gain of the second person outweigh the welfare loss of the first person? If we would like to answer that question we must require that such welfare losses and gains can be measured per individual *and* that they may be compared between the two individuals. It seems to me that these requirements are only

---

[2] The reader will notice that I have used terms that suggest an optical filter. Indeed we may think of the social filter mechanism as looking through a lens at society. Some social groups will be magnified, while others become less important than they should. Another analogue of this mechanism is the Bayesian model, where the objective distribution acts as a priori density, the filter as the sample likelihood, and the income distribution of the reference group as the a posteriori density.

realized if we adopt *conventions* of measurement and comparison. Let us make a further excursion to the physical concept of *temperature*. Whether the change from 15°C to 20°C represents the same change in temperature for an individual as from 20°C to 25°C is impossible to answer. If we assume that it does, it is a pure convention. If we carry out psychophysical experiments, where we measure transpiration or ask the test person at what temperature above 20°C he feels that the change is equal to the first change from 15°C to 20°C, we can construct subjective measures of temperature perception, but such measures present the same problem. They only represent comparable changes *if we agree by convention that they may be compared*. And similar remarks can be made with respect to interpersonal comparability.

The upshot is that there is no natural measure, but that:

- measures have to be accepted by convention;
- a measurement method defines an empirical concept;
- theoretical concepts are of a metaphysical nature;
- a measurement method of an empirical concept is acceptable, if the empirical concept, thus defined, behaves as the theoretical concept it is supposed to measure;
- in case of insufficient conformity between theory and empirical concept either the theory has to be modified or the measurement method and the empirical concept it has been based on have to be modified. Most scientific progress basically consists of a reshaping of theory and/or empirical concepts to improve insufficient conformity between them.

Where do we have to situate our own research, briefly outlined in the previous sections? I believe that it may be situated as follows. We have defined a measurement method and found an empirical concept: the virtual income standards, the values $u_1, \ldots, u_6$, the average log-response μ and the standard deviation σ of log-responses. We have been able to derive interesting empirical laws about those concepts. We did not formally say which theoretical concept we attempt to measure. At this moment we are typically in the situation that *we have found an empirical phenomenon in search of a theoretical metaphysical counterpart*.

We could call that metaphysical concept *welfare* W. Then we would have found that someone's W increases with income and that W is essentially a function of income and some individually determined characteristics $\mathbf{X}$. We would find that $W(y_i; \mathbf{X}) = u_i$ (i = 1, $\ldots$,6) where y_i stands for the response on the IEQ. We would like to equate the empirical W with the metaphysical concept of *welfare*.[3] As long as $W(.)$ empirically behaves as the welfare concept should behave, I do not see much problem with sticking to that convention. However, we certainly cannot *prove* that we are measuring the metaphysical concept of *welfare*. On the other hand, it cannot be disproved either.

---

[3] As in this whole paper the welfare concept is a partial concept: it is only related to income. The concepts of happines, satisfaction, and welfare in the general sense are wider concepts.

There is one thing which makes us reluctant to accept a value W that varies between $-\infty$ and $+\infty$ as a measure of welfare. As human beings we are unable to differentiate our feelings on an unbounded scale. All evaluations and ratings we know of are on finite bounded scales like 1–10 or A–E. This prompts us to normalize welfare between zero and one. So we define

$$W(\ln y_i; \mu, \sigma) = F(u_i) = F[(\ln y_i - \mu)/\sigma]$$

where $F(.)$ is a distribution function, increasing from zero to one, and where the parameters μ and σ are the mean and the standard deviation of the log-answers on the IEQ. We saw in Table 1 that the values of u were practically symmetrical about zero. If we consider them as quantiles of the normal distribution, we see that they roughly correspond with equal probability jumps. That is, $N(u_i) = (2i-)/12$. This does not hold exactly, but to a striking extent. Now, there is a theoretical argument that this is not an accident (see van Praag, 1971; Kapteyn, 1977). The person who responds to the IEQ does this with a certain response strategy. His objective is to give the most informative response. This is clearly not done if all response levels are so near to each other that all income levels would roughly correspond to the same welfare level. On the contrary, the response is given in such a way that the welfare deferences between the levels are maximal. This is realized by choosing the six levels in such a way that each level corresponds with the midpoint of one sixth of the interval $(0,1)$, the range of $W(.)$.[4] It follows that this would imply that $F(.)$ should be taken to be the normal distribution function. Welfare taken as a function of y instead of $\ln(y)$ is then described by a log-normal distribution function.

In view of our earlier interpretation of the IEQ response as a description of the income distribution of the individual's social reference group, we come now to the equality: *welfare evaluation of* y = *percentage below that income in the social reference group*.[5] If we accept this cardinalization, we may formulate welfare comparisons. This cardinalization has a certain plausibility. In van Praag (1968) I formulated the same cardinalization but without any empirical corroboration like the one given here. There I gave other theoretical arguments, which I believe still to be valid, but which I will leave out of the present context.

The same cardinal applications may be based on any other functional increasing specification of $F(.)$. However, the attractive identification of the u-values then gets lost.

---

[4] Exactly speaking we have roughly $W[\ln(y_i)] = (2i - 1)/12$.
[5] This statement has been formulated as a basic hypothesis by Kapteyn (1977) and by Kapteyn, Wansbeek, and Buyze (1978).

9 *Conclusion*

In this paper I have outlined a method and results to get some idea of how individuals evaluate income levels. We saw that this is possible by a fairly simple and intuitively plausible set of questions, the so-called IEQ. The result can only be regarded as ordinal welfare measurement, when we assume that verbal labels have the same emotional connotation to different respondents. If we are willing to apply a plausible cardinalization, such that welfare differences between levels are equalized, we have also found a cardinal welfare measure, useful for normative intra- and interpersonal welfare comparisons.

Obviously the method has to be corroborated still further. Moreover, it may be applied to the measurement of standards for other concepts as well, for example, wealth, amount of education, age, expenditures on specific commodities. Some work has been done in that direction (see for instance van Praag, Dubnoff, and van der Sar, 1985, 1988).

I believe that this is a new and fruitful alley for tackling welfare comparison problems in the sense of positive and normative science.

BIBLIOGRAPHY

ARROW, K.J. (1964). 'The Role of Securities in the Optimal Allocation of Risk-Bearing', *Review of Economic Studies*, 31, 91–6.

ATKINSON A.B. (1970). 'On the Measurement of Inequality', *Journal of Economic Theory*, 2, 244–63.

COHEN STUART, A.J. (1889). *Bijdrage tot de Theorie der Progressieve Inkomstenbelastingen*. The Hague: Nijhoff.

EDGEWORTH, F.Y. (1881). *Mathematical Psychics*. London: Paul.

FRIEDMAN, M. (1957). *A Theory of the Consumption Function*. Princeton, NJ: Princeton, University Press.

HAGENAARS, A.J.M., and VAN PRAAG, B.M.S.(1985). 'A Synthesis of Poverty Line Definitions', *Review of income and Wealth*, 31, 139–53.

HELSON, H. (1964). *Adaptation-Level Theory: An Experimental and Systematic Approach to behaviour*. New York: Harper.

KAPTEYN, A. (1977). 'A theory of Preference Formation'. Ph.D. thesis, Leyden University, Leyden.

—— and VAN PRAAG, B.M.S. (1976). 'A New Approach to the Construction of Family Equivalence Scales', *European Economic Review*, 7, 313–35.

—— WANSBEEK, T.J. and BUYZE, J. (1978). 'The Dynamics of Preference Formation', *Economics Letters*, 1, 93–7.

MINCER, J. (1958). 'Investment in Human Capital and Personal Income Distribution', *Journal of Political Economy*, 66, 281–302.

PARETO, V. (1904), *Manuel d'économie politique*. Paris: Giard and Brière.

RAINWATER, L. (1974). *What Money Buys: Inequality and the Social Meaning of Income.* New York: Basic Books.

ROBBINS, L. (1932). *An Essay on the Nature and Significance of Economic Science,* 1st edn. London: Macmillan.

SAMUELSON, P. A. (1974). *Foundations of Economic Analysis.* Cambridge, Mass.: Harvard University Press.

SARIS, W. E. (1988). *Sociometric Research,* ed. W. E. Saris and I. N. Gallhofer. London: Macmillan.

SEN, A. K. (1973). *On Economic Inequality.* Oxford: Clarendon Press.

—— (1982). *Choice, Welfare and Measurement.* Cambridge, Mass.: M. I. T. Press.

SIMON, H. A. (1979). *Models of Thought.* New Haven, Conn.: Yale University Press, ch. 1.

STEVEN, S. S. (1975). *Psychophysics: Introduction to its Perceptual, Neural and Social Propects.* New York: John Wiley.

SUPPES, P., and WINCK, M. (1954). 'An Axiomatization of Utility based on the Notion of Utility Differences', *Management Science,* 1, 259–70.

VAN DER SAR, N. L., VAN PRAAG, B. M. S., and DUBNOFF, S. (1988). 'Evaluation Questions and Income Utility', in B. Munier (ed.), *Risk, Decision and Rationality.* Dordrecht: Reidal, 77–96.

VAN DOORN, L., and VAN PRAAG, B. M. S. (1988). 'The Measurement of Income Satisfaction', in W. E. Saris and I. N. Gallhofer (eds.), *Sociometric Research.* Houndmills: Mcmillan Press, 230–46.

VAN PRAAG, B. M. S. (1968). *Individual Welfare Functions and Consumer Behavior: A Theory of Rational Irrationality.* Amsterdam: North Holland, 235.

—— (1971). 'The Welfare Function of Income in Belgium: An Empirical Investigation', *European Economic Review,* 2, 337–69.

VAN PRAAG, B. M. S. (1981). 'Reflections on Theory of Individual Welfare Functions', in American Statistical Association, 1981 Proceedings of the Business and Economic Statistics Section, Washington DC.

—— (1988). 'Climate Equivalence Scales: An Application of a General Method', *European Economics Review,* 32, 1019–24.

—— (1989). 'Cardinal and Ordinal Utility: An Integration of the Two Dimensions of the Welfare Concept', forthcoming in *Journal of Econometrics.*

—— DUBNOFF, S. and VAN DER SAR, N. L. (1985). 'From Judgements to Norms: Measuring the Social Meaning of Income, Age and Education', report 8509/E, Econometric Institute, Erasmus University, Rotterdam.

—— and SPIT, J. S. (1982). 'The Social Filter Process and Income Evaluation: An Empirical Study in the Social Reference Mechanism', report 82.08, Center for Research in Public Economics, Leyden University.

—— and VAN DER SAR, N. L.(1988). 'Household Cost Functions and Equivalence Scales', *Journal of Human Resources,* 23/2, 193–210.

—— and VAN WEEREN, J. (1988). 'Memory and Anticipation Processes and their Significance for Social Security and Income Inequality', in S. Maital (ed.), *Applied Behavioural Economics.* Brighton: Wheatsheaf Books, ii. 731–51.

B.M.S. van Praag: The Relativity of the Welfare Concept

Commentary by Siddiq Osmani

Professor van Praag's paper presents in a distilled form the outcome of two decades of research on a novel approach to the evaluation of individual welfare. The basic tool is an 'income evaluation questionnaire' in which people are asked to mention the income levels which in their own judgement correspond to certain prespecified verbal labels such as 'good', 'bad', 'sufficient', etc. This information is then used to develop an interpersonally comparable measure of utility.

Over the years, van Praag and his colleagues have strengthened the foundations of this approach and applied it to a wide variety of issues concerning social policy and social assessment. In their expert hands, the approach has proved amazingly versatile. Van Praag gives a flavour of this versatility by either discussing or referring to many of the applications of the approach. There is, however, one potential application which is not taken up in his paper but which is especially germane to the context of the present volume. It relates to the question: how well can individual utilities, as measured by van Praag, serve as the basis of social welfare evaluation? This question is motivated by van Praag's resurrection of interpersonally comparable utility. While elaborating the mainstream approach to utility, van Praag rightly reminds us that with the denial of interpersonal comparability of utility in the 1930s, welfare economics lost much of its power to compare the goodness of alternative social states. However, as he again correctly notes, several economists, especially those interested in the issues of inequality and poverty, continued to develop the framework for making social welfare judgements by assuming comparability of individual welfare. In doing this, these economists were, in the words of van Praag, 'building the first floor when the foundations are not yet laid'. This is because the underlying presumption of comparable utility remained to be established. Van Praag does not object to this method, for he is quite willing to accept comparable utility as a primitive concept if that is what is needed to make meaningful social welfare judgements, but notes that it would nevertheless 'be nice if we could find some credible method of getting evidence on utility'. This is precisely what he claims to have done; as he says, 'The main message of the paper is then that from attitude questions an ordinal but interpersonally comparable individual welfare concept may be constructed which is "operationally useful"'.

One is therefore led to ask: can the van Praag utilities, interpersonally comparable as they are, serve as the missing foundation of social welfare evaluation? The paper explicitly avoids pursuing this question, being content merely to

Helpful comments from Amartya Sen and Bernard van Praag are gratefully acknowledged without implicating either of them with the views expressed here.

demonstrate that the concept of interpersonally comparable utility has an empirical content. But this is the question I wish to examine here, thus going beyond the paper itself, but building on its empirical findings. My method is to examine closely the concept of utility that emerges from van Praag's method of measurement, and to see if this concept is the appropriate one in the context of social welfare evaluation. My analysis raises some doubts in this regard. In brief, while I accept that van Praag's utility numbers do have the property of interpersonal comparability, I doubt if these numbers represent the concept of individual welfare that is relevant for building a social welfare function.

But first I want to make two preliminary remarks, to clear the way for subsequent discussion. First, by examining whether van Praag's utility numbers can serve as the basis for judging social well-being, we are staying firmly within the 'welfarist' tradition, that is, the tradition in which individual utilities are seen to be the relevant informational basis for arriving at a judgement on social well-being. As is well known, this tradition has recently come under severe attack from Rawls (1971), Sen (1987), and others who have exposed the inadequacy of utility as the basis of social welfare. Our intention here is not to defend the welfarist approach from these attacks, but merely to see whether within its own terms the welfarist approach can make good use of the van Praag utilities.

The second preliminary remark has to do with the cardinality of utility. Van Praag notes that the utility numbers yielded by his measurement method are essentially ordinal in nature, but towards the end of his paper he also proposes a specific method of arriving at cardinal utility. Is this cardinalization essential for the purpose of making social welfare judgements? Van Praag sometimes writes as if it is. For example, after noting that mainstream economics has for a long time accepted Robbins's denial of the existence of a measurable cardinal utility function, he explains its consequence thus: 'Clearly this robbed any normative economics, which has to be based on the evaluation of individual situations and the evaluation of the state of the society as a whole by an aggregate of some sort of individual welfare evaluations, of any foundations.' The suggestion here is that the absence of cardinality precludes the possibility of aggregating individual welfares into social welfare. Similarly, while referring to the practice of those economists who use a utility-based social welfare function, he comments that their analyses are 'either explicitly or implicitly based on a cardinal utility concept', which 'leads to a rather schizophrenic situation in economics as some authors, while on the one hand painstakingly ordinal, in normative studies accept cardinality in the way pictured above, if the need arises,'. Once again, cardinality is seen to be an essential attribute of utilities which enter into a social welfare function.

However, there is nothing essential about cardinality. In fact, it was not Robbins's denial of cardinality as such, but rather his denial of interpersonal comparability, that precluded the possibility of social aggregation. Also, the use of utility-based social welfare functions by the 'painstakingly ordinal' economists does not necessarily imply their tacit acceptance of cardinality, though it does imply their acceptance of interpersonal comparability. Indeed, it is the presence or absence of interpersonal comparability that is crucial. The absence of cardinality does not preclude comparability, nor does its presence ensure it – the two are entirely independent attributes. Recent advances in social choice theory have shown that, of the two, cardinality is not essential in the same way as interpersonal comparability is for permitting meaningful evaluation of social welfare. If utility is assumed to be cardinal but interpersonally non-comparable, then it becomes impossible to evaluate social welfare in a way that will satisfy a set of very reasonable restrictions on the notion of social welfare. On the other hand, with ordinal but interpersonally comparable utilities there would typically exist some reasonable way of evaluating social welfare.[1] Of course, certain methods of evaluation would be ruled out in the absence of cardinality – for example, the utilitarian principle – but other methods will remain open – for example, the Rawlsian leximin. We shall, therefore, leave aside the cardinalized version of van Praag's utility measure, take the measure in its original form, that is, the form of interpersonally comparable ordinal utility, and proceed to examine its usefulness for the purpose of evaluating social welfare.

We begin by asking the question: what do the van Praag utility numbers really mean? To answer this question, it will be helpful to see how van Praag deduces the various properties of his utility numbers. Two of these properties are of special interest in this context: the relativity and comparability of welfare. Relativity refers to the property that the welfare of an individual, to the extent that welfare can be derived from money, depends not on absolute income as is traditionally supposed but on relative income. Comparability refers to the property that the same utility number reflects the same level of welfare for everyone. These two properties are deduced empirically in the following manner.

Each individual is asked to attach certain income levels to a number of verbal labels such as 'good', 'bad', etc. Van Praag then converts these income levels into what he calls utility numbers by following a certain methodology. After studying the data across individuals certain regularities are observed. First, it is found that different people attach different income levels to the same verbal label. That is, what is a 'good' income for one person may not be 'good' for another. In general, the higher a person's current income the higher is his estimate of what a 'good' income is. From this it is deduced that welfare is a relative concept (hence the title of the paper). Second, it is observed that although different people attach different income levels to the same verbal label, when converted into utility numbers all these income levels are mapped into (almost) the same number. In other words, a given verbal label is transformed into the same utility number for everyone; there is a one-to-one correspondence between verbal labels and utility numbers, except for a small random variation. This means that if a certain utility number means 'good' for me it will also mean

---

[1] These issues are discussed in Sen (1970).

'good' for you. From this it is deduced that individual welfares are interpersonally comparable.

It is, however, important to note that behind these deductions there lies an implicit act of faith, without which neither the relativity nor the comparability of welfare can be established, despite the empirical evidence marshalled by van Praag. This act of faith consists in the untested assumption that the same verbal label implies the same *level* of welfare for everyone.

To see the role played by this assumption, take the relativity issue first. Van Praag often writes as if his empirical findings *demonstrate* the intrinsic relativity of individual welfare. But this is not quite so. What his empirical findings show is that the 'good' income for a rich man is higher than the 'good' income for a poor man. Evidently, the conception of 'good' is a relative one. In other words, the empirical evidence proves the relativity of verbal labels. To go on from here to claim that the conception of welfare is also relative, one must then assume that the same verbal label means the same *level* of welfare for everyone. In other words, one must assume a fixed correspondence between verbal labels and welfare levels so that the observed relativity of labels can be interpreted as relativity of welfare. Van Praag clearly makes this assumption, but it remains implicit.

The same assumption is also crucial for deducing the comparability of welfare. The claim that the utility numbers reflect interpersonally comparable welfare levels must be based on the demonstration that the same utility number stands for the same level of welfare for everyone. But van Praag's empirical evidence cannot, on its own, demonstrate this. The evidence merely shows that, given the methodology of converting incomes into utilities, the same utility number implies the same *verbal label* for everyone. In order to claim that the same utility number also reflects the same *level of welfare* for everyone, one must then bring in the assumption that a given verbal label stands for the same level of welfare for everyone—the same act of faith as before. To put it differently, the empirical evidence establishes a one-to-one correspondence between utility numbers and verbal labels, and the act of faith establishes a one-to-one correspondence between verbal labels and welfare; only by combining the two can one claim that there is a one-to-one correspondence between van Praag's utility numbers and individual welfare.

Thus both relativity and comparability of welfare, as deduced by van Praag, depends crucially on an act of faith and not on empirical evidence alone. There is nothing intrinsically wrong with that, for, as van Praag frequently points out, all science must start with some untested primitive concepts. The question is: how plausible is the primitive concept chosen, and are there any alternatives which may be no less plausible but which lead to very different interpretations of the same empirical phenomena?

The way van Praag justifies his particular primitive concept is to argue that the same 'verbal label' must mean the same thing to all people. Among other reasons, he mentions the socio-cultural one that members of the same community must have harmonized their linguistic conventions sufficiently well to mean roughly the same thing when they use a verbal label such as 'good'. In particular, he suggests that the labels must have the same 'emotional content' for everyone. All this sounds plausible enough. But van Praag then takes a further step which is harder to justify. He takes it for granted that the same emotional content means the same *level* of welfare. It is this final step which enables him to equate verbal labels with welfare levels, and this equation in turn allows him to declare that welfare is relative and that his utility numbers reflect interpersonally comparable welfare levels. But there is no a priori reason why the emotional content of verbal labels should be seen in terms of *levels* of welfare. In other words, when you and I describe the respective income levels x and y as 'good', we may have the same emotional perception of these income levels, but the perception need not be that of equal welfare levels. Other interpretations are also possible. For example, x and y may yield different levels of welfare to you and me respectively, but y may give me the same welfare *relative* to what I consider to be the average norm, as x does to you *relative* to what you consider to be the average norm. In this interpretation, verbal labels do have the same emotional content, but this content now consists of ratios rather than levels of welfare.

I shall argue that this is not at all a fanciful interpretation. On the contrary, this will be seen to be the most natural interpretation of van Praag's findings, if we start from the conventional premiss that the level of welfare depends on the absolute level of income. Of course, this premiss contradicts van Praag's conception of the relativity of welfare; but, as we have seen, this property of relativity derives solely from the untested primitive concept that the same verbal label implies the same level of welfare. Since there is no a priori justification for accepting this, there is no compelling reason to accept the relativity property either. We are therefore entitled to substitute for van Praag's primitive concept the more conventional one that welfare depends on absolute income. And once we do that, the verbal labels as well as the utility numbers constructed by van Praag are seen to reflect ratios rather than levels of welfare.

To see how this happens, recall how the utility number is derived by van Praag. It is given by $u_i = (\ln c_i - \mu)/\sigma$, where c_i is the income level attached to the ith verbal label, and μ and σ are respectively the mean and standard deviation of the logarithms of income levels attached by an individual to all the verbal labels. Van Praag has found that except for a random variation, the number u_i attached to the ith verbal label is about the same for all individuals; this is the basis of his contention that the same utility number stands for the same verbal label. Now to see the relationship between u_i and welfare, we make the simplifying assumption that σ is constant across individuals and then normalize it to unity.[2] Also note that μ is really the logarithm of the geometric mean (m) of the incomes $c_i (i = 1, \ldots, n)$ attached to n verbal labels. So the utility number u_i can be seen

---

[2] This assumption simplifies the intuitive exposition without detracting anything from van Praag's basic contentions regarding the relationship between utility numbers and verbal labels.

to be the proportionate difference between c_i and m. Under the conventional premiss that welfare depends on absolute income van Praag's utility numbers can, therefore, be seen to represent the proportionate difference between the welfare derived from a given level of income and the welfare derived from some notion of average income. In other words, these utility numbers reflect some notion of relative welfare. Note that this is not the same thing as saying, as van Praag does, that welfare is relative. For him, welfare is an intrinsically relative concept (in the sense of being a function of relative income), and his utility numbers reflect the absolute *levels* of welfare thus conceived. What I am saying in contrast is that welfare is an absolute concept (in the sense of being a function of absolute income) and that van Praag's utility numbers reflect the *ratios*, and not the levels, of welfare thus conceived.

Now recall the empirically established correspondence between verbal labels and utility numbers, and add the just-described correspondence between utility numbers and welfare ratios. The result is that the same verbal label will now be seen to stand for the same welfare ratio for everyone. Thus the general proposition that verbal labels have the same emotional content for everyone still remains valid, but that content now consists of ratios rather than levels of welfare. This argument illustrates the point made earlier that there is no a priori justification for interpreting the same emotional content of verbal labels as the same level of welfare. It is only by virtue of this interpretation that van Praag is able to claim that his utility numbers reflect interpersonally comparable welfare *levels*. If we reject his interpretation and start instead from the conventional premiss that welfare depends on absolute income, then the very same empirical findings imply that van Praag's utility numbers reflect interpersonally comparable welfare *ratios*.

This interpretation of utility numbers as ratios rather than levels of welfare creates obvious problems for social welfare evaluation. A welfarist social welfare function is typically constructed by aggregating the levels of individual welfare. If the van Praag utility numbers are seen to convey information about the ratios rather than levels of individual welfare, then clearly these numbers cannot be used as the building blocks of a social welfare function. This can only be done if we discard the conventional premiss that welfare depends on absolute income and embrace instead van Praag's own primitive concept, for in that case the utility numbers would indeed reflect levels of welfare. But since van Praag's primitive concept has no obvious superiority over the conventional one, doubts remain about the usefulness of his utility numbers as the foundation of social welfare evaluation. This is not to deny that his method of measuring the so-called 'utility' numbers can none the less be very useful for many practical purposes, as has been amply demonstrated by many interesting applications of his method. What has been questioned here is its relevance for a utility-based evaluation of social welfare.

BIBLIOGRAPHY

RAWLS , J. (1971). *A Theory of Justice*. Cambridge, Mass.: Harvard University Press.
SEN, A.K. (1970). *Collective Choice and Social Welfare*. San Francisco: Holden-Day; republished, Amsterdam: North-Holland, 1979.
—— (1987). *On Ethics and Economics*. Oxford: Basil Blackwell.

Pluralism and the Standard of Living

Paul Seabright

The proper province of a government's economic policy is the enhancement of the standard of living of its citizens. Such a remark, while true, is hardly informative. For in what does the standard of living consist? The intention of this paper is to sketch part of an answer to this question, involving some necessary (though not sufficient) conditions that characterize the concept. In particular, I want to examine how a notion of the standard of living, intended as a criterion of use to governments implementing policy, might be sensitive to a relatively pluralist theory of society. By a pluralist theory I understand an account of how society should be arranged that incorporates the possibility of multiple and non-trivially divergent views of the good life for individual human beings. The rider about non-trivial divergence is important: a theory of society is not pluralist merely because it assigns some citizens to be philosophers and others to be accountants, snake-charmers, or car-park attendants. A genuinely pluralist theory must count it a social good that there may exist multiple views of the individual good that are not subsumable under an encompassing theory of the individual good. This does not imply that a pluralist social theory must be neutral between all or even many theories of the individual good; for it to count as pluralist, it is enough for it to be compatible with the assertion of more than one theory of the individual good. I shall not argue for the correctness of such a point of view. In this paper I want to see instead whether it is possible for a government's economic policies to incorporate it if it is correct. Or does the very notion of an economic policy presuppose that a government has its own comprehensive theory of the individual good? Nevertheless, although I do not consider the correctness of pluralism as such, I shall argue that the possibility of a pluralist economic policy has important implications for the coherence of pluralism even in principle.

The argument proceeds in four stages. In the first I shall argue for the general propriety of allowing a moral or political theory to depend intrinsically on the practical limitations upon implementing its recommendations. By this I mean more than the fatuous point that a theory should not make impossible recommendations. I mean that our choice of a moral or political theory should not always be significantly influenced by our intuitive reactions to what it recommends in impossible or sufficiently unlikely circumstances. In the second stage I shall use this conclusion, along with a series of specific constraints on imple-

Many people have made helpful comments on an earlier version, both participants at the WIDER conference and people at meetings in Cambridge and at the University of East Anglia. The present version has benefited from a number of suggestions made in Derek Parfit's original discussion of the paper, as well as from comments by Tom Baldwin, Jane Heal, Christine Korsgaard, and Martha Nussbaum.

mentation, to help characterize the notion of the standard of living, giving some necessary conditions that any adequate standard must meet. In the third stage I shall draw analogies with other arguments in philosophy and economics that illuminate the connection between this notion and a pluralist theory of society. In the fourth stage I shall use the notion thus characterized to answer some specific questions about living standards and pluralism. These include the question of how the standard of living can incorporate values that are specific to certain cultures without thereby becoming relativist, and the question of whether economic policies need be intrinsically biased towards what is sometimes called commoditization, and to the market economy.

1 The Limitations on Moral Theories

It is a common practice among philosophers and social theorists to test the adequacy of a general theory by searching for possible counter-examples. Robustness against counter-example is definitive of a successful general theory, and on some views definitive of a theory, *tout court*. In ethics and social philosophy, where the data of our theories consist of our intuitive reactions to different situations, this search frequently takes the form of developing elaborately artificial situations designed to abstract away from the messy and confusing detail of every day. Thus we may situate moral dilemmas on Mars or behind a veil of ignorance or on tramlines stacked with Nobel Prizewinners, rather than in the Cabinet or in *EastEnders*[1] or in our own families. The process by which the intuitions in these abstract cases inform our more general judgements has been variously characterized, and John Rawls's notion of 'reflective equilibrium' represents one of the clearest and best known of such accounts.[2] While I have no intention of disputing the frequent usefulness and clarificatory value of such exercises,[3] I do want to argue that we can sometimes reasonably object to the result of such a thought experiment that the situation described is improbable or bizarre. The reason for this is not that I wish to reject the idea that a general theory must be general. 'Not *Fa*' is still and will always be conclusively incompatible with 'For all *x*, *Fx*'. The objection instead is to the idea that the judgements delivered by intuition in improbable cases must always amount to counter-examples.[4]

This line of argument makes best sense within a broadly naturalistic view of ethics. Our ethical intuitions are the product of a long process of both biological and cultural evolution. This evolution has been shaped in a major way by the

---

[1] A soap opera on British television.

[2] Rawls, 1971, esp. 48–51.

[3] Indeed, the exercise of the imagination is an essential component in our moral thinking.

[4] It is of course true that our *initial* reactions to improbable situations may well change on further reflection. It is then trivially true that initial judgements do not always constitute counter-examples. The claim here is the stronger one that *settled* judgements of improbable situations do not always constitute counter-examples.

need to cope with certain recurrent problems and difficulties faced by human beings in society. It has been shaped much less by very rare problems and difficulties that have affected very few people. And, at the risk of labouring the point, I should add that it has not been shaped at all by the need to cope with situations that have never happened or could never happen. It should not be surprising, therefore, if the intuitions we have concerning improbable or impossible situations turn out to be quixotic or mercurial. It is unwise to trust them very far.

At this point it is important to distinguish two conclusions that do not follow from this naturalistic line of reasoning, in order to protect from guilt by association the conclusion that does. First, from the fact that certain moral intuitions have arisen in us as a result of the need to cope with evolutionary contingencies it does not follow that these intuitions are morally defensible ones for us to have: aggression, vindictiveness, and jealousy all have comprehensible evolutionary roots. Instead, what the naturalistic argument illuminates is a question at the heart of the method of reflective equilibrium: do we have any reason to think that an equilibrium exists? Our intuitions can be considered as inputs to this reflective process. Certain requirements of consistency may have been imposed on those of our intuitions that have felt the evolutionary squeeze; others which have never done so may well be wildly inconsistent with what we believe in more familiar contexts. If we require a moral theory *both* to respect the requirements of reflective equilibrium *and* to be applicable to all logically possible situations, we may require the impossible.

A second unwarranted conclusion would be that this evolutionary reasoning implies an anti-objectivist or even just a non-cognitivist account of ethics. Many aspects of reality are too complex for many of reality's inhabitants to understand. The findings of modern physics are certainly beyond the comprehension of a dog, and we have no guarantee that the physical nature of reality will not turn out to be beyond our own comprehension too. To believe that we alone in the animal kingdom had reached the evolutionary plateau that would enable us to comprehend our own environment in its entirety would be a return to the image of ourselves as a chosen species, with no longer a God to be chosen by. So if likewise it turned out that we could not develop ethical theories to cover all possible contingencies without veering into contradictions, that would be a comment upon our moral capacities, not upon the existence or otherwise of objective moral truths.

The conclusion that does follow from this naturalistic argument is that, if we cannot be sure that there exists a moral theory that consistently satisfies our intuitions in all logically possible cases, we had better not throw out all candidates for a theory that happen to fail the test of our intuitions in certain improbable circumstances. We must find ways to choose among those theories that satisfy our intuitions in a sufficiently large number of cases. And here it seems to me inescapable to judge between cases not merely on grounds of number but also on grounds of importance. This is not the place to propose a detailed criterion, but such a criterion will certainly tend, other things being equal, to ascribe greater weight to our intuitions concerning cases that are more central to our everyday practices of judging, evaluating, and acting, than to those that are not.[5]

This issue bears a close relation to an issue in the literature on social choice theory. That literature has been much concerned with the condition of unrestricted domain, which is a condition requiring any reasonable social welfare function or social decision function to apply to any logically possible ordering of individual preferences. To some it seems obvious that the question of what a defensible social decision function should be is independent of the particular decision problems it is applied to in any individual case: if a particular outcome is impossible, it is ruled out of the choice set as infeasible, and if a particular combination of preferences is impossible, it is ruled out as an input to the function. But at all events this infeasibility should not affect the choice of the original function. In other words, on this view you should first decide the moral theory and then apply it to some particular choices; there is no sense in allowing your choice of a moral theory to depend on what choices you will happen to face.

The problem with such a line of argument is that by imposing the condition of unrestricted domain along with other conditions (such as that the function respect transitivity), one effectively requires social preferences over feasible outcomes to be sensitive to what social preferences *would* be over outcomes that are improbable or physically impossible. This might not matter if we knew that social welfare functions compatible with all our intuitions existed. But the social choice literature has documented with depressing thoroughness the circumstances in which *no* social welfare function may exist and satisfy the restrictions that we might intuitively wish to place on it. It is clear that some of our intuitions somewhere may have to give. To insist upon retaining the condition of unrestricted domain is then to admit only those social welfare functions that fail to satisfy some of our other intuitions. The result is paradoxical: the price of requiring a theory to be compatible with all *possible* preferences over states consists in no longer requiring the theory to be compatible with even all *actual* preferences over theories.

The main reason, then, for not necessarily requiring a moral theory to satisfy our intuitions in improbable or impossible circumstances is that a theory compatible with all our intuitions may not exist. A subsidiary reason, familiar from considerations in the philosophy of language, is that it may be dubiously intelli-

---

[5] This is not the same as a procedure that weights cases according to their probability of occurrence. Some cases might have a low probability of occurrence but still be sufficiently like actual cases to be a valuable test of our intuitions. Others might be equally improbable, but so different in nature from actual cases as to be useless to us. Examples of the former occur when we ask questions like: 'If it were possible, by pressing a button, painlessly to kill an unknown and distant individual with no ties to family and friends, would it be wrong to do so?' An example of the latter might be the question: 'Would loyalty be so important a virtue if human beings reproduced asexually and did not age?'

gible to ascribe to creatures capable of intentional action preferences and beliefs bizarrely different from our own. It is not always evident what may count as a genuine possibility, and certain situations may appear intelligible until we inquire closely just what circumstances would make us judge that such a possibility had indeed occurred.[6] This is a particularly powerful argument against the condition of unrestricted domain of preferences in the social choice literature. Here it underlines that in addition to the uncertain *reliability* of our intuitions in improbable or impossible circumstances, we must consider the uncertain *intelligibility* of those hypothetical circumstances themselves.

In the context of the present argument the upshot is this. A political theory, which is one kind of moral theory, deploys a variety of moral concepts in accordance with our intuitions about their application. One with which this paper will be much concerned is the concept of a contract, but there are of course many others, concepts like utility, the good life, self-respect, dignity, obligation, right, the citizen, and so on. I am arguing that it will often be legitimate to characterize a political theory in terms of its adequacy to these concepts as we actually have them, not as we might have had them. For example, it is not in itself an objection to retributive theories of punishment that under conceivable circumstances (those described by Nagel (1976) and Parfit (1976) in their discussions of brain bisection, for instance) the boundaries between persons might be uncertain and the question 'Who committed this crime?' might have no answer. Our theories of punishment have developed to deal with persons as they are. And as they are, persons are distinct entities characterized by physical continuity and a high degree of psychological continuity. If grotesque possibilities become actual we may, of course, need to develop our theories to cope with them. But unless there is some real chance of their doing so we would be unwise to allow our choice of a theory of punishment to be determined by their mere possibility.

There is nothing unusual or original in this form of argument. The emphasis in Rawls's recent work on the political, not metaphysical nature of justice as fairness[7] can best be understood as calling attention to the need to fashion justice to the needs of human communities that already have enough cohesion and common purpose to make justice possible at all. Using a theory of justice to speak to societies so fragmented that they cannot begin to co-operate is a futile exercise, one which therefore teaches us nothing about the kind of justice that more unified communities require. We can say more: if certain rules could never be implemented in any community that was recognizably like our own, then a theory of justice had better respect that constraint, and not seek to judge communities by their degree of resemblance to communities in which such rules are possible.

---

[6] For instance, it may seem logically possible that there should exist a creature all of whose beliefs were false, until one begins to reflect what circumstances could lead us to attribute entirely false beliefs to a language user. We would cease to call such a creature a language user long before that point had been reached.

[7] Rawls, 1985.

2 Constraints and the Standard of Living

It was stated earlier that a government's economic policy should concern itself with the standard of living of its citizens. I want now to turn this around and claim that the way to understand the notion of the standard of living is as that aspect of individuals' well-being that falls within the proper sphere of society's concern. My perspective in making this claim will be broadly contractarian.[8] Society is the institution of co-operation between individuals to their mutual benefit (it may not be only that but it is at least that). In particular, society makes possible the implementation of a framework – involving, for example, property rights and the organization of both production and consumption – without which individuals could not enjoy many of the activities that are central to their well-being. I am not here concerned with the difficult question as to whether an adequate theory of justice must ensure that all individuals are at least as well off in society as they would be on their own (the greatest problem for such a view being posed not by some of the very badly off, whose position is certainly unjust, but by able and law-abiding members of society who in the state of nature would be successful cocaine barons).[9] It is enough for my purposes to observe that in taking part in the institutions of production, consumption, and exchange as they in fact exist, all individuals gain benefits from the co-operation that underlies these institutions. We can therefore reasonably ask what features of these institutions would have emerged from a process of agreement, or more formally of contract, between the individuals concerned, if society had indeed emerged from agreement instead of higgledy-piggledy from history.

Many such features will depend upon how precisely such a contract is specified (for instance, whether individuals are behind a veil of ignorance or aware of some features of their situation in life). For present purposes all that matters is that it is a contract. But – and here lies the connection with the first stage of argument of this paper – it is a contract that is recognizably like contracts made by real people in the real world. In the real world, for example, contracts are frequently made contingent on certain specified circumstances ('if the insured suffers a financial loss the insurer undertakes to indemnify him against such loss'). But the circumstances must always be, at least in principle, publicly verifiable. An insurance company may indemnify an individual against a loss of money, which is verifiable by recourse to the individual's bank, or against a loss of health, which is verifiable by recourse to his doctor. But it will not – it could not – indemnify him against a loss of utility, except in so far as a loss of utility might happen to be dependent on something that is publicly verifiable. So if we are to make sense of a contract at all, we must understand it as something

---

[8] This does not imply that I think the contractarian perspective to be without problems. But the present argument is of strictly limited scope: if contractarianism is correct, and if pluralism is correct, then economic policy-making can be consistently pluralist.

[9] Roemer, 1985, is one important version of such a view.

public, and the contingencies on which it might depend as being public too. Members of society could and perhaps would contract to insure themselves against the hazards of birth and circumstance, but only against the publicly verifiable hazards. They would not contract to insure themselves against all inequalities in *utility*. A contract that did that would be no contract in any sense that we understand the term; it would be a kind of divine intervention.

Similarly, all contracts specify some kind of exchange, and no party can contract to offer something which it is not in his power to supply. This has two aspects. First, I cannot contract to give you something which I cannot ever deliver to anyone. So I cannot offer you my utility or my state of health or my relationships with my friends, though I can offer you my meditation techniques or my patent medicine or my well-thumbed copy of *How to Win Friends and Influence People*. Second, I cannot contract to give you something that must be given freely and without requiring a return if it is given at all. So I cannot make a contract promising you my respect or my love or my agreement with the conclusions of your latest book (I can promise to treat you with respect, but that is something different). And members of society contracting with each other to share the benefits of co-operation cannot make such contracts either. Perhaps this is unfortunate, for the kinds of good we cannot trade by contract include many of the most important elements in the flourishing of human beings. But the fact remains that these goods are outside the sphere of contracts as we know them or even conceivably could know them.

Indeed, from another point of view it is not unfortunate at all, for there would be something distinctly unattractive about even the attempt to think of these goods as within the contractual sphere. One can think of many kinds of motivation that are not only inappropriate for their intended effect but become in the process of conception ridiculous. Human beings need self-respect, and in order to attain self-respect they must have the respect of their fellow human beings. But it would be absurd if they sought to do so by contracting to have respect for each other. In like manner, there can be something by turns comic and sinister about politicians' undertaking to create greater altruism or to improve the quality of family life, as distinct from ensuring that individuals have the means at their disposal to create these conditions themselves. Not only is this something they *cannot* deliver, but they ought not even to try.

In fact, the sphere of contracts consists more or less of rights over scarce[10] physical commodities (including rights of access to such things as library books and land), and of rights to the performance of services, these being publicly verifiable, intentional activities performed by or caused by other human beings. Social contracts must be contracts for the exchange of these commodities or services, contracts that are contingent on publicly verifiable circumstances. And

---

[10] The rider about scarcity reflects the fact that for things that are in indefinite abundance there would be no gains from co-operation and no need to make contracts. Such things (oxygen in the atmosphere, for example) will not be components of the standard of living, though they may become so if the possibility of their scarcity arises (through air pollution, for example).

the standard of living of citizens is represented by the command that they have over these commodities or services, given these circumstances. More precisely, one may say that the standard of living of individuals consists of those components of their well-being the enhancement of which would be the appropriate subject of a social contract between individuals wishing to share the benefits of social co-operation.

It will be evident by now how this account makes room for pluralism. There are a great many aspects of the good life for individuals the enhancement and distribution of which are simply not society's business. This is because, on the contractarian account I am outlining, nothing is society's business unless it could be the subject of an appropriate hypothetical social contract. Thus it is not the business of society at large whether people have happy marriages or believe in God, because these are not the kinds of thing people could contract to do. It may of course be the business of their friends or of their priests, individuals with whom their relationship is not contractual. And it will certainly be society's business whether people have the resources to make happy marriages possible (such as the ability for a couple to work and live in reasonable proximity to each other), and the ability to call on the state's resources to defend them from attacks on their worship of their own God in their own way. But their standard of living represents their command over these resources, and not the outcome that results from it. A pluralist social theory, which allows for the possibility of fundamentally different conceptions of the ends to which these resources may be put, will be superior to a theory which requires society to evaluate social outcomes in every detail, when many aspects of these outcomes are not ones society should be in the business of evaluating at all. The reason they are not is that the kind of world in which these aspects could be the subject of contract would be a world so unlike our own (peopled by individuals completely transparent to each other, and able to trade mental states with each other at will) as to be no fit point of comparison with the world we know.

In describing the standard of living as involving command over resources rather than the outcomes that result, I should make one point clear. The value of command over given resources may well be dependent on circumstances, provided these circumstances are publicly verifiable. Thus it may readily be granted that a disabled person has a lower living standard than a fully healthy person commanding the same resources, because the disability is a publicly verifiable circumstance. Amartya Sen has argued that this shows that the concept of the standard of living must be concerned with evaluating outcomes rather than control over resources,[11] but I hope it is by now clear that, on the present account, it need show nothing of the kind. If standards of living were concerned with evaluating outcomes in their entirety, we should be obliged to state that whenever two individuals derive different levels of happiness from a given

---

[11] He writes (Sen, 1985: 16) that the standard of living 'must be directly a matter of the life one leads rather than of the resources and means one has to lead a life'.

endowment of commodities, their standards of living are different. The present theory differs from Sen's in allowing only some reasons for the divergence of utility levels to count in standard of living comparisons—namely, those that are sufficiently publicly observable to be the basis of a contract. Other claims, such as that one individual may be of a cheerful disposition while another is somewhat morose, may be true without being relevant to the standard of living.

So far a fairly stark contrast has been drawn between those components of the good life for individuals that are, and those that are not, society's business. But it is evident on reflection that there exists a spectrum of possibilities rather than a sharp division. First of all, there is no sharp line between what is and what is not a publicly verifiable event, certain kinds of mild mental disability being a good example of a borderline case. There is nothing wrong with the idea that our conception of the standard of living might be sensitive to developments in diagnostic medicine, for example. But the emphasis on verifiability will tend to impose a burden of proof on borderline cases proposed for inclusion. Two individuals commanding the same resources will be held to have the same standard of living unless a convincing case can be made for their differing in some verifiable respect that might itself be the subject of a contingency clause in a social contract. So two things will need to be established: first, that the difference is verifiable and, second, that it would itself be relevant to the contract. Consider the case of differences in sex: these are (normally) readily verifiable. But are they such as to justify the claim that men and women with the same command over resources differ in standard of living, in a way that society might perhaps wish to correct? This will depend on the degree to which inequalities between the sexes consist of resource inequalities as opposed to inequalities in other respects, and the answer to this is likely to differ between societies and over time. If existing inequalities consisted primarily of unequal access to resources, there would be a less compelling case for adjusting living standard measures to reflect gender differences for given levels of command over resources.

A second kind of borderline problem concerns what kinds of service activity could be the subject of a contract. The problem is most perplexing within associations that are either not contractual or only partly contractual, like families. But here we may distinguish between problems of inclusion and problems of allocation. On the present account the time spent on housework, for example, even though it is frequently performed unpaid and without even a verbal contract, would count as a (negative) component of the standard of living, because it is the kind of activity that households need to perform and some reduction in which they would usually be willing to contract to achieve. Some problem of inclusion still arises because of the difficulty of distinguishing some such activities from those considered hobbies, where the activity is itself valuable. If, for example, I am a keen gardener (the example is hypothetical) I may not be willing to contract for anyone else to do my gardening for me, because it would then in some sense not be my garden any more. But in general there is no doubt that one significant component of poverty in many countries is the time required for unpaid household tasks, a component that the familiar measures of the standard of living routinely ignore.

Separate from the problem of inclusion is a problem of allocation that may arise *between* members of the household. Suppose, for example, that household tasks are shared very unequally. We would be inclined to say that the standard of living of individuals within the household is to that extent unequal. But suppose it were objected that relations within the household are not an appropriate subject for a contract, that there could not be a social contract aiming to equalize time spent on household tasks? This is a difficult area, but if the premiss of the objection were accepted we should have to withdraw the judgement of inequality within the household. Of course, that premiss may be disputed: one of the features of modern feminism has been precisely to draw attention to the tacitly contractual way in which many aspects of relations between the sexes may be understood. Certainly, the theory being advanced here is in no way undermined by the reflection that the concepts of a contract and of what is fit material for contractual exchange are themselves variable and evolving over time.

As the example of household work suggests, the limitation of the notion of the standard of living to the sphere of commodities and services, broadly conceived, does not restrict it to *marketed* commodities and services. In fact, it includes many services of a very general kind. So, for example, the extent to which members of a society enjoy freedom of speech and of association is certainly a part of their standard of living. This is because these freedoms are safeguarded by the resources of society in that people are protected from assaults upon their exercise of free speech or free association. Such freedoms (and the resources to protect them) they could and would contract with each other to guarantee (though not, of course, to an unlimited extent). But the extent to which they *use* these freedoms to say and do worthwhile things is not part of their standard of living, though it may be an important part of what gives value of their lives. Two societies that devote equal effort and resources to television do not differ in their standard of living merely because one society is innovative and creative while the other broadcasts rubbish. One cannot contract to have good taste.

Nevertheless, non-marketed resources do raise problems of a different kind, namely those of valuation. The valuation of marketed resources in measures of the standard of living is commonly made at their market price. How reasonable is this, and how should non-marketed resources be treated? The argument so far has confined itself to considering what aspects of individuals' lives should be counted as part of their standard of living. For all practical purposes, though, what is required is not a complete description of the standard of living of each individual in society, but some aggregation or summary of the information this contains. Two kinds of aggregation are needed: first, aggregation over the many different components of an individual's standard of living, in order to compare individuals with each other. Second, aggregation over the many different individuals in society for the purpose of comparing one society with another or with itself at different times or in different circumstances. The basic conceptual problems these forms of aggregation raise are very similar. All aggregation involves throwing away information. The best way to aggregate cannot be determined independently of the use to which the information is to be put. Different uses may require different methods of aggregation, and different degrees of aggregation: for example, for some purposes we may need to reduce the measure of the standard of living to a single scalar number; for others we may be happy to reduce it to a vector so that we can make comparisons in several dimensions. There is no reason whatever to believe that there is a single optimal aggregate measure of the standard of living either of an individual or of a society.

This point has been obscured by the implicit utilitarianism of much of the economic literature on the standard of living, and the related literature on such questions as the measurement of inequality. It follows from the standard axioms of individual rational choice that individuals choose their consumption so as to equate the ratio of the marginal utility of each commodity to the marginal utility of money with the price of that commodity in money terms. A measure of the standard of living can be constructed adding quantities of commodities traded and using market prices as weights. This measure represents the individual's consumption, and the sum of these measures across all individuals is the national consumption. If—and it is a big if—utility in this sense represents the appropriate maximand for society, and if all consumers have the same marginal utility of money, then a government that acts to maximize the national consumption will thereby maximize the utility of marginal changes in the availability of goods and services to the population.

There are numerous and well-rehearsed problems with this line of reasoning, of which here are six:

1. One may deny that individual consumers maximise anything.
2. Even if they do, one may deny that what they maximize is utility in any interesting sense.
3. Even if it is, one may deny that society should be concerned only with utilities.
4. Even if it should, one may deny that society should be concerned only with the sum of utilities and not with their distribution.
5. Even if it should do that, one may deny that individuals have the same marginal utility of money.
6. Even if they do, one may deny that maximizing utility at the margin is equivalent to global maximization of utility.

The important point in this context is that only if it is true that society's goals can be appropriately represented by the maximization of some one quantity inherent in all commodities, will it follow that there is a single optimal way to aggregate the standards of living either of individuals or of societies.

This paper is concerned with the proper province of government policy, not with what the criteria of that policy should be. So the question of how to aggregate living standards, which requires answers to the latter problem, cannot be addressed fully here. All the same, for many ordinary purposes market prices will provide a useful first approximation to a weighing system for those components of living standards for which markets exist. The reason for this is that if the standard of living comprises those commodities and services that can be exchanged by contract, one cultural indicator of their value will be the amounts of other commodities that citizens would require under the terms of some social contract in order to induce them to exchange. The justification for this need not be utilitarian (and typically will not be, since these amounts represent relative *marginal*, not average utilities). The justification might be directly contractarian: these amounts represent the relative weights that have been agreed as a result of the contractual process. And relative value by this criterion will be related to the amounts of other commodities that citizens in fact require in exchange under the terms of actual contracts. The two will not always or even usually be the same, partly for reasons of market imperfection that are familiar in the economics literature (such as the presence of externalities), and partly because the terms under which individuals make actual contracts are not the terms that would be specified by hypothetical social contracts. Actual contracts reflect substantial inequalities in power and wealth that social contracts might well seek to redress. But here as before the nature of real contracts between real individuals represents an important starting point in the analysis of what social contracts might be.

Non-marketed resources naturally pose greater informational problems than do marketed resources, but the conceptual issues are very similar. Likewise, the valuation of rights such as the right to free speech depends upon what would be the terms of a social contract in which that right was guaranteed: how much of society's resources would be devoted to policing it in the optimal social contract? The more thoroughgoing the right the more expensive its defence, and the higher the valuation placed upon having that right. For those who blanch at the thought of 'valuing' rights in this fashion, I should repeat that the values thus derived represent purely a measure of the weight these rights have in that sphere of life that it is society's business to organize. Their overall importance in and contribution to the flourishing of individual citizens is something that society has no business to put a value upon.

3 *Contractarianism and Pluralism*

That there is a natural affinity between broadly contractarian views of the justification of social theories, and a pluralistic conception of the social good, has a well-established pedigree in the history of social thought. The connection has not always been made explicitly, but one place where it is so made is John Locke's *Letter Concerning Toleration*. On the basis of the claim that 'the commonwealth [is] a society of men constituted only for the procuring, preserving, and advancing their own civil interests', Locke argues that it can be no business of the state what religion its citizens believe in:

it appears not that God has ever given any such authority to one man over another, as to compel any one to his religion. Nor can any power be vested in the magistrate by the consent of the people, because no man can so far abandon the care of his own salvation as blindly to leave to the choice of any other, whether prince or subject, to prescribe to him what faith or worship he shall embrace. For no man could, if he would, conform his faith to the dictates of another. All the life and power of true religion consists in the inward and full persuasion of the mind; and faith is not faith without believing.

The irrelevance of contractual agreement to the procurement of spiritual well-being contrasts with the more material sphere:

For those things that are necessary to the comfortable support of our lives are not the spontaneous products of nature, nor do offer themselves fit and prepared for our use. This part therefore draws on another care, and necessarily gives another employment. But the depravity of mankind being such that they had rather injuriously prey upon the fruits of other men's labours than take pains to provide for themselves, the necessity of preserving men in the possession of what honest industry has already acquired, and also of preserving their liberty and strength, whereby they may acquire what they further want, obliges men to enter into society with one another, that by mutual assistance and joint force they may secure unto each other their properties, in the things that contribute to the comfort and happiness of this life, leaving in the meanwhile to every man the care of his own eternal happiness, the attainment whereof can neither be facilitated by another man's industry, nor can the loss of it turn to another man's prejudice, nor the hope of it be forced from him by any external violence.[12]

Though Locke is not consistent in his demarcation between the contractual and the non-contractual spheres (at some points treating it as coextensive with the distinction between this world and the next, and elsewhere exempting atheists from the right to religious toleration), the idea that there exists such a distinction is central to Locke's argument, as it is to the argument advanced here.

More recently than Locke, Ronald Coase's approach to the analysis of externalities in production and consumption[13] illustrates another natural connection between contractualism and pluralism. Prior to Coase's work, it had been generally accepted that the appropriate response to an externality such as industrial pollution was to tax the polluting firm so as to bring private and social costs into equality at the margin. Coase pointed out that it was not evident that the polluting firm was the right agent to tax, because of the symmetrical character of externalities. For just as another firm downstream of the first might be said to suffer as a result of the actions of the polluting firm, so the polluting firm itself, if taxed, could be said to suffer as a result of the presence of another, a presence that made the pollution more costly in its effects (for the sake of the example, it is assumed that the damage due to the pollution is confined to

---

[12] Locke, 1689: 128–9, 154. I am grateful to Tom Baldwin for directing me to this source.
[13] Coase, 1960. There is a useful discussion by Farrell (1987).

its effect on the downstream firm). The right solution, said Coase, was for the two agents to get together and bargain their way to an optimal outcome. It might be that this outcome would involve, not a reduction in the output of the polluting firm, but a (less costly) move by the other firm to another site where it would be unaffected by the first firm's activities.

One way to characterize Coase's argument is this: using taxes and subsidies to equalize marginal private and social costs will bring about local efficiency, in the sense that no reallocation of resources at the margin will make at least one agent better off without making any other worse off. But locally efficient points may not be globally efficient,[14] because there may exist large resource reallocations (like moving whole factories) that dominate them. In order to ensure that globally efficient points are attained it is necessary for agents to bargain. The analogy with the present argument is that to make non-local comparisons of living standards (comparisons, that is, between individuals or societies that are very different in their values and ways of life), it may be necessary to consider explicitly what would be the terms of a bargain or contract between the different parties. For if we adopt the measures (such as measures of real income) that would be appropriate to local comparisons (within societies, perhaps), we may make incompatible judgements about their standards of living.[15] Each society may have inferior living standards when viewed by the local criteria of the other. To compare them we must consider those terms of a bargain on which the diverse individuals or societies could agree.

4 Living Standards and Pluralism

Economic development has always provoked anxieties about conflicts of value, from fears about the provocation of decadence by riches to more subtle worries about the effect of development on the diversity of cultural traditions. In these matters, economics is often believed, with some justification, to represent philistinism incarnate. The account of living standards outlines here suggests that this need not always be so. First, consider the question whether measures of living standards can be sensitive to the different values of different cultures. In a simple sense they can certainly be so, because living standards have nothing to say about many important areas of human life, which individuals and associations are therefore free to order according to whatever values they hold dear. A more interesting question is whether those elements of individuals' lives that count as part of their standard of living, and the valuation of those elements, might themselves be sensitive to the different values of different cultures.

There is every reason why they should be, and the extent of this sensitivity will depend on the purpose for which the measures of living standards are

---

[14] Indeed, there are particular reasons to fear this in the case of externalities. Dasgupta and Heal (1979: ch. 5) and Starrett (1972) discuss some of the reasons why.

[15] This point is considered explicitly in Christopher Bliss's paper in this volume.

developed. A measure of living standards developed for comparing countries may differ from a measure used in determining the policy of one particular country. This will be so for two kinds of reason. First, different conceptions of the good life will place different emphasis on the commodities and services necessary for their pursuit.[16] Second, different cultures vary to an extent in their views as to what is and what is not the proper subject of a contract. Anyone who has watched an American broadcast of televangelism will be aware that religion has a much more explicitly contractual character in some communities than in others. The point about a social contract is that it must rest on the agreement of all parties. Social contracts within reasonably homogeneous societies will therefore be able to take much more for granted than a social contract involving the citizens of the whole world.

There is no answer to the question 'Which social contract is the right one to make?' Considerations of justice affect relations within villages, within regions, within countries, within the world. To each of these questions a different social contract may be appropriate, and from each of these contractual exercises a different conception of the standard of living may emerge. The degree of divergence between these will depend in a fairly evident way on the degree to which parties to a social contract are required to abstract from the particularities of their own position. If they did not abstract at all the exercise would be futile, but there are grave doubts about the coherence of their abstracting from every value that gives individual character to their judgements – a point that has been familiar since Hegel's criticism of Kant. This is too large a question to explore here, but it may be observed that unless it is possible to delimit a set of values that must be held by all rational beings *qua* rational beings *and* that are sufficiently rich to characterize a social contract, then the outcome of a social contract will be sensitive to the specification of the parties involved. So, therefore, will a contractarian conception of the standard of living. This no more condemns such a conception to relativism than a road map is made relativist because the way to Tipperary depends on where you start from.

Finally, to what extent must governments' attempts to enhance the standard of living bias economic development towards the commoditization of society? Commoditization is a difficult concept to understand and is used in a variety of senses.[17] Most straightforwardly, it refers to the tendency of trade (either trade in general or monetized trade in particular) to penetrate social institutions. Existing measures of national income undoubtedly incorporate a bias towards the measurement of those goods and services that are in fact traded. In the theory advanced here such a bias is quite unwarranted, and involves essentially a confusion between the terms of a social contract and the terms of actual contracts. Nevertheless, it may still be objected that the emphasis in this theory

[16] The commodities and services discussed here therefore represent a much broader spectrum than Rawls's primary goods, which are defined as 'things that every rational man is presumed to want' (Rawls, 1971: 62).

[17] Hart, 1985.

upon those components of the good life that *could be* the subject of contracts incorporates the same bias in a more subtle disguise.

There are two things to say about this objection. The first is that it sometimes incorporates the suggestion that a bias of this kind is in some way responsible for the widely observed tendency of human societies to mediate more and more of their consumption through the market as they become more prosperous. I do not think this is a suggestion to be taken seriously, at least not in this form. For one thing, it is not even true at all levels of development: for example, one may cite the growth of large corporations and their tendency to determine many aspects of their employees' lives either through fringe benefits or as an intrinsic part of their working conditions. Corporations can be viewed as institutions that supersede the market mechanism, as Ronald Coase long ago pointed out.[18] But even barring this exception, the spread of the market is due partly to certain general facts about human beings, about their tastes and about the technologies of production, that make the benefits from specialization in production tend dramatically to outweigh any benefits of specialization in consumption. This case must not be overstated, since it remains one of the most devastating elements of Marx's critique of capitalism that it has tended so to exaggerate specialization in production as to cramp and wither the human potential of all those who perform society's most routine and repetitive tasks. Serious as this criticism is, the causes of such a phenomenon are independent of whether the province of society's concern be restricted to commodities and services in the way I have argued here.

The second thing to say about this objection is that we should indeed be legitimately concerned about the development of our lives in all sorts of ways outside the broad sphere of commodities and services discussed here. If economic development were to lead to all social relations' becoming infected with the mentality of the market, that would be a matter for the gravest concern. We should indeed worry lest prosperity lead to what one might with some licence call the death of the soul (though by any standards the effect of poverty on the soul is of far more pressing concern in the world today). What is denied here is that governments may be legitimately concerned with such matters. It is hard to conceive that a theory which brought these concerns within the province of governments could retain any pretensions to pluralism at all.

---

[18] Coase, 1937. Recent work by Hart and Moore (1988) has developed this in the context of a formal model.

BIBLIOGRAPHY

COASE, RONALD (1937). 'The Nature of the Firm', *Economica*, 4, 386–405.

—— (1960). 'On Problem of Social Cost', *Journal of Law and Economics*, 3, 1–44.

DASGUPTA, P., and HEAL, G. (1979). *Economic Theory and Exhaustible Resources*, Cambridge: Cambridge University Press.

FARRELL, JOSEPH (1987). 'Information and the Coase Theorem', *Journal of Economic Perspectives*, 1, 113–29.

HART, KEITH (1985). 'Commoditisation and the Standard of Living', in Sen, 1985.

HART, OLIVER, and MOORE, JOHN (1988). 'Property Rights and the Nature of the Firm', STICERD Discussion Paper, London: London School of Economics.

LOCKE, JOHN (1689). *A Letter Concerning Toleration*. Oxford: Blackwell. 1956.

NAGEL, THOMAS (1976). 'Brain Bisection and the Unity of Consciousness', in Jonathan Glover (ed.), *The Philosophy of Mind*. Oxford: Oxford University Press.

PARFIT, DEREK (1976). 'Personal Identify', in Jonathan Glover (ed.), *The Philosophy of Mind*. Oxford: Oxford University Press.

RAWLS, JOHN (1971). *A Theory of Justice*. Oxford: Oxford University Press.

—— (1985). 'Justice as Fairness: Political not Metaphysical', *Philosophy and Public Affairs*, 14, 223–51.

ROEMER, JOHN (1985). 'A General Theory of Exploitation and Class', in Roemer (ed.), *Analytical Marxism*. Cambridge: Cambridge University Press.

SEN, A.K. (1985). *The Standard of Living* (The Tanner Lectures). Cambridge: Cambridge University Press.

STARRETT, DAVID (1972). 'Fundamental Nonconvexities in the Theory of Externalities', *Journal of Economic Theory*, 4, 180–99.

Paul Seabright: Pluralism and the Standard of Living

Commentary by Derek Parfit

[I]

In his rich and stimulating paper, Paul Seabright claims that governments should take a narrow view of human well-being. The 'aspect of . . . well-being that falls within the proper sphere of society's concern'—or, for short, the standard of living—consists, he argues, of 'rights over scarce physical commodities' and 'rights to the performance of services'. Seabright admits that, on this narrow view, the standard of living fails to include 'many of the most important elements in the flourishing of human beings'. But these elements, he believes, 'are simply not society's business'. It would be quite illegitimate for a government, when deciding between public policies, to take such things into account.

Seabright's premises are contractualist. 'Nothing is society's business', he writes, 'unless it could be the subject of an appropriate hypothetical social contract'. Since he does not defend this assumption, I shall not question it here. But I shall question Seabright's view about what *could* be covered by such a hypothetical agreement.

At times he suggests that contracts can cover only what we can either exchange, or do. Thus he writes, 'it is not the business of society at large whether people have happy marriages' since this is not the kind of thing that people could 'contract to do'. Nor can the standard of living include such things as the quality of the arts or television, since 'one cannot contract to have good taste'.

On this assumption, it would not be society's business whether people have good health. But Seabright agrees that health is part of the standard of living. He therefore turns, like Dworkin, to the notion of insurance. Though being healthy is not something that we could contract to do, we can insure against bad health.

We can insure against other things too. By appealing to the notion of insurance, a contractualist might reach a much broader view about the proper role of government. If he imagines a sufficiently ideal insurance scheme, there would indeed be few limits.

Seabright rejects this line of thought. He insists that, as contractualists, we should not appeal to an Ideal Insurer. We should imagine only *feasible* insurance schemes; and these would be far more limited in scope. The chief restriction is that, to be feasible, an insurance scheme can cover only publicly verifiable events. This is why, though our health affects our standard of living, the happiness of our marriages does not. We could not reasonably expect to insure against marital disharmony or distress. Nor could we expect to insure against seeing rubbish on television.

Must a contractualist accept this restriction? There are indeed good reasons, to do with verifiability and moral hazard, why we cannot insure against unhappiness. And, to be enforcible, contract law cannot turn on aesthetic judgements. But these points do not apply to many areas of public life. Suppose there are reasons to believe that certain kinds of housing provision, or certain details of family law, increase the incidence of depression in tower block dwellers, or mothers of young children. Why may not planners take such things into account? That one cannot insure against depression may be claimed to be irrelevant. Or consider the question of which buildings, or parts of the countryside, the government should protect. Judgements about beauty cannot be part of contract law. Why should this exclude them from planning decisions? Why may not the standards of verifiability depend on the context, and on the purposes in question?

One relevant difference is precisely that between public planning and private insurance. Thus, in the running of a health service, doctors may try to assess the effects of different treatments on the quality of people's lives. In making this assessment, they may try to gather evidence about such intangibles as comfort, dignity, or *joie de vivre*. Such evidence would fall far below the standards of verifiability that would be required by a private health insurance scheme. But this seems irrelevant.

The point is partly this. In the case of private insurance, what the claimant gains is a loss to the insurance company. Hence the scope for moral hazard; and hence the reasonable requirement that, for a claim to be legally enforcible, the relevant contingency be both well defined and easy to observe. But in areas like health administration, town planning, or education, the question is not whether some insurance company should be forced to bear a loss. The question is which of various policies is, on balance, best. With such a question, there is no need for the same degree of verifiability. In a choice between different policies, there is no special burden of proof which needs to be met. Why should we not here give some weight to *any* evidence which seems to bear on individual well-being? In Sen's words, is it not better to be vaguely right than precisely wrong?

Seabright would reply that this is to misunderstand his argument. He requires verifiability, not because he wants precision, but because of a more general view about the role in moral theory of imaginary cases. He claims that, to be relevant, an imaginary social contract must be '*recognizably like contracts made by real people in the real world*'.[1]

For his defence of this crucial claim, Seabright refers us to the first part on his paper. This attempts to show that 'our choice of a moral or political theory should not . . . be significantly influenced by our intuitive reactions to what

---

[1] In the printed version of his paper, Seabright qualifies this claim. There are, he admits, various differences between 'actual contracts' and 'hypothetical social contracts'. But even so 'the nature of real contracts . . . represents an important starting point in the analysis of what social contracts might be'. In this qualified form, Seabright's claim seems too weak to support his conclusions.

it recommends in impossible or sufficiently unlikely circumstances'.[2]

One of Seabright's points is this. We should not reject a theory simply because it is counter-intuitive in some cases; for all we know, this may be true of *every* theory. This point seems to me correct. But it does not show that we should ignore our intuitions about imaginary cases. It shows only that we should not reject one theory unless we have another theory which seems better.

Seabright makes two other claims. He points out that, if an imagined case is sufficiently bizarre, it may be doubtfully intelligible. Even if we can understand the case, we may fail to realize what it would involve. These are indeed good grounds for doubting our intuitive reactions. But this point applies only to some imaginary cases. It does not cover cases which depart from reality in understandable ways. As Seabright notes, by considering such cases, we can 'abstract away from the messy and confusing detail' of ordinary life. Compare the use, in science, of artificial tests, or impossible thought experiments. If we can clearly imagine what would be involved in such cases, we need some different ground for doubting our intuitive reactions.

Seabright's third point does apply to all imaginary cases. He suggests that, since 'our ethical intuitions are the product of a long process of both biological and cultural evolution', we should expect them to be trustworthy only in the kinds of case in which they arose. These must all be cases which could actually occur.

This claim seems to me too strong. If a case is impossible only because we have imagined away various complicating features, there seems no reason to distrust our reactions to those features that remain. Moreover, as Seabright remarks, we should expect these kinds of evolution to distort our intuitions in various ways. Thus selective pressure favours partiality, tribalism, and aggression. Similarly, when we think about actual cases, we may be influenced by an awareness that some moral claim would threaten our own privileged position. Thinking about non-actual cases may help us to rise above these distorting influences.[3]

Let us now return to Seabright's main argument. How do his claims about imaginary cases support that argument?

They provide, I believe, little support. If we doubt Seabright's argument, this is not because, in some impossible imagined case, we find his moral view counter-intuitive. Since this is not the issue, it is irrelevant whether, and when,

[2] In the printed version of his paper, Seabright inserts the word 'always'. But this makes his claim too weak for his purposes.

[3] In his discussion of these claims, Seabright's only example concerns punishment and personal identity. He writes, 'it is not an objection to retributive theories of punishment that under conceivable circumstances (those described by Nagel and Parfit . . .) the boundaries between persons might be uncertain and the question "who committed this crime?" might have no answer.' 'Our theories of punishment have developed to deal with persons as they are', not as they might be in such bizarre cases. This misunderstands my aim in appealing to such cases. This was to show that we have certain false beliefs about the nature of personal identity, beliefs which apply also to actual cases, or to persons as they are. If retributive theories rest on such false beliefs, this *is* an objection.

we should distrust our intuitions. The question is whether, in a contractualist theory, our imagined social contract *must* be as verifiable as an actual contract. There may be ways to defend this claim; but the issues raised are different.

Consider, for example, Rawls's imagined 'original position'. This is intended as an artificial model to help us to work out the implications of certain assumptions about moral reasoning. If we reject this model, our objection cannot be that, when we consider such a case, we should not trust our moral intuitions. Rawls's argument does not appeal to these intuitions.

There is a further problem. Seabright allows the contractualist model to be, in various ways, unrealistic. Thus he does not exclude a Rawlsian veil of ignorance. The parties to the social contract can be assumed to know nothing about themselves. They are quite unaware of their own aims, abilities, ideals, attitudes to risk, and every other individual feature. An imagined contract between such people is not, in *this* respect, 'recognizably like contracts made by real people in the real world'. Why must it be, in other respects, just like them? Seabright objects that, if we allow the contract to cover unverifiable features—such as the happiness of our marriages—we are imagining individuals who are 'completely transparent to each other'. But he allows us to imagine individuals who are completely opaque to themselves.

Seabright might reply that, even if the contract can be *made* in an unreal world, it must be imagined to *apply* in the real world. This reply is not, I think, sufficient. We should indeed, within a contractualist approach, prefer principles that would be easy to apply. It is in part for this reason that Rawls states his Second Principle in terms, not of well-being, but of primary goods.

Much of Seabright's argument could be recast along these lines. But such an argument could not, I think, yield his conclusion. It could not show that, in every choice between social or economic policies, governments should consider only those facts that could have entered into private contracts or insurance schemes. Such an argument would have to admit that, in different contexts, different degrees of verifiability would be appropriate. Claims about injustice, like claims about rights, need to be simple, and, as far as possible, verifiable. But the grounds for thinking this apply with much less force to a vast range of policy decisions. Besides the examples I have mentioned—health administration, family law, town planning, and the protection of the countryside—there are countless others. If we insist that, in all such cases, we would admit as relevant only verifiable facts—if we echo Mr Gradgrind—we shall not get good decisions. Practical considerations count *against* this narrow view.[4]

---

[4] He gives another argument in passing. Some elements of a person's well-being are not society's business because their value essentially depends on their being the activities or achievements of this person. This is why it would be both comic and sinister for a government to undertake to 'create greater altruism or improve the quality of family life. . . . Not only is this something they *cannot* deliver, but they ought not even to try.'

These claims are plausible, but I believe they exclude little. Though governments cannot *directly* improve the quality of our family life, they can help us to achieve this ourselves, and thus *indirectly*

[II]

I turn to a more particular question raised by Seabright's approach. On his account, the standard of living consists of our command over various goods and services. How should we assess their value?

Seabright at times suggests that the value of goods and services depends on the cost of their provision. Thus he writes: 'the valuation of rights such as the right to free speech depends upon what would be the terms of a social contract in which that right was guaranteed: how much of society's resources would have to be devoted to policing it? The more thoroughgoing the right the more expensive its defence, and the higher the valuation placed upon having that right.'

This seems the wrong test. The value of a right cannot be measured by asking how many resources would have to be devoted to policing it. The right to free speech would then have little value, since the government can 'police' this right simply by ceasing to prosecute people for what they say.

Seabright applies this test to other kinds of goods. Thus he writes: 'Two societies that devote equal effort and resources to television do not differ in their standard of living merely because one society is innovative and creative while the other broadcasts rubbish.' On this view, it is the cost of services, not their effects of quality, which is the measure of their value. But cost seems never to be the measure of value. If it were, we could not *waste* resources.

Later, however, Seabright writes: 'In describing the standard of living as involving command over resources rather than the outcomes that result, I should make one point clear. The value of command over given resources may well be dependent on circumstances . . . Thus it may readily be granted that a disabled person has a lower living standard than a fully healthy person commanding the same resources.' Seabright here concedes that we should assess someone's standard of living, not in terms of the cost of the goods and services which this person commands, but in terms of their value to this person. If you and I have the same resources, but I am disabled, I have a lower standard of living.

This seems to contradict Seabright's earlier claim. If two communities spend equal amounts on television, but one broadcasts rubbish, the value of having television may be, for those in the second community, less. And, if two communities spend as much on education, but one has much worse educated children, the value of their education may be less. On this, which seems the better view, governments should assess their policies in much broader terms.

---

promote this element in our well-being. They can try to make marriages happier by altering family law, promoting creches and flexible work arrangements, and subsidizing marriage guidance counselling. All of these fall within the 'services' which Seabright's formula allows, since one can contract to give or to receive such services.

To exclude such services, Seabright would have to claim that these elements in well-being would lose their value if they were indirectly assisted in this way. On this view, the quality of family life would not really count as higher if its improvement came from state-provided marriage guidance: nor would there be value in greater altruism if this came from state-provided moral education. In the case of virtue, Kant made such a claim; but I doubt that Seabright would agree.

After granting that disablement lowers one's standard of living, Seabright continues, 'Amartya Sen has argued that this shows that the concept of the standard of living must be concerned with evaluating outcomes rather than control over resources, but I hope it is now clear that, on the present account, it need show nothing of the kind.' This is not clear to me. If we believe that a disabled person is worse off than a healthy person with the same resources, Sen seems right to claim that, in our assessment of the standard of living, we look not only at people's control over resources, but also at one aspect of the outcome, namely, what people can *do* with these resources. If people are disabled, their resources enable them to do less.[5]

Seabright continues: 'The present theory differs from Sen's in allowing only some reasons for the divergence of utility levels to count in standard of living comparisons—namely, those that are sufficiently publicly observable to be the basis of a contract.' But this seems inaccurate on three counts. Sen does not allow *all* such reasons to count in the standard of living. What he does count—capabilities and functionings—he does not assess in terms of their effects on utility levels. And both capabilities and functionings *are* publicly verifiable. As before, Seabright's premisses seem to allow a broader conclusion.

[III]

I have not yet mentioned another element in Seabright's view: his appeal to pluralism. This I find enigmatic.

'By a pluralist theory', Seabright writes, 'I understand an account of how society should be arranged that incorporates the possibility of multiple and non-trivially divergent views of the good life for individual human beings.'

How might a theory 'incorporate' this 'possibility'? Is it enough for the theory to admit that there might *be* such divergent views? This would be a very weak constraint. It is hard to imagine a theory which would deny this.

Perhaps by the 'possibility' of divergent views, Seabright means, not that such views might *exist*, but that they might be *correct*. This suggests two readings of his definition.

On one reading, a social theory is pluralist if it admits that divergent views might *all* be correct. But this cannot be right. When Seabright calls these views 'non-trivially divergent', he clearly means that they are incompatible. At most one of them could be correct.[6]

On the second reading, a theory is pluralist if it admits that there are divergent

---

[5] Seabright might reply that, on this approach, we are still *evaluating their control over resources*. But this would make his point trivial. Any view, even the purest hedonism, could be stated in these terms.

[6] Such views, he claims, are 'not subsumable under an encompassing theory of the good'. (We might replace 'correct' by 'reasonable'. Perhaps, to be pluralist, a theory must admit that there are divergent views which could all be reasonably held. But this constraint also seems too trivial.)

views *any one of which* might be correct. This suggests that, to be pluralist, a theory must be *neutral* between these views. And this would be most simply true if this theory does not itself contain any view about the good. Thus Seabright asks 'whether it is possible for a government's economic policies to incorporate [pluralism]. Or does the very notion of an economic policy presuppose that the government has its own comprehensive theory of the individual good?' This seems to imply that, to be pluralist, a theory must not contain its own view about the good.

But this seems not to be what Seabright means. He also writes: 'This does not imply that a pluralist social theory must be neutral between all or even many theories of the individual good; for it to count as pluralist, it is enough for it to be compatible with the assertion of more than one theory of the individual good.' If a pluralist theory, rather than being neutral between all views about the good, is incompatible with many of these views, it must itself contain some view about the good.

Seabright seems to have in mind a theory which is both (*a*) incompatible with some views about the goods and (*b*) compatible with at least two views that are incompatible with each other. I can imagine ways in which (*a*) and (*b*) could both be true. But I am too unclear what Seabright means to take these comments further.[7]

---

[7] Seabright also claims that, to be pluralist, a theory 'must count it a social good that there may exist multiple views of the individual good'. If we delete 'may', this seems to define pluralists as those who welcome the holding by different people of incompatible views about the good.

There are various reasons why a theory might welcome such diversity in people's views. It may hold, with John Stuart Mill, that rivalry between these views will help each view to develop, and make it more intelligently and sincerely held. But from this form of pluralism there seems no argument to Seabright's conclusion on the proper sphere of government. A theory could be in this sense pluralist while allowing a government's decisions to reflect, at any time, the views of the good which are then most widely held. This theory's attitude to competing views would then be like a democrat's attitude to competing political parties.

Life-Style and the Standard of Living

Christopher Bliss

1 Introduction

1.1. The Meaning of the Standard of Living

In a famous, although dubious, definition of economic welfare, Pigou (1952: 11) defines it as 'that part of social welfare that can be brought directly or indirectly into relation with the measuring rod of money'. The aims of this definition, and the almost insuperable difficulties of implementing it, are both echoed when we try to establish a clear and sensible meaning for the term *standard of living*.

This issue is in part semantic. Provided that we make our meaning clear, we can call what we please by the name standard of living. Great departures from standard usage may cause confusion, however. It is perhaps unfortunate that economists, and popular usage, have suborned the term standard of living to a narrowly economic meaning. Because they have done so, we should probably invent a new term if a different meaning is intended. Quality of life already serves that role.

Unfortunately, not all the issues are simply semantic. The question of whether it makes sense to treat the economic quality of a life apart from more general considerations is a real issue. Pigou favoured that separation because he judged that the correlation between what his measuring rod would show, and other, wider, aspects would not be negative. His 'measuring rod of money' turns out in fact to be an estimate of real purchasing power.

This is much narrower than Pigou's definition seems to allow, and gives rise to the question of whether there is anything that might not in principle be brought into relation with the measuring rod of money. If a healthy man would consent to have a leg amputated for $1 million, or change his religion for $200,000, does this provide us with monetary measures of the value that he places on his leg, or on freedom of confession?

A purely practical reply would say that it is a matter of measurement. Bread is traded a great deal and its cost of production may be gauged quite accurately, so the consumption of bread comes within Pigou's definition. The same cannot be said of selling legs or religious allegiance. The common-sense determination of the scope of a standard of living index leaves open the question of whether we would want the standard of living to include nearly everything if we could measure whatever we pleased.

To illustrate some of the issues, consider a rich individual who suffers from an untreatable disease which seriously interferes with the enjoyment of life.[1]

---

[1] Medical economists employ the concept of the *quality of life*, and something like it is an essential ingredient of the cost–benefit analysis of a medical intervention which prolongs the lives of gravely

In this paper I propose not to describe the said individual as having a low standard of living. I shall instead say that he has a high standard of living but he is in poor health.

I recognize and respect a different view argued vigorously by Amartya Sen (see Sen *et al.*, 1987) according to which, to put it simply, the standard of living should embrace all aspects of the quality of life. Not only has this view great appeal but it also enjoys the advantage that it evades awkward delineation problems.

In a developing country, much of the population is in poor health and the endemic bad health is an aspect of the country's low standard of living. In one case, that of the rich man, the ill health is accidental. In the other case, that of the poor country, it is a consequence of material deprivation. In the first case it is excluded from the standard of living, in the second case it is included.

1.2. Measurement and Objectivity

As part of the justification for a narrow focus definition of the standard of living I have mentioned measurement. This leaves open the question of what counts as measurement and of who is to do the measuring. The principle of *positivism*, applied to economics, holds that quantities must be defined in terms of observables.[2] This view is unfashionable at the present time. However, even if it were agreed that quantities should be defined in terms of experiments, some experiments are impossible to implement, or difficult to interpret even if carried out. So we must consider magnitudes that cannot be directly measured.

The positivist approach says that measures should be defined in terms of observables. This is independent of another idea, often encountered in economics, according to which the measure of welfare, and presumably of the standard of living, should be *the preferences of the actors themselves*. My argument will take that idea seriously but will show how it runs into difficulties when preferences are required to bridge large culture or, as I call it, 'life-style' gaps.

The measurement of the standard of living by preferences seems to lead to an objectionable *subjectivism*, in which what should be a scientific measurement is reduced to whatever people think it to be. The opposite view would hold that there is an expertise concerning standard of living measurement, so that there might be an objective sense in which the participants' preferences would be fallible, and the economist would know best.

I believe that expertise in standard of living measurement should be admitted, but only in two instances. First, individual agents can only evaluate small changes in living standards, so the economist's advantage lies in his ability to integrate to obtain a global measure. Second, the individual may not be fully

---

ill patients. One could not substitute the term standard of living for the term quality of life. They plainly mean different things.

[2] The idea is inspired by modern physics in which the results of its application have been most impressive.

informed of his own, or his group's, state. The inhabitants of a poor country, for example, may not realize how unhealthy they are, and the consequences of that ill health, whereas an expert will know. Both these cases are really the same: they involve *imperfect vision* on the part of the individual. They are important, but they should not persuade us to let go of the fundamental point that man, if not the measure of all things, is at least the measure of the standard of living.

1.3. Preferences and the Standard of Living

Above we encountered the idea that the standard of living should be measured by the preferences of the actors themselves. Ignoring the difficulties of finding out those preferences, there remains the important issue of how preference, which is at bottom an ordinal notion, is to quantify the concept of the standard of living, which is surely, to an extent at least, a cardinal concept.

One route out of the difficulty just explained takes the direction of arguing that preference is not simply an ordinal notion. Rather, according to this view, strength of preference is a natural and perfectly legitimate notion. We then have what I shall call *measured preferences*—a preference ordering enforced by values for the power of the preference.

There has been much discussion in the social choice literature of strength of preference, often related to interpersonal comparisons of utility.[3] Strength of preference is different from and weaker than strong cardinality. Thus, if utility may be defined subject to linear transformations, differences are ordered and strength of preference is measurable, say between two changes affecting an individual. Full cardinality, on the other hand, involves *cross-calibration* of settings across individuals.

In my view, strength of preference has meaning only in terms of a *fixed frame*. Hence it makes no sense within a system subject to Arrow's unrestricted domain, for then nothing is fixed and there is no bench-mark for strength of preference. Strength of preference can only be measured in terms of what one is, or is not, willing to surrender to obtain something else.

This is where the argument leads on naturally to choice under uncertainty because that is the field in which von Neumann and Morgenstern (1944), established their well-known utility index. That index is invariant once the utility level 0 has been attached to the worst possible outcome and the utility level 1 to the best possible outcome.[4]

Strangely, the use of the von Neumann–Morgenstern utility index as a measured preference indicator has not proved popular. Thus Sen (1970: 94–9) notes a number of objections to this procedure (see also Harsanyi, 1955). Sen's leading

---

[3] See Sen, 1979, where the connection between interpersonal comparisons of utility and the ordering of differences is made clear. See also von Wright, 1972.

[4] This is equivalent to saying that the index is defined up to a linear transformation, as the values attaching to the worst and best outcomes are arbitrary. Note that the postulate that there exist worst and best outcomes already violates unrestricted domain.

objection claims that gambles may not provide uncontaminated information on preferences. The case of the agent who will not reveal his preferences in a simple lottery experiment, because he regards gambling as sinful, is cited. Much more importantly, how do we know that the curvature of the utility function—which is the specific information which cardinalization provides—does not reflect risk aversion as opposed to strength of preference?

In the modern theory of choice under uncertainty, due to Ramsey, Savage, and von Neumann, there is no room, it would be argued, within a set of consistent preferences over certain and uncertain outcomes, for separate and non-identical quantifications of measured preference[5] and of risk aversion. The two must correspond. Unfortunately, consistent preferences over certain and uncertain outcomes may very well be precisely what actual agents do not have.

2 Fairness, Contract, and the Standard of Living

2.1. The Standard of Living and Fairness

Fairness may be defined in more than one way, for example, as the absence of envy, or in terms of the existence of a consumption bundle such that each individual is indifferent between his own consumption and the said bundle.[6] For our purposes the absence-of-envy definition will serve. Absence of envy directly establishes only a partial ranking, that is, sets of positions evaluated as representing an equal standard of living. However, that partial ranking may be extended to cases of positive envy, and a complete ordering of positions established.

When agents have different tastes, the envy criterion exhibits paradoxical properties. For example A may envy the bundle enjoyed by B, while B envies the bundle enjoyed by A. This can happen when A and B have different tastes. Also, when different tastes are involved, absence of envy does not equate to justice. In a classic example, A divides a cake between himself and B; B greatly prefers nuts to raisins, while A is indifferent between the two. The cake has most of the nuts on one side. A can then cut himself a hugely greater slice than he offers to B, even if he is constrained not to take a slice that B envies. However, B does envy A's positional advantage in being the one who cuts the cake. This example reminds us of the general point that it may be the opportunities that the rich enjoy that are enviable, not necessarily the consumption that they choose.

The concept of fairness was developed within a framework in which tastes, although differing between individuals, are constant for each individual. With standard of living comparison we sometimes need to allow for tastes which are endogenous to the allocation of individuals to positions and consumptions. An illustration would be the migrant. He considers the life of the city factory worker,

---

[5] Strictly, measured preference relative to given best and worst outcomes.
[6] For a full treatment of the concept, see in particular Baumol, 1986; Foley, 1967; and Varian, 1984. Baumol's book provides an extensive list of references.

and as a sophisticated observer he might not envy him unambiguously. He is disgusted by certain aspects of city life, yet he supposes, rightly perhaps, that he would get used to them, that migration would change him.

2.2. Contract Models, Lotteries, and Inequality

There is a connection between fairness and Rawlsian distributive justice[7] but the two are not the same. Consider the 'original position', in which Rawls's social architects agree on the design of the social system. For simplicity, assume that only the economic aspects of the society are at issue. The Rawlsian social architects, yet to be clothed in their personal features and positions, so arrange things that they maximize the lowest standard of living.

It does not follow that the Rawlsian outcome would be free of *ex post* envy. If the president of a major company has to be paid $2 million per annum to give her the incentive to sweat the last drop of efficiency (and with it enormous social benefit) out of her company, then the payment of that salary will command universal support in the original position. After actual positions have been determined, however, the person who has been made company president will be the object of everyone else's envy. Yet *ex ante* there is no envy, for all are in the same position. The question of how the notion of fairness should be applied to processes involving uncertainty is discussed by Diamond (1967).

Rawls's social architects will not surrender the slightest decrease in the welfare of the worst-off one for a large general increase in all others' welfare levels. It seems that this extreme aversion to risk is seen as a typical feature of being in the original position. Imagine that in the original position all have the same tastes and know that they will retain these tastes after the veil of ignorance has been removed. Meanwhile all have an equal probability of occupying any position. Why would they not all vote for arrangements that would maximize the unweighted sum of utilities, since this would measure each one's expected utility prior to knowledge of position?[8]

This solution allows inequalities which are not justified by the interest of the later-to-be-identified worst off. I have no space here to make a case for such a radical rewriting of Rawls's method. Notice, however, that the alternative approach leads naturally to a helpful way of looking at inequality within units whose standards of living are to be compared.

Does an inhabitant of Jamaica envy an inhabitant of the USA? It obviously depends upon which inhabitants, for there are certainly many North Americans who are worse off than the Jamaican middle class. Yet it is absurd to suppose that this fact prohibits us from claiming that the USA has a higher standard of living than Jamaica. One solution to the difficulty is to use a notional lottery to compare positions of inequality. Country A has the same standard of living

---

[7] See Rawls, 1971.

[8] Note, however, that Rawls himself is not a utilitarian and would not accept the idea that expected utilities could be attached to agents in his original position.

as country B if an agent with an equal chance of occupying any position in one country or the other is indifferent as to which country it should be.

One appealing implication of this idea is that national inequality automatically reduces the national standard of living. If country A has the same population and the same total national income as country B, but in country B that income is more unequally distributed, then an agent about to play the lottery that will allocate him a position in country B will envy the agent about to play a lottery that will allocate him a position in country A. For the purpose of this exercise inequality should be measured by the Atkinson index (see Atkinson, 1970).

3 The Classical Theory and Extensions

3.1. The Classical Theory

The classical theory uses the model of consumer choice with a budget constraint to compare different situations. The subject has been treated extensively elsewhere.[9] Here I present only the results required to bring out particular points. A brief but more formal treatment of certain topics will be found in the appendix.

At the heart of the classical model is the theory of the cost of living index number. This measures how much money income in one position would make the subject as well off as he (or she) is in another position. Our starting point is similar. We take two agents in different positions. But then we do not ask, what change would make them equal? Rather we ask, how far apart are they in standard of living space? This small extension leads to large differences.

An agent is defined by a list of features: his income, the prices that he faces, his tastes, etc. We shall refer to a complete list of the agent's features as his *station*. The image of an observer looking out at other stations and forming judgements concerning them, and of each station being occupied by a similar observer, captures well the idea intended. The classical theory assumes uniform tastes in all stations, so a station is fully characterized by prices and a level of income. As tastes are uniform, the stations can be unambiguously ranked in terms of their desirability.

We start with the case of two stations of equal standard of living. As all individuals have the same tastes, the level of utility enjoyed at the two stations must be equal. If utility is not directly observable, we could ask an agent to choose between the stations and count indifference as standard of living equality. The classical index number is an approximation that bypasses the need for that experiment.

Standard of living equality tests side-step an important issue. Is standard of living to be measured in terms of real purchasing power? If it is, then it must be silent on the issue of whether high standards of living in terms of a high real income are proportionately effective in buying economic quality of life.

---

[9] See, in particular, Sen, 1979, which provides numerous references; Deaton and Muellbauer, 1980; Fisher and Shell, 1970; Phlips, 1974; and Samuelson and Swamy, 1974.

For example, if we define an *index number measure* of the difference between the standards of living of two stations as the difference between two price indices, then the difference is expressed in terms of real purchasing power.

Does a real-purchasing-power-index measure capture what we want the standard of living to mean? Suppose, for example, that prices at two stations are the same but that income at the first station is twice as high. Then an agent at the first station may, if he wishes, consume twice the quantity of goods consumed by the agent at the second. When we measure a standard of living difference in terms of quantities of goods we make it a matter of definition that the rich enjoy a hugely higher standard of living than the poor. Perhaps the standard of living should be measured in terms of the utility that it makes possible, rather than the quantities of goods the purchase of which it permits.

A problem with defining the standard of living in terms of utility is that utility is not directly measurable. In order to use it we have, therefore, to establish a procedure for calibrating it. To make precise the common notion of a standard of living, we need to be able to say something about differences in living standards, and on this question ordinal utility is silent. It may be clear that the standard of living in Zaire is lower than the standard of living in Ghana, which in turn is lower than the standard of living in Switzerland. There must also be some meaning to the idea that the standard of living in Switzerland is much higher than in either Zaire or Ghana.[10]

3.2. The Lottery Measure

The obvious objection to measuring standard of living by utility level is that utility is not cardinally measurable. We noted above (Section 2.2), however, that a lottery of stations provides a measure of utility with a genuine cardinal property. Why should it not provide a cardinal measure of the standard of living?

A sensible objection to a lottery index of standard of living would argue that it makes little sense to ask most agents to evaluate a lottery involving a gamble between the highest and the lowest standard of living in the world, as the original definition would entail. Most people are far from either, and to pin everything on such a decision is seemingly to invite a confused and meaningless result. Fortunately, if agents can accurately evaluate lotteries involving local stations, then a chain method can link together their choices to provide a globally accurate measure. This is shown in the appendix.

A standard of living measure on this interpretation is like a map from which the distances of long journeys can be read off. However, no map-maker will have directly measured the distance concerned. Rather, the map will have been constructed from numerous local, line-of-sight measurements.[11] The chain method

---

[10] To say that the idea has meaning is not to claim that it must be true. It could be held that the lift from the abject poverty of Zaire to the less appalling deprivation of Ghana is a much more important step than the rise to the hugely greater Swiss standard.

[11] Traditional cartography is assumed. Today maps are prepared from satellite photographs, and this alters the point completely.

works in the classical model because there is a global map to be reconstructed. To run ahead of our argument, note that when the implications of life-style are taken into account, discontinuities emerge which make it impossible to make local measurements in all directions. This has radical implications for standard of living measurement.

3.3. The General Equilibrium Model

The specification of the consumer in standard expositions of the classical theory is narrower than the treatment of the consumer in modern general equilibrium theory, the *locus classicus* of which is Debreu, 1959. In Debreu's general equilibrium model the consumer is confined to a *consumption set*. This device is important. Indeed, unless it is included the theory of the consumer is just nonsense. The provision of a labour service is, for example, treated as negative consumption in the general equilibrium model. Then only the constraints of my consumption set, and not my preferences, can explain why I am writing this paper, rather than conducting a symphony orchestra, which my preferences certainly rate higher.

A consumption set is an important component of a life-style because the consumption set varies with life-style. In the standard general equilibrium model the consumption set is a fixed characteristic of the agent. As long as it is fixed, including a consumption set makes little difference, and the version of the classical theory developed in the appendix needs only small amendments to cover the general case.

Where comparisons, and especially international comparisons, of standards of living are concerned, we do need to allow for different consumption sets. The consumption set of a typical American and the consumption set of a typical Indian villager may both be fixed, but they will surely be different. Notice that care must be taken to distinguish between the consumption set and prices. Much more is obtainable in the USA, even in a village, than is obtainable in an Indian village. We might regard the unobtainable as having an infinite price, but this makes comparison almost impossible.

In any case, obtainability is not the only issue. The populations of rich countries are better educated and trained than those of poor countries. Even when faced with identical prices for goods and labour services, their standard of living would thus be significantly different. The prices used in the usual cross-national income comparisons do not include wage rates. Income is taken as a proxy for earning power, whether the latter is determined by skill level or wage rates. However, differences between consumption sets can have significant consequences, even when income is given.

Some of these consequences have been explored by Usher (1968) in the context of a comparison of the UK and Thailand. UK consumers, for instance, spend much more heavily on transport services than their Thai counterparts. This cannot be accounted for either by differences in income or by differences in tastes. The difference is in the consumption sets. This is not the way that Usher expresses the point but it is implicit in his argument.

An estimate of the standard of living based on a comparison of expenditure outlays by households which fails to note that much expenditure on transport is consumption set-imposed is seriously biased. The streams of commuters who pour into London every day do not reveal a preference for moving around. Their consumption sets allow them no combination of a good job and affordable housing which is not jointly consumed with a large quantity of transport.

This last case is close to an instance of life-style demonstrated from within the classical model extended to include consumption sets. The commuters of the last example are not forced to commute. They could perhaps obtain poorly paid jobs in their home towns. If they decided to do so it would profoundly affect how they lived and would influence the tastes which they revealed, and not just because of the income shift. The introduction of life-style in Section 5 below is therefore a novelty, but one which springs naturally from received theory.

4   The Determination of Tastes

4.1 Endogenous Tastes

The idea that preferences are fixed and given is probably the least appealing idea that economists have ever come up with. Some writers, including Marxists, have made the criticism of this idea a leading point in their assault on economic theory. Generally speaking, however, economists have not been much concerned by this case. Most would take the point that preferences are governed by upbringing and culture, but would still feel that they can be taken as fixed for many purposes of economic analysis.

Many writers have looked at endogenous preferences.[12] To a remarkable degree, however, this literature neglects to examine the welfare implications of endogenous preferences. As the whole basis of the welfare evaluation of change is unchanging preferences, this is understandable. However, Fisher and Shell (1972) face the problem when they discuss the introduction of new goods in cost of living comparisons. New goods and changes in tastes raise similar problems.

There are further exceptions to my claim that the endogenous preferences literature ignores welfare evaluation. Especially relevant here is von Weizsäcker, 1971, because this paper looks at an example in which migration is what affects the endogenous preferences of the model.[13] In the von Weizsäcker example, a farmer has to consider whether to migrate to the city or not. Relative prices are different in the city but tastes only adapt slowly.

[12] See Deaton and Muellbauer, 1980: 13.6; Dixit and Norman, 1978; Hammond, 1976; Phlips, 1974; ss. 6 and 7; Peleg and Yaari, 1973; Pollack, 1970; von Weizsäcker, 1971; and Yaari, 1977.
[13] Other papers that examine welfare implications include Dixit and Norman, 1978; and Yaari, 1977.

How convenient it would be if we could invoke cardinal utility comparisons between positions. Imagine the farmer saying: 'I moved to the city because I thought that I could earn $3,000, which would have given me 100 miwigs,[14] but in fact I could only earn $2,000. However, I discovered that once accustomed to city life I liked it more than I had expected, so that the $2,000 could buy me 120 miwigs.' Unfortunately, as we know, and as von Weizsäcker agrees, the meaning of an absolute cardinal utility quantity is questionable.

The strictly ordinal approach mostly favoured by economists has been questioned but no clear alternative has been worked out. The problem is a genuine one. Intertemporal comparisons of happiness do not translate readily into orderings or into even hypothetical decisions. What do people think they mean when they assert that one's school days are the happiest days of one's life?

In von Weizsäcker's account the farmer who might migrate applies a method for evaluating the change which is clearly invalid. Specifically, he assumes that his preferences will not change when he takes up residence in the city, when in fact they will. This is the result of applying the short-run indifference curve and it is invalid as a matter of ordinal fact. The farmer's ordinal preferences will change.

However, imagine a farmer who is more clear-sighted. He understands that he will adapt. He might even have a very good idea of the form that this adaptation will take. What is he to do? To be specific, how is he to form intertemporal preferences with which to evaluate such a history? It is hard enough to know how to weight one's future self against one's present self, even if they are the same character. With a fundamental change, the problem looks impossible. Imagine that you are told that you will shortly undergo a profound religious conversion that will radically alter your personality and your values. Meanwhile you have to decide how much to save. If such exercises have meaning, it is only by virtue of the preferences of the present and actual. Forced to weight one's changed self against one's present self one can only allow the present self to act as a benign dictator.[15]

4.2. Regret

The problem discussed by von Weizsäcker is echoed in Hollis's discussion of the Ant and the Grasshopper.[16] The Grasshopper consumes during the summer while the Ant invests. When winter comes the Ant asks the Grasshopper, who is hungry and depressed, whether he is not now sorry. Hollis retails the story as follows: '"Are you not sorry that you sang all summer?" "Very sorry", the

---

[14] The miwig is an absolute unit of pleasure, so called after Martin Hollis's felicitous phrase 'micro watts of inner glow'; see Hollis, 1987.

[15] Peleg and Yaari (1973) show that an optimal policy may not exist if the present self chooses subject to the constraint that a future self will not deviate. I think this point is fascinating but rather technical as it stands. My reason is that a policy may be constructed which cannot be improved by more than a small number, as small as desired.

[16] See Hollis, 1987: appendix to ch. 6.

Grasshopper sighed, "just as I knew that I would be. But now is now—I acted rationally then. It is you who are irrational in resisting your present desire to help me"' (Hollis, 1987: 95).

The Ant's criticism of the Grasshopper seems to amount to an insistence on the priority of long-term preferences over short-term ones. However, there is a crucial difference between this last story and von Weizsäcker's construction. Weizsäcker assumes myopia; indeed he freely employs the term, and myopia is used to explain, for example, the catastrophic path chosen by the lover of variety who switches back and forth, though consuming less and less, until he reaches starvation point. Hollis's Grasshopper, however, is far-sighted. He expects to feel painful regret.

Regret can mean more than one thing. Genuine regret should amount to a preference, if one could be transported back in time, to be constrained to take a different decision. The Grasshopper feels no such regret. He *wishes* that he had food in the cold winter, as how could he not, but if transported back in time he would not wish to be constrained to choose differently.

Are preferences concerning situations of sheer impossibility meaningful? Many feel that they have such preferences. 'If I could be young again I would not marry.' Such preferences, if they mean anything, reflect current views. Fisher and Shell (1972: 4) argue provocatively that the question 'Would you like to live your youth over again having the tastes that you do now?' is more meaningful than the question 'Were you happier when young than you are now?', on the ground that the former question elicits a preference concerning an, admittedly fantastic, choice, while the latter does not.

It is on a test of the form: If you could go back having your present knowledge, would you wish to be constrained? that the non-migrant in von Weizsäcker's example can be convicted of non-optimality. Present or final tastes are allowed to legislate the optimality of past actions.

Eventual non-regret is, however, a dubious criterion, as the Grasshopper understands. The Grasshopper is rigidly rational and consistent. How much worse when changes of taste are involved which are so radical that they amount to a change of personality. We do well to turn away he who says to us: 'Try this, man, it will blow your mind, but I promise that you will never regret having taken it.' But can we prove that we are right to do so?

5 The Concept of Life-style

5.1. The Meaning of Life-style

We come now to the heart of our argument, the idea of life-style. As it stands, the term is not precise, and some of its overtones may be out of place. Bear in mind that formally a life-style involves both a consumption set and preferences.

The first examples that spring to mind are those that correspond most closely to a life-style in the popular sense of the term. The Bohemian (or in modern terminology the 'Hippy') life-style incorporates a happy-go-lucky life of a non-acquisitive kind, which rates contentment and personal fulfilment above the dictates of the work ethic. We can also consider styles corresponding to ways of organizing social life–tribal or patriarchal–as opposed to the nuclear family and individualistic, for example. Or we might consider life-styles that are generated by means of organizing production–rural self-sufficient or nomadic, for example. The Western life-style might be characterized as acquisitive and consumerist, with an emphasis on work as a valuable and fulfilling activity. It might be regarded as embodying a high level of 'rationality'–in the sense of Max Weber rather than the economist's sense.[17] Ultimately the list of life-styles is coextensive with the number of separate types of station, the differences between which complicate the comparison of standards of living.

Life-style, as a joint specification of the consumption set and preferences, is closely related to the productivity of the economy. The strict work discipline of industrial societies may be regarded as a feature of their predominant life-style. This life-style in turn allows for the high productivity which results in enlarged consumption choices as well as narrowing choice with regard to how and how much the subject works.[18]

We can now contrast the formal content of the idea of a life-style with the assumptions of the classical model. The differences are twofold. First, when different life-styles are considered, preferences, prices, and consumption sets are not independent. Second, the choice of a station involves the choice of a consumption set, and also of the prices that will apply for the chosen station. Hence the consumption set is to some extent *chosen by the agent* but chosen jointly with prices.[19]

In assuming that preferences are determined by life-style, I am neglecting the purely individual and idiosyncratic component of preferences. Something like this view has wide support. The classical model adheres to it in assuming tastes to be uniform. Those who stress the social and cultural determinants of taste also set aside the merely individual. Stigler and Becker (1977) argue that many transcultural differences in tastes can be accounted for by relative price differences. I agree with them but would go further. Even more differences in tastes can be accounted for by differences in relative prices and consumption sets. The residual element of strictly individual quirk then looks quite unimportant.

5.2. Life-style and Community

People are not simply individuals. They live socially and their views, their

---

[17] The reference to Weber is not meant to suggest that his concept of rationality is wholly satisfactory. On the contrary, see Runciman, 1972.

[18] Marglin (1974) offers a sinister interpretation of the benefits of work discipline but we take it that the benefits are genuine.

[19] We can define the *super-consumption set* to be the mathematical sum of the various individual consumption sets. However this does not reduce life-styles to a case of the classical theory for two reasons. The super-consumption set is not necessarily convex, and preferences and prices vary across it in a systematic manner.

values, and even their beliefs, as well as their abilities, are formed and sustained within social groupings, families, and communities. Living a life-style and inhabiting a community are not equivalent but they can be closely interrelated. Perhaps the consideration of life-style offers an alternative to the *methodological individualism* that has been held to be a weakness of orthodox social science.

For the case of self-contained, even isolated, collections of similar people, to inhabit a community is to occupy a place together with others and to participate in their social and economic activity. However, even common usage recognizes more complex and ambiguous cases, for example, the Jewish community in France. Often the community does not conduct its economic activity in isolation from the rest of the nation. Neither are the values maintained by that group independent of those that prevail elsewhere.

The attempt to prove that the smaller community is viable within the larger defines the life and the history of certain groupings: the gypsies, the wandering Jews, or the monastic orders. This is partly an issue of economic viability, but value and identity dilution are often more acute problems, as the history of the Jews – both as recorded in the Bible and in later history – well illustrates. These questions are powerfully focused by migration, whether forced or chosen.

5.3. Switches of Life-style

If life-style never changed we should all still be hunter-gatherers. The environment is never static, however, and life and ideas are constantly changing. In the course of this process life-styles undergo translation, sometimes gradually, sometimes abruptly. Some switches reflect a conscious decision to switch, some are unintended implications of other decisions. A family decides to give up farming, or to send a son to college, and thus embarks upon a road which will change their horizons and alter their life-style whether they realize it or not.

Life-style may be changed by force, when on account of changes in prices and the environment a point is reached when the existing consumption set is no longer attainable. We call the last outcome *life-style breakdown*. Even when unforced, the decision is typically made in a cloud of uncertainty, as the forward extrapolation of taste changes is assessed in terms of present tastes.

5.4. Standard of Living Comparisons Across Life-styles

Comparisons of the standards of living of different stations are judgements, and judgements concerning which there is often no higher authority than the concerned actors themselves. That sounds simple, but its application must confront some serious problems. Compare comparisons of standard of living, on the one hand within the classical model, and on the other across life-styles. In the first case we are dealing with judgements, but the content of the judgement is fairly clear. To judge A to be a better standard of living than B is equivalent to deciding that one would rather enjoy the income and prices of A than the income and prices of B.

Of course prices and incomes are not everything, which means that on my narrow definition of standard of living a person need not wish to move from a lower to a higher standard of living. If standard of living is a partial measure of the value of a life, then a high standard of living is something that a rational agent will not invariably pursue.

When we turn to standard of living comparison across life-styles, what an evaluative judgement means becomes a very difficult issue. The monastic life-style may involve a vow of poverty and a positive commitment not to seek a high standard of living. Even in this extreme instance, however, it is not clear that a judgement cannot be made. One does not have to want to live in a fine house to judge a dwelling to be such. However, an enclosed monk might be incapable of appreciating what a rich man's life-style entails, so that not only does he not want it, but he cannot even judge it. Such differences of viewpoint, sometimes in subtle guises, will always intrude themselves into comparisons across life-styles.

In the classical model we 'solved' the problem of myopia by stitching together a chain of locally small steps, each step involving comparison of the relatively adjacent. Then it was not a preposterous act of faith to assume that meaning attached to the integrated sum of such steps. With standard of living comparison across life-styles, however, we may encounter discontinuities, and across boundaries between life-styles there may be nothing adjacent in the relevant sense.

It does not necessarily follow from the lack of clarity in the comparisons that there will be disagreement – at least as far as the ranking of stations in terms of standard of living is concerned. Perhaps the *ordering* will command agreement, and it may even correspond to one defined by a classical real income measure. Even then, however, we should still lack a measure of how far apart are the standards of living of different stations. And when we consider the special nature of the assumptions needed to provide such a quantification in the classical case, we might very well wonder why anyone should suppose that the *difference* between the US standard of living and the standard of living of Burma admits of exact quantification.

6   Migration and the Standard of Living

6.1. The Decision to Migrate

I shall deliberately take a somewhat narrow view of migration, concentrating on migration motivated by economic considerations. The migration motivated by personal safety, or to avoid maltreatment, may be called *flight*. The distinction between economic migration and flight is notoriously difficult to administer. Governments may wish to turn away people in flight, by claiming that would-be migrants are economically motivated. However, migrants do have multiple and ambiguous motives.

When we consider migration defined as movement resulting from a desire for economic betterment, we are almost by definition looking at people who are

trying to improve their standard of living, at least as they perceive it. The literature on the economics of migration takes a rather simple view of the economic
gain which drives migration.[20] This is broadly a higher income, although the
most influential model[21] includes uncertainty concerning the realization of the
improved income which the city promises.

The subtleties of the difference between a city and a rural standard of living
are difficult to quantify. Close investigation has also tended to undermine the
original Todaro view that urban earnings are simply higher and it is only the
risk of unemployment that deters migrants. The comparison of standards of
living in the country and in the city encounters many conceptual problems.
For example, the city may offer better education, on the one hand, but more
expensive, if not frankly inferior, housing, on the other. How to weight these
differences is in part an issue of the city life-style versus the rural life-style
itself.

Migrants are critical assessors of standard of living because they vote with
their feet. Yet they may make mistakes; as von Weizsäcker's farmer is supposed
to do, by underestimating city life in that case; or as a Todaro migrant, unfortunately unemployed in the city, finds out that he has done.

The British Industrial Revolution experienced mass migration from the country to the town, the evaluation of which is every bit as complicated as the evaluation of the, in some respects similar, migrations of the present day.[22] The
majority of migrants do not regret the decision to move. Not all have burnt their
boats, but return to the country is fairly rare.[23] Yet tastes are altered by the
city, and the possibility of return to the old life-style can be forfeited. As
Hobsbawm, referring to the British Industrial Revolution, puts it:

Whether the Industrial Revolution gave most Britons absolutely or relatively more and
better food, clothes and housing is naturally of interest to every historian. But he will
miss much of its point if he forgets that it is not merely a process of addition and subtrac-
tion, but *a fundamental social change*. It transformed the lives of men beyond recognition.
Or, to be more exact, in its initial stages it destroyed their old ways of living and left
them free to discover or make themselves new ones, if they could and knew how.[24]

6.2. Life-style Breakdown

I explained life-style breakdown as the arrival of a point at which the existing
consumption set is no longer attainable. More common is the less drastic *life-style
erosion*. In the latter case a life-style does not become unviable, but it fails to
retain sufficient adherents to survive. The two are closely connected. As a life-
style approaches the point of forced extinction it can become harsher and less
attractive, and people will leave it.

[20] For a survey see Williamson, 1989.
[21] See Harris and Todaro, 1970; and Todaro, 1969.
[22] For a broad review of the human consequences of the British Industrial Revolution, see
Hobsbawm, 1969, esp. ch. 4 and 5.
[23] Although more common in Africa, where the country never loses its attraction.
[24] Hobsbawm, 1969: 61–2.

History and the contemporary world provide examples of life-style erosion or breakdown. Thus, nomadic pastoralism as a way of life is under acute stress, if not in the course of breakdown in various places (e.g. much of the Sahel), due to overgrazing, soil erosion, and the invasion of traditional pasture land by the crops and animals of settled farmers.

Changes such as these pose acute problems for moral or welfare evaluation. It is easy to say that large-scale social transition imposes powerful stresses on those who undergo it, even if it is in some sense a movement towards a better way of life, or to a higher standard of living. This is to look at the moral issue too microscopically. A human life-style is quite like a species of animal in some respects. It can be regarded as a resource, a valuable thing. It would be absurd to take this view to extremes, to want to preserve any way of life for its own sake, however horrible or brutal it might be. The danger in the modern world, however, is of an extreme concentration on a narrow range of life-styles.

The motives that lead people to attack life-styles include the simple and usual motive of self-betterment. The loggers attack the forest to obtain for themselves and their families a better standard of living, longer life, more capabilities, etc. They might not recognize the terminology, but that is what they are doing. Consider the motivation of governments, World Bank officials, and various do-gooders. The intentions with which they are armed are impeccable: better health, longer life, less hunger, etc. Yet there exist life-styles that cannot receive these goods without disappearing. Can we be sure that it is good that they should disappear?

APPENDIX

A.1. Index numbers and the income comparison method

A station is characterized by a normalized price vector **p**, and a level of income in terms of the numeraire. Tastes are uniform and the stations can be unambiguously ranked in terms of their desirability. We assume them indexed by k, with station 1 the best station, and station N the worst.

Income might be simply money income and prices money prices. In that case, assuming money not to be desired for itself, we can normalize by setting income to equal 1, and expressing prices as costs in terms of income.[25] Then hours of work, working conditions, etc., are not taken into account. However, if there is a fixed income at each station, we can normalize as described, and a station will be fully characterized by a vector of already normalized prices, **p**.

Classical standard of living equality exists when the same level of utility is associated with two stations. Equality between stations i and j may be conveniently expressed in terms of the equality of two values of the indirect utility function:

$$V(\mathbf{p}_i) = V(\mathbf{p}_j), \tag{A.1}$$

where the prices normalized on income equal 1. A direct method of testing for the satisfaction of (A.1) follows.

By the mean-value theorem, (A.1) implies that there exists a value z between 0 and 1 such that:

$$-H_k \mathbf{x}_k (\mathbf{p}_i - \mathbf{p}_j) = 0, \tag{A.2}$$

where H_k is the marginal utility of income in station k, $\mathbf{x}_k$ is the vector of net demands in station k, and k is a station defined by prices:

$$z\mathbf{p}_i + (1 - z)\mathbf{p}_j, \tag{A.3}$$

with z chosen to satisfy the condition of the mean-value theorem.

Rearranging (A.2), the unobservable H_k value disappears and we are left with:

$$\mathbf{p}_i \mathbf{x}_k = \mathbf{p}_j \mathbf{x}_k. \tag{A.4}$$

Standard of living equality corresponds to an index of normalized prices being the same. The price index is precise, but as its weights are obtained from a point determined by the mean-value theorem, an approximation may have to be employed. If prices $\mathbf{p}_i$ and $\mathbf{p}_j$ are not too far apart, a good approximation is:[26]

$$\mathbf{x}_k = (\mathbf{x}_i + \mathbf{x}_j)/2. \tag{A.5}$$

---

[25] This way of expressing things is illuminating and is often employed. Thus a reporter might accompany film of a certain country with the commentary: these motor cars would cost the workers making them two years' earnings. The price of a car has been given in terms of years of income, as 2 units.

[26] There are many important points which this simple account ignores. Fisher and Shell (1972), for example, argue that with an intertemporal standard of living comparison the end-weighted Paasche cost of living index number is to be preferred on the grounds that it is more appropriate when new goods are introduced.

The *index number measure* of the difference between the standards of living of two stations i and j is:

$$p_i x_k - p_j x_k, \tag{A.6}$$

where x_k is again determined by the requirement of the mean-value theorem. The move from equality to inequality makes an essential difference. The marginal utility of income cancels out of an equality measure, so that utility equality is perfectly measured by a real income index. A real income index of differences measures differences in real income and is silent on the question of how far utility levels differ.

A.2. The lottery index

The *lottery index* of the standard of living is defined as 100 times the probability of being translated to the best station (station 1), as against being translated to the worst station (station N), which would leave the agent indifferent between staying in his existing station and entering a lottery as specified. Let T_k be the value of the lottery index in station $k(k = 1, \ldots, N)$. It can thus be specified that $T_N = 0$ and $T_1 = 100$.

A chain method is employed to link together local choices to provide a global measure. There are N station (i = 1, \ldots, N), and N − 2 probability values p_j(j = 2, \ldots, N − 1), such that the agent at j is indifferent between station j with certainty and station j + 1 with probability p_j together with station j − 1 with probability $(1 - p_j)$. Then we have:

$$p_2 T_1 + (1 - p_2) T_3 = T_2;$$
$$p_3 T_2 + (1 - p_3) T_4 = T_3;$$
$$p_j T_{j-1} + (1 - p_j) T_{j+1} = T_j; \tag{A.7}$$
$$p_{N-1} T_{N-2} + (1 - p_{N-1}) T_N = T_{N-1}.$$

The system (A.7) can be solved uniquely for the T_j values, given the specification $T_1 = 100$ and $T_N = 0$.[27]

BIBLIOGRAPHY

ARROW , K.J. (1963). *Social Choice and Individual Values*, 2nd edn. New Haven: Yale University Press.

ATKINSON, A.B. (1970). 'On the Measurement of Inequality'. *Journal of Economic Theory*, 2, 224–63.

BAUMOL, W.J. (1986). *Superfairness: Applications and Theory*, Cambridge, Mass., and London: MIT Press.

[27] The sketch of a proof goes like this. Choose a value of T_2. Then all the remaining values of T_i (i = 3,.., N) can be solved sequentially from (A. 7). The right T_2 is the one that results in $T_N = 0$.

DEATON, A., and MUELLBAUER, J. (1980). *Economics and Consumer Behaviour*. Cambridge: Cambridge University Press.

DEBREU, G. (1959). *Theory of Value: An Axiomatic Approach*. New York: Wiley.

DIAMOND, P. (1967). 'Cardinal Welfare, Individualistic Ethics and Interpersonal Comparisons of Utility: A Comment', *Journal of Political Economy*, 75, 765–6.

DIXIT, A., and NORMAN, V. (1978). 'Advertising and Welfare', *Bell Journal of Economics*, vol. 9, no. 1, 1–17.

FISHER, F.M., and SHELL, K. (1972). *The Economic Theory of Price Indices*, New York and London: Academic Press.

FOLEY, D.K. (1967). 'Resource Allocation and the Public Sector', *Yale Economic Essays*, 7, 45–98.

HAMMOND, P.J. (1976). 'Endogenous Tastes and Stable Long-run choice', *Journal of Economic Theory*, 13, 329–40.

HARRIS, J.R., and TODARO, M. (1970). 'Migration, Unemployment and Development', *American Economic Review*, 60, 126–42.

HARSANYI, J. (1955). 'Cardinal Welfare, Individualistic Ethics and Interpersonal Comparisons of Utility', *Journal of Political Economy*, 63, 309–21.

HOBSBAWM, E.J. (1968). *Industry and Empire*. London: Weidenfeld and Nicholson.

HOLLIS, M. (1987). *The Cunning of Reason*. Cambridge: Cambridge University Press.

MARGLIN, S. (1974). 'What Do Bosses Do? The Origins and Function of Hierarchy in Capitalist Production', *Review of Radical Political Economics*, 6.

PELEG, B., and YAARI, M.E. (1973). 'On the Existence of a Consistent Course of Action when Tastes are Changing', *Review of Economic Studies*, vol. 40, no. 123, 391–401.

PHLIPS, L. (1974). *Applied Consumption Analysis*. Amsterdam: North-Holland.

PIGOU, A.C. (1952). *The Economics of Welfare*. London: Macmillan.

POLLACK, R.A. (1970). 'Habit Formation and Dynamic Demand Functions', *Journal of Political Economy*, 78, 748–53.

RAWLS, J. (1971). *A Theory of Justice*. Oxford: Oxford University Press.

RUNCIMAN, W.G. (1972). *Critique of Max Weber's Philopsophy of Social Science*. Cambridge: Cambridge University Press.

SAMUELSON, P.A. (1950). 'Evaluation of Real National Income', *Oxford Economic Papers*, 2, 1–29.

—— and SAMY, S. (1974). 'Invariant Economic Index Numbers and Canonical Duality: Survey and Synthesis', *American Economic Review*, 64, 566–93.

SEN, A.K. (1970). *Collective Choice and Social Welfare*. Amsterdam: North-Holland.

———— (1979). 'The Welfare Basis of Real Income Comparisons', *Journal of Economic Literature*, 17, 1–45.

SEN, A.K., *et al.* (1987). *The Standard of Living*, Cambridge: Cambridge University Press.

STIGLER, G.J., and BECKER, G.S. (1977). 'De gustibus non est disputandum', *American Economic Review*, 67, 76–90.

TODARO, M. (1969). 'A Model of Labour Migration and Urban Unemployment in Less Developed Countries', *American Economic Review*, 59, 138–48.

USHER, D. (1968). *The Price Mechanism and the Meaning of National Income Statistics*. Oxford: Clarendon Press.

—— (1980). *The Measurement of Economic Growth*. Oxford: Basil Blackwell.

VARIAN, H. (1974). 'Equity, Envy and Efficiency', *Journal of Economic Theory*, 9, 63–91.

VON NEUMANN, J., and MORGENSTERN, O. (1944). *Theory of Games and Economic*

Behaviour. Princeton: Princeton University Press.

VON WEIZSÄCKER, C.C. (1971). 'Notes on Endogenous Changes of Tastes', *Journal of Economic Theory*, 3, 345–72.

VON WRIGHT, G.H. (1972). 'The Logic of Preference Reconsidered', *Theory and Decision*, 3, 140–69.

WILLIAMSON, J. (1989). 'Migration and Urbanization', in H. Chenery and T.N. Srinivasan (eds.), *Handbook of Development Economics*. Amsterdam: North-Holland.

YAARI, M.E. (1977). 'Endogenous Changes in Taste: A Philosophical Discussion', *Erkenntnis*, 2, 157–96.

Christopher Bliss: Life-Style and the Standard of Living

Commentary by Amartya Sen

Christopher Bliss has provided an illuminating examination of the concept of the standard of living and the possibility (in fact, the impossibility) of making comparisons when changes in life-styles and preferences are involved. I have some problems with the methodology he uses, which is largely derived and developed from contemporary mainstream economic theory, but even when we disagree—in ways that I shall presently discuss—I do not in the least doubt that his arguments are powerful and demand serious consideration and scrutiny. I would argue that the sceptical position that Bliss outlines can lead to a different conclusion—less destructive than the one he seems to prefer. But any constructive thesis, to be well-founded, must address what Bliss presents as the nihilistic implications of changing preferences and non-comparable life-styles.

1 Conservative Destructivism

Bliss's strategy can be described as one of relying on methodological conservatism (the programme of the first three sections) to draw radically destructive conclusions about living standard comparisons (in the rest of the paper). He begins his essay defending a relatively narrow view of the standard of living, largely in line with standard practice in mainstream contemporary economics. Bliss endorses Pigou's distinction between *economic* welfare and welfare in general, and wrestles—not entirely happily—with Pigou's (1952: 11) pointer to 'economic welfare' as 'that part of social welfare that can be brought directly or indirectly into relation with the measuring rod of money'. Bliss also reveals his sympathy for what he sees as 'the positivist approach' that 'says that measures should be defined in terms of observables'. He explains and defends the case for concentrating on (1) the *set* of commodity bundles (the 'consumption set') from which a consumer can choose one, and (2) the particular commodity bundle that he happens to choose (thereby revealing his 'preference'). He elaborates on his distrust of any notion of utility other than what can be based on observed choices over certain and uncertain prospects. He discusses how—with the assumption of given tastes—the person's preference map can be recovered from observed choices and how index numbers of living standards may be constructed based on such observations. He explains the strategy of 'the classical model', its extensions involving lotteries, and their use in 'general equilibrium' theory. All this—up to and including Section 3—is largely defensive, with a few variations, of the received methodological beliefs in standard neo-classical economics.

What emerges most powerfully from the first three sections of the paper is Bliss's acceptance of the unique relevance, for living standard comparisons, of 'consumption sets' and 'preferences'. If preferences are constant and given, no-nonsense comparisons of real incomes or living standards can be made in the way that neo-classical theory has made familiar. But at this point Bliss abandons the smugness of the standard theory, and proceeds to explain the difficulties arising from different tastes. He discusses, with remarkable clarity, the problems created by taste formation (and the resulting 'endogeneity' of tastes) and by intertemporal variations in tastes (and the resulting 'regrets' regarding past decisions). Given the reliance on standard economic methodology, based on constant-taste comparisons, everything looks very dicey at this point, and Bliss enlivens the dilemmas with excellent discussions of well-chosen illustrations.

Bliss's definition of a life-style involves 'a joint specification of a consumption set and preferences', the two together being identified by Bliss as the person's 'life-style'. When preferences differ over time, or between regions, the standard approach based on constant-preference analysis proves quite unequal to the task of comparing different life-styles. Along with that crumbles the traditional method of comparing living standards. Bliss gives examples of 'differences of viewpoints' that 'will always intrude themselves into comparisons across life-styles'. (p. 430).

It also becomes impossible, within the chosen methodology, to judge whether people who migrate benefit from the migration, for example, to a city, since 'tastes are altered by the city and the possibility of return to the old life-style can be forfeited'. Also, the achievement of 'better health, longer life, less hunger, etc.' may be at the cost of 'the disappearance of old life-styles', for example, when 'the loggers attack the forest', or when development policies are carried out by 'governments, World Bank officials, and various do-gooders'. Bliss's radical scepticism ends with the rhetorical question: 'Can we be so sure that it is good that they should disappear?'

2 Consequences and Methods

Let me comment, first, on one of the implications of Bliss's last argument, which is, in fact, an inescapable consequence of the methodology that Bliss has chosen to adopt. The result of Bliss's argument is *not*, as the rhetorical question may induce one to assume, a censure of the destructive consequences of economic changes that ruin our traditional life-styles. It is only an assertion of 'non-comparability'. Even if it happens to be the case that when the loggers attack the forest, millions of others experience an utter destruction of cherished ways of living and its replacement by a new life-style adapted to the reduced circumstances (in addition to hunger and deprivation generated by the creation of deserts and the loss of livelihood), Bliss's methodology would not permit him to denounce this change on that ground and could not give reason for resisting it. The new situation *vis-à-vis* the old would be simply non-rankable. There is no *decidable* gain or loss in life-styles as people adjust to their reduced circumstances and seek other ways of living, with other preoccupations. We would be permitted the luxury of gently wondering about those lost life-styles ('Can we be sure that it is good that they should disappear?'), but we would not have any basis, on this theory, for demanding, 'Foul, stop it!' One does not have to be an all-out 'green' to miss something assertive in this theory.

It is not only the 'governments, World Bank officials, and various do-gooders' and others (social activists, economic planners, radical political parties) working for a change who need a theory that enables them to make comparisons over alternative social states and life-styles. So do those who *resist* change. Bliss's methodological nihilism undermines *both* support for and rejection of change.

The sources of the impossibility Bliss identifies is clear enough. If a theory that was devised to deal specifically with constant-taste comparisons is to serve as the basis of variable-taste contrasts, we are likely to get an impasse. That is an argument for looking for a different theory. The type of methodological conservatism that Bliss adopts cannot but lead to the radical scepticism with which he ends up.

To recognize this elementary fact must not, however, be seen, in itself, as a rebuttal of Bliss's argument. It *could be* that assertive statements regarding comparisons of life-styles and living standards are indeed insupportable when preferences change, and the arguments of 'the greens', 'the reds', and 'the blues' may all be without foundation. We have to show why methodological conservatism of the kind adopted by Bliss need not be forced on us.

3 *Inadequacy of Constant Tastes*

I will begin with arguing that *even when tastes are constant*, the constant-taste methodology—based on comparisons only of commodity bundles—can give patently wrong answers in comparing living standards. The problem arises from the fact that tastes and preferences, in the sense discussed by Bliss, are defined over bundles of commodities (the elements are ranked in 'consumption sets'), whereas an assessment of living standards has to look beyond that 'space'.

Consider the following case. Person 1 has commodity bundle x and person 2 has y. They have just the same tastes and preferences over this pair, each preferring x to y. (We can easily assume—if we want—that they also have exactly the same ordering over *all* commodity bundles.) But person 1 is handicapped in some way relevant to the life she can lead, for example, she is disabled (and needs expensive prosthesis and care), or is a chronic depressive, or lives under terrible environmental conditions, or has to spend her life nursing a small child or an ill relative. (The variety of ways in which such a handicap can arise indicates how general the problem under discussion is.) The constant-taste comparison will assert that person 1 has the higher standard of living of the two if standard of living is to be seen simply as a matter of commodity bundles. But this can be absurdly wrong if the life that person 1 can lead is severely reduced by the handicap in question. It is deeply misleading to assume that if 'all individuals have the same tastes, the level of utility enjoyed at the two stations must be equal' (p. 422).

Indeed, if we were permitted to *talk* to persons 1 and 2 (and not just to 'observe' their economic choices), they might both agree on a ranking of living standards based on *combinations* of (i) commodity holdings, and (ii) other relevant circumstances of the respective persons, for example, in descending order: $(x, 2)$, $(y, 2)$, $(x, 1)$, $(y, 1)$. In terms of 'observed choices' over commodity bundles both 1 and 2 can be found to choose x over y, and a living standard comparison based only on what would put person 1 (disabled, depressed, environmentally deprived, or overburdened, as she is) above 2, since 1 owns x whereas 2 owns y. But both agree that 2 has a higher living standard (even with y) than 1 has (with x), reflected by the placing of $(y, 2)$ above $(x, 1)$ by both. The constant-taste methodology is caught in a trap created by its own informational parsimony.[1]

4   Capability and the Measuring Rod of Money

This problem with the constant-taste methodology relates to the view that Bliss rejects early on in his paper when he asserts that 'a rich individual who suffers from an untreatable disease which seriously interferes with the enjoyment of life' has 'a high standard of living' though he is 'in poor health'. Bliss's position is based on a clear distinction between living standards, which depend only on commodity bundles, and the broader notion of 'quality of life'. Bliss attributes to me the view that 'the standard of living should embrace all aspects of the quality of life', and while there may be scope for doubting that simple diagnosis (on some related distinctions, see Sen *et al.*, 1987), it is certainly my view that the commodity bundle is informationally quite inadequate to capture the complex notion of the standard of living.

In defence of his position, Bliss points to the distinction between the case in which poor health is 'accidental' (as with the morbid, rich man) and one in which it arises from 'material deprivation' (as in a poor, developing country). In Bliss's view, 'in the first case it is excluded from the standard of living, in the second case it is included'. There is much sense in making a distinction

---

[1] In Bliss's characterization of 'life-styles', we have, in addition to preferences, the person's 'consumption set', i.e. not just the bundle actually chosen by him, but the set of bundles from which he can choose any one. It is easy to extend the example discussed here to cover this broader basis of comparison.

between the two cases, but is the case of the rich man with ill health really so simple?

First consider a case in which the ill health takes the form of the person having to spend much of his income on medical treatment. Despite his being rich with a high income, he may have little money left under these circumstances to buy reasonable food, clothing, shelter, and so on. It would be odd to describe his standard of living as high just because he has a large income, and indeed it would be much more natural to see him as a person with a low living standard even in primarily economic terms.

Next, consider a change—or an alternative scenario—in which the person's ailment is no longer treatable, so that he receives no treatment and suffers terribly, even though he now has more money left to spend on other non-medical commodities. He is clearly *worse off* as a result of this change, and it would be very odd to see the change as one that *raises* his standard of living! If he had a low living standard in the earlier case, his living standard is no higher now (as a result of his ailment ending up being untreatable). But in either case, this person with a poor living standard is precisely the rich man in bad health described by Bliss. It seems not unreasonable to resist Bliss's view that this miserable and deprived person is really enjoying a high living standard.

I would argue that unless we want to tie ourselves in knots, it is wise not to dissociate the notion of the standard of living from the actual standard or characteristics of a person's living, no matter how high his income—or how opulent his consumption set—might be. In fact, this notion of standard of living is not really at odds even with Pigou's (1952) definition of economic welfare as 'that part of social welfare that can be brought directly or indirectly into relation with the measuring rod of money' (p. 11), with which Bliss begins his paper. Since a person's ability to function—what has been called his or her 'capability'— can generally be enhanced by having more money, we can link the deprivation in the space of functionings to deprivation in terms of income. For any specified functioning vector (or some specified index of functionings), we can calculate for each person—given her circumstances—the minimal amount of money that she needs to achieve that functioning vector (or that functioning index). A person with ill health (or other handicaps, such as unfavourable environmental conditions, or exacting obligations to others, or disability) would need *more* money to achieve the same level of functioning.[2] If person 1 has a lower income than she needs (given her circumstances) to achieve that specified level of functionings, while 2 has a higher income than he needs for that level (given his circumstances), then—in this comparison—person 1 has a lower standard of living than person 2, even though in crude, unadjusted terms 1 may have the higher income of the two.

---

[2] This is so if that level of functioning is at all achievable with more money income. If not the person would need, as it were, an infinite income to achieve this level of functioning, so that she would be always short of that required amount.

This is how the broader notion of living standards—related to functionings and capabilities—may be brought 'indirectly into relation with the measuring rod of money'. This 'indirect' use of 'the measuring rod of money' is closely related to the direct use of comparisons in the space of functionings.[3] For the rest of this commentary, I shall not return to this alternative representation in terms of 'the measuring rod of money' and will concentrate instead directly on the achievement and deprivation of the capability to function.

5 Commodities, Capabilities, and Valuation

In evaluating living standards, should preferences be seen in terms of rankings of commodity vectors or of n-tuples of functionings? Bliss does not distinguish between a person's preferences and what he or she has reason to value. That distinction can be important, and I have tried to argue elsewhere (Sen, 1985; Sen et al., 1987) that reasoned valuations provide a basis for the assessment of well-being and living standards in a way that mere preferences do not. However, I shall not further pursue that distinction here.

What is immediately relevant here is the space over which valuations may be defined. If it is accepted that what matters ultimately is a person's capability to function (or, alternatively, the actual functioning n-tuple), then it would be a mistake to concentrate on the person's consumption set (or, alternatively, the chosen commodity bundle). Even if we confine our attention to constant-preference (or constant-valuation) comparisons, the constancy sought has to be that over the functioning space.[4]

The distinction is by no means trivial. The valuation of the commodity bundles (the 'means') to achieve the same functioning n-tuples (the 'ends') can vary greatly with social and cultural conditions. The importance of this type of variation had been noted by both Aristotle and Adam Smith.[5] Indeed, this was the starting point of Smith's analysis of intersocietal variations in *commodities* that are seen as 'necessary', since the same level of basic func-

[3] Formally, just as a person's capability to function is dependent *inter alia* on his or her income, there would be standardly an 'inverse function' relating any given bundle of functionings to the minimal income needed by a particular person to achieve that bundle, given other conditions. What we have to compare in this representation are the different persons' actual incomes *vis-à-vis* the respective 'minimally needed incomes' for specific functioning bundles. If no level of income would permit person 1 to achieve the index value of functioning that 2 can in fact achieve, then person 2 must be seen as having a deficiency in living standard no matter how high an income he or she enjoys. On this, and some related technical problems, see my paper in this volume, and also Sen (1992).

[4] Note that while there is an important issue as to whether to concentrate on capability to function or on achieved functionings, it must be remembered that both are defined in the same space, namely, the space of functionings (on this see Sen, 1992, and my paper in this volume). A functioning n-tuple is a point in that space, whereas a capability set is a set of such points.

[5] On Aristotle, see Martha Nussbaum's paper in this volume; on Adam Smith, see Sen (1984: essay 14); Sen et al. (1987).

tionings requires different commodity bundles in different societies.[6] For example, the commodities needed for the functioning of 'appearing in public without shame' may be very different in, say, India or China than in England or France. Adam Smith put the point thus:

A linen shirt, for example, is, strictly speaking, not a necessary of life. The Greeks and Romans lived, I suppose, very comfortably though they had no linen. But, in the present times, through the greater part of Europe, a creditable day-labourer would be ashamed to appear in public without a linen shirt, the want of which would be supposed to denote that disgraceful degree of poverty which, it is presumed, nobody can well fall into without extreme bad conduct. Custom, in the same manner, has rendered leather shoes a necessary of life in England. The poorest creditable person of either sex would be ashamed to appear in public without them.[7]

Even when life-styles vary greatly, with different preferences over commodity bundles (e.g. particular types of clothing), there may be considerable congruence in the valuation of basic functionings relevant for the analysis of living standards (e.g. the ability to appear in public without shame).

When there is substantial uniformity in the evaluation of functioning bundles or capabilities, it may be possible to make intersocietal comparisons of living standards, even though the preferences in the commodity space are quite different given different social conditions and life-styles. Thus, variations in preference over commodity bundles may not necessarily have the nihilistic implications that Bliss expects. Since there is likely to be much greater stability in treasuring important functionings than in ranking commodity bundles, the distinction could be, in practice, quite substantial (as Adam Smith emphasized).

6 Partial Orders and Assertive Judgements

It is, of course, quite possible that *even* in the space of functionings there will often be some intersocietal variations in evaluation. From here we can go in one of two different directions. The 'objectivist' position – well stated and defended by Aristotle – is to seek a uniformity of valuation of functionings in terms of 'human flourishing', based on reasoning.[8] Such an objective identification could involve the rejection of some of the actual valuations of the functioning space that people may – 'wrongly' – endorse.

The other approach is to leave as incomplete the specific comparisons that are affected by this multiplicity of evaluative orderings. The shared rankings can be separated out from the discordant ones. The 'intersection' of the valuations that people have reasons to endorse will generate partial orderings of functioning n-tuples and capability sets, and these will often be quite extensive.[9] This is one of many fields of social evaluation in which the partial

---

[6] See Smith (1776: 351–2).
[7] Ibid.
[8] On this see Nussbaum (1988, 1990).
[9] On this see Sen (1985); Sen *et al.* (1987).

order – rather than a complete or linear ordering – is the natural ranking format. Despite the incompleteness, this approach is still far from the nihilism in favour of which Bliss argues.

Finally, what about 'the loggers attacking the forest'? The newly created deserts may force people to a different life-style and to different tastes over commodity bundles, but in the space of functionings they may be identifiably more deprived in terms of their abiding valuation of health, security, happiness, and peace. Even if the valuations of these functionings vary a little between persons and over time, there can still be large 'intersections' in the rankings in the appropriate space, and the deprivation may be demonstrable in terms of shared valuations. There will then be good reasons to shout, 'Foul, stop it!', and not just to speculate as to whether we can 'be so sure that it is good' that the old life-style 'should disappear'. Changing tastes over commodity bundles and altering life-styles would not prevent a reasoned judgement against the enforced deprivation of living standards.

Bliss's insightful and foundational questions call for, I believe, a different class of answers than the one he himself endorses. But despite our differences, I cannot emphasize adequately the inescapable need for constructive theories to face Bliss's challenging questions. On that there is complete agreement.

BIBLIOGRAPHY

ARISTOTLE. *The Nicomachean Ethics*. English translation. W.D. Ross, *Aristotle: The Nicomachean Ethics*. Oxford: Oxford University Press, 1925.

NUSSBAUM, M.C. (1988). 'Nature, Function and Capability: Aristotle on Political Distribution,' *Oxford Studies in Ancient Philosophy*, suppl. vol.

—— (1990). 'Aristotelian Social Democracy', in G. Mara and W. Richardson (eds.), *Liberalism and the Good*. New York: Routledge, Chapman and Hall.

PIGOU, A.C. (1952). *The Economics of Welfare*. London: Macmillan.

SEN, A.K. (1984). *Resources, Values and Development*. Oxford: Blackwell, and Cambridge, Mass.: Harvard University Press.

—— (1985). 'Well-being, Agency and Freedom: The Dewey Lectures 1984', *Journal of Philosophy*, 82.

—— et al. (1987). *The Standard of Living*. Cambridge: Cambridge University Press.

—— (1992). *Inequality Reexamined*. Oxford: Clarendon Press.

SMITH, ADAM (1776). *An Inquiry Into the Nature and Causes of the Wealth of Nations*. Republished London: Home University, 1910.

INDEX OF NAMES

INDEX OF SUBJECTS